CONVEYANCING
LAW AND PRACTICE IN SCOTLAND

CONVEYANCING
LAW AND PRACTICE
IN SCOTLAND

by

JOHN M. HALLIDAY

C.B.E., M.A., LL.B. (Glasgow), LL.D. (Edin.).

*Emeritus Professor of Conveyancing in the
University of Glasgow*

Volume II

Feus and Dispositions

Published under the auspices of
THE SCOTTISH UNIVERSITIES LAW INSTITUTE

EDINBURGH
W. GREEN & SON LTD.
1986

First published in 1986

© 1986. THE SCOTTISH UNIVERSITIES LAW INSTITUTE

ISBN 0 414 00789 1
Typeset by Wessex Typesetters
(Division of The Eastern Press Ltd),
Frome, Somerset

Printed in Great Britain
by
The Eastern Press Ltd, London, Reading and Frome

PREFACE

THIS volume deals with transactions relating to the creation and transfer of rights of ownership of heritable property in Scotland. The general scheme of the work is to proceed from contracts of sale and purchase through conveyancing procedures leading to settlement and registration.

The arrangement of topics in a work on conveyancing always presents problems, which have been compounded in the case of the present volume by my predilection for exploring historical and other interesting side roads, by the need to accommodate the dual systems of sasine and registered titles and by the legislature which, with impeccable timing, enacted three important statutes immediately after the entire text had been originally written. I have endeavoured to ameliorate the resulting difficulties for the reader by the provision of a comprehensive index.

I have once more to acknowledge the unstinting help of Professor J.A.M. Inglis and Emeritus Professor A.J. McDonald who have given expert assistance upon many aspects of the text. On matters of registration of title I have relied heavily on the invaluable Registration of Title Practice Book and on the advice of the Keeper of the Registers of Scotland, and in particular the Deputy Keeper Mr. John Robertson, upon many difficult problems. In addition I am indebted to Mr. I.J.S. Talman for reading the whole text and making many valuable suggestions. Miss Candice Blackwood has prepared the table of statutes and assisted in research, Miss Shelagh Barclay and Mrs. Fiona Halliday have with cheerfulness and patient labour produced the typescript and my wife has been responsible for the table of cases and much else besides. To all of them I record my gratitude. Lastly I must thank the publishers, W. Green & Son Ltd., for their excellent services in the printing and production of the volume. However, I remain solely responsible for the text in its final form.

The law is stated as at December 31, 1985.

J.M. HALLIDAY

CONTENTS

LIST OF ABBREVIATIONS

Anton	Professor A.E. Anton, *Private International Law*, 1967.
Bell, *Comm.*	Professor G.J. Bell, *Commentaries on the Law of Scotland and the Principles of Mercantile Jurisprudence*, 7th ed., 1870.
Bell, *Prin.*	Professor G.J. Bell, *Principles of the Law of Scotland*, 10th ed., 1899.
Bell, (Montgomerie)	Professor A.M. Bell, *Lectures on Conveyancing*, 3rd ed., 1882.
Burns	John Burns, *Conveyancing Practice according to the Law of Scotland*, 4th ed., 1957.
Craigie, *Heritable Rights*	John Craigie, *Scottish Law of Conveyancing, Heritable Rights*, 3rd ed., 1899.
Currie	James G. Currie, *Confirmation of Executors in Scotland*, 7th ed., by A.E. McRae, 1973.
Encyclopaedia	*Encyclopaedia of the Laws of Scotland* 1926–1933.
Ersk.	Professor John Erskine of Carnock, *An Institute of the Law of Scotland*, 8th ed., 1871.
Gloag, *Contract*	Professor W.M. Gloag, *Law of Contract*, 2nd ed., 1929.
Gloag and Henderson	Professor W.M. Gloag and Professor R.C. Henderson, *Introduction to the Law of Scotland*, 8th ed., by A.B. Wilkinson and W.A. Wilson, 1980.
Gill	B. Gill, *The Law of Agricultural Holdings in Scotland*, 1982.
Halliday	Professor J.M. Halliday, *Conveyancing and Feudal Reform (Scotland) Act 1970*, 2nd ed., 1977.
McDonald, A.J.	Professor A.J. McDonald, *Conveyancing Manual*, 3rd ed., 1986.
Menzies, *Lectures*	Professor Allan Menzies, *Lectures on Conveyancing according to the Law of Scotland*, revised ed., 1900.
R.T.P.B.	Registration of Title Practice Book, 1981.
Stair	Sir James Dalrymple, Viscount Stair, *Institutions of the Law of Scotland*, Tercentenary ed., 1981.
Walker, *Contract*	Professor D.M. Walker, *Law of Contracts and Related Obligations in Scotland*, 2nd ed., 1985.
Walker, *Prin.*	Professor D.M. Walker, *Principles of Scottish Private Law*, 3rd ed., 1982.
Wood, *Lectures*	Professor J.P. Wood, *Lectures on Conveyancing*, 1903.

TABLE OF CASES

xi

TABLE OF STATUTES

xxix

CHAPTER 15

CONTRACTS FOR SALE AND PURCHASE OF HERITABLE
PROPERTY

A. SALES BY PRIVATE BARGAIN

1

A. SALES BY PRIVATE BARGAIN

Constitution of contract

15–01   Contracts for the sale and purchase of land by private bargain may be in the form of an agreement executed by both parties but much more frequently are concluded by missive letters between the parties or their solicitors. Such contracts are *obligationes literis* and, in order to be enforceable, must be created not only in writing but in writing which is probative or holograph or adopted as holograph,[1] subject to the principles of homologation or *rei interventus* aftermentioned.[2] If the writing is attested or holograph of only one party, either may resile, even the one who has given the formal writing.[3] If missives of sale or purchase are adopted as holograph by laymen it is essential that they have been informed of the meaning and legal effect of these words in making the bargain binding; otherwise they may resile,[4] so the proper practice is to have missives attested unless the signatories are legally qualified or are persons whose business is to deal with heritable property. Where the sale is of a business, the assets of which are preponderatingly moveable but include some heritable items, probative or holograph writing may not be necessary,[5] but the safe course is to have the contract attested or in holograph writing if any heritage is involved. A verbal contract for the sale of goodwill and stock and also of heritage was held unenforceable, even as regards the moveable items, since the contract so far as relating to the heritage required probative writing and the bargain for the purchase of the moveables was inseparable from that of purchase of the heritage.[6] Provisions

---

[1] Walker, *Contract*, 13–22, 13–23. As to what may be construed as a holograph acceptance, see *McGinn v. Shearer*, 1947 S.C. 334.
[2] See paras. 15–15 to 15–21.
[3] *Goldston v. Young* (1868) 7 M. 188; *Malcolm v. Campbell* (1891) 19 R. 278.
[4] *Harvey v. Smith* (1904) 6 F. 511; *Maclaine v. Murphy*, 1958 S.L.T. (Sh.Ct.) 49.
[5] *Allan v. Millar*, 1932 S.C. 620.
[6] *Allan v. Gilchrist* (1875) 2 R. 587.

relating to a contract in respect of a moveable item belonging to third parties, *e.g.* an inn sign, contained in a formal agreement for the purchase of heritable property may be varied by subsequent verbal agreement.[7] It is competent to add to missives the designations of witnesses and a testing clause, even after entry has been taken and the purchaser has attempted to repudiate the contract.[8] If both parties agree that the formal contract does not accurately express the whole terms of the bargain, then parole evidence, including informal documents spoken to in evidence, may be admissible to establish the agreement actually made.[9]

Contracts by agents

15–02 Missives for the purchase and sale of land are frequently entered into by solicitors or other agents. The authority of the agent is a matter of fact and may be proved by parole evidence.[10] The usual and best practice is that an offer to purchase is made by the agent on behalf of a disclosed and identified principal. If the offer is made expressly as agent but the principal is not identified, the seller may be content to rely on the reputation of the agent but he may wish to know, particularly where the price is substantial, that the principal is a person or company of financial standing. If an agent contracts on behalf of an unidentified principal he should for his own protection have written authority to make the offer, although he can still prove the existence of his authority by other competent evidence.[11] Where an agent offers to purchase on behalf of a new company it is essential to verify that the company has been incorporated, since if the offer antedates the incorporation of the company the agent will be personally liable on the contract.[12] If one solicitor acts for both parties he should not sign the missives as agent for either, but should have the offer and acceptance signed by the respective clients and attested.[13]

Consensus

15–03 The acceptance must meet the offer—there must be *consensus in idem* before the contract is binding. Qualifications or new conditions in an acceptance constitute a counter-offer which requires acceptance by the original offerer before the bargain is complete.[14] An acceptance

---

[7] *William Masson Ltd.* v. *Scottish Brewers Ltd.*, 1966 S.C. 9.
[8] *Stewart* v. *Burns* (1877) 4 R. 427.
[9] *Grant's Trs.* v. *Morison* (1875) 2 R. 377; *Grant* v. *Mackenzie* (1899) 1 F. 889. It is now competent to have the document rectified by the court (Law Reform (Miscellaneous Provisions) (Scotland) Act 1985, s. 8).
[10] Walker, *Prin.*, II, 220: *Cameron* v. *Lewis*, 1948 S.L.T. (Notes) 1.
[11] See *Gibb* v. *Cunningham & Robertson*, 1925 S.L.T. 608.
[12] European Communities Act 1972, s. 9(2) (now repealed but provision re-enacted in Companies Act 1985, s. 36(4)).
[13] *Mitchell* v. *Scott's Trs.* (1874) 2 R. 162.
[14] *Dickson* v. *Blair* (1871) 10 M. 41.

subject to a more formal contract being adjusted is not necessarily a condition which is suspensive of agreement provided that all the essential elements of the bargain have been agreed in the documents exchanged.[15] The words "subject to contract" do not have in Scots law the effect of suspending agreement.

> "The only rules of Scots law which it appears to me to be possible to extract from past decisions and general principles are that it is perfectly possible for the parties to an apparent contract to provide that there shall be *locus poenitentiae* until the terms of their agreement have been reduced to a formal contract; but that the bare fact that the parties to a completed agreement stipulate that it shall be embodied in a formal contract does not necessarily import that they are still in the stage of negotiation. In each instance it is a matter of the construction of the correspondence in the light of the facts, proved or averred, on which side of the border line the case lies."[16]

The fact that the price is not specified does not preclude agreement if an agreed method of ascertaining it, *e.g.* by arbitration, is included.[17] Once *consensus in idem* has been reached then, unless the agreement contains a suspensive or resolutive condition which operates, neither party can repudiate without becoming liable in damages for breach of contract.

Unilateral obligation

15–04   It is possible for a person to grant a unilateral probative or holograph obligation undertaking to convey heritable property to another person on payment of a stated price, and that obligation is binding without the need of acceptance by the other person, but it must be clear that the intention as expressed is to undertake an obligation and not to make an offer.[18]

Time for acceptance—withdrawal

15–05   An offer which contains no condition as to the time allowed for acceptance may be withdrawn at any time before acceptance. If an acceptance is posted before a letter withdrawing the offer is received, the contract is complete and the withdrawal comes too late,[19] even although the acceptance has been delayed in the post.[20] If the offer contains no condition as to time, it falls if not accepted within a

---

[15] *Erskine* v. *Glendinning* (1871) 9 M. 656.

[16] *Stobo Ltd.* v. *Morrisons (Gowns) Ltd.*, 1949 S.C. 184, at 192, *per* Lord President Cooper. In the circumstances of this case the phrase was suspensive of obligation, especially since it was used in an improbative document.

[17] *Earl of Selkirk* v. *Nasmith* (1778) Mor. 627; Bell, *Prin.*, s. 92.

[18] See *Malcolm* v. *Campbell* (1891) 19 R. 278; *Haldane* v. *Watson*, 1972 S.L.T. (Sh.Ct.) 8. See also *Anderson* v. *Anderson*, 1961 S.C. 59.

[19] *Thomson* v. *James* (1855) 18 D.1.

[20] *Dunlop* v. *Higgins* (1848) 6 Bell's App. 195.

SALES BY PRIVATE BARGAIN

reasonable period, what is a reasonable period being a matter of circumstances.[21] If an offer contains a condition that it must be accepted, or that missives must be concluded, within a stated time, that does not prevent its withdrawal within the period stated, but it precludes acceptance after the expiry of that period.[22] On the other hand the condition may be so expressed that it constitutes an obligation not to withdraw it within the time specified.[23] An offerer will usually wish to retain his right to withdraw the offer at any time. That objective can be achieved by the use of wording such as, "This offer, if an acceptance is not received by us by (hour and date), will be deemed to be withdrawn"; phraseology such as, "This offer will remain open up to" should be avoided.[24]

Withdrawal—mistake in offer

15–06 If an offer contains a mistake in a material matter, *e.g.* where a solicitor by mistake offers a price greater than his client has authorised, he may correct the mistake and withdraw the erroneous offer by telephone or telex at any time before an acceptance has been dispatched; once the mistake has been communicated to the seller, even although that has not been done in formal writing, the seller cannot accept the original offer.[25] The principle is that a party to negotiations for a contract cannot take advantage of an error by the other party of which he has knowledge.[26]

Conditions for the exclusive benefit of one party

5–07 If the contract contains a condition which is exclusively in the interest of one party, he is entitled to waive compliance with it and still maintain that the contract is binding.[27] In *Dewar & Finlay Ltd.* v. *Blackwood*[28] purchasers were held to be entitled to waive a condition that they obtain unrestricted planning permission for the working of minerals and still enforce the contract. If, however, the sellers have made a counter-stipulation that they can resile if the planning permission is not obtained, or if the other party can demonstrate that a condition was not purely in the interest of the party who introduced it, then the same result does not follow.[29] In *Imry Property Holdings Ltd.*

[21] *Hall-Maxwell* v. *Gill* (1901) 9 S.L.T. 222.
[22] *Heys* v. *Kimball & Morton* (1890) 17 R. 381, 384; *Effold Properties Ltd.* v. *Sprot*, 1979 S.L.T. (Notes) 84.
[23] *Littlejohn* v. *Hadwen* (1882) 20 S.L.R. 5.
[24] *A. & G. Paterson* v. *Highland Rly. Co.*, 1927 S.C. (H.L.) 32, 38.
[25] Gloag, *Contract*, 437, 438.
[26] *Steuart's Trs.* v. *Hart* (1875) 3 R. 192; *Moncrieff* v. *Lawrie* (1896) 23 R. 577 (although the decision was affected by a specialty).
[27] Gloag, *Contract*, 42.
[28] 1968 S.L.T. 196. Dub., *Ellis & Sons Second Amalgamated Properties Ltd.* v. *Pringle*, 1975 S.L.T. 10.
[29] *Ellis & Sons Second Amalgamated Properties Ltd.* v. *Pringle, supra.*

v. *Glasgow Y.M.C.A.*[30] a condition that the offer was subject to the purchasers obtaining all necessary permissions and consents for a proposed development was qualified by a provision that if the permissions were not obtained by a stated date the bargain would be voidable at the instance of either party; it was held that the condition had not been conceived solely in the interests of the purchasers. For suggestions as to the style of a "subject to planning permission" clause see paragraph 15–106 *infra*.

Negotiations in sales by private bargain—practice

15–08   The procedure in negotiating a sale of heritable property by private bargain depends upon the circumstances of the particular transaction and involves professional and commercial judgment. There can be few absolute rules but the following guide lines are suggested.[31]

15–09   (i) **Expected price.** Usually some indication of the price expected will be given in advertisements or particulars of the property or verbally in response to inquiry. It is helpful to prospective purchasers to give such indication; it may obviate expense on legal and survey fees in cases where the price is beyond their financial resources. It is usually inadvisable to overstate the expected price; unnecessary costs of further advertisement may be incurred and prospective purchasers who might have been able to compete at the actual level of price eventually secured may be discouraged. A small understatement of the price expected may promote competition and can be qualified by "offers upwards of."

15–10   (ii) **Confidentiality of offers.** Any offer received should be treated as confidential between the seller and the offerer. It should not be disclosed, nor should indications of price level based upon it be given, to other offerers. "Dutch auctions" are contrary to reputable professional practice.

15–11   (iii) **"Shotgun" offers.** When an offer is received at an early stage of negotiations which is stated to be open for acceptance immediately or within a very brief period, it is a matter of judgment for the seller, depending upon the amount of the offer and his estimate of the value of the property, whether or not to accept forthwith. Subject to those considerations, it is seldom advisable, at least if other parties are showing interest, for the seller to accept the "shotgun" offer immediately or within the period stated. This type of offer represents a legitimate negotiating tactic designed to eliminate the competition which it is in

---

[30] 1979 S.L.T. 261. See also *Aberfoyle Plantations Ltd.* v. *Cheng* [1960] A.C. 115; *T. Boland & Co. Ltd.* v. *Dundas's Trs.*, 1975 S.L.T. (Notes) 80; *George Packman & Sons* v. *Young*, 1976 S.L.T. (Notes) 52.

[31] See articles: A. I. Phillips, "The Psychology of the Negotiator," 1958 *Conveyancing Review* 149; P. W. Richmond, "Is Sale of Heritage by Private Bargain Outmoded?" (1966) 11 J.L.S. 156; A. R. Brownlie, "The Purchase and Sale of Houses," (1971) 16 J.L.S. 139.

the seller's interest to stimulate. If the tactic fails and time is allowed for other parties to offer then, should the original shotgun offer still prove to be the highest received, it is unlikely that the original offerer will decline to extend the period for its acceptance.

5–12 **(iv) Closing date.** When several parties have indicated an interest the seller may bring negotiations to a conclusion by intimating to all of them a closing date for the receipt of offers. It is improper, although probably it does not involve legal liability, for the seller thereafter to accept an offer before the closing date; he has represented to the others that they will have an opportunity of submitting an offer by a specified date which will have a chance of acceptance.

5–13 **(v) Increment and escalating offers.** Increment offers, *i.e.* an offer of £x more than the highest other offer received, should not be accepted. All offers should be confidential and should not be used as a basis for another. Escalating offers, *e.g.* a series of offers containing prices on an ascending scale with instructions that they be opened in turn until one exceeds the highest offer received from any other person, should for the same reason not be accepted. In either case the offerer should be asked to substitute an offer of a fixed amount.

5–14 **(vi) Bridging loans.** Where an offer to purchase is being made on behalf of a person who proposes to finance it with funds from the sale yet to be made of another property, the date of entry should, if practicable, be sufficiently far forward to allow time for the advertisement and sale of the existing property of the offerer to be completed, or at least for a binding contract for the sale of it being signed. Unless there is a concluded bargain for the sale of the existing property, bridging finance for the new purchase may be difficult to obtain. The obtaining of bridging finance is a matter between the purchaser and his bankers; it is usually unwise for his solicitor to become involved, although in special cases the solicitor may be prepared as a service to his client to arrange bridging finance with the solicitor's own bankers.

Rei interventus and homologation

5–15 Contracts for the sale and purchase of heritable property, although improbative or in some respect incomplete, may be validated by *rei interventus* or homologation. These doctrines are most frequently invoked in two sets of circumstances: (1) where the agreement is imperfect in form, not being probative or holograph, but actings have followed of such a character that it would be inequitable to permit either party to resile[32]; or (2) where in the course of exchange of

---

[32] *e.g. Stodart* v. *Dalzell* (1876) 4 R. 236; *Stewart* v. *Burns* (1877) 4 R. 427; *Mitchell* v. *The Stornoway Trs.*, 1936 S.C. (H.L.) 56.

missive letters there has been failure to achieve complete *consensus in idem*, but actings have followed which bar *locus poenitentiae*, so that a stipulation not accepted in writing may nevertheless be implied as binding.[33]

15–16   The classic definitions of *rei interventus* and homologation are stated in Bell's *Principles*[34]:

> "*Rei interventus* is inferred from any proceedings not unimportant on the part of the obligee, known to and permitted by the obligor to take place on the faith of the contract as if it were perfect; provided they are unequivocally referable to the agreement and productive of alteration of circumstances, loss or inconvenience, though not irretrievable."
>
> "Homologation (in principle similar to *rei interventus*) is an act of the obligor or his legal representative approbatory of a preceding engagement, which in itself is defective or informal or unauthorised, either confirming it or adopting it as binding. It may be express, or inferred from circumstances. It must be absolute, and not compulsory, nor proceeding on error or fraud, and unequivocally referable to the engagement; and must imply assent to it, with full knowledge of its extent, and of all the relevant interests of the homologator."

The respective fields of application of those two principles have been defined by Lord Macmillan[35]:

> "Thus the party who seeks to enforce an informal contract against the party who seeks to disown it may found upon his own actings on the faith of the contract, if these actings have been known to and permitted by the other party, in which case he invokes the doctrine of *rei interventus*; or he may found upon the actings of the party seeking to disown the contract as actings which imply confirmation of the contract, in which case he invokes the doctrine of homologation . . . The essence of the matter is the occurrence, subsequent to the informal agreement, of acts on the part of either party which would render it inequitable to hold that there was still a *locus poenitentiae*."

15–17   The requirements of a successful plea of *rei interventus* may be summarised thus:

(a) *There must be an antecedent agreement.* The first requirement is that there is an agreement to which the actings refer.[36] The agreement may be constituted by informal writings,[37] or by a combination of verbal agreement and writings,[38] or it may even be verbal but in that

---

[33] *e.g. Whyte* v. *Lee* (1879) 6 R. 699; *Charles* v. *Shearer* (1900) 8 S.L.T. 273.

[34] ss. 26, 27.

[35] In *Mitchell* v. *The Stornoway Trs.*, *supra* at 63.

[36] *Heiton* v. *Waverley Hydropathic Co. Ltd.* (1877) 4 R. 830; *Mitchell* v. *The Stornoway Trs.*, *supra*; *Stobo Ltd.* v. *Morrisons (Gowns) Ltd.*, 1949 S.C. 184; *East Kilbride Development Corporation* v. *Pollok*, 1953 S.C. 370.

[37] *Stewart* v. *Burns* (1877) 4 R. 427; *Mitchell* v. *The Stornoway Trs.*, *supra*; *Secretary of State for Scotland* v. *Ravenstone Securities Ltd.*, 1976 S.C. 171.

[38] *Stodart* v. *Dalzell* (1876) 4 R. 236.

case the constitution of the agreement can be proved only by the oath of the defender.[39] There has been considerable conflict of judicial opinion on the question of whether, in circumstances where a written offer was made but not accepted, the fact of agreement may be proved by actings of parties, *i.e.* such actings may actually constitute the agreement and not merely perfect an informal agreement.[40] In the latest decision which is directly in point, *Errol* v. *Walker* cited below, it was held that the fact of agreement may be so proved, but the judges admittedly found the earlier authorities confusing and the soundness of the decision must be regarded as dubious.[41]

5–18   (b) *Actings unequivocally referable to the agreement and not unimportant.* The actings must be unequivocally referable to the agreement as if it were perfect. Expenses incurred in making inquiries as to the value of the property and endeavouring to arrange finance are actings of a kind which a purchaser may undertake before entering into an agreement to purchase and are not actings in reliance upon it.[42] "Unequivocally" is not necessarily "exclusively"; the fact that the actings may assist in furthering several transactions does not preclude them being founded upon in respect of one of the transactions.[43] What is "not unimportant" is a question of degree, but entering into possession of a feu, paying feuduties and commencing to build,[44] giving a tenant notice to remove and re-letting,[45] actings by both parties including laying out of ground and removal of a sale ticket[46] and paying the purchase price[47] have been held to be sufficiently important, but not merely making a small payment to account of the price.[48] Taking possession, instructing architects to prepare plans for a hotel, seeking building and planning permissions and commencing material development on the ground were held to be sufficiently important.[49]

5–19   (c) *Known to and permitted by the other party.* In most cases where *rei interventus* has been pleaded the actings have been known to the other party, but if, although not actually known to him, they are such as he might reasonably have expected to take place in pursuance of the agreement, that may be sufficient.[50]

[39] *Allan* v. *Gilchrist* (1875) 2 R. 587.
[40] *Keir* v. *Duke of Atholl* (1815) 6 Pat. App. 130; *Colquhoun* v. *Wilson's Trs.* (1860) 22 D.1035; *Errol* v. *Walker*, 1966 S.C. 93. Cf. *Mitchell* v. *The Stornoway Trs.*, *supra* at 66; *East Kilbride Development Corporation* v. *Pollok*, *supra* at 374, 375.
[41] Walker, *Prin.*, II, 52; article, "Rei Interventus Reconsidered?" (1966) 11 J.L.S. 263.
[42] *Mowat* v. *Caledonian Banking Co.* (1895) 23 R. 270.
[43] *Secretary of State for Scotland* v. *Ravenstone Securities Ltd.*, *supra*.
[44] *Smith* v. *Marshall* (1860) 22 D.1158; *Stodart* v. *Dalzell* (1876) 4 R. 236.
[45] *Stewart* v. *Burns* (1877) 4 R. 427.
[46] *Westren* v. *Millar* (1879) 7 R. 173.
[47] *Foggo* v. *Hill* (1840) 2 D. 1322.
[48] *McLean* v. *Scott* (1902) 10 S.L.T. 447.
[49] *Secretary of State for Scotland* v. *Ravenstone Securities Ltd.*, *supra*.
[50] *Gardner* v. *Lucas* (1878) 5 R. 638 *per* Lord Shand at 656. As to actings not permitted by the other party and not unequivocally referable to a condition as to date of entry which had not been accepted, and so not constituting *rei interventus* see *Law* v. *Thomson*, 1978 S.L.T. 250.

15-20   (d) *Alteration of circumstances, loss or inconvenience.* The principle is that the alteration of circumstances of, or the loss or inconvenience to, the person seeking to maintain the agreement must be such that in all the circumstances it is inequitable that the other party should be permitted to plead that the agreement is not binding. This requirement is closely related to that of the actings being not unimportant—see para. 15–18 and cases cited at notes 44 to 47 and 49. Averments that the purchaser had formed a syndicate to operate minerals were held insufficient to support a plea that an incomplete contract for the purchase of rights under a lease of the minerals and of certain plant and machinery had been validated *rei interventu*.[51] Giving up other businesses was decided to be too remote an alteration of circumstances to found a plea of *rei interventus* as perfecting an improbative lease of minerals.[52]

15-21   *Homologation.* Homologation of an informal agreement may result from express words, or be inferred from actings, of the party who seeks to deny the existence of an enforceable contract. The words or actings must be subsequent to and not *unico contextu* with the original agreement[53] and must be such as unequivocally refer to it and approve of it.[54] The subsequent words or conduct founded on must have been made with full knowledge of the circumstances.[55] The application for transfer of a liquor licence by a purchaser of a licensed business was sufficient to infer his homologation of a condition as to consignation of the price stipulated by the seller but not accepted by the purchaser.[56] Homologation of an uncompleted agreement to feu was implied from subsequent actings of the superiors' factor in assisting the prospective feuar to have building plans approved by the dean of guild court.[53] Incomplete agreements to lease were homologated by allowing the tenant to take possession,[57] retaining possession of a lease signed by the tenant,[58] and application by the tenant for renewal of the licence for a hotel.[59]

Contents of missives

15-22   The provisions which should be inserted in offers for the purchase or sale of heritable property become ever more numerous. It is necessary to take into account not only the common and statute law relating to land and/or leases but also the requirements of local authorities and special statutes relating to particular categories of property or persons

---

[51] *Rigg* v. *Mather* (1902) 10 S.L.T. 426.
[52] *Gardner* v. *Lucas* (1878) 5 R. 638.
[53] *Mitchell* v. *The Stornoway Trs.*, 1936 S.C. (H.L.) 56.
[54] Bell, *Prin.*, s. 27.
[55] *Paterson* v. *Moncrieff* (1866) 4 M. 706; *Donaldson* v. *Tainsh's Trs.* (1886) 13 R. 967.
[56] *Charles* v. *Shearer* (1900) 8 S.L.T. 273.
[57] *Forbes* v. *Wilson* (1873) 11 M. 454.
[58] *Ballantine* v. *Stevenson* (1881) 8 R. 959.
[59] *Station Hotel, Nairn, Ltd.* v. *Macpherson* (1905) 13 S.L.T. 456.

or companies. It is virtually impossible to compile a comprehensive list of all the items which should be included in offers; the check list which follows should not be regarded as exhaustive and additional matters may be required in offers for properties or leases which have individual peculiarities.

15–23 **Check list.** The following list (which is not exhaustive) comprises general items which are appropriate for inclusion in most offers and special items which should be considered in the case of offers for particular categories of property or leases.

Parties

> Identification
> Power of sale
> Consent of spouse—matrimonial homes

Subjects

> Description—tenure, feu or leasehold,
> Principal and ancillary buildings
> Ground—main and separate parts
> Rateable value
> Boundaries:
>> Mutual gables
>> Division walls or fences
>> Sea—foreshore
>> Rivers or lochs—fishings
> Pertinents:
>> Accesses
>> Common areas—parking or service areas
>> Fixtures and fittings
> Services:
>> Electricity
>> Water
>> Gas
>> Sewerage and drainage
> Minerals
> Survey—materials used in construction—site stability—subsidence
>> in property or vicinity

Price

> Date of payment
> Punctual payment essential condition
> Deposit
> Interest if payment late
> Formula to ascertain price
> Apportionment of price between heritage and moveables

Entry

    Fixed or flexible date
    Entry on contractual date of the essence
    Vacant possession

Title

    Pre-emption or redemption clause
    Burdens and conditions
        Feuduty or ground annual allocated or not
        Construction of buildings
        Use
        Minerals—compensation for damage
        Rights of third parties
    Servitudes for benefit of subjects
        Access
        Service area
        Private water supply
        Sewage disposal
    Servitudes burdening subjects—positive and negative
    Rights of way
    Register of Sasines
    Searches—period
    Land Register
        Sale inducing first registration
        Sale of interest already registered
    Searches—companies

Inquiries on collateral matters—local authorities

    Planning
        Existing buildings and use permitted
        New buildings or use—permission
        Conservation area
        Notices or proposals
    Building
        Warrants and certificates of completion for recent buildings
        Listed buildings
    Roads, footpaths and sewers—maintenance
        Proposals—new roads

Apportionments

    Ground burdens—redeemed or not
    Rents
    Rates
    Insurances

Common charges
Continuing charges based on consumption—electricity, gas,
    telephone

Pre-settlement contingencies

Liability for damage by fire, vandalism, etc.
Seller's responsibility
Insurance—adequacy
Right of purchaser to resile

Taxation

Stamp duty
Capital allowances
Value added tax (moveable items included in purchase)
Capital gains tax—roll-over relief
Grants
Enterprise zones

Conditions—missives

Time limit for acceptance
Conditions of missives remaining in force after settlement

Additional matters—particular subjects

(1) *Leaseholds*
    Head lease or sub-lease?
    Landlord's title—infeftment
    Tenant's title
        Period
        Rent and rent reviews
        Permitted use—consent to proposed use
        Restrictions on assignation
        Irritancy—head lease and sub-lease
        Variations or amendments of lease or sub-lease
        Consents granted
        No breach of conditions by tenants
        No sub-tenancies/authorised sub-tenancies
        Other conditions of lease or sub-lease
        Insurance provisions

(2) *Dwelling-houses*
    Matrimonial homes consents, etc.
    Recent buildings or alterations
        National House Building Council indemnity
        Building warrant
        Certificate of completion
        Roads, footpaths and sewers public?

Purchases under tenant's rights legislation
Contents
    Carpets and floor coverings
    Curtains, curtain-rods and pelmets
    Tiled hearths and fenders
    Mantels and overmantels
    Grates
    Gas or electric fires
    Fitted cupboards and wardrobes
    Mirrors
    Picture rails or rods or picture panels
    Stair rods and runners
    Central or off-peak heating system and radiators
    Electric lighting—meter, plugs, bulbs, shades, bowls, chandeliers
    Gas—meter, brackets and lights
    Kitchen fittings and appliances—cooker, refrigerator, deep freeze, dishwasher, washing machine, waste disposal unit
    Bathroom fittings—towel rails, cabinets, showers, bidet
Garden—greenhouses, glass frames, wire fencing, growing trees, shrubs, flowers and vegetables
Flatted dwelling-houses
    Ground burdens allocated or not
    Common parts—roof, walls, *solum*, entrance and stairway
    Garden ground—common—exclusive part
    Share of maintenance—common parts
    Deed of conditions

(3) *Licensed premises—hotels and public houses*
    Sale conditional on transfer of licence
    Special arrangements if entry before transfer of licence
    Premises
      Fire certificate
      Offices, Shops and Railway Premises Act
    Parking area and access
    Houses for staff accommodation
    Service areas
    Goodwill
    Moveable furnishings and equipment
      Hired or leased items
    Wet and dry stocks—valuation
    Insurance—loss of licence
    Supply agreements—tied house?

(4) *Commercial property*
    Details of leases granted
    Estimated free annual yield—present and future
    No breaches by tenants
    No sub-tenancies/sub-tenancies authorised
    Variations or amendments of leases
    Consents granted to tenants
    Prohibition of variations of leases or consents before entry
    Offices, Shops and Railway Premises Act
    Fire certificate
    Floor areas—extent
    Garage accommodation and parking area

(5) *Industrial property*
    Premises (existing or proposed new use)
        Factories Acts
        Fire certificate
        Statutory requirements for particular use
    Usable floor area
    Trade fixtures—machinery, tools or equipment to be purchased
    Water supply—waste disposal—any special requirements?
    Parking accommodation
    Title conditions—any restriction on existing or proposed use?
    Leasehold—see (1) *Leaseholds*, above

(6) *Landed estates and farms*
    Description—area—plan
    Excepted parts
    Shootings and fishings—salmon-fishing rights
    Minerals
    Timber—forestry dedication agreements
    Apportionment—rents and charges
    Water supply, sewerage, drainage—servitude rights required?
    Ancient monuments, archaeological areas, areas of special
      scientific interest
    Buildings of architectural or historic interest
    Conservation area
    Access agreements
    Roads and accesses—maintenance
    Repayable grants
    Farms

        (a) *With vacant possession*
        Tied cottages?
        Growing crops
        Live and dead stock
        Dairy quota
        Fixed plant and machinery

Moveable equipment and implements
Dung
Early access for ploughing, sowing
Apportionment of price
Repairs or improvements instructed before entry
Tax allowances—capital expenditure

(b) *Subject to tenancy*
Terms of leases—period, rent and rent reviews, etc.
Apportionment of rent
Contracting out agreements
Conditions on waygoing
   Compensation for improvements
   Bound sheep stocks
Notice to tenant of change of ownership

I. *Parties*

15–24 Offers to purchase should, in the absence of special instructions to the contrary, be made by or on behalf of identified purchasers.[60] An offer submitted by an agent on behalf of a company which has not yet been formed may involve the agent in personal liability.[61] If any of the parties to the transaction *prima facie* has limited capacity or powers or may contract only after the observance of special procedures[62] it is advisable that these matters should be considered, at least in a preliminary way, at the time of negotiating missives: they will be investigated fully at the stage of examination of title but it is in the interest of all parties that any defects in powers or special procedures required be identified before a binding contract has been made. In a sale of a dwelling-house the seller's solicitor should ensure that any consent or renunciation required in terms of the Matrimonial Homes (Family Protection) (Scotland) Act 1981[63] will be available. The missives should include a provision such as:

> The seller will deliver [on acceptance hereof] [at or prior to settlement] (i) a duly executed statutory form of consent by his/her spouse to the sale of the subjects to the purchaser or (ii) a duly notarised renunciation of occupancy rights of the seller's spouse in the said subjects or (iii) in the event of the seller being or stating that he/she is unmarried an affidavit that the subjects of sale are not a matrimonial home in relation to which a spouse of the seller has occupancy rights, all for the purposes of section 6 of the Matrimonial Homes (Family Protection) (Scotland) Act 1981; and in the event of a statutory form of consent being delivered the seller's spouse will also, if required by the purchaser, sign the Disposition aftermentioned as signifying his/her continuing consent

---

[60] See para. 15–02.
[61] *Ibid.*
[62] See Vol. I Chap. 2.
[63] s. 6(3).

to the dealing implemented thereby. The seller will also deliver evidence that there were no effective occupancy rights of a non-entitled spouse in relation to any sale of the subjects made on or after September 1, 1982.

II. *Subjects of Purchase*

5–25 Offers of purchase or sale frequently have to be framed under pressure of time. Nevertheless it is desirable to ensure that the description of the subjects purchased should comprehend everything that is to be included in the sale: in the event of any subsequent dispute as to what has been sold it is the description in the contract of sale, not the description in the seller's title deeds, that will determine the issue.[63a] It is essential that a solicitor submitting an offer on behalf of a purchaser should ascertain from his client particulars of the heritable property itself and of all items which are to be included in the price tendered, and examine the particulars of the property furnished by the seller. The particulars will often stipulate that they do not form part of the contract of sale, and so any particular items desired by the purchaser should be specified in the offer. Alternatively, if they are included in the particulars furnished, the particulars should be imported into the contract, *e.g.* "together with the whole items and rights specified in the particulars of the subjects provided by the seller."[64] Matters which may require special attention are considered in the following paragraphs.

(a) Tenure

5–26 A contract for the sale of heritable property, without stipulation as to the nature of the tenure, implies that the property is feudal and subject to normal feuing conditions applicable to the type of property sold. If the superiority is to be included, that should be specified. If the property is leasehold, that should be made clear in the contract; if the contract does not do so, the purchaser may resile.[65] As to special matters to be considered in a purchase of leasehold property, see the paragraphs undernoted.[66]

(b) Buildings

5–27 The contract should specify the principal building or buildings and also any ancillary buildings or erections which are to be included in the sale. A self-contained dwelling-house can usually be described adequately by its type (detached villa or bungalow, semi-detached villa, terrace dwelling-house), name and/or street number and town.

[63a] *Houldsworth* v. *Gordon Cumming*, 1910 S.C. (H.L.) 49, 55.
[64] For decisions on purchase of subjects "as advertised," see *Nisbet* v. *Smith* (1876) 3 R. 781, and *Mossend Theatre Co. Ltd.* v. *Livingstone*, 1930 S.C. 90.
[65] *McConnell* v. *Chassels* (1903) 10 S.L.T. 790.
[66] paras. 15–59 and 15–92.

Ancillary buildings should be separately mentioned, *e.g.* garage, carport, garden sheds or outhouses, since these may be portable and not part of the heritable subjects, with a general phrase such as, "all (any) other buildings and erections at present located on the subjects." A flatted dwelling-house should be identified by reference to street number, floor and geographical orientation, *e.g.* "the four apartment flat being the westmost house on the second floor above the ground floor of the building entering from No. 7 Bank Street, Edinburgh." Descriptions such as "2 up left" may be ambiguous; the stairway may turn and "2 up left" viewed from the street may be "2 up right" as approached from the stairway. Ancillary buildings such as a garage, coal cellar, shed or hut belonging exclusively to the flat purchased should also be specified: if any such ancillary buildings are owned or used in common with the proprietors of other flats, the right to ownership or use in common should be stated. Similar principles apply to contracts for the sale of commercial or industrial property. The main building or buildings should be described sufficiently to identify them, with the postal address, and any ancillary buildings should either be separately mentioned or included in a comprehensive phrase, *e.g.* "all other buildings and erections belonging to the seller at present situated in or upon the said area of ground" (the area of ground will already have been described—see paragraph 15–28). Flatted commercial property such as business offices should be described by reference to the principal office premises (floor or floors, geographical orientation and postal address) together with any separate buildings or accommodation, *e.g.* garage accommodation, to which the seller has exclusive or common rights. Buildings on agricultural property may be described as "the farmhouse and steading known as   (situation) together with all buildings and erections comprised therein," and any buildings or erections not plainly included in that description should be separately mentioned. The description of buildings on a landed estate should follow a similar pattern: the principal mansion-house and offices should be described by name and location and any other buildings or erections not clearly comprehended therein should be separately mentioned.

(c) Ground

15–28   It is desirable, and in certain cases essential for a satisfactory description, that the ground included in the sale be specified either by a general description, *e.g.* "the garden ground pertaining thereto as at present occupied by the seller," or by reference to an existing plan included in the titles or prepared specially for the purposes of the sale.[66a] In view of the provisions of the Land Registration (Scotland)

[66a] For an example of a description too indefinite, see *Grant* v. *Peter G. Gauld & Co.*, 1985 S.L.T. 545.

Act 1979[67] it is now in the interests of both parties to a contract of sale to verify that there is no discrepancy between the boundaries of the ground as described in the contract and the occupational boundaries of it as appearing on the Ordnance Survey map of the area. In particular it is in the interests of the seller to ascertain at the stage of negotiation of the missives whether there is any such discrepancy so that an appropriate qualification may be made in the contract.[68] If the area in which the subjects are situated is already operational for the purposes of the Act but the title to it has not yet been registered, an appropriate condition should be inserted in the offer to purchase, *e.g.* "The seller will furnish to the purchaser such documents and evidence including a plan as the Keeper may require to enable the Keeper to issue a Land Certificate in name of the purchaser as the registered proprietor of the whole subjects of offer and containing no exclusion of indemnity in terms of section 12(2) of the Land Registration (Scotland) Act 1979."[69] The seller or his solicitor may verify the coincidence or otherwise of the boundaries as described with those shown on the Ordnance Survey map either by personal comparison[70] or by application to the Keeper on Form P16.[71] If the title to the subjects has already been registered all that is normally necessary is to compare the boundaries as shown on the land certificate with the boundaries of the ground being purchased, unless any part of the subjects is excluded from indemnity or any boundaries are shown by dotted lines on the land certificate plan,[72] in which latter event an application to the Keeper on Form P17 may produce further information.[73] In such a case, *i.e.* where the title of the seller has already been registered in the Land Register and the whole of a registered parcel is being sold, the subjects may be identified in the offer by reference to the title number.

–29 Ground owned in conjunction with a dwelling-house should be specified either generally "together with the garden and amenity ground pertaining thereto as occupied by the seller" or, especially if extensive, by statement of total area. If any part of such ground is not owned by the seller the missives should be qualified appropriately. In sales of flatted dwelling-house property the area or areas of garden ground owned exclusively and/or in common, as the case may be, should be described, with rights of access. Consideration should be given to the inclusion or exclusion of plants, trees, shrubs, flowers and vegetables and greenhouses or conservatories and their contents.

---

[67] ss. 4(2) and 6(1).
[68] R.T.P.B., para. E.30.
[69] R.T.P.B., paras. G.2.08, 2.09.
[70] O.S. sheets may be obtained from the regional or local offices of the Ordnance Survey or agents—(1981) 26 J.L.S. W. 185 and W. 207.
[71] R.T.P.B., paras. E.35 to E.37.
[72] R.T.P.B., para. E.16.
[73] R.T.P.B., para. E.36.

15–30   Where the area of the ground purchased is significant or extensive it should be described by reference to area and a plan. Examples are ground purchased for development, ground forming the site of industrial or commercial buildings and their curtilage, landed estates and agricultural subjects. The area and plan will be definitive of the subjects purchased.[74] A description of land as "occupied by the seller" or, in the case of leasehold, "tenanted by the seller" may exclude land occupied or tenanted as a privilege.[75] If such subjects are not described by reference to a plan, care should be taken to ensure that any areas discontiguous to the principal area are specified and sufficiently identified, *e.g.* parking or storage areas, staff accommodation, courts or yards owned in connection with a hotel or other business, together with rights of access.

(d) Boundaries

15–31   **(i) Common gables.** If the subjects of purchase include a building which has a gable mutual or common to an adjoining building and the gable has been utilised to its full height on both sides, the offer to purchase should stipulate that there are no outstanding charges in respect of the maintenance or, if recently built, construction of the gable. If the gable has been erected by the seller or his predecessors in ownership but has not yet been used, or not used to its full height, by the proprietor of the adjoining property, the seller should reserve the right to recover half of the cost from the adjoining proprietor or any of his successors as and when they make use of it.[76] If the seller or a former owner of the property purchased has previously made use of the gable but has subsequently demolished the upper flats and re-roofed the property at a lower level and there is any risk of the gable becoming dangerous, the purchaser should keep in view as an element in the value of the property purchased that he may become liable for one-half of the cost of demolition of the gable or the upper part of it which is no longer in use on his side.[77]

15–32   **(ii) Division walls or fences.** At the stage of adjustment of missives a purchaser is normally concerned to know (a) that the division walls, fences or hedges which separate the property from adjoining properties are mutual, being erected to the extent of one-half of their breadth on each of the adjacent properties and (b) that there are no outstanding obligations in respect of their erection and repair and maintenance. If a wall or fence has been erected wholly on the adjoining property it is not common property[78] and may be increased in height or altered by

---

[74] *Houldsworth* v. *Gordon Cumming*, 1910 S.C. (H.L.) 49, 55.
[75] *Earl of Ancaster* v. *Doig*, 1960 S.C. 203.
[76] See Burns, 171, 172.
[77] *Trades House of Glasgow* v. *Ferguson*, 1979 S.L.T. 187.
[78] *Hetherington* v. *Galt* (1905) 7 F. 706; *Griffin* v. *Watson*, 1962 S.L.T. (Sh.Ct.) 74.

the adjoining proprietor, possibly with a detrimental effect on the property which is being purchased. If the boundary walls or fences are mutual, the obligation of paying one-half of the cost of their maintenance will usually have been imposed as a real burden upon both adjacent properties. So an offer to purchase should include a provision that the boundary walls and fences (except so far as fronting upon the road or street) are mutual and there are no outstanding obligations for their erection or repair or maintenance.

15–33 **(iii) Sea.** If the subjects of purchase are bounded on any side by the sea or a tidal and navigable river the purchaser may be concerned at the stage of adjusting the contract of sale to inquire whether the foreshore, *i.e.* the land between the high and low water marks of ordinary spring tides,[79] is included or excluded. The ownership of the foreshore may be of considerable financial importance if the removal of sand or gravel[80] or the construction of works for the purpose of industrial operations[81] is contemplated.

15–34 **(iv) Rivers, lochs and fishings.** If the subjects of purchase contain or are bounded by a river the acquisition of the lands will normally include the right of trout-fishing, which is a privilege of the riparian proprietor,[82] but not salmon-fishings, which form a separate feudal estate. If salmon fishings are to be included they should be specified with particulars of their location and extent, whether the rights are exclusive or shared,[83] and any necessary rights of access. Where the subjects are bounded by a loch the location of the line of the boundary, the right to the *solum* and the rights of fishing, whether exclusive or shared, should be investigated and preferably specified in the contract.[84]

(e) Fixtures and fittings

5–35 Fixtures are part of the heritable property and in the absence of special stipulation will pass to the purchaser on a sale of the heritage; fittings are moveable and may be removed by the seller unless otherwise provided in the contract of sale.[85] Whether a particular article is heritable or moveable depends upon the degree of physical attachment, but an item not permanently attached or not attached at all may be heritable if it is essential or material to the use of the heritage or has been specially adapted to it so that it has a special value which it would not have elsewhere.[86] Even when an article has become

---

[79] Bell, *Prin.*, s. 641; *Lord Advocate* v. *Lord Blantyre* (1879) 6 R. (H.L.) 72.
[80] *Agnew* v. *Lord Advocate* (1873) 11 M. 309.
[81] *Luss Estates Co.* v. *B.P. Oil Grangemouth Refinery Ltd.*, 1982 S.L.T. 457.
[82] *Earl of Galloway* v. *Duke of Bedford* (1902) 4 F. 851 (but they may have been let—see para. 15–54).
[83] *Fothringham* v. *Passmore*, 1983 S.L.T. 444, 1984 S.L.T. 401.
[84] *Scott* v. *Lord Napier* (1869) 7 M. (H.L.) 35; *Stewart's Trs.* v. *Robertson* (1874) 1 R. 334; *Meacher* v. *Blair-Oliphant*, 1913 S.C. 417.
[85] *Jamieson* v. *Welsh* (1900) 3 F. 176.
[86] *Dowall* v. *Miln* (1874) 1 R. 1180.

a fixture on the criterion of physical attachment it may be removed on a sale if the object of attaching it was the use or enjoyment of the article and not the improvement of the heritage, *e.g.* trade fixtures.[87, 88] The moral for a purchaser of heritable property is clear; if there could be doubt whether any item which is to be included in the purchase is heritable or moveable, specify it particularly as comprehended in the purchase. Likewise the seller, if he wishes to remove any item which might be heritable, should specifically exclude it from the sale.

15-36   Particular items which may merit special stipulation are listed below, with indications of their classification as heritable or moveable, but much depends upon the degree of attachment which can vary in different properties. Some items have been the subject of judicial decision: the classification of others is based upon normal practice.

15-37   **(i) Dwelling-houses**

Electrical system including meter and wiring to the bulb-holder in the case of lights or to the wall socket in the case of electrical apparatus	Heritable
Electric light bulbs, shades, bowls and chandeliers and electric fires, cookers, washing machine, refrigerator, deep freeze, dishwasher and other electrical apparatus installed for use	Moveable
Electrical central or off-peak heating system including radiators	Heritable
Gas meter and piping	Heritable
Gas brackets and lights,[89] gas fires and cookers	Moveable
Gas or oil-fired central heating system	Heritable but radiators or panels may be moveable
Tiled hearths[89] and fixed fenders, mantels and overmantels	Heritable
Grates[89]	Moveable
Built-in fitted cupboards, cabinets or wardrobes and fitted shelving therein	Heritable

---

[87] *Dowall* v. *Miln, supra*; *Edinburgh and Leith Gas Commissioners* v. *Smart*, 1918 1 S.L.T. 80.
[88] As to what are fixtures or fittings in different relationships of parties see Walker, *Prin.*, III, 11–16. As to industrial plant see full review of authorities in *Scottish Discount Co. Ltd.* v. *Blin*, 1986 S.L.T. 123.
[89] *Nisbet* v. *Mitchell-Innes* (1880) 7 R. 575; *Jamieson* v. *Welsh, supra*.

Built-in kitchen units	Heritable
Mirrors and picture rods[89]	Moveable
Curtains, pelmets, curtain rails or rods and window blinds	Moveable
Waste disposal unit	Moveable
Fitted bathroom units	Heritable, but articles screwed on such as towel rails or mirrors are moveable
Carpets, whether fitted or not, linoleum and other floor coverings, stair rods and runners	Moveable
Keys[90]	Heritable
Pictures, even when inserted as a panel in the wall of a room[91]	Moveable
Television aerials	Moveable

5–38 **(ii) Gardens**

Greenhouses, garden huts or sheds	Heritable or moveable according to nature of construction and degree of attachment[92]
Wire fencing[93]	Heritable
Growing trees, shrubs,[94] vegetables and flowers—but not flowers in pots although sunk in the earth[89]	Heritable
Gravel on paths and turf[94]	Heritable

5–39 **(iii) Commercial or industrial property.** In property of this nature the primary criterion remains the degree of physical attachment, whether the article can be removed without damage to itself or the heritage, but the element of intention is also important, namely, whether the object of installation of the article was its use for the business carried on in the premises or the enhancement of the heritage itself. For illustrative cases see the authorities cited,[95] although it should be kept in view that

---

[90] See *Fisher* v. *Dixon* (1845) 4 Bell's App. 286.
[91] *Cochrane* v. *Stevenson* (1891) 18 R. 1208.
[92] *Christie* v. *Smith's Exrx.*, 1949 S.C. 572.
[93] *Graham* v. *Lamont* (1875) 2 R. 438.
[94] *Burns* v. *Fleming* (1880) 8 R. 226.
[95] *Fisher* v. *Dixon, supra; Syme* v. *Harvey* (1861) 24 D. 202; *Dowall* v. *Miln, supra; Brand's Trs.* v. *Brand's Trs.* (1876) 3 R. (H.L.) 16; *Scottish Discount Co. Ltd.* v. *Blin, supra*; Walker, *Prin.*, III, 14–16; Gloag and Henderson, 556–560; Amos and Ferrard on *Fixtures*; Adkin and Bowen, *Law relating to Fixtures*.

the decisions may be affected by the relationship of the parties between whom the issue arises. If the purchaser intends to continue the business carried on by the seller and wishes to acquire any plant, machinery or other items, whether heritable or moveable, an inventory of all the principal items should be prepared and it should be made clear whether they are to be included along with the heritage in a total price or whether they should be acquired separately at a price stated or determined by valuation. Even if the purchaser intends to use the premises for a different business the same policy should be followed as regards equipment and articles in service areas, *e.g.* canteens and toilets.

15–40   **(iv) Agricultural subjects.** Where a farm is being purchased with vacant possession the offer should specify the whole fixtures in and upon it and all fixed plant and machinery and all live and dead stock, dung and implements as detailed in an inventory or as specified in particulars of the property as prepared by the seller. Dung made on the farm is heritable.[96] So also are growing crops[97] and standing timber.[98] As regards timber, inquiry should be made whether it is subject to a forestry dedication agreement which, when recorded in the Register of Sasines or entered on the title sheet of registered land, is enforceable against a purchaser.[99] If a farm is purchased subject to an existing tenancy the lease should be examined in order to ascertain the provisions with regard to landlord's and tenant's fixtures and the rights therein of parties on the termination of the tenancy. See further, paragraphs 15–130 to 15–133.

(f) Pertinents

15–41   An offer to purchase heritable property should add to the description, "with the parts, privileges and pertinents thereof." A clause of pertinents may carry rights in[1] and property of[2] subjects which do not expressly fall within the description of the property conveyed. In particular, where the principal subject is a flat, the clause of pertinents may comprehend ownership of or common rights in cellars or outhouses not specifically mentioned in the description which have been occupied exclusively or in common during the period of positive prescription.

(g) Common or mutual rights

15–42   It is recommended that an offer to purchase should also include a reference to common or mutual rights, *e.g.* "together with all rights

---

[96] *Reid's Exrs.* v. *Reid* (1890) 17 R. 519 (a case between heir and executor).
[97] *Chalmers' Tr.* v. *Dick's Tr.*, 1909 S.C. 761.
[98] *Munro* v. *Liquidator of Balnagown Estates Co. Ltd.*, 1949 S.C. 49.
[99] Forestry Act 1967, s. 5.
[1] *Meacher* v. *Blair-Oliphant*, 1913 S.C. 417.
[2] *Cooper's Trs.* v. *Stark's Trs.* (1898) 25 R. 1160.

exclusive, common, mutual and others pertaining thereto," which will be followed by a clause of pertinents as suggested in paragraph 15–41. This is an *omnium gatherum* provision which may comprehend a variety of rights, whether common, mutual or otherwise. The clause, however, will embrace only rights which pertain to the property as disclosed on subsequent examination of the title deeds and will not include privileges apparently enjoyed, possibly by informal agreement, but not effectively created as rights in law. Accordingly, if any right apparently enjoyed is of importance to the purchaser it should be particularly specified in addition to the general comprehensive provision.[3]

5–43 If the subject of purchase is a flat in a building or tenement, further provision may be advisable. The title deeds of flatted property frequently contain stipulations that the *solum*, foundations, roof, outer walls or gables (in the case of mutual gables one-half thereof) and common parts of the building are the common property of the proprietors of the flats in the building, the cost of maintenance thereof being shared by all in stated proportions. If the title deeds make no provision on that matter, however, the common law of the tenement applies, with the result that the walls are the exclusive property of the owner of the flat which they enclose and the roof is the property of the owners of the topmost flat or flats, each proprietor being responsible for the maintenance and repair of the parts of the walls or roof owned by him and the proprietors of the remaining flats having a common interest to require that they be maintained so far as reasonably necessary for the support of the upper flats and as a cover for the lower flats.[4] Since repairs to a roof are likely to prove an onerous responsibility the purchaser of a top flat will wish to be assured that the cost of maintenance of the roof is borne by all the proprietors and the purchaser of a lower flat may not wish to incur sole liability for remedying a major defect in the main structure which may happen to occur in a part of it owned by him. In these circumstances a clause may be inserted on the following lines:

> There will be conveyed to the purchaser a right of property in common with the proprietors of other flats in the said building to the roof, main walls, *solum*, entrance, stairways and all other common parts of the said building. The purchaser will be liable for an equitable share of the cost of maintenance, repair, insurance and management of the said common parts and each of the remaining flats (and/or shops) in the said building have been or will be validly burdened with the like obligation.[5]

---

[3] *e.g.* a right of common access or the use of a common parking area—see para. 15–47.

[4] Stair, II, vii, 6; *Smith* v. *Giuliani*, 1925 S.C. (H.L.) 45, 56; *Wells* v. *New House Purchasers Ltd.*, 1964 S.L.T. (Sh.Ct.) 2.

[5] As to the need for the last part of this clause see *Duncan* v. *Church of Scotland General Trs.*, 1941 S.C. 145.

If no such obligations are imposed in the title deeds the seller's acceptance will be qualified appropriately, but the purchaser will have the opportunity of amending the price offered to allow for any contingently greater expenditure on maintenance.

(h) Roads, streets or lanes and footpaths and sewers

15–44   A purchaser is concerned to know whether any road, street or lane and footpath bounding the property and the sewers therein are maintained by the relevant local authority. A condition of offer might be: "The road(s), lane(s), footpath(s) and sewer(s) *ex adverso* and serving the said subjects are maintained by the relevant public authority." It is also in the interests of the purchaser to know whether there are any proposals which will affect the roads or streets, *e.g.* widening of the thoroughfare, which may adversely affect the amenity of the property. That matter will be covered by the general condition regarding notices or proposals under the Town and Country Planning Acts or other statutes which would adversely affect the property.[6]

15–45   In new developments the selling builder normally undertakes responsibility for completing and surfacing the roads, but for practical reasons that work is only completed after houses have been built and sold. Until recently purchasers might have been exposed to the risk of insolvency of the builder before the roads were completed, and safeguards against such a contingency sometimes took the form of a road bond or other financial guarantee that the roads and footpaths would be completed by the builder to the standard required by the roads authority. The Roads (Scotland) Act 1984 and related regulations[6a] now provide that no building works by a private builder shall commence until consent for construction of a road or extension of a road has been obtained from the local roads authority and security for the cost of its construction in the form of a bond or deposit has been lodged with the authority.

15–46   The modern practice is to include in the conveyance to the purchaser the footpaths and, to the extent of one-half of their width, the roads and lanes *ex adverso* the property, subject to the burden of rights of passage and use for the benefit of other properties or the public. If that course is not adopted and the boundary of the property conveyed excludes the street or lane—as "bounded by" the street or lane normally would[7]—the frontagers would usually have a right of common interest therein which would enable them to enforce a right of

---

[6] See para. 15–136, style 15A, cl. 10.
[6a] s. 17(2); Security for Private Road Works (Scotland) Regulations 1985 (S.I. 1985 No. 2080), applicable from April 1, 1986.
[7] *Louttit's Trs.* v. *Highland Rly. Co.* (1892) 19 R. 791.

continuing use for access.[8] The advantage of a conveyance of the *solum* of the street or lane to the frontagers is that if at some future time the line of the street or lane is altered and it is desired to build over it or use it for some other purpose it may be impossible to trace the developer who had retained title to it or he might seek payment for a conveyance of it. If the *solum* has been made the property of the frontagers it would be necessary to obtain a waiver or discharge of the original burden restricting its use for passage but that could be achieved either by agreement of the parties interested to enforce the burden or, in a proper case, by application to the Lands Tribunal for Scotland under section 1 of the Conveyancing and Feudal Reform (Scotland) Act 1970. The plan of the development may indicate that each plot includes the one-half of the street or lane, but if not, or if the plan is not available when missives are being adjusted, the purchaser should stipulate that the road(s) or street(s) and lane(s) *ex adverso* the property will be included to the extent of one-half of their breadth in the conveyance to him.

(i) Accesses and common areas

5–47   Where a driveway or other access from the street or road is not situated wholly within the subjects of purchase, or where there is a common driveway and/or parking area used by the proprietor of the subjects and the proprietor of an adjacent property, it is advisable to stipulate in the offer that valid rights of access and use of and over (specified), all as at present used by the seller, will be conveyed. Uses of parts of adjoining property may have been constituted by informal agreements not enforceable by or binding upon singular successors.[9]

(j) Services

5–48   Electricity and gas supplies are almost always from the public supply, but water supply and sewage disposal may be private or special and may require attention at the adjustment of missives of sale.

5–49   If the property is in a rural area and is not connected to a public water supply it should be ascertained whether the loch, private reservoir, stream, spring or well from which water is drawn is situated within the ground purchased and, if not, that there are valid servitude or other rights to a permanent and sufficient supply. In either case it may be desirable to stipulate that the reservoir, pipes, pumps and other apparatus relating to the supply of water are in good working order and that, if they are situated outwith the subjects purchased, there are rights of access for maintenance. Where the source of supply

---

[8] *Argyllshire Commissioners* v. *Campbell* (1885) 12 R. 1255, 1261; *Boyd* v. *Hamilton*, 1907 S.C. 912. See I. W. Noble, "An Urban Lane" (1982) J.L.S. W. 259.

[9] See *Brown* v. *Baty*, 1957 S.C. 351.

is not situated within the subjects purchased it should be kept in view that superior heritors who share the supply may in dry weather exhaust the supply and also that other consumers may be introduced subsequently with a similar result.[10] Suggested provisions in offers to purchase, adjusted where appropriate to special circumstances, might be: (i) (where the source of supply and all pipes and connections are situated within the subjects of purchase) "There is a private water supply which will be ample at all times for the existing usage of the subjects purchased, and the source thereof and all pipes and works are situated within the said subjects and are in good working order and condition," or (ii) (where the source of supply or any connections or works are not situated wholly within the subjects of purchase) "There will be conveyed to the purchaser valid rights to a supply of water which will be ample at all times for the existing usage of the subjects of purchase, with all necessary rights of access for the maintenance and repair of all works and connections relating thereto, which works and connections are in good working order and condition." If the subjects are being purchased for industrial use and continuance of the water supply is essential to the operations contemplated it may be desirable to make more detailed specification, *e.g.* to stipulate for a minimum supply of a stated volume of water per day.

15–50   Similar problems apply to a private system of drainage and sewage disposal, *e.g.* by septic tank. If the connections to the tank, the tank itself and the outfall therefrom are all situated within the subjects of purchase a condition that the whole system is in good working order and condition may suffice. On the other hand if any parts of the system or outfall are located outwith the subjects of purchase it will be necessary to stipulate also that valid rights to a continuance of the system and all necessary rights of access for maintenance will be conveyed.

(k) Goodwill

15–51   It has not been determined as an abstract proposition that the goodwill of licensed premises, such as a public house or hotel, is wholly heritable,[11] but the general trend of decisions of the courts favours that conclusion[12] in most circumstances. In other types of retail business, such as shops and garages, the position is much more doubtful, the test being whether the goodwill is derived from the situation of the premises or the personality and business expertise of the owner. It is clear that when an offer is being made for a property in which a business is carried on and it is intended that the goodwill of the business should be

---

[10] *Scottish Highland Distillery Co.* v. *Reid* (1877) 4 R. 1118; *McNab* v. *Robertson* (1896) 24 R. (H.L.) 34; *Crichton* v. *Turnbull*, 1946 S.C. 52.
[11] *Leishman* v. *Glen & Henderson* (1899) 6 S.L.T. 328.
[12] *Ross* v. *Ross's Trs.* (1901) 9 S.L.T. 340; *Town and County Bank* v. *McBain* (1902) 9 S.L.T. 485; *Graham* v. *Graham's Trs.* (1904) 6 F. 1015; *Muirhead's Trs.* v. *Muirhead* (1905) 7 F. 496.

included in the sale the goodwill should be separately specified in the offer. The purchase of licensed premises with the goodwill of the business carried on therein will normally be a transfer of business to which the Transfer of Undertakings (Protection of Employment) Regulations 1981[12a] apply and special provision as to the employees may require consideration.[12b]

(l) Property subject to tenancies

5–52 **(i) Dwelling-houses.** An offer to purchase a block of let dwelling-houses should specify the address of the block, the number and size of the dwelling-houses contained therein, a statement of the recoverable rentals and whether the tenancies are regulated or statutory or otherwise.[13] It should be stipulated that none of the rents exceeds any statutory rent limit,[14] that all rent agreements are in writing and are legally enforceable[15] and that the seller will not agree to any change in the rents or conditions of tenancy before the date of entry except with the approval of the purchaser.

5–53 **(ii) Commercial or industrial property.** An offer for the purchase of commercial or industrial property which is subject to leases should specify the various offices or buildings which are the subject of tenancies and their respective floor areas, the leases should be scheduled to the offer and it should be confirmed that there are no sub-leases or subsidiary rights of occupation. To guard against the existence of conditions unduly favourable to tenants the offer should require production of all leases and sub-leases (if any) by the seller within a stated period and the purchaser should reserve the right to resile from the offer within a specified time after such production if the leases or sub-leases or any of them contain provisions which are unacceptable to the purchaser. (The provisions of the leases with which the purchaser will be principally concerned are period, rent and rent reviews, restrictions on use, tenant's obligations as to repair and rebuilding, insurance, irritancy and rights of parties on termination.) For these and other specialities see the undernoted style.[16] Where the purchase is of a long lease and numerous long sub-leases or sub-tenancies have been granted a stipulation should be inserted that the head lease (if not already examined by the purchaser) does not contain provisions unacceptable to the purchaser, that none of the sub-leases or sub-tenancies contravene the provisions of the head lease, and that any consents or variations of them have been disclosed to the purchaser.

[12a] S.I. 1981 No. 1794.

[12b] See Vol. I, para. 8–32.

[13] The former controlled tenancies are now regulated tenancies—Tenants' Rights, Etc. (Scotland) Act 1980, s. 46.

[14] Rent (Scotland) Act 1984, s. 28.

[15] *e.g.* if entered into after January 1, 1973, they comply with the requirements of the Housing (Financial Provisions) (Scotland) Act 1972, s. 42 as amended.

[16] Style 15D, para. 15–139.

15–54   **(iii) Landed estate.** A contract of sale of a landed estate may comprise several categories of property, *e.g.* the principal house, gardens and policies of which vacant possession is being given, the superiority of parts of the estate which have been feued, let farms or houses, etc. The total area should be stated, preferably by reference to a map or plan.[17] The map should indicate the various categories above mentioned, the amounts of the unredeemed feuduties still payable should be stated in a schedule and the leases or tenancy agreements of let subjects should also be specified in a schedule with particulars of the rents receivable. As to let farms see paragraph 15–132 and as to apportionment of rents see paragraph 15–114. The contents of the contract of sale will vary according to the nature of the estate but, where appropriate, the following may require suitable provision: (1) standing timber and dedication agreements under the Forestry Acts 1947 and 1967, (2) salmon fishings (which should be separately specified), (3) sporting leases for shooting or trout fishing (the latter if for not less than a year are now binding on a purchaser[17a]), (4) repayable improvement grants in respect of buildings on the estate, (5) ancient monuments under the Ancient Monuments and Archaeological Areas Act 1979, (6) buildings of architectural or historic interest or areas of special scientific interest, (7) conservation areas, (8) access agreements under Part II of the Countryside (Scotland) Act 1967, and (9) private water supply or drainage systems. If the estate business involves the employment of any person the provisions of the Transfer of Undertakings (Protection of Employment) Regulations 1981 should be considered.[17b]

(m) Licensed premises

15–55   The description of a public house or hotel should contain in addition to the name and postal address any relative ground, including any discontiguous parts such as parking areas, all fixtures and fittings, the goodwill, and the pertinents. Moveable furnishings, equipment, glassware and utensils to be included in the purchase should be detailed in an inventory. Wet and dry stocks will be purchased at wholesale prices and should include only items normally sold or (to allow for old stock) realisable value if less, the amount to be agreed between the parties or determined by a valuer acting as an expert and to be paid within a short period after the amount is so agreed or determined. The contract will be conditional upon transfer of the licence and the purchaser will be entitled to resile if the transfer of the licence is not obtained. When the sale is made between the dates of sittings of the licensing board provision may be made for consignation of a substantial part of the price upon entry, the existing licence holder as agent for the

---

[17] See para. 15–30.
[17a] Freshwater and Salmon Fisheries (Scotland) Act 1976, s. 4.
[17b] See Vol. I, para. 8–32.

purchaser continuing to be responsible for ensuring that the management of the premises by the purchaser complies with statutory requirements for the conduct of licensed premises during the interim period until the licence is transferred. As to other matters relating to transfer of the business and compliance with statutory requirements see the undernoted style and notes thereto.[18]

(n) Minerals

15–56 When land is purchased with a view to exploitation of minerals therein the principal legal matters requiring attention are: (1) description of the area purchased by reference to map or plan, (2) if any part of the land purchased has been feued or leased that the minerals have been reserved with acceptable provisions as to rights to withdraw support both vertical and lateral and that the provisions as to compensation for subsidence damage are acceptable, (3) rights of access or wayleave over any adjoining lands to the nearest public road, (4) the offer being made conditional on planning permission for the mineral development being obtained on terms acceptable to the purchaser.

15–57 In a purchase of the surface or buildings thereon the minerals will be included unless otherwise provided, on the *a coelo usque ad centrum* principle.[19] Frequently minerals will have been reserved to the superior in the original feu grant so that it is usual to provide in contracts of sale of the *dominium utile* that the minerals are included in the sale only so far as belonging to the seller. This provision may be inadequate if (a) the minerals have been reserved with right to enter upon the surface even although compensation is payable, or (b) a right to withdraw support has been reserved without compensation or with a right to compensation which is unduly restricted.[20] The seller should examine the terms of any mineral reservation clause in his title deeds and qualify his acceptance by reference to it, furnishing the relevant deed to the solicitor for the purchaser so that he may advise his client as to acceptance of the title provision.

(o) Feus

15–58 Where the offer is in respect of land to be feued the seller will usually furnish a *pro forma* style of feu grant and the offer will identify the particular feu and state the price and date of entry, and will refer to the style for other conditions with such modifications as may be sought by the prospective feuar in the particular case and as may be acceptable to the prospective superior. It is not permissible to impose a feuduty.[21]

---

[18] Style 15C, para. 15–138.
[19] *Whyte* v. *Lee* (1879) 6 R. 699; *Campbell* v. *McCutcheon*, 1963 S.C. 505.
[20] See para. 21–44.
[21] Land Tenure Reform (Scotland) Act 1974, s. 1.

In a situation where the purchaser is buying property in a new development and the developer has erected buildings and is granting a feu, the purchaser should stipulate that the developer will deliver at settlement a certificate that the whole buildings, fences and roads as completed satisfy the conditions of the feu grant. Ownership of the superiority may change, as where the developer sells to a third party or is sequestrated, and the purchaser should be protected against claims by the new superior for implement of the building conditions of the feu. It may be impracticable to include the roads in the certificate if they have not been completed at the date of settlement—as to that matter see para. 15–45.

(p) Leases

15–59   Where the offer is to take property on lease the proprietor will usually have a standard or *pro forma* style of lease or tenancy agreement which will be furnished to the offerer. The offer will refer to the style for the general conditions of the tenancy and will be specific on matters peculiar to the particular subjects, such as identification of them and of any special or common rights, or negotiable items such as the period, rent, rent reviews, permitted use, obligations as to maintenance and/or renewal or rebuilding, irritancy provisions and rights on termination. The negotiable items will vary according to the nature of the subject, whether residential, commercial, industrial or agricultural and are considered more fully in Volume III. In negotiations for a lease the details of the principal document of title, the proposed lease or tenancy agreement, are adjusted at the stage of missives, which may result in protracted correspondence before a binding contract is concluded, but in this type of transaction the risk of competing offers is usually less and it is preferable that agreement in detail be reached before the parties are contractually bound. If the subjects lie in an operational area for the purposes of registration of title the grant of a long lease will induce first registration and a clause as to title and production of documents to enable a land certificate to be issued should be included in the offer (see R.T.P.B. para. G.2.08).

Where the offer is to purchase an existing lease it should be stipulated that (i) any necessary consents to assignation or any change of use contemplated by the purchaser will be procured by the seller, and (ii) all the obligations of the tenant prestable up to the date of entry have been duly implemented. Where the purchase is of an existing sub-lease it will be necessary to stipulate also that there have been no contraventions of the conditions of the head lease.

Survey

15–60   Whether a purchaser should instruct a survey of the property before submitting an offer, or alternatively insert a condition in the offer that it is subject to a satisfactory survey, is a matter for his own decision. It is suggested that a solicitor, if consulted on the matter, should always advise that a professional survey be obtained: the cost of a survey, even a full structural survey, is relatively small in relation to the expenditure that may subsequently be incurred in remedying serious defects. A private valuation and survey will also be of assistance in assessing the price to be offered in a situation where there may be competitive offers.

5-61 A private valuation and report will found a claim for damages for professional negligence against the surveyor but only in respect of defects which his report should have disclosed. The liability of the surveyor thus depends upon the scope and extent of the survey instructed and may be limited by qualifications embodied in the report. The most satisfactory form of private valuation includes a full structural survey, but that normally requires the employment of both a surveyor and tradesmen, may need the co-operation of the seller in permitting removal of floor boards or other coverings and is costly. Nevertheless it may be advisable, particularly where the building is of substantial value and of considerable age and a defective damp course, concealed dry rot, old electrical wiring or water pipes or deterioration of slates or leadwork of the roof may not be evident on inspection and may be expensive to remedy. For most properties, however, it is sufficient to instruct a private valuation and survey which covers all matters which are evident on a careful visual inspection and examination; there will usually be indications of any serious latent defects which will lead an experienced professional surveyor to recommend a more detailed structural examination of suspected areas which he has been unable to investigate. There is a standard form of R.I.C.S. House Buyers Report and Valuation which may be instructed by prospective purchasers of residential property. Clearly anything less than a full structural survey involves some risk to the purchaser, but in a practical situation where a report is required quickly for the purpose of making an offer the less full and less costly type of report may be all that is possible and affords some safeguard.

5-62 It is inadvisable for a purchaser/borrower to rely upon a valuation/report instructed by the building society or other lender. There is no contractual relationship between the surveyor and the borrower and, although there may now be a duty of care owed by the surveyor to the borrower who he knows may rely upon his report,[22] at least when, as now sometimes happens, the report is disclosed by the building society to the borrower, he has no knowledge or control of the scope or extent of the survey instructed by the lender.

---

[22] *Hedley Byrne & Co.* v. *Heller & Partners* [1964] A.C. 465, 2 All E.R. 575; *Yianni* v. *Edwin Evans & Sons* [1982] Q.B. 438.

III. *Price*

Price—statement or ascertainment

15–63   An agreement on price or upon a method of ascertaining it, *e.g.* by arbitration, is an essential constituent of an enforceable contract of sale.[23] If the price is to be determined by formal arbitration, the award must be in formal and probative writing.[24]

Date of payment

15–64   The usual condition of contract is that the price will be payable on the date of entry in exchange for a valid conveyance or lease and the delivery or exhibition of a good marketable title. There may be provision for a deposit on completion of the missives or for payment by instalments or for a retention of part of the price in respect of works to be completed by the seller or to cover some contingency. In the ordinary case where payment is due on the date of entry the seller cannot require payment on that date if, without fault on the part of the purchaser or his solicitor, the seller is unable to tender a valid conveyance or lease and the purchaser has not entered into possession.[25]

Interest—consignation

15–65   If the price is not paid, in whole or in part, on the pactional date but the purchaser is permitted to take possession of the property, interest is payable on the price so far as not paid from the date of entry by the purchaser until payment.[26] The rate of interest payable, in the absence of any contractual provision on the matter, is the rate of interest currently payable on securities over heritable property of the kind purchased, since the seller in effect has security over the subjects until delivery of a conveyance which will be made only in exchange for payment of the full price. The missives may make provision for payment of interest at a stipulated rate.

15–66   If the purchaser is permitted to enter into possession on the pactional date of entry without making full payment of the price, as where the seller is not at that date able to implement his obligations of delivery of a conveyance or the production of a valid title, he may consign the price on deposit receipt in joint names of both parties or their solicitors and interest on the deposited sum is payable only at the rate earned on the consigned money.[27] Consignation of the price must be in a form

---

[23] Gloag, *Contract*, 40; Walker, *Prin.*, III, 295.
[24] *McLaren* v. *Aikman*, 1939 S.C. 222.
[25] *Bowie* v. *Semple's Exrs.*, 1978 S.L.T. (Sh.Ct.) 9.
[26] *Stirling and Dunfermline Rly. Co.* v. *Edinburgh and Glasgow Rly. Co.* (1857) 19 D. 598, 621; *Greenock Harbour Trs.* v. *Glasgow and South-Western Rly. Co.*, 1909 S.C. (H.L.) 49; *Aitken* v. *Hyslop*, 1977 S.L.T. (Notes) 50.
[27] *Prestwick Cinema Co.* v. *Gardiner*, 1951 S.C. 98.

which will give the seller or his agent a measure of control over it.[28] The right of a purchaser to obtain entry on consignation may be negatived by a condition to that effect in the contract of sale.

15–67   As to post-contractual arrangements regarding payments to account, consignation and liability for interest on the price arising from delays in effecting settlement, see Chapter 23 *infra*.

Apportionment of price

15–68   In a sale of heritable and moveable property for a single comprehensive price it is desirable that there should be agreement between the parties, preferably at the stage of adjustment of the missives, as to the apportionment of the price between the heritable and moveable elements and possibly between the different constituents of the latter such as stock, fittings and equipment. The apportionment may be of significance particularly in relation to taxation. Stamp duty is payable only on the conveyance of heritage and registration dues are based upon the price of the heritable property conveyed. Other possible taxation liabilities to be considered are capital gains tax, value added tax on stock and claw-back of capital allowances for the purposes of corporation tax or income tax. The interests of the seller and the purchaser may conflict and their respective tax advisers should be consulted. It may be impracticable for parties and their advisers to reach agreement on the matter within the time when the contract has to be concluded, in which case provision may be made for apportionment of the price to be agreed between the parties or, failing agreement, by an independent expert.

Time of payment of the price

15–69   In principle the price should be payable at the time when the purchaser enters into possession and enjoyment of the property purchased, but there may be circumstances such as the existence of a suspensive or resolutive condition in which payment or partial payment may be deferred until the condition is purified. There may also be retention of part of the price until the seller has completed works on, or remedied defects in, the property. Unless payment of the price on the pactional date is made an essential condition of the contract, failure by the purchaser to pay punctually on that date will not entitle the seller to rescind the contract.[29] It is necessary for the seller to provide specially that punctual payment on the agreed date is an essential condition if he wishes to be in a position to resile immediately upon failure by the purchaser to make payment promptly. In practice, however, such a provision is unusual, since upon rescission the seller

---

[28] *Grandison's Trs.* v. *Jardine* (1895) 22 R. 925.
[29] *Black* v. *Dick* (1814) Hume 699; *Burns* v. *Garscadden* (1901) 8 S.L.T. 321; *Rodger (Builders) Ltd.* v. *Fawdry*, 1950 S.C. 483, 492.

will still incur delay in re-advertising and re-selling. A more effective compulsitor can be imposed by providing for payment of interest at a realistic rate if payment is delayed, *e.g.*

> The purchaser shall not be entitled to require possession of the said subjects except upon payment in full of the said price on (*the contractual date of entry*) and consignation of the price will not be acceptable. In the event of failure by the purchaser to make payment on the said date in exchange for a valid disposition and delivery or exhibition of a good marketable title he will pay to the seller interest on the said price at the rate of   % per annum from said date until payment. If the purchaser fails to make payment of the price and interest as above stipulated within   (weeks) (months) after the said date he shall be in material breach of contract and the seller will be entitled to cancel the contract constituted by the offer of (*date*) and this acceptance and re-sell the subjects to any person. In such event the purchaser will be liable for all loss resulting from the re-sale including all expenses and outlays incurred by the seller or his agents with interest thereon at the said rate from the said date until the date of settlement of the re-sale.

A clause in those terms may not be acceptable to the purchaser, at least if the rate of interest stipulated is unduly high, but that may be negotiable. The principal value of such a clause is that it enables the seller to re-sell after a stated period and entitles him to interest at an acceptable rate in the meantime.

IV. *Entry and Possession*

Date of entry

15–70   The contract should specify the date of entry or contain provisions which enable it to be ascertained with precision, *e.g.* the date of an architect's certificate of practical completion or a certificate of fitness for occupancy by the local authority when the purchase is of a new house in course of construction, or the date of transfer of the liquor licence by the licensing board either at its next meeting or adjournment thereof or disposal of an appeal therefrom when the purchase is of licensed premises. If the date of entry is to be determined by an architect's certificate it must be clear that the certificate is granted for that purpose and not for some other purpose, and that the certificate of completion is not qualified with regard to work which has still to be carried out.[30]

15–71   There has been an apparent conflict of opinion on the question whether an agreed date of entry is an essential element before there

---

[30] *Sworn Securities Ltd.* v. *Chilcott*, 1977 S.C. 53.

can be a valid contract of sale of heritage.[31] An examination of the authorities cited leads to the conclusion that, even if a precise date of entry is not stated in the writings which constitute the contract of sale but actings of parties have followed from which a date of entry can be implied, a valid contract of sale exists with entry on the implied date which will normally be the date of settlement. Illustrations of such actings are possession following on a verbal contract of feu (*Smith* v. *Marshall*), ceding possession of land and preliminary steps in a project for building a hotel which implied that the date of entry would be the date of settlement (*Secretary of State for Scotland* v. *Ravenstone Securities Ltd.*), and the adjustment and averred execution of a Schedule A conveyance which implied entry at the next term of Whitsunday or Martinmas following its date in terms of section 28 of the Conveyancing (Scotland) Act 1874 (*Sloans Dairies Ltd.* v. *Glasgow Corporation*). On the other hand, in the absence of special circumstances such as subsequent actings of parties which enable a date of entry to be implied, the statement of Lord Maxwell in *Law* v. *Thomson* that in ordinary circumstances there must be an agreed date of entry before there can be a binding contract and that an agreement for a sale "sometime," with no agreed date of settlement from which a date of entry could be implied, is not an agreement which the law would normally recognise[32] seems sound, despite the criticism of it in *Stone* v. *Macdonald*.[33] The moral for solicitors is plain; a contract for sale of heritage should specify the date of entry or contain provisions which enable it to be ascertained as suggested in the preceding paragraph.

Time of the essence

15-72   Whether failure by the seller to give entry, and where stipulated vacant possession, on the contractual date affords a ground for the purchaser to resile is a question which will be determined by the court in the circumstances of the particular case. In certain older decisions rescission was allowed when the period was lengthy (three years)[34] or the property had been purchased for resale and entry was delayed for six months.[35] It is thought that in the ordinary case the attitude of the courts, in consonance with their practice in relation to delay in payment of the price[36] or in production of title,[37] would be to allow a reasonable time to give entry before determining that the contract could be

---

[31] Unnecessary: Montgomerie Bell, *Lectures*, 696; *Encyclopaedia*, Vol. 13, para. 376; *Smith* v. *Marshall* (1860) 22 D. 1158; *Secretary of State for Scotland* v. *Ravenstone Securities Ltd.*, 1976 S.C. 171, 189, 196, 197; *Sloans Dairies Ltd.* v. *Glasgow Corporation*, 1979 S.L.T. 17, 19; *Stone* v. *Macdonald*, 1979 S.C. 363, 369, 370. Contra: *Freeman* v. *Maxwell*, 1928 S.C. 682, 685; *Stobo* v. *Morrisons (Gowns) Ltd.*, 1949 S.C. 184, 194; *Law* v. *Thomson*, 1978 S.C. 343.
[32] *Law* v. *Thomson, supra* at p. 346.
[33] at 370.
[34] *Hunter* v. *Carsewell* (1822) 1 S. 248.
[35] *Kelman* v. *Barr's Tr.* (1878) 5 R. 816.
[36] See cases cited in para. 15-69.
[37] *Raeburn* v. *Baird* (1832) 10 S. 761.

terminated. It is not the usual practice, however, to provide in missives of sale that entry and possession on the agreed date are essential conditions of the bargain. Rescission is not a remedy which is of value to the purchaser since he will then have to find another property: if delay occurs in obtaining entry to the property which the purchaser has originally contracted to buy he can impose a reasonable time limit and meantime be seeking an alternative subject of purchase.

Vacant possession

15–73   If vacant possession is desired the offer should so stipulate. The existence of a tenancy of a house is not a breach of warrandice, even although the warrandice is not qualified by an exception of leases.[38] If the subjects are let and vacant possession is required by the purchaser a clause should be inserted in the offer providing that vacant possession shall be given on the date of entry and that the seller shall be bound to remove any tenant or occupant and to take all steps necessary for that purpose at the seller's expense so that the property will be unoccupied at the date of entry. Before accepting such a provision the seller will require to ensure that the tenant has no rights under a lease or tenancy agreement or under statutes such as the Rent Acts, the Agricultural Holdings (Scotland) Act 1949 or the Tenancy of Shops (Scotland) Acts 1949 and 1964 which may prevent or delay termination of the tenancy.

V. Title

15–74   The contract of sale will impose upon the seller in exchange for the price the obligation to deliver a formal deed in appropriate form (feu disposition, disposition, lease, assignation of lease) to give effect to the contract and to deliver or exhibit a valid marketable title and clear searches. As to a valid title and clear searches, see Chapter 21 *infra*. The forms of clauses imposing the obligation vary depending upon whether (a) the deed of conveyance to the purchaser is to be recorded in the Register of Sasines, or (b) the title of the purchaser is to be registered in the Land Register of Scotland.

(a) Register of Sasines

15–75   **Style of obligation.** If the disposition or other formal deed giving effect to the contract of sale is to be recorded in the Register of Sasines the form of the obligation may be:

> In exchange for the price the seller will deliver a duly executed Disposition (Feu Disposition) (Lease) (Assignation of Lease) in favour of the purchaser or his/her/its nominees and will deliver or exhibit a valid marketable title with clear searches in the Property Register for the period of 40 years prior to the date of acceptance

---

[38] *Lothian and Border Farmers Ltd.* v. *McCutchion*, 1952 S.L.T. 450.

hereof or for such lesser period as the purchaser may agree and in the Personal Register against all relevant interested parties for the period of 5 years prior to the date of acceptance hereof.

5–76 **Periods of search.** The period of positive prescription is now ten years, except where prescription is pled against the Crown in relation to an interest in foreshore or salmon fishings when the period is 20 years.[39] If a valid progress of titles is produced for a period of more than ten years, or more than 20 years for foreshore or salmon fishings, the title of the purchaser should be secure from challenge, but the possibility remains that an undischarged heritable security recorded outwith that period may still be an enforceable real burden if interest has continued to be paid.[40] For that reason it is prudent to stipulate in an offer for a 40-year search, but when the title deeds are examined it may be reasonably safe for the purchaser's solicitor to accept something less. It is essential that the search in the property register covers the period from the date of recording of the last deed of conveyance or notice of title[41] outwith the period of positive prescription, but if the earlier history of the title discloses that there has been a series of transactions for value involving several solicitors it is unlikely that the existence of a heritable security will have been overlooked by neglect and, since each successive proprietor on sale will have incurred liability in warrandice to procure a discharge of the security,[42] it is unlikely that the existence of a security will have been concealed by deliberate fraud. The use in an offer of a phrase such as "the prescriptive period" in relation to the search in the property register should be avoided: it may be construed as meaning only ten years.[43]

5–77 The personal search in the Register of Inhibitions and Adjudications will be for a period of five years back from the date of search, since the effect of the undernoted statutory provisions[44] is that any incumbrances or diligences not disclosed by a search for that period are no longer effective.

(b) Land Register of Scotland

5–78 **Sale transaction inducing first registration.** In circumstances where the sale transaction will induce first registration in the Land Register, as where the subjects (whether feudal or leasehold) are situated in an operational area, searches in the property and personal registers are no longer appropriate. Instead a Form 10 report will be issued by the

---

[39] Prescription and Limitation (Scotland) Act 1973, s. 1.
[40] See Burns, 301.
[41] Prescription and Limitation (Scotland) Act 1973, s. 5(1).
[42] *Briggs' Trs.* v. *Dalyell* (1851) 14 D. 173; *Horsbrugh's Trs.* v. *Welch* (1886) 14 R. 67.
[43] Burns, 180 (when the period of positive prescription was 20 years).
[44] Conveyancing (Scotland) Act 1924, s. 44; Bankruptcy (Scotland) Act 1913, s. 44. As regards sequestrations where the award of sequestration was made on or after April 1, 1986 see Bankruptcy (Scotland) Act 1985, s. 14.

Keeper on application and will cover the Register of Sasines, the Land Register and the Register of Inhibitions and Adjudications. It does not cover the Companies Register of Charges.[45] If subsequently it is desired to continue the report a further report up to a date nearer settlement can be obtained on Form 11. An appropriate style of a clause to be inserted in missives is provided in the *Registration of Title Practice Book*, para. G.2.08—for a detailed explanation of the provisions of the clause see the following paragraphs G.2.09–G.2.13.

15–79   Sale of interest already registered. In the case of a sale of subjects the title to which has already been registered in the Land Register the appropriate clause to be inserted in the missives differs since a land certificate will already exist. A style of clause for insertion in missives in such circumstances is suggested in the *Registration of Title Practice Book*, para. G.3.05, and its provisions are explained in paras. G.3.06 and G.3.07.

Companies

15–80   In addition to the clause requiring clear searches in the property and personal registers where the conveyance or deed is to be recorded in the Register of Sasines the missives should contain a provision for a search in the Companies Register of Charges and Company Files against any incorporated company which has had an interest in the subjects of sale during the period of positive prescription. For each company concerned the period of search in these registers should end, as regards the Register of Charges 22 days, and as regards the Company Files 16 days, after the cessation of the company's interest in the subjects. As to the reasons for selection of those periods see paragraph 21–87; as to the form of clause see the undernoted style.[46] Where registration of the purchaser's title is to be or has been made in the Land Register the answers to inquiries made by the Keeper[47] when a company is a party to the relevant deed creating or dealing with the interest and any subsequent investigations made by the Keeper may dispense with the need to make separate provision for searches in the Companies Register of Charges or the Company Files. As regards companies involved in earlier transactions the land certificate, when issued, will be conclusive of the validity of the purchaser's title.

Qualifications of seller's obligation as to title and searches

15–81   In new building developments the seller may proffer to the purchaser an offer to sell or purchase in a standard form which modifies, sometimes extensively, the obligations of the seller as to delivery of a

---

[45] See para. 15–80.
[46] Style 15C, cl. 16(a), para. 15–138.
[47] Form 1 (first registration), questions 4, 5 and 6; Form 2 (registration of a dealing), questions 2, 3 and 4; or Form 3 (registration of a transfer of part), questions 4, 5 and 6.

valid conveyance, exhibition of a good marketable title and provision of searches. Some of these qualifications are considered below, with suggestions as to how the purchaser and his solicitor should respond.

5–82 **(a) Payments to account or in full before delivery of deed of conveyance.** The standard form of offer may provide for a deposit on completion of the missives, or stage payments as the building work progresses, or payment of the price or the balance thereof upon issue of an architect's certificate of completion notwithstanding that the deed of conveyance is not yet available for delivery. Payment of an initial deposit of relatively small amount may be an acceptable condition, but substantial payments before delivery of the conveyance impose upon the purchaser the unacceptable risk that the seller may be unable to grant and deliver a conveyance by reason of inhibiting diligence or insolvency.[48] A solicitor acting for the purchaser should inform his client of the hazards involved and should advise against acceptance of such conditions. If the purchaser nevertheless agrees to accept them or has already completed missives including these conditions before consulting his solicitor, it is for consideration whether he should withhold the contractually-agreed payments until a conveyance is delivered: the remedy of rescission and damages for breach of contract followed by resale to another purchaser will seldom result in the seller receiving a price for the subjects more quickly than by executing and delivering a conveyance to the original purchaser, and the possible financial loss to the purchaser of incurring liability in damages for breach of contract may be much less than that which could result from making substantial payments and not receiving a conveyance.

5–83 **(b) Production of title deeds.** Numerous sales of individual plots in a building development pose practical difficulties since different solicitors for the purchasers may all require to examine the common writs within a short period. To expedite the conveyancing procedures the seller may stipulate, in cases where the conveyance to the purchaser is to be recorded in the Register of Sasines, that (a) the common writs will be available for examination only in the offices of the seller's solicitor or (b) the purchaser will accept copies of them as sufficient. The former stipulation may be accepted if not unduly inconvenient. The latter should not, since the copies may not disclose vitiations such as erasures in the principal deeds or the execution of them. Sasine extracts, however, are acceptable.[48a]

5–84 If the subjects of sale lie in an operational area for the purposes of registration of title, the seller's title will normally have been registered in the Land Register and the land certificate will have been deposited with the Keeper who will have issued a deposit reference number

---

[48] *Gibson and Hunter Home Designs Ltd.*, 1976 S.C. 23.
[48a] Conveyancing and Feudal Reform (Scotland) Act 1970, s. 45.

which can be quoted to purchasers. A purchaser may then quote the reference number in his application for registration instead of producing the land certificate. Office copies of the title sheet may be obtained by the seller and furnished to purchasers for preparation of the conveyance.[49]

15–85 **(c) Searches.** In cases where the deed of conveyance is to be recorded in the Register of Sasines, the seller's standard form of offer may provide that (a) no searches will be delivered or exhibited, or (b) no interim reports thereon will be furnished. If these provisions have been or have to be accepted it is the duty of the purchaser's solicitor to instruct a search and interim report at his client's expense. If the seller's title has been registered in the Land Register the form of offer may exclude exhibition of a Form 12 Report. In that event the purchaser should apply for it at his own expense.

15–86 **(d) Title as it stands.** If a seller, although he owns the property, fears that there may be technical defects in his title, a stipulation may be inserted in missives that the purchaser will accept the title as it stands. A provision in these terms will not oblige the purchaser to complete the transaction if the seller has no right of ownership of the subjects or if there are irremediable defects in the title which might render it reducible, but if there are curable defects in the title the expense of rectifying them will be borne by the purchaser.[50] The seller will remain liable for any insufficiency of stamp duty on any deeds in the title progress, since section 117 of the Stamp Act 1891 prohibits the insertion of any condition in a contract of sale which precludes the purchaser from objecting to the insufficiency or lack of stamp on a document forming a link in title. Nor does such a condition exempt the seller from his obligation to deliver or exhibit searches, although it may have a bearing on what constitutes a clear search.[51] If the sale induces a first registration in the Land Register and a defect in title results in exclusion of the subjects or any part of them from indemnity, it is thought that the purchaser would require to accept that unless the defect was one that could never be removed by the operation of positive prescription.

Pre-emption clauses

15–87 It is essential for the seller's solicitor, before a contract for sale is concluded, to check that the title deeds do not contain a clause of pre-emption which requires to be observed. The validity of such a clause, the persons obliged to observe its provisions or to enforce them, the nature of the transactions which may constitute a breach of the clause,

---

[49] R.T.P.B., para. D.3.09.
[50] *Carter* v. *Lornie* (1890) 18 R. 353.
[51] Burns, 182.

the statutory provisions relating to the time within which the right of pre-emption must be exercised and the relevant procedures are considered in paragraphs 17–68 to 17–79 *infra*.

15–88   An enforceable clause of pre-emption is inconvenient when a sale of the property is contemplated. The clause usually provides that before a proposed sale the seller must offer the property to the person having the right of pre-emption at the price offered by the prospective purchaser, although it is competent to state in the clause a fixed price[52] or a price to be determined by arbitration.[53] Hence the seller must keep a prospective purchaser waiting for up to 21 days before accepting his offer, during which time the offer may be withdrawn. It may be advisable to accept the offer subject to the right of pre-emption not being exercised, but that qualification requires acceptance by the prospective purchaser.

Often the solicitor for the party bound by the pre-emption provision will be aware from experience that the right is unlikely to be exercised and may be able to procure a declinature quickly, but the procedure of formal offer must be followed. If the existence of the right is overlooked and is discovered only after a contract of sale to a third party has been concluded, the solicitor for the seller may be in an awkward position. If the right has been created a real burden or is a continuing condition of a feu the contract of sale may be reduced, with possible liability to the purchaser in damages. On the other hand, if the right has not been created in a form which will make it enforceable against a singular successor the contract of sale may not be reducible but the seller may be liable in damages to the person in whose favour the right of pre-emption was created. If the right was to purchase at the highest amount offered, however, the damages in either case may not be substantial unless it can be demonstrated that the property was of special value to the purchaser or the person having the right of pre-emption, as the case may be.

Redemption clauses

5–89   A clause of redemption may entitle the superior or other person to purchase heritable property on his own initiative. The validity of such clauses and the statutory limitation of the time for which they may in certain cases be enforceable are considered in paragraph 17–80 *infra*. Clauses of redemption occur comparatively seldom in practice, but if an enforceable right of redemption exists the seller must have regard to its terms and arrange for its waiver before he concludes a bargain for the sale of the property to which it relates.

---

[52] *Preston* v. *Earl of Dundonald's Creditors* (1805) 3 R.L.C. 289.
[53] Burns, 223.

Burdens and conditions of title

15-90 **(a) Feuduty or ground annual.** If any feuduty or ground annual was exigible only from, or has been allocated upon, the subjects of sale then, if not already redeemed, it will become redeemable by the seller on the date of entry.[54] Redemption is not required, however, if the property is part of larger subjects burdened by a *cumulo* feuduty or ground annual which has not been allocated.[55] At the stage of making an offer the purchaser may be unaware of the position as to ground burdens and a stipulation may be inserted on the following lines:

> The subjects will be conveyed free of all pecuniary ground burdens and there will be exhibited before settlement and delivered at settlement either a redemption receipt in the form prescribed in Form 2 of Schedule 1 to the Land Tenure Reform (Scotland) Act 1974 or a duplicate of a notice of redemption in the form contained in Schedule 2 to the said Act with an appropriate acknowledgment endorsed thereon. In the case of the latter there will be delivered within one month after settlement of the transaction evidence that the person entitled to receive same has received payment of the feuduty or ground annual for the period up to the date of redemption and the redemption money.

A briefer version may be used: "Any feuduty [ground annual] or [standard charge] has been or will be redeemed by the seller and a receipt for the redemption payment will be exhibited at or prior to the date of entry or within one month thereafter."

If the property is burdened with an unallocated feuduty or ground annual and the seller does not propose to have it allocated and redeemed he will require to qualify his acceptance and the purchaser may then modify the price to take account of the burden.

15-91 **(b) Conditions of title—buildings.** It is not strictly necessary to insert in an offer a provision that the buildings conform to any relevant building conditions contained in the title deeds. If the existing buildings do not do so, then normally an irritancy will have been incurred and the title is not marketable. Minor disconformities such as small ancillary buildings not authorised by the title conditions may be acceptable in feudal subjects because if the superior seeks to irritate the court will normally allow the feuar an opportunity to purge the irritancy within a specified time.[56] The position is otherwise if the subject of purchase is leasehold property where an irritancy, once incurred, cannot be purged.[57] If the purchaser has any doubt and wishes to insert an express condition in his offer he may do so, *e.g.* "The whole buildings

---

[54] Land Tenure Reform (Scotland) Act 1974, s. 5.
[55] *Ibid.*, s. 5(12) applying s. 4(7).
[56] *Anderson* v. *Valentine*, 1957 S.L.T. 57.
[57] *McDouall's Trs.* v. *MacLeod*, 1949 S.C. 593; *Dorchester Studios (Glasgow) Ltd.* v. *Stone*, 1975 S.L.T. 153; *H.M.V. Fields Properties Ltd.* v. *Tandem Shoes Ltd.*, 1983 S.L.T. 114. But now the court has a discretion as to enforcing the irritancy—Law Reform (Miscellaneous Provisions) (Scotland) Act 1985, s. 5.

and erections on the subjects are in conformity with any relevant conditions in the title deeds."

15–92 (c) Conditions of title—use. It is usually advisable for the purchaser to include an express condition in his offer that the use, or proposed use if change of use is contemplated, is not in contravention of conditions of title. The existing use may constitute a breach of title conditions and the contravention may hitherto have been unnoticed by the superior; if a change of use by the purchaser is intended he will wish to be assured that there is no impediment to it in the title deeds. The matter is of particular importance where the subjects of purchase are leasehold, since commercial leases normally contain strict provisions as to permitted use and the landlord may seek to alter other provisions of the lease as a condition of consenting to the new use of the premises, e.g. he may seek to increase the rent to current level and so anticipate the next rent review date. An appropriate stipulation might be: "There are no conditions or restrictions in the title deeds or elsewhere which might prevent, restrict or render more expensive the development and/or use of the subjects as (specify proposed use)." As to the reason for insertion of the words "or elsewhere" see paragraph 15–103.

Servitudes

15–93 (a) Servitudes for the benefit of the subjects of purchase. If upon inspection of the subjects it appears that there are any rights enjoyed over property belonging to other persons the proper practice is to specify them particularly in the offer to purchase and to add a general phrase which will comprehend any servitude or other rights which may subsequently be found convenient for the enjoyment of the subjects but may not have been observed on inspection. Particular matters for inquiry relate to access, the use of common parking or service areas, private water supply and connecting pipes (*aquaehaustus* and aqueduct), drainage and sewage disposal, access over adjoining land for maintenance of gables or walls erected on the boundary and, in rural subjects, common grazings or pasturage and peat, fuel or divot.

15–94 (i) *Access.* The terms of the offer should cover identification of the particular access, the extent of permitted user, e.g. foot or vehicular passage,[58] and whether the use is restricted to particular purposes.[59] It may also be important to ascertain the parties responsible for maintenance and repair of the access. The obligation of the proprietor of the servient tenement consists only *in patiendo* and he has no obligation to maintain the access[60]; other persons may also have rights to use the access and there may have been different provisions, or no provisions at all, as to contribution to the costs of its maintenance. It is

---

[58] *Smith* v. *Saxton*, 1928 S.N. 59; *Crawford* v. *Lumsden*, 1951 S.L.T. (Notes) 62.
[59] *Carstairs* v. *Spence*, 1924 S.C. 380, 385.
[60] *Allan* v. *MacLachlan* (1900) 2 F. 699.

important to ensure by appropriate wording in the offer that, if there is an existing apparent use of an access, there is a valid legal right to that use; the use may simply be by way of privilege, or may rest upon a purported grant by or to a tenant under a long lease, the validity of which is doubtful,[61] or may be unenforceable if there has been an express grant of another access.[62] Suitable wording might be: "There will be conveyed to the purchaser an unrestricted right of access for pedestrian and vehicular passage to the subjects for all purposes by (specify). The cost of maintenance and repair of said access will be borne by all the users thereof in equitable proportions." If the seller cannot accept a provision in those terms he will require to qualify his acceptance, but the purchaser will know the position at a time when he is not yet contractually bound.

15–95   In circumstances where the purchaser contemplates greater use of the access than hitherto, as by change of use of the subjects or use of the access for adjoining property acquired or being acquired by him, it is important to ensure that the access will be available for the increased use because of the rule against increasing the burden of a servitude[63] and because a servitude right of access cannot be used to reach a property which was not originally a part of the dominant tenement. Specific provision should be inserted in the offer that the access will be available for the greater use proposed. The seller will normally be unable to accept such a provision, but it is preferable that the issue be raised at the missives stage when the seller, who may have a good relationship with the owner of the neighbouring servient tenement, will be anxious in the interests of procuring the sale to co-operate in seeking an enlargement of the servitude right.

15–96   (ii) *Common service areas.* The right to use common service areas, *e.g.* for parking or garaging, is usually created as a right of common property[64] rather than by way of servitude. If the right is in the nature of a servitude, provisions similar to those regarding access[65] as to specification, responsibility for maintenance and, if appropriate, increased user should be included in the offer.

15–97   (iii) *Water supply and pipes.* Where a water supply to the subjects is private and there are servitude rights to draw water from,[66] or to lead it through pipes situated in or on,[67] land belonging to other persons, the

---

[61] *Metcalfe* v. *Purdon* (1902) 4 F. 507; *Safeway Food Stores Ltd.* v. *Wellington Motor Co. (Ayr) Ltd.*, 1976 S.L.T. 53.
[62] *McEachen* v. *Lister*, 1976 S.L.T. (Sh.Ct.) 38.
[63] Ersk., II, ix, 4; Bell, *Prin.*, s. 988; *Mags. of Dunbar* v. *Sawers* (1829) 7 S. 672; *J. White & Sons* v. *J. & M. White* (1906) 8 F. (H.L.) 41; *Irvine Knitters Ltd.* v. *North Ayrshire Co-operative Society Ltd.*, 1978 S.C. 109.
[64] See para. 15–47.
[65] See para. 15–95.
[66] *Crichton* v. *Turnbull*, 1946 S.C. 52.
[67] *Robson* v. *Chalmers Property Investment Co. Ltd.*, 1965 S.L.T. 381; *Murray* v. *Medley*, 1973 S.L.T. (Sh.Ct.) 75; *More* v. *Boyle*, 1967 S.L.T. (Sh.Ct.) 38.

rights should be specified in the offer as included in the conveyance with provision as to access for and contributions to maintenance and, if greater usage is contemplated, provision as to the right to increase the use.

5–98 (iv) *Pasturage*. Frequently in rural areas there may be servitude rights of pasturing sheep or cattle, frequently in common with other members of a community.[68] The right and (if known) its extent, *i.e.* if limited as to the number of stock, should be specified in the offer, together with a stipulation for any necessary right of access.

5–99 (v) *Peat, fuel and divot*. A right to dig peat for fuel or to take clods for building or fencing from land belonging to another are recognised servitudes.[69] Again the right should be expressly included in the offer, together with a right of access although that would normally be implied.[70]

5–100 (vi) *Servitude rights not particularly specified*. The *omnium gatherum* clause suggested at paragraph 15–41 *supra* will embrace servitude rights effeiring to the subjects of purchase, but only those to which the seller has a legal right. Hence the desirability of mentioning specifically any apparent servitude right which is of importance.

(b) Servitudes burdening the subjects of purchase

5–101 (i) *Positive servitudes*. Some positive servitudes which burden the subjects may be evident on inspection, *e.g.* access roads or paths over the subjects which serve other properties. If the purchaser contemplates continuance of the existing use of the property the only matter for inquiry or stipulation in the offer is to ensure that the expense of maintenance and repair of the access is borne equitably by all users and that the proprietor of the subjects of purchase is not contractually bound in terms of the servitude right to bear an undue proportion of such expense. Many servitude rights may not be obvious on inspection, *e.g.* underground electricity or telephone cables or gas or water pipes or drainage or sewage pipes serving other properties which pass through the subjects of purchase. The existence of such rights may not be material if no change of use of the subjects is contemplated, but if the purchaser proposes to make any building additions or developments the existence of the servitude rights may preclude or restrict the works or render them more expensive, either by reason of the terms of the servitude right or the statutory rights of public undertakings.[71]

5–102 (ii) *Negative servitudes*. These, such as *non aedificandi* or *altius non*

---

[68] Bell, *Prin.*, s. 1013; *Campbell* v. *McKinnon* (1867) 5 M. 636.
[69] Bell, *Prin.*, s. 1014; *Watson* v. *Sinclair*, 1966 S.L.T. (Sh.Ct.) 77; *Grierson* v. *Sandsting School Board* (1882) 9 R. 437.
[70] *Dingwall* v. *Farquharson* (1797) 3 Pat. App. 564.
[71] *e.g.* Telegraph Act 1878, s. 8; Pipe-lines Act 1962, s. 27; Gas Act 1972, s. 39(2).

tollendi, will not be evident on inspection and may not even appear in the titles of the servient tenement. If the buildings on the subjects have existed without alteration for a considerable time it may be assumed that there has been no contravention of a negative servitude but if the buildings or extensions to them are of recent construction or if any new building developments are contemplated by the purchaser, an appropriate provision should be inserted in the offer.

15–103   (iii) *Stipulation in the offer.* The clause suggested in paragraph 15–92 *supra* is designed to cover *inter alia* the risk of the existence of any positive servitudes which would render development more expensive or of the existence of any negative servitudes which would preclude development. Hence the inclusion of the words "or elsewhere" in the clause. Although a clause in these terms may be adequate in most cases where building development is envisaged, the provisions may require to be specially adapted to the circumstances of the particular property. For example, operations by the owner of the servient property such as digging peat or tree-planting may be precluded by the existence of a servitude of pasturage[72] and afforestation may diminish the volume of water from a natural supply percolating through the area planted.

15–104   *Rights of way.* These will normally be evident on inspection unless the right is to a footpath which is used infrequently. The clause suggested in paragraph 15–92 might protect the purchaser against the existence of a right of way which restricted development, but if there is any reason to suspect that a right of way over the subjects of purchase exists an express provision that there are no rights of way over any part of the property may be inserted.[72a]

VI. *Collateral Assurances*

(1) *Building regulations*

15–105   The construction of new buildings or alterations or additions to buildings or a change of use of a building require to be authorised by the relevant buildings authority,[73] which will issue a warrant for the construction or change of use if satisfied that the building or the use to which it is put complies with the requirements of the current Building Standards (Scotland) Regulations. Where the subjects of purchase comprise buildings recently constructed or there have been recent alterations or additions to buildings or change of use, an offer should provide that the seller will produce evidence of compliance with these requirements. See Style 15A, Note 2, para. 15–136.

---

[72] *Ferguson* v. *Tennant*, 1978 S.C. (H.L.) 19.
[72a] See *Armia Ltd.* v. *Daejan Developments Ltd.*, 1979 S.C. (H.L.) 56.
[73] Building (Scotland) Act 1959, s. 6, as amended by Building (Scotland) Act 1970.

(2) *Planning*

–106   A purchaser will wish to be assured that the buildings on the subjects have been constructed in accordance with planning consent and that the use of them is also authorised under the planning statutes.[74] He will also be concerned to ensure that for the future there are no notices, proposals or development plans that will adversely affect the property or will frustrate or restrict either the continuance of the existing use or any new use contemplated. It is also of importance to ascertain whether the property includes any listed buildings which may restrict development. For suitable provisions (although the wording may require adjustment for special types of property) see Style 15A, clause 10 and Note 2, para. 15–136.

Where land is being purchased for development the Styles Committee of the Law Society of Scotland suggest[74a] an appropriate clause might be as follows:

> The contract, of which this missive forms part, shall be subject to the condition that within   calendar months from the conclusion of the contract, or such longer period as the parties may agree, our client obtain detailed planning permission and local authority warrant for a   all in accordance with the plans signed as relative hereto. Such permission and warrant shall be [to our client's entire satisfaction] [free of unduly onerous conditions] [for a minimum floor area of   square feet and parking facilities for at least   cars and shall meet the following additional requirements of our client   and shall not be subject to unduly onerous conditions]. Our client undertakes to apply for the said permission and warrant as soon as practicable after conclusion of the contract and to pursue such application diligently; your client shall do nothing which might frustrate the purification of this condition. Unless our client obtains such permission and warrant within the said period or earlier withdraws this condition, which he shall be entitled to do at any time, the contract shall be at an end.

(3) *Fire precautions*

–107   Fire certificates are required under the Fire Precautions Act 1971[75] for certain designated classes of premises which include hotels and boarding-houses, nursing homes, clubs and premises open to the public but excepting churches and certain kinds of premises such as offices, shops, factories and mines or quarries which are covered by other legislation.[76] If the subjects include premises designated for the purposes of the Act the offer should contain a requirement of production by the seller of a fire certificate, since alterations to satisfy

---

[74] The principal current statutes are the Town and Country Planning (Scotland) Act 1972 and the Town and Country Planning (Scotland) Act 1977.
[74a] (1980) 25 J.L.S. W. 129.
[75] s. 1.
[76] *Ibid.*, s. 2.

the requirements of regulations under the Act may involve expensive reconstruction. See para. 15–138, Style 15C, clause 12(b).

(4) *Offices, shops, factories*

15–108   The Offices, Shops and Railway Premises Act 1963 imposes certain requirements in respect of premises as defined in section 1 of the Act as to overcrowding, temperature, ventilation, sanitary conveniences, etc., and also as to fire precautions. The Factories Act 1961 and the Health and Safety at Work etc., Act 1974 also contain provisions imposing requirements relating to the construction of factory buildings and facilities therein. It is important in a purchase of any subjects which comprise buildings affected by these statutes to know that the requirements of the Acts are satisfied, and an appropriate condition should be inserted in the offer. See para. 15–138, Style 15C, clause 12(a).

(5) *Dwelling-houses recently constructed*

15–109   If the purchase is of a dwelling-house which has been built within ten years before the date of purchase the purchaser should seek to ensure that indemnity against *inter alia* structural defects will be available by production and delivery by the seller of a Scottish House-Purchaser's Insurance Policy issued by the National House-Building Council in respect of the subjects of purchase. See para. 15–136, Style 15A, clause 13.

(6) *Business premises*

15–110   Where a purchase of heritable property involves also the acquisition of a business carried on therein it may be necessary to have regard to statutory requirements or special agreements which affect it and to insert appropriate provisions in the contract of sale. The statutory regulations may be of general application such as the provisions of the Transfer of Undertakings (Protection of Employment) Regulations 1981,[77] or peculiar to the particular business such as the transfer of a liquor licence,[78] or there may be solus agreements in relation to petrol stations or licensed premises. Some of these special statutory provisions are considered in paragraphs 15–107 and 15–108, but the solicitor for the purchaser should inquire of his client as to the matters peculiar to the particular business which should be referred to in an offer.

---

[77] S.I. 1981 No. 1794.
[78] See para. 15–55.

VII. *Apportionments*

(1) *Ground burdens*

-111   Allocated feuduties or ground annuals will be redeemed by the seller,[79] but unallocated ground burdens may remain and provision should be made for their apportionment between the seller and the purchaser as at the date of entry. The amount of the unallocated part exigible from the subjects of purchase and the amount of the *cumulo* burden should be stated.[80]

(2) *Local rates*

-112   In the case of owner-occupied property local rates should likewise be apportioned as at the date of entry. In most cases the local authority will apportion the rates on being advised of the change of ownership[80a]: if not, the seller should pay the rates for the whole of the current year which includes the date of entry and recover the post-entry proportion from the purchaser at settlement, since, as the person appearing on the valuation roll, the seller is responsible for payment.

(3) *Electricity, gas, telephone and other periodic charges based on consumption*

-113   Accounts for the period up to the date of entry should be instructed and paid by the seller. If that is inconvenient or overlooked apportionment of the charges between seller and purchaser may be agreed if there has been no abnormal usage.

(4) *Rents receivable*

-114   In the case of a purchase of let property the contract should specify the first rents which the purchaser is to receive. In the absence of any such provision in missives the rents receivable by a purchaser will depend upon statutory provisions defining the effect of the clause of assignation of rents in the subsequent disposition[81] or the implied effect of a disposition without such a clause.[82] These provisions are not always simple in their application[83] and it is preferable to regulate the matter by specific provision in the contract of sale.

---

[79] See para. 15–90.

[80] The decisions in *Bremner* v. *Dick*, 1911 S.C. 887 and *Morrison* v. *Gray*, 1932 S.C. 712 may still have some relevance for, although a purchaser may now be assumed to know that a continuing ground burden is unallocated, the amount of the contingent liability for the *cumulo* burden may be material.

[80a] See Local Government (Scotland) Act 1947, ss. 241, 242, as to power of local authority to apportion liability.

[81] Titles to Land Consolidation (Scotland) Act 1868, s. 8.

[82] Land Registration (Scotland) Act 1979, s. 16(3)(*a*).

[83] See para. 22–13.

(5) *Fire insurances*

15–115   The older practice was to have the existing insurance policy endorsed in favour of the purchaser, who refunded to the seller the proportion of the annual premium referable to the period of the year subsequent to the date of entry. The modern practice, which is recommended, is for the purchaser to instruct insurance cover immediately upon completion of the contract of sale and indeed many solicitors have arrangements with insurers which automatically provide cover for all properties purchased during the periods between completion of contract and settlement of the transaction, the premium, based on the number and size of the transactions, being adjusted annually. The seller will normally cancel the existing insurance policy only upon settlement but any element of double insurance lasts only for the relatively short period between contract and settlement and avoids the risks outlined in the following paragraph.

15–116   During the period between the completion of missives and entry by the purchaser the subjects of sale may be destroyed or damaged by fire, bursting or overflowing of water pipes or tanks, vandalism, etc. If the contract of sale has been perfected and is not subject to any suspensive condition, *e.g.* the obtaining of planning permission, the risk of loss or damage to the property is borne by the purchaser on the principle that he has a *jus ad rem*,[84] unless the damage has been attributable to negligence on the part of the seller.[85] In practice such risks should not normally be accepted by a purchaser who is placed in the position of an insurer of property over which he has no control, and so an appropriate provision should be inserted in the contract of sale, which expressly imposes the risk upon the seller. See paragraph 15–136, Style 15A, clause 11 and paragraph 15–138, Style 15C, clause 15. Notwithstanding such a provision, however, the purchaser should effect insurance immediately upon completion of the contract as recommended in paragraph 15–115 *supra*; it may be arguable in view of the terms of the contract whether he has an insurable risk, but insurers would not in the circumstances deny liability on that ground.

VIII. *Matrimonial Homes*

15–117 The provisions of the Matrimonial Homes (Family Protection) (Scotland) Act 1981 are considered more fully in paragraphs 21–23 to 21–26 *infra*. The sale of heritable property which is a matrimonial home, whether feudal or leasehold, but excepting schedule conveyances under section 80 of the Lands Clauses Consolidation (Scotland) Act 1845, is a "dealing" in the sense of section 6 of the 1981 Act. A stipulation should now be made in contracts for the sale of dwelling-

---

[84] *Sloans Dairies Ltd.* v. *Glasgow Corporation*, 1979 S.L.T. 17.
[85] *Meehan* v. *Silver*, 1972 S.L.T. (Sh.Ct.) 70.

house property that the seller should produce (a) a consent to the sale by the non-entitled spouse in the statutory form,[86] or (b) a duly notarised renunciation by the non-entitled spouse of his or her occupancy rights in the subjects of sale, or (c) in the event of the seller being or stating that he or she is unmarried an affidavit sworn or affirmed by the seller that the subjects of sale are not a matrimonial home in relation to which a spouse of the seller has occupancy rights.[87] Since the separate statutory form of consent may be mislaid an additional precaution is to stipulate that the non-entitled spouse should sign the conveyance or assignation, as the case may be, consenting to the transaction. The like consent, renunciation or affidavit is also required in respect of any previous dealing to which the Act applied.[88] If a sale is by an executor the person who would have been entitled to succeed to the property and/or his or her spouse should sign a consent thereto or grant a renunciation or affidavit as appropriate.

IX. *Endurance of Missives*

118 The decision in *Winston* v. *Patrick*[89] has elicited the expression of views in legal journals that it may be advisable to insert in missives of sale of heritable property a clause to the effect that the contract embodied in the missives shall remain in force except in so far as it has been implemented by the disposition which follows, or even that a similar provision should be inserted in the disposition itself.[90] It is suggested that a condition of this kind should not be accepted by a seller either in the missives or the disposition, save in special contracts, *e.g.* a purchase of commercial or industrial property which is being built by the seller.[91] If there are material provisions of the missives which have not been implemented settlement should be postponed, and if settlement proceeds a specific agreement identifying the outstanding matters should be entered into, in order to preserve the obligations of the seller in respect of them. Where the sale will or may induce first registration in the Land Register of Scotland or is a sale of an interest already registered therein, it is recommended that the obligation to exhibit or deliver a valid marketable title should be expressed as remaining in force notwithstanding delivery of the disposition, since the purchaser may require to obtain further information from the seller to support the application for registration.[92]

---

[86] Prescribed in the Matrimonial Homes (Form of Consent) (Scotland) Regulations 1982 (S.I. 1982 No. 971 (S. 129)).

[87] 1981 Act, s. 6(3)(*a*) and (*e*) as amended by the Law Reform (Miscellaneous Provisions) (Scotland) Act 1985, s. 13(6). For styles of consent or renunciation or affidavit see paras. 21–29, 21–30 and 21–31.

[88] *i.e.* dealings on or after September 1, 1982.

[89] 1981 S.L.T. 41.

[90] (1981) 26 J.L.S. 414; (1982) 27 J.L.S. 37; (1982) 27 J.L.S. W. 323.

[91] See para. 15–119.

[92] See R.T.P.B., paras. G.2.08 and G.3.05.

X. *Special Contracts*

(1) *Purchase of site and buildings to be erected by seller*

15–119   In commercial developments it is not uncommon for the seller to offer a package deal comprising the sale or long lease of a site and the construction of purpose-built premises upon it. Such transactions are normally effected by separate but interlinked contracts for the sale of the site and construction of the buildings. In addition to the usual clauses in a contract for the purchase of heritage there are certain special provisions which require attention.

(a) The problem of payments by the purchaser to account before receiving a conveyance occurs in an acute form.[93] If payment is deferred until the buildings are complete and a conveyance is delivered the seller will require to finance the construction costs and will build in an addition to the total price to cover that service. Alternatively the purchaser may make an initial payment of the value of the undeveloped site in exchange for a valid conveyance and undertake to make stage payments as the work of construction progresses. The difficulties of the latter course are that the seller may be unable to obtain the consent of a heritable creditor to the release of the site from his security in exchange for a relatively small payment and he is exposed to the risk of insolvency of the purchaser. The latter problem may be resolved by the grant of a standard security by the purchaser to secure his obligations of payment under the contract, but that involves further documentation in respect of a temporary period. Much depends upon the financial status of the respective parties and the negotiating strength of each.

(b) The purchaser should have rights of inspection by himself or his architects or surveyors while building work is in progress.

(c) Payment of the price should be dependent upon satisfactory completion of the buildings and provision should be made for deduction at settlement of the amount of all retentions under the building contract.

(d) Provision should be made for an assignation to the purchaser of the seller's rights to enforce warranties under the building contract against sub-contractors and others, and also rights against the seller's professional advisers in relation to the design and construction of the buildings.

(e) The conditions of the contract for the sale of the land and the building contract should remain in force notwithstanding delivery of a conveyance.[94]

(2) *Purchases under Tenants' Rights, Etc. (Scotland) Acts*

15–120   The Tenants' Rights, Etc. (Scotland) Act 1980, as amended by the

---

[93] See para. 15–82.
[94] See *McKillop* v. *Mutual Securities Ltd.*, 1945 S.C. 166.

Tenants' Rights, Etc. (Scotland) Amendment Act 1980, sections 53 to 55 of the Local Government and Planning (Scotland) Act 1982 and the Tenants' Rights, Etc. (Scotland) Amendment Act 1984, confers on certain tenants in the public housing sector a right to purchase their dwelling-houses at a price discounted in relation to the period for which their tenancy has subsisted by procedure and subject to conditions prescribed. The discount is recoverable on early resale to an extent related to the period between the service of the tenant's notice of acceptance of the offer to purchase and the subsequent disposal of the house by him. The purchasing tenant may also apply to the selling authority for a loan to assist him in making the purchase. (References to sections in paragraphs 15–121 to 15–129 are to the principal 1980 Act unless otherwise stated.)

15–121 (a) **Tenants entitled to purchase.** The tenant or any one of joint tenants must have been in occupation of a dwelling-house or a succession of dwelling-houses provided by any of the bodies specified in section 1(10) of the 1980 Act as extended by section 2(1) of the 1984 Act for a period of not less than two years.[95] Where the spouse of a tenant or joint tenant occupies the dwelling-house as his only or principal home, the right to purchase cannot be exercised without the consent of such spouse.[96] Occupation of the dwelling-house may have been rent-free and may include occupation as the child of a tenant who has succeeded to the tenancy, but the occupation by the child is reckonable for the purpose of calculating the two-year period only in relation to a period when the child is over the age of 16.[97] (Originally the landlords had discretion as to inclusion in the reckoning of the period of occupancy by the child, but that discretion has been taken away.[98])

15–122 (b) **Dwelling-houses which may be purchased.** The right of purchase is conferred only in respect of dwelling-houses let under a secure tenancy.[99] A secure tenancy is one where the dwelling-house is let as a separate dwelling, the tenant is an individual and the dwelling-house is his only or principal home and the landlord is one of the public bodies specified in section 10(2) of the 1980 Act.[1] Where the tenancy is held jointly by two or more individuals it is sufficient if one of them occupies the dwelling-house as his only or principal residence.[2] Certain tenancies are excluded, notably where the period of tenancy exceeds 20 years (*i.e.* is a long lease), or the premises are occupied under a contract of employment which requires the tenant to occupy the dwelling-house for the better performance of his duties, or where the

---

[95] Substituted by 1984 Act, s. 1(1)(*a*) instead of three years in 1980 Act, s. 1(3).
[96] s. 1(2).
[97] s. 1(12)(iii).
[98] 1984 Act, s. 1(1)(*c*).
[99] s. 1(3).
[1] s. 10(1): see para. 15–123 for list of bodies referred to.
[2] s. 10(3).

tenancy or accommodation is temporary, or where the dwelling-house is let with agricultural land exceeding two acres or consists of or includes business or licensed premises.[3] A specially-built park-keeper's house situated within a public park was held to have been occupied by a foreman gardener for the better performance of his duties under a contract of employment so that he was not entitled to purchase it.[4] A dwelling-house which is one of a group which has been provided with facilities specially designed or adapted for the needs of elderly or disabled persons cannot be purchased,[5] but a dwelling-house which has facilities substantially different from those of an ordinary dwelling-house and which has been designed or adapted for occupation by an elderly person having special needs for such accommodation, if not excluded by being one of a group, may be purchased subject to special provisions enabling the landlord to apply to the Secretary of State for authority to refuse to sell.[6]

15–123   (c) **Landlords obliged to sell.** The obligation to sell to a qualified tenant is imposed upon (i) an islands or district council or a joint board or joint committee thereof or the common good of an islands or district council or any trust under the control of an islands or district council; (ii) a development corporation established under an order made, or having effect as if made under the New Towns (Scotland) Act 1968; (iii) the Scottish Special Housing Association; (iv) the Housing Corporation; (v) a registered housing association within the meaning of the Housing Act 1974; (vi) a housing co-operative within the meaning of section 5 of the Housing Rents and Subsidies (Scotland) Act 1975; or (vii) any housing trust which was in existence on November 13, 1953, or any authorised society within the meaning of the Housing Act 1914.[7] Regional councils are not included in the list in section 10(2) although they are included in the list of landlords in section 1(10) occupancy of whose houses may qualify a tenant to purchase. It was decided that a single-tier islands council was obliged to sell his dwelling-house to a teacher employed by them despite the anomaly that a teacher whose dwelling-house was let from a regional council would not have been entitled to purchase it, but that anomaly has now been removed.[8] The landlord must be the heritable proprietor of the dwelling-house,[8a] but "heritable proprietor" includes a landlord who has a right to land which would entitle him to grant a

---

[3] s. 10(4) and Sched. 1.
[4] *Douglas* v. *Falkirk District Council*, 1983 S.L.T. (Lands Tr.) 21. See also *Kinghorn* v. *City of Glasgow District Council*, 1984 S.L.T. (Lands Tr.) 9.
[5] s. 1(11)(c).
[6] 1980 Amendment Act, s. 1.
[7] s. 10(2).
[8] *Hill* v. *Orkney Islands Council*, 1983 S.L.T. (Lands Tr.) 2: now superseded in principle by 1984 Act, s. 4.
[8a] s. 1(11).

disposition under section 3 of the Conveyancing (Scotland) Act 1924,[8b] but does not include a lessee under a long lease.[8c]

-124 (d) Price. The tenant is entitled to purchase at a price determined by deducting a discount from the market value.[8d] The market value is fixed either by a qualified valuer or the district valuer on the basis of a sale in the open market with vacant possession on the date of service of the application to purchase.[9] The selling authority may elect that the valuation be made either by a qualified valuer or the district valuer, but if the former is chosen the tenant must be consulted and approve of the valuer selected. Once the market value has been so determined the Lands Tribunal has no jurisdiction to alter it.[10] The discount to be deducted from the market value is 32 per cent of the valuation plus an additional 1 per cent for every year beyond two of continuous occupation by the tenant or by any one of the joint tenants or by his spouse immediately preceding the date of service of the application to purchase subject to a maximum of 60 per cent (formerly 50 per cent).[11] As to recovery of discount on early re-sale and security for repayment thereof see the paragraph undernoted.[12]

-125 (e) Procedure—refusals of offers. A tenant who seeks to exercise his right to purchase must serve on the landlords a notice in prescribed form.[13] If the landlords dispute the tenant's right to purchase a notice of refusal must be served within one month, or, if on inquiry the landlords consider that information contained in the application is incorrect in a material respect, within two months of the service of the application.[14] A notice of refusal must state the grounds of refusal and the tenant may apply to the Lands Tribunal within one month thereafter for a finding that he has a right to purchase.[15] If the landlords do not serve a notice of refusal they must within two months of service of the application to purchase serve on the tenant an offer to sell which contains (i) the market value, (ii) the discount, (iii) the price, (iv) any conditions which the landlords intend to impose under section 4 of the Act, and (v) an offer to sell to the tenant and any joint purchaser named in the application at the price and on the conditions above referred to.[16] As to the date of application when there were

---

[8b] 1980 Amendment Act, s. 2(*f*).

[8c] *Graham and Robertson* v. *Motherwell District Council*, 1985 S.L.T. (Lands Tr.) 44.

[8d] Where the house was first let under a secure tenancy after May 15, 1975, the price may be the lesser of the outstanding debt incurred in providing it or the market value—s. 1(7); *Murdoch* v. *Gordon District Council*, 1985 S.L.T.(Lands Tr.) 42.

[9] s. 1(5) and (12).

[10] *Thomson* v. *City of Edinburgh District Council*, 1982 S.L.T. (Lands Tr.) 39; *MacLeod* v. *Ross and Cromarty District Council*, 1983 S.L.T. (Lands Tr.) 5.

[11] s. 1(5) as amended by 1984 Amendment Act, s. 1.

[12] para. 15–129.

[13] The form of notice is prescribed in the Right to Purchase (Application Form) (Scotland) Order 1980 (S.I. 1980 No. 1388 (S. 109)).

[14] s. 3(1) and (2).

[15] s. 3(3) and (4).

[16] s. 2(2).

subsequent correspondence and actings on detailed matters, see the cases cited.[17] Where the tenant (i) considers that a condition in the offer is unreasonable, (ii) wishes to have a new condition included, or (iii) wishes to include or to exclude a joint purchaser thus altering the application, he may within one month after service of the offer request the landlords in writing to vary the offer or make a new offer as the case may be. If the landlords refuse to accede to the request by serving an amended or new offer within one month of service of the request, the tenant may within one month, or with the written consent of the landlords two months, thereafter refer the matter to the Lands Tribunal for determination.[18] If the landlords fail to progress an application properly or timeously, as by failure to serve a notice of refusal or an offer to sell which conforms to the requirements of section 2(2) of the Act within the time limits specified in the Act, the tenant may refer the matter to the Lands Tribunal, and if they find that there has been such failure the Tribunal may themselves issue notices and take such other steps as are required to complete the statutory procedure.[19] If there has been such failure an order under section 7(3) of the Act must be made by the Tribunal if the tenant so requests and effectively displaces the landlords, and the Tribunal themselves have to undertake the procedures required by the Act and may give any consents and exercise any discretions as the landlords could have done.[20] If the tenant fails to accept the offer or an amended offer to sell within two months the offer lapses: originally the tenant was not entitled to make a new application to purchase until 12 months after the last date on which he could have accepted it but that restriction has now been removed.[21]

15–126   **(f) Conditions of sale.** An offer to sell under the provisions of the Act must contain conditions which are reasonable and in particular the conditions shall (i) ensure that the tenant shall have as full enjoyment or use of the dwelling-house as owner as he had as tenant, (ii) secure to the tenant such additional rights as are necessary for his reasonable enjoyment and use of the house as owner including common rights in any part of the building of which it forms part and impose on the tenant any necessary duties relative to the rights so secured, (iii) include such terms as are necessary to entitle the tenant to receive a good and marketable title. It is not permissible to require the tenant to make any deposit.[22] A condition which imposes a new or increased charge for the provision of a service in relation to the house must

---

[17] *Snedden, Wighton and McNaughton* v. *Stirling District Council*, LTS/TR/1981/120, LTS/TR/1981/82 and LTS/TR/1981/141.

[18] s. 2(3) and (4).

[19] s. 7, as amended by Local Government and Planning (Scotland) Act 1982, s. 55.

[20] *Fraser* v. *City of Glasgow District Council*, 1982 S.L.T. (Lands Tr.) 46; *Fullerton* v. *Monklands District Council*, 1983 S.L.T. (Lands Tr.) 15. The powers to consent and exercise any discretion are conferred by the Local Government and Planning (Scotland) Act 1982, s. 55.

[21] s. 2(6) and (10): 1984 Amendment Act, s. 3.

[22] s. 4 and Local Government and Planning (Scotland) Act 1982, s. 53.

provide for the charge being in reasonable proportion to the cost to the landlords of providing the service. No condition can be imposed which has the effect of requiring the tenant to pay any expenses of the landlords in connection with the sale. No right of pre-emption can be reserved to the landlords or any other person except in sale of a dwelling-house having facilities substantially different from those of an ordinary dwelling-house and designed or adapted for occupation by an elderly or disabled person, but such a right may be imposed if the Secretary of State makes an order to that effect as regards dwelling-houses in an area which has been designated as a rural area by the islands or district council concerned, and in this latter case the period within which the right of pre-emption can be exercised is restricted to ten years after the date of conveyance to the tenant.[22a] As to conditions which have been decided by the Lands Tribunal to be reasonable or otherwise see the cases undernoted.[23] Some of the more important general principles decided by the Tribunal are:

(i) The conveyance may be in the form of a feu disposition with an irritancy clause.

(ii) A clause of reservation of minerals to the selling authority as superiors is permissible subject to compensation for damage to the surface or buildings from exercise of the reserved right, the amount of such damage to be determined, failing agreement, by arbitration.

(iii) A provision that the sale is subject to conditions in the title deeds should be qualified by a declaration that there are no such conditions of an unusual or onerous nature other than any specifically referred to in the offer.

(iv) A restriction to use as a private dwelling-house for one family only is permissible if qualified to the effect that the superiors may consent to use for more than one family or for a trade, profession or business, such consent not to be unreasonably withheld, but consent is not required for the carrying on of a trade, profession or business by the occupier alone which does not detract from the use as a private dwelling-house nor involve the public at large resorting to the premises.

(v) Subdivision may be prohibited except with the consent of the superiors (not to be unreasonably withheld).

(vi) An obligation in proper terms to keep the subjects insured and to apply the moneys received under the policies in repair and reinstatement is permissible.

In practice most local authorities offer to grant a feu disposition of the dwelling-house with conditions set out in a recorded deed of

---

[22a] s. 4(4) to (8).

[23] *J. M. Wilson* v. *Renfrew District Council*, LTS/TR/1981/436; *J. R. Wilson* v. *Renfrew District Council*, LTS/TR/1981/444; *Keay* v. *Renfrew District Council*, 1982 S.L.T. (Lands Tr.) 33; *Pollock* v. *Dumbarton District Council*, 1983 S.L.T. (Lands Tr.) 17; *MacLeod* v. *Ross and Cromarty District Council*, 1983 S.L.T. (Lands Tr.) 5; *Thomson* v. *Midlothian District Council*, LTS/TR/1981/768; *McKean* v. *City of Glasgow District Council*, LTS/TR/1981/801; *Clark, Craigie, Smith and Tulloch* v. *Shetlands Islands Council*, LTS/TR/1981/599, 597, 598 and 594.

conditions varying in relation to the nature of the property, *e.g.* low-rise flatted property, high-rise flatted property. Apart from the provisions required by the Act or approved by the Lands Tribunal as above detailed, additional conditions sometimes provide for (i) the right of the landlords to cancel the sale if there is undue delay, not attributable to the landlords, in making payment of the price, (ii) imposing the risk of destruction or damage prior to the date of entry upon the tenant–purchaser, (iii) prohibition of assignation before settlement, (iv) reservation of rights of servitude or wayleave for common pipes or cables serving other houses, (v) no searches being provided (which should be qualified in the acceptance at least to the extent that searches, if obtained by the purchaser, will be clear), and (vi) provisions as to recovery of discount on re-sale within five years which remain enforceable notwithstanding settlement, and the granting of a standard security therefor. In the case of semi-detached or detached dwelling-houses similar provisions are normally incorporated in the feu disposition of the particular house with restrictions to use as a dwelling-house, maintenance and use of garden ground and fences, permission to erect a garage with consent of the selling authority, and prohibition of nuisance.

15–127   **(g) Completion of contract of sale.** When an offer of sale has been made to the tenant in terms which he is willing to accept or if any dispute as to the terms of the offer has been decided by the Lands Tribunal, the tenant must serve a notice of acceptance on the landlords within two months of (i) service of the offer, or (ii) service of any amended offer or the latest amended offer, or (iii) determination by the Tribunal if that does not require the service of an amended offer, or (iv) where a loan application has been made to the landlords, the service of an offer of loan, or (v) where an application is made to the court under section 5(7) in respect of a loan, the decision of the court, whichever of those is the latest.[24] The contract for sale is then constituted.

(h) Loans and securities

15–128   (i) *Loans by landlords to tenants.* Where a tenant–purchaser has applied for but been unable to obtain a sufficient building society loan he may, within one month after the service of the offer to sell or any amended offer or a determination of the Lands Tribunal which does not require the service of an amended offer, whichever is the latest, apply in a prescribed form[25] for a loan of an amount not exceeding the price to assist him in making the purchase. Where the landlord is a development corporation or the Scottish Special Housing Association,

---

[24] s. 2(6). As to loans see para. 15–128.
[25] s. 5. The form of application is prescribed in the Right to Purchase (Loan Application) (Scotland) Order 1980 (S.I. 1980 No. 1492 (S. 119)). The terms of loan are regulated by the Right to Purchase (Loans) (Scotland) Regulations 1980 (S.I. 1980 No. 1430 (S. 115)).

application should be made to that body; in all other cases application should be made to the islands or district council for the area in which the house is situated. Evidence as to matters stated in the application (gross and net income, liabilities under credit sales or other fixed outgoings and inability to obtain a building society loan) must accompany the loan application. The landlords or other body to whom the application has been made must within two months of the date of service of the application either (a) issue an offer of loan specifying a maximum amount of loan calculated in prescribed terms,[25] or (b) refuse the application on the ground that information contained in it is incorrect in a material respect. The applicant who wishes to accept the loan offer must do so with his notice of acceptance of the offer to sell the dwelling-house. If a loan application is refused the applicant may within two months of the refusal raise proceedings by summary application in the sheriff court for declarator that he is entitled to a loan and, if the sheriff grants the application, the declarator will have effect as if it were an offer of loan of the amount specified in the declarator.[26] If an applicant has received an offer to sell but is unable to obtain a loan of the amount for which he has applied he may, within two months of service on him of the offer of loan or the declarator of the sheriff, whichever is the later, serve on the landlords a notice that he wishes to have a fixed price option which will enable him to serve a notice of acceptance within two years of his application to purchase. The notice must be accompanied by payment of £100, recoverable if he purchases within that period or, if he does not, on the expiry of that period, or if the landlords for any reason recover possession of the house, or if the tenant dies without purchasing.[27]

-129   (ii) *Securities for discount recoverable on early re-sale.* Where a purchaser sells or otherwise disposes of the dwelling-house purchased at a discount in terms of the Act within five years after notice of acceptance of the offer to sell, he is liable to repay to the landlords a proportion of the discount reducing from 100 per cent by 20 per cent per annum in relation to the length of the period between acceptance of the offer to sell and the subsequent sale or disposal.[28] The landlords may take security for repayment of any recoverable discount over the dwelling-house by way of a standard security. Originally it was provided that such a standard security might be created with priority immediately after a standard security in respect of a loan granted for the purchase of the house plus interest and expenses and outlays (including interest thereon) reasonably incurred by the prior lender in exercise of any powers conferred in his standard security, or, but only with the consent of the landlords, after a standard security for any other loan.[29] (That

[26] s. 5.
[27] s. 2(8) and (9).
[28] s. 6(1) and (3).
[29] s. 6(5).

provision was necessary since a building society may only grant loans on first mortgage.[30]) The scope of a permissible prior security has now been enlarged to include also securities for any loans granted for the improvement of the dwelling-house.[31] It may be advisable for the selling authority to stipulate in the offer for sale that the purchaser should intimate to the authority any standard securities granted subsequently in respect of improvements and, if required, to produce evidence that the moneys thus secured have been applied in making improvements to the dwelling-house.

(3) Agricultural subjects

15–130   **(a) Farms sold with vacant possession.** A style of offer for a farm and the stock, crop and implements being purchased with vacant possession is suggested (para. 15–140, Style 15E). Matters for attention are:

(i) The subjects should be described by the name of the farm, the approximate total area and a plan either prepared for the purpose or supplied in the particulars of sale.[32] If any part of the farm or buildings is reserved from the sale it should be specified and delineated on the plan.

(ii) Where stock, crop and implements are included in the sale the stock (by total numbers and description), the implements and any hay, straw or silage should be specified in an inventory to be taken over either at stated prices or prices ascertained by valuation.

(iii) Mineral rights may be important, particularly where the minerals consist of sand or gravel the removal of which may destroy the surface.

(iv) Growing crops are heritable,[33] so that a general specification of crops will include them.

(v) Growing timber also is heritable but becomes moveable when felled.[34] It should be ascertained whether there are plantations subject to forestry dedication agreements under the Forestry Acts 1947 and 1967: these if recorded are enforceable against successors in ownership of the land.[35]

(vi) Salmon fishings should be separately specified. At common law, trout fishing and shooting tenancies are not binding on a purchaser, but written contracts for consideration and for not less than a year giving a right to fish for trout now are.[36]

(vii) Water supply and drainage.

(viii) Tied cottages.[37]

---

[30] Building Societies Act 1962, s. 32.
[31] Local Government and Planning (Scotland) Act 1982, s. 54.
[32] *Johnston's Trs.* v. *Kinloch*, 1925 S.L.T. 124; *Houldsworth* v. *Gordon Cumming*, 1910 S.C. (H.L.) 49.
[33] *Chalmers' Tr.* v. *Dick's Tr.*, 1909 S.C. 761.
[34] *Munro* v. *Liquidator of Balnagown Estates Co. Ltd.*, 1949 S.L.T. 85.
[35] Forestry Act 1967, s. 5(3).
[36] *Beckett* v. *Bisset*, 1921 2 S.L.T. 33 (shootings). *Earl of Galloway* v. *Duke of Bedford* (1902) 4 F. 851, now superseded by Freshwater and Salmon Fisheries (Scotland) Act 1976, s. 4.
[37] See Protection from Eviction Act 1977, s. 4.

(ix) Ancient monuments or archaeological areas and rights of access thereto.[38]

(x) Sites of special scientific interest.[39]

(xi) Buildings of architectural or historic interest.[40]

(xii) Whether located in a conservation area (which may render permission for developments more difficult to obtain).[41]

(xiii) Access agreements or orders.[42]

(xiv) Repayable improvement grants.

(xv) Private access road to the subjects, whether shared and responsibility for maintenance.

(xvi) Any servitude rights or rights of way.

Other matters for attention in particular circumstances may be (i) occupancy rights of a non-entitled spouse under the Matrimonial Homes (Family Protection) (Scotland) Act 1981,[42a] and (ii) in the case of dairy farms the dairy produce quota.[42b]

-131 Depending upon the date of entry special arrangements may be necessary to allow the purchaser early access for carrying out certain farming operations, e.g. ploughing and sowing. Alternatively the purchaser may provide the seed and pay an agreed figure to the seller for the cost of carrying out the work of ploughing and sowing. Another special matter which may cause difficulty is the apportionment of subsidies or livestock compensating allowances. Agreement should be reached on such matters between purchaser and seller, usually as a separate arrangement left on correspondence rather than incorporated in the formal missives.

-132 **(b) Farms subject to tenancies.** Where the purchase is of an estate which includes let farms it is essential to examine the leases of each farm and the leases should be scheduled in the offer to purchase, including any contracting-out agreements permissible[43] under section 5(3) of the Agricultural Holdings (Scotland) Act 1949. If there are bound sheep stocks the basis of valuation thereof on outgoing may have important financial consequences and may vary with the provisions or the dates of the leases.[44] The offer should make specific provision as to the first rents which the purchaser is to receive—see paragraph 15–114. Since the purchaser will inherit liability to make compensation for improvements made by a tenant under Part I and Part II of Schedule 1

---

[38] Ancient Monuments and Archaeological Areas Act 1979.

[39] Countryside Act 1968, s. 15.

[40] Town and Country Planning (Scotland) Act 1972, s. 53.

[41] *Ibid.*, s. 262 as substituted by Town and Country Amenities Act 1974, s. 2(1).

[42] Countryside (Scotland) Act 1967, ss. 13, 14, as amended.

[42a] See paras. 21–23 to 21–26.

[42b] Dairy Produce Regulations 1984 (S.I. 1984 No. 1047).

[43] Agreements which attempt to contract out of mandatory provisions of the statute may be unenforceable: *Johnson* v. *Moreton* [1980] A.C. 37.

[44] Sheep Stocks Valuation (Scotland) Act 1937, s. 1; Hill Farming Act 1946, s. 28; *Tufnell and Nether Whitehaugh Co. Ltd.*, 1977 S.L.T. (Land Ct.) 14. See Gill, *Agricultural Holdings*, 233 *et seq.*

to the 1949 Act,[45] it is important that he should have information as to the potential amount which may become due upon termination of the tenancy; the seller should have records of such improvements since he will have consented to or been notified of them.[46] The purchaser should stipulate in the offer that the only improvements for which he will be liable are those disclosed in writing by the seller. Provision should also be made in the offer for the seller giving formal notice to quit to any tenant where possession of the farm is to be a condition of the bargain.

15–133   (c) **Farms where tenancy is terminating.** In circumstances where an existing tenancy is terminating and the landlord is selling with vacant possession the first essential matter for the seller is to ensure that there will be no legal impediment to the tenant removing. If the tenant has given appropriate notice to quit or the landlord has obtained a decree of removing or of irritancy the legal position is clear enough, but, if the landlord has served notice to quit and the tenant has not served a counter-notice or has failed to contest the notice successfully on one of the grounds in section 25(2) of the Agricultural Holdings (Scotland) Act 1949, the notice to quit may nevertheless be nullified by the curious provisions of section 31 of the Act.[47] Moreover, if a counter-notice has been served by the tenant the landlord may have no title to apply for consent of the Land Court to the operation of the notice to quit if he has contracted to sell the farm.[48] In any such circumstances the landlord, although he may negotiate for a sale of the farm, should not conclude the contract of sale until the tenant has actually quitted the farm.

15–134   Other matters to which the parties should have regard are (a) the rights of the outgoing tenant to remove fixtures or buildings erected by him under section 14 of the 1949 Act and its provisions as to notices and counter-notices, (b) arrangements as to the purchaser having access for operations such as ploughing and sowing (the lease may provide for this matter and the provisions of the contract of sale should correspond to the landlord's rights therein), (c) the obligations of the landlord to pay compensation for improvements and for growing crops and dung, hay and straw, all of which should be made the responsibility of the purchaser under the contract of sale, and (d) where there are bound sheep stocks the estimated compensation payable will have to be taken into account in determining the price offered.[49]

---

[45] 1949 Act, s. 48.
[46] *Ibid.*, ss. 50, 51.
[47] See as to corresponding provisions in older English statutes, *Blay* v. *Dadswell* [1922] 1 K.B. 632 and *Rochester and Chatham Joint Sewerage Board* v. *Clinch* [1925] Ch. 753.
[48] *Stewart* v. *Moir*, 1965 S.L.T. (Land Ct.) 11; *Gordon* v. *Rankin*, 1972 S.L.T. (Land Ct.) 7.
[49] See para. 15–132.

(4) Options

–135 In major development projects options to purchase heritable property are now frequently used. The adoption of options and cross-options may be convenient to attain various objects, *e.g.* to acquire right to purchase the site if all necessary planning and building permissions are obtained, to embody a contract between the developer and the finance house which is funding the project, and to permit of flexibility in adjusting the operative date or dates for the purpose of minimising liability to capital gains tax by the use of suspensive conditions.[50] The documentation varies in accordance with the nature of the proposed development and the relationship of the parties. An option to purchase land must be constituted by probative or holograph writing,[51] but the exercise of an option does not require probative writing,[52] nor does a collateral arrangement such as a contract to perform building works.[53] In practice the documents relating to developments which constitute the options are executed formally and, although it is not strictly necessary, the exercise of the options is usually made by probative or holograph writing.

Style 15A

Offer for semi-detached villa for purchaser's own occupation

–136 On behalf of our client [*name and address*] we hereby offer to purchase from your client [*name and address*] the semi-detached villa [*name, street number and town or other identifying description*] together with the garden ground pertaining thereto and [*the garage and*] all other buildings or erections thereon as at present occupied by your client, and also the fixtures and fittings on and in the said villa and others, the whole parts and pertinents thereof and the whole rights, exclusive, common and mutual pertaining thereto (all of which are herein together called "the subjects") and that on the following terms and conditions:—

1. The price will be £   payable on the date of entry aftermentioned. [*As to qualification by the seller if prompt payment is to be of the essence see paragraph 15–69.*]

2. Entry and vacant possession will be given on [*date*] or such other date as may be mutually agreed.

3. The price will include [*any particular fixtures, fittings or moveable items in house and garden to be included in price—see paragraphs 15–37 and 15–38*]. If a central heating system is included: "The said central heating system with all pipes, radiators, time clock and other appurtenances thereof will be in good working order at the date of entry and any defects in the said

---

[50] Capital Gains Tax Act 1979, ss. 19, 137.

[51] *Hamilton* v. *Lochrane* (1899) 1 F. 478; *Scott* v. *Morrison*, 1979 S.L.T. (Notes) 65, 66; *Stone* v. *MacDonald*, 1979 S.C. 363, 368.

[52] *Sichi* v. *Biagi*, 1946 S.N. 66; *Scott* v. *Morrison, supra*; *Stone* v. *MacDonald, supra*.

[53] *Hamilton* v. *Lochrane, supra*.

system, if notified to your client within   days after the date of entry, will be rectified forthwith at your client's expense."

4. The road, footpath and sewer [*and lane, if any*] *ex adverso* the subjects have been taken over and are maintained by the local authority.

5. The minerals will be included in the sale only in so far as your client has right thereto. If any of the minerals are reserved there are adequate provisions in the title deeds for compensation for damage to the subjects arising from mineral workings past or future.

6. The gable(s) and the boundary walls or fences (other than on the street boundary) are mutual and are maintained jointly with the proprietors of the adjoining properties, and there are no outstanding liabilities for their repair or maintenance. Your client will be responsible for all repairs to the subjects or any such mutual items which have been instructed or become necessary prior to the date of entry.

7. There are no unduly onerous conditions in the title nor any servitudes or rights of way affecting the subjects. The conditions of title have been implemented or, so far as continuing, have been punctually performed.

8. [*Clause as to redemption of feuduty or ground annual as in paragraph 15–90, suitably adapted.*]

9. The rateable value of the subjects is [£   ]. The rates and any other periodic charges, other than charges based on consumption, will be apportioned as at the date of entry.

10. There are no outstanding notices, orders or proposals under the Town and Country Planning (Scotland) Acts or any other public or local statute or regulation or order adversely affecting or likely to adversely affect the subjects.

11. Until the date of entry your client will maintain the subjects in their present condition and will accept liability for damage thereto, however caused, notwithstanding any rule of law to the contrary.

If at the date of entry the subjects are not substantially in their present condition our client will be entitled to resile from the contract of which this offer forms part, without any liability.

12. There will be delivered to us prior to the date of entry (a) a duly executed statutory form of consent by your client's spouse to the sale of the subjects to our client or (b) a duly notarised renunciation of occupancy rights in the subjects granted by your client's spouse or (c) in the event of your client being unmarried an affidavit sworn or affirmed by the seller that the subjects of sale are not a matrimonial home in relation to which a spouse of the seller has occupancy rights, all within the meaning of the Matrimonial Homes (Family Protection) (Scotland) Act 1981 as amended by the Law Reform (Miscellaneous Provisions) (Scotland) Act 1985, and in the event of your delivering to us a statutory form of consent as aforesaid your client's spouse will also, if required by us, sign the disposition aftermentioned as signifying his/her continuing consent to the dealing implemented thereby. If there has been any previous dealing with the subjects to which the said Act applied the appropriate consent, renunciation or affidavit in respect of that dealing will be produced or exhibited to us.[54]

---

[54] As to sales by an executor see para. 15–117.

13. [There will be exhibited before and delivered at settlement to our client a Scottish House Purchaser's Insurance Policy of the National House-Building Council with the Council's Standard Notice of Insurance Cover and the relative Scottish House Purchaser's Agreement in respect of the subjects purchased. Your client warrants that any defects or wants of repair affecting the subjects which have become or may become apparent prior to the date of entry have been or will be timeously notified in terms of the said Policy and Agreement.][55, 55a]

14. In exchange for the price your client will deliver a duly executed disposition in favour of our client or his/her nominees and will deliver or exhibit a good marketable title and clear Searches in the Property Register for 40 years prior to the date of acceptance hereof or for such lesser period as our client may agree and in the Personal Register against all relevant parties for the period of five years prior to the date of acceptance hereof.[56]

15. This offer unless previously withdrawn will be deemed to have been withdrawn unless an acceptance thereof is received by us by [hour] on [date].

NOTES

1. If there is any possibility that the subjects are a listed building and that would be unacceptable to the purchaser a clause may be inserted as follows:

"The subjects are not situated in a conservation area and are not listed as being of architectural or historic interest nor are they the subject of a preservation order."

2. If the building has been erected or any alterations thereon or additions thereto have been made within, say, ten years a clause may be inserted as follows:

"Before the date of entry your client will produce evidence that all necessary planning and building consents and warrants have been obtained in respect of all buildings and works forming part of the subjects (including alterations or additions thereto) and have been complied with. If such evidence is not produced our client will be entitled to resile from the contract of which this offer forms part without any liability."[57]

3. If there is any doubt as to the subjects being in an area zoned for residential purposes add at the beginning of clause 10 of the style:

"The subjects are in an area zoned for residential purposes in the approved Development Plan now current and".

---

[55] Appropriate where house inspection by council was applied for on or after January 1, 1980.

[55a] Consider in the case of relatively new houses an assignation of rights against the builder and in the case of older houses an assignation of any specialist guarantees, *e.g.* in respect of woodworm, dry rot, etc.

[56] For alternatives to this clause (a) where the sale induces first registration in the Land Register see R.T.P.B., para. G.2.08, or (b) where the title is already registered in the Land Register see R.T.P.B., para. G.3.05. As to periods of search see paras. 21–73, 21–84.

[57] *Winston* v. *Patrick*, 1981 S.L.T. 41, and see para. 15–118.

Style 15B

Offer for tenement flat for purchaser's own occupation

15–137   On behalf of our client [*name and address*] we hereby offer to
purchase from your client [*name and address*] the flat being the
westmost house on the second floor above the ground floor [*or
otherwise as the case may be*] of the tenement building [*street
number and town*] together with [*specify any garage, store, cellar
or other erection or plot of ground owned exclusively for use by
proprietor of flat purchased*] as at present occupied by your client
and also the fixtures and fittings on and in the said flat and others,
the parts, privileges and pertinents thereof and the whole rights
exclusive, common and mutual pertaining thereto (all of which are
herein together called "the subjects") and that on the following
terms and conditions:—

1. to 5. [*As in Style 15A, clauses 1–5, adapted as appropriate.*]

6. There will be conveyed to our client in the disposition
aftermentioned a right of property in common with the proprietors
of other flats [*and shops*] in the said building to the roof, main
walls, *solum*, entrance, stairways and all other common parts of
the said building and all rights of access required for maintenance
and the proper enjoyment and use of the subjects. Our client as
proprietor of the subjects will be liable for an equitable share of
the cost of maintenance, repair, insurance and management of the
common parts of the said building and the remaining flats [*and
shops*] in the said building are validly burdened similarly. There
are no outstanding obligations in respect of the maintenance or
repair of the said common parts and your client will be responsible
for all repairs to the subjects and his/her share of the maintenance
or repair of the said common parts which have been instructed or
become necessary prior to the date of entry.

7. [*As in Style 15A, clause 7.*]

8. The subjects are burdened with an annual feuduty [ground
annual] of £   , being an unallocated proportion of a *cumulo*
feuduty [ground annual] of £   .

9. [*As in Style 15A, clause 9, adding a reference to apportionment
also of feuduty or ground annual.*]

10. The subjects are in an area zoned for residential purposes in
the approved Development Plan and are not listed for treatment
under the Housing (Scotland) Acts. There are no outstanding
notices, orders or proposals under the Town and Country Planning
(Scotland) Acts or any other public or local statute or regulation
or order adversely affecting or likely to adversely affect the
subjects.

11 to 15. [*As in Style 15A, clauses 11–15, so far as appropriate.*]

Style 15C

Offer for licensed hotel (limited companies)

15–138   On behalf of our clients [*name and address*] (hereinafter called
"the Purchaser") we hereby offer to purchase from your clients
[*name and address*] (hereinafter called "the Seller") the property
known as [*name and address of hotel*] together with the ground

attached extending to [*area*][58] or thereby all as delineated within red boundaries on the plan [*annexed and signed as relative hereto or as annexed to Particulars furnished by the Seller*] (which plan is demonstrative only and not taxative); Together also with (1) the whole fixtures and fittings thereon and therein (2) the business of a licensed hotel, including the goodwill thereof, carried on in the said property and (3) the parts, privileges and pertinents of the whole subjects of offer and the whole rights of access and all other rights exclusive, common and mutual effeiring thereto (all as the same, being the whole property and others described in the Particulars of Sale, a copy of which is annexed and signed as relative hereto, are hereinafter called "the subjects"), and that on the following terms and conditions:—

1. The price will be £   payable on the date of entry aftermentioned and will be apportioned between heritable and moveable items as agreed between the Purchaser and the Seller or, failing such agrement being reached within three weeks after the date of entry, as determined by an expert to be chosen by the parties or, in the event of failure to agree, to be appointed by the Chairman for the time being of the Royal Institution of Chartered Surveyors (Scottish Branch) on the application of either party.[59]

2. The whole contents of the subjects, including the fixtures and fittings above mentioned and all furniture, furnishings, effects, equipment and utensils of every kind including without prejudice to that generality [*any particular items*] will be included in the sale and in the said price. An inventory of said contents will be prepared by the Seller and agreed with the Purchaser within three days of acceptance of this offer. All the said contents belong absolutely to the Seller and none is subject to hire purchase, leasing or similar agreement.[60]

3. Entry and vacant possession of the subjects will be given on the first working day after the Licensing Board approve the transfer of the licence aftermentioned or on such other day as may be mutually agreed.[61]

4. The wet and dry stocks (as those terms are normally interpreted in the licensing trade) so far as of a usable and saleable nature commensurate with a good hotel business will be taken over by the Purchaser as at the date of entry at a value to be agreed between the Purchaser and the Seller based on the lower of the wholesale cost price to the Seller and the realisable value thereof. In the event of failure to agree the value shall be fixed by an independent expert to be appointed by the parties whose decision shall be final and binding on the parties: the cost of such valuation shall be borne by the parties equally between them. The value of the stocks so agreed or fixed, with any Value Added Tax due thereon, will be paid by the Purchaser to the Seller within seven days of the value thereof being ascertained as aforesaid.

5. [*As in Style 15A, clause 9.*]
6. [*As in paragraph 15–90 supra, suitably adapted.*]
7. [*As in Style 15A, clause 5.*]

---

[58] Specify any separate areas, staff accommodation or common parking areas—see para. 15–30.
[59] See para. 15–68.
[60] See note 1 to this style.
[61] See note 2 to this style.

8. There are no unduly onerous conditions in the title and in particular there are no conditions or restrictions therein which might prevent, limit or restrict the use of the subjects as a licensed hotel. There are no servitudes, wayleaves or rights exercisable by third parties affecting the subjects.

9. There is in existence for the subjects a [full 7 day] [restricted] hotel licence issued under the Licensing (Scotland) Act 1976 for the current period held by the Seller or its nominee. This offer and any contract of sale following thereon is conditional on the said licence being transferred to the Purchaser or its nominee at the meeting of the Licensing Board of [date of next meeting of the Board]. The Seller will and, in the event of the licence being held in name of the Seller's nominee, ensure that its nominee will:—

(a) not, during the currency thereof, surrender the said licence or cause it to be forfeited,

(b) co-operate in an application for transfer of the said licence to the Purchaser or its nominee and lodge the said licence with a suitable letter of consent to the application with the clerk to the Licensing Board timeously and

(c) lodge all such other applications as may be permitted under the said Act with the clerk to the Licensing Board as may reasonably be requested by the Purchaser including, without prejudice to the foregoing generality, applications for consent to alterations and for alterations of the permitted hours provided that the Purchaser shall meet the cost thereof.

In the event of the said application for transfer of said licence not being granted at said meeting of the Licensing Board the Purchaser shall, at its own discretion, have the right to resile from the contract of which this offer forms part without any compensation due to or by either party.

10. The Seller (i) will be entitled to collect all sums due to it prior to and at the date of entry and (ii) will discharge all debts due by it and all claims made against it in connection with the business carried on in the subjects prior to and including the date of entry and will free and relieve the Purchaser of all such debts and claims. The Seller will use its best endeavours to ensure that the transfer of the business to the Purchaser is effected smoothly and will, on acceptance of this offer, furnish to the Purchaser details of all bookings made in respect of the said business for dates subsequent to the date of entry [and the Purchaser will be entitled to require the Seller to cancel any such bookings which it does not wish to accept]. As from the date of acceptance of this offer and conclusion of a contract of purchase following hereon the Seller will furnish to the Purchaser details of all applications for bookings for dates subsequent to the date of entry to enable the Purchaser to deal with them as it may decide.

11. The Seller will supply to the Purchaser with its acceptance of this offer a list of the persons employed in the business carried on in the subjects and particulars of the conditions of their employment and the Purchaser shall in terms of the Transfer of Undertakings (Protection of Employment) Regulations 1981 and subject to the exclusion relating to occupational pension schemes in Regulation 7 thereof take over these employees so far as still employed in said business at the date of entry, all in terms of the said Regulations. The wages, national insurance contributions and

holiday pay of such employees will be apportioned between the Seller and the Purchaser as at the date of entry. The Seller will not as from the date of this offer take on or engage any additional employees in the said business without the written consent of the Purchaser.

12. Prior to the date of entry there will be exhibited and, if the Purchaser so requires, delivered to the Purchaser certificates or other evidence that:—

(a) the subjects conform to the requirements of the Offices, Shops and Railway Premises Act 1963, the Health and Safety at Work etc. Act 1974 and any subsequent amendments or modifications or alterations thereof and of any regulations, instruments and orders affecting the subjects whether issued thereunder or otherwise;

(b) a current valid Fire Certificate for the whole of the subjects has been issued unconditionally;

(c) there are no outstanding notices, orders or proposals by the local or any other authority or body requiring repairs or other works to be carried out on or in the subjects;

(d) the current permitted use of the subjects within the meaning of the Town and Country Planning (Scotland) Acts is as a licensed hotel;

(e) the subjects are not affected by any existing planning scheme or proposals by the planning authorities and are not listed as being of architectural or historic interest and do not lie within a conservation area; and

(f) the roads, footpaths and sewers *ex adverso* the subjects have been taken over and are maintained by the local authority and there are no road widening or other road proposals affecting the subjects.

13. (a) Copies of any notices affecting the subjects issued after the date of this offer and before the date of entry will be delivered to the Purchaser within seven days of receipt thereof by the Seller.

(b) Copies of all planning permissions, building warrants and certificates of completion issued in respect of the construction of or any alteration on or addition to the subjects within ten years prior to the date of this offer will be delivered to the Purchaser prior to the date of entry together with evidence that the conditions of all such permissions or warrants have been complied with.

14. The Seller warrants that there will at the date of entry be no agreements for the continuing supply of beverages, alcoholic or otherwise, to the subjects with any supplier thereof.

15. Until the date of entry the Seller will maintain the subjects and contents in their present condition and will accept liability for loss or damage, however caused, and will use its best endeavours to ensure that there is no material change in the business conducted in the subjects. If at the date of entry there is any material deterioration in the condition of or change in the subjects or the said business the Purchaser will be entitled to resile from the contract of which this offer forms part without any liability.

16. At the date of entry the Seller will, in exchange for the price:—

(a) exhibit or deliver to the Purchaser a good marketable title to the subjects and (i) clear searches in the Property Register for 40 years prior to the date of acceptance hereof or for such lesser period as the Purchaser may agree and in the Personal Register against all relevant parties for the period of five years prior to the date of acceptance hereof and (ii) a clear search in the Companies Register of Charges and Company Files against all limited companies interested in the subjects within the period of search in the Property Register brought down to 22 days and 16 days respectively after the companies concerned ceased to be infeft in the subjects or any part thereof;[62]

(b) deliver a duly executed disposition of the subjects in favour of the Purchaser or its nominees.

17. With regard to the said business the Seller will at the date of entry:—

(a) deliver to the Purchaser the books and records of the business and all material correspondence including without prejudice to that generality all books and correspondence relating to functions held in the subjects and all correspondence plans and documents relating to the subjects or any extensions or alterations thereto, but under reservation to the Seller of a right of access thereto when reasonably required for a period of 6 months after the date of entry, and

(b) deliver to the Purchaser an undertaking, in terms of a draft to be prepared by the Purchaser's solicitors, that neither the Seller nor any of its directors will trade, whether as a company or individual or partnership or be engaged in any manner of way in business as a hotelier or restaurateur within a radius of
miles from the subjects for a period of   years from and after the date of entry.

18. [As in Style 15A, clause 15.]

NOTES

1. If any items are on hire-purchase or rental the purchaser should stipulate for the option either to require the seller to terminate the relevant agreements or to take over the agreements as from the date of entry.

2. If entry is taken before the licence has been transferred (which is not normally advisable) equitable arrangements will require to be made, e.g. on the date of entry the purchaser will deposit in joint names a sum of up to one-half of the price of which £x will be agreed to represent rent for the subjects and use of the furnishings and equipment for the period from the date of entry to seven days after the next meeting of the Licensing Board, and will pay for the wet and dry stocks at agreed value. If the licence is duly transferred to the purchaser the deposited amount (with all interest accrued thereon) will be payable to the seller within seven days after the decision of the Licensing Board together with the balance of the price with interest thereon at a stipulated rate from the date of entry until payment. If a transfer of the licence is not obtained and the purchaser resiles under clause 9 of the offer then within seven days after such decision £x of

---

[62] See paras. 15–78 and 15–79 for variations where title is about to be or has been registered in Land Register. As regards companies see para. 21–87.

the deposited sum will be paid to the seller and the balance of the deposited sum with all interest accrued on the whole deposited sum will be paid to the purchaser, the seller will take over the wet and dry stocks valued as at that date and the purchaser will be responsible for the proportion of rates, wages, etc., in respect of the period of his occupation from the date of entry until outgoing. The major risk in such an arrangement is the possibility of insolvency of either party before the decision of the licensing board is obtained. That risk may be minimised (a) by expressing the deposit as in trust for performance of the contract in accordance with its terms and (b) by delivery of the executed disposition to the purchaser at the date of entry with an exchange of formal letters to the effect that the deed is to be held by the purchaser until full payment of the price and interest in terms of the contract has been made when the purchaser shall be entitled to record or register it but otherwise, if such payment is not duly made, in trust for the seller to whom it will be re-delivered.

3. If the purchase is made conditional upon a structural survey a provision on the lines of clause 10 of Style 15D may be inserted.

Style 15D

Offer for commercial property subject to leases (limited companies)

139   On behalf of our clients [*name and address*] (hereinafter called "the Purchaser") we hereby offer to purchase from your clients [*name and address*] (hereinafter called "the Seller") the property known as [*name and/or address of property*] as delineated within red boundaries on the plan (or Ordnance Survey Sheet) annexed and signed as relative hereto (which plan is demonstrative only and not taxative),[63] the landlords' fixtures and fittings therein and thereon, the parts, privileges and pertinents of the whole subjects of offer and the whole rights of access exclusive, common and mutual effeiring thereto (all hereinafter called "the subjects") and that on the following terms and conditions:—

1. The price will be £   payable on the date of entry aftermentioned.

2. Entry and vacant possession, subject only to and with the benefit of the Leases aftermentioned, will be given on [*date*] or such earlier date as may be mutually agreed.

3. It is an essential condition of this offer that the subjects comprise the office premises and approximate areas thereof (and the parking facilities) and are currently let under leases all as specified in the Schedule annexed and executed as relative hereto.

4. It shall be shown prior to the date of entry that:—

(i) There are no outstanding notices, orders or proposals under the Town and Country Planning (Scotland) Acts or any other public or local statute or regulation or order adversely affecting or likely to adversely affect the subjects;

---

[63] Specify any separate areas or common parking or service areas if not within the main building—see para. 15–30.

(ii) The existing use of the subjects as office accommodation [*or otherwise as the case may be*] is the permitted use, free from conditions, for the purposes of the Town and Country Planning (Scotland) Acts [and that unconditional planning permission exists for the use of the whole of said car parking area for not less than   cars];

(iii) The subjects comply with the Offices, Shops and Railway Premises Act 1963 and the Health and Safety at Work etc. Act 1974; and

(iv) The roads, footpaths and sewers *ex adverso* the subjects have been taken over and are maintained by the local authority.

5. There shall be exhibited prior to the date of entry:—

(i) Current unconditional Fire Certificates in respect of all the component parts of the subjects; and

(ii) In respect of all works carried out on the subjects within the past ten years all necessary planning consents and all necessary building warrants and certificates of completion under the Building (Scotland) Acts.

6. The Seller warrants that no blue asbestos, high alumina cement, wood-wool slabs or calcium chloride have been used in any part of the structure of the subjects. This warranty shall remain in force after the date of entry notwithstanding that settlement of the transaction has taken place.

7. The Seller (i) warrants that the subjects are in good tenantable order, condition and repair and undertakes, in the event of any part of the subjects not being in that state, to effect before the date of entry any remedial works necessary to put the whole of the subjects in that condition (ii) accepts liability to maintain the subjects in that condition during the period until the date of entry and to restore any damage to the subjects, however caused, during that period (iii) will be responsible for implementing any statutory notices relating to the subjects issued before the date of entry and (iv) undertakes to keep the subjects insured until the date of entry against fire and all other usual risks for their full reinstatement value and to exhibit the policy or policies of insurance endorsed to show the interest of the Purchaser within seven days of acceptance of this offer.[63a] In the event of the subjects suffering material damage, however caused, before the date of entry which is not restored before that date the Purchaser will be entitled to resile from the contract of which this offer forms part, without liability, and for this purpose damage will be deemed to be material if in the opinion of the Purchaser's surveyors Messrs. [   ] a hypothetical tenant of the subjects under a lease would be entitled to an abatement of rent of 5 per cent or more in respect of the damage.

8. There are no conditions in the title deeds or elsewhere which might prevent, limit or restrict the use of the subjects for their present purpose and there are no servitudes or wayleaves adversely affecting the subjects or any part thereof.

9. [Clause as to redemption of feuduty or ground annual as in paragraph 15–90 *supra*.]

10. This offer is conditional upon the Purchaser obtaining (i) a

---

[63a] The purchaser may effect its own insurance but this provision may be useful in any interim period—see para. 15–115.

structural report in relation to the subjects which is to its satisfaction and (ii) information satisfactory to the Purchaser as to the financial standing of the present tenants of the subjects. Access to the subjects will be given to the Purchaser's surveyor immediately after conclusion of the missives for the purpose of making his inspection and, if this condition is not withdrawn in its entirety within 14 days from conclusion of the missives, the contract which includes this offer shall terminate without liability on either party.

11. As regards the Leases specified in the said Schedule:—

(i) All of the said Leases are head leases and there are no sub-leases or sub-tenancies or subsidiary rights of occupation of any part of the subjects;

(ii) There have not been and will not prior to the date of entry be any amendment, alteration or variation, formal or informal, of the said Leases between the landlords and the tenants thereunder [*except as stated in the said Schedule*];

(iii) The tenants are not in breach of any of their obligations thereunder and there are no claims against the landlords outstanding, and the Seller will relieve the Purchaser of any such claims arising prior to the date of entry;

(iv) Any applications for the consent of the landlords under said Leases which are now outstanding or which may be submitted prior to the date of entry shall be exhibited to the Purchaser, and the Seller shall not grant or refuse the same save in accordance with the instructions of the Purchaser; and

(v) The Seller shall exhibit to the Purchaser not later than seven days after acceptance of this offer the said Leases or official extracts or copies thereof and all permissions, warrants, consents and certificates of completion issued in relation to any part of the subjects and all documents relating to consents or approval sought or given under the said Leases. If any of the said Leases and related documents contain any unusual provisions which are not acceptable to the Purchaser, the Purchaser may within 14 days after receipt of such Leases or documents resile from the purchase without liability.

12. The Seller will formally intimate the transfer of ownership to all tenants in the subjects immediately after the date of entry and will exhibit to the Purchaser within seven days thereafter evidence of such intimation.

13. [*As in Style 15A, clause 14.*]

14. [*As in Style 15A, clause 15.*]

SCHEDULE

[Specify each separately let office, shop, etc., in the subjects, its approximate floor area and the current lease thereof by reference to parties, dates and recording date and the current rents payable in respect of each.]

Style 15E

Offer for farm with vacant possession

On behalf of our client [*name and address*] we hereby offer to purchase from your client [*name and address*] the farm and lands of [*name of farm and county*] as at present owned and occupied by your client and extending to   acres or thereby all as more particularly described in the Particulars supplied by [*you*] [*your client*] and delineated on the plan annexed thereto, [*but under exception of the parts hereinafter specified*][64] together with the farmhouse and other buildings, the fittings and fixtures in and upon the same, the fixed plant and machinery and fixed equipment, the whole metals and minerals including sand and gravel, the whole timber standing or fallen, the growing crops, the shootings and fishings [*if salmon fishings specify the same precisely stating whether right exclusive or joint*], the live and dead stock, dung and implements all as stated in the said Particulars [*as specified in the inventory thereof annexed and signed as relative hereto*], the whole rights, uses, servitudes, wayleaves, access rights, existing water supply and drainage systems and rights relating thereto, and the whole pertinents of the subjects (the whole of the foregoing being hereinafter called "the subjects") and that on the following terms and conditions:—

1. The price will be £   payable on the date of entry aftermentioned. [*If a deposit is made, specify same and date payable, the balance of the price being payable on the date of entry.*]

2. The said price will be apportioned as to £   on the heritable property and £   on the stock, crop and implements.

3. Entry and vacant possession of the subjects will be given on [*date*].

4. The rateable value of the farmhouse is £   , of the farm cottages is £   and of the shootings is £   . The rates will be apportioned between the seller and the purchaser as at the date of entry.

5. Any feuduty and standard charge have been or will be redeemed by the seller and receipts for the redemption payments will be exhibited at or prior to the date of entry within one month thereafter.

6. Your client will have no claim for improvements to buildings or other fixed equipment or in respect of unexhausted manures nor any other claim arising at waygoing.

7. [*As in Style 15A, clause 10.*]

8. Your client will pay and so free and relieve our client of all outstanding accounts for repairs or improvements instructed or due by your client prior to the date of entry.

9. There are no grants in respect of buildings on the subjects which are or may be repayable in whole or in part to the local authority or any other person or body, or otherwise, if there is any such grant, your client will make repayment thereof before the date of entry.

10. It is a condition of this offer that the water supply to the farmhouse, cottages and other buildings on the subjects is ample for those properties and is private to the subjects and not shared and that the drainage of the whole buildings on the subjects is to a septic tank or tanks within the boundaries of the subjects [*or otherwise as the case may be*].

11. There is no right of access, right of way, wayleave or other servitude right over or affecting the subjects [*other than (specify)*].

---

[64] See note (a).

12. Your client will assign to our client the benefit of any income tax allowances remaining due in respect of capital expenditure on the subjects and will make available all necessary schedules, figures and vouchers in connection with claims for such allowances.[65]

13. [*As in Style 15A, clause 11.*]

14. [*As in Style 15A, clause 12.*]

15. [*As in Style 15C, clause 11.*]

16. [*As in Style 15A, clause 14.*]

17. Your client will provide an Ordnance Survey Sheet, in duplicate, showing the subjects to be recorded in the Register of Sasines along with the Disposition to be granted in favour of our client or his nominees. [*If the subjects lie in an operational area for purposes of registration of title the reference to recording in the Register of Sasines will be omitted.*]

18. [*As in Style 15A, clause 15.*]

Inventory of Plant, Equipment, Implements, etc.

NOTES

(a) If any parts of the subjects are to be excepted specify by reference to plan on which the excepted parts should be distinctively coloured or edged with hatching.

(b) In the case of a dairy farm include stipulation as to dairy produce quota—see para. 15–130.

B. Sales by Auction

-141   In current practice sales of heritable property by public roup are much less common than formerly. It is no longer obligatory for sales by heritable creditors to be made by public exposure[66] and almost all sales by proprietors are now effected by private bargain. Nevertheless a seller may prefer to sell publicly, as in the case of a proprietor whose title has a remediable defect and who wishes to impose the cost of rectifying it upon the purchaser by the familiar provision in articles of roup that the title be taken as it stands, or a trustee in sequestration who wishes to avoid the procedure required under the Bankruptcy (Scotland) Act 1913[67] for a sale by private bargain, or if the sale is by a heritable creditor and the possibility of subsequent foreclosure is anticipated.

-142   Public sales are normally conducted under articles of roup, prepared and executed in probative form by the seller, which contain all the conditions of sale, and the contract is constituted by signature of a minute of enactment and preference, also executed in probative form,

[65] Capital Allowances Act 1968, s. 68 as amended by Finance Act 1978, s. 39.

[66] Conveyancing and Feudal Reform (Scotland) Act 1970, ss. 25, 35.

[67] s. 111. In sequestrations commencing after April 1, 1986 sale procedure is much simpler—Bankruptcy (Scotland) Act 1985, s. 39.

by the judge of the roup and the successful bidder and also, to preserve recourse against him on failure of the highest bidder to complete, by the second-highest bidder.

15–143   Various styles of articles of roup are in use, *e.g.* (a) comprehensive articles which contain the whole conditions in a single document, or (b) a brief form which contains only a description of the subjects and the exposer and the place, date and time of the exposure, to which there are annexed schedules of the special conditions of sale such as the upset price, date of entry, etc., and general conditions of sale. The principal elements are (1) a description of the subjects, usually a formal conveyancing description which the seller proposes to incorporate in the disposition implementing the sale, (2) an identifying description of the exposer which, if he is selling under powers contained in a heritable security, describes the security deed, (3) the place, date and time of the exposure, (4) the upset price and the term of entry, (5) the procedure at the auction such as the minimum amount of bids and a requirement that the successful bidder shall execute a minute of enactment and preference or minute of sale binding himself to the purchase, (6) provisions as to the purchaser making a deposit or finding caution within a short period after the auction with a right of recourse, in the option of the exposer, against preceding offerers if the highest offerer fails to provide a deposit or satisfactory caution, (7) the obligation of the exposer to grant a disposition in implement of the sale and the writs which will be delivered therewith, (8) a provision that offerers will be held to have satisfied themselves as to the sufficiency of the titles, the extent of the subjects and the burdens affecting them and that the seller's title to the subjects will be accepted as it stands, (9) a clause preserving the conditions in the articles, notwithstanding delivery of the disposition, in any subsequent difference between the parties, (10) the nomination of the judge of the roup (normally by a separate minute completed just before the sale incorporated in advance by the articles), and (11) an arbitration clause.

In addition there may be special qualifications which offerers will be required to accept, *e.g.* unusual exceptions from warrandice in the disposition to be granted by the seller or as to searches to be exhibited or delivered. In relation to modern legislation it may be desirable to include special conditions:

(i) *Redemption of ground burdens.* The seller would undertake to redeem any allocated feuduty or ground annual; if the burden is unallocated the purchaser would require to accept liability for future payments. (It is thought that a provision on such matters is strictly unnecessary; if the burden is allocated the seller is obliged under section 5 of the Land Tenure Reform (Scotland) Act 1974 to redeem the burden and section 21 forbids contracting out, whereas if it is unallocated the purchaser's obligation to accept liability will be covered by the condition (8) above mentioned.)

(ii) *Matrimonial homes.* If the seller has any reason to doubt that his or her spouse will co-operate a condition may be inserted that, if the necessary consent or renunciation by the spouse is not delivered or exhibited before the date of entry, the seller will be entitled to cancel the sale without liability for damages.[67a]

(iii) *Land registration.* If the sale induces first registration the condition as to title will be altered appropriately, possibly with a further condition that, if there is an exclusion from indemnity which the arbiter shall determine is not material the purchaser will require to accept the title but if there is such an exclusion which the arbiter shall determine is material the seller will be entitled to cancel the sale without liability for damages.

–144 After appropriate advertisement,[68] on the day of the exposure the articles of roup, along with the title deeds, are laid on the table and bidding may commence at the upset price or more. The seller may not bid nor employ any person to do so on his behalf; that is white bonneting and is illegal,[69] and it is doubtful whether the seller can reserve a right to bid.[70] The judge of the roup may not bid since he is the seller's agent until the fall of the hammer.[71] Nor may a sole residuary legatee when property forming part of the residue of the trust estate is exposed by the trustees, since in substance he is the seller,[72] but one of several residuary legatees may do so since he is not identical with the sellers and so it is not a case of *idem emptor et venditor.*[73] On similar reasoning the owner cannot bid at a sale by a heritable creditor since the selling creditor is truly an agent for the owner selling under the mandate to do so contained in his security and any surplus will accrue to the owner.[74] One of several heritable creditors exposing the property may bid,[75] and it is competent to reserve in the articles that right to one of several co-proprietors who are selling.[76] If a bid is made by one of a body of trustees exposing the property it may be open to challenge by a beneficiary on the ground that he is *auctor in rem suam*, but a competing bidder cannot object.[77] At a public sale by a trustee in sequestration any creditor may purchase, but not the trustee or any commissioner or any solicitor

---

[67a] Unnecessary where the sale is by a trustee in bankruptcy or a heritable creditor.

[68] In sales by a heritable creditor under a bond and disposition in security there are statutory requirements as to advertisement: Conveyancing (Scotland) Act 1924, s. 38 as substituted by Conveyancing and Feudal Reform (Scotland) Act 1970, s. 36.

[69] *Grey* v. *Stewart* (1753) Mor. 9560.

[70] See article, 1967 S.L.T. (News) 231 and authorities cited.

[71] *Anderson* v. *Croall & Sons Ltd.* (1903) 6 F. 153, 159.

[72] *Faulds* v. *Corbet* (1859) 21 D. 587.

[73] *Shiell* v. *Guthrie's Trs.* (1874) 1 R. 1083.

[74] *Jamieson* v. *Edinburgh Mutual Investment and Building Society*, 1913 2 S.L.T. 52.

[75] *Wright* v. *Buchanan*, 1917 S.C. 73.

[76] *Thom* v. *Macbeth* (1875) 3 R. 161.

[77] *Aberdein* v. *Stratton's Trs.* (1867) 5 M. 726.

employed by the trustee or a partner of such solicitor.[78] Bidders must not act unfairly, as by collusively agreeing that one would be preferred and the others would refrain from bidding.[79]

15–145   The articles of roup usually provide that the successful bidder must within a short period find caution for payment of the price and, in the event of his failure to do so, the exposer shall be entitled either to cancel the sale and retain the property or to require the immediately lower offerer to implement his offer. In deciding whether the caution offered is acceptable the seller must exercise his discretion fairly,[80] but he may refuse to accept as cautioner a party who is not subject to the jurisdiction of the Scottish courts.[81] A provision in the normal form does not entitle the preceding offerer to insist upon purchase if the highest offerer fails to find caution; the condition is for the benefit of the seller who may elect to accept the higher offer without satisfactory caution.[82]

15–146   The articles of roup normally provide that the offerers will be held to have satisfied themselves as to the validity and sufficiency of the exposer's title which will be accepted as it stands. Such a condition will not oblige the purchaser to accept a title which excludes a material or substantial part of the subjects offered,[83] but it will preclude withdrawal where the excluded area is relatively small.[84] The condition will not bind the purchaser to proceed if the title is incurably defective in a material matter, but if the defect is remediable the purchaser cannot withdraw and must rectify the defect at his own expense.[85] If the articles stipulate that the purchaser will accept the subjects with any burdens contained in the title deeds the offerer must accept the title offered with a special pecuniary burden.[86] A "title as it stands" condition in articles would not, on the application of the foregoing principles, excuse failure to furnish a consent, renunciation or affidavit under section 6 of the Matrimonial Homes (Family Protection) (Scotland) Act 1981 in relation to the sale of a dwelling-house exposed for sale with vacant possession, since the purchaser would not be entitled to obtain occupancy in a question with the spouse of the seller.[87] On the other hand if the subjects of sale lie in an operational area for the purposes of registration of title and there is a discrepancy

---

[78] Bankruptcy (Scotland) Act 1913, s. 116. In sequestrations commencing after April 1, 1986 it is incompetent for the permanent trustee or an associate of his or for any commissioner to purchase—Bankruptcy (Scotland) Act 1985, s. 39(8).
[79] *Murray* v. *Mackwhan* (1783) Mor. 9567.
[80] *Menzies* v. *Barstow* (1840) 2 D. 1317; *cf. Kennedy* v. *Ramsay's Trs.* (1847) 9 D. 1333.
[81] *Davidson* v. *Kerr*, January 19, 1815, F.C.
[82] *Walker* v. *Gavin* (1787) Mor. 14193.
[83] *Hamilton* v. *Western Bank of Scotland* (1861) 23 D. 1033.
[84] *Morton* v. *Smith* (1877) 5 R. 83; *Young* v. *McKellar Ltd.*, 1909 S.C. 1340.
[85] *Carruthers* v. *Stott* (1825) 4 S. 34.
[86] *Davidson* v. *Dalziel* (1881) 8 R. 990.
[87] s. 6(1)(*b*).

in boundaries which is unacceptable to the Keeper, the remedial action required, or if need be the exclusion of a relatively small area from indemnity, would require to be undertaken or accepted by the purchaser.

-147   At the conclusion of the bidding the highest offerer and the judge of the roup sign a minute of enactment and preference annexed to the articles, which is attested. If no offer of the upset price or more is received the judge of the roup signs a minute of adjournment appended to the articles; such a minute does not require attestation.

-148   The articles usually incorporate an arbitration clause referring to arbitration all questions as to the meaning and interpretation of the articles or the implement thereof, and questions as to the sufficiency of the exposer's title are normally within the scope of the arbitration clause.[88] The judge of the roup has no power to decide questions as to the *bona fides* of a bid, *e.g.* where white bonneting is alleged, arising after the sale is over; his function is restricted to the proper conduct of the proceedings at the sale.[89]

---

[88] *Watt and Anderson* v. *Shaw* (1849) 11 D. 970.
[89] *Strachan* v. *Auld* (1884) 11 R. 756.

CHAPTER 16

FEUDAL TENURE—HISTORY AND DEVELOPMENT

Transmission on Death of Vassal
A. Intestate Succession

B. Testate Succession

Alteration of Feus

Extinction of Feudal Estates

II. STATUTORY ALTERATIONS—1845 TO 1974

Prescription

III. REGISTRATION OF TITLE

Introductory

16–01   The basic land tenure of most land in Scotland is feudal and a brief account of its origins and development is essential to a proper understanding of the modern system of land rights.[1] The history of the system may be conveniently divided into three periods, *viz.*—(1) its origins and development up to 1845, (2) the statutory reforms of the period 1845 to 1974, and (3) the fundamental alterations made by the Land Registration (Scotland) Act 1979.

I. ORIGINS AND DEVELOPMENT BEFORE 1845

Origins of feudal system

16–02   The feudal system originated in Western Europe in the period which followed the overthrow of the Roman Empire. It was introduced in Scotland in a comparatively developed form during the reigns of David I and his successors, and feudalisation of land tenure in the most politically important parts of the kingdom had been effected by the close of the twelfth century.[2] During the succeeding 600 years the system, which had been introduced primarily as an instrument of royal policy, gradually lost its political significance but remained as the pattern of land tenure.

Nature of feudal relationship

16–03   As originally developed in Western Europe the feudal system involved the concept of a grant of lands by an overlord or chief in exchange for military services. This principle was not peculiar to feudalism; possession of land in return for services was familiar in Anglo-Saxon or Celtic Scotland,[3] but the distinctive feature of the feudal system was that the services were owed, not merely by the vassal personally, but in some sense by the land itself—they were constituted inherent conditions of the grant of the land and the grantee's right to the land depended upon performance of the services which were real burdens upon the land prestable from any proprietor who succeeded to it or acquired it.[4] Its basic principles thus were (1) a

---

[1] For fuller accounts see Craigie, *Heritable Rights*, Chap. 1; Menzies, *Lectures*, 456 *et seq.*; Montgomerie Bell, *Lectures*, 561 *et seq.*

[2] *Introduction to Scottish Legal History* (Stair Society), 147, 148; Cosmo Innes, *Studies of Early Scottish History*, 93; G.W.S. Barrow, *Regesta Regum Scottorum*, 4, 5.

[3] *Sources and Literature of Scots Law* (Stair Society), pp. 194, 339 *et seq.*

[4] *Ibid.*, pp. 194, 195.

personal relationship between superior and vassal inferring an obligation of fidelity and performance of services on the part of the vassal and his successors in ownership of the land and a corresponding duty of protection by the superior in the vassal's enjoyment of the land, and (2) a grant of the land which was conditional upon performance of the services by the vassal and his successors.

The feudal system in Norman times

-04 By the time of the Norman Conquest the feudal system had been established in Normandy with well-defined formalities of procedure. A new vassal was formally invested by a solemn act of homage whereby he acknowledged himself vassal of his overlord and swore fidelity and service. He was then put in possession of the lands to be held from his superior. The services of the vassal involved *auxilium et concilium*—service in the superior's forces and attendance at the superior's court. *Auxilium* also implied special pecuniary aid on certain occasions such as the knighting of the superior's son or the marriage of his daughter. Failure on the part of the vassal to perform the services due constituted a breach of the relationship and consequent forfeiture of the land to the superior. The mutual contract inherent in the feudal relationship imposed reciprocal obligations on the superior of protecting the vassal in the enjoyment of the land and of rendering him justice in the superior's courts.

The feudal system in Scotland

-05 Such was the structure of the system which was introduced by David I, and during the twelfth century it became the predominating system of land tenure in Scotland. Its introduction was an act of deliberate policy as one of the props of a strong monarchy, already of proven value in England. The policy was actively continued by his successors and the greater security of holding under a powerful overlord made it acceptable to the vassals of the Crown and of the great barons. The fundamental theory of the system was that all lands originally belonged to the sovereign. As Professor Montgomerie Bell puts it[5]: "The Sovereign could not, in the nature of things, have any superior. His own right, *jure coronae*, was allodial, and free of all obligation and condition. He was the source or fountain from whom all feudal rights flowed." He made grants of lands to be enjoyed by the grantees as vassals of the sovereign on condition of performance of services varying with the kind of grant, and the lands were held by the vassal only while he performed those services. In addition there was a personal relationship between the sovereign as superior and his vassal, the latter being bound by oath to fulfil the services which he had promised and

---

[5] *Lectures*, 562.

the former to protect the vassal in the enjoyment of the lands which he had bestowed. The rights flowing from the ownership of land were thus divided, the vassal having the right of possession, use and enjoyment of it on condition of performing certain services, the *dominium utile*, while the sovereign as superior retained the radical right of ownership, the *dominium directum*. Since the superior retained this right of ownership and the *dominium utile* was a kind of usufruct to which the maxim *salva rei substantia* applied, the superior continued to have a direct interest in the land and in any action which might affect its value adversely. Similarly the vassal, in his turn, could grant sub-feus of parts or a sub-feu of the whole of the land, involving the same type of relationship and creating a further new feudal estate, the vassal now being in the position of superior *quoad* the person to whom he made the subordinate grant, and so on in a chain of sub-feus downwards from the Crown. So if the sovereign feued land to A, and A sub-feued the whole or part of the land to B, in a question between the Crown and A, the Crown was superior and A was vassal, but in a question between A and B, A was superior and B was vassal. If at any stage in the chain a vassal failed to perform the services to his superior upon which the grant of feu was conditional, his estate in the land was liable to forfeiture with the result that any sub-feus granted by the vassal which were derived from it were also forfeited. Alternatively A, instead of sub-feuing, could convey the whole or part of his estate in land to B, in which event no new feudal estate would be created but B would come into the place of A as regards the land conveyed and, subject to acceptance by the superior, would become vassal to the superior in the whole or part of the land conveyed and would become personally liable to the superior for performance of the services stipulated in the feu to A.

16–06   From the foregoing outline there emerge three fundamental characteristics of the system of feudal tenure:

(1) The grant of lands in feu created a new estate in land, the *dominium utile*, which was perpetual so long as the vassal fulfilled the conditions imposed in it but was terminable upon any breach of them.

(2) It involved a direct personal relationship between the superior and the vassal whereby the vassal was obliged personally to perform the services which he had promised and when, upon transmission or conveyance, another person took his place, the new vassal was subject to the same personal obligation since it was implied in the feudal relationship.

(3) The superior was not wholly divested of ownership but retained the *dominium directum* whereby he continued to have a direct interest in preventing any act which might impair or diminish the value of the land.

Feudal Tenures

(1) Ward holding

–07   The original and highest type of feudal tenure was ward holding, the obligation of the vassal being to perform military services. It was known as ward holding from the most important casualty involved in the tenure, namely, ward. In the majority of feudal tenures the superior was entitled to require additional services or casualties on the occurrence of certain events.[6] In ward holding the principal casualties were:

(i) Ward. Since the condition of the grant was military service, which could not be performed by a minor, the superior during the minority of the vassal's heir had custody of the heir's person and the right to receive the full rents from the land as compensation for the loss of the service. The right continued until the heir, if male, became 21, or, if female, became 14.

(ii) Marriage. In view of the obligation to perform military service the superior was concerned to ensure that an heir succeeding to the vassal's estate married into a friendly house. Hence arose the right of the superior to choose a husband or wife for an unmarried vassal who succeeded to the estate and to receive what the heir got with such husband or wife by way of provision or tocher. It was computed originally at three years' and later at two years' free rent of the land and was greater if the vassal married to a person of whom the superior did not approve.[7]

(iii) Recognition. Originally land held on ward tenure was not freely transferable by the vassal since the military service due depended on the vassal's prowess in arms. Accordingly if a vassal alienated more than half of his lands without the superior's consent the whole of the land which had been feued to him was liable to recognition or forfeiture to the superior.

(iv) Non-entry. If an heir of full age succeeded on the death of the vassal but neglected for a year and a day thereafter to enter formally with the superior he became liable to forfeit the holding, but later it came to be recognised that he could enter at any time on payment of the casualty of non-entry which was the retour (the annual value of the lands according to a valuation made during the time of Cromwell) from the date of his ancestor's death. Ward holding and its casualties were abolished after the 1745 Rebellion by the Tenures Abolition Act 1747.

---

[6] See para. 16–12.
[7] See *Drummond* v. *Stuart* (1678) Mor. 8541.

(2) Feu-farm or feu-holding

16–08   This type of holding took the form of a perpetual grant of land on condition of payment of a feuduty (originally by performance of agricultural services, when the tenure was called soccage, and later by payments in grain or in kind and ultimately by payments in money). It developed comparatively late in Scotland, possibly because of the unsettled conditions of the country in the earlier feudal period, but was encouraged for the improvement of agriculture by the Act 1457 c.71 whereby the Crown undertook to restrict its claim when lands fell into ward to the feu-farm dues only. This is the tenure that became the most important form of land holding.

(3) Blench-farm or blench-holding

16–09   In early times this type of grant was made in recognition of some distinguished service and was considered an honourable holding. The tenure was "blench" because the return was small or nominal, given merely as an acknowledgment of the superiority, *e.g.* a penny Scots if asked only. Later this form of tenure came to be used where a full price had been paid in exchange for the grant but it was desired to create the relationship of superior and vassal to enable more effectively the enforcement of other conditions, but more recently that result was achieved by a grant in feu-farm for a nominal feuduty.

(4) Mortification or mortmain

16–10   This tenure was used when land was granted to the Church in return for *preces et lacrymae* (prayers and masses for the soul of the granter). The land was mortified in that there were no casualties falling to the superior since the Church never died. The tenure was abolished at the Reformation, but the abolition extended only to religious purposes: it is still technically competent to have lands mortified for charitable or benevolent purposes although in practice the object is achieved by a grant in feu-farm for a nominal return.

Burgage tenure

16–11   Strictly this was not a feudal tenure: it was a special form of tenure by which lands situated within a royal burgh were held. The growth of trade and commerce led to the establishment of burghs because persons engaged in trade tended to associate themselves together in communities, frequently around royal castles, for reasons of security. The Crown sought to encourage such communities, not only as a source of wealth to the kingdom, but as an element of strength against the power of the great feudal lords, and so conferred upon them important trading privileges and made grants of land to them which were held directly of the Crown. Hence came the tenure of burgage whereby land in a burgh was held, usually through the magistrates, direct from the Crown, sometimes for no money return but more frequently for a burgh mail and on condition of watching and warding, *i.e.* defence against assaults on the community from without and the preservation of order within the burgh. The fact that the magistrates were not themselves superiors led to the practice of the creation of ground annuals in burghs whereby, without creating a new feudal estate, a reserved money rent was charged. Writs relating to burgage property were recorded in the burgh register. It is possible that burgage tenure existed in Scotland from early times but when feudal tenure became normal the documentation of burgage grants was sometimes given a quasi-feudal form, but important distinctions remained; in burgage there were neither feuduties nor casualties nor was subinfeudation permitted, the burgess being free to alienate his property but unable to grant a feu. The distinctions between feudal and burgage tenure were abolished by the Conveyancing (Scotland) Act 1874,[8] and burgh registers were discontinued progressively under the provisions of the Burgh Registers (Scotland) Act 1926.[9]

Booking. In Paisley there was a special form of burgage tenure known as Booking with special rules and a special register kept by the town clerk. Conveyances of land were followed by minutes of booking of which extracts were given out by the town clerk. The forms of conveyances of lands formerly held on the tenure of booking were assimilated to those used in feudal tenure by the 1874 Act[10] although the Register of Booking remained until discontinued under the provisions of the Burgh Registers (Scotland) Act 1926.[11]

Casualties in feu-farm tenure

5–12   Since feudal grants were perpetual it was natural that the superior should seek to obtain from time to time some benefits beyond the annual services. The fact that he had a continuing direct interest in the lands to secure the performance of the services provided a basis for the exaction of further services or casualties on the occurrence of particular events, and casualties were a feature of the system in the earlier period. The more important casualties peculiar to ward holding have already been noticed[12]; the principal casualties in feu-farm or feu-holdings were:

(i) Non-entry. This was a casualty exigible when a vassal's heir neglected to renew his investiture as vassal to the superior. It was a fundamental principle of the feudal system that a superior was entitled to have a

---

[8] s. 25.
[9] s. 1.
[10] s. 26.
[11] s. 5.
[12] para. 16–07.

vassal duly bound to perform the services due, and until the heir duly entered with the superior the lands were in non-entry. The superior could then raise an action of declarator of non-entry to have it found that the bygone non-entry duties since the death of the last vassal until the date of citation belonged to him and that the full rents of the lands also belonged to him.

(ii) Relief was the casualty payable by an heir as the consideration to the superior for granting to him investiture in the lands, the amount being one year's feuduty. So in his first year the heir paid twice the feuduty, once in respect of the ordinary feuduty for that year and once in respect of the casualty of relief.

(iii) Composition was the fine payable to the superior by a purchaser or singular successor in order to obtain recognition as vassal. Originally, owing to the element of *delectus personae* in the relationship of superior and vassal, alienation of the *dominium utile* was not permitted without the superior's approval, but the Tenures Abolition Act 1747 ordained superiors to enter purchasers or disponees on payment of a fine or composition, which was one year's rent of the lands as they were let at the time.

(iv) Liferent escheat was forfeiture of the vassal's interest in the lands during his lifetime and was incurred if the vassal remained a year and a day at the horn, *i.e.* a rebel unrelaxed after denunciation for a crime (which might be no more than non-payment of a civil debt), or had been sentenced to death but had escaped. In such circumstances the superior became entitled to the fruits of the lands. The casualty was abolished by the Tenures Abolition Act 1747 in cases where the denunciation was only in respect of a civil debt.

(v) Disclamation was a casualty incurred if a vassal disowned his superior's right in breach of his duty of loyalty. The penalty was forfeiture of the land feued. This casualty is long since obsolete.

(vi) Purpresture was a casualty incurred if the vassal encroached on any part of the superior's land. Again the penalty was forfeiture but this casualty also is now obsolete.[13]

By 1845 the only casualties which remained in feu holdings were (1) non-entry, (2) relief, (3) composition, and (4) liferent escheat in the case of criminal or capital offences.

Allodial Tenures

(1) Crown property

16–13   Since in feudal theory the Crown is the source of all feudal rights,

---

[13] For an interesting account of the nature of this casualty see *Donald & Sons* v. *Esslemont & Macintosh Ltd.*, 1923 S.C. 122 per Lord President Clyde at 133.

land and rights belonging to the Crown can have no superior and are allodial. Crown property and rights comprise (i) the patrimonial estates of the Crown consisting of lands, castles and palaces and the principality of Scotland belonging to the eldest son of the monarch, (ii) the superiority of lands feued by the Crown, and (iii) all rights reserved by the Crown out of lands feued to subjects, *e.g.* rights to mines of gold and silver and salmon fishings. The reserved rights are *regalia minora*, rights of property in the Crown which are reserved unless specially granted, as distinct from *regalia majora*, rights vested inalienably in the Crown on behalf of the public.

(2) Church property

6–14   Churches, manses, glebes and churchyards of the Church of Scotland were until comparatively recently allodial. After the Reformation it was necessary to provide property for the new Protestant churches. The burden of doing so was laid upon the heritors of the parish and the necessary land was set aside by designation of the presbytery without any grant from the Crown and without the sanction of or confirmation by the Crown. The Church of Scotland (Property and Endowments) Act 1925[14] provided for the transfer of churches and manses of parishes *quoad omnia* (with certain exceptions) to the General Trustees of the Church to the same effect as if a complete feudal title holding of the Crown in free blench farm for payment of a penny Scots yearly if asked only had been duly constituted in favour of the General Trustees. The 1925 Act[15] also provided for the transfer of glebes of such churches to the General Trustees and of churchyards to the parish council of the district but with no corresponding provision as to their being held feudally of the Crown, so that glebes and churchyards are usually still allodial.

(3) Udal tenure

6–15   Udal tenure is peculiar to Orkney and Shetland. The title to udal land consisted of natural possession, provable by witnesses, and no written evidence was required. Upon marriage of the daughter of Christian I, King of Denmark, to James III of Scotland, these islands were pledged in security of her dowry. It has many times been said that the right of redemption was afterwards renounced; that is unclear but at least centuries of Scottish possession and administration have created a title of Scottish sovereignty both *de facto* and *de jure*.[16] In 1611 an Act of the Privy Council of Scotland[17] professed to discharge the

---

[14] s. 28(3).
[15] ss. 30, 32.
[16] *Sources and Literature of Scots Law* (Stair Society), 448, 449; *Lord Advocate* v. *University of Aberdeen*, 1963 S.C. 533.
[17] R.P.C., ix, 181.

foreign laws within Orkney and Shetland, but an earlier Act of the Scottish Parliament in 1567[18] providing that the islands should enjoy their own laws has not been repealed, so that technically owners continue to hold their property by the same title as before. Udal tenure therefore remains unless the owners have elected to feudalise their holdings by obtaining charters from the Crown, but that has now been done to a considerable extent.

Special Tenures

(1) Land acquired under certain statutes

16–16   Lands acquired compulsorily by a Schedule A conveyance in terms of section 80 of the Lands Clauses Consolidation (Scotland) Act 1845 confer a "complete and valid feudal title" but, since the due registration of the conveyance dispensed with the need of entry with the superior which was then requisite to a completed feudal title, the Act really created an anomalous type of tenure which was not strictly feudal.[19] Lands acquired compulsorily under later statutes which incorporate the relevant provisions of the 1845 Act[20] are in the like position.

(2) Kindly tenants

16–17   The King's Kindly Tenants of the four towns of Lochmaben which formed part of former demesne lands of the monarch hold their lands on a tenure which, though neither feudal nor allodial, gives them a right amounting to full proprietorship. They were enrolled in the rental book of the King's steward or of their lord and this, or a copy of the entry, constituted their only title; it was a hereditary right of a perpetual character.[21]

Conveyancing Procedures in Feudal Property—Constitution of Feus

Proper investiture

16–18   The method of creating a feu right in the earliest period was a solemn ceremony on the ground in presence of other vassals of the superior who, from being bound to attend his courts and being of equal rank, were *pares curiae*. The superior delivered to the new vassal earth and stone from the ground as a token of possession and the vassal pledged his fidelity and undertook the services upon which the grant of

---

[18] A.P.S., c.48, iii, 41.
[19] *Magistrates of Elgin* v. *Highland Rly. Co.* (1884) 11 R. 950; *Duke of Argyll* v. *London, Midland & Scottish Rly. Co.*, 1931 S.C. 309.
[20] *e.g.* Acquisition of Land (Authorisation Procedure) (Scotland) Act 1947; Town and Country Planning (Scotland) Act 1972, s. 102; Building (Scotland) Act 1959, s. 15.
[21] Stair, II, ix, 21; Bell, *Prin.*, s. 1279; *Royal Four Towns Fishing Association* v. *Assessor for Dumfriesshire*, 1956 S.C. 379.

feu was conditional. The *pares curiae* were witnesses to the oath of fidelity, the conditions of the tenure and the fact of sasine or possession having been granted by the superior. This was proper investiture, sasine having been given *propriis manibus* by the superior. Later it became the practice to have a written memorandum of the transaction and a *breve testatum* was prepared recording briefly the grant and delivery of sasine: it was sealed by the superior and the *pares curiae* but the attestation by the superior was not essential, the certificate of a notary public or of two witnesses from among the *pares curiae* being accepted as sufficient evidence.

Improper investiture

–19   It was often inconvenient for the superior to attend the ceremony personally and so the *breve testatum* came to be prepared beforehand and a warrant or precept was included in it, addressed to the superior's bailie and authorising him to give possession or sasine to the vassal. The bailie, having done so, sealed the warrant with his own seal or wrote out and sealed a separate declaration of the fact. This was improper investiture, since it was not performed by the superior *in propria persona*.

Charter and sasine

–20   About the fifteenth century the *breve testatum* was superseded in practice by the superior granting a written charter accompanied by a separate precept directing his bailie to give sasine. Later the precept came to be incorporated in the charter itself. The charter in its later form contained the following clauses: (1) narrative clause containing the names and designations of the granter and grantee and the cause of granting; (2) dispositive clause comprising the words of alienation and disposition in feu farm, destination, description of the subjects and the reservations, conditions and burdens; (3) tenendas clause stating the tenure; (4) reddendo clause stating the feuduty payable; (5) clause of warrandice; (6) assignation of writs and rents; (7) obligation to free and relieve of public burdens; (8) clause of registration for preservation; (9) precept of sasine; and (10) testing clause.

–21   By the sixteenth century it had become the practice that the procedure of investiture and sasine following upon the charter was performed by agents for both parties, the superior's bailie and a procurator appointed by the vassal, in presence of a notary public and two witnesses. The notary then expede an instrument of sasine recording the ceremony, which was executed by the notary and the witnesses. The content of the instrument of sasine was: (1) the invocation, "In the name of God, Amen"; (2) the date; (3) narrative of the compearance of the parties, notary, witnesses, the procurator of the grantee and the superior's bailie; (4) narrative of the relevant parts of the charter; (5) narrative of the requisition by the procurator requiring the bailie to execute his office and delivery by the bailie of the precept to be read and published followed by the engrossment of the precept *verbatim*; (6) narrative of delivery of sasine by the bailie by handing over appropriate symbols—for land, earth and stone, for fishings, net and coble, etc.; (7) clause specifying the taking of instruments; (8) declaration that these things were done on the ground of the lands between two specified hours on the date of the instrument in presence of the witnesses named and designed; and (9) the notary's docquet (in Latin) asserting the authenticity of the facts set forth in the body of the instrument. The instrument was signed and sealed by the notary and subscribed by the witnesses. By the time of Stair in the latter part of the seventeenth century it was an established rule that the formal delivery of sasine required writing for its proof and the notary's instrument was by that time an essential part of the procedure—the rule was *nulla sasina, nulla terra*.[22] The importance of the instrument of sasine was that it provided the evidence required to make the vassal's right real, since the charter gave no more than a personal right.

Registration

16–22   Originally the records of instruments of sasines were engrossed in the notary's protocol books but by a series of statutes passed in the sixteenth and seventeenth centuries[23] a system of public registration of instruments of sasine was established. Of these the most important were the Registration Act 1617,[24] the Real Rights Act 1693,[25] the Register of Sasines Act 1693[26] and the Act 1696 c. 18. The main features of the system of registration as established by the statutes were: (1) A general register of sasines was established in Edinburgh and also particular registers of sasines for different districts. (2) Writs[27] had to be recorded within 60 days of their date to make faith in questions with third parties, but writs recorded outwith that time limit were effective in a question with the granter or his heirs and successors. (3) In a competition of title, preference depended upon the order in which writs appeared on the register. (4) The keepers of the various registers were required to keep minute books showing the day and hour of presentation of writs and the names and designations of the parties. Each minute required to be signed by both the keeper and the ingiver, and the time of signature of the minute was the time at which registration was deemed to have been effected. Upon registration the

---

[22] Stair, II, iii, 16.
[23] For an account of these see Craigie, *Heritable Rights*, 56–62.
[24] 1617 c.16.
[25] 1693 c.13.
[26] 1693 c.14.
[27] The writs to be so recorded were all instruments of sasine and also reversions, regresses, bands and writs for making reversions and regresses, assignations thereto, discharges of the same, renunciations of wadsets and grants of redemption.

keeper placed a certificate on the writ that it had been recorded with a reference to the relevant page of the register and returned the writ to the ingiver. Similar provision was made by the Act 1681 c.11 for registration of writs relating to burgage lands in registers kept by the town clerk of each burgh.

Voluntary Transfer of Feudal Subjects

Conveyances

16–23   Originally the feudal law did not admit of the right of a vassal to transfer his land voluntarily on account of the element of *delectus personae* involved in holdings conditional upon military service. In a more settled society that impediment to the commerce of land became unacceptable—it was essential that, as the most valuable asset, it should be capable of being made security for loans without the creditor having to rely on the superior to enforce the security. The Diligence Act 1469[28] conferred on a creditor the right to apprise his debtor's lands for payment of the debt and ordained the superior to accept the creditor as vassal on payment of one year's rent. Later, apprisings were superseded by adjudications and the Adjudications Act 1672[29] gave to adjudgers the same rights as apprisers *quoad* the superior and payment of one year's rent to the superior became the established casualty of composition. These statutes overcame the difficulty so far as creditors were concerned and the ingenuity of conveyancers made use of them to secure the right of entry to purchasers on a voluntary sale. If the superior was unwilling to receive a purchaser, the selling vassal granted a security over the lands and the purchaser went through the procedure of apprising or adjudication and compelled the superior to accept him on tendering one year's rent. The charter granted by the superior was known as a charter of apprising, or later as a charter of adjudication, upon which formal delivery of sasine followed and an instrument of sasine was expede and recorded.

Alternative methods of conveying lands on sale

16–24   Where the superior was willing to accept the purchaser the strictly correct feudal procedure was for the selling vassal to resign the lands into the hands of the superior who then granted a charter (known as a charter of resignation since it proceeded on resignation by the selling vassal) in favour of the purchaser upon which sasine followed. But another method came into use at an early date—the seller granted a conveyance to the purchaser on which sasine followed and thereafter the purchaser obtained from the superior a charter of confirmation. This method was also effective—the purchaser got sasine or possession

---

[28] 1469 c.36.
[29] 1672 c.19.

from the seller, who as an infeft proprietor of the feu could give it, and the charter of confirmation was evidence of the other necessary element, entry with and recognition by the superior.

Early practice—base infeftment

16–25   Before the registers of sasines were established it was possible for a fraudulent seller to grant conveyances to two purchasers because the instrument of sasine, although theoretically a public document, was not recorded in any public register. In order to check such frauds the Act 1540 c. 105 provided that if a purchaser obtained peaceable possession of the lands for a year and a day his title excluded the title, even though earlier in date, of any other person who had obtained private delivery of sasine but had not taken possession. Accordingly a purchaser wished to obtain sasine immediately after the purchase had been effected so that he might enter into possession of the lands immediately and the statutory period of a year and a day might commence to run. An elaborate process was devised which later became the foundation of the *a me vel de me* holding and ultimately of the modern disposition. The documentation involved was: (1) A contract of sale creating a binding bargain whereby the seller undertook in exchange for the price to infeft the purchaser in the lands and grant the necessary writs. (2) A charter of alienation of the lands by the seller in favour of the purchaser whereby the lands were to be held by the purchaser from the seller as his superior (*de me*) for a nominal feuduty, *i.e.* a sub-feu creating a new feudal estate. (3) A precept of sasine (either separate or incorporated in the charter of alienation) whereby the seller authorised delivery of sasine to the purchaser as his vassal. (4) A second alternative charter of alienation whereby the seller conveyed the lands to the purchaser to be held direct of the seller's superior (*a me de superiore meo*). (5) A procuratory of resignation (either separate or incorporated in the last mentioned charter of alienation) whereby the seller constituted the purchaser his procurator to appear before the superior and resign the lands so that a charter of resignation might be granted by the superior to the purchaser. (6) A precept of sasine referable to the last mentioned charter of alienation (which might be separate or incorporated in that charter) authorising delivery of sasine. When these deeds had been delivered to the purchaser he took delivery of sasine and an instrument of sasine was expede which did not specify the manner of holding and could be attributed to either the precept referable to the *de me* charter or the precept referable to the *a me* charter. Immediately upon sasine being taken the purchaser entered into physical possession of the lands and after a year and a day his title was secure, at least as regards the *de me* holding. Normally the purchaser wished to attribute his possession to the second charter but until he entered with or was confirmed by the superior he could, for the purpose of defeating competition, claim that the seller was his superior. The temporary superiority ended when the superior granted a charter of confirmation which could be obtained if necessary by the use of the apprising or adjudication device.

Disposition a me vel de me

—26   In course of time the various writs required to effect a sale of land came to be incorporated in a single deed, the disposition *a me vel de me*, and by the latter part of the seventeenth century it comprised the following clauses: (1) narrative clause, (2) dispositive clause containing words of conveyance, destination, description of the lands and burdens, (3) obligation to infeft by two alternative methods of holding *a me vel de me*, (4) procuratory of resignation, (5) assignation of writs and rents, (6) obligation to free and relieve of public burdens, (7) clause of warrandice, (8) clause of consent to registration, (9) precept of sasine in terms sufficiently indefinite to be attributable to either the *a me* or *de me* holding, and (10) testing clause. The transfer of lands was facilitated by statutes designed to remove impediments to the operation of the system without making fundamental changes, notably (1) the Real Rights Act 1693 already mentioned,[30] which made rights to land preferable according to the date of registration of the sasines in the appropriate register of sasines, (2) the Act 1693 c.35 which provided that procuratories of resignation and precepts of sasine, hitherto personal to the parties, continued valid after the death of the granter or the grantee, and (3) the Tenures Abolition Act 1747,[31] which gave a purchaser the right to compel entry with the superior by resignation on tendering the fees and casualties of entry.

Summary of practice in sales before 1845

—27   To sum up, the practical situation in sales of land in the pre-1845 period was:

(1) If there was no difficulty in securing immediate entry with the superior and the purchaser was ready to pay the casualty of composition, he could take a disposition with an obligation to infeft *a me* only. In practice, however, that method had disadvantages. The purchaser could not obtain sasine and register his title until he had operated the procuratory of resignation in the disposition and then obtained a charter of resignation from the superior containing a precept of sasine and had taken sasine upon it, so that the commencement of the period of possession for a year and a day desirable to protect the purchaser against fraud by the seller was necessarily delayed. Further, the purchaser had to pay the casualty of composition almost immediately in order to obtain sasine.

---

[30] In para. 16–22.
[31] ss. 12, 13.

(2) Accordingly the disposition *a me vel de me* became normal in practice. The purchaser could elect the way in which he would complete his title. If he considered that there was no risk of fraud on the part of the seller and was ready to pay the casualty of composition, he operated the procuratory of resignation and became infeft *a me*. If, however, as was more usual, he wished immediate infeftment and was in no hurry to pay the composition, he operated the seller's precept of sasine in the disposition, took infeftment speedily and registered his title, holding from the seller (*de me*). Then, when he was ready to pay the composition, he obtained a charter of confirmation from the superior and completed entry with the superior; the sasine previously obtained on the indefinite precept and evidenced by the instrument of sasine which had followed upon it could now be attributed to the *a me* holding.

(3) Where the holding was *de me* it was known as private or base infeftment as distinct from holding on resignation or confirmation from the superior which was public infeftment.

(4) Where sasine was taken on the seller's precept a sub-feu was in effect created, the seller being a mid-superior interjected between the true superior and the purchaser entitled to the *dominium utile*. The mid-superiority was a temporary estate defeasible at the will of the purchaser who could terminate it at any time upon obtaining a charter of confirmation.

(5) The true superior could not object to base infeftment—he still had an entered vassal, the seller, to whom he could look for performance of the conditions of the holding, although the seller was entitled to be relieved of such obligations by the purchaser. If, however, the seller died before the purchaser had obtained a charter of confirmation the feu was in non-entry with the effect of compelling the purchaser to enter.

Transmission on Death of Vassal
A. Intestate Succession

Right of heir to succeed

16–28   In former times when a vassal died the personal feudal relationship had to be renewed by his heir and a new investiture was required. The relationship between superior and vassal being essentially contractual a new party could not come into the place of either without the consent of the other. From as far back as Norman times, however, the right of the heir to succeed had been recognised in feudal law, but it was a personal right, and only became a real right to the lands when the heir renewed the investiture in his own person by taking a formal oath of fidelity in presence of the *pares curiae* and being given formal sasine. The casualties of ward and relief involved recognition of the heir's right to succeed.

Precept of clare constat

-29   In course of time written titles became common and the procedure
for completion of an heir's title to lands ultimately came to be by way
of service and precept of *clare constat*. The Crown always insisted on
service of an heir. In the case of subject-superiors, however, the heir
was usually known to the superior or his bailie and possession was given
by a written precept from the superior to his bailie authorising him to
put the heir formally in possession. The precept was called a precept of
clare constat from its opening words "Clare constat," and an instrument
of sasine was taken upon it as evidence of possession having been
given.

Completion of heir's title—lands held of the Crown

-30   **(1) Ancestor infeft and entered.** Where the ancestor died infeft and
entered in lands held of the Crown a service was always required.
Briefly the method was that the heir applied to Chancery for a brieve
of inquest, a direction to a sheriff to hold an inquiry before a jury to
determine that the claimant was truly the heir. Where the ancestor was
infeft the service was a special service and, although it determined
various matters, the important ones were (1) the fact that the ancestor
died infeft in certain lands, and (2) that the claimant was the heir to his
ancestor in these lands. The jury's finding was reported or retoured to
Chancery and an extract of it called a retour was issued from Chancery.
Thereupon a precept of sasine was issued from Chancery for infefting
the heir in the subjects, upon which he took sasine.

-31   **(2) Ancestor base infeft.** Where the ancestor died base infeft in lands
held of the Crown, *i.e.* where A, an entered vassal of the Crown,
disponed to B with an obligation to infeft *a me vel de me* and B took
infeftment but died without having obtained a charter of confirmation,
the heir first made up title to the mid-superiority by means of a general
service. This was similar to the procedure for a special service, *i.e.*
brieve from Chancery, inquest and retour, but it did not establish that
the ancestor was infeft, only that the claimant was his nearest and
lawful heir. The retour of service gave the heir the right to use the
unexhausted procuratory of resignation in the disposition to B, and in
virtue of that he obtained a charter of resignation from the Crown.
Having taken infeftment on that he recorded an instrument of sasine
and so completed a title to the mid-superiority of the lands in which his
ancestor had died base infeft. He then as superior granted a precept of
clare constat in his own favour for infefting himself as heir in the
dominium utile and expede an instrument of sasine. Being thus infeft in
both mid-superiority and *dominium utile* he consolidated these by
granting as vassal a procuratory of resignation *ad remanentiam* in his
own favour as superior and expede and recorded an instrument of

resignation *ad remanentiam*. He thus became full vassal to the Crown in the lands.

16–32   **(3) Ancestor having personal or unfeudalised rights.** Where the ancestor died with only a personal or unfeudalised title to lands held of the Crown, *e.g.* where A, a vassal entered with the Crown, disponed to B, but B took no steps to take infeftment so as to obtain a real right, his heir first of all had to expede a general service as indicated above in order to obtain the right to use the unexecuted warrants in B's disposition. He could then either (1) take base infeftment by expeding and recording an instrument of sasine proceeding on the precept of sasine in B's disposition and the general service in his own favour and obtain a charter of confirmation, or (2) obtain a charter of resignation from the Crown in virtue of the procuratory of resignation in B's disposition and the general service in his own favour, followed by infeftment proceeding on the precept of sasine contained in the charter of resignation.

Completion of heir's title—lands held of subject-superior

16–33   **(1) Ancestor infeft and entered.** Where the ancestor died infeft and entered in lands held of a subject-superior the heir completed title by (1) obtaining (if the superior insisted upon it) a retour of general service to establish his character as heir, and (2) obtaining a precept of *clare constat* and expeding thereon and recording an instrument of sasine.

16–34   **(2) Ancestor base infeft.** Where the ancestor died base infeft in lands held of a subject-superior the heir made up his title in the same way as if his ancestor had been infeft and entered except that, instead of obtaining a precept of *clare constat*, he got a combined charter of confirmation and precept of *clare constat*. The charter confirmed the ancestor's base infeftment, and the precept was a warrant for infeftment.

16–35   **(3) Ancestor having personal or unfeudalised right.** Where the ancestor died having only a personal or unfeudalised title the procedure was similar to that in the same case where lands were held of the Crown on a personal title, substituting the subject-superior for the Crown.

Services

16–36   As regards services the following important principles applied. (1) A special service was competent only if the ancestor had been entered with the superior and was infeft: since only an entered vassal and consequently his heir could be known to the superior, the superior was obliged to grant a precept of *clare constat* only upon a special service retour. (2) The finding of the jury was declaratory only: it conveyed nothing and only when the precept was obtained and infeftment followed did the heir take a real right in the lands. (3) A retour of special service was personal to the heir: if he died before obtaining infeftment it fell and the next heir required a new service. A retour of general service was different: it established simply a fact of relationship and the benefit of it was available to the heir's successors.

Precepts of clare constat

6–37   As regards precepts of *clare constat*: (1) The ancestor had to be entered with the superior: if the ancestor was not so entered the superior did not legally know him and did not know his heir. (2) It was essential that the superior was infeft in the superiority estate, although a precept of *clare constat* granted by an uninfeft superior could be validated if the superior subsequently became infeft. (3) Precepts of *clare constat* were excepted from the provisions of the Act 1693 c.35 and so infeftment upon them could be taken only during the lifetimes of both the superior and the vassal. The Lands Transference Act 1847 altered that position as regards the death of the superior but the precept remained, and still remains, personal to the heir in whose favour it is granted. (4) A precept of *clare constat* was always granted *periculo petentis*: the superior did not warrant the right of the heir to succeed.

B. Testate Succession

Special disposition mortis causa

6–38   It was a fundamental concept of feudal conveyancing that a person could only alter the succession to heritage by a *de presenti* conveyance. No other expression would suffice than the use of the word "dispone," and the only way in which a man could disinherit his heir was by executing a conveyance of his lands to someone else. Accordingly, one method of bequeathing land was to grant a disposition of it to become operative on the granter's death—a *de presenti* conveyance *mortis causa*. It was in the same form as an ordinary disposition but under reservation of the granter's liferent and dispensing with delivery. It could be absolute or conditional or subject to trust purposes. After the granter's death the grantee could then complete title as a disponee in the ordinary way.

General disposition mortis causa

6–39   But there were difficulties in the above method, if, for example, the granter sold part of the lands after executing the disposition, or acquired other lands afterwards. Accordingly the method was adopted of making a general disposition *mortis causa* which contained no description of specific lands. Where the granter was not infeft, *e.g.* was holding under an unrecorded disposition, the grantee could complete his title readily enough because the general disposition *mortis causa* contained an assignation of writs. That carried to the disponee of the general conveyance *mortis causa* the open procuratory and precept in the unfeudalised disposition held by the deceased, which could be used to take infeftment and enter with the superior. But if the granter of the general conveyance was himself infeft the matter was not so easy. In that case the procedure was as follows:

(a) If the disponee was also the heir to the lands, so that the general conveyance effected no change in the succession, the heir completed title by service as before explained, passing over the general disposition, and nobody had any interest to object.

(b) If the disponee was not the heir, but the heir was willing to co-operate in giving him a title, the heir completed title by service and then granted a voluntary conveyance to the disponee.

(c) If the disponee was not the heir, and the heir was unwilling to co-operate or was not available, a complicated process was involved whereby the heir was charged to enter on the ground that the general disposition *mortis causa* created an obligation on the heir to make up titles and grant a disposition. If he failed to do so an action of constitution and adjudication was taken, whereby the obligation was constituted against the *hereditas jacens*, the lands were adjudged to the disponee in implement of that obligation, and the decree of adjudication was a warrant to the disponee upon which he could obtain sasine.

Alteration of Feus

Charters of novodamus

16–40   When it was desired to enlarge or alter the original feu grant, or where the vassal's title deeds were destroyed or lost or his title was defective, the older practice was to insert a clause of novodamus effecting the change in a charter of resignation by the superior. Originally the charter of resignation containing the clause of novodamus had to be preceded, like any other charter of resignation, by a formal resignation by the vassal but later that was not invariably done, partly because in circumstances where the vassal's title was defective or lost a proper resignation was impracticable, and also because in one of its aspects it was possible to regard the novodamus as a new grant. Later the practice became to dispense with resignation and the superior simply granted a charter of novodamus, a fresh grant of the feu or the enlarged feu on the new terms, and the need for a preceding resignation was formally removed by section 3 of the Conveyancing Amendment (Scotland) Act 1887. Since a charter of novodamus was normally granted at the request of the vassal it was granted at the vassal's risk and a clause *salvo jure meo et cujuslibet* was always inserted.

Extinction of Feudal Estates

Voluntary extinction—resignation ad remanentiam

6–41   Where it was desired to extinguish a feudal estate by restoring the *dominium utile* to the superior—the process of consolidation—the method used in early times was personal appearance by the vassal before the *pares curiae* where he formally resigned the lands into the hands of the superior *ad perpetuam remanentiam* (to remain for ever) as distinct from resignation *in favorem* (for regranting to another). Later it became customary for the vassal to execute a disposition in favour of the superior containing a procuratory of resignation *ad remanentiam*, but no obligation to infeft and no precept of sasine, because the object of the disposition was not to create or transfer a feudal estate but to extinguish one. The procurator then appeared before the superior or his commissioner and resigned the lands in the hands of the superior *ad remanentiam* by delivering, technically staff and baton, in fact a pen, all in presence of a notary and witnesses. The notary then expede an instrument of resignation which was recorded in the register of sasines and completed the consolidation.

Involuntary extinction

6–42   A feudal estate could also be extinguished without the vassal's consent as a result of actions by the vassal which involved the penalty of forfeiture of the *dominium utile* or irritancy of the feu.

6–43   **(1) Conventional irritancies.** As already mentioned there were certain old feudal casualties such as recognition[32] and disclamation and purpresture[33] which involved forfeiture of the feu by the vassal. These casualties became extinct at an early date but were replaced in the later period by an express clause inserted in feu grants which imposed a conventional irritancy enforceable if the vassal contravened conditions of the grant. If any such breach occurred the superior was entitled to raise an action of irritancy or tinsel of the feu, and the effect of a decree in favour of the superior was to annul the feu and all sub-feus, securities and other subordinate rights which had been granted by the vassal and the lands reverted unencumbered to the superior. If the superior adopted this drastic remedy, however, he could not claim unpaid arrears of feuduty.

6–44   **(2) Statutory irritancy ob non solutem canonem.** From very early times it had been the practice to insert in feu grants a condition that, if the feuduty remained unpaid for two years, the superior had the right to annul the feu by an action of irritancy or tinsel of the feu. By the

---

[32] para. 16–07.
[33] para. 16–12.

Feuduties Act 1597 it was made a statutory condition of all feus that the vassal should forfeit his feu if the feuduty remained for two years[33a] unpaid, with the same result as if a conventional irritancy to that effect had been contained in the feu grant.

II. STATUTORY ALTERATIONS—1845 to 1974

Defects of the older system

16–45   The rigidity of the system as it had developed before 1845 in the matters of entry with the superior and sasine involved a plurality of charters and writs by progress to effect a single transaction. Moreover the procedure of formal delivery of sasine on the ground of the lands was unacceptably inconvenient as the volume of transactions, particularly in cities and towns, markedly increased. During the period between 1845 and 1974 fundamental alterations were made by statute in order to simplify the procedures, particularly with regard to the two basic requirements for a real right in land, (1) sasine and registration and (2) entry with the superior.

Sasine and registration

16–46   The first step was taken by the Infeftment Act 1845[34] which rendered it unnecessary to go to the lands or deliver symbols: infeftment was now effected by production to the notary of the warrants of sasine and relative writs upon which the notary expede an instrument of sasine which was then recorded. Shorter forms of precept of sasine and instrument of sasine were authorised, and the requirement of the Registration Act 1617 that sasines be recorded within 60 days was abolished, and registration could now be effected at any time during the life of the grantee. The Lands Transference Act 1847[35] introduced short forms of clauses which could be inserted in conveyances of land and defined their import. The Titles to Land (Scotland) Act 1858[36] introduced direct registration of the deed itself in terms of a warrant of registration endorsed on the feu charter or disposition and such registration was declared to have the same effect as a recorded instrument of sasine. Where a conveyance of lands was contained in a deed granted also for other purposes, *e.g.* a marriage contract or a deed of trust or settlement, it was made permissible to record only such parts as the granter desired to be recorded if a clause of direction was inserted in the deed indicating the parts which it was desired to record.[37] Precepts of sasine were made unnecessary[38] and conveyances

---

[33a] Now five years—Land Tenure Reform (Scotland) Act 1974, s. 15.
[34] 8 & 9 Vict. c.35.
[35] 10 & 11 Vict. c.48.
[36] 21 & 22 Vict. c.76, s. 1.
[37] *Ibid.*, s. 3.
[38] *Ibid.*, s. 5.

to a superior containing a clause of resignation *ad remanentiam* could be recorded direct.[39] Accordingly precepts of sasine and instruments of sasine were rendered obsolete; direct recording of a deed of conveyance now became equivalent to the recorded instrument of sasine in the old form. The Act of 1858 was repealed by the Titles to Land Consolidation (Scotland) Act 1868 but its main provisions were re-enacted. Similar provisions were made *mutatis mutandis* in relation to burgage tenure by other statutes.[40]

Entry with the superior

5–47   The process of entering with the superior by a procuratory of resignation followed by a charter of resignation or alternatively a charter of confirmation was simplified and shortened by the Land Transference Act 1847 and the Titles to Land (Scotland) Act 1858 which were consolidated in the Titles to Land Consolidation (Scotland) Act 1868, which provided shortened and combined forms of charters of resignation and confirmation and introduced brief writs of resignation and confirmation which could be endorsed by the superior on dispositions. These are now matters of history since the law was radically altered by the Conveyancing (Scotland) Act 1874[41] which abolished the necessity for renewal of investiture and most of the charters and writs by progress and substituted the concept of entry by implication of law. The leading provisions of the Act which effected this radical change were contained in section 4 and may be summarised thus:

(1) In the completion of the title of any person having a right to lands, whether by succession, bequest, gift or conveyance, it would not be necessary to obtain from the superior any charter, precept or other writ by progress, and it would not be competent for the superior to grant any such charter, precept or writ by progress except (i) charters of novodamus, (ii) precepts or writs from Chancery, (iii) precepts or writs of *clare constat* or (iv) writs of acknowledgment.[42]

(2) Every proprietor duly infeft in lands was deemed, as at the date of registration of his infeftment in the appropriate register of sasines, duly entered with the nearest superior whose estate of superiority would, according to the law before the Act, have not been defeasible at the will of the proprietor so infeft, to the same effect as if the superior had granted a writ of confirmation, and that whether the superior's own title or that of any over-superior had been completed or not, but such implied entry did not confer or confirm any rights more extensive than those contained in the original charter or feu right of

[39] *Ibid.*, s. 4.
[40] Lands Transference Burgage Act 1847 (10 & 11 Vict. c.49); Titles to Land Burgage Act 1860 (23 & 24 Vict. c.143).
[41] 37 & 38 Vict. c.94.
[42] s. 4(1).

the lands or in the last charter or other writ by which the vassal was entered therein. The entry so implied did not validate a sub-feu where subinfeudation had been effectually prohibited. Notwithstanding such implied entry the proprietor last entered in the lands and his heirs and representatives continued personally liable to the superior for payment of the feuduties and performance of the whole obligations of the feu until notice of the change of ownership of the feu had been given to the superior. A form of notice of change of ownership was scheduled to the Act[43] and evidence of the notice having been given could be preserved either by (i) keeping a copy of the notice certified by the sender as having been delivered or posted by him in presence of two witnesses who also signed the certificate or (ii) an acknowledgment of receipt by the superior or his agent either on a duplicate of the notice or in the form of a separate acknowledgment, and the superior or his agent was required on receiving such intimation in duplicate with a fee of five shillings to return one copy of the notice with an acknowledgment of intimation endorsed thereon subscribed by him.[44] Such implied entry did not prejudice or affect the right of the superior to any casualties, feuduties or arrears thereof due at or prior to the date of such entry and all rights and remedies of the superior under the existing law or under the conditions of the feu right, including irritancy, were preserved, and all the obligations and conditions in the feu rights continued available to the superior.[45] If the former vassal omitted to serve notice of change of ownership promptly and was required by the superior to pay feuduty which the new vassal should have paid, all the remedies competent to the superior for recovery of feuduties were held to be assigned to the former vassal.[46]

(3) Non-entry was abolished but an alternative form of action, declarator and for payment of any casualty, was substituted.[47]

Commentary on section 4 of 1874 Act

16–48   The principal effects of the reforms contained in this section may be summarised.

(1) Direct registration of a charter or disposition had already been made equivalent to a recorded sasine in the old form; the 1874 Act made it equivalent also to entry with the superior.

(2) Under the old law a superior himself had to have a completed title before he could receive a vassal and similarly the title of an over-superior required to be complete, so that where entry purported to be given by an uninfeft superior the title of the vassal and those of all vassals subordinate to him in the feudal chain were invalidated. Implied

---

[43] Sched. A.
[44] s. 4(2).
[45] s. 4(3).
[46] s. 4(2).
[47] s. 4(4).

entry removed that danger since it is valid whether the title of the superior or that of any over-superior has been completed or not.

(3) The words "not defeasible at the will of the proprietor so infeft" make it clear that the superior with whom entry is implied is the true superior, not a mid-superior created by the *a me vel de me* manner of holding where the disponee had taken infeftment in a *de me* holding and his title had not been confirmed by the superior. The effect of implied entry was to abolish mid-superiorities of that kind and the use of the *a me vel de me* method ceased.

(4) As entry now takes place on registration of a disposition to a new vassal, without intervention by the superior, the superior has no opportunity, as he formerly had, of ensuring that no provisions have been inserted in the vassal's title which are inconsistent with the conditions of the feu or that the conveyance to the vassal fails to refer to the conditions of the holding. Accordingly, it is provided that implied entry does not enlarge the rights of the vassal under the original feu grant or the last charter or writ by progress.

(5) Under the old law entry of a new vassal with the superior relieved the previous vassal of his personal liability to pay feuduty and perform the other obligations of the feu grant. That effect under implied entry would have been inequitable since the superior might have had no notice of the change and be unaware of the person who was now liable as vassal. Hence the provisions of the Act that the previous vassal is to continue liable until implied entry has taken place by registration of the new vassal's title and notice of the change has been given to the superior. It is therefore important in the interests of the previous vassal that the notice is given immediately on conclusion of the relevant transaction. It may be observed that *two* things are necessary to relieve the previous vassal of liability for implementing the obligations of the feu, namely, (a) registration of the new vassal's title and (b) service of the notice of change of ownership.

(6) The service of the notice of change of ownership does not relieve the former vassal of obligations of the feu which arose before its date, only obligations which continue or arise after that date.[48]

Reddendo—feuduties and services

49   During the period between 1874 and 1974 statutory reforms were made designed first to simplify the nature and amount of the return for feudal grants, to eliminate casualties and ultimately to eliminate payment of feuduties altogether. The principal stages by which these objectives have been achieved are outlined in the succeeding paragraphs.

---

[48] *Marshall* v. *Callander and Trossachs Hydropathic Co.* (1895) 22 R. 954; (1896) 23 R. (H.L.) 55.

16–50   **(1) Commutation and subsequent abolition of carriages and services.**
The 1874 Act[49] provided that where carriages and services were due
from the vassal and had for five years been commuted into an annual
money payment, that payment would thereafter be deemed to be the
annual value of such carriages and services. If they had not been so
commuted either the superior or the vassal was given the right to
apply to the sheriff to have the annual value thereof determined and
that sum became the amount which had to be paid and accepted in lieu
of the former carriages and services. A memorandum (where
commutation was effected by agreement) or the extract decree of the
sheriff (where effected by such decree) was recorded in the Register of
Sasines. The Conveyancing (Scotland) Act 1924[50] went further and
provided that carriages and services which had not been commuted
before January 1, 1935, would cease to be exigible.

16–51   **(2) Feuduties payable in kind.** The 1924 Act[51] enacted that in all feus
granted on or after January 1, 1925, the feuduty must be payable in
money. In the case of prior feus where the feuduty was payable in
grain or other fungibles commutation into money could be effected by
agreement and the recording of a memorandum of the agreement in
the Register of Sasines. If such an agreement had not been made
before December 31, 1932, the annual feuduty payable thereafter was
fixed as a sum of money representing the average annual value of the
feuduty payable in kind for the 10 years preceding that date, and either
party could require the other to enter into and record a memorandum
of agreement to that effect or could apply to the sheriff for a decree to
the like effect and record an extract of it in the register of sasines.

16–52   **(3) Casualties.** The 1874 Act[52] permitted redemption of casualties other
than fixed duplicands, in the option of the vassal only, upon fixed
terms of compensation which the superior could elect to receive either
in the form of a lump sum or by way of conversion into an additional
amount of annual feuduty. The Feudal Casualties (Scotland) Act 1914
provided for the redemption of casualties, including fixed duplicands,
before January 1, 1930,[53] on terms of compensation prescribed[54] with
the compulsitor that any casualties not so redeemed would be
extinguished. The creation of casualties in future feus was prohibited,
but it remained permissible to stipulate for a permanent increase or
reduction of feuduty.[55] These provisions applied also to ground
annuals.[56]

---

[49] ss. 20, 21.
[50] s. 12(7).
[51] s. 12(1)–(6).
[52] ss. 15–18.
[53] s. 4.
[54] s. 5.
[55] s. 18.
[56] s. 3.

5–53   **(4) Allocation of feuduties.** Where land feued was subdivided allocation of the *cumulo* feuduty might be authorised by the superior in the feu grant or by the original vassal under a power to do so conferred in the grant. In the absence of such provisions it was open to the parties to effect allocation by agreement either by a charter of novodamus or by a separate or endorsed memorandum under the 1874 Act[57] as amended by the 1924 Act.[58] The Conveyancing and Feudal Reform (Scotland) Act 1970[59] entitled the proprietor of any part of a feu to serve a notice of allocation of the feuduty on the superior specifying the amount apportioned on his part of the feu. If not objected to by the superior that amount becomes effectually allocated: if the superior objects an allocation is made by the Lands Tribunal for Scotland by order in such manner as the Tribunal consider reasonable. The provisions of the 1970 Act apply also to allocations of ground annual.[60]

5–54   **(5) Redemption and abolition of feuduties.** The Land Tenure Reform (Scotland) Act 1974 prohibited the imposition of feuduty after September 1, 1974,[61] save in the case where the proprietor of the land had entered into an obligation to do so before November 8, 1973, and the deed was executed before November 8, 1975,[62] and the like prohibition extended to the imposition of a ground annual.[63] As regards existing feus no increase in the amount of the feuduty can be created in a charter of novodamus.[64] An existing allocated feuduty or ground annual may be redeemed voluntarily by the proprietor of the land on terms stated in the Act,[65] and must be redeemed compulsorily by the seller on sale of the property[66] or by the acquirer on compulsory acquisition of it.[67] The provisions of the Act with regard to redemption do not apply to unallocated feuduties or ground annuals, but these may in the option of the proprietor of the land be allocated under the provisions of the 1970 Act as a preliminary step. As a result of the 1974 Act feuduties and ground annuals are gradually being redeemed and no new ones may be created.

Special and general conveyances—notarial instruments and notices of title

5–55   Under the old feudal law a voluntary transfer of lands could be effected only by a special conveyance containing words of *de presenti*

---

[57] s. 8.
[58] s. 13.
[59] ss. 3–5.
[60] s. 6.
[61] s. 1.
[62] s. 7(1).
[63] s. 2.
[64] s. 3.
[65] s. 4.
[66] s. 5.
[67] s. 6.

conveyance of lands properly described with the inclusion of the necessary executorial or feudal clauses such as a precept of sasine and procuratory of resignation. The Titles Act of 1858[68] (feudal property) and the Titles Act of 1860[69] (burgage property) enabled persons who had a right to lands by a general conveyance, which did not contain the description of the lands or the necessary executorial clauses of a special conveyance, or by an assignation of an unrecorded conveyance or by service or adjudication or otherwise to obtain a recorded title and real right to the lands without the intervention of the granter or his representatives or recourse to judicial proceedings by expeding and recording a notarial instrument which established his right by production of the last recorded title and the subsequent writs whereby he acquired that right. These provisions were re-enacted by the Titles to Land Consolidation (Scotland) Act 1868[70] and the facility of completing title by notarial instrument was extended to a grantee or legatee acquiring right to lands under a will even if the will contained no *de presenti* conveyance but contained with reference to the lands words which, if used in a will relating to moveables which was duly executed in the manner required or permitted by the law of Scotland, would be sufficient to confer on the executor or legatee a right to claim or receive the same.[71] The Conveyancing (Scotland) Act 1924[72] authorised the use of notices of title as an alternative form of document to notarial instruments. The Succession (Scotland) Act 1964[73] amended section 20 of the 1868 Act, broadly to the effect of restricting the right to complete title to executors in cases of testate succession.

Deduction of title

16–56   It was a fundamental concept of feudal tenure that sasine could be given to another only by a person who was himself infeft—the rule of *non dat qui non habet*. Accordingly if a person who had a right to land but had not completed title by infeftment proposed to grant a conveyance of the land to another the grantee could obtain a recorded title either (a) by the granter first completing his own title and then granting a special conveyance or (b) by granting a general conveyance or assigning the unrecorded conveyance in his own favour when the grantee could complete title by expeding and recording a notarial instrument under the provisions of the 1868 Act. Section 3 of the Conveyancing (Scotland) Act 1924 short-circuited the procedure by providing that where a person having right to lands but whose title thereto had not been completed by being recorded granted a disposition

---

[68] ss. 12, 13 and 14.
[69] ss. 8, 9 and 10.
[70] ss. 19, 22 and 23.
[71] s. 20.
[72] s. 4.
[73] s. 34 and Sched. 2.

of the lands containing a clause whereby he deduced his title from that of the person last infeft and the disposition was duly recorded in the appropriate Register of Sasines, the title of the grantee would be in all respects in the same position as if he had expede and recorded a notarial instrument according to the existing law and practice. That section did not involve a departure in principle from the former law; it simply provided by a statutory fiction that the requirements of the existing law were deemed to be satisfied by the shorter procedure authorised by the 1924 Act.

Automatic infeftment in certain cases

5–57   The Act 13 and 14 Vict. c.13[74] relating to heritable property conveyed for religious or educational purposes, as extended to trusts for the support of ministers or the maintenance of churches, schools, etc., and made applicable to feuduties by the Act 23 and 24 Vict. c.143,[75] contained provisions, substantially re-enacted by the Titles to Land Consolidation (Scotland) Act 1868,[76] whereby lands acquired and heritable securities created for religious or educational purposes, the title to which was taken in the names of office-bearers of or trustees for the body and duly recorded, vested the lands automatically also in their successors in office. The Conveyancing (Scotland) Act 1874[77] provided that when by the tenor of the title to an estate in land held in trust duly completed the office of trustee was conferred upon the holder of a place or office or the proprietor of any estate and his successors therein, any person subsequently becoming a trustee by appointment or succession to such place or office should be deemed to have a valid and complete title by infeftment without the need of any deed of conveyance or other procedure.

Prescription

5–58   **(1) Positive prescription.** The Prescription Act 1617,[78] on the narrative "And his Majesty according to his fatherly care, which his Majesty hath, to ease and remove the griefs of his subjects, being willing to cut off all occasion of pleas, and to put them in certainty of their heritage in all time coming," introduced the concept of positive prescription of heritable rights. It enacted that heritable infeftments followed by possession peaceably without lawful interruption for 40 years would not be challengeable except for falsehood. In calculating the period of 40 years, years of minority and less age of the parties against whom the prescription was used were not counted. The necessary infeftments

---

[74] ss. 1 and 3.
[75] s. 32.
[76] s. 26.
[77] s. 45.
[78] 1617 c.12.

comprised charter and sasine or, in the case of heirs, instruments of sasine standing together for 40 years and proceeding upon retours of service or precepts of *clare constat*. The Conveyancing (Scotland) Act 1874[79] provided that any *ex facie* valid irredeemable title to an estate in land recorded in the appropriate register of sasines followed by continuous possession peaceably without lawful interruption for 20 years was equivalent to 40 years' possession under the Act of 1617; years of minority or less age were not counted in that period but if such possession had continued for 30 years no deduction or allowance for years of minority or less age would be made. The Conveyancing (Scotland) Act 1924[80] provided that 20 years of the requisite possession following on an *ex facie* valid irredeemable recorded title would be sufficient in all cases, no allowance being made for years of minority or less age. The period of 40 years possession was still required if it followed upon a redeemable recorded title as in the case of an adjudication for debt or if positive prescription was pled to establish a right to a servitude or a public right such as a right of way. The Conveyancing and Feudal Reform (Scotland) Act 1970[81] substituted 10 years' possession for the 20 years in the 1924 Act, except in relation to any claim as against the Crown to ownership of foreshore or salmon fishings when the period remained 20 years. The Prescription and Limitation (Scotland) Act 1973 used new terminology but in effect left the provisions of the 1924 Act as amended by the 1970 Act unaltered in relation to positive prescription as regards ownership of land based on recorded titles[82] but (a) as regards registered leasehold titles provided that the period of the requisite possession was 10 years[82] but (b) as regards interests of lessees having an unregistered title, allodial land and any other interest in land based on an unrecorded title which was sufficient foundation for positive prescription provided that the period of such possession was 20 years.[83] As regards positive servitudes and public rights of way the period of possession necessary was reduced to 20 years.[84]

16–59 **(2) Negative prescription.** The negative prescription of obligations applied in relation to land rights mainly as regards the extinction of heritable securities by non-payment of principal or interest without any other acknowledgment of the debt for the period of negative prescription. That period was originally 40 years,[85] which was left unchanged by the 1874 Act, but was reduced to 20 years by the 1924 Act without deduction for periods of minority or less age.[86] The 1973

---

[79] s. 34.
[80] s. 16.
[81] s. 8(1).
[82] s. 1.
[83] s. 2.
[84] s. 3.
[85] Prescription Act 1617.
[86] s. 17.

Act in effect left the period of 20 years unchanged in relation to heritable securities and rights relating to heritable property,[87] but rights to arrears of periodical payments of feuduty, ground annual, rent, etc., from land were extinguished by the new short negative prescription after five years.

Other reforms

6–60   The foregoing account describes only the principal reforms made during the period between 1845 and 1974 in relation to the ownership of feudal land. Reforms made during that period in relation to leasehold subjects, heritable securities, succession and entails are noted subsequently under the relevant subject headings.

III. REGISTRATION OF TITLE

Establishment of Land Register of Scotland

6–61   The Land Registration (Scotland) Act 1979 established the Land Register of Scotland under the management and control of the Keeper of the Registers of Scotland.[88] Registration of title is being introduced by a phased process, one area after another, and will replace the recording of deeds in the Register of Sasines as the principal means of creating real rights in land. In areas which have become operational the interest in land in certain kinds of transaction can only be created real by registration in the Land Register; these include grants of feus and transfers of land for valuable consideration.

Effect of Registration of Title

6–62   The Register of Sasines is a register of deeds and the validity of the title conferred by the recorded deed depends upon the sufficiency of the progress of title deeds which precedes it, at least until the operation of positive prescription has rendered the recorded title unchallengeable. Accordingly it is necessary to examine the progress of titles back to the last recorded title prior to the commencement of the relevant period of positive prescription. Under the system of registration of title the Keeper, upon an application for first registration, satisfies himself that the antecedent progress of title is in order and, if so satisfied, issues a land certificate without exclusion of indemnity with the effect of vesting the person named in the certificate in a real right to the registered interest in the land[89] fortified by an indemnity from the Keeper.[90] An uninfeft proprietor of an interest in land which has

---

[87] Sched. 1, para. 2(*c*) and (*e*) and s. 8.
[88] s. 1.
[89] s. 3(1).
[90] s. 12.

been registered does not require to expede and record a notice of title; if the necessary links or midcouples evidencing his right are produced to the Keeper the title of the proprietor will be registered.[91] For each registered interest in land a title sheet will be prepared containing (i) a description of the land based on the Ordnance Survey map and, where the interest is that of the proprietor of the *dominium utile* or the lessee under a long lease and the land appears to the Keeper to extend to two hectares or more, its area as calculated by the Keeper, (ii) the name and designation of the person entitled to the interest and the nature of the interest, (iii) any subsisting entry in the Register of Inhibitions and Adjudications adverse to the interest, (iv) any heritable security over the interest, (v) any enforceable real right pertaining to the interest or subsisting real burden or condition affecting the interest, (vi) any exclusion of indemnity in respect of the interest, and (vii) such other information as the Keeper thinks fit to enter in the register.[92] The Keeper will enter in the title sheet a summary of any real burden or condition affecting the registered interest and may note any overriding interest; he does not require to enter an over-feuduty or over-rent but may do so.[93] The Register of Sasines continues effective for certain restricted purposes.[94]

Practice

16–63   In areas which have not yet become operational under the 1979 Act the existing system of heritable conveyancing will continue with recording of deeds in the Register of Sasines, subject to provisions which simplify the form and clarify the effect of certain deeds.[95] When an area has become operational the new system of registration of title will gradually supersede recording in the Register of Sasines as transactions which induce registration under the Act occur or titles are registered voluntarily as a matter of convenience of practice. Once an interest has been registered the official copy of the title sheet will give notice of all the important matters relating to the title which hitherto have had to be ascertained by examination of the relevant deeds, the interest may be described by reference to the number of the title sheet and the title of the registered proprietor is fortified by indemnity.[96]

---

[91] s. 3(6).
[92] s. 6(1).
[93] s. 6(2)–(4).
[94] s. 8.
[95] ss. 15–19.
[96] The account given in paras. 16–61 to 16–63 is a brief outline of the fundamental changes in principle made by the 1979 Act. For a more detailed treatment see Chaps. 17 to 24.

CHAPTER 17

FEUS

I. NARRATIVE CLAUSE

II. DISPOSITIVE CLAUSE

III. TERM OF ENTRY

IV. TENENDAS

V. REDDENDO

I. Narrative Clause

Granters

Capacity and power

-01   The capacity and power of particular persons and bodies to grant feus have already been considered.[1] A trustee in bankruptcy, or a liquidator or receiver in relation to limited companies, will not normally be concerned in granting feus and will dispose of heritable property by way of outright sale, but if exceptionally feuing is preferred he must observe the procedures requisite in the sale of heritable property.[2]

-02   **Fiduciary fiars.** Fiduciary fiars may by application to the court obtain authority to exercise the powers of trustees at common law or under the Trusts Acts, which may include power to feu.[3]

-03   **Heirs of entail.** The rights of an heir of entail in possession to grant feus under powers contained in the various Entail Acts are summarised in the undernoted texts.[4] Further, an heir of entail in possession may feu land for housing purposes to a local authority or housing association without the consent of the next heir and without restriction as to the extent of the ground feued.[5] In general the provisions of the statutes which authorised the granting of feus by heirs of entail in possession prohibited the taking of a grassum and contemplated the imposition of feuduty, but, since the Land Tenure Reform (Scotland) Act 1974[6] prohibits the imposition of feuduty, disposal of land by an heir of entail in possession will now be effected by disposition under the conditions of the entail statutes applicable to sales. It seems doubtful whether an heir of entail in possession may grant a feu for a lump-sum consideration in circumstances where the enabling statute has not been repealed and prohibits the taking of a grassum,[7] even on the basis that the price received is treated as capital and invested for behoof of the heir in possession and succeeding heirs of entail. The 1974 Act provides in relation to redemption of feuduties that where the feuduty redeemed is subject to an entail the redemption money will be treated as capital.[8]

-04   **Glebes.** As regards glebes which have been transferred to the General

---

[1] See Vol. I, paras. 2–09 (tutors), 2–23 (minors), 2–56 (trustees), 2–82 (judicial factors) and 2–100 to 2–102 (companies).

[2] See Vol. I, paras. 2–86 to 2–92 (trustee in bankruptcy), 2–104 and 2–108 (liquidator) and 2–111 (receiver). As to permanent trustee in bankruptcy see Bankruptcy (Scotland) Act 1985, s. 39. As to liquidators, s. 623(4) of the Companies Act 1985 should now be read with the references to ss. 108–113 and 116 of the Bankruptcy (Scotland) Act 1913 superseded by references to s. 39(3), (4), (7) and (8) of the Bankruptcy (Scotland) Act 1985—see Sched. 7, para. 21(1) to the last-mentioned Act.

[3] Trusts (Scotland) Act 1921, s. 8(2); *Pottie* (1902) 4 F. 876.

[4] Burns, 220–222; *Encyclopaedia of the Laws of Scotland*, Vol. 6, 232–235.

[5] Housing (Scotland) Act 1966, s. 203.

[6] s. 1.

[7] *e.g.* Entail (Scotland) Act 1914, s. 4.

[8] ss. 4(6), 5(12) and 6(6).

Trustees of the Church of Scotland under the Church of Scotland
(Property and Endowments) Act 1925, the General Trustees may feu a
glebe or part thereof subject to the obligation of first giving to the
heritor or heritors of adjoining lands the opportunity of purchasing or
taking the same in feu at such price and on such terms as may be
agreed upon by the General Trustees and the heritor or heritors or as
may, failing agreement, be determined by an arbiter appointed by the
sheriff on the application of either party.[9]

Infeftment

17–05   The granter of a feu right is normally designed as "heritable
proprietor of the subjects [and others] hereinafter disponed." He
should be infeft,[10] but a grant of a feu by a person who is not infeft
may be validated by accretion on his subsequent infeftment,[11] even
although it occurs after the death of the grantee,[12] and operates to
perfect the title of the grantee retrospectively to the date of the
grantee's infeftment under the original grant of feu.[13] Accretion does
not operate, however, where subsequent infeftment is taken by the
heir or executor or trustees of the granter[14] or by assumed trustees
when the feu was granted by the trustees by whom they were assumed,
none of whom were ever infeft[15] or by the trustee in bankruptcy of the
granter.[16] Nor does accretion operate if the warrandice in the feu grant
was less than absolute.[17]

Consenters

17–06   Where a feu grant is made with the consent of a heritable creditor
the consent may be to the effect of either (i) disburdening the land
concerned, both superiority and *dominium utile*, of the security, or
(ii) disburdening the *dominium utile* only, but preserving the security over
the superiority. In post-1974 feu grants the former is more usual, since
no direct financial benefit is retained in the absence of an obligation to
pay feuduty. As regards earlier feus where it was intended to disburden
only the *dominium utile*, the correct conveyancing method was to
express the creditor's consent "for all interests competent to him in the
dominium utile of the subjects hereby disponed," and to insert before
the term of entry a declaration that the *dominium utile* was disburdened

---

[9] 1925 Act, s. 37.
[10] The right of an uninfeft proprietor to grant deeds relating to lands under s. 3 of the Conveyancing
(Scotland) Act 1924 is restricted to the deeds specified in the section which do not include feu
charters or original grants of a feu.
[11] Stair, III, ii, 2; Ersk., II, vii, 3.
[12] *Lockhart* v. *Ferrier* (1837) 16 S. 76.
[13] *Neilson* v. *Murray* (1738) Mor. 2895, 7773.
[14] *Keith* v. *Grant* (1792) Mor. 2933; *Redfearn* v. *Maxwell*, March 7, 1816, F.C.
[15] *Martin* v. *Wight* (1841) 3 D. 485.
[16] Bankruptcy (Scotland) Act 1913, s. 100; Bankruptcy (Scotland) Act 1985, s. 31(3).
[17] Ersk., II, vii, 4; *Douglas* v. *Wedderburn* (1664) Mor. 7748.

of the security which was restricted to the *dominium directum* over which all rights and claims of the creditor were reserved entire.[18]

Consideration

7–07   A deed containing a grant of land in feu executed after September 1, 1974, cannot impose a feuduty,[19] unless permitted under a transitional provision where the deed was granted before November 8, 1975, in implement of an obligation entered into before November 8, 1973, by the person who was then proprietor of the land and there has been included in the deed or in a memorandum endorsed thereon a statement to that effect by or on behalf of the granter in a prescribed form.[20] If a feu grant which purports to impose a feuduty in contravention of the Act has been recorded in the Register of Sasines the deed remains enforceable in other respects but no feuduty is payable,[21] and the granter or his successor may be required by any person having an interest to grant an appropriate corrective deed which can be recorded in the Register.[22] In practice, feus are now granted for a lump sum price. The various prestations of the grant also form part of the consideration.

II. Dispositive Clause

Ruling clause

7–08   In conveyances of land the dispositive clause is the ruling clause: it is the measure of the grant as regards the matters with which it deals, *e.g.* the subjects conveyed and the destination to the grantee. The rule of construction is that the dispositive clause, if clear, cannot be controverted, added to or restricted by other clauses which are inconsistent with it.[23] But if the dispositive clause is ambiguous, reference may be made to other clauses to assist in construing it.[24]

Conveyance

7–09   The usual words of conveyance are "in feu farm dispone," but may be rendered "sell and in feu farm dispone" when the grant is for a price. The words "in feu farm" identify the purpose of the deed in creating a new feudal estate. The word "dispone," formerly essential, is no longer necessary in a deed or writing conveying heritage, provided

---

[18] See Craigie, *Heritable Rights*, 84, 85.
[19] Land Tenure Reform (Scotland) Act 1974, s. 1(1).
[20] *Ibid.*, s. 7(1) and Sched. 4.
[21] *Ibid.*, s. 1(2).
[22] *Ibid.*, s. 7(2).
[23] *Grahame* v. *Grahame*, June 20, 1816, F.C.; *Chancellor* v. *Mosman* (1872) 10 M. 995; *Cooper Scott* v. *Gill Scott*, 1924 S.C. 309. *Cf. Largs Hydropathic Ltd.* v. *Largs Town Council*, 1967 S.C. 1.
[24] *Lord Advocate* v. *McCulloch* (1874) 2 R. 27; *Orr* v. *Mitchell* (1893) 20 R. (H.L.) 27; *Dick-Lauder* v. *Leather-Cully*, 1920 S.C. 48.

that other words importing conveyance or transference, or a present intention to convey or transfer, are contained in it.[25] In practice, however, the word "dispone" continues in common use in such deeds.

Grantee—destination

17–10   It was, and to some extent still is, customary to insert after the name and designation of the grantee a destination designed primarily to regulate the succession to the feu upon the death of the grantee. Sometimes the destination was intended to effect a special line of devolution of the subjects other than that which would have been regulated by the general law of testate or intestate succession: such destinations were often complex and their interpretation was governed by particular rules of law developed over centuries.[26] They are relics of the older law before 1868, when succession to heritage could be directed only by a *de presenti* disposition; their continued use has been judically discouraged[27] and is not recommended. More commonly the destinations inserted were not intended to alter the succession, *e.g.* "and to his heirs and assignees whomsoever" or, after the Succession (Scotland) Act 1964, "and to his executors and assignees whomsoever." In the Institutional writers[28] and older judicial decisions[29] and in judicial *dicta* in more recent cases[30] the term "assignees" was interpreted as a reference to assignees whose right had not been feudalised by infeftment, but there are conflicting authorities which extend the meaning of the term to include singular successors.[31] Since destinations of the latter kind do not alter the succession their insertion is now of little importance in that connection, but they may still be of significance in relation to the ascertainment of persons obliged to perform the obligations and conditions of a feudal grant which are often expressed as binding upon "the said disponee and his foresaids."[32] It is suggested that in feu grants (1) the grant should be expressed in favour of the grantee *simpliciter* or the grantee and his executors and assignees whomsoever; (2) if it is desired to secure early infeftment of the grantee the deed should be expressed as not being a warrant for infeftment after a specified date; and (3) the continuing obligations and conditions (as distinct from conditions merely personal) should be expressed simply as obligations and conditions of the grant, since in feudal theory all successors in ownership of the *dominium utile* are bound to implement them, or as binding upon "the feuars" defined as

---

[25] Conveyancing (Scotland) Act 1874, s. 27.
[26] See Craigie, *Heritable Rights*, 517–583.
[27] *Hay's Tr.* v. *Hay's Trs.*, 1951 S.C. 329 *per* Lord President Cooper at 334.
[28] Stair, II, iii, 5; Ersk., II, vii, 5; Bell, *Prin.*, s. 727.
[29] *e.g. Magistrates of Inverkeithing* v. *Ross* (1874) 2 R. 48.
[30] *Marshall's Tr.* v. *Macneill & Co.* (1888) 15 R. 762 *per* Lord President Inglis at 769; *Magistrates of Banff* v. *Ruthin Castle Ltd.*, 1944 S.C. 36 *per* Lord Justice-Clerk Cooper at 69.
[31] *Hamilton* v. *Dunn* (1853) 15 D. 925; *Christie* v. *Jackson* (1898) 6 S.L.T. 245.
[32] See G. L. Gretton, "Heirs, Executors and Assignees" (1984) 29 J.L.S. 103.

including the grantee and his successors in ownership of the subjects feued.

Particular grantees

7–11   Where lands are acquired in feu by tutors for a pupil, by a minor, whether or not he has a curator, or by a factor or attorney for his principal, the grant should be in favour of the pupil, the minor or the principal respectively.[33] Where lands are acquired by a partnership the grant should be in favour of the partners and the survivors of them as trustees for the firm.

Description of lands

7–12   The description of lands in feu grants and other conveyances and of reservations or exceptions therefrom are considered in Chapter 18 *infra*.

Qualifications of the grant—real conditions and burdens

7–13   Qualifications of grants of feu and real conditions and burdens are considered in relation to conveyances of land generally in Chapter 19 *infra*.

III. TERM OF ENTRY

Date of entry

7–14   The date of entry should always be specified. The statutory form for conveyances of land runs, "With entry at the term of   " but, if the date of entry is not a recognised term, may run, "With entry at   (*date*)." If the date of entry is prior to the date of execution of the deed the clause may be, "With entry as at   (*date*) notwithstanding the date(s) hereof." If no date of entry is specified the date of entry will be the first term of Whitsunday or Martinmas after the date or last date of execution of the feu grant, unless it appears from the deed that another term of entry was intended.[34]

IV. TENENDAS

Function

7–15   The function of the tenendas clause is to specify the superior of whom the lands are held and to state the tenure by which they are held. It normally runs: "To be holden the said subjects of and under

---

[33] *Scott* (1856) 18 D. 624; *Yule* v. *Alexander* (1891) 19 R. 167.
[34] Conveyancing (Scotland) Act 1874, s. 28.

me (us) and my (our) successors as immediate lawful superior(s) thereof in feu farm, fee and heritage for ever." Although the clause is in some sense superfluous, in that the words of conveyance in the dispositive clause have already established that the grant is of a feu and the presumption of law is that it is a holding *de me*, *i.e.* from the granter and his successors, it is almost invariable practice to insert it in an original grant of a feu.

Cannot alter or enlarge the grant

17–16   As already stated,[35] the dispositive clause, if clear, determines the measure of the grant, but if the dispositive clause is ambiguous the tenendas clause may be invoked to explain it and may raise a presumption of inclusion in the grant of items to which a right of ownership may be established in favour of the grantee by evidence of subsequent possession.[36] A limitation or restriction sought to be inferred from the provisions of a statutory form of tenendas clause in a conveyance was held to be ineffective.[37]

V. REDDENDO

Function and content

17–17   The *reddendo* clause in a feu grant specifies the return to be made to the superior as the consideration for the grant. Originally that return consisted of a payment in kind or in money, but latterly only in money,[38] together with performance of the prestations of the grant. The Land Tenure Reform (Scotland) Act 1974 prohibited the imposition of feuduties after September 1, 1974, subject to a transitional provision during a period which has now expired,[39] and the only permissible considerations now are a price and performance of the prestations of the grant; in pre-1974 grants these prestations remain enforceable notwithstanding that the feuduty has been redeemed in terms of the Act.[40] If a deed which purports to impose or increase a feuduty in contravention of the 1974 Act has been recorded in the Register of Sasines the person who granted the deed or his successor may be required by any person having an interest to grant any appropriate corrective deed capable of being recorded in the Register.[40a]

---

[35] para. 17–08.
[36] *Lord Advocate* v. *Sinclair* (1867) 5 M. (H.L.) 97; *Lord Advocate* v. *McCulloch* (1874) 2 R. 27 (both cases relating to salmon fishings).
[37] *Kemp* v. *Magistrates of Largs*, 1939 S.C. (H.L.) 6.
[38] See paras. 16–50 and 16–51.
[39] See paras. 16–54 and 17–07.
[40] 1974 Act, ss. 4(3), 5(3) and 6(2)(*b*).
[40a] *Ibid.*, s. 7(2).

Feuduties—enforcement, allocation and redemption

7–18   There still remain feuduties imposed in pre-1974 grants which have not yet been redeemed. The current position as to the enforcement of payment, allocation and redemption of such feuduties is considered in paragraphs 17–19 to 17–50 *infra*.

Remedies for Recovery of Feuduties

(1) Personal action

7–19   The superior and the vassal are parties to a contract of tenure, a continuing personal contract automatically renewed between successors of the respective parties. If the contract has been created by a unilateral deed such as a feu charter or feu disposition, delivery of the deed and acceptance of it by the vassal impose a contractual obligation upon the vassal to pay the stipulated feuduty and to perform the other obligations imposed upon him by the deed[41]; if the original feu has been created by a bilateral deed such as a feu contract the vassal is similarly bound by the terms of the deed which he has signed upon delivery and acceptance of it. To enforce that obligation the superior may raise a personal action against him. Moreover, if the feu was constituted by a feu contract which contained a consent to registration for execution, summary diligence to enforce the personal obligation to pay feuduty is competent against the original vassal.

7–20   **Liability of successors.** When a vassal dispones the *dominium utile* to another and the disponee takes infeftment, the new vassal becomes personally liable for payment of feuduties which become exigible thereafter. The liability of the former vassal for feuduties payable prior to the change of ownership remains prestable until he serves a notice of change of ownership on the superior, but he has no liability for feuduties becoming due subsequently.[42] It should be noted that (i) since these results accrue only when *both* the new vassal has completed his infeftment *and* the former vassal has given notice of the change of ownership to the superior, failure to carry out either of these requirements before the next payment of feuduty after the pactional date of entry has become due will result in the former vassal remaining liable to the superior for that payment, but he will be entitled to recover the amount from the new vassal[42]; and (ii) although the new vassal is not *personally* liable to the superior for arrears of feuduty payable by the former vassal he is concerned to ascertain that there are no such arrears outstanding, since they may form a ground for irritancy of the feu by the superior which remains available to him notwithstanding the change of ownership.[43]

---

[41] *Hunter* v. *Boog* (1834) 13 S. 205.
[42] Conveyancing (Scotland) Act 1874, s. 4(2).
[43] *Ibid.*, s. 4(3).

17–21   Liability of representatives of deceased vassal. If the obligation to pay feuduty is imposed in terms of the grant upon the vassal only, or upon the vassal and his heirs, executors and successors whomsoever (or after 1964 upon the vassal and his executors and successors whomsoever), and the heirs or executors do not take up the feu, their liability for payment of feuduties extends only to payments due before the death of the vassal.[44] If, however, the obligation to pay feuduty is expressed as binding upon the vassal and his heirs, executors and successors whomsoever conjunctly and severally, that phrase implies liability upon each of the parties named *in solidum* and the executors remain liable for payment also of feuduties becoming due after the death of the vassal, whether they take up the feu or not and even after they have conveyed the lands to a singular successor who is duly infeft and entered with the superior.[45]

17–22   Liability of sub-feuars. A sub-feuar is personally liable for the over-feuduty to the extent only of the amount of the sub-feuduty payable to his own immediate superior; the over-superior is entitled to enforce for his own benefit the obligations undertaken by the sub-feuar to his immediate superior.[46] But apart from personal liability the sub-feuar may be affected by irritancy of the whole feu on the ground of non-payment of the over-feuduty, and may in practice require to pay the whole over-feuduty in order to protect his property.[47]

17–23   Rights of relief of parties paying feuduty for another. As already noted,[48] a vassal who has disponed the *dominium utile* to another person and has paid feuduties due by the disponee may recover the amount so paid from the disponee, and, if the liability of the disponer arises from failure to serve notice of the change of ownership timeously, he has the remedies available to the superior for enforcing that right of relief.[49] But parties who pay feuduty for another but who are not entitled to found on section 4(2) of the 1874 Act, although they may be entitled to relief at common law, cannot require the superior to assign his remedies for recovery of feuduty to enforce that right of relief, for the reason that it may prejudice the superior in recovering future feuduties.[50]

(2) Hypothec

17–24   The superior retains a right of property in the lands feued, the *dominium directum*, although he has parted with the *dominium utile*

---

[44] *Aiton* v. *Russell's Exrs.* (1889) 16 R. 625.
[45] *Police Commissioners of Dundee* v. *Straton* (1884) 11 R. 586.
[46] *Sandeman* v. *Scottish Property Investment Co.* (1881) 8 R. 790.
[47] *Sandeman* v. *Scottish Property Investment Co.* (1885) 12 R. (H.L.) 67.
[48] at para. 17–20.
[49] 1874 Act, s. 4(2).
[50] *Guthrie and McConnachy* v. *Smith* (1880) 8 R. 107.

which carries the right of possession. Accordingly he has the remedy available in law to a proprietor who does not have possession, that of hypothec, which he may exercise by sequestration for recovery of feuduty.[51] It extends over crop and stock in agricultural subjects and *invecta et illata* in urban subjects. The right is available only in security and for payment of the last or current feuduty. Where the subjects have been let, the superior's hypothec prevails over that of the landlord, since the landlord can only let under burden of the feuduties payable from the subjects.[52] It is competent against a limited company even after commencement of liquidation or the appointment of a receiver, since the superior is merely making effectual a pre-existing security.[53] It is used comparatively seldom in practice since the remedy of poinding of the ground attaches substantially the same assets and is wider in scope as extending to all arrears of feuduty, subject only to a statutory restriction in the case of a trustee in bankruptcy or a liquidator.[53a]

(3) Poinding of the ground

17–25   Since the feuduty has been created a *debitum fundi* by the feu grant the superior may attach the moveables on the land, whether belonging to the vassal or his tenants, by an action of poinding of the ground for payment of the current feuduty and all arrears. The moveables belonging to tenants, however, may only be poinded to the extent of their rents due and unpaid.[54] Since the right to poind the ground is available only to a person having a real right in the land it cannot be exercised by a superior after he has parted with ownership of the superiority.[55]

17–26   **Competition and preference of poindings.** Heritable creditors under a bond and disposition in security or a standard security also may poind the ground, their rights being preferable, not in accordance with the dates of raising the respective actions, but in accordance with the dates of their respective infeftments in their securities,[56] since each heritable creditor is not creating a preference but simply exercising a preference that is already his. It follows that a superior using this form of diligence has preference over poindings of the ground by any heritable creditor holding a security over the *dominium utile*, since the infeftment of the superior is prior in date.[57] There is a statutory limitation of the

---

[51] *Yuille* v. *Lawrie and Douglas* (1823) 2 S. 155.
[52] Craigie, *Heritable Rights*, 190.
[53] *Anderson's Trs.* v. *Donaldson & Co. Ltd. (in liquidation)*, 1908 S.C. 38.
[53a] See para. 17–26.
[54] *Brown* v. *Scott* (1859) 22 D. 273.
[55] *Scottish Heritages Co. Ltd.* v. *North British Property Investment Co. Ltd.* (1885) 12 R. 550.
[56] *Athole Hydropathic Co. Ltd. (in liquidation)* v. *Scottish Provincial Assurance Co.* (1886) 13 R. 818 at 822.
[57] *Royal Bank* v. *Bain* (1877) 4 R. 985 at 990.

superior's preference in a competition with a trustee in bankruptcy; no poinding of the ground which has not been carried into execution by sale of the effects 60 days before the date of sequestration is available in a question with the trustee except to the extent of the current half-year's feuduty and one year's arrears.[58] There is a similar limitation in a competition with the liquidator of a limited company.[59,60] A claim of the Crown to income tax, capital gains tax and corporation tax is preferable to the right of a superior under a poinding of the ground to the extent of one year's arrears of tax.[61] A claim by a local authority for rates enjoys a similar preference.[62]

(4) Adjudication

17–27   As creditor in a *debitum fundi* the superior may adjudge the land for payment of arrears of feuduty,[63] but in practice this remedy is seldom used, since an adjudication for debt may be redeemed within the legal period of 10 years, whereas by the procedure of irritancy[64] the superior may obtain an irredeemable title to the land.

(5) Irritancy or tinsel of the feu

17–28   The most drastic remedy available to a superior to compel payment of feuduty is the right to irritate the feu. The effect of a decree of irritancy is to annul the feu right; the relationship of superior and vassal is extinguished and the land and all buildings thereon revert to the superior disburdened of all real rights derived from the vassal including sub-feus, heritable securities over the *dominium utile* and tenancies whether created by the vassal or any sub-feuar, and no compensation is payable by the superior regardless of the value of the land feued and buildings thereon.[65] The superior recovers the land, however, subject to any statutory real burden imposed upon it, since it is not a burden created by the vassal but one which passes with possession of the land whoever takes it.[66]

17–29   **Legal basis of irritancy.** The superior's right to irritate a feu may be based on statute, the Feu-duty Act 1597,[67] which provides that any vassal or feuar who fails to pay the feuduty for two years will "amit and

---

[58] Bankruptcy (Scotland) Act 1913, s. 114; Bankruptcy (Scotland) Act 1985, s. 37(6).
[59] Companies Act 1985, s. 623(5).
[60] The statutes express the limitation in relation to poindings of the ground by heritable creditors, but a superior is a heritable creditor for feuduty by virtue of his infeftment in the superiority: *Campbell* v. *Edinburgh Parish Council*, 1911 S.C. 280.
[61] Taxes Management Act 1970, s. 64.
[62] *North British Property Investment Co. Ltd.* v. *Paterson* (1888) 15 R. 885; *Campbell* v. *Edinburgh Parish Council*, *supra*. These cases were decided under older statutes; the relevant statutory provision is now s. 248 of the Local Government (Scotland) Act 1947.
[63] *Sandeman* v. *Scottish Property Investment Co.* (1885) 12 R. (H.L.) 67 *per* Lord Watson at 71.
[64] See para. 17–28 *et seq.*
[65] *Cassels* v. *Lamb* (1885) 12 R. 722; *Sandeman* v. *Scottish Property Investment Co.*, *supra*.
[66] *Pickard* v. *Glasgow Corporation*, 1970 S.L.T. (Sh.Ct.) 63.
[67] Act 1597 c.250.

tine" his feu. Normally the right to irritate the feu on the ground of non-payment of feuduty for a specified period of years is also created conventionally by an irritant clause in the feu grant itself. Whether the right of irritancy is based upon the statute or created conventionally, the minimum period of arrears is now five years.[68] The title to pursue an action of irritancy lies in the superior alone; it is not available to the executor or an assignee of the superior and cannot be founded upon failure to pay feuduties which became due either before he became superior or after he ceased to be superior.[69] The creditor in a heritable security over the superiority estate cannot sue unless the form of the security was such as to divest the superior from the superiority estate, leaving only a *jus crediti* to require a reconveyance.[70]

7–30 **Declarator of irritancy.** To enforce an irritancy by the superior, whether based on the 1597 Act or on a conventional provision in the feu grant, it is necessary to raise an action of declarator.[71] To protect the interests of persons deriving right from the vassal, the action of declarator must not only be served on the last-entered vassal but intimated as the court may direct to sub-feuars, heritable creditors and others who appear to have some real right in or security over the vassal's estate or any part thereof, and who from a search in the Register of Sasines against the vassal's estate for 20 years immediately prior to the raising of the action or from an examination of the relevant title sheet in the Land Register of Scotland are disclosed as having such interest.[72] The decree becomes final when an extract of it has been recorded in the appropriate Register of Sasines.[73] It follows that failure to pay feuduties for five years does not bring the feu to an end; it merely makes it voidable at the instance of the superior.[74]

7–31 **Purging the irritancy.** The irritancy can be purged by the vassal or any other person having an interest paying the arrears of feuduty to the superior at any time before an extract decree of declarator of the irritancy has been recorded in the Register of Sasines,[73] but persons other than the vassal who make the payment cannot require the superior to assign his rights against the vassal.[75] Interest on the arrears of feuduty may be demandable if the feu grant has so provided with the rate of interest being specified, but not otherwise.[76]

---

[68] Land Tenure Reform (Scotland) Act 1974 s. 15.

[69] *Maxwell's Trs.* v. *Bothwell School Board* (1893) 20 R. 958, 964.

[70] *Campbell* v. *Bertram* (1865) 4 M. 23, 28.

[71] Bell, *Prin.*, s. 701; *Lockhart* v. *Shiells* (1770) 2 R.L.C. 244.

[72] Conveyancing Amendment (Scotland) Act 1938, s. 6(1) as amended by the Land Registration (Scotland) Act 1979, Sched. 2, para. 3.

[73] Conveyancing (Scotland) Acts (1874 and 1879) Amendment Act 1887, s. 4; Conveyancing Amendment (Scotland) Act 1938, s. 6(4).

[74] *Inglis* v. *Wilson*, 1909 S.C. 1393.

[75] *Guthrie and McConnachy* v. *Smith* (1880) 8 R. 107.

[76] *Maxwell's Trs.* v. *Bothwell School Board, supra* at 965.

17–32 **Forfeiture of arrears of feuduty upon irritancy**. If a decree of declarator of irritancy has been pronounced and has become final the superior forfeits his claim to arrears of feuduty, since in principle the feu right has been annulled.[77] It was a common practice to insert in feu grants a clause contracting out of this result by stipulating that the conventional irritancy was without prejudice to the legal rights and remedies of the superior to require payment of bygone feuduties due prior to the irritancy being incurred, but the effectiveness of such a clause has been doubted judicially.[78]

17–33 **Vassal's right to withhold feuduty**. If the superior has failed to perform an essential condition of the contract of feu, the vassal may be entitled to withhold payment of the feuduty.[79]

Allocation of Feuduties

Subdivided feus

17–34 When a vassal has sub-feued parts of the feu to different persons, the owners of each separate part may not incur *personal* liability to the superior for payment of the *cumulo* feuduty imposed on the whole feu save to the extent of the amount of the feuduty imposed in the sub-feu upon their own part.[79a] There is no direct contractual relation between them and the superior which creates personal liability for the *cumulo* feuduty but the superior may enforce for his own interest payment of the sub-feuduty payable from each separate part.[80] On the other hand the feuduty imposed in the original feu grant is a *debitum fundi* upon the whole of the land, and the real conditions such as erection and maintenance of buildings are enforceable against the whole land feued or any part of it unless limited in the feu grant, and the real remedies such as poinding of the ground and declarator of irritancy are available for that purpose. It is no defence to an action based on the superior's real right that the defender has paid the sub-feuduty due from his own part or the amount of feuduty apportioned by disposition thereon and that he has implemented the building conditions of the original feu grant in respect of his own part.[81] Even if the superior is sympathetic, an action of declarator of irritancy restricted to that part of the feu in respect of which the owner is in breach of the obligations of the feu

---

[77] *Magistrates of Edinburgh* v. *Horsburgh* (1834) 12 S. 593.

[78] *Malcolm* v. *Donald*, 1956 S.L.T. (Sh.Ct.) 101 at 105, 106.

[79] *Ainslie* v. *Magistrates of Edinburgh* (1842) 4 D. 639; *Arnott's Trs.* v. *Forbes* (1881) 9 R. 89. Contrast *Thom* v. *Chalmers* (1886) 13 R. 1026.

[79a] The position is otherwise if the vassal dispones parts of the feu to different persons, when each of the disponees remains liable for the *cumulo* feuduty subject to a right of relief against co-disponees in favour of any who pays more than his apportioned share (Menzies, 833; *Wemyss* v. *Thomson* (1836) 14 S. 233).

[80] *Sandeman* v. *Scottish Property Investment Co.* (1881) 8 R. 790.

[81] *Cassels* v. *Lamb, supra.*

grant is incompetent,[82] unless a limitation to that effect has been inserted in the grant.

Vassal's risk

7–35   The risk to each owner of a separate part is evident. That risk may be less if the building and other conditions of the feu have been implemented in respect of all the separate parts, since every owner will have an incentive to pay his sub-feuduty or apportioned part of the *cumulo* feuduty in order to preserve valuable property, but it is not wholly eliminated. If the buildings on any part are destroyed or seriously damaged by fire, subsidence or other cause and there is no or inadequate insurance cover, the owner of them may be unable or unwilling to incur the cost of their replacement or repair. If the subjects feued consisted of a single flatted tenement the owner of each flat would normally be entitled, either under the common law of the tenement or by conditions imposed in dispositions of each flat or a deed of conditions applicable to the tenement, to compel the proprietor of any other flat to comply with the feuing obligations as regards that flat, but where the land feued had been subdivided into plots upon which separate buildings had been or were to be erected the owners of each plot, although they might have a *jus quaesitum tertio* to require performance of the feuing obligations by the owner of any other plot, would have no defence to an irritancy by the superior in the event of failure by such other owner to implement, *quoad* his part, building conditions of the feu grant which were fenced with an irritant and resolutive clause. Again, if the owner of any part defaulted in paying the proportion of the *cumulo* feuduty apportioned on his part, the owners of the remaining parts might require to make the payment in order to avoid irritancy of the whole feu and they might not be entitled to an assignation of the superior's remedies to assist them in recovering it.[83] For these reasons it is clearly in the interests of the owner of a part of a larger feu to obtain an allocation of an appropriate proportion of the *cumulo* feuduty upon his property.

Effect of allocation of feuduty

7–36   When a proportion of the *cumulo* feuduty has been validly allocated on a part of the original feu, the proprietor of that part is liable thereafter only for the proportion thus allocated. Moreover, although he remains liable for performance of the building and other conditions of the original feu grant *quoad* his own part of the feu, he is not affected by a failure to implement these conditions in respect of other

---

[82] *Fothringham* v. *Anderson*, 1950 S.L.T. (Sh.Ct.) 25.
[83] *Guthrie and McConnachy* v. *Smith* (1880) 8 R. 107. *Cf. Nelson's Trs.* v. *Tod* (1904) 6 F. 475 at 485.

parts of the land originally feued. In effect, the position is as if his part were the subject of a separate feu grant relating to it alone. Allocation has certain disadvantages for the superior, *viz.*—(1) There is increased administrative expense in collecting several feuduties instead of one. (2) The security for the feuduty is restricted. (3) There could be complex problems when a *cumulo* feuduty over flatted property is allocated over individual houses, *e.g.* if two houses were seriously damaged by fire and one owner was willing to repair but the other was unable to do so, would it be an effective defence to an action of declarator of irritancy against the first owner that it was impossible to implement the obligation to repair because of the need for remedial work on both houses? Burns[84] suggests that adequate insurance in which the superior's interest should be *primo loco* is the best practical solution.

Allocation by agreement—augmentation

17–37 Before the enactment of the Conveyancing and Feudal Reform (Scotland) Act 1970[85] allocation of feuduties could only be effected by agreement between the superior and the vassal. In practice the superior, because of the disadvantages mentioned above,[86] would agree to allocation only if the appropriate proportion of the *cumulo* feuduty was augmented by a stipulated amount, such augmentation being an additional feuduty enforceable by the same compulsitors.

Methods of allocation before March 1, 1971

17–38 Allocation could be effected before the enactment of the 1970 Act by the following methods:

(1) By provision in original feu grant. The superior might undertake in the feu grant to allocate the *cumulo* feuduty in specified amounts over identified plots or confer power on the vassal to do so, subject to the condition that the vassal had first implemented the whole conditions of the grant by completing the prescribed buildings on every plot.[87] Any such condition had to be strictly observed if an allocation by the vassal under such a delegated power was to be valid.[88]

(2) By charter of novodamus. This was the appropriate feudal method of altering any of the conditions of a grant of feu and was a competent method of allocating feuduty. If the only alteration was allocation of feuduty, however, the charter of novodamus for that purpose was largely superseded in practice by the simpler memoranda of allocation aftermentioned.

---

[84] at 267.
[85] Operative as regards allocation on March 1, 1971.
[86] para. 17–36.
[87] See *Mitchell's Tr.* v. *Galloway's Trs.* (1903) 5 F. 612.
[88] *Pall Mall Trust* v. *Wilson*, 1948 S.C. 232.

(3) By endorsed memorandum. Section 8 of the Conveyancing (Scotland) Act 1874 introduced a simpler method of allocation by way of a memorandum in the form of Schedule D to the Act endorsed on the deed forming the vassal's title either before or after it was recorded in the Register of Sasines. If the memorandum was endorsed on the vassal's title before it was recorded, the memorandum would normally be recorded along with it, but if afterwards the memorandum did not require to be recorded. In either case the allocation and any augmentation which it imposed were binding upon all having interest, but did not prejudice or affect the rights of heritable creditors whose securities existed at the date of the allocation unless they were parties thereto. As to allocations made by an insolvent vassal by memorandum under the Act see the undernoted case.[89]

(4) By separate memorandum. Section 13 of the Conveyancing (Scotland) Act 1924 made provision for allocation by a separate memorandum in the form of Schedule H to the Act, recorded in the Register of Sasines, which would be binding on heritable creditors and all others having interest, but again with the proviso that the allocation should not prejudice or affect the rights of existing heritable creditors who were not parties thereto.

(5) By actings of the superior. Allocation may be inferred from actings by the superior. If a feuduty of £20 is payable from a feu on which two houses are erected and the superior by memorandum allocates £10 on one house, it is evident that effectively the balance of £10 is also allocated on the other. Where a feu had been subdivided into four lots and the superior granted a charter of confirmation in favour of the owner of one lot under burden of a feuduty (being the amount previously apportioned on it), thus allocating that proportion of feuduty, it was held in *Nelson's Trs.* v. *Tod*[90] that the superior could not succeed in an action of poinding of the ground against the owner of another of the lots for recovery of arrears of the *cumulo* feuduty, on the ground that by allocating a portion of the feuduty on one lot he had deprived the defender of the right of relief which would otherwise have been available against the owner of that lot. Doubts as to the soundness of that decision were expressed *obiter* in *Pall Mall Trust* v. *Wilson*,[91] where it was distinguished particularly on the ground that the allocation by the vassal in respect of two lots was not made strictly in accordance with the power of allocation conferred on him by the feu charter.

Statutory allocation

7–39 The introduction of a right in the vassal to have a *cumulo* feuduty

---

[89] *British Linen Co.* v. *Ogg* (1904) 11 S.L.T. 756.
[90] (1904) 6 F. 475.
[91] 1948 S.C. 232 at 241, 249.

allocated by notice in accordance with the provisions of sections 3 to 5 of the Conveyancing and Feudal Reform (Scotland) Act 1970, and the prohibition imposed by section 3 of the Land Tenure Reform (Scotland) Act 1974 of any increase in the total amount of an existing *cumulo* feuduty by charter of novodamus or other deed having equivalent effect, have resulted in rendering the earlier methods of allocation by agreement virtually obsolete, although still technically competent so long as the total amount of the *cumulo* feuduty is not increased. Where a feuduty was validly imposed in a pre-1974 grant with power to the vassal to allocate it in dispositions of the individual plots forming part of the land feued, the opinion is expressed that it remains competent to allocate the *cumulo* feuduty on the various plots after September 1, 1974, so long as the amount thereof is not increased: section 1 of the 1974 Act prohibits the *imposition* of a feuduty and the dispositions are merely allocating a feuduty already imposed.

Allocation by notice

17–40   In terms of the 1970 Act the proprietor of any part of land burdened by a *cumulo* feuduty may serve notice in a prescribed form upon the superior or his factor or agent allocating the portion of the *cumulo* burden which has been apportioned on that part. The superior may within 21 days of receipt of the notice send to the Lands Tribunal for Scotland an application in prescribed form objecting to the amount of the portion of *cumulo* feuduty proposed to be allocated in terms of the notice, and the tribunal will then after a hearing allocate the *cumulo* feuduty upon all parts of the burdened land in such manner as they consider reasonable. The allocation effected by a notice to which the superior has not objected has the effect that the part on which allocation is made will, in relation to the rights and obligations of the proprietors of the remainder of the feu relating to payment of the remainder of the feuduty, be treated as if it had never been part of the feu and as if the feuduty allocated on it had never formed part of the *cumulo* feuduty. An order of the tribunal allocating the whole of the *cumulo* feuduty (which must not alter the total amount of the existing *cumulo* feuduty) supersedes for all purposes any existing apportionment of that feuduty.[92] Registration of the documents evidencing the allocation in the Register of Sasines is not required by the 1970 Act,[93] but in registered titles the Keeper of the Land Register will enter the amount of the allocated feuduty in the title sheet of the *dominium utile* as a real burden.[94] For a fuller discussion of procedure in allocation by notice see the undernoted text.[95]

---

[92] 1970 Act, ss. 3–5.
[93] See Halliday, C. & F.R.A. 1970, 57.
[94] Land Registration (Scotland) Act 1979, s. 6(1)(*e*) and (2).
[95] Halliday, C. & F.R.A. 1970, 50–58.

Redemption of Feuduties

(1) Voluntary Redemption

Redemption before September 1, 1974

7–41 Prior to the enactment of the Land Tenure Reform (Scotland) Act 1974 a feuduty could be redeemed by agreement between the superior and the vassal; but in view of the requirement of a reddendo to satisfy feudal theory the correct method was for the superior, in exchange for the redemption money, to grant a charter of novodamus which substituted a nominal feuduty. Although less consonant with strict theory, a simple discharge or receipt was sometimes accepted. These methods are still competent.[96] Occasionally a right to redeem the feuduty was conferred on the vassal in the feu grant.[97] Usually, however, the object of the vassal was to get rid of restrictive conditions in the grant, which would not be accomplished merely by redemption of the feuduty: that could only be achieved by purchase of the superiority, usually followed by consolidation.

Voluntary redemption under the Land Tenure Reform (Scotland) Act 1974

7–42 Section 4 of the 1974 Act conferred upon a vassal the right to redeem the feuduty exigible in respect of his feu at any term of Whitsunday or Martinmas, by notice given to the superior or his agent in accordance with the provisions of the section.

7–43 **What feuduties are redeemable.** For the purposes of voluntary redemption under section 4 or compulsory redemption under section 5 "feuduty" is defined as including "any *cumulo* feuduty which is unallocated and any part of a *cumulo* feuduty which has been allocated."[98] The definition is not very happily framed and it has been suggested that it may authorise redemption of an unallocated feuduty.[99] It is thought, however, that on a proper construction of the section the results are:

(1) Where a feuduty has been constituted over an area of ground which is subdivided into several plots or subjects which come into separate ownership the feuduty becomes a *cumulo* feuduty, since it is now a burden on properties owned by several proprietors. If no allocation of the *cumulo* feuduty has been made on any of the several subjects it is an unallocated *cumulo* feuduty. All of the proprietors of the burdened subjects may then jointly redeem the feuduty, but no one

---

[96] 1974 Act, s. 3(1).
[97] *e.g.* as in *Gibb* v. *Inland Revenue* (1880) 8 R. 120.
[98] 1974 Act, ss. 4(7) and 5(12).
[99] Professor P. N. Love, (1976) 21 J.L.S. 364.

of them may redeem the portion of the feuduty apportioned, but not allocated, upon his property.

(2) Where portions of the *cumulo* feuduty have been allocated on some, but not all, of the several subjects, then (a) each proprietor on whose property the allocation has been made may redeem the portion of the feuduty allocated on his property, but (b) the unallocated remainder of the feuduty is an unallocated *cumulo* feuduty and may be redeemed by all the proprietors of the subjects in respect of which there has been no allocation acting jointly, but no one of them may redeem the portion of the *cumulo* feuduty apportioned, but not allocated, on his property.

(3) Where portions of the *cumulo* feuduty have been allocated on all the several subjects except one, each proprietor on whose property allocation has been made may redeem the portion allocated upon it and so also may the proprietor on whose property there has been no formal allocation.

(4) Where the feuduty is not a *cumulo* feuduty but one constituted over a feu which has not been subdivided, the proprietor may redeem it: subsection (1) of section 4 provides that any proprietor of a feu may redeem the feuduty which is exigible from it, and the definition in subsection (7) is expressed as being inclusive and is not exhaustive. If any proprietor is not entitled to redeem by reason of the fact that his proportion of a *cumulo* feuduty has not been allocated he may overcome the difficulty by having his proportion allocated by notice or under an order of the Lands Tribunal by the procedure authorised in sections 3 to 5 of the Conveyancing and Feudal Reform (Scotland) Act 1970, and may then redeem the portion of the feuduty so allocated.

17–44   **Persons who may redeem.** For the purposes of voluntary redemption by notice under section 4 or compulsory redemption under section 5 of the Act the proprietor of the feu (or *dominium utile*) includes not only an infeft proprietor but also a person having right to the land but whose title thereto is not complete.[1] A person having right to the land is clearly used in the sense of that expression in section 3 of the Conveyancing (Scotland) Act 1924 as indicating a person who may at his own hand and without the intervention of another complete title to the land, but excludes a person who has only a *jus crediti* to require a conveyance. So if land has been conveyed to trustees under a trust disposition and settlement with directions to convey it to a specified beneficiary but that has not yet been done, the persons entitled to redeem the feuduty voluntarily are the trustees (whether or not they have completed title to the land), not the beneficiary. If land has been sold under missives it is the seller, not the purchaser, who is obliged to pay the redemption money in terms of section 5.[2] Where the feu is

---

[1] 1974 Act, s. 7(3).
[2] That is made clear expressly in s. 5(4).

subject to a heritable security constituted by *ex facie* absolute disposition, the person entitled or obliged to redeem the feuduty is the debtor in the security, except where the creditor is in possession of the land.[3] In the excepted case where the heritable creditor is in possession and sells either under powers in the security or with the concurrence of the debtor, it would appear that as a practical matter the obligation to redeem the feuduty rests on the heritable creditor.

–45   Procedure. The proprietor of the *dominium utile* gives to the superior or his agent a notice of redemption in or as nearly as may be in the form contained in Form 1 of Schedule 1 to the 1974 Act not later than the term of Whitsunday or Martinmas at which he proposes to redeem the feuduty.[4] The notice may be given at any time up to the term when redemption is to be made; the Act does not require that it must be given at any specified period prior to the term. It is not necessary that the notice be given by registered post or recorded delivery. The sum payable on redemption is the amount which would, if invested in 2½ per cent Consolidated Stock at the middle market price at the close of business last preceding the date occurring one month before the term when redemption is effected, produce an annual sum equal to the feuduty, together with any arrears of feuduty and, if the feu grant has so provided, interest on such arrears.[5] On redemption the superior or his agent grants a receipt in the form specified in Form 2 of Schedule 1 to the Act.[6]

Notice of redemption[7]

–46   *(Address of person sending notice, and Date)*
To *(name and address of superior or his agent)*
Take notice that, in terms of section 4 of the Land Tenure Reform (Scotland) Act 1974, I wish to redeem at the term of [Whitsunday] [Martinmas] *(year)* the feuduty of £   per annum exigible in respect of *(sufficient identification of the land in respect of which the payment to be redeemed is exigible).*
(Signed) AB
or
CD,
Agent for AB.

Form of receipt[8]

–47   I hereby acknowledge to have received from *(name of proprietor)* the sum of £   *(amount of redemption money)* in redemption (in terms of section 4 of the Land Tenure Reform (Scotland) Act

---

[3] 1974 Act, s. 7(3).
[4] 1974 Act, s. 4(2)(*a*).
[5] *Ibid.*, s. 4(2)(*b*). The redemption factor or number of years' purchase of the annual feuduty based upon the statutory formula is published for each term in the *Journal of the Law Society of Scotland.*
[6] *Ibid.*, s. 4(4).
[7] *Ibid.*, Sched. 1, Form 1.
[8] *Ibid.*, Sched. 1, Form 2.

1974) of the feuduty of £   per annum exigible as at (*date of notice of redemption*) in respect of (*sufficient identification of the land in respect of which the payment being redeemed is exigible*).
Dated this   day of   19   .
(*Signed*) XY
or
YZ
Agent for XY.

17–48   Effect of redemption. The effect of redemption of the feuduty is only to extinguish for the future the liability to make payment of the periodic sum. In all other respects the conditions of the tenure remain unaltered. If it is desired to extinguish these conditions it is necessary to purchase and obtain a disposition of the superiority and thereafter to consolidate the two estates of *dominium directum* and *dominium utile*. Since by that process the feuar is acquiring the additional benefit of freedom from the former feudal conditions the price payable is normally greater than the statutorily fixed price for redemption of the feuduty.

(2) Compulsory Redemption on Sale

When redemption is compulsory

17–49   Under the Land Tenure Reform (Scotland) Act 1974 an allocated feuduty must be redeemed where the property which it burdens is sold with a date of entry on or after September 1, 1974. Feuduties which must be redeemed comprise (a) the feuduty created over a single plot sold, (b) part of a *cumulo* feuduty which has been allocated upon the plot sold, and (c) an over-feuduty created over or allocated upon a superiority which has been sold. It is unnecessary to redeem a feuduty which has not been allocated on the land sold, *e.g.* land subject to a proportion of a *cumulo* feuduty which has been apportioned but not allocated upon that land. If land which is burdened with an allocated feuduty is sold in lots, the *cumulo* feuduty being apportioned but not allocated on each lot sold, it is submitted that there is no obligation to redeem: as at the date when entry is taken to each lot there is no allocated feuduty applicable to that lot. Nor is redemption compulsory when each lot is sold subsequently, unless in the interim a proportion of the *cumulo* feuduty has been allocated upon it, and each lot remains liable for the *cumulo* feuduty subject to the right of partial relief against the proprietors of the other lots created by the arrangement as to apportionment. If, however, a *cumulo* feuduty has been allocated on all except one of the lots into which the original feu has been subdivided, then on sale of any of the lots the proportion of the *cumulo* feuduty must be redeemed, since in the case of the excepted lot there has been an implied allocation. Redemption is compulsory only on *sale*: it is not necessary on the occasion of any other disposal or passing of land such as by gift or on death. The date upon which the feuduty is redeemed is the date when entry is taken under the contract of sale or under the conveyance implementing a sale (if there has been no preceding contract): if the date of entry is prior to the date of completion of the contract of sale or the date of execution of the disposition (where there has been no preceding contract) the date of redemption is the date of completion of the contract or the date of execution of the disposition, as the case may be.[9]

Procedure

17–50 On the date of redemption the feuduty exigible is deemed to have been redeemed.[10] On that date the person who was the proprietor of the feu immediately before the date of the contract of sale (or the date of execution of the disposition where there was no contract), *i.e.* the seller or his representatives, is obliged to pay to the superior the redemption money being an amount ascertained as in the case of voluntary redemption explained in paragraph 17–45 *supra*.[11] At any time after the completion of the contract of sale or (if there was no such contract) the date of execution of the disposition the proprietor of the feu for the time being or his agent may give notice to the superior or his agent in the form contained in Schedule 2 to the Act that the feuduty will be or is redeemed at the date of redemption.[12] In the normal case the redemption money is duly paid to the superior by the seller on the redemption date, usually without the seller having given the notice above-mentioned.

Commentary on compulsory redemption of feuduty

7–51 (1) Upon voluntary redemption the feuduty is redeemed only when notice has been given and the redemption money paid.[13] Compulsory redemption on the other hand is deemed by statutory fiction to have taken place, usually on the date of entry of the purchaser, whether the redemption money has been paid or not.[14]

(2) For the protection of the superior the redemption money in a case of compulsory redemption, if it has not been paid on the date of redemption, is, with interest thereon from the date of redemption until payment, secured in favour of the superior as a real burden on the land feued binding on the proprietor of the feu for the time being in the same manner and subject to the same remedies as the feuduty redeemed.[15]

---

[9] 1974 Act, s. 5(1) and (2).
[10] *Ibid.*, s. 5(1).
[11] *Ibid.*, s. 5(4).
[12] *Ibid.*, s. 5(6). Often a purchaser stipulates in the missives of sale that the seller will give such a notice, since it places a time limit on the existence of the real burden for the redemption money.
[13] *Ibid.*, s. 4(3).
[14] *Ibid.*, s. 5(1).
[15] *Ibid.*, s. 5(5).

(3) This security for the redemption money ceases to burden the feu on the expiry of two months after the giving of the notice of redemption mentioned in paragraph 17–50 *supra* or after the date of redemption, whichever is later, and the feu is also disburdened of any arrears of feuduty which have accrued up to and including the date of redemption.[16] Until a notice of redemption is given the two months period will not commence to run, since the later date is indeterminable. In effect, therefore, the provisions as to giving the notice of redemption provide machinery whereby a purchaser who is not satisfied that the redemption money has been paid to the superior may, as the proprietor of the feu after the date of entry, give the notice and so ensure that the land will be freed of the burden two months thereafter, subject to any extension of time by order of the court as aftermentioned.[17]

(4) After the expiry of the said period of two months the only persons against whom court action may be taken (a) for recovery of the redemption money is the former proprietor of the feu immediately before the contract of sale was completed or the execution of the disposition (where there was no contract), and (b) for recovery of arrears of feuduty accrued up to and including the date of redemption is any person who was liable therefor immediately before the date of redemption, again subject to the superior's rights aftermentioned.[17]

(5) If before the end of the said period of two months the superior has obtained warrant to cite the defender in an action against any of the persons mentioned in (4) above for recovery of the redemption money or arrears of feuduty, the court may at any time within the two months period (whether or not the defender has been actually cited) order that the land shall continue to be burdened for such additional period as is reasonable to enable the superior to recover the sum sued for in the action, and the additional period may be extended by further order of the court. The purchaser will only be liable to pay the redemption money or arrears in the last resort if the court is satisfied that it is not reasonably practicable to recover the redemption money from the seller or the arrears of feuduty from the seller or other person liable therefor before the sale.[18] An extract of any order of the court extending the period of the security must be recorded in the Register of Sasines before the expiry of the said period of two months or of the period specified in any existing order.[19] In practice this means that an extract of any order extending the period of the burden, or of any subsequent order prolonging that period, must be recorded immediately after it has been obtained. The warrant of registration will be signed by or on behalf of the superior.

---

[16] *Ibid.*, s. 5(6).
[17] *Ibid.*, s. 5(6).
[18] *Ibid.*, s. 5(7).
[19] *Ibid.*, s. 5(8).

Notice of redemption

–52   A notice of redemption may be served by the person who is the proprietor of the feu for the time being, *i.e.* by the seller before entry has been taken or by the purchaser thereafter. On receipt of the notice in duplicate the superior or his agent if so requested must return one copy with an acknowledgment thereon subscribed by him.[20] The practice of serving the notice in duplicate with a request for an acknowledgment should be adopted but, in order to guard against failure by the superior to acknowledge it, the notice should be sent by registered post or recorded delivery since giving the notice is important as establishing the *terminus a quo* the period of two months may run. The statutory form[21] of the notice is:

> (*Address of sender, and Date*)
> To (*name and address of superior or his agent*)
> Take notice that, in terms of section 5 of the Land Tenure Reform (Scotland) Act 1974, the feuduty of £   (*amount*) per annum exigible in respect of (*sufficient identification of the land in respect of which the feuduty was exigible*) as at (*date of redemption*) [will be deemed to be redeemed] [is deemed to have been redeemed] at that date by reason of entry having been taken to the said subjects [under an obligation to convey] [*or, as the case may be,* under a deed conveying] the said subjects by [*name(s) of obligant(s) or person(s) conveying as the case may be*] dated [*give date(s) of obligation or of execution of deed as the case may be*].
> (*Signed*) AB
> *or* CD,
> Agent for AB.

Persons liable to pay redemption money

–53   Upon compulsory redemption the person primarily liable to pay the redemption money is the person who was the proprietor of the feu immediately before the completion of the contract of sale or the execution of the disposition (where there was no contract), *i.e.* the seller.[22] For this purpose the definition of "proprietor" is the same as that already considered in relation to voluntary redemption.[23] It is possible, however, if the period of two months while the redemption money remains secured over the land feued, or any extensions of that period by order of the court, remains unexpired, and the superior satisfies the court that it is not reasonably practicable to recover the redemption money from the seller or his representatives, that the purchaser may have to pay the redemption money in order to relieve his land of the continuing burden of it. The purchaser will normally protect himself against that risk by a clause in the contract of sale on

---

[20] *Ibid.*, s. 5(9).
[21] *Ibid.*, Sched. 2.
[22] *Ibid.*, s. 5(4).
[23] *Ibid.*, s. 7(3): see para. 17–44.

the lines of that suggested in paragraph 15–90 *supra* with the additional precaution, if a receipt for the redemption money is not produced at or prior to settlement, of obtaining the personal obligation of the seller's solicitor to exhibit such a receipt.

Heritable creditors

17–54 Both voluntary and compulsory redemption under the provisions of the 1974 Act are expressed as binding on all persons having interest, but with the proviso that the redemption shall not prejudice the rights of existing heritable creditors (unless in the case of voluntary redemption they are parties to the redemption), but the superior is liable to indemnify any proprietor of the feu against liability arising after redemption from such rights.[24] Clearly heritable creditors over the superiority may be prejudiced if the superior does not apply the redemption money to any extent in reduction of the creditors' secured loans. In that event, if the heritable creditors subsequently enforce their security by real action, the proprietor of the feu who has voluntarily redeemed the feuduty, or the purchaser in the case of compulsory redemption, may require to pay the annual feuduty which has been redeemed in order to protect his property, and the indemnity of the superior in such circumstances may be of little value. It is suggested that the person redeeming the feuduty should obtain an assurance from the superior that there are no heritable securities over the superiority, possibly supported, in transactions involving substantial amounts, by examination of a search over the superiority. If any heritable securities over the superiority are disclosed it would be advisable to seek from the creditors a consent to the redemption which presumably would be granted upon an arrangement with the superior for application of the redemption money or some part of it in reduction of the creditors' loan. *Quaere*, in the case of compulsory redemption, whether the person liable to pay the redemption money could insist on such consent? The Act requires redemption of the feuduty on sale, in the circumstances where that is automatic, on the conditions of the Act, which leave the purchaser in the position of having to rely on the indemnity of the superior.

Apportionment

17–55 When redemption takes place on a date between the terms of payment of the feuduty the seller is liable to pay to the superior, in addition to the redemption money, the proportion of the current feuduty from the last term to the date of redemption accruing on a day-to-day basis under the Apportionment Act 1870.

---

[24] *Ibid.*, ss. 4(5) and 5(10).

Increasing feuduty

56   The 1974 Act does not make special provision for redemption either voluntarily or compulsorily of a feuduty which increases permanently by a stated amount at specified intervals (permissible in terms of section 18 of the Feudal Casualties (Scotland) Act 1914). Assume that in terms of a feu charter executed in 1970 the feuduty is £100 per annum until 1980, increasing to £150 thereafter until 1990 and to £200 after 1990, and that the land feued is sold in 1984. How is the redemption money payable on sale in 1984 to be calculated? It is submitted that it would be incorrect to treat a payment of redemption money based on £150, the feuduty exigible at the date of redemption, as a complete discharge of the burden of the feuduty, a method that would plainly be unfair to the superior. It appears that on a strict interpretation of section 5 of the Act, (i) the feuduty deemed to be redeemed is that exigible at the date of redemption, *i.e.* £150 (subs. (1)); (ii) no payment will be exigible in respect of a feuduty after the date of redemption thereof but the feu continues in force otherwise as if the feuduty were not redeemed (subs. (3)); and (iii) since the only feuduty that has been redeemed is £150, then in 1990 when a further feuduty of £50 becomes payable in terms of a condition of the feu which otherwise continues, *i.e.* otherwise than in respect of the feuduty which has been redeemed, the additional feuduty of £50 will be a burden on the feu payable until redeemed voluntarily or automatically on sale.

(3) Redemption on Acquisition of Land by Authority possessing Compulsory Purchase Powers

Compulsory redemption under section 6 of 1974 Act

57   Section 6 of the Act makes special provision for the compulsory redemption of feuduty which burdens land acquired by an authority possessing compulsory purchase powers. The principle of automatic redemption as in the case of sales under section 5 of the Act applies, but there are important differences.

58   **Transactions inducing compulsory redemption.** Redemption of feuduty is compulsory where an authority possessing compulsory purchase powers (the acquiring authority) takes entry to a feu from which the feuduty is exigible. The acquisition need not be for valuable consideration; nor need it have been made by exercise of the authority's powers of compulsory acquisition; if an authority which possesses these powers takes entry to land burdened by a feuduty, whether the land is acquired by way of gift, or purchase by agreement, or by the use of compulsory powers, the feuduty is automatically redeemed.[25]

---

[25] 1974 Act, s. 6(1). S. 107 of the Lands Clauses Consolidation (Scotland) Act 1845 (which permitted bodies acquiring land under compulsory powers to continue paying the feuduty upon it unless called upon by the superior to redeem it) is superseded.

17–59 Feuduty need not have been allocated. In contradistinction to the position where redemption of feuduty is compulsory on sale under section 5 of the Act, the feuduty on land acquired by the acquiring authority must be redeemed whether it has been allocated or not. If the land acquired is part only of a feu subject to a *cumulo* feuduty, the portion of the feuduty settled on the land acquired by the provisions of section 109 of the Lands Clauses Consolidation (Scotland) Act 1845 or by paragraph 32 of Schedule 24 to the Town and Country Planning (Scotland) Act 1972 (in the case of acquisition by means of a general vesting declaration) must be redeemed. The balance of the *cumulo* feuduty remains a burden on the unacquired part of the feu.[26]

17–60 Liability for and assessment of redemption money. The redemption money is payable, not by the seller as in a sale under section 5 of the Act, but by the acquiring authority.[27] The complex and difficult problems of valuation of superiorities under section 20 of the Land Compensation (Scotland) Act 1963[28] are superseded by substituting the simpler formula for ascertaining the redemption money based on the yield from $2\frac{1}{2}$ per cent Consolidated Stock prescribed in section 5(4) of the 1974 Act in relation to sales under that section.[29]

17–61 Date of redemption. Where acquisition is by way of notice to treat or deemed notice to treat under the Lands Clauses Consolidation (Scotland) Act 1845 or other statute having similar effect, the date of redemption is the date when entry is taken under the notice to treat.[30] Where acquisition has been by means of a general vesting declaration within the meaning of Schedule 24 to the Town and Country Planning (Scotland) Act 1972, the date of redemption is the date of vesting of the land in the acquiring authority under paragraph 7 of that Schedule, *i.e.* the end of the period stated in the general vesting declaration after which such vesting would take place.[31]

17–62 Notice of redemption. The provisions of the 1974 Act whereby for the protection of the superior the feuduty remains a burden on land sold for a limited period until the redemption money is paid do not apply to acquisitions by an acquiring authority under section 6, since the authority is a responsible body which will implement the obligation to make the payment. Instead, in order to certiorate the superior of his right to the redemption money, the acquiring authority must, not later than the date of redemption, give to the superior or his agent a notice of redemption in the form contained in Schedule 3 to the Act and pay the redemption money with interest from the date of redemption.[32]

---

[26] 1974 Act, s. 6(7).
[27] *Ibid.*, s. 6(2)(*c*) and (4).
[28] For an illustration of such problems, see *Blythswood Friendly Society* v. *City of Glasgow District Council*, 1979 S.C. (H.L.) 1.
[29] 1974 Act, s. 6(2)(*c*) and (4).
[30] *Ibid.*, s. 6(2)(*a*).
[31] *Ibid.*, s. 6(4).
[32] *Ibid.*, s. 6(5).

The statutory form of notice is:

> (*Name and addres of authority sending notice and Date*)
>
> To (*name and address of superior or his agent*)
> Take notice that, in terms of section 6 of the Land Tenure Reform (Scotland) Act 1974, the feuduty of £ (*amount*) per annum exigible in respect of (*sufficient identification of the land in respect of which the feuduty was exigible*) as at (*date of redemption*) will be deemed to be redeemed at that date [to such extent (if any) as may be settled under section 109 of the Lands Clauses Consolidation (Scotland) Act 1845 as applied by virtue of section 6 of the said Act of 1974].
>
> (*To be signed on behalf of the acquiring authority*)

Over-feuduties

–63 The 1974 Act is silent as regards over-feuduties, but it seems reasonably clear that on sale of a superiority from which an allocated over-feuduty is exigible that over-feuduty must be redeemed. There can, however, be complex problems, not considered in the Act, where an over-feuduty is not as yet redeemed since the superiority has not been sold but allocated sub-feuduties have been redeemed voluntarily under section 4 or compulsorily on sale under section 5 of the Act. The problems stem from the fact that redemption of a feuduty leaves intact all the other conditions of the feu. When the immediate superior receives the redemption moneys in respect of the sub-feus he is under no obligation to apply them in redeeming the over-feuduty. If subsequently he defaults for five years in payment of the over-feuduty the over-superior, although he cannot recover payment from the sub-feuars by personal action since that right exists only to the extent of the sub-feuduties and these have been extinguished by redemption, may still irritate the feu to his vassal, the immediate superior of the sub-feuars, and annul also the sub-feus derived from it. It would appear that in those circumstances the sub-feuars might be compelled to pay the arrears of the over-feuduty in order to protect their properties, although they would have a right of indemnity from their immediate superior *quantum valeat*. The possibility is not remote: once the immediate superior has received the redemption moneys in respect of all the sub-feus he has no immediate financial interest left and no incentive to continue to pay the over-feuduty.

VI. EXECUTORY CLAUSES

Assignation of writs

–64 It is no longer necessary to insert in a feu grant a clause of assignation of writs. Any feu grant shall, unless specially qualified, import an assignation to the grantee of the title deeds and searches to the effect of maintaining and defending the right of the grantee in the feu, and the superior shall be held to be obliged for that purpose to make the title deeds and searches forthcoming to the grantee on all necessary occasions at the grantee's expense.[33] The obligations of the parties thus imported without the need of an express clause effectively reproduce the terms of the clause of assignation of writs which previously was customarily inserted in a feu grant. In practice, the former clause is now omitted as unnecessary unless some special variation is required.

Assignation of rents

17–65   Likewise the 1979 Act dispenses with the need to incorporate in a feu grant a clause of assignation of rents. In its absence the deed, unless specially qualified, imports an assignation of the rents payable (i) in the case of backhand rents, at the legal terms following the date of entry, and (ii) in the case of forehand rents, at the conventional terms following that date.[34] The statutory provision produces substantially the same general result as the import of a clause of assignation of rents as defined in section 8 of the Titles to Land Consolidation (Scotland) Act 1868.[35] Unless some variation in the statutory provision is required the clause is now almost always omitted.

Obligations of relief

17–66   A clause of obligation of relief from feuduties and public burdens is now also no longer required. In the absence of any such clause a feu grant, unless specially qualified, imports an obligation on the granter to relieve the grantee of all feuduties, ground annuals, annuities and public, parochial and local burdens exigible in respect of the feu prior to the date of entry and of all feuduties payable by the granter to his superiors from and after the date of entry.[36] It is recommended that, in the absence of any special reason for modifying the statutory effect of such an obligation, it should be omitted. If for any reason the obligation is expressed, care should be taken to restrict its terms to relief from burdens exigible for periods prior to the date of entry; as to the dangers and possible liabilities of an obligation of relief expressed as applicable to future burdens see the cases undernoted.[37]

---

[33] Land Registration (Scotland) Act 1979, s. 16(2).
[34] 1979 Act, s. 16(3)(*a*).
[35] The effect is considered in detail in para. 22–13 in relation to dispositions.
[36] 1979 Act, s. 16(3)(*b*).
[37] *Dunbar's Trs.* v. *British Fisheries Society* (1878) 5 R. (H.L.) 221; *Scott* v. *Edmond* (1850) 12 D. 1077; *Latto* v. *Mags. of Aberdeen* (1903) 5 F. 740; *North British Rly. Co.* v. *Mags. of Edinburgh*, 1920 S.C. 409.

Warrandice

-67 The warrandice in a feu grant follows the ordinary rules[38] and when a price is payable should be absolute.

VII. SPECIAL CLAUSES

Clause of pre-emption

-68 A clause of pre-emption is valid[39] subject to certain statutory restraints imposed by the Conveyancing Amendment (Scotland) Act 1938, s. 9 and the Conveyancing and Feudal Reform (Scotland) Act 1970, s. 46. The statutory limitation as regards clauses of pre-emption in feu grants now is:

> "Any condition or provision whether made before or after 17th May 1938 to the effect that the superior of any feu shall be entitled to a right of pre-emption in the event of a sale thereof or of any part thereof by the proprietor of the feu (*whether or not that right purports to be exercisable on more than one occasion*[40]) shall, with all irritant clauses applicable thereto, be in all time coming null and void, and not capable of being enforced as regards such feu or part thereof, as the case may be, unless the person in right of the superiority (whether or not his title thereto is complete) shall within 21[41] days or such shorter period as may be specified in the charter stipulating for such right of pre-emption after an offer has been made to him by the proprietor for the time being *accept the offer.*[42]"

Detailed provisions are made in the 1938 Act with regard to the procedure in delivering or sending the offer and evidence of its having been so delivered or sent.[43] Section 13 of the Land Tenure Reform (Scotland) Act 1974 applied the limitations of the 1938 and 1970 Acts, formerly applicable only to rights of pre-emption contained in feu grants, to rights of pre-emption created in any deed or writing executed after September 1, 1974, in favour of any person of an interest in land in the event of a sale thereof or of any part thereof by the proprietor for the time being.

-69 **Statutory limitations.** The statutory limitations apply as follows: (1) If the right of pre-emption was created in a feu grant, whenever made, then (a) if the offer was made on or after September 17, 1938, but before November 29, 1970, the provisions of the 1938 Act only apply; but (b) if the offer has been or is made on or after November 29, 1970,

---

[38] See Vol. I, paras. 4–28 to 4–52.

[39] *Preston* v. *Earl of Dundonald's Creditors* (1805) 3 R.L.C. 289.

[40] The words in parenthesis were added by the 1970 Act.

[41] Substituted by the 1970 Act for "40" in the 1938 Act.

[42] The italicised words substituted by the 1970 Act for "intimate his intention to exercise such offer" in the 1938 Act.

[43] 1938 Act, s. 9(2).

the provisions of the 1938 Act as amended by the 1970 Act apply. (2) If the right of pre-emption was created in any other deed, *e.g.* a disposition, and only if that deed has been or is executed after September 1, 1974, the provisions of the 1938 Act as amended by the 1970 Act apply with the appropriate adaptations of wording made by section 13 of the 1974 Act.

17–70 Terms of clause. A right of pre-emption limits the freedom of a proprietor of land to dispose of it and is not *inter naturalia* of a feu and even less so of a disposition. Accordingly, it will be strictly construed *contra proferentem* and must be carefully framed if it is to be effective. In particular there must be precise definition of (1) the persons by whom and against whom the right is enforceable, (2) the occasion on which the right will become exercisable, (3) the price payable on exercise of the right or the method by which it is to be ascertained, (4) the time within which an offer must be accepted, and (5) whether the right is a contractual bargain or a real burden on the land.

17–71 *Persons by whom and against whom right enforceable.* The frame of the clause on this matter depends upon the intentions of parties. If the right is simply to be a personal bargain then it may be expressed as between the parties, without more, or possibly, if it is intended to subsist after the death of either, as between the parties and their respective executors and representatives. If, however, the right is to be enforceable by successors in the ownership of the respective interests of the parties in the land, the wording presents greater difficulty. It has been held that a right expressed in a feu disposition as binding upon the vassal and his heirs and assignees was enforceable against a singular successor,[44] but it is suggested that it would be preferable if the right is created against the vassal and his executors, assignees and successors in ownership of the feu in favour of the superior and his executors, assignees and successors in ownership of the superiority, and that it be expressly created a real burden. Where the right is created in a disposition something more is required, because who are the successors of the disponer and in the ownership of what land? If the disponer owns or has interests in other land in the vicinity, the right should be created in favour of himself and his executors and successors in the ownership of specified land. If, however, the disponer does not own or have interests in any other land in the vicinity, it is thought that it is impossible to create the right as a continuing burden since there is no praedial interest to enforce it.

17–72 *Occasion on which right exercisable.* The right of pre-emption may be expressed as arising on sale. If it has not been made a real burden or expressed as binding on any successors in ownership, the effect may be that the right is not enforceable if the subjects are transferred by gift or

---

[44] *Christie* v. *Jackson* (1898) 6 S.L.T. 245.

transmitted on death. A provision frequently encountered is that the subjects shall not be "sold or disposed of" to a third party until they have been offered to the holder of the right of pre-emption at the price offered by the third party. It would appear that this provision is still only enforceable in the event of a sale; if a gratuitous transfer *inter vivos* is contemplated or if the proprietor of the subjects dies, whether testate or intestate, there is no price ascertained at which the subjects can be offered to the person having the right of pre-emption. A clause in these terms expressed as binding upon the grantee and his executors and assignees would, however, be binding upon the executors of the proprietor if and when they proposed to sell the subjects. If it is desired that the right should be exercisable on gratuitous disposal or on the death of the proprietor, it would be necessary to provide for a method of determining the price, *e.g.* by independent valuation.

-73   There was some doubt whether under the provisions of section 9 of the 1938 Act the right was exercisable on more than one occasion. That doubt is removed in circumstances where the 1970 Act applies; it is now clear that if on one occasion the offer is made and not accepted the right ceases to be exercisable thereafter.

-74   It has been decided that a clause in a feu charter which prohibited sale or alienation of the subjects by the vassal until she had made the first offer to the superior was not infringed by the grant of a lease for 19 years with an obligation to renew for further periods of 19 years unless the lessor took over the buildings at valuation.[45] It is thought, however, that the granting of a lease for a longer period would amount to a disposal[46] and would be an occasion for exercise of a right of pre-emption expressed as arising on alienation or on disposal.

-75   *Price payable on exercise of right of pre-emption.* It is usual to provide that the price payable on exercise of a right of pre-emption is that offered by any other person. It would appear, however, that it is permissible to provide that the subjects, before sale to any other person, must be offered to the holder of the right of pre-emption at a stipulated price[47] or at a price fixed by arbitration.[48] Clearly the existence of a right of pre-emption may be an impediment to the conclusion of an advantageous sale, since a third party offering a satisfactory price may be unwilling to agree to leave his offer standing for a period of up to 21 days before receiving an unqualified acceptance. In practice it is advisable to ascertain the intentions of the holder of the right of pre-emption before advertising the subjects for sale, but this may not always be practicable if the decision as to exercise of the right

---

[45] *Lumsden* v. *Stewart* (1843) 5 D. 501.
[46] *Petrie's Trs.* v. *Ramsay* (1868) 7 M. 64.
[47] *Preston* v. *Earl of Dundonald's Creditors, supra.*
[48] Burns, 223.

is dependent upon the price which will require to be paid. The proprietor of the subjects is not entitled, after a contract of sale has been made, to start a competition between the third party offering and the person entitled to the right of pre-emption.[49]

17–76 *Time limit for acceptance of offer.* A right of a pre-emption created in a feu grant of whatever date or created in any other kind of deed executed after September 1, 1974, becomes null and void in all time coming unless the person entitled to exercise the right accepts an offer made to him by the proprietor of the subjects within 21 days or any shorter period specified in the clause of pre-emption.[50] It is thought that the relevant dates are the dates of receipt of the offer and of the acceptance, not the dates of their signature or despatch. If the offer by the proprietor is withdrawn by him and the withdrawal is received within the permitted period for acceptance before an acceptance or refusal of the offer has been despatched, that does not constitute an offer for the purposes of the statutory provisions.[51]

17–77 *Right of pre-emption as real burden.* If the clause creating a right of pre-emption is to be of maximum effect, it should be created real by inclusion in the dispositive clause and framed in terms that it is binding upon successors in the ownership of the subjects. Even so, it will not be enforceable if the person in whose favour it is constituted does not have a praedial interest to do so, nor will it be effective if the subjects are acquired compulsorily by a body having the requisite power,[52] but, certainly if it is a real burden, it will be enforceable against a heritable creditor enforcing a power of sale. An attempt to enforce a right of pre-emption over part of a larger property failed on the ground that the right had not been repeated as a burden in the conveyance of that part.[53] A right of pre-emption is a land obligation in terms of section 1(2) of the Conveyancing and Feudal Reform (Scotland) Act 1970, but cannot be varied by the Lands Tribunal if imposed directly by statute as distinct from an obligation imposed under enabling powers contained in a statute.[54]

17–78 *Procedure.* An offer by the proprietor to the person entitled to the right of pre-emption may be made by delivering it to that person or his agent or factor or by sending it by registered letter to such person, agent or factor at his last known address or, if such person is not known or cannot be found, to the Extractor of the Court of Session. It is sufficient evidence that the offer was duly made if an acknowledgment

---

[49] *Pickett* v. *Lindsay's Trs.* (1905) 13 S.L.T. 440.
[50] 1938 Act, s. 9 as amended by 1970 Act, s. 46 and 1974 Act, s. 13.
[51] See *J.M. Smith Ltd.* v. *Colquhoun's Tr.* (1901) 3 F. 981 for an analogous case in relation to shares of a company.
[52] Town and Country Planning (Scotland) Act 1972, s. 108.
[53] *McLean* v. *Kennaway* (1904) 11 S.L.T. 719, 12 S.L.T. 117.
[54] *Mrs Ann M. Macdonald*, 1973 S.L.T. (Lands Tr.) 26.

of receipt is endorsed on the offer or a copy of it by the addressee or, if the offer was made by registered letter, a certificate subscribed by the proprietor or his solicitor that the offer was duly posted with the Post Office receipt for the registered letter attached.[55] The acknowledgment and certificate may be in the form of Form No. 2 and Form No. 3 respectively of Schedule L to the Conveyancing (Scotland) Act 1924 with the substitution of the word "Offer" for the word "Premonition."[56] The offer, being an offer to sell heritable property which requires acceptance, should be probative or holograph.[57]

–79 *Style—clause of pre-emption*

(*To be inserted in dispositive clause and declared a real burden fortified by irritant and resolutive clause*)
It shall not be in the power of the said CD or his assignees or successors in ownership of or having power of sale of the subjects hereby disponed or any part thereof to sell, alienate or dispose of the said subjects or any part thereof to any person (except under statutory authority or compulsion) until he or they have first offered the same in writing to [me or my successors as superiors thereof] [me or my successors as proprietors of (*specified lands*)] for the time being at such price and on such other conditions as any other person shall have offered for the same, and I or my foresaids shall be bound to intimate in writing acceptance or refusal of the offer within   days[a] after the offer shall have been received.

NOTE
[a] The period must not exceed 21 days.

Clause of redemption

–80 A clause of redemption in a conveyance of land which reserves a right to the granter to repurchase it is legal,[58] even when the price payable may not be the full value of the subjects.[59] If a right of redemption is created in a deed executed after September 1, 1974, however, and it purports to be exercisable on the happening of an event which is bound to occur or the occurrence of which is within the control of the person for the time being entitled to exercise the right or of a third party, the right is exercisable only within 20 years of the date of its creation.[60]

---

[55] 1938 Act, s. 9(2) as amended by 1974 Act, s. 13(3).
[56] 1938 Act, s. 9(2).
[57] See *Stone* v. *MacDonald*, 1979 S.C. 363 at 368.
[58] *Viscount Strathallan* v. *Lord Grantley* (1843) 5 D. 1318.
[59] *McElroy* v. *Duke of Argyll* (1902) 4 F. 885.
[60] Land Tenure Reform (Scotland) Act 1974, s. 12.

Styles of Feu Grants

Skeleton charter

17–81   I, AB, (*designed*), heritable proprietor of the subjects and others
hereinafter disponed (I and my successors in the superiority
thereof being hereinafter called "the superiors") in consideration
of the price of £   paid to me by CD, (*designed*), and of the
whole prestations hereinafter specified or referred to hereby sell
and in feu farm dispone to the said CD and his executors and
assignees whomsoever [but excluding assignees before infeftment
on these presents and under the declaration that the same shall
not be a valid warrant for such infeftment after the expiry of
        months from the date hereof][a] (the said CD and his
successors in the ownership of the said subjects being hereinafter
called "the feuars") heritably and irredeemably ALL and WHOLE
(*description of subjects*)[b] (which subjects are hereinafter referred
to as "the feu"); Together with free ish and entry therefrom and
thereto, the pertinents thereof and my whole right, title and
interest, present and future, in and to the *dominium utile* thereof;
Excepting and Reserving always (First) to the National Coal
Board constituted by the Coal Industry Nationalisation Act 1946
the whole coal, mines of coal and other minerals in or under the
feu and interests therein now vested in the said Board by virtue of
the said Act and (Second) to the superiors the whole metals,
minerals and substances capable of being worked commercially in
and under the feu other than those vested in the said Board as
aforesaid with full power to the superiors and any persons to
whom they may communicate the right to work, win and carry
away the same but without entering on the surface of the feu [and
to remove support from the feu and buildings thereon by the
working of any subjacent or adjacent metals, minerals or substances
belonging to the superiors], the superiors or such other persons
being bound to pay to the feuars for all damage to the surface of
the feu and the buildings and erections thereon that may be
occasioned by any such workings as such damage shall, failing
agreement, be determined by an arbiter to be mutually chosen or
failing agreement to be appointed by the Sheriff of   on the
application of either party: But the subjects hereby disponed are
so disponed always with and under so far as valid, subsisting and
applicable to the said subjects the reservations, burdens, conditions,
obligations and others specified in (*refer to prior deeds*) and
hereinafter contained (which so far as herein contained are
hereinafter referred to as "the feuing conditions") (*Insert
reservations, burdens, conditions etc. imposed by this deed*)[c]; (*Clause
of pre-emption if any*)[d]; declaring that if the feuars contravene or
fail to implement any of the feuing conditions these presents and
all that may have followed thereon shall in the option of the
superiors become null and void and the feuars shall forfeit their
whole right, title and interest in and to the said subjects hereby
disponed which with all buildings thereon shall revert and belong
to the superiors free and disencumbered of all burdens as if these
presents had not been granted; all of which feuing conditions are
hereby declared to be real burdens and conditions on and of the
said subjects hereby disponed and are appointed to be inserted in

any infeftment that may follow hereon and inserted or effectually referred to in all future conveyances or transmissions of the said subjects or any part thereof on pain of nullity: With entry at   : To be holden the said whole subjects of and under me and my successors as immediate lawful superiors thereof in feu farm, fee and heritage for ever: And I grant warrandice: (*Stamp clause if required*). (*To be attested*) (*Stamp duty as conveyance on sale*)

NOTES

[a] As to situations in which this clause may be desirable see Chapter 24.

[b] As to description of subjects see Chapter 18.

[c] The conditions and burdens will vary with the nature of the subjects and the intentions of parties—see Chapter 19.

[d] See paras. 17–68 to 17–79.

Charter—individual house to be erected by feuar

7–82

[*As in skeleton charter to first feuing condition*] (1) [*Buildings and Maintenance*] The feuars shall be bound to erect and complete on the feu before   and thereafter to maintain and uphold in all time coming and if necessary rebuild a detached dwelling-house and garage conform to the plans and elevations which have been signed by me or on my behalf and by the said CD. The house and garage shall be built of (*specify materials of walls and roofs*) at a cost of not less than £   . Any additional ancillary buildings shall be built only on sites, of materials and according to plans which have received the written approval of the superiors before construction is commenced. No exterior or structural alterations shall be made to the said dwelling-house, garage or ancillary buildings or erections without the prior written consent of the superiors and, where necessary, of the relevant planning and building authorities.

(2) [*Use*] The said dwelling-house shall be used as a single private dwelling-house only, and for no other purpose, and shall never be sub-divided nor occupied by more than one family. The said garage and any ancillary buildings which may be erected shall be occupied and used only by the occupier of the said house or his family residing there and shall never be let or occupied or used separately from the said dwelling-house nor be used for the purposes of any trade or business. No other buildings or erections of any kind whatever, except the walls or fences enclosing it, shall ever be erected on the feu, and the same so far as not occupied by the said dwelling-house, garage and any permitted ancillary buildings or erections and any driveway or entrances shall be laid out and used and kept in a neat and tidy condition as garden ground and for no other purpose.

(3) [*Walls and Fences*] The feuars shall enclose the feu in front with a parapet wall and railing similar to those already erected in front of the plot of ground immediately to the west, and at the rear and on the east they shall erect fences similar to the fence already existing on the west, which fences they may erect one-half on the adjoining ground, and they shall be entitled to recover one-half of the cost thereof from the adjoining feuars when the adjoining areas are feued, but they shall have no claim in respect thereof against the superiors. In respect that the boundary fence already

erected on the west has been erected one-half on the feu, the feuars shall be bound forthwith to repay to the adjoining feuar one-half of the cost thereof. The said parapet wall and railing and fences to be erected by the feuars shall be completed before   . The feuars shall in all time coming maintain the said parapet wall and railing at their own expense, and they shall maintain the said fences jointly with the adjoining feuars or at their sole expense so far and so long as there is no adjoining feuar.

(4) [*Roadway, Footpath and Services*] In respect that I have already formed the roadway and footpath opposite the feu (which to the extent of the footpath and one-half of the roadway are situated within the boundaries of the feu) with all necessary sewers, drains, pipes and cables and that the said CD has paid to me the sum of £   being the share of the cost thereof applicable to the feu, [I undertake to complete the surfacing of the said roadway and footpath opposite the feu to the standard required by the local authority for taking over the same for future maintenance at public expense and the feuars shall be bound, if required, to concur in any application for such taking over.]ᵃ *or* [the feuars shall be bound, if and when the local authority so require, to complete the surfacing of the said roadway and footpath so far as within the feu to the standard required by the local authority for taking over the same for future maintenance at public expense]. Unless and until each of the said roadway and footpath so far as within the feu is so taken over the feuars shall be bound to allow free passage for pedestrian and vehicular traffic over the said roadway and pedestrian traffic only over the said footpath. The feuars shall make at their own expense or permit to be made by the relevant public authority all necessary connections to or from the sewers, drains, pipes and cables in the said roadway for the purpose of providing services to the said dwelling-house and other buildings or erections on the feu.

(5) [*Insurance*] The feuars shall be bound to keep the said dwelling-house and all other buildings and erections on the feu insured against loss or damage by fire [flood and storm and tempest] with a reputable insurance company for the full replacement value thereof [including site clearance charges and professional fees] and to produce to the superiors from time to time when required the policy of insurance and receipts for payment of the premiums, and in the event of the said dwelling-house or other buildings or erections or any part thereof being destroyed or damaged by fire or otherwise the feuars shall be bound to restore the same within one year after such destruction or damage to the condition and value thereof immediately prior to such destruction or damage, and the whole sums to be received from the insurance company with any additional sum that may be required for the purpose shall be expended to the satisfaction of the superiors in restoring the said dwelling-house and other buildings and erections to their former condition and in accordance with the provisions herein contained, any new plans and specifications being first approved by the superiors in writing.

(6) [*Deviation from Feuing Plans*] The superiors shall be entitled to make or permit to be made such alterations or deviations as they may think fit upon the feuing plan(s) of the lands of   in which the feu is situated or the roads or drains thereof, or even to

depart entirely therefrom, and in the event of the superiors doing so the feuars shall have no right or title to object thereto and shall have no claim in respect thereof. [*Clause of pre-emption, if any*] [*Irritant and resolutive clause and declaration that real burdens as in skeleton charter*] [*Continue from term of entry to the end as in skeleton charter*] (*To be attested*) (*Stamp duty as conveyance on sale*)

NOTE
[a] If this alternative applies it may be prudent for the feuars to require a road bond to guarantee performance of the superiors' obligation. The risk is now alleviated by regulations made under section 17 of the Roads (Scotland) Act 1984. (The Security for Private Road Works (Scotland) Regulations 1985, S.I. 1985 No. 2080 (S. 159).)

Charter—individual house erected by builder-superior

7–83

[*As in skeleton charter to first feuing condition with appropriate modifications of description to include the house identified by name and/or postal address, garage and relative offices and fixtures and fittings*]

(1) [*Maintenance of Buildings*] The said house, garage and offices shall be maintained by the feuars in good order and repair and if necessary rebuilt in all time coming and no external or structural alterations shall be made thereto without the prior written consent of the superiors and, where necessary, of the relevant planning and building authorities.

(2) [*Use*] The said house shall be used as a single private dwelling-house for one family only and for no other purpose and the said garage and offices shall be used only by the occupier of the said house or his family residing there and shall never be let or occupied or used separately from the said house nor be used for the purposes of any trade or business. No other buildings or erections of any kind whatever, except the walls or fences enclosing it, shall be erected on the feu, and the same so far as not occupied by the said house, garage and offices and any driveway or entrances shall be used and kept as garden ground and for no other purpose.

(3) [*Walls and Fences*] The wall enclosing the feu fronting the said Road and the fences enclosing the feu on the other three sides shall be maintained in good order and repair and when necessary renewed or replaced, the expense thereof being borne in the case of the said wall at the sole expense of the feuars and in the case of the said fences at the mutual expense of the feuars and the respective proprietors of the ground adjoining the feu. [*Insurance clause and reservation of right to superiors to alter feuing plan as in clauses (5) and (6) in para. 17–82*] [*Clause of pre-emption, if any*] [*Irritant and resolutive clause and declaration that real burdens as in skeleton charter*] [*Continue from term of entry to the end as in skeleton charter*] (*To be attested*) (*Stamp duty as conveyance on sale*)

Deed of feuing conditions—building development—detached, flatted and four-in-a-block houses with garages

7–84

We, AB Limited, (*designed*), heritable proprietors of ALL and WHOLE that area of ground (*description of whole area in development*) WHEREAS we are about to feu the said area of ground in separate plots for the erection of detached and/or flatted dwelling-houses and/or four-in-a-block dwelling-houses and it is desirable to execute these presents in order to define (without prejudice to the insertion in individual conveyances of further special provisions) the rights, interests, obligations and liabilities of the proprietors of the individual houses in the development THEREFORE we hereby DECLARE and PROVIDE as follows:—

FIRST   In this Deed
Definitions   "Block" means a building containing Flats or Four-in-a-Block Houses as may be appropriate in the context.

"Common Parts" in relation to a Block means (i) the solum, foundations, outside walls, gables, roof and any chimney vents and stalks of the Block and any internal division walls between any dwelling-house and any of the other Common Parts, (ii) the Plot upon which the Block is erected so far as not occupied by the solum of the Block or by any Garage, (iii) the drains, soil and rain water pipes, water supply pipes, tanks, cisterns, rhones, gutters, conductors, gas and electric mains, and all pipes, cables, wires and transmitters and connections so far as used in common by the Proprietors of more than one dwelling-house in the Block and (iv) the whole parts and pertinents, fixtures and fittings of or in connection with that Block which are used in common by the Proprietors of more than one dwelling-house and (v) where the Block is a tenement of Flats, the entrance vestibule and elevators and relative machinery and the stairs, landings, stair railings and the walls and ceilings enclosing the same.

"Detached House" means a detached dwelling-house situated on a Plot owned exclusively by the Proprietor thereof.

"Factor" means a factor appointed in terms of sub-clause (9) of Clause THIRD of this Deed.

"Flat" means a flatted dwelling-house in a Block.

"Four-in-a-Block House" means one of the dwellinghouses forming part of a Block containing four dwelling-houses.

"Garage" means a garage owned exclusively by any Proprietor.

"Plot" means a plot of ground on which a Detached House or a Block is erected and the curtilage or garden ground appertaining thereto, and includes any footpath or part of roadway within the Plot.

"Proprietor" means the owner for the time being of any Detached House, Flat or Four-in-a-Block House and, where two or more persons own the same, includes both or all of them and any obligations hereby imposed on them shall bind them jointly and severally.

"Superiors" means us and our successors for the time being in the superiority of the Whole Area as and when feued.

"Whole Area" means the whole of the said area of ground including all Plots and public open spaces thereon.

References to dwelling-houses shall include Detached Houses, Flats and Four-in-a-Block Houses.

References to the male shall include the female.

Detached Houses

SECOND

Buildings

So far as regards each Detached House and the Plot on which it is erected:—

(1) Each Plot shall be used solely for the purpose of erection thereon of not more than one self-contained dwelling-house with relative offices (which may include a Garage which may be a double garage but one garage only) all of which the Proprietor thereof shall be bound to complete both inside and outside so as to be ready and certified for occupation within one year of his own date of entry and the Proprietor shall be bound first to submit to the Superiors such plans and specifications as they may reasonably require and to obtain their prior written approval before building is commenced as to design, type, roof, size, accommodation, materials, colour, minimum value, site and building lines, method of construction and all other relevant particulars. No additional buildings or erections nor alterations thereto shall be made without the prior written consent of the Superiors having been obtained. Every building or alteration thereto shall conform in all respects to any Local Authority, Town and Country Planning or other relevant statutes and regulations in that behalf and all gas or electric installations shall comply with the requirements of the British Gas Corporation or the relevant Electricity Board.

Note. The building may be constructed by the Builder-Superior before the date of entry in conformity with the provisions of the clause, but the obligation is imposed on the Proprietor to allow flexibility in the case where the Proprietor acquires an unbuilt on Plot and to define his obligations under sub-clause (3) of this clause and Clause FIFTH for rebuilding in the event of destruction or damage by fire or otherwise.

Garden Ground

(2) Each Plot so far as not occupied by buildings as aforesaid or roadways, access drives or footpaths shall be laid out and maintained as ornamental garden or pleasure ground in front and as such or as a vegetable garden and drying green at the rear of the Detached House and for no other purpose whatever, and shall be maintained as such in a neat and tidy condition in all time coming.

Maintenance

(3) The Proprietor of each Plot shall maintain all buildings and erections thereon in good order and repair and if necessary rebuilt in all time coming and in the event of damage or destruction shall repair, restore and re-erect the same in all respects in accordance with the provisions of sub-clause (1) of this Clause.

Flats and Four-in-a-Block Houses

THIRD

So far as regards each Flat or Four-in-a-Block House and the Plot on which the Block containing it has been erected by the Superiors:—

Common Parts—
Ownership

(1) Each Proprietor of a Flat or Four-in-a-Block House shall have an equal pro indiviso right of property in common with the other Proprietors of Flats or Four-in-a-Block Houses, as the case may be, in the same Block to the Common Parts of the said Block.

Maintenance of
Common Parts

(2) Each Flat or Four-in-a-Block House shall be held by the Proprietor thereof in all time coming under the obligation jointly with the other Proprietors of Flats or Four-in-a-Block Houses, as the case may be, in the same Block of upholding and maintaining in good order and repair and from time to time when necessary renewing and restoring the Common Parts of the said Block and of cleaning, repainting and decorating the said Common Parts. All expenses and charges incurred under the foregoing obligation and of any other work done or services rendered in respect of the said Common Parts shall be payable by the whole Proprietors of Flats or Four-in-a-Block Houses, as the case may be, in the same Block in equal proportions.

Reference to Factor

(3) In the event of any Proprietor of a Flat or Four-in-a-Block House in a Block considering it necessary or desirable that any repairs or renewals or decoration or other works should be executed to the Common Parts of the Block or to the Plot on which it is situated and of a majority of the Proprietors of the Block present in person or represented at a meeting convened and held in accordance with sub-clause (8) of this Clause refusing to sanction such repairs, renewals, decoration or other works or in the event of any such Proprietor considering that any repairs or renewals or decoration or other works upon the Common Parts ordered or sanctioned at any such meeting are unnecessary or undesirable he shall be entitled to refer the question to the Factor, and, in the event of the Factor deciding that all or any of such repairs, renewals, decoraton or other works are necessary or desirable, the Factor shall have power to order them to be executed forthwith and the expense thereof shall be borne by all of the Proprietors of the Flats or Four-in-a-Block Houses, as the case may be, in the said Block in equal proportions. Any Proprietor shall be bound to intimate in writing his intention so to refer the question to the Factor within fourteen days of the date of the meeting at which it was decided to execute or not to execute the said repairs, renewals, decoration or other works, failing which his right to refer the question shall be lost. The decision of the Factor shall be final and conclusive.

Maintenance of Flats or Four-in-a-Block Houses

(4) Each Proprietor of a Flat or Four-in-a-Block House shall maintain and when necessary renew the same and the fittings therein, the window frames and glass in the windows thereof and any stairs and stairway exclusively serving the same in a good state of repair and decoration and shall take all appropriate steps to prevent damage to the fabric of the Block of which the Flat or House forms part, and in particular by control of vermin and immediate treatment of any wood rot or infestation in the floors, skirting boards, joists, doors, walls, ceilings, mouldings and others and by the repair of any damage to the water supply pipes, soil and water pipes and gas or electric cables, pipes or appliances within his own Flat or House, and in the event of failure by any Proprietor to take timeous and adequate measures to prevent or repair such damage he shall be

liable for any additional damage to other parts of the Block arising from such failure. If in the opinion of the Factor it is necessary or desirable for the protection, appearance or general amenity of a Block that any works of repair, maintenance, renewal or decoration be carried out in or upon any Flat or Four-in-a-Block House therein he may serve notice upon the Proprietor thereof requiring the performance of such works as are specified in the notice within a period stated therein. The Proprietor to whom such notice is sent shall be entitled within twenty-one days of its receipt to appeal to the Arbiter appointed in terms of Clause ELEVENTH hereof to decide whether the works specified or any of them are necessary or desirable for the purposes above mentioned and, if the Arbiter considers that such works or any of them are necessary or desirable, to determine the period within which they shall be performed. In the event of failure by the Proprietor to perform these works within the period stated in the Factor's notice or in the determination of the Arbiter, as the case may be, the Factor shall be entitled to have the work carried out and to have any access convenient or necessary for that purpose and to recover the cost thereof from the Proprietor.

Alterations (5) No alterations or additions shall be made on or to any of the Blocks or any Flat or Four-in-a-Block House therein without the prior written consent of the Superiors, and in particular without prejudice to that generality the cutting or boring of holes in common or party walls or in the plasterwork, plasterboard or other facing thereof is expressly prohibited, and any alterations to any of the Blocks shall conform in all respects to any Local Authority, Town and Country Planning or other relevant statutes and regulations in that behalf and all gas or electric installations shall comply with the requirements of the British Gas Corporation or the relevant Electricity Board.

Colour Scheme (6) The Proprietors in each Block shall be bound to adhere to a common colour scheme in respect of the exterior parts of that Block and the Flats or Four-in-a-Block Houses therein, the Common Parts thereof and all woodwork, window frames, rhones, gutters and others. In the event of any disagreement amongst the Proprietors as to the colour of the exterior parts of the Block or as to the necessity for redecorating or painting the Block or any part thereof the Proprietors or

**Curtilage or
Garden Ground**

any of them shall submit the matter to the Factor whose decision shall be final and binding on all Proprietors.

(7) The Plot on which a Block is erected shall, so far as not occupied by the Block or Garages, access areas, forecourts, roadway, driveways, footpaths and drying greens (which greens shall be situated to the rear of the Block), shall be kept and used as ornamental or garden ground and for no other purpose. No fences, division walls or any form of trellis or draught boarding or screening shall be erected thereon without the prior written consent of the Superiors and no vehicles of any kind shall be left or parked thereon. No clothes poles or clothes lines shall be erected on any part thereof (excepting only on drying greens) nor shall clothes or clothes lines be attached to or suspended from any part of the exterior walls or down pipes, and no garbage cans, ash buckets or any other refuse receptacles shall be left or deposited on any part thereof other than in the common bin shelter.

**Proprietors'
Meetings**

(8)(a) The Proprietor of any Flat or Four-in-a-Block House or the Factor shall be entitled at any time to convene a meeting of all the Proprietors of dwellinghouses within the same Block which meeting shall be held at such reasonably convenient time and place as the convener of the meeting may determine, of which time and place of meeting not less than seven days' notice in writing shall be given by or on behalf of the convener to all the other Proprietors of dwellinghouses in the said Block.

(b) At any meeting so convened any Proprietor who is entitled to attend may be represented by any other person as mandatory appointed by written mandate to attend, vote and act on behalf of the Proprietor giving the mandate.

(c) The Proprietor entitled to attend or his mandatory present at such meeting shall be entitled to one vote for each dwelling-house owned by such Proprietor.

(d) It shall be competent at any such meeting, by a majority of the votes of the Proprietors or their mandatories present, (i) to order to be executed and thereafter to have executed any repairs, renewals, painting or decoration of the Common Parts of the Block, (ii) to make any regulations which may be considered necessary with regard to the insurance of the Block, and the amount thereof, and (iii) to make any regulations which may be considered necessary with regard to the preservation, cleaning, use or enjoyment of the Common Parts of the Block, which regulations shall be binding on all those concerned.

Factor

(9)(a) The Proprietors shall at any such meeting have power to appoint a Factor who shall take charge of all such matters in relation to the management of the Block as may competently be dealt with at any meeting convened and held as herein provided and to delegate to the Factor such rights or powers as may be exercisable by a majority of the Proprietors present or represented at such meeting with responsibility for instructing and supervising repairs to and maintenance of the Common Parts of the Block, and to fix the remuneration payable to the Factor for his services (which shall be payable by the Proprietors to the Factor in equal proportions) and the duration of his appointment and also to terminate the appointment of the Factor and to appoint another in his place [declaring that so long as we remain the owners of any part of a Block the powers contained in this sub-clause (9)(a) shall be exercisable by us alone]. (b) The Factor shall, unless otherwise determined at a meeting at which he is appointed or at any subsequent meeting of the Proprietors of dwellinghouses in the Block, duly convened and held as aforesaid, be entitled, during the continuance of his appointment, to exercise the whole rights and powers which may competently be exercised at or by any such meeting subject to any limit of expenditure which may be fixed by the said Proprietors at any such meeting but excepting any matters relating to the appointment of the Factor, the duration of his appointment and his remuneration. (c) The Factor shall be entitled during the continuance of his appointment to collect from the Proprietors of the dwellinghouses in the Block the proportions payable by them respectively of (i) the premiums necessary for maintaining the insurances provided for in Clause FIFTH hereof, (ii) the expenses and charges incurred in maintenance of the Common Parts in terms of sub-clause (2) of this Clause and (iii) any other sums for which the Proprietors of dwellinghouses in the Block may become liable in terms of or in furtherance of the provisions herein contained, and the Factor shall be entitled to make payment of the said premiums, expenses, charges, remuneration and others to the insurance company or other person or persons entitled to receive payment thereof, and in the event of any of the said Proprietors failing to make payment of his proportion of the said premiums, expenses, charges, remuneration or other sums for which he is liable within one month after payment of the same is demanded by the Factor the proportion due by such Proprietor shall bear interest at a rate equivalent to four per cent per annum above the base lending rate of the Bank of   or   per cent per annum, whichever be the greater, from the date of demand until payment and the Factor (without prejudice to any rights or remedies of the other Proprietors) shall be entitled to sue for and recover the same and interest thereon in his own name.[60a]

FOURTH
Use and
Prohibitions

All dwellinghouses and Whole Area
So far as regards the Whole Area and all Plots and dwellinghouses thereon:—
(1) Each dwelling-house shall be used solely as a private dwelling-house and for no other purpose whatever and none of the dwellinghouses shall ever in any way be sub-divided or occupied by more than one family at a time. Each Garage shall be used only as a private garage for the sole use of a Proprietor or occupant of his dwelling-house and shall not be let separately therefrom nor used for any commercial or trading purpose.
(2) The Proprietors and parties occupying any of the dwellinghouses are hereby expressly prohibited from carrying on therein or in any other part of the Whole Area any trade, business, manufactory or profession, or from using them or any of them or causing them or any of them to be used for any purpose which might in the opinion of the Superiors be deemed a nuisance and that whether or not such trade, business or profession is incidental to the ordinary residential use thereof, and notwithstanding any rule of law to the contrary.
(3) Nothing may be done on any part of the Whole Area or in any building or erection thereon that may, in the sole opinion of the Superiors, be deemed a nuisance or likely to occasion disturbance to other Proprietors of parts of the Whole Area or proprietors of subjects adjoining the Whole Area or their tenants or assignees.

[60a] As to possible additional provisions, see notes to style in para. 19–37.

(4) No Proprietor of any dwelling-house or Plot upon which it is erected shall permit any trailer, boat, caravan or commercial vehicle (other than the normal tradesmen's delivery vans or removal contractors' vehicles) to enter or remain within the Whole Area or to be parked upon such Plot.

(5) Every Proprietor and his tenants and occupiers are hereby expressly prohibited from keeping in a dwelling-house or on the Plot on which it is erected poultry, ducks, pigeons, rabbits, bees or other livestock or from breeding animals and shall not be entitled to keep more than one dog or cat and that only provided that such animal shall not prove to be a nuisance to other Proprietors; and it is hereby expressly provided that all dogs shall be kept under control within the Whole Area and shall at no time be allowed to run unfettered within the same or to foul the footways, other footpaths or accessways, common amenity areas or public open spaces.

(6) No trees, hedgerows or shrubs on or overhanging any part of the Whole Area shall be cut down, lopped, damaged or removed from any part thereof unless they have become dangerous or overgrown, without the prior consent in writing of the Superiors.

FIFTH
Insurance

(1) The proprietors of the whole dwelling-houses in each Block shall be bound to concur with each other in effecting with a reputable insurance company and keeping in force in respect of such Block and relative Garages and outhouses (if any) (i) a policy of insurance against property owners' liability in the names of such Proprietors for their respective rights and interests or of the Factor on their behalf for the sum of £   for any one accident or such greater sum as may from time to time be fixed at a meeting of the Proprietors of dwellinghouses in that Block convened and held as herein provided and (ii) a policy of insurance against loss or damage by fire, explosion, flood, escape of water, storm and tempest and such other risks as may from time to time be determined at a meeting of the Proprietors of dwellinghouses in that Block convened and held as herein before provided for the full reinstatement value thereof to include site clearance charges and professional fees.

(2) The Proprietor of each Plot on which a Detached House is erected shall be bound to

keep his dwelling-house and any Garage and all other buildings erected on or forming part of his Plot insured with a reputable insurance company against loss by fire and other risks normally covered by a homeowner's comprehensive policy for the full replacement value thereof including site clearance charges and professional fees.

(3) The Superiors shall be entitled from time to time to require production of the foregoing policies of insurance or any of them and receipts for payment of the premiums.

(4)(a) In the event of any Block, Garage or outhouses or any part thereof being destroyed or damaged by any cause, whether an insured risk or not, or

(b) in the event of any Detached House, Garage or any other buildings on the Plot on which it is erected being so destroyed or damaged

all the Proprietors of the Block or the Proprietor of the Detached House, as the case may be, shall be bound to restore or rebuild the same and to repair the damage within one year of the occurrence of such destruction or damage but without making any alteration in or deviation from the original design and dimensions of the said Block or Detached House or Garage except with the consent in writing of the Superiors and, in the case of a Block, of all Proprietors in the said Block and other persons having an interest therein. All sums which may be received from the insurance company under a policy in respect of loss or damage to buildings shall be applied forthwith in restoring or repairing such buildings. In the event of the cost of any such restoration or repairs exceeding the sum recovered from the said insurance company in respect of such loss or damage any further sum required to meet the said cost shall be paid (i) in the case of a Block by the proprietors of the dwellinghouses therein in equal proportions, and shall be recoverable, if necessary, in an action at the instance of the Proprietor of any one or more of the said dwellinghouses or the Factor, each and all of whom shall have authority to sue for and recover all such proportions, so far as unpaid, for and on behalf of all persons having an interest in the restoration and repair of the said Block, and in the event of the sum recovered from the said insurance company in respect of loss or damage to the buildings of the said Block or outhouses exceeding the cost of restoration or repair any surplus shall be divided among the Proprietors of the said dwellinghouses as at the date of loss in equal proportions and (ii) in the case of a Detached House shall be paid to the Proprietor thereof at the date of such loss.

SIXTH
Boundaries
and Fences

Fences or walls so far as forming divisions between adjoining Plots shall be erected as to one half of their width on each of such adjoining Plots and shall thereafter, except as aftermentioned, be maintained and kept in good order and repair by the adjoining Proprietors in all time coming, declaring that no Proprietor shall ever have a claim against the Superiors in respect of the maintenance, restoration or re-erection of any such fences or walls. Where part of a boundary is formed by a wall of a Garage and there is no adjoining garage on the adjacent Plot, the maintenance of such wall shall be the sole responsibility of the owner of the Garage. No alterations shall be made on boundary fences or walls without the prior written consent of the Superiors and the erection of additional gates or accesses in boundary walls or fences is expressly prohibited.

SEVENTH
Roads and
Services

All necessary roadways and footpaths adjoining the same and all sewers, drains, pipes, cables and other transmitters and connections shall be constructed by us but once so constructed (a) the Proprietor or all the Proprietors of a Plot shall be bound and obliged to maintain unbuilt on and in good order and repair any such roadway and footpath so far as within the Plot unless and until the same or any of them are taken over for maintenance by any public authority, in any application for which the said Proprietor or Proprietors shall be bound to concur, and to allow to all other Proprietors of Plots free passage over such roadway for pedestrian and vehicular traffic and over such footpath for pedestrian traffic only and (b) the Proprietor or Proprietors of a Plot shall be bound and obliged to maintain and repair such sewers, drains, pipes, cables and other transmitters and connections so far as the same do not become the responsibility of any public authority, the expense thereof being borne equally by the Proprietor or Proprietors of the property served thereby, and, where any of such sewers or others passes through another Plot or other Plots, the Plot or Plots through which the same passes shall be subject to a servitude right of wayleave for the same in favour of the Plots served thereby.

EIGHTH
Public Open
Spaces

In respect that we may form certain portions of the Whole Area as public open spaces being such portions as are not included in any Plot, the same shall be formed, laid out and planted by us and once so formed shall remain open and unbuilt upon in all time coming, each and every Plot being held under burden of the Proprietors of dwellinghouses thereon maintaining as public open spaces in neat and tidy condition the said portions and any erections thereon, footpaths traversing the same and any trees, shrubs, flowers and grass planted or to be planted therein and (so far as belonging to us and not exclusively conveyed to the owner of a Plot) the boundary walls and fences thereof, and the expenses thereof being borne equally by all the Proprietors of dwellinghouses situated within the Whole Area unless and until the said portions and others or any part of them are conveyed to or are taken over by any public authority for maintenance; declaring that no Proprietor of a dwelling-house shall ever have a claim against the Superiors in respect of such maintenance.

NINTH
Reserved
rights

(a) There are reserved to the Superiors and those Proprietors of dwellinghouses erected on the Whole Area having right thereto or served thereby power to use all rights of way, land and other drains, pipes, cables, services and servitudes with power and liberty to make connections or to grant to the Proprietors of any Plot, local authority or statutory undertaker power and liberty to lay or to make connections with drains, sewers, electric, telephone or television cables, gas and water mains together with all necessary rights of access for the purpose of inspection, repair or renewal thereof subject always to an obligation to restore the surface of the ground damaged thereby.

(b) There are reserved to the Superiors (one) all rights of access which may be necessary to complete building and other work and also to plant any trees or shrubs which may form part of the amenity scheme, (two) power to grant rights of access and egress and other servitudes or wayleaves over any of the roads or footpaths or parts held in common by the Proprietors of dwelling-houses or any of them, and (three) power to allocate to the Proprietor of any one dwelling-house interested therein the exclusive right to the use and enjoyment of a parking space notwithstanding that rights of common property therein may already have been granted to other Proprietors.

(c) Where the Proprietor of any dwelling-house is entitled or obliged to maintain any part whether solely or in common with others he and his duly authorised tradesmen and others shall have all necessary rights of access whenever reasonably required for the purpose of inspecting, maintaining and renewing the same, subject always to making good damage caused thereby.

TENTH
Title

Any Proprietor shall be bound, when called upon by the Superiors to do so, to produce his title including all deeds within the period of prescription and the original feu writ or disposition granted by us free of charge to the Superiors.

ELEVENTH
Arbitration

All questions, differences and disputes which may arise among the Proprietors or any of them regarding (1) their rights and interests in the Whole Area or any part thereof, (2) the necessity for executing any works, whether common or not, or the liability for the cost thereof, (3) the reasonableness or expediency of any order, regulation, decision, determination or appointment made at any meeting of Proprietors convened and held as aforesaid and (4) all other questions so far as depending upon or otherwise arising out of or in respect of these presents in any manner of way (except in all cases any question which may be referred to the Factor in terms of sub-clause (3) or (6) of Clause THIRD hereof), shall be referred (in a case arising under sub-head (3) of this Clause within fourteen days of the meeting in question) to the amicable decision of the Sheriff Principal of   or any of the Sheriffs at   or any other suitable person appointed by the said Sheriff Principal or any of said Sheriffs as Arbiter, and whatever the said Arbiter shall determine shall be final and binding in all matters of law as well as of fact upon all concerned, and the Proprietors concerned shall be bound to implement and fulfil to each other the decisions, findings and decrees of the said Arbiter, with power to the said

Arbiter to take skilled advice and order execution or performance of works and to apportion the cost thereof among the said Proprietors, to vary or annul any such order, regulation, decision, determination or appointment, and to find all or any of them liable in the expenses of the arbitration, and to decern accordingly. The application of section 3 of the Administration of Justice (Scotland) Act 1972 is expressly excluded.

TWELFTH
Deviations
Jus Quaesitum
Tertio

There is reserved to the Superiors full power to alter or even to depart entirely from the plans and feuing plan of and to deal with the Whole Area or any part thereof and the development thereof as may be required by the Superiors from time to time including alterations in types of Plot, feu, dwelling-houses, the layout, breadths, levels, gradients and the materials used for the construction of buildings, roads, footpaths, drains, sewers and others, and as regards the whole or any part of the Whole Area to waive, alter, modify, or dispense with observance of any conditions, restrictions and others herein set forth and in the event of such alteration or deviation by the Superiors, no Proprietor shall have a right to object thereto or have any claim in respect thereof; [and subject to the foresaid reservation there is hereby conferred on the Proprietor of each dwelling-house a *jus quaesitum tertio* for enforcement of the provisions of these presents in a question with any other Proprietor in so far as he shall from time to time have an interest to enforce the same.]

THIRTEENTH
Irritancy and
Declaration

It is hereby expressly provided and declared that if any Proprietor shall contravene or fail to implement any of the reservations, burdens, conditions and others herein written his dwelling-house and all property and parts held by him exclusively and in common in connection therewith shall in the option of the Superiors revert and belong to the Superiors free and unencumbered as if the original feu writ or other conveyance had never been granted by the Superiors, and the whole reservations, burdens, conditions and others herein contained shall be real liens, burdens and servitudes upon and affecting the said Whole Area and any part thereof so far as the same apply thereto, and as such are appointed to be inserted in any infeftment that may follow upon the said original feu writ or other conveyance and also inserted or validly referred to in all deeds or instruments

relating to any part of the Whole Area
otherwise the same shall be null and void.
(*To be attested*) (*Stamp 50p*)

Style—feu disposition—detached dwelling-house (following on deed of conditions—paragraph 17–84)

17–85   We, AB Limited, (*designed*), heritable proprietors of the subjects
and others hereinafter disponed, in consideration of the sum of
£   paid to us by CD, (*designed*), and of the other prestations
hereinafter specified or referred to, Do Hereby in feu farm
DISPONE to the said CD and his executors and assignees
whomsoever [but excluding assignees before infeftment on these
presents and under the declaration that the same shall not be a
valid warrant for such infeftment after the expiry of   months
from the date hereof,] heritably and irredeemably ALL and
WHOLE that plot of ground in the Parish of   and County
of (*description*), all as the said plot of ground is shown within
boundaries coloured red and marked   on the plan
annexed and executed as relative hereto (which plan is
demonstrative only and not taxative); Which plot of ground forms
part and portion of ALL and WHOLE that area of ground lying
within the said Parish and County being the area of ground more
particularly described in and disponed by and delineated and
coloured green on the plan annexed and executed as relative to
Disposition by XY Limited in our favour dated   and
recorded in the Division of the General Register of Sasines
applicable to the County of   on   both days of   ;
Together with the rights of property, rights common, mutual and
sole, rights of access and whole other rights so far as effeiring
thereto specified and contained in Deed of Conditions by us
dated   and recorded in the said Division of the General
Register of Sasines on   both days of   Nineteen
hundred and   ; Together also with (one) the dwelling-house
forming Number   Road,   , and the garage and whole
other buildings and erections upon the plot of ground hereby
disponed, (two) free ish and entry therefrom and thereto, (three)
the parts and pertinents thereof and (four) our whole right, title
and interest, present and future, in and to the *dominium utile*
thereof; But the subjects hereby disponed are so disponed always
with and under, so far as valid, subsisting and applicable to the
subjects hereby disponed, the reservations, burdens, conditions,
obligations, restrictions, declarations, rights of access, wayleaves,
servitudes and others specified and contained in (First) (*specify
any prior deed imposing real burdens or obligations*), (Second) the
said Disposition by XY Limited in our favour dated and recorded
as aforesaid and (Third) the said Deed of Conditions dated and
recorded as aforesaid: WITH ENTRY as at the   day of
          Nineteen hundred and   notwithstanding the date
hereof: TO BE HOLDEN the said whole subjects hereby disponed
of and under us and our successors as immediate lawful superiors
thereof in feu farm fee and heritage for ever: And we grant
warrandice: (*Stamp clause*) (*To be attested*) (*Stamp as conveyance on
sale*)

Style—feu disposition—flatted or four-in-a-block dwelling-house (following on deed of conditions—paragraph 17–84)

-86 WE, AB LIMITED, (*designed*), heritable proprietors of the subjects and others hereinafter disponed, in consideration of the sum of £ paid to us by CD, (*designed*), and of the other prestations hereinafter specified or referred to, Do Hereby in feu farm DISPONE to and in favour of the said CD and his executors and assignees whomsoever [but excluding assignees before infeftment on these presents and under the declaration that the same shall not be a valid warrant for such infeftment after the expiry of months from the date hereof,] heritably and irredeemably ALL and WHOLE that [flatted] [four-in-a-block] dwelling-house containing four [*or otherwise*] apartments in the Parish of and County of being [the westmost dwelling-house on the second floor above the ground] [the eastmost dwelling-house on the ground floor] of the block erected on the plot shown within boundaries coloured red and marked on the plan annexed and executed as relative hereto (which plan is demonstrative only and not taxative) and being part of a block of [eight] [four] dwellinghouses erected on the said plot; Which plot is part and portion of ALL and WHOLE that area of ground within the said Parish and County being the area of ground more particularly described in and disponed by and delineated and coloured green on the plan annexed and executed as relative to Disposition by XY Limited in our favour dated and recorded in the Division of the General Register of Sasines applicable to the County of on both days of Nineteen hundred and ; Together with (one) the garage coloured and marked No. on the said plan, and the solum thereof, and (two) the rights of property, rights common, mutual and sole, rights of access and whole other rights so far as effeiring to the said dwelling-house and garage specified and contained in Deed of Conditions by us dated and recorded in the said Division of the General Register of Sasines on both days of Nineteen hundred and ; Together also with (one) free ish and entry to the subjects hereby disponed, the pertinents thereof and our whole right title and interest, present and future in and to the *dominium utile* thereof; But the subjects hereby disponed are so disponed always with and under so far as valid, subsisting and applicable to the subjects hereby disponed, the reservations, burdens, conditions, obligations, restrictions, declarations, rights of access, wayleaves, servitudes and others specified and contained in (First) (*Specify any prior deed imposing burdens or conditions*), (Second) the said Disposition by XY Limited in our favour dated and recorded as aforesaid, and (Third) the said Deed of Conditions dated and recorded as aforesaid: WITH ENTRY as at the day of Nineteen hundred and notwithstanding the date hereof: TO BE HOLDEN the said whole subjects hereby disponed of and under us and our successors as immediate lawful superiors thereof in feu farm fee and heritage forever: And we grant warrandice: (*Stamp clause*) (*To be attested*) (*Stamp as conveyance on sale*)

General considerations—building developments

17–87   In the case of building developments involving significant numbers of dwelling-houses, possibly of different types, of the kind envisaged in the styles in paragraphs 17–84 to 17–86 *supra*, there are certain considerations which should be kept in view.

(1) The general scheme of development envisaged is that each plot on which a detached house is erected and all buildings thereon will be owned exclusively by the proprietor of the detached house and that each plot on which flats or four-in-a-block houses are erected so far as unbuilt-on will be owned in common by the owners of all the flats or four-in-a-block houses erected on the plot. The footpath and roadway so far as within a plot will be owned similarly with an obligation of maintenance until taken over by the local authority. Walls or fences between plots will be owned in common by the adjoining proprietors with special provision as to garage walls forming part of a boundary. The public open spaces will be laid out by the builder-superior and are defined simply as the parts of the whole area not occupied by plots, and ownership of them is not given to the proprietors of the plots or dwelling-houses although the burden of maintenance of them is imposed upon the owners of dwelling-houses in the whole area. That leaves flexible the exact parts of the development which will ultimately be public open spaces. The deed of conditions is framed on the basis that in the case of flats or four-in-a-block houses there will be a separate row of garages, one garage and the solum thereof being conveyed with the relevant dwelling-house and the solum of the row of garages being excluded from the common parts. If the garages form part of the block in which the dwelling-houses are situated appropriate alterations will be required. Internal division walls which separate a dwelling-house in a block from any of the common parts are made common property of all the proprietors of dwelling-houses in the block; internal division walls which separate two dwelling-houses are not specifically mentioned and the ordinary rule of common law will apply to the effect that they are the mutual property of the proprietors of the two dwelling-houses concerned.

(2) The plan annexed to the deed of conditions should show the boundaries of the individual plots identified by distinctive numbers but should not indicate the types of dwelling-houses to be erected on each plot. In the course of the development the builder-superior may find that certain types of dwelling-houses are more readily marketable than others and alter the scheme of development accordingly, and the original plan will not require alteration if the types of dwelling-houses on each plot have not been shown thereon. If the superior subsequently exercises his power to alter the original plan of development by varying the boundaries of plots as shown on the original plan, it is suggested that this be effected by a short supplementary deed of conditions with a new plan attached, and prints or photocopies of the new deed and

plan should be furnished to feuars of the plots affected and also to all subsequent feuars. If the land is situated within or straddles an area which is operational for the purposes of registration of title the deed of conditions and relative plan should be registered in the Land Register of Scotland at the outset of the development: that will enable the boundaries of the area of the proposed development to be verified by the Keeper in relation to the Ordnance Map and will simplify references to that area by parcel number in subsequent feu grants. If the land is situated wholly outwith an operational area it is advisable to check its boundaries with the Ordnance Map to ensure as far as possible that no alterations will be required when in due course the development area will become part of an operational area for registration of title.

(3) It is always advisable to reserve to the superior power to alter the plan and to alter or dispense with the conditions as regards the whole or any part of the area of the development. The superior at some stage may not wish or may be unable to complete the development and it will facilitate the sale of the undeveloped part if the superior can disburden it of the conditions (see clause TWELFTH of deed of conditions, paragraph 17–84).

(4) It is a matter of policy for the superior to determine whether a right to enforce conditions of the deed of conditions should be conferred on co-feuars (see clause TWELFTH of deed of conditions, paragraph 17–84). In general it is thought equitable that co-feuars should have that right: a contravention of a condition may be of little consequence to the superior but may significantly affect a neighbouring dwelling-house or its owner.

(5) The style of deed of conditions in paragraph 17–84 is necessarily complex. If separate parts of the area of a development are restricted to dwelling-houses which are all of the same type a separate deed of conditions for each such part will be a simpler document. The latter method, however, is less flexible. If subsequently a change is desired in the type of dwelling-house to be erected on a particular part that may be practicable by the exercise of the superior's power to alter plans and conditions, but further documentation will then be required.

Style—charter—industrial buildings[61]

–88 *[As in skeleton charter up to first feuing condition]*
Buildings   (1) The feuars shall be bound to erect and complete on the feu before   and thereafter to maintain and uphold in all time coming and if necessary rebuild substantial

---

[61] Feus of commercial and industrial property are now less frequently encountered, long leases being the more favoured method. It is an ironical reflection that the progressive casting-off of the yoke of feuduties under the Land Tenure Reform (Scotland) Act 1974 has resulted in the imposition of a burden much more galling, a reviewable rent that goes ever upward with the added threat of extrusion on the expiry of the term of the lease. Feus of industrial property are, however, still in use in particular circumstances.

industrial buildings constructed of stone or brick or concrete or other material conform to plans and specifications thereof to be approved of in writing by the superiors before construction is commenced and all buildings so far as fronting   Street shall be constructed of stone or artificial stone or of brick or concrete roughcast or harled with stone or artificial stone facings (*or other materials and finish agreed*).[62] No high alumina cement or blue asbestos shall be used in the construction of the said buildings.

Compliance with requirements

(2) In the construction and installation of the said buildings and the erection and installation of fixed plant and machinery thereon or therein the feuars shall obtain and in all respects comply with all conditions attached to planning permissions and building warrants and all other necessary consents and shall comply with all relevant statutory requirements and orders or regulations made by public, local or other competent authorities.

Use

(3) The buildings and all erections on the feu shall be used for the purpose of   and for no other purpose except with the prior written consent of the superiors [which consent shall not unreasonably be withheld]. No pungent, dangerous or obnoxious vapours or substances shall be emitted into the atmosphere.

Pipes, cables and services

(4) In respect that there already exist under, on or above the feu electricity cables, telephone wires and/or cables, gas and water supply pipes, drains and sewers (a) there are reserved to the superiors and others deriving right from them a heritable and irredeemable servitude right to continue to use, repair, replace or relay the same or any of them and a right of access thereto and of opening up the ground for such purpose but under liability of restoring the surface and (b) there is conferred on the feuars a heritable and irredeemable servitude right to make connections to and use the same or any of them, provided always that (i) the use thereof by the feuars shall not overload or exceed the existing capacity of any such cables, wires, pipes, drains or sewers and (ii) the feuars shall not discharge into such drains or sewers or into any other drains and sewers or into any running water any pungent or deleterious waste material or gas or effluent.

---

[62] If the nature of the buildings is to be specified with more precision a schedule may be annexed with details.

Access road

[(5) The feuars shall have a servitude right to use now and in all time coming for the purpose of access to and egress from the feu by pedestrian and vehicular traffic the private road leading through other land belonging to the superiors to the feu from the public road from   to   , as the said private road is delineated and coloured blue on the said plan, provided always that the feuars shall maintain the same at their own expense in good order and repair to the satisfaction of the superiors,[63] declaring that the superiors shall be entitled in their sole discretion at any time to carry out maintenance on the said road by themselves or others whom they may employ for the purpose and to recover the cost thereof from the feuars.]

Insurance

(6) The feuars shall be bound to keep the buildings and all other erections and installations on the feu constantly insured against loss or damage by fire, explosion, flood, lightning and storm and tempest with a reputable insurance company for the full reinstatement value thereof and to produce to the superiors from time to time when required the policy or policies of insurance and receipts for payment of the premiums; and in the event of the said buildings and/or other erections and installations being destroyed or damaged the feuars shall be bound to restore the same within two years after such destruction or damage, and the whole sums to be received from the insurance company with any additional sum that may be required for the purpose shall be expended to the satisfaction of the superiors in restoring the said buildings and others to their former condition in accordance with the provisions herein contained, any new plans and specifications being first approved by the superiors in writing.

[*Irritant and resolutive clauses and declaration as to real burdens and conditions, term of entry, etc., to end as in skeleton charter*]

NOTE

For special kinds of industrial businesses other detailed provisions may be required.

---

[63] Appropriate where the feuars will be the sole or main users of the road; if otherwise, provision for maintenance in accordance with user as determined by superiors.

Particular clauses

Common parts

17–89   *(a) Two semi-detached houses*

All main water supply pipes, drains and down pipes, sewers, gas and electric main pipes or cables, telephone wires or cables, and all transmitters and connections serving both the plot of ground hereby disponed and the adjoining plot of ground to the [west] thereof and the two semi-detached houses built thereon and the division walls or gables and boundary walls and fences between the said two plots and houses shall, so far as not belonging to any public or supply authority, be mutual to and shall be maintained mutually at equal expense of the proprietors of the said two plots.

(b) Terrace houses

(1) All main water supply pipes, drains and down pipes, sewers, gas and electric main pipes or cables, telephone wires or cables and all transmitters and connections serving more than one of the dwelling-houses in the said terrace shall, so far as not belonging to any public or supply authority, be mutual to and shall be maintained mutually at equal expense of the proprietors of the dwelling-houses served thereby and (2) all division walls or gables and boundary walls or fences between the said plot of ground hereby disponed and an adjoining plot of ground and the houses built thereon shall so far as used in common be the mutual property of the two proprietors of the said plots and houses separated thereby and shall be maintained mutually at equal expense of the said two proprietors.

17–90   **Pipes, cables, etc., passing through several feus**

In respect that there are or may be constructed in or over the feu drains, sewers and water, gas, electricity, telephone or other pipes or cables which serve more than one property (all or any of which drains and others are comprehended within the phrase "service connections") there is reserved to the superiors and others deriving right from them a heritable and irredeemable servitude right to lay, use and maintain and when necessary repair or relay any service connections in or over the feu or any part thereof with right to free access over and to open up the ground of the feu for such purposes, and that without the feuars having any claim for compensation, provided always that the persons exercising the right shall restore any damage to the surface of the feu caused by their operations. In so far as there are any service connections which serve the feu and are or may be constructed in or over other ground feued or that may be feued by the superiors we confer upon the feuars a corresponding heritable and irredeemable servitude right to lay, use and maintain such service connections and when necessary repair or relay the same in or over such feus with the like rights of access to and opening up the ground of such other feus and on the same conditions as are hereinbefore provided.

17–91   **Road to be formed by superiors—proportion payable by feuar**

In respect that the superiors are to form the roadway of

Street of   feet in width with footpaths, kerbstones, gutters, gratings and surface water drains [*modify as required for type of street*] and also the main [drain] [sewer] therein and to connect it with the public sewer in   Street, the feuars shall be bound, as soon as these works shall have been certified by the superiors' architect to have been completed so far as required in connection with the feu, to pay to the superiors the sum of £   in respect of the proportion applicable to the feu of the superiors' expenditure upon the construction of said works, which sum, with interest thereon at the rate of   per cent per annum from the date of the architect's certificate of completion as aforesaid until paid, is hereby created a real burden on the feu. In the event of the proportion applicable to the feu of said expenditure as such proportion shall be conclusively determined by a certificate of the said architect exceeding the said sum of £   , the amount of the excess shall also be paid by the feuars to the superiors with interest thereon at said rate from the date of the certificate last mentioned until paid.[64]

Infeftment

7–92   As to the procedure for completing the infeftment of a feuar by recording in the Register of Sasines or registration of his interest in the Land Register see Chapter 24 *infra*.

Registered conveyancing

7–93   **First registration.** A feu charter or feu disposition which induces first registration in the Land Register of Scotland should be framed in the same style as for a feu charter or feu disposition which is to be recorded in the Register of Sasines but with such amplification of the description as may be required to enable the subjects to be identified on the Ordnance Map.[65]

7–94   **Registered interests.** A feu charter or feu disposition of land or a part of it the title to which has already been entered in the Land Register should be in similar form to that of a feu grant which is to be recorded in the Register of Sasines subject to the variations suggested in this paragraph.

(1) Granter. It is still necessary under common law that the granter be infeft, although a feu grant by an uninfeft superior may be validated by his subsequent infeftment.[66] That requirement is not dispensed with by the provisions of section 3(6) of the Land Registration (Scotland) Act 1979, since the interest being registered is a different interest. When a feu is granted out of a registered interest where the granter is not infeft, the feuar's application for registration on Form 3 should be

---

[64] Since the amount of a real burden must be specific, only the proportion of the expenditure as originally estimated is created real; liability for the excess is made a contractual obligation.
[65] See paras. 18–64 to 18–70.
[66] See para. 24–63.

preceded or accompanied by an application on Form 2 completed by the uninfeft superior together with the links in title connecting him with the last registered proprietor. If such an application is not made the Keeper will normally register the feuar's interest but will exclude indemnity in respect of the superior's lack of infeftment.[67]

(2) Description of subjects. Where the feu grant relates to the whole of the superior's interest it is unnecessary to insert a new description—reference to the title number of the whole interest is all that is required.[68]

(3) Burdens and conditions. The resolutive clause requiring the burdens and conditions to be inserted in any future conveyances, transmissions or infeftments on pain of nullity is not required, since the burdens and conditions will be entered in the title sheet of the feuar's interest.[69] It is suggested, however, that the declaration that they are real burdens and conditions should be inserted in order to certiorate the Keeper of their character. It may be advisable for the superior to require as a condition of granting the feu that the land certificate including the burdens or conditions should be exhibited to him. It is still appropriate to include the clause creating a conventional irritancy on breach of any of the provisions and conditions of the feu grant.[70]

Executory clauses. The clauses of assignation of writs, assignation of rents and obligation of relief may, apart from specialties in any particular case, be omitted.[71]

Style of feu disposition out of registered interest

17–95   We, AB Limited, *(designed)*, heritable proprietors of the subjects hereinafter disponed (we and our successors in the superiority thereof being hereinafter called "the superiors") in consideration of the price of £   paid to us by C, *(designed)*, and of the whole prestations hereinafter specified or referred to hereby sell and in feu farm dispone to the said C and his executors and assignees whomsoever [but excluding assignees before infeftment on these presents and under the declaration that the same shall not authorise registration of the interest of the said C in the Land Register of Scotland after the expiry of   months from the date hereof] (the said C and his foresaids being hereinafter called "the feuars") heritably and irredeemably ALL and WHOLE that plot of ground in the County of   *(particular description by boundaries and annexed plan or by reference to any Deed of Feuing Conditions and plot number on plan annexed thereto)* being part of the land described in and registered under Title Number   (which subjects hereby

---

[67] See R.T.P.B., para. G.3.22(c). See also para. 24–63.
[68] R.T.P.B., para. G.3.22(c).
[69] 1979 Act, s. 15(2).
[70] R.T.P.B., para. G.3.22(c).
[71] 1979 Act, s. 16(2) and (3)(*b*).

disponed are hereinafter referred to as "the feu"); Together with free ish and entry therefrom and thereto, the pertinents thereof and our whole right, title and interest, present and future, in and to the *dominium utile* thereof[71a]; [*reservation of minerals if appropriate*]; But the subjects hereby disponed are so disponed always with and under the reservations, burdens, conditions, obligations and others following, videlicet:— (*Insert reservations, burdens, conditions, etc., imposed by the deed*)[71b]; (*Clause of pre-emption, if any*); declaring that the said burdens, conditions and others shall be real burdens and conditions on and of the feu and that if the feuars contravene or fail to implement any of them these presents and all that may have followed thereon shall in the option of the superiors become null and void and the feuars shall forfeit their whole right, title and interest in and to the said subjects hereby disponed which with all buildings thereon shall revert and belong to the superiors free and disencumbered of all burdens as if these presents had not been granted: With entry on : To be holden the said subjects hereby disponed of and under us and our successors as immediate lawful superiors thereof in feu farm, fee and heritage for ever: And we grant warrandice: (*Stamp clause, if required*) (*To be attested*) (*Stamp as conveyance on sale*)

VIII. Charter of Novodamus

History

–96   Originally the proper method of effecting alterations in the conditions of a feu was by the vassal resigning the lands into the hands of the superior who then granted a charter of novodamus, a new grant in feu incorporating the alterations. Since a charter of novodamus, although in one aspect a charter by progress, was in another a new grant, it was excepted from the general abolition of charters and writs by progress in the Conveyancing (Scotland) Act 1874[72] and is still competent. Although technically the superior should be reinvested by resignation as a preliminary to the granting of a charter of novodamus, that was made unnecessary by statute.[73] In consonance with the policy of prohibiting the imposition of feuduties embodied in the Land Tenure Reform (Scotland) Act 1974, it was enacted[74] that a feuduty could not be increased by a charter of novodamus nor, if granted in respect of two or more feuduties, could it effect an increase in the total amount of feuduty payable.

[71a] If any rights are given to the feuars in addition to those set out in the superior's title sheet specify same in detail.

[71b] If any conditions contained in a Deed of Feuing Conditions executed before April 4, 1979 or in any such Deed executed on or after that date in which section 17 of the 1979 Act is disapplied are to apply to the new feu, it is necessary to include a reference to the Deed.

[72] s. 4(1).

[73] Conveyancing (Scotland) Acts (1874 and 1879) Amendment Act 1887, s. 3.

[74] s. 3

Use

17–97 **(1) Lost or defective titles.** Where the title to the *dominium utile* has been lost or is defective a new progress of title may be started by the grant by the superior of a charter of novodamus. The superior should be reasonably satisfied that the grantee has right to the lands but the charter should *not* include a statement that he is so satisfied; the charter should be granted *periculo petentis* with warrandice either simple or from fact and deed only. Since the effect of a novodamus is to commence a new progress of title to the *dominium utile*, that title is not fortified by positive prescription until the expiry of 10 years' possession after infeftment on the charter of novodamus.

17–98 **(2) Alteration of feuing conditions.** Where the vassal wishes to use the land for a purpose which would contravene a condition of the feu and the superior is willing to co-operate but wishes to impose restrictions upon the new user, a charter of novodamus is appropriate. If all that is contemplated is a waiver of an existing condition, however, that may be effected more simply and cheaply by a minute of waiver. A minute of waiver or any deed recorded in the Register of Sasines, whether before or after April 4, 1979, whereby a land obligation (as defined in section 1(2) of the Conveyancing and Feudal Reform (Scotland) Act 1970) is varied or discharged, is binding upon the singular successors of persons in right of or bound under the obligation. The same result arises from a minute of waiver the terms of which are registered in the Land Register.[75]

17–99 **(3) Additional land.** Where it is desired to add further land to an existing feu a charter of novodamus may be used, but it may be clearer and more satisfactory to have a resignation *ad rem* of the existing feu and a new feu grant of the whole of the increased area.

Effects of novodamus on existing rights of parties

17–100 **(a) Superior.** Except in so far as it is intended that existing conditions of the feu be altered, it is essential in the interests of the superior that all the reservations and conditions of the original grant are either repeated *ad longum* or validly imported by reference in the charter of novodamus. Where a reservation of coal had been contained in the original charter but was not repeated in the novodamus, the vassal was held entitled to the coal.[76] Unless it appears that there was an intention to alter its meaning a phrase, or similar phrase, in the original and novodamus charters will be accorded the same significance, but *in dubio* the terms of the novodamus will rule.[77]

---

[75] Land Registration (Scotland) Act 1979, s. 18.
[76] *Cadell* v. *Allan* (1905) 7 F. 606.
[77] *Magistrates of Inverkeithing* v. *Ross* (1874) 2 R. 48.

7–101 **(b) Vassal.** In certain circumstances there may be disadvantage to the vassal in accepting a novodamus which, as is usual, repeats all the conditions of the original grant other than any which the parties have agreed to alter. If there have been departures from the original conditions, either as regards the feu itself or in many other feus from the superior in the neighbourhood, so that the superior may have become barred by acquiescence from enforcing the conditions, the acceptance of a novodamus which repeats them may negative the plea of acquiescence which might formerly have been available to the vassal.

7–102 **(c) Heritable creditors.** If the original feu is burdened with heritable securities, a novodamus entered into without the consent of the heritable creditors will not affect their securities which may be enforced against the feu by sale under the original feuing conditions, so rendering the novodamus nugatory. A heritable creditor should be wary of consenting to a novodamus for his interest and should only do so if his standard security is varied by a variation under section 16 of the Conveyancing and Feudal Reform (Scotland) Act 1970, and then only if it appears from a search that there have been no intervening encumbrances or diligences which might affect the priority or validity of his security. If the novodamus involves the addition of ground to that originally feued a variation of the security is incompetent: the security should be reconstituted over the new extended feu, and again only if it is clear from a search that there have been no intervening encumbrances that will affect the priority of the new security and no diligences which may affect its validity. The heritable creditor should also be satisfied, if the security is reconstituted anew, as to the solvency of the debtor-vassal (at least if there are changes in the terms of security), to obviate any question as to the new security being in respect of a prior debt. The consent to a novodamus by heritable creditors over the superiority is also necessary if it is to be binding upon them.

Infeftment and searches

7–103 Infeftment of the superior is necessary to the grant of a novodamus, just as in the case of the grant of an original charter, with the distinction that the subsequent infeftment may not effect accretion since the novodamus will not normally have been granted with absolute warrandice. Although in practice the precaution is frequently omitted, it is recommended that searches should be obtained against both the superiority and property when a novodamus is being granted to ensure that there are no heritable creditors over either estate and no diligences such as inhibitions against either party. The granting and accepting of a novodamus is a voluntary transaction and, if it could be shown that the new conditions were less beneficial to either party than the original

ones, there could be an argument that the novodamus was prejudicial
to an inhibitor.

Style—charter of novodamus—lost or defective title[77a]

17–104   I, AB, (*designed*), immediate lawful superior of the subjects
hereinafter disponed, considering that it is represented to me by
CD, (*designed*), that he is proprietor of the *dominium utile* thereof,
but that [his titles thereto have been lost] [in the progress of his
title deeds thereto there is a defect which is not remediable except
at disproportionate expense] and in these circumstances he has
requested me to grant these presents which I have agreed to do in
the terms underwritten and without any alteration in the original
grant, conditions and tenure, therefore I now in feu farm fee and
heritage for ever dispone and confirm to the said CD and his
executors and assignees whomsoever [*continue as in the original
charter except as to warrandice*] And I grant warrandice against
future facts and deeds only; and the said CD agrees by acceptance
hereof that this charter is granted at his risk and that he and his
successors shall be bound to relieve me and my successors of all
liability which may be incurred by the granting hereof. (*To be
attested*) (*Stamp 50p*)

Style—charter of novodamus altering feuing conditions[77b]

17–105   I, AB, (*designed*), immediate lawful superior of ALL and WHOLE
the subjects in the Parish of   and County of
described and disponed in Feu Charter (hereinafter called "the
Charter") by CD in favour of EF dated   and recorded in
the Division of the General Register of Sasines for the County of
              on   of which subjects the *dominium utile* is now
vested in GH, (*designed*), whose title is recorded in the said
Division of the General Register of Sasines on   , Considering
that it has been agreed between me and the said GH as testified by
his signature hereto that the permanent alterations hereinafter
specified shall be made in the feuing conditions of the said
subjects, Therefore I of new in feu farm fee and heritage for ever
dispone and confirm to the said GH and his executors and
assignees whomsoever (hereinafter called "the feuars") the said
subjects with and under the reservations, conditions, obligations
(*list words as in the original charter*) contained in the Charter
subject to the following alterations, namely, (1) The feuars may
erect on the portion of the said subjects (*description of portion to
which alteration applies*) and thereafter maintain blocks of
dwellinghouses of not more than two storeys in height, each
containing not more than four dwellinghouses to be used and

[77a] This Style is appropriate where the titles to both the superiority and the property are recorded in
the Register of Sasines. If either or both of the titles are registered in the Land Register the wording
should be amended appropriately. If the title to the property has been registered with exclusion of
indemnity the Keeper may be prepared to remove the exclusion on registration of the Charter of
Novodamus.

[77b] Note 77a aplies to this style also. Although not now necessary to precede the Charter of
Novodamus by a disposition *ad rem* it may clarify the position where registration of title is involved if
such a disposition is granted followed by the Charter of Novodamus setting out the conditions as now
altered.

occupied by one family only, with relative garages to be used only by the occupants of said dwellinghouses for private motor vehicles and not for any trade or business purposes, and that on sites and of materials and in accordance with plans and elevations to be approved in writing by me or my successors before building is commenced and (2) The feuars may erect on the portion of the said subjects (*description of portion to which alteration applies*) and thereafter maintain not more than four shops of not more than one storey in height to be used and occupied as retail shops only, and that on sites and of materials and in accordance with plans and elevations to be approved in writing by me or my successors before building is commenced, declaring that the whole clauses in the Charter shall be read and construed and shall operate as if the alterations hereby made had been contained in the Charter: To be holden the said subjects of and under me and my executors and successors as immediate lawful superiors thereof in feu farm, fee and heritage for ever: [*Warrandice, etc., in style in paragraph 17–104 supra to the end*].

(*To be attested*)   (*Stamp 50p*)

Style—minute of waiver of feuing condition[78]

106   I, AB, (*designed*), immediate lawful superior of ALL and WHOLE the subjects in the Parish of   and County of described and disponed in Feu Charter (hereinafter called the "Charter") by me in favour of EF Limited, (*designed*), dated   and recorded in the Division of the General Register of Sasines for the County of   on   of which subjects the *dominium utile* remains vested in the said EF Limited (*or otherwise as the case may be*), Whereas the Charter provided in Clause   thereof that a strip of ground within the said subjects (*description of strip*) should remain open and unbuilt upon in all time coming and should be used jointly with the proprietor of adjoining lands belonging to CD, (*designed*), to the north of the said subjects for the construction of an access road to be formed to the extent of one-half of the breadth thereof on the said strip all in terms of and under the conditions in the said Clause, and whereas it has now been agreed that such access road will not be required, I hereby at the request and with the consent of the said EF Limited and with the consent also of the said CD for his whole right and interest in the premises hereby waive and cancel the said Clause   of the Charter and whole conditions thereof to the same extent and effect as if the said Clause had never been contained in the Charter but that the said strip of ground had been held by the said EF Limited subject to the whole provisions and conditions applicable to the remainder of the said subjects disponed by the Charter: (*continue with warrandice generally as in style in paragraph 17–104*) (*To be attested*) (*Stamp duty nil*)[78a]

---

[78] See para. 17–95.
[78a] Finance Act 1985, s. 85 and Sched. 24(1).

IX. Division and Interjection of Superiority

Division of Superiority

17–107 The vassal may subdivide the *dominium utile* by sub-feuing or disponing different parts to other parties but the superior cannot split the superiority into different parts, whether in fee[79] or liferent,[80] so that different portions of it are held by different persons, but there is no objection to several persons owning the whole of the superiority estate in *pro indiviso* shares.[81] Division of the superiority may be effected, however, if the superior has reserved the right to do so in the relevant feu grant (which is rarely done) or with the consent of all the feuars concerned.[82] The right of a feuar to object may be extinguished by the long negative prescription, now of 20 years, but failure to object to a division among liferenters does not cut off the right of objection to a subsequent division of the superiority among several fiars.[83]

Interjection of Superiority

17–108 A vassal may also object to the interjection of a mid-superiority between the superiority and the property,[84] *i.e.* the superior may not feu the superiority and thereby remove the vassal a stage further from the Crown in the feudal hierarchy. The ratio of the rule seems somewhat antique today, but it remains the law. As in the case of division of a superiority the objection could be barred by a reserved power in a feu grant or lost by the consent of the vassal or by acquiescence by the vassal for the period of the negative prescription. The objection does not apply to the grant of a heritable security over the superiority: the heritable creditor on default may obtain right to collect the feuduties, but that is not the creation of a mid-superiority but merely a burden exacted by the creditor instead of the superior.[85]

X. Voluntary Extinction of Feu—Consolidation

Resignation

17–109 The historical method of extinguishing a feu by procuratory of resignation *ad perpetuam remanentiam* or by disposition containing such a procuratory has already been described.[86] Simplification of the

---

[79] *Montrose* v. *Colquhoun* (1782) 6 Pat.App. 805.
[80] *Graham* v. *Westenra* (1826) 4 S. 615.
[81] *Cargill* v. *Muir* (1837) 15 S. 408.
[82] Montgomerie Bell, *Lectures*, 754.
[83] *Stewart* v. *Houston* (1823) 2 S. 300.
[84] *Stewart* v. *Lord Abbotshall* (1610) Mor. 15012.
[85] *Home* v. *Smith* (1794) Mor. 15077.
[86] See para. 16–41.

procedure was effected by various statutes between 1845 and 1858.[87] It was essential that the titles of both superior and vassal should be complete. Section 11(2) of the Conveyancing (Scotland) Act 1924 provides that where an infeft superior has acquired the property or mid-superiority and the disposition in his favour contains a clause of resignation *ad perpetuam remanentiam* the recording of the disposition in the Register of Sasines is deemed to have the effect of consolidating the property or the mid-superiority, as the case may be, with the superiority. It should be noted that (1) the superior must be infeft in the superiority, (2) the disposition itself must be recorded, (3) the method is available only where the superior acquires the property or mid-superiority, not in the converse situation, and (4) on recording of the disposition consolidation is automatically effected. The clause of resignation should be inserted immediately after the clause of entry in a disposition which is otherwise in ordinary form, and runs: "And I resign the (lands and others) *or* (subjects) hereby disponed *ad perpetuam remanentiam.*"

Minute of consolidation

–110 **(1) Separate minute.** Consolidation may also be effected by separate minute executed and recorded in the Register of Sasines by a person who is infeft in both estates.[88] As to the description of the lands in the minute, (a) if the consolidation is of an entire feu the lands may be described as in the original feu grant, (b) if there are different descriptions of the lands in the two titles, insert that in the superiority title adding "which subjects are otherwise described as," and insert the description in the property title, and (c) if the description in the property title includes a larger area than that being consolidated, the latter not being separately described, insert a description of the lands being consolidated and add "which subjects form part of," and add a description by reference of the larger area.

(2) Annexed minute. Alternatively, where a person is already infeft in the superiority or the property and acquires the other of them by disposition, he may annex to the disposition a minute of consolidation which is recorded in the Register of Sasines along with the disposition, and when the disposition and minute are so recorded consolidation of the two estates is effected.[89]

Consolidation by separate or annexed minute is competent whether the superior acquires the property or the vassal acquires the superiority.

---

[87] For an account of these, see Burns, 384; Craigie, *Heritable Rights*, 407–425.
[88] Conveyancing (Scotland) Act 1874, s. 6 and Sched. C.
[89] Conveyancing (Scotland) Act 1924, s. 11(1) and Sched. G.

Prescription

17–111   Consolidation of the estates of superiority and property may be effected in certain circumstances by the operation of prescription. It is essential that the title to the superiority is a title to the lands, *e.g.* a conveyance of the lands themselves, the fact that it is truly a conveyance of the superiority only being established from subordinate clauses such as an assignation of feuduties or the exception of feu rights from warrandice. In such a case the principle that the dispositive clause rules determines that the actual land is conveyed; the references to feuduties or feu rights in subordinate clauses merely indicate that there are burdens of feu grants existing upon it. If the title to the lands is expressed as to "the superiority" or "the *dominium directum*" of the lands (which is technically not the proper method), there is no room for consolidation by prescription because possession of the *dominium utile* would not be upon a recorded deed which was sufficient in respect of its terms[90] to constitute a title to the superiority.

17–112   **(1) Consolidation by possession of dominium utile.** If A is superior holding on a recorded title to the lands and B is vassal, but A actually possesses the lands openly, peaceably and without judicial interruption for a continuous period of 10 years, positive prescription gives A a title to the lands disburdened of the feu and so effects consolidation.[91] Within a further period of 10 years B may challenge on the ground that the obligation of warrandice in the feu grant in his favour does not prescribe for 20 years,[92] but that gives only a personal claim for loss of the property.

17–113   **(2) Consolidation by vesting of titles in one person.** Where A holds a title to the superiority (*ex facie* the lands) and also acquires a title to the property, consolidation does not thereby automatically result,[93] but if A possesses the lands thereafter for a continuous period of 10 years openly, peaceably and without judicial interruption the *dominium utile* merges in the higher title of the superiority so that A holds the *dominium plenum*.[94] Consolidation does not operate in such circumstances, however, if the respective titles to the two estates contain different destinations: in that case the heirs called under the different destinations succeed to the superiority and the property respectively when the succession opens even after the period of prescription has run.[95]

---

[90] Prescription and Limitation (Scotland) Act 1973, s. 1(1)(*b*).
[91] See *Middleton and Paterson* v. *Earl of Dunmore* (1774) Mor. 10944; *Lord Elibank* v. *Campbell* (1833) 12 S. 74.
[92] 1973 Act, s. 7.
[93] *Bald* v. *Buchanan* (1787) 2 R.L.C. 210.
[94] *Wilson* v. *Pollok* (1839) 2 D. 159.
[95] *Zuille* v. *Morrison*, March 4, 1813, F.C.

–114 **(3) Consolidation—limited and unlimited titles.** Where a person owns both the superiority (*ex facie* the lands) and the property and one of the titles is absolute and unfettered but the other is limited, *e.g.* by an entail, the question of whether consolidation operates by prescription depends upon certain presumps as affected by the intention of the person. (a) If the superiority title is unlimited but the property title is limited by an entail and possession of the lands for the prescriptive period follows infeftment in the superiority, the presumption is in favour of freedom so that consolidation is effected on the expiry of the period of positive prescription to the effect that the limitation of the property title is extinguished.[96] (b) If the superiority title is entailed but the property title is not, then the presumption for freedom operates against consolidation,[97] with the result that the property does not merge in the superiority and become subject to the fetters of the entail. These presumptions may, however, be negatived by actions of the person or his successors in ownership of both estates which indicate a different intention. For example, in case (a) if the successors keep up separate titles to both estates consolidation will not operate; they have demonstrated by their actions that they have not ascribed possession solely to the superiority title.

Effects of consolidation

–115 When consolidation is effected by resignation or by minute the effect has been judicially stated to be that the *dominium utile* is not destroyed but is restored to the superior for the purpose of enjoyment.[98] On the contrary the effect has been described by Lord President Inglis as extinguishing and destroying the *dominium utile*.[99] The theoretical distinction is important in relation to (a) different destinations in the superiority and property titles, and (b) rights attached to and burdens upon the property title. As regards destinations the general rule is that, when consolidation takes place by resignation or minute, the destination in the higher title of the superiority rules.[1] So, if that result is not desired and the destination in the superiority title can be evacuated, steps should be taken to evacuate the destination before consolidation is effected. As regards rights attached to the property title it was held in the *Earl of Zetland* case[98] that a right of salmon fishing in the property title was not lost when that title was consolidated by resignation of the lands and fishings with the superiority, the title to which contained no such right.[2] It is suggested that when there are any

[96] *Bruce* v. *Bruce-Carstairs* (1770) Mor. 10805.
[97] *Earl of Glasgow* v. *Boyle* (1887) 14 R. 419.
[98] *Earl of Zetland* v. *Glover Incorporation of Perth* (1870) 8 M. (H.L.) 144 *per* Lord Chancellor at 151, Lord Westbury at 154.
[99] *Park's C.B.* v. *Black* (1870) 8 M. 671 at 675.
[1] *Park's C.B.* v. *Black, supra; Hay* v. *Paterson*, 1910 S.C. 509.
[2] It may be observed that since salmon fishings are a separate feudal subject there was no coincidence of subjects in the two titles as is basic to the theory of consolidation.

special rights attached to the *dominium utile* title, consideration should be given as to the desirability of effecting consolidation or of allowing it to happen by prescription. It is clear that where either the superiority or property title is burdened with heritable securities, consolidation does not affect these.[3]

Style—consolidation by separate minute[4]

17–116 I, AB, (*designed*), heritable proprietor both of the immediate superiority and of the [property] [mid-superiority] of ALL and WHOLE (*describe or refer to the lands*), hereby consolidate the [property] [mid-superiority] of the said lands with the immediate superiority thereof. (*To be attested*) (*Stamp nil*)[4a]

Style—consolidation by annexed minute[5]

17–117 I, AB, designed in the foregoing disposition, proprietor both of the superiority and of the [property] [mid-superiority] of the lands described in the foregoing disposition, hereby consolidate the [property] [mid-superiority] of the said lands with the superiority thereof. (*To be attested*) (*Stamp nil*)[4a]

NOTE.
The warrant of registration need not mention the minute.

Consolidation—registered titles

17–118 The Land Registration (Scotland) Act 1979 refers to the absorption of one interest by another, and absorption includes the merging of an interest in the *dominium utile* with the interest of the immediate superiority.[6]

Absorption or consolidation by resignation or minute

17–119 If the higher right of fee (superiority) is registered in the Land Register and the lower fee (property) is not, absorption requires registration of the lower fee in the Land Register. On the other hand if the higher fee is recorded in the Register of Sasines then, whether the lower fee is recorded in the Register of Sasines or is registered in the Land Register, the deed which effects consolidation is recorded in the Register of Sasines. In the latter event if the lower fee is registered in the Land Register the title sheet for the lower fee is cancelled, removed from the Land Register and returned to the Register of Sasines by an application under section 2(4) of the 1979 Act which permits the Keeper to close the title sheet and so give effect to the consolidation in the Land Register. For details of the procedure where consolidation is

---

[3] *Fraser* v. *Wilson* (1824) 2 Sh.App. 162.
[4] Conveyancing (Scotland) Act 1874, Sched. C.
[4a] Finance Act 1985, s. 85 and Sched. 24(1).
[5] Conveyancing (Scotland) Act 1924, Sched. G.
[6] ss. 2(1)(*a*)(iv), 2(4)(*a*) and (*b*) and 8(2)(*b*).

effected by disposition with a minute of consolidation annexed or by disposition containing a clause of resignation *ad perpetuam remanentiam* or by separate minute in various circumstances, see the *Registration of Title Practice Book*, paragraphs D.4.28 and D.4.29. Where a transfer merely vests an interest in a person already infeft in a higher or lower fee without effecting consolidation, the normal rules of recording in the Register of Sasines or registration in the Land Register will apply. It is suggested[7] that if in such a case subsequent consolidation is considered a possibility consideration should be given to effecting it as part of the transfer, since that course may secure some abatement in registration fees.

Consolidation by prescription

–120 **(a) Superiority title recorded in Register of Sasines.** If the title of the superior (*ex facie to the lands*) is recorded in the Register of Sasines consolidation may still be effected by prescription even if the lands are situated in an operational area for the purposes of registration of title, whether the title to the property is recorded in the Register of Sasines or registered in the Land Register. On expiry of the prescriptive period during which the superior has had full possession of the lands he may, if the title to the property has been registered in the Land Register, apply on Form 2 to the Keeper for cancellation of the title sheet of the vassal's interest in the property. The application must be supported by documents and evidence sufficient to satisfy the Keeper that consolidation has been effected, such as the superior's title and affidavits of uninterrupted possession.

–121 **(b) Superiority title registered in Land Register.** If the superiority title is registered in the Land Register prescription will not operate to effect consolidation, since (i) the superior's interest will be shown in his registered title as relating to the *dominium directum*[8] and so is not habile to support a title acquired by possession of the *dominium utile*, and (ii) section 1 of the Prescription and Limitation (Scotland) Act 1973 was amended by section 10 of the 1979 Act *quoad* interests registered in the Land Register to the effect that the possession must follow on an interest registered with exclusion of indemnity and there would not normally be any such exclusion in the registered title to the superiority or, if it also was registered in the Land Register, the title to the *dominium utile*. If consolidation was desired in circumstances where the vassal had abandoned the property and the superior had possession for the period of positive prescription thereafter, the appropriate procedure would be for the superior to acquire title to the property by an *a non domino* title to the *dominium utile* and, when

---

[7] R.T.P.B., para. D. 4.27.
[8] 1979 Act, s. 6(1)(*b*).

prescription had operated, to expede a minute of consolidation and make application for registration of the minute accompanied by evidence of prescriptive possession of the property.[9]

XI. Involuntary Extinction of Feu—Irritancy

Conventional irritancies

17–122   A feu right may be extinguished by the superior enforcing a conventional right of irritancy when the vassal is in breach of any of the obligations imposed on him by the contract of feu. Irritancy on the ground of failure to pay feuduty, based either on statute or breach of the obligation in a feu grant, has already been considered[10]: this section relates to irritancies imposed conventionally in the event of contravention of other obligations of the grant. The right to enforce an irritancy does not operate so as to make the feu right void, but only voidable at the instance of the superior[11]; the vassal's right is extinguished only when the superior has obtained from the court a decree of declarator of irritancy and an extract of the decree has been recorded in the Register of Sasines or, in the case of registered titles, entered in the Land Register.[12] The title to sue lies in the superior alone; his executor or assignee cannot raise an action of declarator of irritancy.[13]

Procedure

17–123   An action of declarator of irritancy may be raised in the Court of Session or in the sheriff court having jurisdiction in the district where the property forming the subject in dispute is situated.[14] In actions in the Court of Session the provisions as to service and intimation in the case of actions where the ground is non-payment of feuduty have been considered in paragraph 17–30 *supra*. The relevant statutory provisions[15] relate in terms only to actions of declarator of irritancy for non-payment of feuduty, but it is thought that for the protection of persons deriving right from the vassal the court would probably direct the like service and intimation where the ground of action was breach of any

---

[9] R.T.P.B., paras. D. 4.30 and D. 4.31.

[10] paras. 17–28 to 17–32.

[11] *Inglis* v. *Wilson*, 1909 S.C. 1393.

[12] The statutory provision to this effect applies to irritancies *ob non solutem canonem* (Conveyancing (Scotland) Acts (1874 and 1879) Amendment Act 1887, s. 4), but it is thought that the superior would be safe to rely on the decree in a question with *bona fide* third parties dealing with the vassal only after the extract decree was recorded or registered (Conveyancing (Scotland) Act 1924, s. 46; *Mulhearn* v. *Dunlop*, 1929 S.L.T. 59).

[13] *Maxwell's Trs.* v. *Bothwell School Board* (1893) 20 R. 958 at 964.

[14] Sheriff Courts (Scotland) Act 1907, s. 5, as amended (Civil Jurisdiction and Judgments Act 1982, Sched. 14).

[15] Conveyancing Amendment (Scotland) Act 1938, s. 6(1) as amended by the Land Registration (Scotland) Act 1979, Sched. 2, para. 3.

other conventional obligation.[15a] In actions in the sheriff court the relevant rule[16] requires that in any action of declarator of irritancy by a superior against a vassal the superior shall call as parties the last-entered vassal and such heritable creditors and holders of postponed ground burdens as are disclosed by a search for 20 years prior to the raising of the action. In current practice the usual course in any action of declarator of irritancy, whether in the Court of Session or the sheriff court, is to intimate the action to sub-feuars, heritable creditors and others who appear to have some real right in or security over the vassal's estate or any part thereof and who from a search in the Register of Sasines against the vassal's estate for 20 years prior to the raising of the action or from an examination of the relevant title sheet in the Land Register of Scotland are disclosed as having such interest.

Purging the irritancy

–124 Irritancies following on a breach of an obligation *ad factum praestandum*, unlike those following upon a failure to pay feuduty, are not automatically purgeable, but the court will normally allow purgation by performance of the obligation where there are circumstances which justify the exercise of the court's discretion in favour of the vassal.[17] In a case where the vassal was bound to erect a dwelling-house and had failed to do so within seven years the court refused to imply an obligation to implement the condition "within a reasonable time," and indicated that the correct procedure was to obtain from the court an order ordaining the vassal to erect the dwelling-house within a specified time.[18] Because of its drastic effect irritancy is a remedy of last resort; other remedies may in practice be more immediately effective, *e.g.* failure to implement an obligation *ad factum praestandum* may be enforced by seeking an order of court ordaining performance within a stated time,[19] or use of the property for a prohibited purpose may be restrained by interdict.[20] On the other hand a vassal should avoid any risk of incurring an irritancy and in practice should, before commencing building operations or use of the property which is or may be in breach of a feuing condition, seek a waiver of the condition by agreement with the superior or in appropriate cases obtain a variation or discharge of the condition from the Lands Tribunal for Scotland under section 1 of the Conveyancing and Feudal Reform (Scotland) Act 1970.

[15a] Intimation must be made to heritable creditors: Rules of Court, rule 76.
[16] Rule 103(4) of Sheriff Courts (Scotland) Act 1907 as substituted by Act of Sederunt (Ordinary Cause Rules Amendment) 1983, (S.I. 1983 No. 1546) (S. 146).
[17] *Precision Relays Ltd.* v. *Beaton*, 1980 S.L.T. 206.
[18] *Anderson* v. *Valentine*, 1957 S.L.T. 57.
[19] *Middleton* v. *Leslie* (1892) 19 R. 801; *Anderson* v. *Valentine, supra.*
[20] *Colquhoun's C.B.* v. *Glen's Tr.*, 1920 S.C. 737; *Howard de Walden Estates Ltd.* v. *Bowmaker Ltd.*, 1965 S.C. 163.

Effect of irritancy

17–125   A decree of declarator of irritancy has the effect that the feu reverts to the superior unaffected by subordinate rights granted by the vassal, without compensation. The feu right and all derivative rights such as heritable securities and sub-feus granted by the vassal become null and void and the land becomes the property of the superior unencumbered by the vassal's right and all that has flowed from it.[21] That result does not follow if the superior has expressly consented to sub-feus or heritable securities,[22] and the fact that two separate properties were included in a single feu contract does not entitle the superior to irritate the whole feu where failure to implement building conditions has occurred only in respect of one of the properties.[23] A decree of irritancy does not carry to the superior personal claims competent to the vassal against third parties, even although they are connected with the lands, *e.g.* a claim vested in the vassal to compensation under the Lands Clauses Consolidation (Scotland) Act 1845.[24] No compensation is payable to the vassal or persons deriving right from him as a result of an irritancy, but the superior, having elected that remedy, cannot claim damages against the vassal for breach of the feuing conditions.

If the titles of sub-feuars have been registered in the Land Register application must be made to register the effect of the extract decree of irritancy against the title sheets of the sub-feuars and the decree should bear the title numbers of these interests.

Conventional limitations upon right of irritancy

17–126   Where the feu is of a large area to be developed by building on several plots, the right of irritancy may be qualified to protect the proprietors of plots in respect of which the feuing conditions have been implemented. The style of deed of feuing conditions in paragraph 17–84 *supra* (clause THIRTEENTH) expresses the irritancy as applicable only to the proprietor of the plot in respect of which a breach of conditions has occurred, but if the original feu grant contains a clause of irritancy applicable to the whole feu as in the style of skeleton charter in paragraph 17–81 *supra* it may be desirable to insert a qualification thus:

> Providing always that the right of the superiors under this clause shall extend only to forfeiture of the part or parts of the said subjects in respect of which such contravention or failure has occurred and the remainder of the said subjects shall not be affected thereby.

---

[21] *Cassels* v. *Lamb* (1885) 12 R. 722; *Sandeman* v. *Scottish Property Investment Co.* (1885) 12 R. (H.L.) 67.
[22] *Sandeman* v. *Scottish Property Investment Co.*, *supra*, per Lord Watson at 74.
[23] *Welsh* v. *Jack* (1882) 10 R. 113.
[24] *Caledonian Rly. Co.* v. *Watt* (1875) 2 R. 917.

Protection may also be desired against the risk of irritancy in the event of a builder-vassal becoming insolvent when building operations are partly completed for the benefit of heritable creditors over the builder's interest or the trustee in bankruptcy or liquidator of the builder or a receiver appointed over assets of the builder which include that interest. The adjustment of a protective clause is a matter for negotiation but a reasonable proviso might be:

Provided that (a) in the case of a breach, non-observance or non-performance by the feuar of any of the feuing conditions herein stipulated which is capable of remedy the superior shall not exercise such option of irritancy and forfeiture unless and until he shall first have given notice to the feuar and to every creditor in any existing standard security, floating charge or debenture which has been notified to the superior requiring the same to be remedied and intimating his intention to exercise his option of irritancy and forfeiture in the event of such breach, non-observance or non-performance not being remedied within such period as may be stated in the notice (being such reasonable period as the superior may prescribe) and the feuar or any such creditor shall have failed to remedy the same within said period and (b) in the event of [the feuar being sequestrated] [the feuar going into liquidation (other than for reconstruction or amalgamation)] [a receiver being appointed over the assets of the feuar] the superior shall allow the [trustee in bankruptcy of the feuar] [the liquidator of the feuar] [such receiver] a period of one year (*or other reasonable period*) in which to dispose of the feuar's interest under these presents and shall be entitled to exercise the said right of irritancy and forfeiture only if the said [trustee] [liquidator] [receiver] shall have failed to dispose of the feuar's said interest at the end of the said period, provided always that the said [trustee] [liquidator] [receiver] shall personally accept full responsibility for performance of all the said feuing conditions outstanding at the date of [such sequestration] [such liquidation] [his appointment] and arising before such disposal or the end of the said period as the case may be.

CHAPTER 18

DESCRIPTION OF LAND CONVEYED

Introductory

18–01   This chapter deals with (1) the relationship between the contract of sale and the conveyance which implements it, (2) the description of the subjects in conveyances, and (3) the rights which are carried by conveyances of particular subjects.

1. RELATIONSHIP BETWEEN CONTRACT OF SALE AND CONVEYANCE

Ascertainment of subjects to be conveyed

8–02   If a question arises as to the subjects which are to be conveyed in a feu grant or disposition in implementation of a contract of sale, it is determined by a proper construction of the contract and may not necessarily correspond with the description of the subjects in the existing title deeds of the seller. The *locus classicus* of this principle is the following *dictum* of Lord Kinnear in *Houldsworth* v. *Gordon Cumming*[1]:

> "It is manifest, therefore, that if a question arises as to the description to be inserted in a disposition, the first thing to be settled is what is the exact subject sold; and that is to be determined, not by the existing titles, but by the contract of sale, interpreted, as every document whatsoever must, more or less, be interpreted, by reference to the surrounding circumstances."

In accordance with that principle it was held that the subjects to be conveyed were those delineated on a plan furnished to the purchaser although the titles of the estate embraced a somewhat larger area. The principle was applied in *Johnston's Trs.* v. *Kinloch*,[2] where the agreement for sale described the subjects as "all the lands and buildings of Burrowine and Whitehills, in the Parish of Culross, Fife, as held at present by the purchaser (as tenant), subject to the titles of the same," and the disposition described them in much the same language with the addition of their general description in old title deeds, and the contention of the purchasers that they were entitled to an identifying description by map or other more definite description was rejected. The rule is that the seller can be required to convey the subjects as described in the contract, with only such modifications in wording as may be appropriate to a formal conveyance.

Inconsistency between contract and conveyance

8–03   Once a disposition or other formal deed of conveyance has been granted and accepted, however, the later formal deed supersedes the earlier contract in the determination of the subjects conveyed, just as the contract supersedes prior, less formal, communications between the parties.[3] The rule applies only when the disposition has been delivered and accepted; until then the contract embodied in missives determines the matter.[4] There are circumstances in which the rule is inapplicable,

---

[1] 1910 S.C. (H.L.) 49 at 55.
[2] 1925 S.L.T. 124.
[3] *Lee* v. *Alexander* (1883) 10 R. (H.L.) 91; *Orr* v. *Mitchell* (1893) 20 R. (H.L.) 27; *Edinburgh United Breweries Ltd.* v. *Molleson* (1894) 21 R. (H.L.) 10, *per* Lord Watson at 16; *Butter* v. *Foster*, 1912 S.C. 1218; *Norval* v. *Abbey*, 1939 S.C. 724. *Cf. Lord Glasgow's Trs.* v. *Clark* (1889) 16 R. 545 and *dicta* in *Baird* v. *Alexander* (1898) 25 R. (H.L.) 35, but these cases do not subvert the rule. *Wigan* v. *Cripps*, 1908 S.C. 394, a decision inconsistent with the rule, was doubted in *Butter* v. *Foster, supra.*
[4] *Morrison* v. *Gray*, 1932 S.C. 712.

e.g. (1) where the parties have agreed to exclude it to the effect that the antecedent articles of roup determine the burdens or the extent of the subjects[5] or the relevant clause of the missives was repeated in the disposition,[6] (2) where the contract includes the sale of moveable and heritable items the function of the disposition is to convey the heritable items and the contract so far as relating to moveable items continues to regulate the rights of the parties since the disposition implements only part of the contract,[7] (3) where the contract includes both the sale of heritable property and a collateral agreement to construct a building, the acceptance of a disposition of the heritage does not supersede the obligations of the seller to implement the construction agreement,[8] (4) where the language of the disposition on the relevant matter is obscure or ambiguous, reference to the preliminary document is permissible to explain it,[9] or (5) where there was a written agreement in the missives or a separate document that a provision in the missives would remain in force notwithstanding delivery of the disposition.[9a] The rule above referred to is simply a rule of construction; if the formal deed clearly does not accurately give effect to the bargain which the parties intended, it may be reduced on the ground of essential error.[10]

2. DESCRIPTION OF SUBJECTS IN CONVEYANCE

Descriptions before and after registration of title

18–04   Until a title to land has been registered under the ongoing process of registration of title the description to be inserted in a conveyance continues to be regulated by common law and the relevant conveyancing statutes. Upon an application for first registration additional particulars may be required in certain cases in order to enable the subjects to be delineated on the title plan based on the Ordnance Map. Once the title has been registered the description of the registered interest in subsequent dealings will be considerably simplified, the essential element being the reference to the registered title number, and the older forms of description are superseded. Even after registration of the title, however, the description in the former title deeds may be

---

[5] *Wood* v. *Mags. of Edinburgh* (1886) 13 R. 1006; *Young* v. *McKellar Ltd.*, 1909 S.C. 1340.

[6] *Fraser* v. *Cox*, 1938 S.C. 506.

[7] *Jamieson* v. *Welsh* (1900) 3 F. 176.

[8] *McKillop* v. *Mutual Securities Ltd.*, 1945 S.C. 166. It may be doubtful whether a provision in the contract is separate from the sale. In *Bradley* v. *Scott*, 1966 S.L.T. (Sh.Ct.) 25 it was held that a condition that there were no outstanding notices for repairs was a collateral stipulation which was not superseded by the disposition, whereas in *Winston* v. *Patrick*, 1981 S.L.T. 41, a condition warranting that all statutory and local authority requirements had been fulfilled was held to have been superseded by the disposition.

[9] *Duke of Fife* v. *Great North of Scotland Rly. Co.* (1901) 3 F. (H.L.) 2.

[9a] *Winston* v. *Patrick, supra* at 49.

[10] *Glasgow Feuing and Building Co.* v. *Watson's Trs.* (1884) 14 R. 610; *Anderson* v. *Lambie*, 1954 S.C. (H.L.) 43.

relevant to determine issues regarding items from which indemnity may have been excluded on registration or overriding interests which have not been noted in the title sheet.

EXISTING LAW AND PRACTICE—UNREGISTERED LAND

Common Law Descriptions

Identification—common law

18–05   The objectives of a conveyancer in framing the description of lands for insertion in a conveyance have been stated succinctly by Professor Montgomerie Bell: "Secure that the description shall embrace everything intended to be disponed; that it shall not contain anything not intended to be disponed; and that the subjects disponed shall be capable of clear and absolute identification."[11] The description must identify the lands so as to distinguish them from all other lands: that is all that the common law requires. Formerly a conveyance of all lands belonging to the granter with a precept of sasine was sufficient, without further specification, to confer a feudal title, since the notary could identify the lands by reference to the granter's own titles and the instrument of sasine which followed specified them in more detail.[12] The requirement of common law is still the same—a description in any mode which secures the identification of the lands is enough.[12a] So, even although the description in a disposition has omissions or errors in details, it is sufficient if the remainder of the description identifies the subjects conveyed.[13]

Requirements—Register of Sasines

18–06   While at common law a notary could explicate a general descriptive phrase by reference to the granter's title, the Keeper of the Register of Sasines is under no obligation to do so and will not normally accept a deed where the description is too general.[14] Accordingly a description of the lands in a deed submitted for recording must be sufficiently detailed to enable the record of it to be allocated to the appropriate search sheet.

Methods of description—common law

18–07   (a) **General description.** A general description is one which describes the lands without reference to measurement or boundaries, usually

---

[11] *Lectures*, 588.
[12] *Graham* v. *Hyslop* (1753) 2 R.L.C. 31.
[12a] *Smith* v. *Wallace* (1869) 8 M. 204, *per* Lord Deas at 214.
[13] *Murray's Tr.* v. *Wood* (1887) 14 R. 856; *Matheson* v. *Gemmell* (1903) 5 F. 448.
[14] *Macdonald* v. *Keeper of General Register of Sasines*, 1914 S.C. 854.

specifying the name by which they are known, and dependent for their definition upon the owner's possession of them and the operation of positive prescription.[15] If the lands are known in the locality and defined by possession, that is a valid description.[16] An example of such a description is a barony title where lands, possibly both contiguous and discontiguous, have been erected into a single estate by the Crown. Such a title may carry discontiguous lands, although normally these would require separate specification.[17] In particular a barony title may more readily include foreshore and salmon fishings.[18]

18–08 *Practice.* A general description of lands has the advantage that the owner may be enabled to acquire by possession for the period of positive prescription ground or rights not inconsistent with it,[19] which a more detailed description might clearly exclude.[20] On the other hand it has the disadvantage that the draftsman of the conveyance may not know that the description truly describes the subjects of the contract between the parties unless he makes careful inquiry in the area, which may not always be convenient. There is particular danger of error if additional lands have been acquired by the seller or where part only of the lands is intended to be sold, and the error may be of a major character.[21] It is suggested that conveyances of a barony title should always, and of lands described by a general description should usually, repeat the existing general description. If the purchaser desires further definition of the subjects, the general description may be followed by "which subjects above described, and without prejudice to the scope and generality of that description, include"—and insert the more particular description by reference to boundaries or plan, any plan being declared to be demonstrative only and not taxative. In the case of a sale to a tenant a description of the subjects "as possessed by" the tenant is dangerous; the lease may exclude minerals or fishing or sporting rights.

18–09 **(b) Particular description—bounding title.** A particular description or bounding title is one where the subjects are limited by boundaries, either in whole or in part expressly or by implication. Its effects are: (1) No corporeal right of property in land can be acquired beyond the boundaries, even by exclusive possession for the period of positive prescription,[22] subject to the qualification that a right may be acquired

---

[15] As to possession explicative of a general (barony) title, see *Lord Advocate* v. *Wemyss* (1899) 2 F. (H.L.) 1, *per* Lord Watson at 9, 10.

[16] *Johnston's Trs.* v. *Kinloch*, 1925 S.L.T. 124 (the possession in that case being that of a tenant).

[17] *Argyle* v. *Campbell* (1668) Mor. 9631.

[18] See para. 18–28.

[19] *Dalrymple* v. *Earl of Stair* (1841) 3 D. 837.

[20] *Young* v. *Carmichael* (1671) Mor. 9636; *St. Monance Mags.* v. *Mackie* (1845) 7 D. 582.

[21] *Mansfield* v. *Walker's Trs.* (1835) 1 S. & McL. 203; *Houldsworth* v. *Gordon Cumming*, 1910 S.C. (H.L.) 49; *Anderson* v. *Lambie*, 1954 S.C. (H.L.) 43.

[22] *North British Rly. Co.* v. *Moon's Trs.* (1879) 6 R. 640; *Reid* v. *McColl* (1879) 7 R. 84; *North British Rly. Co.* v. *Hutton* (1896) 23 R. 522.

by prescriptive possession to a proper pertinent of the subjects conveyed which may be corporeal heritable property situated outwith the bounds of the title,[23] but (2) incorporeal rights of property such as salmon fishings may be acquired over areas beyond the bounds of the title to the riparian lands by prescriptive possession,[24] and (3) so also may servitude rights which by definition are *jura in re aliena*.[25]

-10 *Illustrations of bounding titles.* The number of ways in which a bounding title may be created are almost infinite, but the following illustrate some of the more usual: (i) by physical boundaries such a wall,[26] street,[27] river,[28] the sea,[29] or the lands of another,[30] (ii) by a plan on which the boundaries are delineated, (iii) by measurements and orientation of boundaries, (iv) by measurement of superficial area, when extrinsic evidence as to its location is competent,[31] (v) by specified boundaries on three sides with a statement of superficial area which enables the position of the remaining boundary to be determined,[32] (vi) by any combination of boundaries, measurements and plan sufficient to identify the actual land, (vii) by a conveyance of part of lands by a bounding description which renders the remainder bounded to the effect of excluding the part conveyed,[33] (viii) in the case of a flat, described as such, the vertical and horizontal boundaries thereof at common law,[34] or (ix) by a reference to lands as lying in a particular parish or county.[35]

-11 *Particular boundaries.* The limits imposed by certain kinds of boundaries, as interpreted judicially, are:

Road. The general rule is that bounded "by" a road excludes the whole *solum* of the road,[36] but where a proprietor conveys two pieces of ground, one on either side of a public road, and describes each as bounded by the road, there is a presumption in the absence of special circumstances or indications of a contrary intention that the boundary is the *medium filum* of the road.[37]

Lane. Bounded "by" a lane excludes the lane,[38] but there may be an implied right of access over it.[39]

---

[23] *Cooper's Trs.* v. *Stark's Trs.* (1898) 25 R. 1160, *per* Lord McLaren at 1169; *Nisbet* v. *Hogg*, 1950 S.L.T. 289.
[24] *Earl of Zetland* v. *Tennent's Trs.* (1873) 11 M. 469.
[25] *Liston* v. *Galloway* (1835) 14 S. 97; *Beaumont* v. *Lord Glenlyon* (1843) 5 D. 1337.
[26] *Kerr* v. *Dickson* (1842) 1 Bell's App. 499.
[27] *Duke of Buccleuch* v. *Mags. of Edinburgh* (1864) 2 M. 1114.
[28] *Menzies* v. *Marquess of Breadalbane* (1901) 4 F. 55.
[29] *Cadell* v. *Allan* (1905) 7 F. 606.
[30] *Reid* v. *McColl, supra.*
[31] *Brown* v. *North British Rly. Co.* (1906) 8 F. 534.
[32] *Stewart* v. *Greenock Harbour Trs.* (1866) 4 M. 283.
[33] *North British Rly. Co.* v. *Hutton* (1896) 23 R. 522.
[34] *Watt* v. *Burgess' Tr.* (1891) 18 R. 766.
[35] *Gordon* v. *Grant* (1850) 13 D.1.
[36] *Logie* v. *Reid's Trs.* (1903) 5 F. 859 at 862; *Houston* v. *Barr*, 1911 S.C. 134.
[37] *Mags. of Ayr* v. *Dobbie* (1898) 25 R. 1184.
[38] *Argyllshire Commrs. of Supply* v. *Campbell* (1885) 12 R. 1255.
[39] *Boyd* v. *Hamilton*, 1907 S.C. 912.

Wall. Bounded "by" a wall normally excludes the wall and solum thereof, the boundary being the inside face of the wall.[40]

Mutual wall. The boundary may be regarded as the centre line of the wall, each proprietor having a right of property in his own half to its centre line and a common interest in the other half. Alternatively the boundary may be the inner face of the wall on each side, the wall and its solum being owned *pro indiviso.* It has been stated that neither owner may alter the wall without the consent of the other,[41] but if the former view (which is rather favoured by Rankine[41a]) is adopted, operations may be carried out by one proprietor on his own half of the wall so long as they do not prejudice the common interest of the other proprietor.[41b]

Gable wall. Bounded "by" a gable wall excludes the wall.[42]

Canal. Bounded "by" a canal excludes both the canal and the towpath.[43]

Sea,[44] *sea-shore,*[45] *tidal river*[46] or *lowest ebb.*[47] The boundary extends to the low-water mark of ordinary spring tides, including the foreshore, subject to the rights of the public such as navigation, drying nets and white fishing and probably walking for recreation.[48]

Full sea, sea flood, flood mark. The boundary is the high-water mark of ordinary spring tides, excluding the foreshore.[49]

Sea beach, sea shore. In certain older cases conflicting views were expressed as to whether "sea beach" or "sea shore" were equivalent to "the sea" (so that the foreshore was included), or whether they were equivalent to the high-water mark of ordinary spring tides (so that the foreshore was excluded). In *Magistrates of Musselburgh* v. *Musselburgh Real Estate Co. Ltd.*[50] judicial opinions were almost equally divided on the question, and while this ambiguity remains the use of either phrase should be avoided.

Lateral boundary seawards. As between two estates on the coast each of the lateral boundaries seawards, both in respect of foreshore and salmon fishings, is a perpendicular line drawn seawards from the end of the land boundary to a straight line drawn parallel to the average direction of the coast.[51]

---

[40] *Smyth* v. *Allan* (1813) 5 Pat. App. 669.
[41] Burns, 329.
[41a] *Land-Ownership,* 620.
[41b] *Gray* v. *MacLeod,* 1979 S.L.T. (Sh.Ct.) 17.
[42] *Campbell* v. *Paterson* (1896) 4 S.L.T. 79.
[43] *Fleming* v. *Baird* (1841) 3 D. 1015.
[44] *Cadell* v. *Allan* (1905) 7 F. 606.
[45] *Culross Mags.* v. *Geddes* (1809) Hume 554.
[46] *Todd* v. *Clyde Trs.* (1840) 2 D. 357.
[47] *Smith* v. *Lerwick Harbour Trs.* (1903) 5 F. 680.
[48] *Hope* v. *Bennewith* (1904) 6 F. 1004.
[49] *Smart* v. *Mags. of Dundee* (1797) 3 Pat. App. 606; *Berry* v. *Holden* (1840) 3 D. 205; *Mags. of St. Monance* v. *Mackie* (1845) 7 D. 582; *Keiller* v. *Mags. of Dundee* (1886) 14 R. 191. See also *Hunter* v. *Lord Advocate* (1869) 7 M. 899.
[50] (1904) 7 F. 308.
[51] *McTaggart* v. *McDouall* (1867) 5 M. 534; *Keith* v. *Smyth* (1884) 12 R. 66.

Lateral boundary in river estuary. The same principle applies as in the case of a lateral boundary seawards, except that the perpendicular is drawn to a line which represents the general direction of the *medium filum* of the river at low water.[52]

Navigable and tidal river. The foreshore is included and the rule for ascertaining the lateral boundaries is as stated above. If additional ground accrues by *alluvio* that is added to the property,[52a] even although the ground was described by superficial and lineal measurements.[53]

Non-tidal river. Where land is described as bounded by a river which is non-tidal but navigable, or non-tidal and non-navigable, or merely a stream, the boundary is the *medium filum*.[54] If the river is divided by an island into a main and subsidiary channels the *medium filum* is the centre line of the *alveus* from bank to bank, not the centre line of the main channel.[55]

Fresh-water loch. Subject to the determination of priority of ownership by the title deeds of the riparian proprietors and possession for the period of positive prescription, the presumptions in the absence of any evidence to the contrary are (i) a loch completely surrounded by the lands of one proprietor belongs to him as a pertinent of the lands; (ii) where a loch is bounded by the lands of two or more proprietors, each proprietor has an exclusive right to his part of the solum but a proportional *pro indiviso* right to the whole water; and (iii) as between a person who has a title of ownership to the whole of a loch and other proprietors of properties bounded by it the boundary is the medium water-line between the summer and winter levels of the loch, the ground down to that line being the exclusive property of the owners of adjoining lands and the ground beyond that line being the exclusive property of the proprietor of the loch.[56]

-12   *Plans.* It was for long the practice to describe new plots of ground, and sometimes existing areas of which it was desired to give more precise definition, by reference to a plan annexed, which could also be used to indicate, in distinctive colouring or by hatching, areas conveyed as common or affected by servitudes of access or wayleave. The Conveyancing (Scotland) Act 1924[57] authorised recording of such plans, signed as relative to the writ submitted for registration, in the Register of Sasines. The writ with the principal plan must be accompanied by a duplicate of the plan, docqueted with reference to

---

[52] *Laird* v. *Reid* (1871) 9 M. 699; *Darling's Trs.* v. *Caledonian Rly. Co.* (1903) 5 F. 1001.
[52a] *Hunter* v. *Lord Advocate* (1869) 7 M. 899.
[53] *Blyth's Trs.* v. *Shaw Stewart* (1883) 11 R. 99.
[54] *Wishart* v. *Wyllie* (1853) 1 Macq. 389; *Gibson* v. *Bonnington Sugar Refinery Co. Ltd.* (1869) 7 M. 394; *Mags. of Hamilton* v. *Bent Colliery Co. Ltd.*, 1929 S.C. 686.
[55] *Menzies* v. *Marquess of Breadalbane* (1901) 4 F. 55.
[56] Craigie, *Heritable Rights*, 113. As to competing titles to a loch, see *Meacher* v. *Blair Oliphant*, 1913 S.C. 417.
[57] s. 48.

the writ and authenticated in the same manner as the principal plan.
The ingiving of the duplicate plan is noted in the Register, and the
Keeper will mark the principal plan with an acknowledgment of receipt
of the duplicate. As to procedure: (1) the principal plan should bear a
docquet on the following lines—"This is the plan referred to in the
foregoing [feu disposition] [disposition] by A in favour of B dated
        ," signed but not attested by the granter or parties; the duplicate
plan should bear a docquet such as, "This is a duplicate of the plan
referred to in, and annexed and signed as relative to, the [feu
disposition] [disposition] by A in favour of B dated   ," similarly
signed; (2) the testing clause should refer to the plan, *e.g.* "together
with the plan annexed and [signed] [executed] as relative hereto"
(although such a reference is not required by the Act); and (3) no
reference to the plan need be made in the warrant of registration.[58]

18–13 *Inconsistencies between boundaries.* In the description of lands in a
conveyance there may be inconsistencies between (1) the boundaries as
described in the deed and as shown on a plan, (2) the lengths of
boundaries as stated in the deed and as delineated on a plan, (3) the
superficial measurement as stated in the deed and shown as enclosed
on a plan, or (4) the superficial measurement and the boundaries as
stated in the deed. If the matter becomes an issue the court will
endeavour to ascertain the true intention of parties, and may admit
extrinsic evidence as to the circumstances of the transaction and
evidence of possession. Absolute rules as to which alternative is to
prevail cannot be formulated since circumstances differ, but from the
decisions of the courts certain broad presumptions may be deduced:
(a) Where boundaries and plan conflict and a measurement of
superficial area is given, the plan will be preferred if it accords with the
measurement.[59] (b) Where boundaries and measurements or plan
(neither being stated to be taxative) conflict the boundaries, if clear,
prevail, the measurements or plan being held to be demonstrative.[60]
So, if the boundaries are clear, a greater area specified by measurements
which are not taxative will not convey more than that enclosed by the
boundaries,[61] nor will a lesser area in the measurements limit that
within the boundaries.[62] (c) Where the boundaries enclose less than a
measurement which is taxative, the purchaser may be entitled to resile
if the shortfall is substantial but not otherwise.[63] (d) Where the
measurement alone is stated it is taxative if the boundaries can be
identified otherwise.[64]

---

[58] See article: 1968 S.L.T. (News) 210.
[59] *North British Rly. Co.* v. *Moon's Trs.* (1879) 6 R. 640.
[60] *Fleming* v. *Baird* (1841) 3 D. 1015; *Blyth's Trs.* v. *Shaw Stewart* (1883) 11 R. 99.
[61] *Currie* v. *Campbell's Trs.* (1888) 16 R. 237.
[62] *Douglas* v. *Lyne* (1630) Mor. 2262; *Currie* v. *Campbell's Trs.*, *supra per* Lord Young at 240.
[63] *Hepburn* v. *Campbell* (1781) Mor. 14168; *Gray* v. *Hamilton* (1801) Mor. App. Sale No. 2;
Montgomerie Bell, *Lectures*, 599.
[64] *Brown* v. *North British Rly. Co.* (1906) 8 F. 534.

-14   (c) Description by reference—common law. Although descriptions by reference tend to be thought of in relation to statutory descriptions by reference discussed *infra*,[65] it should be remembered that it was always competent at common law to identify subjects conveyed by reference to an earlier recorded deed in which they were sufficiently described.[66] The fundamental principle of common law which requires no more than identification may be invoked where an intended statutory description by reference has been blundered, but contains sufficient information to distinguish the subjects from any others and so is a valid description at common law.[67]

Statutory Descriptions by Reference

Description by general name

-15   The earliest form of statutory description by reference was a description by general name. At common law it was competent to insert in a Crown charter a clause of union which enabled sasine to be taken on any part of several lands, even although discontiguous, which sufficed as sasine for the whole.[68] Such union was implied in a barony title without the need of a clause of union, and so a description of lands by the name of the barony embraced the whole lands comprised in it. Section 15 of the Titles to Land (Scotland) Act 1858 introduced description of lands which had been particularly described in a prior recorded writ by specifying a leading name of the lands and a reference to the particular description. That provision was subsequently repealed[69] but substantially re-enacted[70] to the effect that, where several lands are comprehended in one conveyance in favour of the same person or persons, a clause may be inserted declaring that the whole lands conveyed and therein particularly described shall be designed and known in future by one general name. When that deed has been recorded it is sufficient in all subsequent deeds relating to the lands to use the general name only, specifying the county or burgh and county and the recorded conveyance which contained the declaration of the general name, all in the terms of Schedule G to the 1868 Act. These provisions are now largely obsolete, since the statutory description by reference after described[71] is simpler and does not require the specification of a general name. The facility is still used occasionally,

---

[65] paras. 18–15 *et seq.*
[66] *Cattanach's Tr.* v. *Jamieson* (1884) 11 R. 972, *per* Lord President Inglis at 975; *Matheson* v. *Gemmell* (1903) 5 F. 448, *per* Lord McLaren at 451.
[67] An example of frequent occurrence is a description by reference to a deed which does not contain a full particular description but only another description by reference: provided the subjects can be identified from that further reference the description is sufficient.
[68] Menzies, *Lectures*, 550.
[69] Titles to Land Burgage (Scotland) Act 1860, s. 34.
[70] Titles to Land Consolidation (Scotland) Act 1868, s. 13.
[71] para. 18–16.

however, when a number of parcels of land are being included under the name of a single estate.[72]

Description by reference under statute

18–16   The statutory description by reference which is now widely used is based on section 61 of the Conveyancing (Scotland) Act 1874 and section 8 of the Conveyancing (Scotland) Act 1924 and the relative Schedule D. The essential elements to be specified are:

(1) Name of county, or in the case of lands held burgage, the burgh and county in which the subjects are situated. The county is the geographical county, not the county of a city nor a registration area such as the county of the Barony and Regality of Glasgow. It may be helpful, however, in such cases to mention both the geographical county and the registration area, e.g. "in the County of Lanark and for registration purposes in the County of the Barony and Regality of Glasgow." The county specified is that prior to the Local Government (Scotland) Act 1973, not the new region or district thereby established.

(2) The prior recorded deed which contains a particular description of the subjects in terms which are sufficient to identify the deed with specification of the division of the Register of Sasines in which it is recorded and the date of registration. Examples of identifying references to deeds are given in Schedule D.

The following points should be noted:

(a) The prior deed referred to must be a recorded deed which contains a particular description of the subjects, not merely a description by reference, although the latter may be sufficiently identifying as a common law reference.

(b) It is no objection that the deed referred to, having given a particular description of the subjects, goes on to describe them as part of larger subjects which it merely describes by reference.

(c) In specifying the parties to the deed referred to it is sufficient to state their names without designations and where there are several parties acting in the same category it is sufficient to give the name of the first person adding "and others." Where parties act in a fiduciary capacity it is enough to state the capacity without giving individual names, *e.g.* the "Trustees of John Smith."

(d) Although specification of the date of execution of the deed referred to is not required it is usual to include it (as in the examples in Schedule D) and, if there are several dates, it is enough to give the first date, adding "and subsequent dates."

(e) The recording date of the deed referred to, and the division of

---

[72] Burns (333) points out that even for this purpose the use of the statutory facility is unnecessary, but few conveyancers would be content to rely on the general name without reference to a description in prior titles, and specification of the new general name adds little to the ordinary statutory description by reference.

the Register of Sasines in which it is recorded, must be stated. It is competent for the better identification of the deed to state the number of the volume of the Register and of the folio on which it has been recorded. (This further reference may be useful, for example, when trustees or executors have recorded several notices of title to different subjects in the same division of the Register on the same day).

(f) It is desirable to include a short description of the subjects, *e.g.* the postal address, which may suffice to identify the property at common law, as a safeguard against the omission of or error in any of the statutory requirements. Such an omission or error is not necessarily fatal if there are other particulars sufficient to identify the deed.[73]

An obviously false statement in the testing clause of a deed with regard to an erasure in the recording date of another deed referred to in the description having been made before subscription vitiated that reference but the subjects were otherwise sufficiently identified.[74]

(g) Where a part only of subjects described in a former conveyance is being conveyed for the first time as a separate subject it should be described at length, and then stated to be part of the larger subjects from which it has been separated which may be described by reference in the statutory form.

(h) Where a part of subjects which have been described in a former conveyance is being retained and is being excepted from a conveyance of the remainder, the conveyance may be of the whole subjects described by reference in the statutory form under exception of the retained part described at length.

(i) If several subjects have been particularly described in the deed referred to under separate heads and one or more of them are being subsequently conveyed, they may be distinguished in the description by reference in the subsequent conveyance as the subjects (first) or (second and third), as the case may be, described in the deed referred to.

Nature of Rights in Heritable Subjects and References to Particular Rights in Conveyances

Heritable subjects which can be conveyed

-17 The vast majority of heritable subjects which are conveyed are corporeal property such as land or buildings or flats in buildings and in conveyances of such property there are often carried also certain incorporeal rights, either particularly specified or included as pertinents. There are, however, certain incorporeal rights which in feudal theory may exist as separate feudal estates and can be the subject of separate

---

[73] *Matheson* v. *Gemmell* (1903) 5 F. 448 (name of party); *Murray's Tr.* v. *Wood* (1887) 14 R. 856 (omission of recording date).
[74] *Cattanach's Tr.* v. *Jamieson* (1884) 11 R. 972.

conveyances. Examples are *regalia minora*, such as salmon fishings, ports and harbours, ferries, and mines of gold and silver, and teinds may be separated from the lands from which they are due and become a separate feudal estate. When any such incorporeal rights are conveyed along with land they should be separately specified in the deed of conveyance since they may not be within the category of pertinents. As to separate conveyances of these incorporeal rights, see the relevant subject-headings *infra*.[75]

Land and buildings—vertical and horizontal limits

18–18   Land and buildings may be divided both in the vertical and horizontal planes. So an area of land may be subdivided vertically into any number of smaller areas held on separate titles, and may also be subdivided horizontally into any number of layers or strata each of which likewise may be the subject of separate infeftment.[76] Similarly a building may be subdivided both vertically and horizontally into separate flats or separate houses on each flat.

Rights of proprietor of heritable subjects

18–19   A conveyance of heritable property carries to the grantee certain rights implied by law in ownership of the subjects conveyed, unless excluded or restricted by conditions of title, by servitudes or public rights or by statute.

(1) Exclusive possession. He is entitled to exclusive possession of the property owned and may prevent encroachment or trespass by appropriate legal process. The right may be excluded by valid leases or rights of tenancy granted by the proprietor himself or persons whom he represents or by predecessors in title (who will normally have excepted such rights from warrandice in a conveyance of the property). Moreover, leases technically do not exclude possession except physically; the proprietor drawing rent still has civil possession.[77]

(2) Unrestricted use. In principle the proprietor of heritable property may use it for any purpose which he pleases, but this right is frequently restricted by conditions of his title, by the existence of servitudes or public rights such as rights of way, by restraints imposed by the law of neighbourhood or by statutory provisions regulating the use to which the property is put.

---

[75] See para. 18–49.

[76] There are practical limits to the principle. The Keeper of the Register of Sasines refused to record souvenir plots of such insignificant size that they were not separately identifiable on a plan (Keeper's Report, 1969), and he may refuse an application for registration of a souvenir plot under the system of registration of title (Land Registration (Scotland) Act 1979, s. 4(2)(*b*)).

[77] Walker, *Prin.*, III, 100.

(3) Support. The proprietor of heritable property is entitled to support for it, both vertically and laterally, from neighbouring properties and may interdict other persons from withdrawing it or claim damages if that has occurred.[78] Again this right may be varied or restricted by conditions in title deeds or by rights conferred by statute.[79]

(4) Access. The proprietor of heritable property has rights of access to and egress from it, either granted expressly in or implied by law from the terms of the conveyance or, where no other access is practicable, as a servitude of necessity.[80]

(5) Land—vertical extent. Where land conveyed is described by reference to surface boundaries only and no reference is made to subjacent or superjacent strata, *e.g.* a conveyance of land without any reservation of minerals, the grantee has ownership of it *a coelo usque ad centrum*. So if the underlying minerals are to be excluded they must be expressly reserved in the contract of sale of the land[81] and excepted from the conveyance.[82] On the same principle encroachment upon the superjacent air space, even for a temporary period, may be restrained by interdict.[83] The right to minerals may be expropriated by statute.[84]

Special subjects

-20 **(1) Tenements of flatted property.** A tenement of flatted property may be divided in ownership horizontally into separate flats and vertically upon each floor into separate houses or offices. From early times it was recognised that such a division of ownership of parts within a single building involved special rules which have been incorporated in the law of the tenement. As it is described by Stair[85]:

> "When divers owners have parts of the same tenement, it cannot be said to be a perfect division, because the roof remaineth roof to both, and the ground supporteth both; and therefore, by the nature of communion, there are mutual obligations upon both—viz., that the owner of the lower tenement must uphold his tenement as a foundation to the upper, and the owner of the upper tenement must uphold his tenement as a roof and cover to the lower; both which, though they have the resemblance of servitudes, and pass with the thing to singular successors; yet they are rather personal obligations, such as pass in communion even to the singular successors of either party."

Subject to any provisions contained in title deeds, the main principles

---

[78] *Ibid.*, 105–109; N. R. Whitty, (1982) 27 J.L.S. 497 and (1983) 28 J.L.S. 5.
[79] *e.g.* Mines (Working Facilities and Support) Act 1966.
[80] See Chap. 20.
[81] *Whyte* v. *Lee* (1879) 6 R. 699; *Crofts* v. *Stewart's Trs.*, 1927 S.C. (H.L.) 65; *Mossend Theatre Co.* v. *Livingstone*, 1930 S.C. 90; *Campbell* v. *McCutcheon*, 1963 S.C. 505.
[82] See paras. 19–01 to 19–06.
[83] *Brown* v. *Lee Constructions Ltd.*, 1977 S.L.T. (Notes) 61 and authorities there cited.
[84] *e.g.* Petroleum (Production) Act 1934, s. 1; Coal Act 1938, s. 3.
[85] II, vii, 6.

which have been established with regard to the ownership of separate parts within a single building may be summarised as follows: (1) Each proprietor has an exclusive right of ownership of the air space and erections wholly within his own part. (2) The solum and foundations are owned exclusively by the proprietors of the ground flats so far as underlying the parts of the ground floor respectively owned by each, subject to the right of common interest aftermentioned.[86] (3) The outside walls of the building are owned exclusively by each proprietor, section by section so far as enclosing his part, subject to the said right of common interest.[87] On the *ratio* in *Taylor* v. *Dunlop*[88] (where an attic or garret above the top floor was held to be the property of the owner of the top flat), it would appear that the proprietors of the top flats also own the outside walls so far as enclosing the portion of an attic or garret above their respective parts of the top floor, but *quaere* if it is not used exclusively by such proprietors but merely houses water tanks or apparatus which serve the whole building? The outside walls so far as extending below the ground flats to the foundations are the property respectively of the proprietors of the ground floor flats bounded by such walls. (4) Inside division walls so far as separating parts owned exclusively by two proprietors may be regarded as the common property of the two proprietors or alternatively as owned by each *ad medium filum*, although the latter seems the more logical.[89] So far as such walls separate a part owned exclusively and a common part of the tenement, *e.g.* stairs or landings, the rule is probably similar, ownership *ad medium filum* respectively by the individual proprietor and by the proprietors of the common part. (5) Where two tenements share a mutual gable the proprietors in each tenement own the gable *ad medium filum* respectively, with a right of common interest in the other half.[90] (6) The horizontal division between floors is the centre line of the joists or the middle of the floor/ceiling in concrete construction.[91] (7) The roof is the property of the owners of the top flats so far as extending above their respective parts and also the air space or garret between the top floors of the flats and the roof,[92] but again subject to a right of common interest therein as aftermentioned. So far as extending over common parts, *e.g.* the stair, the roof is the common property of all the proprietors of the stair.[93] (8) Conflicting views have been expressed whether chimney vents and chimney stalks (i) are the exclusive property of the owners of the parts of the building which they

---

[86] *Johnston* v. *White* (1877) 4 R. 721; *Calder* v. *Merchant Co. of Edinburgh* (1886) 13 R. 623; *W.V.S. Office Premises Ltd.* v. *Currie*, 1969 S.C. 170.

[87] *Dennistoun* v. *Bell* (1824) 2 S. 784; *Todd* v. *Wilson* (1894) 22 R. 172.

[88] (1872) 11 M. 25.

[89] See K.G.C. Reid, "Law of the Tenement" (1983) 28 J.L.S. 472.

[90] *Trades House of Glasgow* v. *Ferguson*, 1979 S.L.T. 187.

[91] *McArly* v. *French's Trs.* (1883) 10 R. 574.

[92] *Taylor* v. *Dunlop, supra; Sanderson's Trs.* v. *Yule* (1897) 25 R. 211.

[93] J.G.S. Cameron, *Conveyancing Review*, II, 102; Reid, *op. cit.* at 475.

respectively serve or (ii) as regards vents within outside walls are the property of the respective owners of the sections of the walls through which they pass and as regards chimney stalks are the common property of all the proprietors who have vents therein.[94] (9) Common passages and stairs are the common property of all the proprietors of parts of the tenement.[95] (10) Curtilage ground of the tenement is owned by the proprietors of the ground flats so far as *ex adverso* their respective properties, again subject to the right of common interest.[96]

-21   The ownership of each part of the tenement is burdened by a right of common interest in favour of the proprietors of other parts of the tenement. Every proprietor of a part of the tenement is entitled to rely upon support for his property from below, shelter from above and the absence of water penetration through outer walls owned by any other proprietor which adversely affects his part. Any proprietor, however, is entitled to make alterations on a part of the tenement which is his exclusive property, so long as he does not adversely affect that of another or damage the efficacy of the part owned by him in providing the support or shelter involved in common interest.[97] On the other hand, where common parts of a tenement are expressly created as common property, no alterations can be made without the consent of all the proprietors who own them in common.

-22   In conveyancing practice there are two methods which may be used in conveyances of flatted property in a tenement. The first is to convey the subjects acquired with such variations from the law of the tenement as have been agreed, but leaving many matters to be regulated otherwise by that law. The second is to specify, either in the conveyance itself or in a deed of conditions applicable to the whole tenement, the rights of ownership and relative obligations affecting the parts of the tenement which have been created common property and to include provisions for the administration of the tenement as a whole, leaving only comparatively minor matters to be determined by the law of the tenement. Both methods are still employed, but the second is now most commonly favoured and in the case of commercial buildings is almost universal. Its main advantages are: (1) It spreads the burden of maintenance of the main structure of the building, roof, external walls and internal bearing walls, etc., equitably over all the proprietors of parts, either in agreed proportions or in accordance with gross annual values. (2) It facilitates efficient management of the building, usually by empowering a factor to instruct relatively minor repairs to common parts and by enabling major repairs to be authorised by a majority of

---

[94] *Whitmore* v. *Stuart & Stuart* (1902) 10 S.L.T. 290.
[95] *Anderson* v. *Dalrymple* (1799) Mor. 12831; *W.V.S. Office Premises Ltd.* v. *Currie, supra.* See Reid, *op. cit.* at 475.
[96] *Calder* v. *Merchant Co. of Edinburgh, supra.*
[97] *Todd* v. *Wilson* (1894) 22 R. 172. Cf. *Gellatly* v. *Arrol* (1863) 1 M. 592.

the proprietors. (3) It may provide for the use of all parts of the building and its curtilage ground (which is usually made common property) with the object of preserving their appearance and amenity.[98] (4) It ensures that all parts of the building are covered by a common policy of insurance.

(2) Water rights

18–23   *(a) Surface water.* Surface water and water percolating underground, not confined in a particular channel, may be appropriated by the owner of the land upon or through which it passes, whether or not that affects the interest of his neighbours. The same principle applies to stagna, *i.e.* pools or marshes which have no permanent stream flowing into them nor, except in time of heavy rain, an outlet emanating from them, and also to a stream which rises, has its course and falls into the sea all within the lands of a single proprietor. Since these water rights are *partes soli* they do not require special mention in a conveyance of the land.[99]

18–24   *(b) Non-navigable rivers and streams.* If the land conveyed includes the watercourse and both banks, ownership of the *alveus* or bed of the stream is carried by a conveyance of the land without the need of separate mention. If the river or stream forms a boundary of the land conveyed, the disponee, in the absence of any relevant qualification, will acquire ownership of the bank on his own side and the *alveus* to the *medium filum.* He may use the water for primary purposes but not for manufacturing purposes or irrigation unless he has acquired a right to do so by prescriptive use, and he must allow the water to pass downstream without significant diminution in volume and without pollution.[1]

18–25   *(c) Navigable non-tidal rivers.* The position as to ownership of the *alveus* and banks is the same as in the case of non-navigable rivers, but the public have a right of use for the navigation of any craft or vessel.[2, 3] A riparian proprietor has the same rights to use the water as in the case of a non-navigable river, but may not alter the *alveus* so as to affect adversely the right of navigation.

18–26   *(d) Navigable and tidal rivers.* The *alveus* is vested in the Crown in trust for the public,[4] and also the foreshore unless it has been included in terms of a grant to a riparian proprietor.[5]

---

[98] See style in para. 19–37.
[99] Walker, *Prin.*, III, 111.
[1] *Ibid.*, III, 113–115.
[2] *Orr Ewing* v. *Colquhoun's Trs.* (1877) 4 R. (H.L.) 116; *Wills' Trs.* v. *Cairngorm Canoeing and Sailing School Ltd.*, 1976 S.C. (H.L.) 30.
[3] Walker, *op. cit.*, III, 113.
[4] *Lord Advocate* v. *Hamilton* (1852) 1 Macq. 46.
[5] *Lord Advocate* v. *Lord Blantyre* (1879) 6 R. (H.L.) 72; *Buchanan* v. *Lord Advocate* (1882) 9 R. 1218.

(3) Fishings

27   *(a) Fishings other than salmon fishings.* The right to fishings, other than salmon fishings, in non-tidal rivers is a natural incident of ownership available to the riparian proprietors and passes with a conveyance of land which includes the banks. The right of white fishing in tidal rivers is akin to that in the sea; it is vested in the Crown in trust for the public.[6] As regards inland lochs (i) if surrounded completely by the lands of one proprietor he has an exclusive right to the loch and fishings,[7] or (ii) if enclosed by lands belonging to several proprietors they have a common right to fish over the whole loch.[8] (As to ownership of the solum of a loch see paragraph 18–11 *supra*.) The position is apparently similar in relation to an artificial reservoir, subject to any special provisions of statute relating to it.[9] The right to fishings of this kind is a pertinent of the riparian lands and does not require to be separately specified in a conveyance of them, although it sometimes is specially mentioned; where it is so mentioned the safe practice is to repeat that in subsequent conveyances. The right is not capable of being created as a separate feudal estate and indeed until recently could not be made the subject of a lease which was valid against singular successors,[10] but the law has now been altered by the Freshwater and Salmon Fisheries (Scotland) Act 1976[11] to the effect that a tenant under a written lease of fishings, including trout fishings, granted for consideration for a period of not less than a year, will now have the protection against singular successors given by the Leases Act 1449.

28   *(b) Salmon fishings.* The right to fish for salmon is *inter regalia*, is a distinct feudal estate and requires separate conveyance: it is not carried by a grant of riparian lands with parts and pertinents.[12] A right to salmon fishings may be acquired by (i) an express grant from the Crown of lands with salmon fishings,[13] (ii) a Crown grant of lands with fishings followed by prescriptive possession of the salmon fishings,[14] (iii) a barony title, with or without a general clause of fishings, followed by prescriptive possession of salmon fishings,[15] (iv) a separate grant from the Crown of the salmon fishings alone,[16] (v) a feu grant, with pertinents and mention of fishings in the tenendas clause, of land which had formed part of a barony title which included fishings, where

---

[6] *Orr Ewing* v. *Colquhoun's Trs.*, *supra.*
[7] *Montgomerie* v. *Watson* (1861) 23 D. 635.
[8] *Menzies* v. *Wentworth* (1901) 3 F. 941.
[9] *Kilsyth Fish Protection Association* v. *McFarlane*, 1937 S.C. 757.
[10] *Earl of Galloway* v. *Duke of Bedford* (1902) 4 F. 851.
[11] s. 4.
[12] *McKendrick* v. *Wilson*, 1970 S.L.T. (Sh.Ct.) 39.
[13] *Baroness Gray* v. *Richardson* (1876) 3 R. 1031; 1877 4 R. (H.L.) 76.
[14] *Stuart* v. *McBarnet* (1868) 6 M. (H.L.) 123.
[15] *Lord Advocate* v. *Lord Lovat* (1880) 7 R. (H.L.) 122.
[16] *Hogarth* v. *Grant* (1901) 8 S.L.T. 324.

salmon fishings had been enjoyed by the grantee for more than the period of positive prescription,[17] or even (vi) a disposition from a subject with fishings followed by prescriptive possession of salmon fishings.[18] In practice a conveyancer taking a title to salmon fishings must be satisfied that the right has been created in the granter or his authors in an appropriate mode and must ensure that the right is specifically conveyed in the disposition to his client. As to the extent of the right of riparian proprietors to fish over a river, see *Fothringham* v. *Passmore*[19] and earlier authorities there cited.

18–29   **(4) Game.** Game are *ferae naturae* and so are not the property of any person. The owner of land, however, has the right to take or kill game upon it, but it is a personal privilege, not a right which is inherent in or necessarily attached to ownership of the land. The proprietor of land may grant a lease of shootings over it and if the lease is of land together with shooting rights it will have the protection of the Leases Act 1449, but a lease of shootings as a separate and independent heritable right or burden is not enforceable against a singular successor in the ownership of the lands.[19a] An agricultural tenant has no right at common law to kill game on land leased to him[20] but has a statutory right, which cannot be contractually withheld, to kill rabbits and hares to protect his crops.[21]

18–30   **(5) Sea-bed and undersea minerals.** The Crown has a right of property in the sea-bed which can be alienated subject always to the public rights of navigation and white fishing.[22] The minerals under the sea-bed also belong to the Crown but may be alienated,[23] and they may be acquired under a barony title to the land *ex adverso* followed by working of the minerals for the period of positive prescription.[24]

18–31   **(6) Foreshore.** The foreshore (land between the high and low-water marks of ordinary spring tides) is also owned by the Crown, but may be alienated by express grant from the Crown[25] or acquired by a Crown grant which is habile to include it followed by possession for the relevant period of positive prescription[26] or by such possession upon a barony title of lands bordering the sea even although the foreshore was not expressly included in the grant.[27] In all cases, however, ownership

---

[17] *Lord Advocate* v. *McCulloch* (1874) 2 R. 27.
[18] *Lord Advocate* v. *Sinclair* (1867) 5 M. (H.L.) 97.
[19] 1984 S.L.T. 401.
[19a] *Beckett* v. *Bisset*, 1921 2 S.L.T. 33.
[20] *Welwood* v. *Husband* (1874) 1 R. 507.
[21] Ground Game Act 1880 as amended by Agriculture (Scotland) Act 1948, ss. 48, 50 and Crofters (Scotland) Act 1955, s. 27.
[22] *Crown Estate Commissioners* v. *Fairlie Yacht Slip Ltd.*, 1976 S.C. 161.
[23] *Cunninghame* v. *Assessor for Ayrshire* (1895) 22 R. 596.
[24] *Wemyss* v. *Lord Advocate* (1896) 24 R. 216, rev. (1899) 2 F. (H.L.) 1.
[25] Bell, *Prin.*, ss. 642–644.
[26] *Young* v. *North British Rly. Co.* (1887) 14 R. (H.L.) 53; *Marquess of Ailsa* v. *Monteforte*, 1937 S.C. 805.
[27] *Agnew* v. *Lord Advocate* (1873) 11 M. 309; *Buchanan and Geils* v. *Lord Advocate* (1882) 9 R. 1218; *Luss Estates Co.* v. *B.P. Oil Grangemouth Refinery Ltd.*, 1982 S.L.T. 457.

of the foreshore is subject to the rights of use by the public for navigation and recreation.[28]

(7) Roads and streets

-32   *(a) Public highways.* In general the solum of public roads and streets is owned by the proprietors of adjacent property unless it has been acquired from them[29]; if the property on either side is owned by different proprietors the boundary is the *medium filum.*[30] The regional or islands council is the roads authority having the responsibility of maintenance of public roads[31] and members of the public have the right of passage over them. Trunk roads and special roads are usually constructed on land acquired for the purpose by the Secretary of State for Scotland.[32] Streets and pavements within a burgh which have been taken over by the roads authority are in a position similar to public roads; the solum is owned by the proprietors of adjoining property but the streets and pavements are maintained by the regional or islands council.[33] Public roads or streets cannot be encroached upon by proprietors of adjoining property,[34] but the regional or islands council may acquire land from such proprietors or other persons in connection with construction or improvement of a public road.[35] When a public road or street is stopped up, the solum vests in the owners of land adjoining it subject to any prior claim based on title.[36]

-33   *(b) Private roads or streets.* Private roads or streets and footpaths belong to the owner of the ground on which they are constructed, who remains responsible for their maintenance until they are taken over by the regional or islands council as public. The council normally requires that the road or street and footpath are made up to an acceptable standard by the private owner or owners at his or their expense before being taken over, so that it is important in the examination of title of a newly-built property which is being purchased to ascertain whether the road or street and footpath have been so taken over. Frequently the purchase of a house in a scheme of development involving many houses is being completed when the roads have not yet been completed and surfaced, in which case the purchaser may wish to be protected against liability for the costs of completion by retention of part of the

---

[28] *Hope* v. *Bennewith* (1904) 6 F. 1004; *Marquis of Bute* v. *McKirdy & McMillan Ltd.*, 1937 S.C. 93. District and islands councils now have powers to regulate use of the seashore (Civic Government (Scotland) Act 1982, s. 121).

[29] *Galbreath* v. *Armour* (1845) 4 Bell's App. 374; *Kelvinside Estate Co.* v. *Donaldson's Trs.* (1879) 6 R. 995.

[30] *Magistrates of Ayr* v. *Dobbie* (1898) 25 R. 1184.

[31] Local Government (Scotland) Act 1973, s. 133; Roads (Scotland) Act 1984, ss. 1, 151.

[32] Roads (Scotland) Act 1984, ss. 5, 6, 7.

[33] "Road" now includes "street" and "footway" includes "pavement"—Roads (Scotland) Act 1984, s. 151.

[34] *Donald* v. *Esslemont & MacIntosh*, 1923 S.C. 122.

[35] Roads (Scotland) Act 1984, s. 104.

[36] *Ibid.*, s. 115.

price or by an obligation by the selling builder supported by a guarantee or road bond, but much depends upon the negotiating strengths of the parties.[36a]

18–34   **(8) Drains and sewers.** A pipe or drain situated within the curtilage of private property, so far as it serves only the building or any buildings or yards appurtenant to buildings within the same curtilage, belongs to and is maintainable by the owner of that property; beyond that point ownership of it and of the sewer into which it leads is vested in the local authority, normally the regional or islands council, who are responsible for maintenance of it.[37] In effect (i) if a pipe or drain serves only one building and ancillary buildings or yards within the curtilage of the property then, up to the point where it crosses the street or road boundary of the property, it is owned and maintained by the proprietor of the property, but (ii) if a pipe or drain, while still within the curtilage of one property, is joined by another pipe or drain serving an adjoining property or adjoining properties, then the junction itself and the common pipe or drain from the junction to the sewer belong to and are maintainable by the local authority. The local authority have extensive powers to control the discharge of trade effluents into sewers.[38]

18–35   **(9) Ports and harbours, ferries, fairs and markets, royal forests, gold and silver mines and treasure trove.** All of these belong to the Crown, but may be communicated by express grant to a subject. For fuller particulars see the undernoted text.[39]

18–36   **(10) Coal and petroleum and natural gas.** Coal and mines of coal and minerals worked in association therewith are now vested in the National Coal Board under the Coal Industry Nationalisation Act 1946—see paragraph 19–08 *infra.* Petroleum and natural gas occurring in their natural state are now owned by the State by virtue of the Petroleum (Production) Act 1934—see Volume 1, paragraphs 8–59 to 8–70 *supra.*

Discontiguous lands

18–37   Where the subjects of a conveyance comprise two or more parcels of discontiguous lands, then, unless (a) they have been erected into a barony estate[40] or (b) they have been comprehended in a description

---

[36a] The Security for Private Road Works (Scotland) Regulations made under s. 17 of the Roads (Scotland) Act 1984 (operative from April 1, 1986) now provide that in the case of private developments no building works shall commence until any construction consent required for a private road which has not been constructed and security in respect of it in the form of a bond in favour of the local roads authority or a deposit lodged with the authority has been provided (S.I. 1985 No. 2080 (S. 159)).

[37] Sewerage (Scotland) Act 1968, ss. 16, 59.

[38] *Ibid.*, ss. 24–38.

[39] Walker, *Prin.*, III, 40–47.

[40] See para. 18–07.

by general name,[41] the various parcels should be separately described. This is peculiarly important if any discontiguous part is held merely as a pertinent.[42]

Parts and pertinents

-38   There are few topics in the field of heritable conveyancing upon which judicial decisions and *dicta* are more confusing than the significance of the addition of parts and pertinents, or simply pertinents, to a description of the subjects in a conveyance. On the one hand it was stated by Lord Justice-Clerk Hope[43]: "A grant of the lands of A is as extensive as a grant of A with parts and pertinents." On the other hand in numerous cases where pertinents have been expressed in a conveyance the fact has been judicially emphasised and decisions pronounced apparently based on the effect of the expression,[44] and in *Duke of Argyll* v. *Campbell*[45] Lord Johnston spoke of the "distinction between a title which is capable of being construed as including a subject, and one which cannot be so construed but of which the subject may be a pertinent." From the various decisions it is possible to draw certain broad conclusions, *viz.*—(1) An incorporeal heritable right such as a servitude will more readily be included as a pertinent than corporeal heritable subjects such as land or buildings, since the latter may be plainly excluded by the description of the principal lands conveyed. (2) Corporeal subjects may be included as pertinents of lands described generally[46]; that is normally impossible if the subjects lie outwith the limits of a bounding title.[47] (3) Corporeal subjects will more readily be included as part and pertinent if they are contiguous to the principal subjects[48] than if they are not, although discontiguity is not conclusive.[49] (4) Heritable subjects or rights will more easily be included as pertinents if their use[50] or legal quality[51] is accessory to the principal subjects. (5) Possession, particularly where it exceeds the period of positive prescription, is an important element in the determination of whether a subject has become part or pertinent.[52] For a list of items which have been admitted as pertinents in the circumstances of the relative cases, see the undernoted text.[53]

---

[41] *e.g.* as in para. 18–15.
[42] See Burns, 334.
[43] In *Gordon* v. *Grant* (1850) 13 D. 1 at 7.
[44] *e.g. Cooper's Trs.* v. *Stark's Trs.* (1898) 25 R. 1160; *Meacher* v. *Blair-Oliphant*, 1913 S.C. 417.
[45] 1912 S.C. 458 at 491.
[46] *Dalrymple* v. *Earl of Stair* (1841) 3 D. 837; *Agnew* v. *Lord Advocate* (1873) 11 M. 309.
[47] *Gordon* v. *Grant, supra*; *Magistrates of St. Monance* v. *Mackie* (1845) 7 D. 582; *Lord Advocate* v. *Hunt* (1867) 5 M. (H.L.) 1. *Cf. Cooper's Trs.* v. *Stark's Trs.*, *supra*, *per* Lord McLaren at 1169.
[48] Ersk., II, vi, 3.
[49] *Forsyth* .v *Durie* (1632) Mor. 9629; *Glendonwyne* v. *Gordon* (1716) Mor. 9643; *Lord Advocate* v. *Hunt*, *supra*.
[50] *McArly* v. *French's Trs.* (1883) 10 R. 574.
[51] *Meacher* v. *Blair-Oliphant, supra.*
[52] *Cooper's Trs.* v. *Stark's Trs.*, *supra*; *Meacher* v. *Blair-Oliphant*, *supra.*
[53] *Encyclopaedia of the Laws of Scotland*, Vol. 10, 576, 577.

18–39   In practice it is recommended that in all cases a description of heritable subjects in a conveyance should expressly include parts and pertinents or, at least, pertinents. The reference to pertinents should be inserted *after* the specification of parish or county so that they are not limited geographically,[54] although if they are outwith the area covered by the division of the Register of Sasines in which the conveyance is recorded there will not be a recorded title to them.[55]

Joint property

18–40   Joint property, of which the most important example is property owned by trustees, is held by a single undivided title to the whole. Upon the death or resignation of any trustee his interest accresces automatically to the surviving or remaining trustees or trustee.[56] None of the joint owners has a severable interest which he can alienate *inter vivos* or *mortis causa* or burden, and dealings with the property may be carried out only by all the joint proprietors or in the case of trustees by a majority and quorum of them. Where the heritable property of a partnership is vested in named partners as trustees for the firm by a recorded title then, so long as any one or more of those infeft trustees survives, whether or not he remains a partner, the title to the property remains vested by accretion in him or them notwithstanding changes in the personnel of the partnership. Accordingly a disposition of the property or a security over it may be granted by the survivors or survivor of the original trustees without the need of deduction of title, although the transaction is usually entered into with consent of all the current partners who are joined as parties to the deed. When a partner who was infeft as a trustee resigns, consideration should be given to the preparation of a minute of resignation and possibly a deed of assumption and conveyance in favour of additional trustees, and, if the number of the infeft trustees is reduced by death to one, new trustees should be assumed to prevent the trust lapsing on his death.[57]

Common property

18–41   Where property is owned in common by several proprietors, each has a title to his own *pro indiviso* share which he may convey or dispose of by *inter vivos* or testamentary deed and which passes on his death to his executors.[58] So long as the property is owned in common, decisions relating to it must be taken by all the proprietors,[59] any of

---

[54] *Gordon* v. *Grant, supra.*
[55] *Hepburn* v. *Duke of Gordon* (1823) 2 S. 525.
[56] *Magistrates of Banff* v. *Ruthin Castle Ltd.*, 1944 S.C. 36; *Munro* v. *Munro*, 1972 S.L.T. (Sh.Ct.) 6.
[57] See Vol. I, para. 11–74.
[58] *Schaw* v. *Black* (1889) 16 R. 336; *Magistrates of Banff* v. *Ruthin Castle Ltd., supra.* For rather special cases, see *Munro* v. *Munro*, 1972 S.L.T. (Sh.Ct.) 6 and *Steele* v. *Caldwell*, 1979 S.L.T. 228.
[59] *Grozier* v. *Downie* (1871) 9 M. 826; *Price* v. *Watson*, 1951 S.C. 359.

whom may forbid alteration or extraordinary use of the property[60] but not necessary repair or restoration.[61] Any proprietor may require division of the lands by agreement or, in the absence of agreement, raise an action for their division[62] or, where division would reduce the value of each party's share, sale and division of the price.[63] The sale may be by private bargain after adequate advertisement.[64] The existence of a heritable security does not necessarily prevent the exercise of a right of division and sale.[65] It is competent for a proprietor of common property to bar himself contractually from exercising his right of division and sale.[66] Almost certainly the right may not be exercised where it subsists in property which is necessarily ancillary to the ownership of more valuable property which is not being disposed of along with it, as in the case of a right of common property in the roof, walls or stairs of flatted property in a tenement owned in connection with a flat therein, although it is highly improbable that any proprietor would seek to do so or that any person would buy it if he did. The position may be different if the ancillary property owned in common is capable of being used separately from the principal subject, as in the case of amenity ground held in common by proprietors of adjacent houses.[67]

Common gables

8–42   A common gable is a species of common property with special conditions based on custom and not easily reconcilable with feudal theory.[68] In urban areas the builder of a property may erect it to the extent of one-half on his own ground and the other half on his neighbour's ground and so construct it that it may be used by his neighbour when he comes to build as a gable common to both properties. Until his neighbour makes use of the gable the builder has a right of property in the one-half of it built on his own ground and the right to prevent any other person from using it until he makes payment of one-half of the cost of its erection,[68a] but when that payment is made

---

[60] *Taylor* v. *Dunlop* (1872) 11 M. 25; *Sutherland* v. *Barbour* (1887) 15 R. 62.

[61] *Deans* v. *Woolfson*, 1922 S.C. 221.

[62] *Grant* v. *Heriot's Trust* (1906) 8 F. 647 at 658; *Morrison* v. *Kirk*, 1912 S.C. 44. As to the court's discretion where the property is a matrimonial home, see Matrimonial Homes (Family Protection) (Scotland) Act 1981, s. 19.

[63] *Thom* v. *Macbeth* (1875) 3 R. 161; *Morrison* v. *Kirk, supra.*

[64] *Campbell* v. *Murray*, 1972 S.C. 310.

[65] *Morrison* v. *Kirk, supra.*

[66] *Morrison* v. *Kirk, supra.* at 47.

[67] *Grant* v. *Heriot's Trust, supra.*

[68] *Wallace* v. *Brown*, June 21, 1808, F.C.; *Lamont* v. *Cumming* (1875) 2 R. 784 at p. 787; *Sinclair* v. *Brown Bros.* (1882) 10 R. 45 at p. 50; *Robertson* v. *Scott* (1886) 13 R. 1127. *Cf. Jack* v. *Begg* (1875) 3 R. 35 at p. 41.

[68a] There may be a question, arising from the use of the word "value" in certain decisions, whether it is one-half of the original cost of construction of the gable or its value at the time when it is used by the adjoining owner that has to be paid—see W.M. Gordon, (1980) 25 J.L.S. 141. It is submitted that the former is correct: the right to claim a specific sum of money does not alter with changes in the value of money.

the owner of the adjoining ground is free to use the gable which then is owned by each proprietor to the extent of the one-half on his own land with a common interest in the whole.[69] The second builder may "take band," *i.e.* insert binding stones and beams into the gable and make fireplaces and vents therein and may even heighten and widen it,[70] but on condition of paying to the first builder one-half of the cost of erecting the original gable. Subject to any contractual provision imposed in the title deeds, the right to claim payment is one of recompense,[71] and is a real right which passes to singular successors of the original builder[72] without special mention in the conveyance.[73] Where a common gable has been built but has not yet been used by the neighbouring proprietor the right to claim payment of the half cost of its erection should be specifically reserved in any conveyance of the original property.[74] Similarly the obligation to pay transmits against singular successors in the ownership of the burdened property.[75] The person who uses the gable is liable to pay one-half of the cost of only so much of the gable as he actually uses,[76] but, once a gable has been used to its full height on both sides and paid for, it becomes the property of the two proprietors and one does not cease to be liable for one-half of the cost of maintenance of the whole gable even although he subsequently demolishes his property wholly or partially.[77]

18-43 The practice rules in relation to common gables between property A (on which the gable was originally erected) and the adjoining property B may be stated briefly:

(1) If A is sold before the gable has been used to its full height by the owner of B, reserve in the disposition the right to claim the half cost of the gable, *e.g.*

> "Reserving to me and my executors and representatives right to recover the one half or other appropriate proportion of the cost of all common or mutual gables, walls, [roads], drains and others constructed in connection with the said subjects from other persons who may use the same or become liable for any part of the cost thereof, and that without prejudice to the right of my said disponee and his foresaids to continue to use the same without payment."

(2) If B is being purchased and the gable has not yet been used for buildings on B (i) check whether there is any obligation in the title

---

[69] This is the view of Lord Rutherfurd Clark in *Robertson* v. *Scott, supra* at 1132, and is probably the most satisfactory theory but other dicta in the same case are not altogether consistent with it; see *Trades House of Glasgow* v. *Ferguson*, 1979 S.L.T. 187 at 190.

[70] *Lamont* v. *Cumming, supra* at 788; *Robertson* v. *Scott, supra*; *Bryce* v. *Norman* (1895) 2 S.L.T. 471.

[71] *Sinclair* v. *Brown Bros., supra* at 52.

[72] *Hunter* v. *Luke* (1846) 8 D. 787; *Rodger* v. *Russell* (1873) 11 M. 671.

[73] *Law* v. *Monteith* (1855) 18 D. 125 at 130.

[74] *Calder* v. *Pope* (1900) 8 S.L.T. 149. *Cf. Earl of Moray* v. *Aytoun* (1858) 21 D. 33.

[75] *Law* v. *Monteith, supra; Rodger* v. *Russell, supra* at 673.

[76] *Sanderson* v. *Geddes* (1874) 1 R. 1198.

[77] *Trades House of Glasgow* v. *Ferguson*, 1979 S.L.T. 187.

deeds to use and pay for one-half of the gable within a particular period and (ii) advise the purchaser of the potential liability to pay one-half of the cost of the gable when and to the extent that he uses it.

(3) If A or B is being purchased and buildings thereon have been recently constructed, check that there is no outstanding liability for the cost or maintenance of the common gable.

Division walls and fences

-44   A wall or fence forming the boundary between two plots of ground, if erected one-half on each side of the boundary, is the mutual property of the two proprietors; if erected wholly on one side of the boundary it is the property of the owner of the ground on which it is erected. A mutual wall or fence cannot be altered except with the consent of both owners,[78] and both are equally liable for its maintenance and, when necessary, renewal. Such a wall cannot be converted into a common gable except by consent of both proprietors.[79] As to march fences see the undernoted text.[80]

Commonty, common grazings and runrig

-45   See Walker, *Principles*, Volume III, pages 131–138.

Teind and stipend[81]

-46   Teinds are burdens on the fruits of lands, not *debita fundi*. As a separate tenement they should in theory be expressly mentioned in a conveyance of lands but in most cases they will be held to be carried by a conveyance of the relevant land without special mention.[82] Where there is a title to teinds, in the case of extensive rural areas, however, it is suggested that a reference to them, *e.g.* "together with the teinds," be inserted in a conveyance. Since the standardisation of stipends under the provisions of the Church of Scotland (Property and Endowments) Act 1925[83] most teinds have been surrendered or surplus teinds sold to the heritors, so that it is now seldom that teinds have any significant value.

-47   Stipends, formerly a burden on the teinds, have now been standardised and are fixed money payments payable half-yearly to the General Trustees of the Church of Scotland (standard charges) which are real burdens on the lands from the teinds on which the stipend was exigible. They are preferable to all other securities or burdens except incidents of tenure and may be recovered by the General Trustees in the same

---

[78] *Lamont* v. *Cumming* (1875) 2 R. 784 at 790.
[79] *Jack* v. *Begg* (1875) 3 R. 35.
[80] Walker, *Prin.*, III, 131.
[81] See *Encyclopaedia of the Laws of Scotland*, Vol. 14, 350; Walker, *Prin.*, III, 152 *et seq.*
[82] *Watt's Trs.* v. *King* (1869) 8 M. 132.
[83] ss. 16–18.

manner as feuduties.[84] In the rare cases where the teinds have not been surrendered or sold the heritor of the lands from which they are due may deduct the amount of the standardised stipend from the payment of the teinds.[85] Standard charges or stipends are not redeemable voluntarily under section 4 of the Land Tenure Reform (Scotland) Act 1974, but standard charges (not stipends) are compulsorily redeemable on a sale of the burdened lands under section 5 or 6 of the Act. In practice the burden of standard charge may be disregarded in transactions relating to urban property, but can be significant in transactions relating to large areas of rural land.

Entailed estates[86]

18–48   An entail could formerly be created in a charter or disposition of the superiority or *dominium utile* of lands whereby the succession thereto was settled on a series of heirs, not being the heirs-at-law, with clauses prohibiting alienation, contracting of debts affecting the estate and alteration of the succession prescribed by the entail, fenced with irritant and resolutive clauses. The deed creating the entail required to be recorded in the Register of Tailzies as well as in the Register of Sasines. Since 1914 the creation of new entails is incompetent[87] and entails for conveyancing purposes are now relevant only in relation to the powers of heirs in possession and disentail under pre-1914 entails. The Register of Tailzies remains open for purposes other than the creation of entails, particularly in relation to the registration of instruments of disentail. Almost all entailed estates have now been disentailed and there have been few recent statutory provisions or judicial decisions on the subject, which has become a matter of largely historical interest. As regards subsisting pre-1914 entails: (1) as to statutory relaxations of the fetters of entails and the powers of heirs of entail in possession, reference may be made to the undernoted texts[88]; (2) as regards procedure and consents required for disentail see Burns, pages 416 *et seq.*; and (3) as to special provisions relating to entails in succession, see Volume IV of this work.

Subjects which may require express mention in conveyances

18–49   **(1) Salmon fishings,** if conveyed as a separate estate, will be the principal subject of the conveyance, and should be described with particulars of their geographical extent and the rights, whether sole or exclusive, together with any necessary servitudes or rights of access.

---

[84] 1925 Act, s. 12.
[85] *Ibid.*, s. 17.
[86] *Encyclopaedia of the Laws of Scotland*, Vol. 6, p. 195; Walker, *Prin.*, III, 134.
[87] Entail (Scotland) Act 1914, s. 2.
[88] Menzies, *Lectures*, 719 *et seq.*; Montgomerie Bell, *Lectures*, 1012 *et seq.*; Wood, *Lectures*, 319 *et seq.*; Craigie, *Heritable Rights*, 694 *et seq.*, and texts cited in n. 86, *supra.*

Even if the conveyance is of riparian lands, the title to which includes or may be construed to include salmon fishings, the fishings should be specifically mentioned although their extent and the nature of the rights may be described by reference to an earlier deed. In Orkney and Shetland it appears that salmon and sea-trout fishings are not *inter regalia* even although the title to the particular subjects has been feudalised,[89] but the safe course is to mention them in a conveyance.

(2) Foreshore. It may be evident from the terms of the existing title that foreshore is included,[90] but if the title is dubious and possession of the foreshore has in fact been enjoyed it would be advisable to incorporate foreshore by express mention in a conveyance, so that subsequent possession during the prescriptive period (20 years) could be attributed to a title sufficient in respect of its terms to be a clear foundation.

(3) Other regalia minora. Such of these as are capable of alienation, *e.g.* ports and harbours, ferries, fairs and markets, royal forests, gold and silver mines and treasure trove, and have been granted should be mentioned expressly in conveyances.

(4) Fixtures and fittings. Where items are clearly heritable fixtures which are carried with a conveyance of the heritable subjects it is unnecessary to mention them specially, although a general reference to them is often included. It is technically inappropriate to mention in a conveyance items which are plainly moveable: the contract of sale will determine those which are included in the sale,[91] but in doubtful cases mention may be made of them in the conveyance.[92]

(5) Claims for compensation or damages. In principle a purchaser of heritable property takes it as it stands with all the incidental rights belonging to it as a piece of property, but a claim for compensation or damages in respect of injury caused to the property before the sale does not pass to the purchaser with the conveyance of the property.[93] That broad statement, however, leaves certain detailed questions unanswered, *e.g.* (1) When does the claim arise in circumstances where the cause of injury has commenced before the sale and continues after it, so that it can only be quantified with precision after the sale? (2) Is the relevant date of sale that of the contract, or of entry, or of delivery of the conveyance? As to the first question the general rule is that the whole loss, past and anticipated, must be recovered in a single action,[94] but in the case of continuing injury it is competent to claim for loss suffered to

---

[89] *Lord Advocate* v. *Balfour*, 1907 S.C. 1360.
[90] See paras. 18–11 and 18–31.
[91] *Jamieson* v. *Welsh* (1900) 3 F. 176.
[92] For items which are heritable or moveable, see paras. 15–35 to 15–37.
[93] *Burrell* v. *Simpson* (1876) 4 R. 177, *per* Lord President Inglis at 180; *Caledonian Rly. Co.* v. *Watt* (1875) 2 R. 917. See also *Stevenson* v. *Steel Co. of Scotland Ltd.* (1899) 1 F. (H.L.) 91.
[94] *Stevenson* v. *Pontifex and Wood* (1887) 15 R. 125.

date reserving claims for loss yet to be sustained.[95] As to the second question Burns[96] considers different possible views, but it is suggested that the date of completion of the contract is the relevant date, since the risk of damage to the property passes on completion of the contract[97] and so also should the right to compensation. In practice, (a) if the claim has arisen before the completion of the contract it does not pass with the conveyance and requires to be specially assigned if the grantee is to have the benefit of it, but if the right is to be retained by the granter it may be advisable expressly to reserve it in order to obviate any question as to title to sue, (b) if the claim arises after completion of the contract the seller must expressly reserve it if that is the basis of the bargain, and (c) if the claim is a continuing one for damage which has accrued partially before the contract but will continue after it, probably the most convenient arrangement is to assign the granter's rights in the conveyance with an appropriate addition to the price possibly variable depending upon the amount ultimately recovered.

(6) Collateral obligations and rights of relief against parties other than the superior. Obligations of relief, *e.g.* from stipend, if contained in a feu grant, continue enforceable against the superior by successive vassals as parties to a continuing contract of feu and do not require special assignation.[98] Collateral obligations or rights of relief undertaken by any other party in respect of land, unless they have been created real, require to be specially assigned,[98a] and may not be assignable to a number of different persons.[99] The rule does not apply to a general disposition, as to trustees for creditors or testamentary trustees, since that carries the whole rights of the granter, but if testamentary trustees grant a special disposition to a legatee of property bequeathed to him the right to enforce the collateral obligations should be expressly assigned.

(7) Minerals under railways. These are excluded from conveyances of land for railways (unless expressly conveyed) under the Railways Clauses Consolidation (Scotland) Act 1845.[1]

(8) Rights to lairs in churchyards. These are not carried to singular successors by a conveyance of the land to which the right of sepulture attached, and are in any event subject to the law of churchyards.[2]

---

[95] *Jackson* v. *Cowie* (1872) 9 S.L.R. 617.
[96] at 337.
[97] *Sloan's Dairies Ltd.* v. *Glasgow Corporation*, 1977 S.C. 223.
[98] *Welwood's Trs.* v. *Mungall*, 1921 S.C. 911.
[98a] See Conveyancing (Scotland) Act 1874, s. 50 and Sched. M—not required in deeds relating to an interest registered in the Land Register (Land Registration (Scotland) Act 1979, s. 15(4)).
[99] *Moore* v. *Paterson* (1881) 9 R. 337, although the facts were special.
[1] s. 70; *North British Rly. Co.* v. *Budhill Coal and Sandstone Co.*, 1909 S.C. 277.
[2] *Steel* v. *Kirk Session of St. Cuthbert's Parish* (1891) 18 R. 911.

(9) Teinds. See paragraph 18–46, *supra.*

Rights incapable of alienation

3–50 **(1) Regalia.** All the *regalia majora* and such of the *regalia minora* as are held in trust for the public, *e.g.* rights in navigable rivers and highways.[3]

(2) Water rights. A right of drawing water from a stream or of trout fishing in a stream or loch cannot competently be created a real right in a conveyance of lands not abutting on the stream or loch to the effect that it is binding upon a singular successor of the granter of the conveyance or other person having a title and interest to challenge.[4] Likewise a purported reservation of such rights in a conveyance of the riparian lands would be ineffective as a real burden, with the possible exception of the case where the conveyance is a feu right when the granter as superior retains an interest in the *dominium directum* of the riparian lands conveyed. A right of trout fishing cannot be created a servitude or real burden in favour of non-riparian lands,[5] but a written lease of trout fishings for more than a year granted for consideration to any person is now a right in heritable property valid against a singular successor of the granter.[6]

(3) Shootings. A right of shooting cannot be conveyed as a heritable tenement separate from the land over which it is exercised.[7]

(4) Family pew. A family pew or seat in the parish church cannot be conveyed separately from the estate to which it is a pertinent.[8]

Styles of description

3–51 **Boundaries.** The normal practice is to commence with the street or road boundary and then proceed to describe the other boundaries continuing in a clockwise direction. Each boundary should be described, where there is an existing physical feature, by a precise definition of the line of the boundary in relation to that feature, *e.g.* the inner or outer face or the centre line of a wall or gable. Lengths of boundaries should be specified if accurately known and should correspond with the lengths shown on any annexed plan.

3–52 **Measurements.** Measurements of superficial area or lengths of boundaries in the case of new descriptions should be in metric measure in pursuance of EEC Directive of September 27, 1976 (76/770/EEC). However, where a plot of ground is being split out from an existing

---

[3] Montgomerie Bell, *Lectures*, 606.
[4] *Patrick* v. *Napier* (1867) 5 M. 683; *Marquis of Breadalbane* v. *West Highland Rly. Co.* (1895) 22 R. 307.
[5] *Harper* v. *Flaws*, 1940 S.L.T. 150.
[6] Freshwater and Salmon Fisheries (Scotland) Act 1976, s. 4.
[7] *Beckett* v. *Bisset*, 1921 2 S.L.T. 33.
[8] *Stephen* v. *Anderson* (1887) 15 R. 72; *Paterson* v. *Brown*, 1913 S.C. 292.

larger area which has been described in Imperial Measure in the title deeds, it may be more convenient to use Imperial Measure in describing the plot. All superficial or lineal measurements should be qualified by "or thereby" which will cover minor variations.[9]

A. First Description as Separate Subject

Building plot—full description by boundaries and plan

18–53   ALL and WHOLE that plot of ground containing   (area) or thereby bounded on the north by the centre line of a proposed new street   wide to be known as   Street along which it extends   or thereby and on the east, south and west by other ground belonging to [me] [us] along which it extends [along the centre line of mutual fences to be erected by the said disponee or his foresaids or the proprietors of the adjoining plots at joint equal expense and ranges thereof] [*or otherwise as the case may be*] on the east   or thereby, on the south   or thereby and on the west   or thereby as the said plot of ground is delineated and edged red on the plan annexed and [subscribed] [executed] as relative hereto; which plot of ground is part of that area of ground in the [Parish of   and] County of   described and disponed in [*specify prior deed*] dated   and recorded in the Division of the General Register of Sasines for the County of   on   ; Together with the whole buildings [erected] [to be erected] thereon, [the fixtures and fittings therein and thereon], the whole parts and pertinents of the subjects hereby disponed and [my] [our] whole right, title and interest, present and future, [therein] [in the *dominium utile* thereof].

Building plot—short description

18–54   All and WHOLE that plot of ground delineated and edged red [and marked No.   ] on the plan annexed and [subscribed] [executed] as relative hereto [which plan is demonstrative only and not taxative]; which plot of ground is part of [*refer to larger area and continue to end as in style in paragraph 18—53 supra*].

NOTES

1. If the plan is of the individual plot conveyed it is essential that it shows some identifiable fixed point of reference so that its location can be established; otherwise it may be a "floating rectangle" whose location is uncertain.

2. If the plot is numbered on a plan showing several houses that plan must show a road or street of fixed location.

3. The postal address of the plot, if known, should be stated.

Building plot—description—one road boundary

18–55   ALL and WHOLE that plot of ground bounded on the north by

[9] *Hetherington* v. *Galt* (1905) 7 F. 706.

the centre line of [the proposed new road to be known as]
Road   metres wide along which it extends   or thereby
as the said plot of ground is delineated and edged red on the plan
annexed and [subscribed] [executed] as relative hereto: which plot
of ground [*continue to end as in style in paragraph 18–53 supra*].

NOTE. See notes to paragraph 18–54 *supra.*

Plot with new detached dwelling-house thereon

8–56   [*Describe plot as in style in paragraph 18–53, 18–54 or 18–55
including description of larger subjects of which it forms part*];
Together with the [villa] [bungalow] known as (*name or street
number and town*) erected on the said plot of ground, the fixtures
and fittings thereon and therein, the whole parts and pertinents of
the subjects hereby disponed and [my] [our] whole right, title and
interest, present and future, [therein] [in the *dominium utile*
thereof].

Flatted dwelling-house

8–57   ALL and WHOLE that flatted dwelling-house containing
apartments being [the westmost dwelling-house on the second
floor above the ground floor] [the eastmost dwelling-house on the
ground floor] of the [block] [tenement] erected on the plot
[*describe fully or by statutory reference*]; Together with [*describe or
refer to exclusive and common rights of property etc. as in style in
paragraph 17–86 supra or paragraph 18–62 infra*].

NOTES

1. Describe the flat conveyed with reference to its orientation
geographically. References to "left" or "right" may be ambiguous since
the stair may turn and a flat which is left as looked at from the street
may be otherwise as looked at from the stair landing.

2. Describe the level of the house as above the ground floor. Flats in
normal parlance are described as on the ground, first, second or third
floors.

3. When the last flat to be disposed of is being conveyed it may be
desirable to convey the entire subjects under exception of the flats and
common rights already conveyed described by reference to the relevant
dispositions or feu grants, with specification of exclusive ownership of
the last flat. This is a safeguard against inadvertent omission.

Dwelling-house forming part of former larger dwelling-house subdivided

8–58   ALL and WHOLE that plot of ground lying on the south side of
Road, Rothesay containing   or thereby Metric
Measure and bounded as follows:— On the north by the said
Road along which it extends   metres or thereby
measured along the north or outer face of a stone wall; on the east
by the centre line of a mutual division wall separating the said plot
from the adjoining property Ekadasha,   Road, Rothesay

along which it extends   metres or thereby following the
curve; on the south by the lands of   Farm, Rothesay along
which it extends   metres or thereby measured along the
south or outer face of a brick wall; and on the west by the centre
line of a mutual division wall between the said subjects hereby
disponed and the dwelling-house No. 26   Road, Rothesay
and range thereof northwards and southwards along which together
it extends   metres or thereby, as the said plot is delineated
and edged blue on the plan annexed and subscribed as relative
hereto [which plan is demonstrative only and not taxative]; which
plot forms part of ALL and WHOLE that plot or area of ground
containing   square yards or thereby Imperial Measure
(Metric Measure) in the Parish of   and County of
Bute described and disponed in Feu Disposition by AB in favour
of CD dated   and recorded in the Division of the General
Register of Sasines for the County of Bute on   both in the
year 18   upon which the house known as   ,
Road, Rothesay was erected; Together with the dwelling-house
known as No. 26A   Road, Rothesay and relative garage,
the fixtures and fittings therein, the parts and pertinents thereof
and my whole right title and interest, present and future, therein.

NOTE. The foregoing description is appropriate where there is a
complete division with separate accesses and services. More commonly
the original access driveway will continue to be used by both houses
and should be shown hatched on the plan and made common property.
Also the electricity, gas, water supply and telephone cables or pipes
and drains will, up to the point of division at or in the houses, serve
both houses: rights of use of these in common so far as serving both
houses should be created in the titles of each house. Again the garden
ground may not be divided into areas exclusive to each house; parts of
it, *e.g.* a front lawn, may be common property and will be distinctively
coloured on the plan. It will usually be found more convenient and
economical to prepare a single plan of the whole ground of the original
feu, with appropriate distinctive colourings, which can be annexed to
the disposition of each house.

Industrial or commercial property

18–59 A first description of industrial or commercial property may be
required where unbuilt-on land is conveyed upon which a factory or
commercial buildings are to be erected. The ground conveyed will be
described particularly by boundaries and reference to plan as in
paragraph 18–53 *supra*.

Another occasion on which a first description is required may be
when an existing factory or commercial development consists of several
buildings part of which is being disposed of. In such cases the part
conveyed should be described particularly by measurement of area and
boundaries and should be delineated on a plan. The description of
each boundary should be detailed, *e.g.* "bounded on the north partly

by the north or outer face of the wall of a building erected on the subjects hereby disponed and partly by range thereof eastwards until it reaches the point marked A on the plan aftermentioned along which together it extends   metres or thereby." Special matters for which provision should be made include (i) the use of buildings which will continue to be used by the property conveyed and the remainder of the property retained, *e.g.* for central heating, (ii) access roadways or parking facilities to be used in common, (iii) fixtures and any fittings which are or may be moveable, (iv) where the outer wall of a building forms a boundary, right of access over the subjects conveyed or retained as the case may be for maintenance, and (v) wayleaves for or common rights in electric, gas, water and telephone cables, pipes or wires and drains with, where necessary, rights of access for maintenance.

B. Subsequent Description of Subjects previously particularly Described

Landed estate

8–60 **(a) Repetition of existing general description**

ALL and WHOLE the lands and estate of   in the County of   with (*repeat exactly as in existing title including any references to salmon or other fishings and teinds and adding, if not already specified therein, parts and pertinents and all rights and privileges attaching to the lands and fittings and fixtures in the mansion house and other buildings on the estate so far as belonging to the granter and whole right, title and interest*).

NOTE. If the purchaser wishes or in terms of the missives of sale requires a description by reference to a plan, the full description as in the existing title should be inserted, followed by: "declaring without prejudice to the generality of the foregoing description and the whole subjects, rights and interests comprehended therein that the subjects hereby disponed include (*description by reference to annexed plan*)."

(b) Description by reference to former title

ALL and WHOLE the lands and estate of   in the County of   described and disponed by Disposition by AB in [my favour] [favour of CD] dated   and recorded in the Division of the General Register of Sasines for the County of   on   ; Together with the salmon fishings as therein described, the teinds thereof, the fixtures and fittings in the mansion house of   and in all other buildings on the said lands and estate so far as belonging to me, the parts, privileges and pertinents of the subjects hereby disponed and my whole right, title and interest, present and future, in and to the said subjects.

NOTE. The reference to salmon fishings and teinds, if they are already included in the former description, is probably unnecessary.

Variations. In some cases the purchaser may wish particulars of feuduties or rentals to be included in the description in (a) or (b) above. This may be done, but again without prejudice to the general description. As to a style, see Burns, pp. 348, 349.

Detached dwelling-house

18–61　　ALL and WHOLE that dwelling-house with the solum thereof and relative ground known as 3　　　　Road, Edinburgh in the County of Midlothian being the subjects described and disponed in [Feu Charter by AB in favour of CD] *or* [Disposition by EF in my favour] dated　　　　and recorded in the Division of the General Register of Sasines for the County of Midlothian on　　　　; Together with the fixtures and fittings in and upon the said subjects so far as I have right thereto, the parts and pertinents of the said subjects and my whole right, title and interest present and future in and to the said subjects and others.

or

ALL and WHOLE that plot of ground containing　　　　or thereby Metric Measure in the County of Midlothian described and disponed in Feu Disposition by AB in my favour dated　　　　and recorded in the Division of the General Register of Sasines for the County of Midlothian on　　　　; Together with the dwelling-house known as 3　　　　Road, Edinburgh and relative buildings erected thereon, the fixtures and fittings therein so far as belonging to me, the parts and pertinents of the subjects hereby disponed and my whole right, title and interest, present and future, therein.

Flatted dwelling-house

18–62　　ALL and WHOLE that dwelling-house being the westmost flat on the second floor above the ground floor of the tenement No.　　　　High Street, Ayr in the County of Ayr being the dwelling-house described and disponed in Disposition by XY Construction Company Limited in my favour dated　　　　and recorded in the Division of the General Register of Sasines for the County of Ayr on　　　　; Together with (1) the whole rights of property, rights exclusive, mutual and common and whole other rights so far as effeiring to the said dwelling-house specified and contained in Deed of Conditions by the said XY Construction Company Limited dated　　　　and recorded in the said Division of the General Register of Sasines on　　　　, (2) the whole fixtures and fittings in the said dwelling-house so far as belonging to me, (3) the parts and pertinents of the subjects hereby disponed and (4) my whole right, title and interest, present and future, therein.

Superiority

18–63　　ALL and WHOLE [the lands and estate of X] [that area of ground containing 2.45 hectares or thereby] in the County of　　　　described in Disposition by AB in our favour (*or as the case may be*) dated　　　　and recorded in the Division of the General Register of Sasines for the County of　　　　on　　　　; Together with the teinds so far as we have right thereto and our whole right, title and interest, present and future, in and to the subjects and others hereby disponed.

NOTES

1. The conveyance is of the lands themselves without reference to superiority or *dominium directum*. The fact that it is the superiority of the subjects that is conveyed will appear from the assignation of feuduties and the exception of feu rights from warrandice.

2. No mention is made of buildings or pertinents. As *partes soli* the interest of superiority is automatically in them also, but since the vassal has right of possession of them specification of them might be confusing.

3. If minerals have been reserved in the feu grants a conveyance of the superiority described as above would convey the reserved minerals also.[10] If that is not intended a specific reservation should be made.

4. As to inclusion of a list of feuduties see para. 18–60, note of variations.

DESCRIPTIONS—REGISTRATION OF TITLE

A. First Registration

Mapping

8–64   The description of lands in a conveyance where the transaction induces first registration in the Land Register, or where it is intended to apply for voluntary registration, must satisfy the requirements already outlined of a sufficient description at common law or under statute. In addition, since the Land Register is based on the Ordnance Map, it is necessary that sufficient information is given to the Keeper, either in the description of the lands in the deed itself or separately, to enable the subjects to be identified on the Ordnance Map.[11] Frequently there will be sufficient information contained in the title deeds submitted with the application for registration to enable the location of the subjects to be so identified but, if not, the applicant should submit further particulars, preferably accompanied by a plan or sketch showing the boundaries of the subjects as actually occupied.[11a]

Particular subjects

8–65   Reference may be made to paragraph B.3.01 of the Registration of Title Practice Book for guidance as to the descriptions to be inserted in simple cases, and to paragraph E.39 as regards plans and information to be furnished in more complicated cases. In addition the following suggestions are offered.

---

[10] *Orr* v. *Mitchell* (1893) 20 R. (H.L.) 27.
[11] Land Registration (Scotland) Act 1979, s. 4(2)(*a*).
[11a] Any informal plan or sketch should be signed—see para. 18–68.

18–66   **(a) Large areas described only by general description.** Where the subjects conveyed consist of a large area and are described in the existing title deeds only by a general description without reference to a plan, as in the case of a landed estate or agricultural subjects, a plan will often have been furnished in the course of negotiations for the purchase. In such circumstances the purchaser may be entitled to require a conveyance of the lands as delineated on the plan,[12] and it will facilitate registration of the title if a supplementary description by reference to the plan is included in the deed.[13]

18–67   **(b) New building developments.** It is strongly recommended that, when a new building development involving the creation of a number of separate plots is contemplated, advantage should be taken of the facility of having a plan of the whole layout approved by the Keeper before applications are made to have the new units registered. Reference should be made to paragraphs E.44 to E.52 of the Registration of Title Practice Book and to Notes on Approved Estate Plans and Voluntary Registration of Developing Estates, obtainable on application to the Keeper.

18–68   **(c) Special rights and burdens.** It is emphasised that plans, whether formal or informal, submitted in relation to an application for first registration should delineate any particular parts of the subjects in which common or special rights or burdens or conditions have been or are being created or imposed. That is essential in order that the particular parts so affected may be delineated on the title sheet plan.[14] Informal plans should be docketed with a certificate signed by the applicant or his solicitor that the property described in the deed, or any particular part of it, is that delineated on the plan.

18–69   **(d) Rights described in deed of conditions.** A deed of declaration of conditions, duly recorded, commonly deals with two distinct matters, namely (i) it sets out the rights to common parts of a tenement building or curtilage ground of the proprietors of the various parts, and (ii) it specifies the real burdens or conditions applicable to the various parts. If the deed of conditions was granted on or after April 4, 1979, then the burdens and conditions become real upon recording of the deed in the Register of Sasines or registration of them in the Land Register unless the deed contained an express statement to the contrary (1979 Act, s. 17). But a deed of conditions does not operate as a conveyance of the various common or other rights which it sets out. So, when a disposition is being prepared of a flat or portion of a tenement, it is necessary to convey such rights expressly either by description *ad longum* or by reference to the deed of conditions, and this is required also if the disposition is being submitted for first registration so that the

---

[12] *Houldsworth* v. *Gordon Cumming*, 1910 S.C. (H.L.) 49.
[13] See paras. 18–08 and 18–60.
[14] R.T.P.B., para. E.39(vii).

Keeper may describe the subjects accurately in the title sheet. A comparable situation arises where a villa property has been subdivided and common rights have been created in division walls or fences, pathways or avenues or garden ground in the disposition of the sold part. If the retained part is subsequently sold the disposition must convey the common rights described *ad longum*.

8–70 **(e) Boundaries.** The procedure adopted by the Keeper in relation to the mapping of boundaries of the subjects upon first registration is described in paragraphs E.16 to E.24 of the Registration of Title Practice Book. If the existing title deeds do not identify the precise line of a boundary or boundaries in relation to any physical object such as a wall, fence or hedge, it will be of assistance to the Keeper and will facilitate registration if further information is provided with the application regarding the situation of the physical object in relation to the subjects which are to be registered, *e.g.* whether a wall, fence or hedge is mutual or has been erected wholly within or wholly outwith the subjects. For example, in old title deeds the subjects may have been described as "bounded on the west by the property of John Smith" without any reference to a plan, in which case information from the applicant as to the practice as regards maintenance of a dividing wall may indicate whether it is mutual or otherwise. Again, a plot in a new development may be delineated on a plan without any specification of the physical feature on the boundary (which may not have been erected when the title was granted), in which case the applicant may know where a wall or fence has in fact been erected in relation to the boundary on the plan. Another situation, not uncommon in practice, is that the actual boundary was the centre line of an old wall or hedge which has become ruinous or dilapidated and it has been simpler and less expensive to erect a new fence within the line of the old wall or hedge. It is suggested that a copy of any information furnished to the Keeper on such matters should be retained with the land certificate, since the boundaries as indicated by the arrow system on the title plan will be excluded from indemnity in the land certificate under section 12(3)(*d*) of the 1979 Act, and the information may be useful in the event of a dispute subsequently arising as to the precise line of the boundary.

Time element

8–71 It is important that any supplementary information necessary should be submitted with the application or be furnished promptly on any subsequent request by the Keeper, because if all the evidence required for registration is not made available within 60 days the Keeper may reject the application with the result that priority in registration of the title may be affected.[15]

---

[15] Land Registration (Scotland) Rules 1980 (S.I. 1980 No. 1413) (S. 114), r. 12.

Preliminary inquiries

18–72   **(a) Form 10 and Form 11 reports.** A Form 10 report will normally be instructed by the seller's solicitor before conclusion of a contract of sale and will be supplemented by a Form 11 report obtained as nearly as possible to the date of settlement.[16] As regards the description of the subjects in Form 10 it is evident that it must be sufficient to enable the Keeper to identify them in the Register of Sasines and on the index map.[17]

(b) Form P16. If it desired to compare, usually at the pre-contract stage, the boundaries as shown in the title deeds or as indicated by occupation with those delineated on the Ordnance Map and the relevant section of the Ordnance Map is not readily available to the seller or his solicitor, a report on Form P16 may be obtained from the Keeper.[18] This facility is valuable in certain circumstances, as when a large area is being sold the boundaries of which are not clear from the title deeds or when an area is being sold for the purpose of development. In such cases it is prudent for the seller to have the boundaries checked in relation to the Ordnance Map so that missives of sale may be framed by reference to a plan which will correctly indicate the boundaries and will be acceptable for the registration of the purchaser's title. In very many cases, however, where the sale is of a single subject and the area and boundaries are identifiable from a plan or description in the existing title deeds which corresponds generally with the subjects as actually occupied it is unnecessary, and is perhaps inadvisable, to instruct a P16 report. If upon consideration of the application for registration a discrepancy is disclosed between the description of the property in the title deeds or as occupied or as delineated on the Ordnance Map, the difficulty may be overcome in the case of a minor discrepancy by the Keeper exercising his discretion within the concept of "or thereby." If a P16 report is obtained and discloses some slight discrepancy but the report indicates that the discrepancy should not cause any problem on registration, it would be premature and may ultimately prove to have been unnecessary for the seller to embark upon negotiations with neighbours for rectification. If a P16 report is not obtained and a material discrepancy is discovered upon application for registration, the rights of parties and the measures which may be adopted are considered in paragraph 18–73 *infra.*

Boundary discrepancies disclosed on first registration

18–73   Upon an application for first registration a discrepancy may be disclosed between the description of the property in the title deeds and

---

[16] R.T.P.B., paras. G.2.15 and G.2.16.
[17] See R.T.P.B., paras. E.38 and F.07.
[18] *Ibid.*, paras. E.33 and E.34.

the subjects as occupied and delineated on the Ordnance Map, and the discrepancy may be sufficiently material that the difficulty cannot be solved by the exercise of the Keeper's discretion within the latitude permitted by "or thereby." In such cases:

(a) Where the area described in the title deeds is greater than that enclosed within the occupational boundaries the Keeper will normally register the interest as described in the title deeds but may exclude indemnity in respect of that part of the subjects outwith the occupational boundaries.[19] That raises no difficulty. The buyer will almost always have purchased the subjects as described by an address and as inspected, *i.e.* those included in the occupational boundaries, and he is not entitled to require a conveyance of anything more.[20]

(b) In the converse case where the area described in the title deeds is significantly less than that enclosed by the occupational boundaries, the Keeper may be unable to include the additional area since there is no title to support the application for registration. In such a situation:

(i) The seller may agree with the adjoining proprietor who has a title to the additional area that the boundary be adjusted to correspond with the occupational boundary in accordance with section 19 of the 1979 Act. For details of procedure see the undernoted paragraph.[21]

(ii) If for any reason that course is impracticable the seller may grant a disposition of the additional area in favour of the purchaser who may apply for registration of a title to it. The Keeper will normally register the interest but with exclusion of indemnity since the disposition was *a non domino*. On the expiry of 10 years of continued unchallenged possession after the date of registration the purchaser may seek rectification of the Land Register to have the exclusion removed and the risk of a successful earlier challenge may be covered by an insurance indemnity. If the disposition is granted in part implement of the sale with a narrative disclosing the facts it will induce first registration of the additional area in the Land Register, but if granted simply for certain good causes and considerations the application should be for voluntary registration.[22] For further particulars as to the style of dispositions *a non domino* see paragraph 18–88 *infra*.

B. Dealings with Registered Interests

(1) Dealing with Whole Registered Interest

Description

–74   Once an interest in land has been registered in the Land Register the

---

[19] R.T.P.B., para. E.31.
[20] *Houldsworth* v. *Gordon Cumming*, 1910 S.C. (H.L.) 49.
[21] para. 18–84.
[22] See R.T.P.B., para. H.1.08.

land is sufficiently described in any subsequent deed which effects a
dealing with the whole interest, *e.g.* a disposition of it, by reference to
the number of the title sheet of the interest. No further description is
necessary but a short description may usefully be inserted which in
appropriate cases may be taken from the front cover of the land
certificate. Where the subjects comprise or include superiorities or the
landlord's interest in registered leases a schedule of feus or leases may
be annexed to the deed; if not, an up-to-date list of them should
accompany the application for registration of the dealing on Form 2.[23]
Note that the descriptions of the subjects required for dispositions of
land to be recorded in the Register of Sasines are not relevant and the
various statutory provisions authorising brief forms of description of
lands have no place in relation to dealings with registered interests and
are disapplied by the 1979 Act.[24]

Style

18–75 A form of description of land in a deed dealing with a registered
interest is prescribed in Schedule B to the Land Registration (Scotland)
Rules 1980[25] and a style based upon that form may run: "ALL and
WHOLE the subjects known as [the northmost house on the ground
floor 26 Canal Street, Renfrew] [Braeside Farm, Parish of Lesmahagow]
being the subjects registered under Title Number   ."

(2) Transfer of Part of Registered Interest

Description of part

18–76 In a disposition of part of a registered interest there is no need to
describe the subjects in the way required for a description of lands in a
conveyance which is to be recorded in the Register of Sasines,[26] but it
is necessary to describe it in terms sufficient to enable the Keeper to
identify it on the Ordnance Map and to specify the title number of the
registered interest of which it forms part. In most cases the part
conveyed should be described by reference to an accurately-scaled
plan, and boundaries should be consistent with the title plan of the
larger registered area. The following matters also require attention:

(i) Common and other rights relating to the part conveyed already
specified in a deed of conditions require to be conveyed.[27]

---

[23] See R.T.P.B., para. B.3.02.
[24] s. 15(1). The provisions disapplied are: (1) Titles to Land Consolidation (Scotland) Act 1868,
s. 13 and Sched. G; (2) Conveyancing (Scotland) Act 1874, s. 61; (3) Conveyancing (Scotland) Act
1924, ss. 8 and 24(2) and Scheds. D and J; and (4) Conveyancing and Feudal Reform (Scotland) Act
1970, Sched. 2, note 1.
[25] S.I. 1980 No. 1413 (S. 114).
[26] 1979 Act, s. 15(1).
[27] See para. 18–69.

(ii) Where *pro indiviso* rights in common with other property are conferred in the disposition of the part the portions of the subjects in which such rights subsist should be clearly identified and, where practicable, shown on the annexed plan. Any such rights, *e.g.* to *solum*, should be consistent with those in the registered titles of the other subjects concerned.

8–77 **Styles—transfer of part**

(1) *Dwelling-house in flatted tenement—deed of conditions*[27a]

ALL and WHOLE the southmost dwelling-house on the ground floor of the tenement known as 36 Canal Street, Renfrew, being part of the subjects registered under Title Number   together with the rights of common property in the *solum*, walls, roof and other parts of the said tenement and relative ground effeiring to the said dwelling-house as described in Deed of Conditions by AB dated   and entered in the Land Register of Scotland as relating to the subjects registered under the said Title Number.

(2) *Plot of ground in feuing development*

ALL and WHOLE that plot of ground with the dwelling-house and garage erected thereon known as 15 Baker Road, Kilmacolm containing   square metres or thereby bounded on the north by the centre line of the said Baker Road and on the east, south and west by the centre lines of mutual fences, as the said plot is delineated and edged red and marked "No. 15" on the plan annexed and signed [executed] as relative hereto and is part of the subjects registered in the Land Register of Scotland under Title Number   .

(3) *Flatted dwelling-house forming part of former villa*

ALL and WHOLE the dwelling-house and others hereinafter described being part of the subjects known as Hazel Villa, Roger Street, Kilbarchan registered under Title Number   (which villa has now been converted into a block of three self contained flats known as 15 Roger Street, Kilbarchan), namely, (One) the dwelling-house comprising the first or mid floor of the said block (Two) the exclusive right to the area of ground situated to the rear of the said block coloured green on the plan annexed and subscribed as relative hereto and the garage erected thereon (Three) a right in common with the proprietor of the top flat of said block to the stairway leading to the first floor and top flats of the said block and the solum and outer walls and roof of the said stairway as the same are coloured blue on the said plan (Four) a right in common with the proprietors of the other two dwelling-houses comprised in the said block to (a) the solum on which the said block (excluding the said stairway) is erected and the foundations, gables and outside walls, roof and chimney stacks of the said block and the common drains, soil and rainwater pipes, gutters, rhones, electric, gas and water pipes and cables and fittings so far as serving the whole of said block (b) the garden

[27a] Appropriate where deed of conditions already entered in Land Register.

ground situated to the front and sides of the said block coloured yellow on said plan (c) the drive and pathways coloured brown on said plan, and (d) the front wall and a *pro indiviso* one half share of the mutual walls and fences on the other three sides of the whole area delineated on the said plan (Five) the whole fittings and fixtures in and upon the subjects conveyed exclusively to my said disponee and his foresaids and (Six) the parts and pertinents of the subjects hereby disponed and my whole right, title and interest, present and future, in and to the said subjects hereby disponed.

NOTES

(a) The plan will be of a copy of the certificate plan of the registered interest, scaled up if necessary.[28]

(b) The description is framed on the assumption that the certificate plan of the registered interest does not include one half of the roadway. If that is included the common property should include it also.

(c) It is assumed that the walls and fences on the side and back boundaries as shown on the title plan are common or mutual with the owners of the adjoining land, and the certificate plan so indicates. If not the provisions as to these features in the description should be adjusted appropriately.

Preliminary consultation with Keeper

18–78   In view of the problems associated with the adjustment of a disposition which transfers part of a registered title, particularly in the case of flatted property, it is desirable, if time permits, to submit to the Keeper a draft of the proposed disposition. That will enable the subjects conveyed to be checked in relation to boundaries, rights conferred in a deed of conditions, common and *pro indiviso* rights to solum and other common parts and the quotation of the correct title number where amalgamations or divisions of the parent title have occurred.

Transfers of land where title partly recorded and partly registered

18–79   Where a disposition on sale conveys land the title to part of which is recorded in the Register of Sasines and the title to the remainder has been registered in the Land Register, the transaction will induce first registration of the former part and a transfer of a registered title or part thereof as regards the latter. In such a case the description should clearly distinguish the two parts by reference to a plan and the former part should be described in the way required for first registration and supported by the furnishing of a prescriptive progress of titles, whereas the latter should be described appropriately as a transfer of or part of a

---

[28] See R.T.P.B., para. E.42.

registered title with a reference to the number of the title sheet of the parent title.

Errors or Discrepancies in Descriptions—Remedial Procedures

8–80 In the field of conveyancing, as in the wider world, perfection is not always to be found. In this paragraph some of the more common problems are considered, with suggestions for appropriate remedial measures.

(a) Errors not resulting in failure in identification

8–81 Deeds may include errors in the description of the subjects, *e.g.* a bungled reference for description to a previous recorded deed, which nevertheless contain sufficient information to identify the subjects so as to distinguish them from any others. In such cases all that should be done is to insert an accurate description of the subjects in any conveyance that is being prepared which should be linked with the former defective description, *e.g.*

> ALL and WHOLE (*correct description ad longum or by accurate reference to former recorded deed*) which subjects are those described and disponed in (*previous deed containing erroneous description*) in which [the western boundary was *per incuriam* described as the eastern boundary] [the recording date of the Disposition by A (*designed*) in favour of B (*designed*) was *per incuriam* stated as 1st November 1974 instead of 15th November 1974] (*or as the case may be*).

(b) Error in or omission from subjects conveyed

8–82 Where by mistake the wrong subjects have been conveyed, as by an error in orientation whereby the eastmost flat in a tenement has been described as westmost, or where in a subdivision of villa property part of the garden ground has not been conveyed to any of the proprietors of the subdivided property, the granter of the defective deed has not been divested of the eastmost flat or the omitted part of the garden ground, as the case may be. He remains *in titulo* to grant a corrective or supplementary disposition which should be obtained and recorded in the Register of Sasines. Searches against the granter should be continued in the property and personal registers to ensure that there is no intervening impediment. If the granter of the defective deed is deceased when the error is observed it will be necessary for his executor to procure an eik to confirmation to include the property or the omitted part as estate held in trust in order to provide the necessary title linkage. If the granter was a limited company which has been wound up, the flat or part of the garden ground will have vested in the Crown as *bona vacantia*, but the Queen's and Lord Treasurer's

Remembrancer will normally be prepared to grant the necessary disposition on payment of his conveyancing charges.[29]

(c) Common and exclusive rights—flatted property

18–83   Sometimes by conveyancing error mutually inconsistent rights of common and exclusive property have been created in the solum or parts of the buildings or curtilage of flatted property. Technically the appropriate remedial procedure is to have an agreement by all parties concerned incorporating conveyances to achieve the agreed correct rights of ownership of the affected parts and to record it in the Register of Sasines. Where the error is disclosed upon an application for first registration of title the Keeper may be prepared to accept some less formal document, provided that it is signed or executed by all parties having interest.

(d) Discrepancies in boundaries

18–84   Where the titles to two adjoining properties A and B disclose a discrepancy as to the common boundary between them, the proprietors may utilise the provisions of section 19 of the Land Registration (Scotland) Act 1979 by reaching agreement as to the line of the boundary and executing a plan which delineates it. Then,

(i) Where the title deeds of both A and B are recorded in the Register of Sasines a probative agreement as to the boundary with the plan delineating it annexed should be executed by both proprietors and recorded in the Register of Sasines. For a suggested style see paragraph 18–85 *infra*.

(ii) Where the interest of the proprietor of A has been registered in the Land Register and the interest of the proprietor of B is about to be registered on an application for first registration, the plan with a docquet thereon executed by both proprietors referring to the agreement reached may be submitted for registration in the Land Register. A formal deed recording the agreement as in (i) above is not required. For a suggested style of docquet see paragraph 18–86 *infra*.

(iii) Where the interest of the proprietor of A has been registered in the Land Register but the title deed of B is recorded in the Register of Sasines and no application for registration of the title to B in the Land Register is pending, a formal agreement with plan as in (i) above should be executed and submitted for recording in the Register of Sasines with a request to the Keeper that it should be registered also in the Land Register as affecting the registered interest in A. The agreed boundary will then bind both proprietors and their singular successors and all other persons having interest, *e.g.* superiors and heritable creditors.

---

[29] Companies Act 1985, ss. 654, 656.

Style—section 19(2) agreement

8–85   We, (first) CD, (*designed*), heritable proprietor of ALL and
WHOLE (*description of land full or by reference to recorded deed*)
and (second) EF, (*designed*), heritable proprietor of (*description
of land full or by reference to recorded deed*) WHEREAS the said
subjects belonging to me the said CD are situated to the west of
and immediately adjacent to the said subjects belonging to me the
said EF but the title deeds of our respective subjects disclose a
discrepancy in the line of the common boundary between them
AND WHEREAS in pursuance of section 19 of the Land
Registration (Scotland) Act 1979 we have agreed to and have
executed a plan of that boundary which plan is annexed and
executed as relative hereto THEREFORE we agree, that the
common boundary on the east of the said subjects belonging to me
the said CD and on the west of the said subjects belonging to me
the said EF is that delineated and coloured red on the said plan [*if
there is a physical feature on the agreed boundary add* being the
centre of a mutual wall erected thereon *or otherwise as the case
may be*] to the effect provided by the said section.
(*To be attested*)

Stamp duty nil.

NOTE. If the interest of one proprietor is registered in the Land
Register the description of his interest should refer to the land
certificate number.

Style—section 19(3) docquet

8–86   We agree in terms of section 19 of the Land Registration (Scotland)
Act 1979 that the red line (*or as the case may be*) on this plan
delineates the boundary between the subjects registered under Title
Numbers   and   respectively.
(*To be executed by both proprietors*)

(e) Superiority or property?

8–87   Where the superiority and the property are owned by the same
person but the two estates have not been consolidated the description
of the land in a disposition of either estate may be identical, and the
fact that the conveyance is of the superiority or the property may have
to be established by reference to other parts of the deed.[30] For the
purpose of resolving such an ambiguity the principal *indicia* are: (1) In
a disposition of the superiority buildings should not be specified since,
in the absence of any qualification of warrandice, a right of possession
and occupancy may, in certain categories of property, be implied.[31]
(2) In a disposition of a superiority the feuduties and rents should be
assigned. This test may not always be available if no clause of
assignation of rents or feuduties is expressed[32] or because the feuduty

---

[30] See para. 18–63.
[31] See para. 18–63.
[32] Land Registration (Scotland) Act 1979, s. 16(3).

has been redeemed. (3) In a disposition of a superiority feu rights should be excluded from warrandice. (4) Reference may be made to the narrative clause to resolve an ambiguity in the dispositive clause.[33] If the title to either the superiority or the property is registered in the Land Register a reference to the title number will establish whether the interest is of the superiority or the property.

Disposition a non domino

18–88   If a corrective disposition or a section 19 agreement is required but for some reason is unobtainable the best practical solution may be for the seller simply to grant a disposition in favour of the purchaser even although he has no proper title to do so, and procure an insurance indemnity to cover the risk of a successful challenge being made before the purchaser's title has been rendered unchallengeable by positive prescription. A purchaser cannot be compelled to accept such a title since his contract was to obtain ownership of the property supported by a valid title and he need not agree to accept compensation in money if he should be evicted from it, but in many cases he will accept the solution if in the circumstances the risk of challenge is remote. The disposition must contain nothing which indicates the defect since for the purpose of prescription the deed must be sufficient in respect of its terms to constitute a title. The amount of the insurance indemnity should be sufficient to cover any future increase in the value of the property within the succeeding period of 10 years including the value of any proposed development. As to the use of a disposition *a non domino* in registration of title see paragraph 18–73 *supra*.

---

[33] *Orr* v. *Mitchell* (1893) 20 R. (H.L.) 27.

CHAPTER 19

RESERVATIONS AND REAL BURDENS AND CONDITIONS IN CONVEYANCES OF LAND

A. RESERVATION OF MINERALS

B. REAL BURDENS AND CONDITIONS

A. RESERVATION OF MINERALS

Reservation of minerals

–01   A conveyance of land may contain a reservation of any part of the subjects which is capable of separate infeftment. Since a conveyance of land, unless qualified, confers on the grantee ownership *a coelo usque ad centrum*, it is necessary expressly to reserve or except from the

subjects conveyed minerals which are to be retained by the granter.[1]
Such reservations are truly exclusions from the subjects conveyed and
are commonly found in feu grants.

Severance in ownership of surface and minerals

19–02   A severance in ownership of the surface and underlying minerals
may be effected (1) by a feu grant or other conveyance of land
reserving the minerals,[2] (2) by a feu grant or conveyance of the
minerals only,[3] or (3) by separate grants of surface and minerals to
different persons. Once severance occurs there are two separate feudal
tenements which can be dealt with by conveyance or lease. The owner
of the surface is entitled to the uninterrupted possession and enjoyment
of the surface and such support, both subjacent and adjacent, as will
maintain the ground at its natural level and in certain circumstances for
support of buildings thereon. Accordingly the owner of the minerals,
unless he has reserved the right expressly or by implication, cannot
enter on the surface to enable him to work the minerals nor withdraw
support from the surface by working minerals subjacent or adjacent to
it. When minerals are being reserved from a feu grant or other
conveyance it is necessary (1) to specify clearly all minerals which are
to be reserved, (2) to reserve any rights to enter on the surface that
may be required to enable the minerals to be worked, and (3) to
reserve the right to withdraw support, vertical and lateral, from the
surface by the working of subjacent or adjacent minerals.

Minerals included in reservation

19–03   In practice a clause of reservation is framed to include all metals and
minerals within the land conveyed,[4] although special mention may be
made of particular substances which are known to exist in the area in
workable deposits of potential commercial value. It is important to
ensure that the general description "metals and minerals" includes all
substances which it is intended to reserve. Whether a substance is a
mineral or not has been the subject of much litigation, but major
elements in the decisions are: (1) The question is one of fact depending
on the circumstances of each particular case.[5] (2) An important
circumstance is what was in the contemplation of the parties at the
time, and that may be ascertained by reference to whether the
particular substance was referred to as a mineral in the vernacular of

---

[1] Certain minerals are excluded from private ownership of land under the *a coelo* rule since they
are vested in the Crown (see para. 18–36), or statutory bodies (see para. 19–08).
[2] The reservation is ineffective if not made in the original feu grant but only in a subsequent writ by
progress (*Kerse Estates Ltd.* v. *Welsh*, 1935 S.C. 387).
[3] *White* v. *Dixon* (1883) 10 R.(H.L.) 45.
[4] See style, para. 17–81.
[5] *Caledonian Rly. Co.* v. *Symington*, 1912 S.C.(H.L.) 9.

the mining or commercial world or of landowners at the time when the deed containing the reservation was framed.[6] (3) A mineral is something different from the ordinary subsoil of the district, something exceptional in quality and value.[7] So the draftsman of a reservation of minerals should specify by name any substances which it is desired to reserve and add a general phrase such as, "all other metals, minerals or substances (capable of being worked commercially)." Substances which have been the subject of litigation are sand,[8] sandstone,[9] freestone,[10] whinstone,[11] oil shale[12] and fireclay.[13]

Rights to work and to enter on surface

–04 A reservation of minerals probably implies a right to work them by underground operations only and a reservation of the right to work minerals will generally be held to imply a reservation of the minerals themselves.[14] But a reservation of minerals with power to work them will not imply a right to enter upon the surface. If it is necessary to interfere with the surface for the purpose of sinking shafts or driving mines or having a wayleave for an access road or mineral railway, rights to do so must be reserved specifically from a conveyance of the surface.

Rights to withdraw support

–05 A reservation of minerals with power to work does not necessarily imply a right to withdraw support from the surface by the working of subjacent or adjacent minerals.

(a) Where the surface ground is in its natural state. In this situation the surface owner is entitled to support unless he has given it up, *e.g.* by accepting a title subject to a reservation of minerals with express power to withdraw support. If the right of support has not been relinquished the surface owner may restrain the working of minerals which take away support by interdict and may claim damages for any loss sustained on the principle of *sic utere tuo ut alienum non laedas*.[15]

(b) Where there are buildings. Where the ground is not in its natural state, as where buildings have been erected, the surface owner, to

---

[6] *Caledonian Rly. Co.* v. *Glenboig Union Fireclay Co. Ltd.*, 1911 S.C.(H.L.) 72; *Marquis of Linlithgow* v. *North British Rly. Co.*, 1912 S.C. 1327.

[7] *Caledonian Rly. Co.* v. *Symington, supra*; *Borthwick Norton* v. *Gavin Paul & Sons*, 1947 S.C. 659.

[8] *Borthwick Norton* v. *Gavin Paul & Sons, supra.*

[9] *North British Rly. Co.* v. *Budhill Coal and Sandstone Co. Ltd.*, 1910 S.C.(H.L.) 1.

[10] *Caledonian Rly. Co.* v. *Symington, supra*; *Duke of Hamilton* v. *Bentley* (1841) 3 D. 1121.

[11] *Forth Bridge Rly. Co.* v. *Incorporation of Guildry of Dunfermline*, 1910 S.C. 316.

[12] *Marquis of Linlithgow* v. *North British Rly. Co., supra.*

[13] *Caledonian Rly. Co.* v. *Glenboig Union Fireclay Co. Ltd., supra.*

[14] *Duke of Hamilton* v. *Dunlop* (1885) 12 R.(H.L.) 65.

[15] *Bank of Scotland* v. *Stewart* (1891) 18 R. 957, *per* Lord Adam at 966.

maintain a right of support for the buildings, must be able to found upon either a contract, express or implied, or a right of support for the buildings acquired by prescription. If the buildings were erected before the subjacent or adjacent land was granted to another, the owner of the buildings has an implied right of support for the buildings as they stood at the time of the severance,[16] but where buildings are erected after the severance there may be no claim in respect of damage caused by the additional loading of the surface,[17] unless the owner of both surface and minerals has conveyed the surface with an obligation to erect buildings[18] or where the erection of buildings would reasonably have been contemplated at the time of severance.[19] A right of support for buildings may also arise from prescription[20] but as the right is of the nature of a servitude, the burden of which cannot be increased except with the consent of the proprietor of the servient tenement (the subjacent or adjacent land), any extension of the buildings upwards or outwards has a prescriptive right of support only when the period of 20 years has run after the date when the extension was made.

Variation of rights to withdraw support by contract—practice

19–06   It is competent to vary the rights of support of the surface owner by contract,[21] but a provision which purports to limit the common law right of support must be clear since the burden of showing an intention to remove the ordinary right of support rests on the party maintaining that proposition.[22] But it is permissible to frame a clause of reservation of minerals in a feu grant in such express terms that, even when the feuar was bound to erect and maintain a dwelling-house on the feu, the superior's liability for damage by mineral workings was excluded.[23] In practice, when a conveyance of the surface is being granted, the extent to which power to withdraw support is reserved is a matter for negotiation, but the objective of the granter should be to retain power to withdraw support from the surface both vertically and laterally by the working of subjacent and adjacent minerals. If damages are to be paid it should be made clear (i) whether they are to be limited to damage to existing buildings or not,[24] (ii) how any damages payable are to be assessed, and (iii) whether liability should rest only on any persons who actually work the minerals, *e.g.* mineral tenants.

---

[16] *Caledonian Rly. Co.* v. *Sprot* (1856) 2 Macq. 449; *Dalton* v. *Angus* (1881) 6 App.Cas. 740; *Lord Advocate* v. *Reo Stakis Organisation Ltd.*, 1980 S.L.T. 237.

[17] *Geddes's Trs.* v. *Haldane* (1906) 14 S.L.T. 328.

[18] *North British Rly. Co.* v. *Turners Ltd.* (1904) 6 F. 900.

[19] *Neill's Trs.* v. *Dixon* (1880) 7 R. 741.

[20] *Dalton* v. *Angus, supra.* The period is still 20 years: Prescription and Limitation (Scotland) Act 1973, s. 3.

[21] *Rowbotham* v. *Wilson* (1860) 8 H.L.Cas. 348; *White* v. *Dixon* (1883) 10 R.(H.L.) 45; *Barr* v. *William Baird & Co.* (1904) 6 F. 524.

[22] *White* v. *Dixon, supra, per* Lord Blackburn at 47.

[23] *Buchanan* v. *Andrew* (1873) 11 M.(H.L.) 13.

[24] *Barr* v. *William Baird & Co., supra.*

Rights to compensation

9–07   The right to enforce liability for withdrawal of support, whether implied by law or under a conventional obligation, is available to the owner of the surface at the time when subsidence damage occurs.[25] The right to claim damages arises on each occasion of subsidence.[26] A singular successor in the ownership of the surface may only claim damages for subsidence which has occurred before his acquisition of the surface if the right to do so has been specifically assigned to him on the ordinary rule that a claim of damages is personal to the owner of the land at the relevant time.[27] The claim is prestable against the party who caused the subsidence, usually the party who actually worked the minerals, and in a mineral reservation clause in feu grants and in a lease of the minerals the superior normally ensures that only the mineral tenant will be liable. Where subsidence occurs from the working of coal and associated minerals the National Coal Board have now liability for damage under statutes.[28]

Statutory provisions regarding minerals

9–08   **Coal Act 1938 and Coal Industry Nationalisation Act 1946.** The ownership of coal and mines of coal and minerals worked in association with coal is now vested in the National Coal Board by virtue of the Coal Act 1938 and the Coal Industry Nationalisation Act 1946. A statement in a clause of reservation of minerals that the coal and associated minerals are reserved to the Board is unnecessary, but it is still the practice to include it so that the clause is comprehensive and accurate.

9–09   **Coal Mining (Subsidence) Act 1957.** Liability for subsidence damage arising from the working of coal and other minerals worked therewith is imposed on the National Coal Board by the Coal Mining (Subsidence) Act 1957. Where damage caused by subsidence arises after July 31, 1957, from such working to any buildings, sewers, pipes, drains and water, gas, electricity and similar services to land, the Board may either remedy the damage or contribute the amount necessary to repair the damage to any person executing remedial works in which the subsidence damage is included. If the cost of executing remedial works would in the opinion of the Board exceed the amount of depreciation in the value of the property caused by the damage or if the property is a dwelling-house which is likely to be the subject of a clearance order under the Housing Acts, the Board have the option of making a payment equal to the amount of the depreciation caused by the subsidence damage.

---

[25] *Barr* v. *William Baird & Co.*, *supra*.
[26] *Geddes's Trs.* v. *Haldane* (1906) 14 S.L.T. 328.
[27] *Caledonian Rly. Co.* v. *Watt* (1875) 2 R. 917.
[28] See paras. 19–09, 19–10.

19–10   Coal Industry Act 1975. This Act confers on the National Coal Board a right to withdraw support to enable coal to be worked after giving public notice in the *Edinburgh Gazette* and local newspapers and serving copies of the notice on the local planning authority.[29] Where damage arises from the exercise of the right, the Board must either pay proper compensation or, with the consent (not to be unreasonably withheld) of the person who would otherwise be entitled to compensation, make good the damage. The Act also contains provisions as to the construction of buildings on land to which a notice relates: notice of the proposed construction must be given to the Board, who may make proposals for the construction of foundations of the buildings to minimise subsidence damage.[30]

19–11   Mines (Working Facilities and Support) Act 1966. This Act enables persons to obtain power to work minerals in circumstances where it is not reasonably practicable to obtain the right by private arrangement, usually because there are numerous persons from whom a right to withdraw support would require to be obtained. The procedure is by application to the Secretary of State for Industry who, if satisfied that there is a *prima facie* case, refers the matter to the Court of Session. The court will determine whether a right to work the minerals should be granted, and will decide whether in the national interest a right to withdraw support should be conferred having regard to the comparative values of the minerals and the surface buildings.[31]

19–12   Town and Country Planning (Scotland) Act 1972; Town and Country Planning (Minerals) Act 1981. Mining operations are a development requiring planning permission under these Acts.[32]

B. REAL BURDENS AND CONDITIONS

Personal rights and obligations and burdens and conditions running with the lands

19–13 In deeds relating to land, rights and obligations may be created which are either (a) personal or contractual, binding upon the parties to the deed and their personal representatives only, or (b) burdens or conditions which run with the lands and are enforceable against the proprietor of the lands which they burden or affect and/or singular successors in the ownership thereof. Rights and obligations may fall within category (a) if the terms of the deed or the nature of the obligation indicate that only the parties and their representatives are to

---

[29] s. 2.
[30] s. 2, Sched. 1.
[31] See *Archibald Russell Ltd.* v. *Nether Pollok Ltd.*, 1938 S.C. 1.
[32] 1972 Act, s. 19; 1981 Act, s. 19.

be affected or if the obligation is insufficiently specific or in any other respect fails to satisfy the legal requirements for the constitution of a continuing real burden or condition. In *Tailors of Aberdeen* v. *Coutts*[33] obligations imposed in a disposition to pay a proportion of the cost of erecting railings were held not to be binding on singular successors, since the amount payable was indefinite. The same principle was applied in *Magistrates of Edinburgh* v. *Begg*.[34] Rights and obligations which fall within category (b) and run with the lands may be classified broadly as (1) inherent conditions of feus, (2) real burdens for money, and (3) real conditions, although the distinctions amongst them tend to be blurred by the use of the term "real burdens" as descriptive of any or all of them.[35]

Inherent conditions in feu grants

9–14   In a feu grant there are certain conditions which are essential to the feudal contract by tenure, *e.g.* the reserved superiority necessarily resulting from the creation of a new feudal estate in the vassal in terms of the tenendas clause and originally payment of a return under the reddendo clause, although the latter is now prohibited in new feus by the Land Tenure Reform (Scotland) Act 1974. Further, since a feu creates a continuing personal contract between superior and vassal and their respective successors, natural incidents of such a contract which have the qualities of permanency, immediate connection with the subjects and natural relation to the objects of the grant are inherent conditions of that contract and continue binding without requiring to be declared real or to be contained in the dispositive clause of the grant as a burden upon the title.[36] In addition there may be accidental or conventional obligations, not essential to the tenure nor inherent conditions of the feu; these can be created real only if they comply with the requirements of law for the constitution of real burdens or conditions in any conveyance of land.[37]

Real burdens

9–15   A real burden in the strict sense of the term is a money payment created over or reserved in a conveyance of lands and cannot be

---

[33] (1840) 1 Rob.App. 296 at 306, 307; 3 R.L.C. 269, 273.
[34] (1883) 11 R. 352. See also *Williamson* v. *Begg* (1887) 14 R. 720, *per* Lord President Inglis at 723, and *Peter Walker & Son (Edinburgh) Ltd.* v. *Church of Scotland General Trs.*, 1967 S.L.T. 297.
[35] For a fuller discussion see Craigie, *Heritable Rights*, 145 *et seq.*; McDonald, *Manual*, 2.5; K.G.C. Reid, "What is a Real Burden?" (1984) 29 J.L.S. 9; *Tailors of Aberdeen* v. *Coutts* (1834) 13 S. 226, rev. 2 S. & McL. 609; affd. 1 Rob.App. 296; 3 R.L.C. 269; *Stewart* v. *Duke of Montrose* (1860) 22 D. 755; *Mags. of Arbroath* v. *Dickson* (1872) 10 M. 630; *Marquis of Tweeddale's Trs.* v. *Earl of Haddington* (1880) 7 R. 620; *Anderson* v. *Dickie*, 1915 S.C.(H.L.) 79; *Wells* v. *New House Purchasers Ltd.*, 1964 S.L.T. (Sh.Ct.) 2.
[36] *Stewart* v. *Duke of Montrose, supra, per* Lord Deas at 803, 804; affd. (1863) 1 M.(H.L.) 25; *Hope* v. *Hope* (1864) 2 M. 670 (obligation of relief by superior).
[37] See paras. 19–18 *et seq.*

enforced by a personal action in the absence of an obligation for payment specially undertaken. In the absence of such an obligation the burden is enforceable only against the lands by real diligence.[38] Where the real burden is a periodical payment which was imposed in a feu grant, *e.g.* the obligation to pay feuduty, the continuing personal obligation by tenure implied in the feudal relationship entitles the superior to enforce payment by personal action or by irritancy in addition to the remedies of real diligence, but where the real burden is created or reserved in any other deed, such as a disposition, then only the remedies of real diligence directed against the lands are available to enforce payment. The legal requirements for the constitution of a valid real burden effective against singular successors in the ownership of the burdened land are similar to those required for the creation of a valid real condition and are considered in paragraphs 19–18 to 19–34 *infra*.

Real conditions

19–16   A real condition, as distinct from a real burden, is an integral part of the grant which imposes it and may be enforced by personal action against the proprietor of the lands affected for the time being at the instance of a person entitled to enforce it. Where the condition is imposed in a feu grant the superior and his successors can enforce the obligation by personal action against the vassal in the lands for the time being: where the condition is imposed in a disposition then the title to enforce it by personal action by persons other than the disponer or his personal representatives may be more difficult to establish.[39] A real condition may be positive, imposing an obligation to make a payment or *ad factum praestandum*, or negative, imposing a prohibition or restriction on construction of buildings or use of the land or buildings. The legal requirements for the constitution of a valid real condition are considered in the immediately succeeding paragraphs.

Statutory restrictions upon the creation of real burdens and conditions

19–17   *In limine* it should be kept in view that: (a) section 9 of the Conveyancing and Feudal Reform (Scotland) Act 1970 prohibits on or after November 29, 1970, the grant of any right over an interest in land for securing a sum of money which is a debt as defined in subsection (8) of that section except in the form of a standard security[39a]; (b) sections 1 and 2 of the Land Tenure Reform (Scotland) Act 1974 prohibit after July 31, 1974, the creation of a real burden of feuduty or ground

---

[38] See para. 19–62.

[39] *Marquis of Tweeddale's Trs.* v. *Earl of Haddington* (1880) 7 R. 620, *per* Lord Deas at 634; *Wells* v. *New House Purchasers Ltd.*, 1964 S.L.T. (Sh.Ct.) 2. See para. 19–48 for a fuller discussion.

[39a] The Act prohibits the *grant* of a heritable security for a debt. It does not in terms prohibit the creation of a real burden for debt by *reservation*, but the 1974 Act aftermentioned precludes the creation of a real burden which involves a periodical payment.

annual or any other periodical payment in respect of the tenure or use of land or under a land obligation, other than a payment in respect of a lease, liferent or other right of occupancy or a payment of teind, stipend or standard charge, a payment in defrayal of or contribution towards some continuing cost related to land or a payment under a heritable security. The requirements for the creation of a real burden in the succeeding paragraphs apply only for the purpose of testing the validity of real burdens created before the relevant date of either of those statutes or real burdens or conditions within any of the categories permitted by the statutes thereafter.

Constitution of real burdens and conditions

9–18   In any conveyance of lands, burdens and conditions which are to be created real must satisfy certain essential requirements. These requirements were comprehensively stated in *Tailors of Aberdeen* v. *Coutts*,[40] a case which related to real burdens imposed in a disposition, but many of the requirements laid down are applicable also to real conditions and have been so regarded in many subsequent decisions. The requirements, as modified or explained in later cases or by statute, are summarised in the following paragraphs.

9–19   **(1) Burdens or conditions must affect lands.** In the *Tailors of Aberdeen* case[40a] it was laid down that

> "To constitute a real burden or condition, either in feudal or burgage rights, which is effectual against singular successors, words must be used in the conveyance which clearly express or plainly imply that the subject itself is to be affected and not the grantee and his heirs alone . . . It is not essential that any *voces signatae* or technical form of words should be employed. There is no need of a declaration that the obligation is real, that it is a *debitum fundi*, that it shall be inserted in all the future infeftments or that it shall attach to singular successors. It is sufficient if the intention of the parties be clear, reference being had to the nature of the grant, which is often of great importance in ascertaining its import."

The intention to create an obligation which will affect singular successors is more easily implied if the obligation is of a continuing character. An obligation to maintain buildings and keep them insured against loss by fire and pay the premiums is the kind of obligation that may well be binding on singular successors.[41] On the other hand an obligation to pay a proportion of the cost of forming a road which had in fact been made by the superior several years before the singular successor of the vassal acquired the property was held on the wording of the feu charter to be a personal contract not binding upon the

---

[40] (1840) 1 Rob.App. 296 at 306, 307; 3 R.L.C. 269, 273.
[40a] 1 Rob.App. 296 at 306, 307.
[41] *Clark* v. *City of Glasgow Life Assce. Co.* (1854) 17 D.(H.L.) 27.

successor.[42] An obligation by a superior, who was the heir in possession under an entail, to take a disponee of adjoining land bound to pay one-half of the value of a boundary wall and thereafter to maintain it at mutual expense, being in essence an obligation to insert a clause in a deed, was held to be a personal undertaking, not a real condition.[43] A declaration that it should not be lawful to sell or feu ground except under certain conditions as to the type of buildings to be erected thereon was construed as a personal prohibition, not a real condition.[44, 45]

19–20   **(2) Lands affected must be specified.** The land which is burdened must be precisely identified. A description of subjects alleged to be burdened as "the ground occupied as a lawn" between the ground feued to A and the mansion house was held to be insufficiently definite.[46] In *Williamson* v. *Begg*[47] Lord President Inglis expressed the opinion that neither a general disposition without a description of the lands conveyed nor a notarial instrument following thereon could create a real burden on lands but in *Cowie* v. *Muirden*[48] the House of Lords decided that a real burden could be constituted by a notarial instrument in the form of Schedule L to the Titles to Land Consolidation (Scotland) Act 1868, provided that the burden was declared in the dispositive clause of the general disposition upon which the notarial instrument followed.

19–21   **(3) Burden or condition must appear in full or be validly referred to in dispositive clause.** Since the dispositive clause is the ruling clause which determines the measure of the grant a real burden or condition which qualifies the grant must appear in that clause and in order to satisfy the requirements of precision and to give notice of the qualification on the Register of Sasines (or now on the Land Register) the burden or condition must appear *ad longum* in the title of the burdened lands. In *Kemp* v. *Magistrates of Largs*[49] a restriction upon use of lands was held not to be a real restriction since *inter alia* it did not occur in the dispositive clause but in a statutory form of tenendas clause. As to reference in the dispositive clause of a conveyance to a burden or condition contained in full in another recorded deed see paragraph 19–24 *infra*.

19–22   **(4) Burden or condition must enter infeftment of burdened property— registration.** The requirement that a real burden or condition must

---

[42] *Mags. of Edinburgh* v. *Begg* (1883) 11 R. 352.
[43] *Jolly's Exrx.* v. *Viscount Stonehaven*, 1958 S.C. 635.
[44] *Anderson* v. *Dickie*, 1915 S.C.(H.L.) 79.
[45] For other cases where intended real burdens did not clearly affect the land, see *Baird's Trs.* v. *Mitchell* (1846) 8 D. 464 and *Davidson* v. *Dalziel* (1881) 8 R. 990.
[46] *Anderson* v. *Dickie, supra.*
[47] (1887) 14 R. 720.
[48] (1893) 20 R.(H.L.) 81.
[49] 1939 S.C.(H.L.) 6. See also *Liddall* v. *Duncan* (1898) 25 R. 1119.

enter the records was emphasised in the House of Lords by Lord Macmillan[50]:

> "I need not remind your Lordships of the importance of the requirement that any burden or restriction to be effectual must enter the records. In Scotland the purchaser of land buys on the faith of the records. He obtains for his protection a search of the Registers, and is entitled to rely on the land being unaffected by any burdens or conditions other than those contained in the deeds found on record to relate to the subject-matter of his purchase."[51]

Where a condition contained in articles of roup stipulated that the purchaser should build a house according to a particular elevation but the charter and sasine following upon the sale did not contain the condition, it was decided that a singular successor was not bound by the condition and could alter the elevation.[52] Again, where a contract was made amongst proprietors of land in the New Town of Edinburgh which contained conditions as to the buildings to be erected and the contract was referred to in subsequent recorded deeds, since the conditions were not set out at length and so did not enter the Register of Sasines it was held that a singular successor was not bound by the conditions.[53] It is not sufficient that the burdens or conditions enter the record *ad longum* in the title of other property[54] or are contained in a recorded agreement which was merely a personal contract not containing any conveyance.[55] An attempt to circumvent the rule that a real condition must enter the record of the burdened property on the ground that it was a servitude *altius non tollendi* failed,[56] but partly on the ground that it was not a properly constituted servitude.

–23 *Reference to burden or condition in recorded deed.* Prior to 1847 real burdens and conditions had to be inserted at length in successive deeds. Thereafter various statutes permitted short statutory references to burdens and conditions which were already contained *ad longum* in earlier infeftments relating to the property.[57] The current law as to references to burdens or conditions of title is now regulated by the Conveyancing (Scotland) Act 1874,[58] the Conveyancing (Scotland) Act 1924,[59] and the Conveyancing Amendment (Scotland) Act 1938[60] and, as regards certain deeds executed on or after April 4, 1979, the Land

---

[50] In *Kemp* v. *Magistrates of Largs, supra* at 13.
[51] The statement was made in the context of an alleged real condition; it requires qualification in a more general context in relation to inherent conditions of a feu grant and servitudes.
[52] *Croall* v. *Mags. of Edinburgh* (1870) 9 M. 323.
[53] *Liddall* v. *Duncan, supra.*
[54] *Botanic Gardens Picture House* v. *Adamson*, 1924 S.C. 549.
[55] *Campbell's Trs.* v. *Corporation of Glasgow* (1902) 4 F. 752.
[56] *Morier* v. *Brownlie & Watson* (1895) 23 R. 67.
[57] For an account of these statutes, see Craigie, *Heritable Rights*, 154–159.
[58] s. 32 and Sched. H.
[59] s. 9 and Sched. E.
[60] s. 2(1).

Registration (Scotland) Act 1979.[61] The principal provisions are summarised in paragraphs 19–24 and 19–25 *infra*.

19–24   *Deeds recorded in Register of Sasines.* (i) Reservations, real burdens, conditions, provisions, limitations, obligations and stipulations affecting lands may be validly imported into any deed relating to such lands by reference to a deed applicable to such lands, or to the estate of which such lands form part, recorded in the appropriate Register of Sasines, in which such reservations, burdens, etc., are set forth at full length. Such a reference may be in the form of Schedule H to the Conveyancing (Scotland) Act 1874.[62] Note that the deed referred to must be a deed applicable to the lands conveyed or to a larger estate of which they form part. If a large house is being subdivided particulars of any burdens and conditions imposed on the severance must be inserted in full in the dispositions of *both* parts; it is not permissible to insert them at length in one disposition and refer to them in the other.

(ii) The prior deed referred to for burdens may be described in the way permitted by the Conveyancing (Scotland) Act 1924 in the case of deeds referred to for a description of lands.[63]

(iii) If conditions or clauses affecting land have been duly referred to in the title of the proprietor for the time duly recorded in the Register of Sasines, it is not competent to object to the title on the ground that the conditions or clauses were not repeated or referred to in any prior deed affecting the land.[64] If in the course of examination of title an omission to refer to a prior writ which imposed a real burden or condition is observed, the defect is automatically rendered unobjectionable if the reference is effectively made in a later recorded writ in the progress or in a disposition then being prepared when it is duly recorded.

(iv) If such an omission is observed at a time when no new deed is contemplated, the proprietor of the land may grant and record a deed of acknowledgment in the form of Schedule E to the 1924 Act which has the effect of putting right the omission.[65]

(v) It is unnecessary to repeat or refer to conditions or clauses imposing real burdens or conditions in any deed constituting, transmitting or dealing with a heritable security other than a disposition granted in virtue of a power of sale under such a security or a decree of foreclosure.[66]

19–25   *Interests registered in Land Register.* (i) A conveyance in a transaction

---

[61] ss. 15(2) and 17.
[62] s. 32.
[63] Conveyancing Amendment (Scotland) Act 1938, s. 2(1).
[64] 1924 Act, s. 9(3).
[65] 1924 Act, s. 9(4).
[66] 1924 Act, s. 9(1).

which induces first registration must comply with the foregoing requirements regarding reference to real burdens and conditions.

(ii) Once an interest has been registered the real burdens and conditions affecting it or a summary of them will be entered on its title sheet and thereafter it is unnecessary in deeds which effect a dealing with the interest to insert or refer to the real burdens and conditions. The requirement of feudal law that real burdens or conditions must be repeated or referred to in the dispositive clause of a recorded conveyance is now superseded as regards a deed relating to a registered interest by a statutory provision that such a deed imports full insertion of any real burden or condition[67] and the provisions of the older conveyancing statutes which permitted importation of such burdens or conditions by reference are disapplied.[68]

(iii) As to practice in relation to references to real burdens and conditions in cases where there are registered and unregistered interests in the lands concerned, including cases where the lands affected are partly within and partly without operational areas, see the Registration of Title Practice Book, para. D.1.22.

-26 **(5) Burden or condition must be precisely specified.** It is essential that a real burden or condition must be expressed with precision. The principle is that a proprietor of land must be able to ascertain from the Register of Sasines or the Land Register the exact terms of any real burden or condition which affects his property and these terms must be ascertainable from recorded deeds or the registered title of his own land or larger areas which comprehend it without having to refer to the titles of other land or to unrecorded or unregistered deeds. The application of this principle to real burdens and real conditions is considered in the following paragraphs.

Real burdens

-27 *Amount must be definite.* An obligation to pay money, if it is to be a valid real burden, must be for a definite amount.[69] If, however, an obligation *ad factum praestandum* is imposed the implement of which may involve expenditure of an uncertain amount, that is enforceable as a real condition,[70] and an obligation to purchase and transfer stock, although the cost would vary according to the price in the stock market, likewise was sustained as a valid real burden since the obligation was *ad factum praestandum*.[71] So when an obligation is being imposed upon feuars to incur an expense of unascertained

---

[67] Land Registration (Scotland) Act 1979, s. 15(2)(*b*).
[68] *Ibid.*, s. 15(2)(*a*).
[69] See para. 19–13 and authorities there cited.
[70] *Tailors of Aberdeen* v. *Coutts*, *supra* (obligation to form a foot pavement); *Clark* v. *City of Glasgow Life Assce. Co.* (1854) 17 D.(H.L.) 27 (obligation to maintain fire insurance cover).
[71] *Edmonstone* v. *Seton* (1888) 16 R. 1.

amount, *e.g.* the cost of forming a road, the safe method is to impose a direct obligation upon the feuars to perform the work with reservation of the right to the superior to do so and charge a proportion of the cost to the feuars. If singular successors are involved before the work is carried out the obligation to do so may be enforced against them.

19–28 *Real burdens for future or contingent obligations.* It is clear that a personal obligation to create a real burden for payment of money on the happening of some future event, whether certain to occur or not, can be constituted contractually or testamentarily.[72] It is essential that the obligation is expressed in terms which clearly indicate that a real burden is intended, *e.g.* that it is to be binding on singular successors in the ownership of the land upon which the burden is to be created[73] and that the event upon which the burden is to become enforceable is clearly specified in unambiguous terms.[74] Whether it is competent in a conveyance of lands to create a real burden not immediately prestable but only to become exigible on the occurrence of a contingent future event was described as a question of difficulty.[75] It is suggested that there is no legal impediment to that course provided that the event is described with the necessary precision. In *Ewing's Trs.* v. *Crum Ewing*,[74] where a real burden was purported to be created upon lands in the event of a sale of the estate, the court decided that the contingency was too indefinite to form the subject of a real burden since there was no provision as to what was to happen if part only of the estate was sold, but it was not suggested that, in the absence of such ambiguity, the creation of a real burden would have been incompetent. In former practice, before the abolition of casualties, it was customary to impose expressly as a real burden in a feu charter the obligation to pay composition in the event of a sale.

19–29 *Identification of creditor.* In conformity with the rule that a real burden must be specific it is necessary that the creditor in the burden, whether a party to the deed or another person, is clearly identified[76] but it is sufficient if the burden is created in favour of unnamed children of a named person.[77]

Real conditions

19–30 *The requirement of precision.* A real condition which imposes obligations or restrictions upon land which will be binding upon each successive owner of it should be expressed in clear and unambiguous terms. It

---

[72] *Falconar Stewart* v. *Wilkie* (1892) 19 R. 630.
[73] *Davidson* v. *Dalziel* (1881) 8 R. 990; *Buchanan* v. *Eaton*, 1911 S.C.(H.L.) 40.
[74] *Ewing's Trs.* v. *Crum Ewing*, 1923 S.C. 569.
[75] In *Falconar Stewart* v. *Wilkie* (1892) 19 R. 630, *per* Lord Ordinary (Kyllachy) at 634.
[76] Ersk., II, iii, 50; *Stenhouse* v. *Innes and Black* (1765) Mor. 10264.
[77] *Erskine* v. *Wright* (1846) 8 D. 863.

must not be indefinite either as to the land affected[78] or the nature of the restriction, which cannot be one which is determinable as a matter of taste or by a subjective test on which there could be legitimate difference of opinion.[79] Nor can a limited right of occupation based on an assumption that buildings would continue to be used for a particular purpose be sustained as a real condition.[80] On the other hand an obligation *ad factum praestandum* to erect buildings within a time limit which has expired[81] or is unspecified[82] will not thereby be rendered nugatory; the court will ordain implement within a reasonable time specified.

-31 *The presumption for freedom—strict construction.* The presumption of law is in favour of freedom of an owner of land to use his property as he wishes and so any real condition which fetters such use will be construed strictly and a restriction which is not plainly expressed will not readily be implied.[83] The reports of decided cases[84] abound in illustrations of the rule that a real condition will be construed strictly in accordance with its terms and that obligations which are not expressly imposed or operations or uses which are not expressly prohibited, even although intended to be so, will not limit the freedom of action of the owner of the land affected. In *Heriot's Hospital* v. *Ferguson*[85] a feu charter stipulated that it would not be lawful without the consent of the superiors to dig for stones, coal, sand or any other thing within the ground nor to use the same in any other way than by the ordinary labour of plough and spade. It was held that the latter restriction was simply explicative of the former and did not prohibit the erection of buildings. A restriction to the erection of "villas or dwelling-houses" did not prohibit the erection of tenements since these were included in the latter category.[86] In *Wyllie* v. *Dunnett*[87] a feu charter obliged the vassal within two years to erect a dwelling-house with suitable offices conform to a plan and elevation to be approved by the superior and provided that "no buildings of any other description" should be erected without the written sanction of the superior. A dwelling-house and offices were duly erected and some years later the vassal proposed to build a stable. It was decided that he was entitled to do so without the consent of the superior since a stable fell within the description of

---

[78] *Anderson* v. *Dickie*, 1915 S.C.(H.L.) 79; *Scottish Temperance Life Assce. Co.* v. *Law Union and Rock Insce. Co.*, 1917 S.C. 175.

[79] *McNeill* v. *Mackenzie* (1870) 8 M. 520; *Murray's Trs.* v. *Trs. for St. Margaret's Convent*, 1907 S.C.(H.L.) 8.

[80] *Kirkintilloch Kirk Session* v. *Kirkintilloch School Board*, 1911 S.C. 1127.

[81] *Magistrates of Glasgow* v. *Hay* (1883) 10 R. 635.

[82] *Anderson* v. *Valentine*, 1957 S.L.T. 57. See *Middleton* v. *Leslie* (1892) 19 R. 801.

[83] *The Walker Trs.* v. *Haldane* (1902) 4 F. 594 *per* Lord Low (Ordinary) at 596; *Anderson* v. *Dickie, supra, per* Lord Dunedin at 89.

[84] See para. 19–32.

[85] (1773) 3 Pat.App. 674.

[86] *Bainbridge* v. *Campbell*, 1912 S.C. 92.

[87] (1899) 1 F. 982.

offices: the prohibition would require to have been against the erection of "other buildings of any description," not "buildings of any other description." In *Carswell* v. *Goldie*[88] a feu contract provided that the vassal should erect a dwelling-house "with relative offices which may include a garage," and also that the plans of all buildings to be erected should first be approved by the superiors. The house and garage were duly erected and subsequently, without obtaining the approval of the superiors, the vassal erected another garage. It was held in the Outer House that the reference to a garage did not impose a limitation to the building of one garage only, since relative offices could include a garage. On appeal that construction was approved by the Inner House but, since the prior approval of the superiors was necessary and that had not been obtained, it was held that an irritancy had been incurred.

19–32   Certain rules which are important to conveyancers in framing real conditions may be derived from the principle of strict construction, *viz.–*

(a) *A positive obligation will not readily be construed as implying a restriction.* Where an obligation to erect self-contained villas to yield a net rental of double the feuduty had been implemented by the erection of villas on part of the ground, it was held that there was no restriction on the remainder of the ground that only self-contained villas be erected and a singular successor was entitled to build tenements.[89] An obligation to use ground in all time coming for a pier and harbour did not infer a prohibition against the use of part of it for other purposes.[90]

(b) *An obligation to build will not imply an obligation to maintain.* In *Peter Walker & Son (Edinburgh) Ltd.* v. *Church of Scotland General Trustees*[91] it was held that an obligation to build a house, unless expressed so as to be plainly a real burden on singular successors, would not imply an obligation on such successors to maintain it, and singular successors were entitled to demolish a house built in 1809 and to substitute a different type of building.

(c) *A restriction on building will not imply a restriction on use.* An obligation in a feu contract to build a self-contained lodging and maintain it was construed as referring only to construction and not to use, so that conversion of a house by internal structural alteration did not contravene the conditions of the feu contract.[92] A provision that the vassal was entitled only to erect self-contained lodgings or dwelling-houses and offices and that these should not be converted into shops, warehouses or trading places of any description was held not to preclude the use of one of the houses as an office for clerical work by

---

[88] 1967 S.L.T. 174; revd. 1967 S.L.T. 339.
[89] *Fleming* v. *Ure* (1896) 4 S.L.T. 26.
[90] *Kemp* v. *Magistrates of Largs*, 1939 S.C.(H.L.) 6.
[91] 1967 S.L.T. 297. See also *Boswell's Trs.* v. *Hunter* (1904) 12 S.L.T. 406.
[92] *Porter* v. *Campbell's Trs.*, 1923 S.C.(H.L.) 94; also *Buchanan* v. *Marr* (1883) 10 R. 936 and *Miller* v. *Carmichael* (1888) 15 R. 991.

the staff of a post office—the restriction applied to structure only and not to use, and no structural alteration was involved.[93]

9–33 *Particular restrictions.* For the purpose of framing real conditions or considering the validity of real conditions in existing title deeds the most convenient approach to an examination of the relevant decisions is by reference to subject-matter. The following list of authorities is not exhaustive but may be of assistance.

SITE OF BUILDINGS

Identification of site of buildings to be erected

> *Naismith* v. *Cairnduff* (1876) 3 R. 863.
> *Scottish Temperance Life Assce. Co.* v. *Law Union and Rock Insurance Co.*, 1917 S.C. 175.

Building up to boundaries—building line

> *Trustees of Free St. Mark's Church* v. *Taylor's Trs.* (1869) 7 M. 415.
> *Dennistoun* v. *Thomson* (1872) 11 M. 121.
> *Crawford* v. *Darroch*, 1907 S.C. 703.

Prohibition of building and area affected

> *Russell* v. *Cowpar* (1882) 9 R. 660.
> *Lawson* v. *Wilkie* (1897) 24 R. 649.
> *Clark & Sons* v. *School Board of Perth* (1898) 25 R. 919.
> *Anderson* v. *Dickie*, 1915 S.C.(H.L.) 79.
> *Thomson* v. *Liddell's Motor Service*, 1928 S.N. 42.
> *Lawrence* v. *Scott*, 1965 S.C. 403.

Underground passage

> *Gray* v. *Malloch* (1872) 10 M. 774.

STYLE AND CONSTRUCTION OF BUILDINGS

Height of buildings

> *Alexander* v. *Stobo* (1871) 9 M. 599.
> *Banks & Co.* v. *Walker* (1874) 1 R. 981.
> *McEwan* v. *Shaw Stewart* (1880) 7 R. 682.
> *Cochran* v. *Paterson* (1882) 9 R. 634.
> *The Walker Trs.* v. *Haldane* (1902) 4 F. 594.

---

[93] *Mathieson* v. *Allan's Trs.*, 1914 S.C. 464.

Proprietors of Royal Exchange Buildings, Glasgow v. *Cotton*, 1912
  S.C. 1151.
Dykehead and Shotts Co-operative Society v. *Public Trustee*, 1926
  S.C. 157.

Buildings similar or not inferior to others

  Morrison v. *McLay* (1874) 1 R. 1117.
  Sandeman's Trs. v. *Brown* (1892) 20 R. 210.
  Middleton v. *Leslie* (1894) 21 R. 781.
  Assets Co. v. *Ogilvie* (1897) 24 R. 400.
  Oswald v. *Wilson* (1898) 6 S.L.T. 69.

Materials of buildings

  Beattie v. *Ures* (1876) 3 R. 634.
  Waddell v. *Campbell* (1898) 25 R. 456.
  Street v. *Dobbie* (1903) 5 F. 941.

Building conform to plans and elevations

  The Walker Trs. v. *Haldane* (1902) 4 F. 594.

Description of style too vague

  McNeill v. *Mackenzie* (1870) 8 M. 520.
  Murray's Trs. v. *Trustees for St. Margaret's Convent*, 1907 S.C.
    (H.L.) 8.
  Gammell's Trs. v. *Land Commission*, 1970 S.L.T. 254.

CHARACTER AND USE OF BUILDINGS

Villas

  Millar v. *Trustees for Endowment Committee of Church of Scotland*
    (1896) 23 R. 557.

Villas or dwelling-houses

  Moir's Trs. v. *McEwan* (1880) 7 R. 1141.
  Minister of Prestonpans v. *Heritors* (1905) 13 S.L.T. 463.
  Bainbridge v. *Campbell*, 1912 S.C. 92.

Self-contained villas, lodgings or dwelling-houses

  Buchanan v. *Marr* (1883) 10 R. 936.
  Miller v. *Carmichael* (1888) 15 R. 991.
  Montgomerie-Fleming's Trs. v. *Kennedy*, 1912 S.C. 1307.
  Mathieson v. *Allan's Trs.*, 1914 S.C. 464.

Colquhoun's C.B. v. *Glen's Tr.*, 1920 S.C. 737.
Porter v. *Campbell's Trs.*, 1923 S.C.(H.L.) 94.
Macdonald v. *Douglas*, 1963 S.C. 374.

Dwelling-houses

Graham v. *Shiels* (1901) 8 S.L.T. 368.
Gordon v. *Campbell's Trs.* (1902) 10 S.L.T. 315.
Botanic Gardens Picture House v. *Adamson*, 1924 S.C. 549.
Howard de Walden Estates Ltd. v. *Bowmaker Ltd.*, 1965 S.C. 163.

Private dwelling-houses

Ewing v. *Hastie* (1878) 5 R. 439.
Colville v. *Carrick* (1883) 10 R. 1241.
Brown v. *Crum Ewing's Trs.*, 1918 1 S.L.T. 340.

Dwelling-houses and offices—stables, garages

Murison v. *Wallace* (1883) 10 R. 1239.
Colville v. *Carrick* (1883) 10 R. 1241.
Thom v. *Chalmers* (1886) 13 R. 1026.
Wyllie v. *Dunnett* (1899) 1 F. 982.
The Walker Trs. v. *Haldane* (1902) 4 F. 594.
Shand v. *Brand* (1907) 14 S.L.T. 704.
Carswell v. *Goldie*, 1967 S.L.T. 339.

Water supply

Anstruther's Trs. v. *Burgh of Pittenweem*, 1943 S.L.T. 160.

Works of defence

Ardgowan Estates Ltd. v. *Lawson*, 1948 S.L.T. 186.

Petrol pumps

Ben Challum Ltd. v. *Buchanan*, 1955 S.C. 348.

PROHIBITIONS

Liquor—public houses

Ewing v. *Campbells* (1877) 5 R. 230.
Earl of Zetland v. *Hislop* (1882) 9 R.(H.L.) 40.
Menzies v. *Caledonian Canal Commissioners* (1900) 2 F. 953.

Shops or trading places

> Graham v. Shiels (1901) 8 S.L.T. 368.
> Mathieson v. Allan's Trs., 1914 S.C. 464.
> Williamson & Hubbard v. Harrison, 1970 S.L.T. 346.

Particular business

> Phillips v. Lavery, 1962 S.L.T. (Sh.Ct.) 57.

Nuisance

> Anderson v. Aberdeen Agricultural Hall Co. (1879) 6 R. 901.
> Manson v. Forrest (1887) 14 R. 802.
> North British Rly. Co. v. Moore (1891) 18 R. 1021.
> Sandeman's Trs. v. Brown (1892) 20 R. 210.
> Crichton's Trs. v. Corporation of Glasgow (1892) 1 S.L.T. 325.
> Mannofield Residents Property Co. Ltd. v. Thomson, 1983 S.L.T. (Sh.Ct.) 71.

Subdivision

> Girls' School Co. Ltd. v. Buchanan, 1958 S.L.T. (Notes) 2.

Planting or growing trees

> Hunter v. Fox, 1964 S.C.(H.L.) 95.

19–34   (6) Real conditions must not be contrary to law or public policy nor useless or vexatious nor inconsistent with nature of property. The classic statement of the law with regard to those negative conditions is contained in *Tailors of Aberdeen* v. *Coutts*[94] as follows:

> "The burden or condition must not be contrary to law, or inconsistent with the nature of this species of property; it must not be useless or vexatious; it must not be contrary to public policy, for example, by tending to impede the commerce of land, or create a monopoly. The superior or the party in whose favour it is conceived must have an interest to enforce it."

Illustrations of conditions contrary to law would be a prohibition of alienation without the superior's consent[95] or of subinfeudation,[96] or a clause conferring a conveyancing monopoly on the superior's agent.[96a] A condition which required every singular successor to grant his personal obligation to the superior for performance of the prestations of the feu grant would be superfluous; that is already implied in the feudal contract by tenure. Examples of unenforceable monopolies were a

---

[94] (1840) 1 Rob.App. 296 at 307.
[95] Tenures Abolition Act 1747, s. 10.
[96] Conveyancing (Scotland) Act 1874, s. 22; Conveyancing Amendment (Scotland) Act 1938, s. 8.
[96a] Conveyancing (Scotland) Act 1874, s. 22.

stipulation that feuars of former barony lands should have their work done by the barony blacksmith,[97] or that owners of land within a barony should purchase ale only from a brewery within it.[98] A real condition which purported to create an exclusive right of shooting over other lands which remained the property of the disponer was held to be inconsistent with the nature of the species of property.[99] Interest to enforce a real condition is considered more fully later,[1] but it is contrary to public policy as impeding the commerce of land to permit the imposition of a real condition for personal reasons or commercial advantage: the interest to enforce must be a patrimonial interest in property.[2] Difficult questions may arise where a restriction is protecting both a commercial interest and a patrimonial interest in property, as in the case of a prohibition of the sale of liquors which is protecting the goodwill of licensed premises nearby, since such goodwill is heritable.[3]

Framing real burdens and conditions—practice

–35 (1) The granter of the deed imposing the burdens or conditions should have a recorded or registered title. That is essential if the deed is a feu grant or deed of conditions. It is thought that it is competent to impose such burdens or conditions in a disposition by an uninfeft granter who deduces title in terms of section 3 of the Conveyancing (Scotland) Act 1924. Upon the disposition being recorded the grantee is deemed to have expede and recorded a notarial instrument to which the provisions of section 146 of the Titles to Land Consolidation (Scotland) Act 1868 apply, and it would seem impossible for the grantee who has accepted a disposition incorporating the burdens or conditions and caused them to be inserted at length in his recorded title or entered in the title sheet of his registered title to contend that they have not been effectively created real.[4]

(2) It is now incompetent to grant a heritable security for debt except by way of a standard security[5] or to create a real burden on land for a periodical payment of money, subject to certain exceptions.[6]

(3) The burden or condition must be inserted *at length* in the *dispositive clause* of a conveyance of the burdened land or an estate of which it forms part, or in a notice of title following thereon, or in a deed of conditions applicable to such land or estate under section 32 of the Conveyancing (Scotland) Act 1874.

---

[97] *Yeaman* v. *Crawford* (1770) Mor. 14537.
[98] *Orrock* v. *Bennet* (1762) Mor. 15009.
[99] *Beckett* v. *Bisset*, 1921, 2 S.L.T. 33.
[1] See paras. 19–41 *et seq.*
[2] *Aberdeen Varieties Ltd.* v. *James F. Donald (Aberdeen Cinemas) Ltd.*, 1939 S.C. 788; 1940 S.C.(H.L.) 52; *Phillips* v. *Lavery*, 1962 S.L.T. (Sh.Ct.) 57.
[3] *Co-operative Wholesale Society Ltd.* v. *Usher's Brewery*, 1975 S.L.T. (Lands Tr.) 9.
[4] *Cowie* v. *Muirden* (1893) 20 R.(H.L.) 81 at 88.
[5] Conveyancing and Feudal Reform (Scotland) Act 1970, s. 9.
[6] Land Tenure Reform (Scotland) Act 1974, s. 2. See para. 19–17.

(4) A real condition must be precise on all relevant matters such as the description and character of the obligation or restriction imposed, the ground to which it is applicable and any event on the occurrence of which the condition is to apply. Since purchasers buy on the faith of the registers the courts will not readily adopt a construction of a real condition which will give effect to the intention of parties but does violence to the ordinary meaning of the words used, as they might do in the case of an ordinary contract.[7]

(5) If the condition relates to the construction of buildings it should contain a stipulation that the plans and specifications must be approved by the superior or other party entitled to enforce the condition before the work of construction is commenced,[8] and a prohibition of any buildings or erections other than those sanctioned. A specific obligation to maintain the buildings should be included.

(6) If the condition involves an obligation to pay or contribute to the cost of works a sum of money of uncertain amount, an obligation to construct the works should be imposed with a reserved right to construct the works and require payment of the cost when ascertained.[9]

(7) Since a real condition can be enforced only by a person having a patrimonial interest in land, it is advisable in the case of a real condition created in a disposition to identify the land in respect of which the interest subsists, particularly where the condition may be vulnerable to attack on the ground that it was imposed for commercial advantage.[10]

(8) Although it is not necessary that the condition be declared real or fenced with irritant or resolutive clauses, the best practice is to insert such a declaration and clauses in order to demonstrate the intention of parties.

(9) The conveyance or notice of title containing the condition must be recorded in the Register of Sasines or the condition must be inserted in the title sheet of a registered interest, in order to be effective as real. If contained in a deed of conditions authorised by section 32 of the 1874 Act the conditions will become effective immediately on recording of the deed in the Register of Sasines or registration of the conditions in the Land Register unless the deed expressly otherwise provides.[11]

Deeds of conditions

19–36   A proprietor of lands may execute and record in the Register of Sasines a deed setting forth the reservations and real burdens and

---

[7] *Hunter* v. *Fox*, 1964 S.C.(H.L.) 95.
[8] *Carswell* v. *Goldie*, 1967 S.L.T. 174; revd. 1967 S.L.T. 339.
[9] See para. 19–27.
[10] See para. 19–34.
[11] Land Registration (Scotland) Act 1979, s. 17.

conditions under which he is to feu or otherwise deal with or affect his lands or any part thereof.[11a] Thereafter the reservations and real burdens and conditions in the deed may be effectually imported by reference to it in any subsequent conveyance of the land or part thereof.[11b] This facility is widely used in prescribing feuing and building conditions in an estate which is about to be developed and in setting out the common rights and obligations of the respective owners of flats in a tenement building which are about to be sold separately. There was some doubt whether conditions specified in a deed of conditions became real on the recording of the deed or only on the recording of a subsequent conveyance which imported the conditions by reference, the general view being that they became real only in the latter event. As regards deeds of conditions executed after April 4, 1979, that doubt is removed by section 17 of the Land Registration (Scotland) Act 1979 which provides that a land obligation[11c] specified in such a deed becomes a real obligation affecting the land to which it applies on the recording of the deed of conditions in the Register of Sasines or on the obligation being registered in the Land Register unless it is expressly stated in the deed that the provisions of the section are not to apply to the obligation. If a deed of conditions is executed at the commencement of a housing development without any express statement of disapplication, each purchaser of a house has the assurance that the conditions will apply throughout the whole development. On the other hand the developer will be unable, except with the consent of the owners of all the houses already sold, to depart from the original scheme of development. That may be disadvantageous if it is desired to change the scheme of development and may detract from the value of the undeveloped land if it has to be sold before the development is completed, since the purchaser would be bound by the conditions in the original deed of conditions. It is suggested that the deed of conditions should be executed only in respect of an area where there is no likelihood of the scheme of development being altered. Alternatively, the deed of conditions should contain a statement expressly disapplying section 17 of the 1979 Act and the conditions should be applied in the conveyances of individual plots when sold with a provision that there is reserved to the granter a right to vary them as regards any part of the area of the development. As to reference to deeds of conditions in subsequent conveyances see note to paragraph 19–39 *infra*.

[11a] The deed may be an agreement to which the proprietor of the land is a party—*Gorrie & Banks Ltd.* v. *Burgh of Musselburgh*, 1973 S.C. 33.

[11b] Conveyancing (Scotland) Act 1874, s. 32.

[11c] The phrase "land obligation" includes real conditions; see Conveyancing and Feudal Reform (Scotland) Act 1970, s. 1(2).

Styles

19–37 *Deed of conditions—flatted tenement—no express statement deferring applicability*

We X Company Limited, (*designed*), heritable proprietors of the Property aftermentioned, WHEREAS we are about to sell or otherwise deal separately with the eight dwelling-houses comprised in the Property and it is desirable to set forth in writing the rights appertaining to each of the said dwelling-houses and the real burdens, conditions and provisions under which the same shall be held by the respective proprietors thereof THEREFORE we provide and declare as follows:—

Definitions

1. In this Deed—

(a) "Property" means ALL and WHOLE the steading of ground in the City of Glasgow and County of Lanark containing (*area*) or thereby described and disponed in Feu Contract between AB and CD dated   and recorded in the Division of the General Register of Sasines for the County of the Barony and Regality of Glasgow on   both in the year   together with the building comprising eight dwelling-houses known as Copland Road, Glasgow and all other buildings erected on the said steading and the whole fittings and fixtures situated on the said steading and in or upon the said building and other erections.

(b) "Tenement" means the building comprising the said eight dwelling-houses.

(c) "Dwelling-house" means any one of the said eight dwelling-houses in the Tenement and the fixtures and fittings therein.

(d) "Common Parts" means (i) the solum, foundations, gables, outside walls and roof and chimneystalks of the Tenement (ii) the entrance close, passage and common staircase of the Tenement with the stairs, stair landings, stair railings in and walls and ceilings enclosing the said close, passage and staircase and the hatchway leading to the roof (iii) the back court and ashbin shelter, the boundary walls and railings of and all other erections on the said back court (iv) the pavement *ex adverso* the Tenement (v) the common drains, soil and rain water pipes, tanks, cisterns, gutters, rhones, conductors, electric mains, cables, pipes and wires serving the Property and (vi) the whole parts and pertinents, fixtures and fittings of or in connection with the Property which are common to the proprietors of all or two or more Dwelling-houses.

(e) "Common Charges" means the whole expenses incurred from time to time in respect of the repair, maintenance and renewal and any authorised improvement of the Common parts or any portion of them.

(f) "Proprietor" means the proprietor for the time being of any one Dwelling-house and where two or more persons own any Dwelling-house means both or all of such persons who shall be liable jointly and severally for any obligations relating to such Dwelling-house.

(g) "Factor" means the person, firm or company responsible for the general management and administration of the Property appointed in accordance with the provisions of clause 5 of this Deed.

Dwelling-houses

2. (a) Each Dwelling-house shall be held by the Proprietor thereof in all time coming subject to the conditions of this Deed.

(b) Each Dwelling-house shall be maintained by the Proprietor thereof at his own expense in good order and repair. No structural or external alterations shall be made to any Dwelling-house or to any part thereof except with the prior consent in writing of the Factor. In order to preserve uniformity in the external appearance of the Tenement no change shall be made in the colour scheme or mode of decoration or finish of the exterior of any Dwelling-house except with the prior approval in writing of the Factor.

(c) Each Proprietor shall be bound to allow access to the Dwelling-house owned by him to the Factor or any other Proprietor or to the tradesmen employed by the Factor or such other Proprietor for the purpose of carrying out any necessary repairs to or renewals of the Common Parts or any portion thereof.

(d) (i) The proportion of any feuduty, ground annual and other periodic charge which has been allocated on a Dwelling-house shall be paid by the Proprietor thereof punctually when due.

(ii) The proportion of any unallocated feuduty, ground annual and any other periodic charge payable from the Property which has been apportioned on a Dwelling-house shall be added to the Common Charges and included in the statement thereof and shall be payable by the Proprietor of such Dwelling-house in the same way as provided in Clause 3 of this Deed.

(e) Each Dwelling-house shall be used and occupied in all time coming as a private dwelling-house and for no other purpose whatever.

(f) There shall not be kept in or about any of the Dwelling-houses or in any other part of the Property any animal or bird or other livestock (except one bird in a cage) without the consent in writing of a majority of the Proprietors of the remaining Dwelling-houses and the permission to keep such animal or bird or livestock shall cease in the event of such consent being withdrawn.

Common Parts

3. (a) The Common Parts shall be owned by all the Proprietors of Dwelling-houses as their common property.

(b) Each Proprietor shall be liable jointly with the remaining Proprietors for the repair and maintenance and, where necessary, renewal or improvement of the Common Parts or any portion thereof and for payment of the Common Charges in the proportion of one eighth share for each Dwelling-house.

(c) The Factor shall have full power and authority to instruct and have executed from time to time such works as he in his judgment shall consider necessary or desirable for the repair, maintenance and renewal of the Common Parts or any portion thereof, provided always that in the case of a major work (being a work the cost of which is estimated by the Factor to exceed £   or such other amount as may from time to time be fixed by the Proprietors) the Factor shall, before instructing the same, report the matter to a meeting of the Proprietors called for the purpose as hereinafter provided.

(d) As soon as reasonably practicable after the thirty first day of

May in each year the Factor shall prepare a statement of the Common Charges incurred in respect of the year ended on that date (hereinafter called "the property year") and shall furnish a copy thereof to each of the Proprietors. Each Proprietor shall pay to the Factor the proportion of the Common Charges payable in respect of his Dwelling-house as follows:— (i) On the first day of each of the four months of February, May, August and November in the property year a sum, notified by the Factor to each Proprietor from time to time, approximately equivalent to a one fourth proportion of the share of the Common Charges estimated by the Factor as payable by such Proprietor in respect of that year (hereinafter called "the quarterly instalment") and (ii) within fourteen days after the receipt from the Factor by each Proprietor of a copy of the statement of the Common Charges for that year the amount (if any) by which the share of the Common Charges ascertained in accordance with that statement exceeds the total of the four quarterly instalments paid for that year. Any amount by which said total exceeds the amount ascertained in accordance with said statement shall be retained by the Factor and taken into account by him in determining the monthly instalments for the succeeding year. The Factor shall have power to sue for and recover by legal process the amount of any monthly instalment or other sum due and payable in terms of this Deed which has not been paid.

Insurance

4. (a) The Property shall be kept insured against fire, storm damage and other risks normally covered by a comprehensive insurance of residential property for the full replacement value thereof under a common policy in name of the Proprietors. The Proprietors shall be kept insured against property owners' liability arising from ownership of the Property the indemnity for which shall be not less than £   in respect of any one accident. The said insurances shall be effected by the Factor on behalf of the Proprietors and the premiums payable in respect thereof shall be payable by the Proprietors in the proportion of one eighth share for each Dwelling-house. The amount of such premiums shall be added to the Common Charges and included in the statement thereof and shall be payable by the Proprietors in the same way as provided in respect of Common Charges in Clause 3 of this Deed.
(b) The amount of the replacement value for which the said insurance of the Property shall be effected shall be determined from time to time by the Proprietors and the minimum amount of the indemnity in respect of property owners' liability may be increased from time to time by the Proprietors.
(c) Any amount recovered from the insurers under the comprehensive insurance of the Property in the event of a claim shall be applied in the repair and reinstatement of the damage to the Property.

Factor

5. (a) The Factor shall be appointed and his appointment may be renewed or terminated by the Proprietors who shall determine his remuneration and the terms and conditions of his appointment.

(b) The Factor shall be responsible for the general management and administration of the Property and, without prejudice to that generality, he shall have the powers conferred on him and shall perform the duties imposed on him by this Deed and exercise any other functions assigned to him in relation to the Property by the Proprietors.

Meetings of Proprietors

6. (a) A meeting of the Proprietors to decide any matter relating to the Property falling to be determined by the Proprietors in terms of this Deed or otherwise (including regulations as to the use of the back-court or other Common Parts) may be called by the Factor on twenty one days' notice in writing specifying the business of the meeting and the place, date and time of the meeting, and the Factor shall convene such a meeting to be held within thirty days of receipt by him of a requisition therefor signed by any two or more Proprietors.

(b) At any such meeting (i) any Proprietor may be represented by any other person as his mandatory appointed by written mandate to attend, vote and act on behalf of the Proprietor granting the mandate, (ii) the Proprietors of any five or more Dwelling-houses present in person or represented by a mandatory shall be a quorum, (iii) the chairman of the meeting shall be appointed by those present and entitled to vote, and (iv) all matters shall be determined, where necessary, by a majority of the Proprietors or their mandatories present and voting.

(c) All decisions and regulations regularly made at any such meeting shall be binding upon all the Proprietors whether or not present in person or represented and whether or not consenting to any such decision unless any Proprietor shall within fourteen days of the making of such decision refer the matter to arbitration in accordance with clause 7 of this Deed.

Arbitration

7. (a) All questions, disputes or differences which may arise between or among the Factor, the Proprietors or any of them arising directly or indirectly from the provisions of this Deed or generally in relation to the Property shall be referred to the decision of   as Arbiter, whom failing, by declinature or otherwise, of an Arbiter to be appointed by the Sheriff Principal of   on the application of any person interested.

(b) The Arbiter may appoint an assessor and may order the execution of works and allocate the expenses of works and may make an award of the costs of the reference and decern accordingly.

(c) The decision of the Arbiter shall be final and binding upon the parties and upon all Proprietors.

(d) The application of section 3 of the Administration of Justice (Scotland) Act 1972 is hereby expressly excluded.

Real Burdens and Conditions

8. The whole conditions, provisions, obligations, stipulations and others contained in this Deed are hereby created real burdens and conditions affecting the Property and any part thereof and shall be

binding upon all Proprietors and their respective executors and successors in all time coming [and shall be inserted or validly referred to in all conveyances and instruments of or affecting the said Dwelling-houses or any of them or any part of the Property otherwise the same shall be null and void.]

(*To be attested*)   *Stamp duty 50p.*

NOTES

(a) Provision may be made for proprietors making an initial deposit to finance common charges, *e.g.*

Each of the Proprietors will deposit with the Factor in respect of his or her Dwelling-house the sum of £   or such other sum as may be agreed between the Factor and the proprietors from time to time. This sum will be deposited immediately upon acquisition of the Dwelling-house as a contribution to finance the cost of Common Charges. The deposit will be returned when any Proprietor or his or her representatives cease to own the Dwelling-house. No interest shall be payable on the deposit.

(b) In the event of any proprietor defaulting in making payment of his or her appropriate share of common charges provision may be made for reimbursement thereof to the factor by the other proprietors if the defaulting proprietor's share proves irrecoverable, *e.g.*

In the event of the share of Common Charges of any Proprietor remaining unpaid after a demand for payment has been issued by the Factor and a decree of court has been obtained therefor the Factor shall be entitled, on expiry of the period of twenty one days after the date of such decree or, in the case of an instalment decree, after the date when the last instalment became due, to receive from the remaining Proprietors the amount of such share and expenses awarded by the court so far as the same have not then been paid by the defaulting Proprietor, each Proprietor contributing one seventh part thereof. The remaining Proprietors shall be entitled to recover the amount so contributed from the defaulting Proprietor.

19–38 *Deed of feuing conditions—housing development—no express statement deferring applicability—reserved power to vary conditions*

See paragraph 17–84 *supra.*

Express statement deferring applicability

19–39   Where it is intended that the conditions should not apply immediately but only when incorporated by reference in subsequent feu grants or dispositions an express statement as now required by section 17(1) of the Land Registration (Scotland) Act 1979 may be included thus: (a) insert after the words of declaration "but subject to clause hereof," and (b) insert at the end of the deed an additional clause: "We hereby provide and declare that the provisions of section 17 of the Land Registration (Scotland) Act 1979 shall not apply to [the subjects above described] [the following part of the subjects above described, namely, (*describe part in respect of which application is deferred*)]."

Note on registration of deeds of conditions

(a) Sasine Register. Where a deed of conditions applies immediately on recording it will be referred to in subsequent conveyances which are recorded in the Register of Sasines or which will induce first registration in the Land Register. The reference will be in accordance with the existing practice in referring to deeds for burdens. Where the deed of conditions was executed before April 4, 1979, or if executed on or after that date contains an express statement disapplying section 17, then in any subsequent conveyance recorded in the Register of Sasines or inducing first registration in the Land Register when it is intended that the deed of conditions should apply reference to the deed for burdens must be made: *contra*, if it is intended that the deed of conditions should remain inapplicable.

(b) Land Register. In the case of an interest already registered in the Land Register where the deed of conditions appears in the burdens section of the title sheet it is unnecessary to refer to it in any subsequent conveyance or transfer of part: it will be imported automatically. In the case of an interest already registered in the Land Register but the deed of conditions has disapplied section 17 thereto, then in any subsequent conveyance where it is desired that the deed of conditions should apply to the subjects conveyed it is necessary to import the conditions in the deed of conditions by reference in order to create the burdens therein real. Normally the deed of conditions will already have been entered in the Land Register in respect of other subjects to which section 17 did apply, in which case the reference will be: "but always with and under the reservations, burdens, conditions and others in the Deed of Conditions in entry   of the Burdens Section of Title Number   ."

Transfer, transmission and discharge of real burdens

●─40   As mentioned in paragraph 19–17 *supra*, it has for some years been incompetent to create by way of reservation in a conveyance real burdens for money, whether obligations for debts or, with certain exceptions, for periodical payments. Accordingly, the occasions of transfer, transmission and discharge of money burdens reserved in conveyances are relatively few and will decrease. For procedure and styles of transfer, transmission or discharge of such burdens, reference may be made to Burns, pages 501–504.

Enforcement of Real Burdens and Real Conditions

(a) Title and Interest to Enforce

Both title and interest necessary

19–41   A person seeking to enforce a real burden or condition must have a title to do so. Moreover, since the presumption of law has always been in favour of the freedom of a proprietor to deal with his land, there must exist a praedial interest in land to enforce a burden or condition which restricts that freedom. That interest must exist not only when the burden or condition is imposed but also when it is sought to be enforced, and so a burden or condition validly created may cease to be enforceable by reason of acquiescence in breaches of it or actions which bar the enforcement of it, or simply by change of circumstances which render it of no continuing usefulness in protecting a patrimonial interest in land. The determination of questions as to title and interest to enforce real burdens and conditions depends to some extent upon the relationship of the parties concerned.

19–42   **As between superior and vassal.** Once a valid real burden or condition has been created in a feu grant or deed of feuing conditions there is usually no doubt as to the *title* of the superior to enforce it. The continuing contract by tenure entitles the superior and his successors to enforce the continuing conditions of the feu against the feuar and his successors.

As regards *interest* to enforce, the fact that the superior has inserted a condition in the feu grant raises a presumption that he has an interest to enforce it.

> "*Prima facie*, the vassal, in consenting to be bound by a restriction, concedes the interest of the superior; and so the onus is on the vassal who is pleading a release from his contract to allege and prove that owing to some change of circumstances any legitimate interest which the superior may originally have had in maintaining the restriction has ceased to exist."[12]

In the cases cited[12] a prohibition of the sale of liquors was sustained as enforceable despite averments of altered circumstances in the district. A condition as to the use of a particular kind of slate was sustained although the vassal offered to prove that another kind which he proposed to use was of better quality.[13] In two recent cases the interest of a superior to enforce restrictions as to use of property as dwelling-

---

[12] *Earl of Zetland* v. *Hislop* (1882) 9 R.(H.L.) 40, *per* Lord Watson at 47; *Menzies* v. *Caledonian Canal Commissioners* (1900) 2 F. 953.
[13] *Waddell* v. *Campbell* (1898) 25 R. 456.

houses has been sustained since, although there had been departures from the restriction, the area had not lost its substantially residential character.[14] For various circumstances in which the interest of a superior to enforce feuing conditions has been sustained see the cases undernoted.[14a]

As between co-feuars

9–43 *Title. Prima facie* a feu grant which imposes real burdens and conditions is a contract between the superior and feuar who are parties to the transaction: to any other feuar from the same superior it is *jus tertii* and he has no title to sue upon it. But a contract of feu may be so framed as to create in a third party a right to enforce it for his benefit, a *jus quaesitum tertio*. These principles in their application to the rights of co-feuars to enforce feuing conditions *inter se* were expressed by Lord Watson in the leading decision of *Hislop* v. *MacRitchie's Trs.*[15] thus:

> "The fact of the same condition appearing in feu-charters derived from a common superior, coupled with a substantial interest in its observance, does not appear to me to be sufficient to give each feuar a title to enforce it. No single feuar can, in my opinion, be subjected in liability to his co-feuars, unless it appears from the titles under which he holds his feu that such similarity of conditions and mutuality of interest among the feuars either had been or was meant to be established."[16]

Lord Watson went on to state that the circumstances in which each feuar had an implied right to enforce a common condition fell within one of two categories, namely (1) where the superior feued out his land in separate lots upon a uniform plan, or (2) where the superior feued out a considerable area with a view to its being subdivided and built upon, without prescribing any definite plan, but imposing certain general restrictions which the feuar was bound to insert in all sub-feus or dispositions to be granted by him.[17]

9–44 (1) In the first place it is clear that, when a superior has feued out an area by separate grants, the mere fact that the several feuars hold of a common superior and the feu grants contain identical or similar conditions does not entitle any one of the feuars to enforce the conditions contained in the feu grant to another.[18] In order to establish the mutuality which will enable a feuar to enforce a restriction against

---

[14] *Macdonald* v. *Douglas*, 1963 S.C. 374; *Howard de Walden Estates Ltd.* v. *Bowmaker Ltd.*, 1965 S.C. 163.

[14a] *Naismith* v. *Cairnduff* (1876) 3 R. 863; *Calder* v. *Police Comrs. of North Berwick* (1899) 1 F. 491; *Marquis of Linlithgow* v. *Paterson* (1903) 11 S.L.T. 486; *J. & F. Forrest* v. *Governors of George Watson's Hospital* (1905) 8 F. 341; *North British Rly. Co.* v. *Clark*, 1913, 1 S.L.T. 207.

[15] (1881) 8 R.(H.L.) 95 at 102.

[16] See also *Nicholson* v. *Glasgow Blind Asylum*, 1911 S.C. 391, *per* Lord Dunedin at 399–401.

[17] *Hislop* v. *MacRitchie's Trs.*, *supra* at 103.

[18] *Hislop* v. *MacRitchie's Trs.*, *supra*; *Guthrie* v. *Young* (1871) 9 M. 544; *Bannerman's Trs.* v. *Howard & Wyndham* (1902) 10 S.L.T. 2; *Thomson* v. *Mackie* (1903) 11 S.L.T. 562.

a co-feuar it is necessary to find in the latter's title something to show that the restriction was to be enforceable by a *tertius*, and then have recourse to the titles of the other co-feuars to ascertain whether there has been established such a community among them as will entitle any of them to enforce the restriction in a question with the others.[19] Such mutuality may be established by (i) express stipulation by the superior in the respective feu grants,[20] (ii) reasonable implication from reference in the feu grants to a common plan or scheme of building[21] or to leaving ground for the formation of a street or lane serving several feus,[22] but it is not enough that the reference to a common plan was inserted merely for the purpose of identifying the plot feued,[23] or (iii) mutual agreement amongst the feuars themselves.[24] It should be noted that the right of a feuar to enforce a condition directly against co-feuars which is implied from mutuality is separate from and independent of the superior's right.[25] Accordingly a subsequent waiver of the condition by the superior does not preclude a co-feuar from enforcing it.[26]

19–45   (2) Where the superior has feued out a large area which is subsequently subdivided into separate lots, the right of a sub-feuar or disponee of any lot to enforce the conditions of the feu against the others rests on the principle that the sub-feuars or disponees who have acquired their titles with notice that the original superior who is their common author has imposed conditions upon the whole area must be taken as consenting that the conditions shall be mutual for the benefit of all sub-feuars and disponees within the area and that all having an interest will be entitled to enforce them.[27]

19–46   (3) The effect upon the title of one co-feuar to enforce a condition of title against another of a reserved right to the superior to alter the condition depends upon whether (a) the right of the co-feuar is implied from mutuality or community of rights, or (b) is expressly conferred upon co-feuars by the feu grants. In the former case a reservation to the superior of a right to dispense with the condition was held to be destructive of mutuality,[28] whereas in the latter case it was held that the right expressly conferred was an independent and substantially

[19] *Nicholson* v. *Glasgow Blind Asylum, supra* at 400.
[20] *McGibbon* v. *Rankin* (1871) 9 M. 423; *Sutherland* v. *Barbour* (1887) 15 R. 62; *Governors of Muirhead College* v. *Millar* (1901) 38 S.L.R. 835; *Maguire* v. *Burges*, 1909 S.C. 1283.
[21] *Johnston* v. *The Walker Trs.* (1897) 24 R. 1061.
[22] *Mackenzie* v. *Carrick* (1869) 7 M. 419; *Glasgow Jute Co.* v. *Carrick* (1869) 8 M. 93.
[23] *Murray's Trs.* v. *Trs. for St. Margaret's Convent* (1906) 8 F. 1109, 1907 S.C.(H.L.) 8.
[24] Not a case of *jus quaesitum tertio* but of direct contract amongst the feuars.
[25] *Hislop* v. *MacRitchie's Trs., supra* at 102.
[26] *Glasgow Jute Co.* v. *Carrick, supra; Lawrence* v. *Scott*, 1965, S.C. 403.
[27] *Hislop* v. *MacRitchie's Trs., supra* at 104; *Robertson* v. *North British Rly. Co.* (1874) 1 R. 1213 (criticised, but on other grounds, in *Hislop, supra*). For illustrations of the application of this principle see *Beattie* v. *Ures* (1876) 3 R. 634, *Fergusson* v. *McCulloch*, 1953 S.L.T. (Sh.Ct.) 113, and *Smith* v. *Taylor*, 1972 S.L.T. (Lands Tr.) 34. For decisions where in special circumstances the principle was not applicable, see *Campbell* v. *Bremner* (1897) 24 R. 1142, *Girls' School Co. Ltd.* v. *Buchanan*, 1958 S.L.T. (Notes) 2, and *Williamson & Hubbard* v. *Harrison*, 1970 S.L.T. 346.
[28] *Turner* v. *Hamilton* (1890) 17 R. 494.

different right from that of the superior and was not affected by a reserved right to the superior to deviate from the conditions which was subsequently exercised by charter of novodamus.[29]

–47 *Interest.* There is also a difference between the position of a superior and a co-feuar as regards interest to enforce real conditions. The interest of a superior is presumed,[30] but the interest of a co-feuar must be proved. It must be real and substantial and normally involves questions of amenity. The interests which will be sufficient vary with the circumstances of each case.[31]

–48 **As between disponer and disponee.** The *title* of the granter of a disposition to enforce real conditions imposed in it upon the disponee is clear; it rests on the contract embodied in the disposition. The title to enforce it against singular successors of the disponee rests on the law of real burdens and conditions which, when validly created in a conveyance, are binding upon such successors. It is less clear whether successors of the disponer can enforce the conditions, because the question immediately arises as to who are the successors of the disponer in the patrimonial interest which the conditions were designed to protect. In *J. A. Mactaggart & Co.* v. *Harrower*[32] a disposition imposed a building restriction but did not specify the lands in favour of which it was imposed, but the plot disponed was in fact part of a larger area belonging to the disponer and in subsequent dispositions of other parts of that area the right to enforce the restriction was expressly assigned. It was held that the grantees of the subsequent dispositions were entitled to enforce the restriction in virtue of the assignations, but opinions were reserved upon the question whether apart from the assignations the grantees of the later dispositions would have had a title to enforce the restriction. The question may now be regarded as settled by the decision in *Braid Hills Hotel Co. Ltd.* v. *Manuels*[33] to the effect that an assignation is not required where the lands benefited by the restriction are identifiable and the disposition expresses the right as enforceable by successors in ownership of identified lands. As regards the *interest* of the granter of a disposition to enforce a real condition imposed in it, *prima facie* the disponee concedes the interest of the disponer by reason of entering into the contract contained in the disposition, and the onus rests on the disponee to establish that the disponer no longer has any interest to enforce the condition.[34]

---

[29] *Lawrence* v. *Scott*, 1965 S.C. 403. See also *Thomson* v. *Liddell's Motor Service*, 1928 S.N. 42.

[30] See para. 19–42.

[31] Sufficient interest—*Glasgow Jute Co.* v. *Carrick, supra*; *McGibbon* v. *Rankin, supra*; *Alexander* v. *Stobo* (1871) 9 M. 599; *Beattie* v. *Ures* (1876) 3 R. 634; *Ewing* v. *Hastie* (1878) 5 R. 439; *Hill* v. *Millar* (1900) 2 F. 799; *Mactaggart & Co.* v. *Roemmele*, 1907 S.C. 1318. Insufficient interest— *Campbell* v. *Bremner* (1897) 24 R. 1142; *Maguire* v. *Burges*, 1909 S.C. 1283.

[32] (1906) 8 F. 1101.

[33] 1909 S.C. 120.

[34] *Scottish Co-operative Wholesale Society* v. *Finnie*, 1937 S.C. 835.

19–49 **As between co-disponees.** The *title* of a co-disponee to enforce a real condition created in the title of another co-disponee from their common author has effectively been considered in the preceding paragraph. If the condition has been validly created over land now owned by one disponee from a common author, any co-disponee is *in titulo* to enforce the condition if it was imposed expressly for the benefit of the land which he now owns or if there has been created the necessary mutuality of interest in maintaining the condition, and no express assignation of the right to enforce it is required.[35] *Interest* to enforce is a matter of circumstances which will be determined upon considerations of the same kind as those relevant in the case of co-feuars.[36]

Obligations by superior or disponer to impose real conditions in other titles

19–50 Where a superior or disponer has undertaken to insert similar real conditions in other feu grants or dispositions, but fails to do so, the original feuars or disponees cannot enforce the conditions against the subsequent feuars or disponees since the real conditions have not entered the recorded or registered titles of the latter,[37] but the original feuars or disponees may be entitled to recover damages from the superior.[38] The original feuars or disponees are entitled, however, to require the superior or disponer to comply with the contractual stipulation and insert the conditions in other feu grants or dispositions, unless the superior or disponer can obtain a declarator from the court relaxing the obligation in special circumstances.[39]

Loss of interest to enforce

19–51 A real condition which has been validly created may subsequently become unenforceable through (1) personal bar, (2) acquiescence, or (3) change of circumstances which results in absence of interest to enforce. These are distinct *nomina juris*, although the distinction has not always been clearly recognised. Personal bar is an equitable plea based upon actings by the person entitled to enforce the condition which would result in prejudice to the person bound by the condition if it were subsequently enforced. Acquiescence also involves actings by the person entitled to enforce the condition, as by permitting breaches of it by other proprietors bound by it without objection, which raise a

---

[35] *Braid Hills Hotel Co. Ltd.* v. *Manuels, supra; Nicholson* v. *Glasgow Blind Asylum*, 1911 S.C. 391.
[36] See para. 19–47, *supra.* As to the interest of co-disponees, see *Gould* v. *McCorquodale* (1869) 8 M. 165; *Taylor's Trs.* v. *McGavigan* (1896) 23 R. 945; *Proprietors of Royal Exchange Buildings, Glasgow* v. *Cotton*, 1912 S.C. 1151; *Botanic Gardens Picture House* v. *Adamson*, 1924 S.C. 549.
[37] *Walker & Dick* v. *Park* (1888) 15 R. 477; *Morier* v. *Brownlie & Watson* (1895) 23 R. 67; *Magistrates of Edinburgh* v. *Trs. of St. John's Church*, 1915 S.C. 248.
[38] *Leith School Board* v. *Rattray's Trs.*, 1918 S.C. 94.
[39] *Dixon's Trs.* v. *Allan's Trs.* (1868) 7 M. 193; (1870) 8 M.(H.L.) 182; *Dalrymple* v. *Herdman* (1878) 5 R. 847.

presumption that there is now no interest to enforce it. Change of circumstances does not necessarily involve any actings by the person entitled to enforce the condition and is not an equitable plea; it is based on a principle of land law that a proprietor is presumed to be free to use his property as he wishes without a restraint which has ceased to serve any useful purpose. That personal bar is a distinct plea involving prejudice has been recognised in some judgements,[40] but acquiescence and change of circumstances have not always been distinguished, largely because the two pleas often concur in respect that continued acquiescence frequently infers lack of interest to enforce. As an example of what was judicially described as a bald case of loss of interest through change of circumstances, see *Wingate's Trs.* v. *Oswald.*[41]

-52 Personal bar, acquiescence and loss of interest to enforce—general principles. Where decisions depend upon the particular circumstances of the individual cases, and in many cases different grounds of decision are involved, an attempt to extract principles is a perilous enterprise and may be misleading, but it may nevertheless be helpful to readers to group the relevant decisions under the major grounds involved.

-53 *(1) Onus of Proof.* Since the presumption is that a superior or disponer who, or whose authors, have inserted a real condition or restriction in a feu grant or disposition has an interest to enforce it, the onus of establishing that no such interest remains rests upon the person who challenges its enforceability.[42]

-54 *(2) Acquiescence is more readily inferred against a superior than a co-feuar.* Where both the superior and co-feuars have a title to enforce a real condition or restriction, the interest to enforce will more readily be lost from acquiescence in breaches of it by the superior than by a co-feuar. The superior has *prima facie* an interest to object to any breach, whereas a co-feuar may only have an interest to object if the particular breach affects his own property.[43]

-55 *(3) Acquiescence insufficient to infer loss of interest to enforce.* Although a superior or co-feuars have acquiesced in departures from a restriction which are minor or of a less objectionable kind than the departure now

---

[40] *Johnston* v. *The Walker Trs.* (1897) 24 R. 1061, *per* Lord Adam at 1074; *Howard de Walden Estates Ltd.* v. *Bowmaker Ltd.*, 1965 S.C. 163, *per* Lord Ordinary (Kissen) at 171 (reversed on appeal but not on the matter of personal bar).

[41] (1902) 10 S.L.T. 517.

[42] *Earl of Zetland* v. *Hislop* (1882) 9 R.(H.L.) 40; *Sutherland* v. *Barbour* (1887) 15 R. 62; *Menzies* v. *Caledonian Canal Comsrs.* (1900) 2 F. 953; *Scottish Co-operative Wholesale Society* v. *Finnie*, 1937 S.C. 835.

[43] *Gould* v. *McCorquodale* (1869) 8 M. 165; *McGibbon* v. *Rankin* (1871) 9 M. 423; *Mactaggart & Co.* v. *Roemmele*, 1907 S.C. 1318.

proposed, there is no inference that the restrictions are entirely abolished: acquiescence goes no further than the thing acquiesced in.[44]

19–56 *(4) Acquiescence which involves loss of interest to enforce.* Where a superior had relaxed a restriction against use as a public house in respect of one part of the feu, it was held that he was not thereby debarred from enforcing the restriction upon another part of the feu.[45] In recent cases where there had been a number of departures from a restriction to residential property the superior was nevertheless held to be entitled to enforce it, the test being whether the residential nature of the neighbourhood had been lost.[46] On the other hand there have been cases where there have been so many unchallenged contraventions that the interest to object by both superiors and co-feuars has been lost.[47]

19–57 *(5) Abandonment of common feuing plan.* Where the superior abandons the feuing plan whereby mutuality was to be created in respect of a significant part of the whole area, the right to enforce the feuing conditions by the superior or co-feuars is lost.[48]

19–58 *(6) Personal bar.* A superior may be barred from enforcing a real obligation against the feuar or his successors if the superior is himself in breach of an obligation which is its counterpart.[49] A superior who permits, without objection, substantial breaches of feuing conditions which have involved the feuar in considerable expense may be barred from enforcing them,[50] but permitting or authorising breach of conditions on one part of a feu does not necessarily bar enforcement of them as regards the remainder of the feu.[51]

19–59 *(7) Relaxation of conditions by superior.* When a right to enforce real conditions or restrictions has been validly created in favour of a superior or disponer and also co-feuars or co-disponees, waiver or relaxation of the condition or restriction by the superior or disponer does not affect the independent right of the co-feuars or co-disponees to enforce it.[52]

---

[44] *Stewart* v. *Bunten* (1878) 5 R. 1108 (co-feuar); *Johnston* v. *The Walker Trs.* (1897) 24 R. 1061 (superior); *North British Rly. Co.* v. *Clark*, 1913, 1 S.L.T. 207 (superior). See also *Magistrates of Edinburgh* v. *Macfarlane* (1857) 20 D. 156.

[45] *Ewing* v. *Campbells* (1877) 5 R. 230. See *Marquis of Linlithgow* v. *Paterson* (1903) 11 S.L.T. 486.

[46] *Macdonald* v. *Douglas*, 1963 S.C. 374; *Howard de Walden Estates Ltd.* v. *Bowmaker Ltd.*, 1965 S.C. 163.

[47] *Browns* v. *Burns* (1823) 2 S. 298 (superior); *Campbell* v. *Clydesdale Banking Co.* (1868) 6 M. 943 (superior); *Fraser* v. *Downie* (1877) 4 R. 942 (co-feuars); *Johnston* v. *MacRitchie* (1893) 20 R. 539 (co-feuars); *Liddall* v. *Duncan* (1898) 25 R. 1119 (superiors and co-feuars); *Paterson* v. *Glasgow and South-Western Rly. Co.* (1902) 9 S.L.T. 429 (superior); *Robertson's Trs.* v. *Bruce* (1905) 7 F. 580 (co-feuars).

[48] *Calder* v. *Merchant Co. of Edinburgh* (1886) 13 R. 623; *Richardson* v. *Borthwick* (1896) 3 S.L.T. 303. Cf. *Cheyne* v. *Taylor* (1899) 7 S.L.T. 276.

[49] *Stevenson* v. *Steel Co. of Scotland Ltd.* (1899) 1 F.(H.L.) 91.

[50] *Ben Challum Ltd.* v. *Buchanan*, 1955 S.C. 348.

[51] *Ewing* v. *Campbells, supra.*

[52] *Glasgow Jute Co.* v. *Carrick* (1869) 8 M. 93; *Dalrymple* v. *Herdman* (1878) 5 R. 847.

–60 *(8) Tenant has no title to challenge superior's interest to enforce.* A tenant has no title to challenge the interest of the superior to enforce a feuing condition; he has no direct contractual relationship with the superior.[53]

(b) Remedies for Enforcement

Superior and vassal

–61 Where a real burden or condition has been created in a feu grant the superior may enforce it by the various remedies already discussed,[54] including the drastic compulsitor of irritancy, and these remedies are available to successors of the superior by reason of the continuing feudal contract by tenure.

Disponer and disponee

–62 Where real burdens or conditions have been imposed in a disposition, so that there is no continuing relationship between the parties, enforcement of the burdens or conditions is less easy, partly because the remedies available for the enforcement of real burdens or conditions as such are limited,[55] and partly because, when successors are involved, there may be problems in establishing a title and interest to sue.

(a) Real burdens for money. A real burden for money imposed in a disposition does not constitute a proper feudal estate since the creditor is not infeft in the burdened property in security of the sum due; he has simply a *debitum fundi* upon the land conveyed to the disponee. So, in the absence of special provisions creating a personal obligation or conferring special powers of enforcement, the disponer has no right of personal action for payment, no title to raise an action of maills and duties and no power to compel sale of the burdened property. He has only the remedies characteristic of a *debitum fundi*, an action of poinding of the ground and/or adjudication. If there are arrears of interest on the debt a poinding of the ground must precede adjudication, in order to make the arrears also a real debt entitled to the preference accorded to an adjudication on a *debitum fundi* over an adjudication by an unsecured creditor.[56] Successors of the disponer require an assignation of the real burden in order to entitle them to enforce it: the burden continues to affect the lands after ownership of them has passed to singular successors of the disponee, but they have no personal obligation to make payment.[57]

---

[53] *Eagle Lodge Ltd.* v. *Keir and Cawder Estates Ltd.*, 1964 S.C. 30.
[54] In Chap. 17, *supra.*
[55] See para. 19–15.
[56] Bell, *Comm.*, I, ss. 753, 754.
[57] *Royal Bank* v. *Gardyne* (1853) 1 Macq. 358.

(b) Real conditions. Where the real condition imposes a prohibition or restriction, breach of it may be restrained by an action of interdict. Such an action may be raised by the disponer or a person to whom the right to enforce has been expressly assigned[58] or upon whom the right has been expressly conferred in terms of the disposition which imposed the condition,[59] and who has a praedial interest to do so. Where the condition imposes a positive obligation, *e.g.* to erect buildings, it may be enforced by an action *ad factum praestandum* at the instance of the disponer or his executors or representatives against the disponee or his executors or representatives, but when it is not of a continuing character it is not generally enforceable against singular successors of the disponee.[60]

Moreover, whether the real burden imposes a restriction or a positive obligation, the court may in appropriate circumstances award damages in lieu of enforcing interdict or pronouncing a decree *ad factum praestandum*.[61] It is evident that the remedies for enforcement of real conditions in dispositions may not be effective in practice, particularly when singular successors are involved, and it is preferable to create the feudal relationship in the documentation which imposes them.

Registered interests

19–63   Although real burdens or conditions are entered in the burdens section of the title sheet and the right to them in the property section there is no indemnity payable for inability to enforce a real burden or condition unless the Keeper expressly assumes responsibility for its enforceability.[62]

C. Variation and Discharge of Land Obligations

Conveyancing and Feudal Reform (Scotland) Act 1970

19–64   Sections 1 and 2 of this Act provide for the variation and discharge of land obligations by the Lands Tribunal for Scotland[63] and rules regulating its procedure are prescribed.[64]

---

[58] *North British Rly. Co.* v. *Birrell*, 1916, 1 S.L.T. 46. The point was not contested in later stages of the action: 1918 S.C.(H.L.) 33.
[59] *Braid Hills Hotel Co. Ltd.* v. *Manuels*, 1909 S.C. 120.
[60] *Marshall's Tr.* v. *Macneill & Co.* (1888) 15 R. 762.
[61] *Grahame* v. *Magistrates of Kirkcaldy* (1882) 9 R.(H.L.) 91; *Jack* v. *Begg* (1875) 3 R. 35; cases not relating to real conditions but illustrative of the equitable discretion of the court to award damages in lieu of enforcing a legal right.
[62] 1979 Act, s. 12(3)(g).
[63] Lands Tribunal Act 1949, s. 10(2).
[64] Lands Tribunal for Scotland Rules 1971 (S.I. 1971 No. 218) (S. 35), as amended by Lands Tribunal for Scotland (Amendment) Rules 1977 (S.I. 1977 No. 432).

Land obligations

9–65   A land obligation is defined for the purposes of sections 1 and 2 of the Act by section 1(2) as an obligation which (a) relates to land, (b) is enforceable by a proprietor of an interest in land by virtue of his being such proprietor, and (c) is binding upon a proprietor of another interest in that land, or of an interest in other land, by virtue of his being such proprietor. It includes a future or contingent obligation, an obligation to defray or contribute to some cost, an obligation to refrain from doing something and an obligation to permit or suffer something to be done or maintained. An interest in land is defined in section 2(6) of the Act as meaning any estate or interest in land which is capable of being owned or held as a separate interest and to which a title can be recorded in the Register of Sasines. In relation to registered interests a land obligation becomes real when it is included in the title sheet of a registered interest in land which it affects[65] or is registered in pursuance of a deed of conditions which does not expressly state that the obligation is not to become real,[66] and a registered variation or discharge of a land obligation is binding on the singular successors of the party entitled to enforce the obligation and of the person on whom the land obligation was binding.[67]

9–66   **Obligations included.** Land obligations as defined in the 1970 Act include real burdens and conditions which are inherent conditions of a feu grant[68] or satisfy the conditions for their creation[69] and enforceability.[70] The statutory definition, however, is wider and extends to servitudes,[71] rights of pre-emption conferred upon the proprietor of an interest in land[72] and obligations in registered leases.[73]

9–67   **Obligations excluded.** Obligations relating to non-registrable leases and public rights such as rights of way are not within the definition nor are certain special kinds of obligations which are expressly excluded by the 1970 Act.[74] A qualification that the consent of the superior was required before a co-feuar could enforce a *jus quaesitum tertio* is not itself a land obligation and it is incompetent for the Tribunal to vary such a qualification.[74a] Nor is an irritancy clause itself a land obligation.[74b]

---

[65] Land Registration (Scotland) Act 1979, s. 3(1).
[66] *Ibid.*, s. 17.
[67] *Ibid.*, s. 18.
[68] See para. 19–14.
[69] See paras. 19–18 *et seq.*
[70] See paras. 19–41 *et seq.*
[71] *Devlin* v. *Conn*, 1972 S.L.T. (Lands Tr.) 11.
[72] *Macdonald*, 1973 S.L.T. (Lands Tr.) 26; *Ainslie Walton* v. *Farquharson*, January 26, 1978; *McQuiban* v. *Eagle Star Insurance Co.*, 1972 S.L.T. (Lands Tr.) 39.
[73] But an exclusion of assignees in a long lease is not a land obligation (*George T. Fraser Ltd.* v. *Aberdeen Harbour Board*, 1985 S.L.T. 384).
[74] Sched. 1.
[74a] *Reid* v. *Stafford*, 1979 S.L.T. (Lands Tr.) 16.
[74b] *Highland Regional Council* v. *MacDonald-Buchanan*, 1977 S.L.T. (Lands Tr.) 37.

19–68   **Benefited and burdened proprietors.** The 1970 Act also defines the terms "benefited proprietor" and "burdened proprietor" in relation to land obligations.[75] A benefited proprietor means the proprietor of an interest in land who is entitled, by virtue of his being such proprietor, to enforce the obligation. Examples of benefited proprietors include a superior, the granter of a disposition which imposed the obligation, a person entitled to enforce the obligation on the principle of *jus quaesitum tertio*,[76] or sub-feuars in relation to obligations imposed in the title of their common author.[77] It is not necessary that the benefited proprietor be the person who originally contracted under the deed which imposed the obligation; persons who had acquired the superiority with the object of obtaining a *locus* to object to an application were found entitled to do so.[77a] A burdened proprietor means the proprietor of an interest in land upon whom, by virtue of his being such proprietor, the obligation is binding. Where an interest in land is held by two or more persons jointly or in common the benefited or burdened proprietor in relation to a land obligation affecting the interest means either all those persons or any of them.

Jurisdiction of Lands Tribunal

19–69   The jurisdiction of the Lands Tribunal in relation to the variation or discharge of land obligations is limited. The Tribunal must *in limine* be satisfied that the circumstances exist in which jurisdiction is conferred upon them by the 1970 Act. In particular (1) the land obligation which is the subject of the application must be legally enforceable by the proprietor of an interest in land, (2) the applicant must be a burdened proprietor upon whom the obligation is binding, and (3) the facts of the case must fall within one or more of the sets of circumstances specified in paragraph (*a*), (*b*) or (*c*) of section 1(3) of the Act. It would probably be incompetent for the Tribunal to grant an order, even with the consent of parties, which would in effect be purely declaratory of the rights of parties in relation to a land obligation, but that does not mean that the Tribunal cannot refuse an application *on its merits* under section 1(3)(*c*) of the Act if the Tribunal consider that the existence of the land obligation as framed does not in fact impede the particular use of the land which is intended.[78] Moreover, the Tribunal may adjudicate upon the title of a person who claims to be a benefited proprietor as distinct from a person who is entitled to be

---

[75] s. 2(6).
[76] *Main* v. *Lord Doune*, 1972 S.L.T. (Lands Tr.) 14; *Solway Cedar Ltd.* v. *Hendry*, 1972 S.L.T. (Lands Tr.) 42; *Sinclair* v. *Gillon*, 1974 S.L.T. (Lands Tr.) 18.
[77] *Smith* v. *Taylor*, 1972 S.L.T. (Lands Tr.) 34. For a special case where the right of a superior to waive a land obligation was held not to be a land obligation but simply a qualification attached to one in which a co-feuar applicant was a benefited and not a burdened proprietor, see *Reid* v. *Stafford*, 1979 S.L.T. (Lands Tr.) 16.
[77a] *McArthur* v. *Mahoney*, 1975 S.L.T. (Lands Tr.) 2.
[78] *Solway Cedar Ltd.* v. *Hendry*, 1972 S.L.T. (Lands Tr.) 42 at 44.

heard merely as an affected person, a distinction which may be important in relation to compensation.[79] So, in *Co-operative Wholesale Society* v. *Usher's Brewery*[80] the Tribunal considered that, while it would be incompetent for them to decide that a restriction was totally unenforceable on the ground that it was contrary to public policy as being imposed for the protection of a commercial and not a praedial interest, it was within the province of the Tribunal to decide that, in the particular case, objectors were benefited proprietors having a sufficient patrimonial interest to enforce the restriction. Again, in *James Miller & Partners Ltd.* v. *Hunt*[81] the Tribunal decided that an obligation to build was not spent upon the expiry of a stipulated time limit and that there was still a subsisting enforceable land obligation which made the application competent.

9–70 Onus of proof. The burden of establishing that the facts of the case fall within one or more of the circumstances specified in paragraphs (*a*), (*b*) or (*c*) of section 1(3) of the Act rests upon the applicant.[82]

9–71 The Tribunal's discretion. Even if the applicant succeeds in discharging that onus, however, he is not necessarily entitled to an order varying or discharging the land obligation. Section 1(3) provides that the Tribunal "may" vary or discharge the obligation on being satisfied that "in all the circumstances" one or more of the grounds specified in paragraphs (*a*), (*b*) or (*c*) have been established. In *Main* v. *Lord Doune*[83] it was observed:

> "But on the basis of the evidence led before them and their inspection a Tribunal may judicially determine whether a contractual right to maintain a particular environment should be upheld or modified. Unlike the amended s. 84(1)(*aa*) of the Law of Property Act 1925, which has appended under subs. (1A) its own specific guidelines, we are merely directed by the opening words of s. 1(3) to have regard to 'all the circumstances'. This appears to be a looser style of legislation requiring us to give consideration to such circumstances as the Tribunal consider relevant."

The Tribunal has frequently exercised this discretion by looking at the whole picture, rather than confining themselves narrowly to whether the ground of application had been affirmatively proved.[84] The discretion of the Tribunal is of a judicial character and so, if in the

---

[79] *Smith* v. *Taylor*, 1972 S.L.T. (Lands Tr.) 34 at 35.
[80] 1975 S.L.T. (Lands Tr.) 9.
[81] 1974 S.L.T. (Lands Tr.) 9.
[82] *Murrayfield Ice Rink Ltd.* v. *Scottish Rugby Union*, 1972 S.L.T. (Lands Tr.) 20 at 21; on appeal 1973 S.L.T. 99 at 105; 1973 S.C. 21; *Bolton* v. *Aberdeen Corporation*, 1972 S.L.T. (Lands Tr.) 26 at 28.
[83] 1972 S.L.T. (Lands Tr.) 14 at 18.
[84] See *Murrayfield Ice Rink Ltd.* v. *Scottish Rugby Union, supra*; *Manz* v. *Butter's Trs.*, 1973 S.L.T. (Lands Tr.) 2; *McArthur* v. *Mahoney*, 1975 S.L.T. (Lands Tr.) 2.

exercise of their discretion the Tribunal proceeds upon improper or wrong principles, their decision is subject to review by the Court of Session.[85]

19–72 Limits of Tribunal's jurisdiction. The jurisdiction of the Tribunal extends only to the variation or discharge of obligations imposed upon a burdened proprietor which affect his land. It is not permissible for the Tribunal, when varying an obligation upon the land of the burdened proprietor, to impose incidentally an extended obligation upon other land in which the burdened proprietor has an interest. So in *Murrayfield Ice Rink Ltd.* v. *Scottish Rugby Union, supra,* it was made clear that, where an additional car park belonging to the respondents was used to a limited extent by the burdened proprietor on a servitude right basis, it would have been incompetent for the Tribunal, in varying the obligations upon the land of the burdened proprietor, to enlarge the servitude right affecting the respondents' land in order to facilitate the use of the applicants' land which they proposed.

19–73 Applications to Lands Tribunal and irritancy proceedings. Where a feuing condition has been contravened and an action of declarator of irritancy at the instance of the superior is proceeding in the courts and the feuar at the same time is applying to the Lands Tribunal for variation or discharge of the condition which he has contravened, it is competent for the Tribunal to consider the application since until the feu right has in fact been irritated there still exists an enforceable land obligation which it is within the Tribunal's jurisdiction to vary or discharge. It is for the court to determine whether a decree of declarator of irritancy should be pronounced in respect of a past breach of a land obligation when a variation or discharge of the obligation by the Tribunal has intervened, but in reaching a decision the court may be assisted by the decision of the Tribunal.[86] An irritancy clause is not itself a land obligation in terms of section 1(2) of the Act but a condition relating to the enforcement of one under section 1(6).[87]

Grounds for variation or discharge of land obligations

19–74 (a) Obligation unreasonable or inappropriate—section 1(3)(a). Under section 1(3)(*a*) of the Act the Tribunal must be satisfied that, by reason of changes in the character of the land affected by the obligation or of the neighbourhood thereof or other circumstances which the Tribunal may deem material, the obligation is or has become unreasonable or inappropriate.

---

[85] *Murrayfield Ice Rink Ltd.* v. *Scottish Rugby Union, supra.*

[86] *Ross and Cromarty District Council* v. *Ullapool Property Co. Ltd.*, 1983 S.L.T. (Lands Tr.) 9. See also *James Miller & Partners* v. *Hunt*, 1974 S.L.T. (Lands Tr.) 9; *Devlin* v. *Conn, supra; Mr. & Mrs. G. Volante* v. *Lord Burton*, Oct. 18, 1976 (L.T.S./APP/1/135); *Bruce* v. *Modern Homes Investment Co. Ltd.*, 1978 S.L.T. (Lands Tr.) 34.

[87] *Highland Regional Council* v. *MacDonald-Buchanan*, 1977 S.L.T. (Lands Tr.) 37.

–75 *Changes in the character of the land affected.* Circumstances in which the Tribunal have discharged or varied land obligations either mainly or partly on account of changes in the character of the land or buildings upon it were:

(1) Where nine smallholdings, a use to which the land was restricted, were in the interest of better management being amalgamated into two holdings, a variation was granted to permit the sale of the dwelling-houses which had become surplus to requirements.[88]

(2) A prohibition of buildings other than a public hall, reading room and library was discharged when the need for those facilities had been fulfilled by a new community centre and the old public hall on the burdened land had been demolished.[89]

(3) A restriction to use of land for a garage was varied when the bus service for which it had been originally used was discontinued and private car hiring had also ceased, so that the basis on which the original restriction rested had gone, and a limited number of dwelling-houses was permitted.[90]

(4) In *Macdonald*[91] the Tribunal indicated the view that a right of pre-emption exercisable if the land was to be used for a purpose other than agriculture would have become unreasonable and inappropriate in circumstances where planning permission to develop the land and neighbouring holdings for housing had been granted and a house had been erected on part of the land concerned, but the application was refused on technical grounds. A limitation of £2 per annum, imposed in 1877, upon the contribution by each dwelling-house to the cost of upkeep of common central gardens was held unreasonable and inappropriate in view of the greatly increased cost of maintenance, but the Tribunal decided that they were not empowered to override a minority of the burdened proprietors who refused to join in the application.[91a]

–76 *Changes in the character of the neighbourhood.* What is a neighbourhood for the purposes of section 1(3)(*a*) of the 1970 Act may differ in different cases and may be difficult to determine.[92] Clearly, however, it will include all the properties of proprietors benefited by the land obligation of which variation or discharge is sought and also the properties of persons who may appear to the Tribunal to be affected by the obligation or its proposed variation within the meaning of section 2(2) of the Act. Where an application was made for the variation of a prohibition of the sale of alcoholic liquors to permit the use of the

---

[88] *Secretary of State for Scotland* v. *Howard de Walden Estates Ltd.*, Jan. 16, 1973.
[89] *County Council of the County of Stirling* v. *Paterson's Representatives*, Feb. 11, 1974.
[90] *Robertson* v. *Fraser*, Dec. 6, 1974.
[91] 1973 S.L.T. (Lands Tr.) 26.
[91a] *Young*, 1978 S.L.T. (Lands Tr.) 28.
[92] *Bolton* v. *Aberdeen Corporation*, 1972 S.L.T. (Lands Tr.) 26 at 28.

premises for off-sales, the relevant neighbourhood was regarded as the whole of an isolated village (Gairloch).[93] Where the prohibition of which discharge was sought was against the sale of spirituous liquors in hotel premises in a major tourist centre (Pitlochry), the entire High Street of the town was treated as the neighbourhood.[94] Where the variation granted was to permit the use of a schoolhouse for residential purposes, the neighbourhood was a large estate in which the numbers of schoolchildren had greatly declined.[95] In cases relating to obligations affecting shops in housing estates, the neighbourhood was regarded as the whole estate,[96] or the particular sector of the estate which the shop was designed to serve.[97] Where variation was sought to permit the use of a former private dwelling-house as a licensed hotel, an area comprising six streets was taken as the neighbourhood in one case[98] and the inner area of a residential district in another.[99] In cases involving residential property the whole street,[1] or one side of a street but not the other,[2] or an enclave of houses having a distinctive character,[3] has been regarded as a neighbourhood. In rural areas it may be a group of smallholdings[4] or a small low-density housing scheme.[5] In one special case relating to a servitude of access the neighbourhood was simply the dominant tenement.[6]

19–77   The kind of change in the character of a neighbourhood which is relevant to support an application for variation or discharge of a land obligation is one which has occurred subsequent to the creation of the obligation and has altered the quality or amenity of the neighbourhood in such a way that the protection which the obligation affords is no longer reasonable or appropriate. Many applications under section 1(3)(a) relate to land obligations which restricted use of property to residential purposes and variation or discharge has been sought to permit commercial or other non-residential use, frequently on the ground that other properties in the neighbourhood which had formerly been residential were now used for other purposes.[7]

19–78   *Other circumstances which the Tribunal may deem material.* Other circumstances which the Tribunal may take into account in determining whether there has been a relevant change in the character of the land

---

[93] *Owen* v. *Mackenzie*, 1974 S.L.T. (Lands Tr.) 11.
[94] *Manz* v. *Butter's Trs.*, 1973 S.L.T. (Lands Tr.) 2.
[95] *Highland Regional Council* v. *MacDonald-Buchanan*, 1977 S.L.T. (Lands Tr.) 37.
[96] *Co-operative Wholesale Society* v. *Usher's Brewery*, 1975 S.L.T. (Lands Tr.) 9.
[97] *Bolton* v. *Aberdeen Corporation, supra.*
[98] *Morris* v. *Feuars of Waverley Park*, 1973 S.L.T. (Lands Tr.) 6.
[99] *Pickford* v. *Young*, 1975 S.L.T. (Lands Tr.) 17.
[1] *Sinclair* v. *Gillon*, 1974 S.L.T. (Lands Tr.) 18.
[2] *Main* v. *Lord Doune*, 1972 S.L.T. (Lands Tr.) 14.
[3] *Mercer* v. *MacLeod*, 1977 S.L.T. (Lands Tr.) 14.
[4] *Macdonald*, 1973 S.L.T. (Lands Tr.) 26.
[5] *Solway Cedar Ltd.* v. *Hendry*, 1972 S.L.T. (Lands Tr.) 42.
[6] *Devlin* v. *Conn*, 1972 S.L.T. (Lands Tr.) 11.
[7] *Main* v. *Lord Doune, supra*; *Morris* v. *Feuars of Waverley Park, supra*; *Sinclair* v. *Gillon, supra*; *Pickford* v. *Young, supra.*

or the neighbourhood include alteration in social habits which may justify the relaxation of a prohibition against the sale of liquors[8] or a variation to permit use of shop premises as a fish and chicken bar,[9] the fact that an area had become ripe for development for housing,[10] and a decline in the number of children of school age in a small local area which rendered a restriction to use of property as a school and schoolhouse no longer appropriate.[11]

-79 *The obligation has become unreasonable or inappropriate.* Even although an applicant establishes that there have been changes in the character of the land or the neighbourhood or other circumstances which the Tribunal may deem material, he must also convince the Tribunal that the obligation has become unreasonable or inappropriate. In *McArthur* v. *Mahoney*[12] it was contended that, where the original purpose for which the obligation had been imposed had disappeared so that its substratum was gone, the Tribunal had no discretion as to amenity or otherwise and were bound to discharge the obligation. The Tribunal held that they had an overriding discretion to refuse to discharge or vary the obligation on amenity grounds or because it still served some other useful purpose, and that in reaching that decision they were entitled to take into account the representations of affected persons.

-80 **(b) Obligation unduly burdensome compared with benefit—section 1(3)(b).** The weighing of burdensomeness of a land obligation in comparison with its benefit depends so much upon the particular circumstances of the case that it is difficult to extract general principles from the decisions of the Tribunal, but the following elements may be identified. (1) Section 1(3)(b) applies principally to positive obligations involving performance,[13] but it also applies to negative obligations which impose a restriction.[14] (2) In assessing burdensomeness the Tribunal will not be influenced by circumstances purely personal to the applicant[15]; the question is whether a land obligation should be permanently varied or discharged, and the Tribunal are not empowered to grant an order in the form of a personal licence.[16] (3) An obligation will not be regarded as unduly burdensome if the applicant can still use his property profitably although its existence impedes some more

---

[8] *Manz* v. *Butter's Trs.*, *supra*; *Owen* v. *Mackenzie*, *supra*.
[9] *Di Mascio* v. *Pickard*, Aug. 7, 1972.
[10] *Keith* v. *Texaco Ltd.*, 1977 S.L.T. (Lands Tr.) 16.
[11] *Highland Regional Council* v. *MacDonald-Buchanan*, *supra*.
[12] 1975 S.L.T. (Lands Tr.) 2.
[13] *Bachoo* v. *George Wimpey & Co. Ltd.*, 1977 S.L.T. (Lands Tr.) 2 at 5.
[14] *Murrayfield Ice Rink Ltd.* v. *Scottish Rugby Union*, 1972 S.L.T. (Lands Tr.) 20, affd. 1973 S.L.T. 99; *Bolton* v. *Aberdeen Corporation*, 1972 S.L.T. (Lands Tr.) 26; *McQuiban* v. *Eagle Star Insce. Co.*, 1972 S.L.T. (Lands Tr.) 39.
[15] *Bachoo* v. *George Wimpey & Co. Ltd.*, *supra*; *Nicolson* v. *Campbell's Trs.*, 1981 S.L.T. (Lands Tr.) 10.
[16] *Main* v. *Lord Doune*, *supra*.

profitable use[17] or prevents the maximisation of its realisable value,[18] but if the property is virtually derelict and cannot be sold without removal of the restriction that is a proper case for discharge of the obligation.[19] (4) If there is virtually no benefit to the person entitled to maintain the obligation a comparatively small degree of burdensomeness will justify the Tribunal in discharging it, since there is nothing to be weighed in the balance against the burden.[20] (5) It is not a benefit in terms of the subsection that a superior might have been able to obtain a payment for granting a waiver of the obligation; the Tribunal are required to compare the burdensomeness of the obligation with any benefit which the superior might obtain from its performance, not any benefit which, apart from the Act, he might derive from its waiver.[21] (6) In assessing benefit the Tribunal may take into account loss of amenity to the property of the benefited proprietor,[22] but it is not relevant for the purposes of subsection (3)(b) to consider the benefit to affected persons or third parties who are not benefited proprietors.[23]

19–81   (c) **Existence of obligation impeding some reasonable use of land—section 1(3)(c).** The ground stated in this subsection is wider and essentially different from those in the previous two subsections (3)(a) and (b). Subsection (3)(a) looks back to past history and the continuing reasonableness of the relevant land obligation in changed circumstances, subsection (3)(b) involves a weighing in the balance of benefit and burdensomeness of the obligation, but subsection (3)(c) is potentially wider in its application, since it looks forward to the future and requires the Tribunal to determine simply whether some reasonable proposed new use of the land is being impeded.[24] It is not necessary for an applicant to establish that the existence of the obligation would prevent the land from being put to reasonable use at all; that would involve reading "some" as "any." The task of the Tribunal is to decide whether, in the relevant circumstances of the particular case, some reasonable use is being impeded.[25] Some of the relevant circumstances which have been canvassed in decided cases are considered in the following paragraphs.

---

[17] *Smith* v. *Taylor*, 1972 S.L.T. (Lands Tr.) 34; *Sinclair* v. *Gillon*, 1974 S.L.T. (Lands Tr.) 18; *Co-operative Wholesale Society* v. *Usher's Brewery*, 1975 S.L.T. (Lands Tr.) 9; *Lothian Regional Council* v. *George Wimpey & Co. Ltd.*, 1985 S.L.T. (Lands Tr.) 2; *Grampian Regional Council* v. *Viscount Cowdray*, 1985 S.L.T. (Lands Tr.) 6.
[18] *Murrayfield Ice Rink* v. *Scottish Rugby Union, supra.*
[19] *West Lothian Co-op. Society* v. *Ashdale Land and Property Co. Ltd.*, 1972 S.L.T. (Lands Tr.) 30.
[20] *McQuiban* v. *Eagle Star Insce. Co., supra; Manz* v. *Butter's Trs., supra.*
[21] *West Lothian Co-op. Society Ltd.* v. *Ashdale Land and Property Co. Ltd., supra; McVey* v. *Glasgow Corporation*, 1973 S.L.T. (Lands Tr.) 15.
[22] *Murrayfield Ice Rink* v. *Scottish Rugby Union, supra; McArthur* v. *Mahoney, supra.*
[23] *Manz* v. *Butter's Trs., supra.*
[24] *Leney* v. *Craig*, 1982 S.L.T. (Lands Tr.) 9, 11; *Ross and Cromarty District Council* v. *Ullapool Property Co. Ltd.*, 1983 S.L.T. (Lands Tr.) 9 at 13.
[25] *Murrayfield Ice Rink* v. *Scottish Rugby Union, supra; Smith* v. *Taylor, supra* at 36.

-82 (i) *The need for the proposed use.* The desirability of the use proposed as satisfying some social need in the area is a relevant consideration. Examples are the need for provision of a nursery school,[26] the change in social habits which resulted in hotel visitors expecting to have alcoholic refreshment with their meals,[27] the need for caravanners and campers to purchase alcoholic drinks locally,[28] the desirability for office workers to have a convenient coffee shop,[29] or the continuing demand for hotel accommodation in the area[30] or for an additional housing development.[31]

-83 (ii) *Beneficial utilisation of land.* The strongest case for variation or discharge is where a land obligation permits only buildings of a certain kind and there is no longer a market for such buildings or they could now be constructed only at uneconomic cost, so that in effect the obligation renders the land derelict and incapable of development.[32] More arguable are cases where variation or discharge of an obligation is sought to permit the building of an additional house or an extension of an existing house on garden or amenity ground, since in these circumstances the Tribunal have to take into account the effect upon the neighbourhood and neighbouring properties and conservation of the architectural and visual character of the area.[33]

-84 (iii) *Planning permission.* In general the fact that planning permission has been granted for the use proposed is helpful to an applicant's case but, although a significant factor, it is not conclusive. The relevance of a grant of planning permission was discussed in *Main* v. *Lord Doune*[34] and again considered in depth in *Mercer* v. *MacLeod.*[35] Planning permission is granted in the context of public interest, whereas the Tribunal are concerned primarily with matters of private right, and as a matter of procedure planning applications may be granted without the views of affected persons being considered, whereas applications for variation or discharge of land obligations are considered by the Tribunal usually after taking into account representations by affected persons. There have been several decisions in which the Tribunal have refused applications even although the applicant had obtained planning permission for the proposed use.[36]

---

[26] *Main* v. *Lord Doune, supra.*
[27] *Manz* v. *Butter's Trs., supra.*
[28] *Owen* v. *Mackenzie. supra.*
[29] *Sinclair* v. *Gillon, supra.*
[30] *Smith* v. *Taylor, supra.*
[31] *Keith* v. *Texaco Ltd., supra.*
[32] *West Lothian Co-op. Society Ltd.* v. *Ashdale Land and Property Co. Ltd., supra.*
[33] *Robinson* v. *Hamilton,* 1974 S.L.T. (Lands Tr.) 2; *Gorrie and Banks Ltd.* v. *Musselburgh Town Council,* 1974 S.L.T. (Lands Tr.) 5; *Mercer* v. *MacLeod,* 1977 S.L.T. (Lands Tr.) 14; *Ness* v. *Shannon,* 1978 S.L.T. (Lands Tr.) 13; *Bachoo* v. *George Wimpey & Co. Ltd.,* 1977 S.L.T. (Lands Tr.) 2; *Scott* v. *Fulton,* 1982 S.L.T. (Lands Tr.) 18.
[34] 1972 S.L.T. (Lands Tr.) 14.
[35] 1977 S.L.T. (Lands Tr.) 14.
[36] *Solway Cedar Ltd.* v. *Hendry,* 1972 S.L.T. (Lands Tr.) 42; *Bachoo* v. *George Wimpey & Co. Ltd., supra; Mercer* v. *MacLeod, supra.*

19–85   (iv) *Licence for proposed use.* The fact that the applicant has obtained the appropriate type of licence for the premises may be a pointer to the reasonableness of the proposed use, but is not conclusive since the licensing authority are not so much concerned with the amenity questions to which the Tribunal must have regard.[37]

19–86   (v) *Amenity.* The most common ground of objection to applications is the loss or impairment of the amenity of an environment which the obligation was designed to preserve. The attitude of the Tribunal has been put thus: "Parliament has not yet indicated that control of a particular environment may not continue to be exercised (in supplement of public control) by private obligation. It has only provided that if it is so exercised such exercise must now be reasonable."[38] It would be a somewhat difficult task to analyse the various elements of amenity in separate categories, since normally the Tribunal have to evaluate a complex of considerations and determine the weight to be attached to each of them. Relevant matters are the value of protecting the residential character of an area against the intrusion of commercial or non-residential projects, the damage to visual aspects of an area and of the prospect from properties within it, and the maintenance of the architectural unity of a district or enclave having special value as a conservation area[39]; also special damage to properties immediately adjacent to or in the vicinity of the land in respect of which the application is made, such as loss of privacy from being overlooked[40] or apprehended nuisances such as cooking smells and noise, increased traffic in the area and parking problems.[41]

Works commenced before application to Tribunal

19–87   Where an applicant has commenced or partially carried out building operations in breach of a land obligation before an application for its variation or discharge is made, the attitude of the Tribunal is to deal with the application without regard to the presence of the new or partially completed building in deciding whether any of the conditions of section 1(3) of the Act have been satisfied, since to do otherwise would enable applicants to benefit from self-created changes in breach of their land obligations.[42]

---

[37] See *Owen* v. *Mackenzie, supra* (liquor licence); *Co-operative Wholesale Society* v. *Usher's Brewery, supra* (liquor licence); *Bolton* v. *Aberdeen Corporation, supra* (betting shop); *Main* v. *Lord Doune, supra* (nursery school).

[38] *Bolton* v. *Aberdeen Corporation, supra* at 29.

[39] For a fuller examination see Halliday, *Conveyancing and Feudal Reform (Scotland) Act 1970*, 31–34; see also *Bachoo* v. *George Wimpey & Co. Ltd., supra; Mercer* v. *MacLeod, supra; Ness* v. *Shannon, supra; Leney* v. *Craig*, 1982 S.L.T. (Lands Tr.) 9; *Scott* v. *Fulton, supra.*

[40] *Smith* v. *Taylor, supra; McArthur* v. *Mahoney, supra; Bachoo* v. *George Wimpey & Co. Ltd., supra.*

[41] *Smith* v. *Taylor, supra; Morris* v. *Feuars of Waverley Park, supra; Leney* v. *Craig, supra.*

[42] *Bruce* v. *Modern Homes Investment Co. Ltd.*, 1978 S.L.T. (Lands Tr.) 34; *Ross and Cromarty District Council* v. *Ullapool Property Co. Ltd.*, 1983 S.L.T. (Lands Tr.) 9.

Additional or substituted provisions

–88   The power of the Tribunal to vary or discharge a land obligation includes power to add or substitute any provision, other than an award of compensation, which the Tribunal consider reasonable as the result of the variation or discharge. The provision must be acceptable to the applicant, but the Tribunal may refuse to vary or discharge the obligation without the provision.[43] Any provision so added or substituted will be enforceable in the same manner as the obligation which has been varied or discharged.[44] The Tribunal have frequently exercised the power to add or substitute provisions when making a variation order. Examples are restrictions upon the number and height of dwelling-houses permitted on former amenity ground and the provision of screening by trees,[45] restrictions as to the height of buildings for light industry,[46] restriction to buildings for which the applicant had already obtained the authority of the dean of guild court,[47] the provision of remedial works including a retaining wall when a building had been erected too close to an adjoining property,[48] and the provision of double glazing to minimise noise nuisance and provision for extraction of kitchen fumes at chimney-head level.[49] Limitations on the nature of the permitted use have also been imposed[50] in one case with alteration of the location of the permitted building.[51] Any new or substituted provision imposed by the Tribunal must be directly related to the variation or discharge order sought: in a rather special case where superiors had feued land subject to a restriction to use of the site as a school and, upon discharge of the restriction being sought to enable use of the site for housing development, the superiors, a building company, wished a right of pre-emption in their favour to be introduced in order that they might undertake the housing development themselves, but the applicants did not consent, the Tribunal decided that the introduction of a right of pre-emption was not directly related to the existing land obligation and discharged it *simpliciter*.[52]

Compensation

–89   In terms of section 1(4) of the 1970 Act the Tribunal may direct the applicant to pay to a benefited proprietor such sum as the Tribunal

---

[43] 1970 Act, s. 1(5).

[44] *Ibid.*, s. 1(6).

[45] *Crombie* v. *George Heriot's Tr.*, 1972 S.L.T. (Lands Tr.) 40; *Robinson* v. *Hamilton, supra*; *Gorrie and Banks Ltd.* v. *Musselburgh Town Council, supra*.

[46] *West Lothian Co-op. Society Ltd.* v. *Ashdale Land and Property Co. Ltd., supra*.

[47] *Smith* v. *Taylor, supra*.

[48] *Bruce* v. *Modern Homes Investment Co. Ltd., supra*.

[49] *Leney* v. *Craig, supra*.

[50] *Main* v. *Lord Doune, supra*; *Sinclair* v. *Gillon, supra*; *Co-operative Wholesale Society* v. *Usher's Brewery, supra*.

[51] *Ross and Cromarty District Council* v. *Ullapool Property Co. Ltd., supra*.

[52] *Strathclyde Regional Council* v. *Mactaggart & Mickel Ltd.*, 1984 S.L.T. (Lands Tr.) 33.

think just under one, but not both, of two heads, namely (i) a sum to compensate for any substantial loss or disadvantage suffered by the proprietor as benefited proprietor in consequence of the variation or discharge of the land obligation, or (ii) a sum to make up for any effect which the obligation produced, at the time when it was imposed, in reducing the consideration then paid or made payable for the interest in land affected by it. The Tribunal have discretion to refuse to vary or discharge an obligation under section 1(3)(c) if they consider that, due to exceptional circumstances related to amenity or otherwise, money would not be an adequate compensation for any loss or disadvantage to a benefited proprietor which would result. It is clear from the terms of section 1(4) that a claim of compensation is available only to a benefited proprietor and that an affected proprietor has no such claim.[53] The circumstances in which compensation has been awarded by the Tribunal under the above heads are fully discussed in the undernoted text.[54] In *Keith* v. *Texaco Ltd.*[55] the Tribunal reaffirmed the principle of earlier decisions[56] that compensation would not be awarded under section 1(4)(i) for the removal of a power to obtain money in return for granting a minute of waiver and also refused compensation under section 1(4)(ii) on the ground that it had not been established that any deduction had been made in the original sale price to reflect the presence of the land obligations. Compensation was awarded under section 1(4)(i) in respect of reduction in the value of the properties of benefited proprietors in *Smith* v. *Taylor*,[56a] *Ness* v. *Shannon*[57] and *Leney* v. *Craig*.[58] The Tribunal may award interest on compensation at the same rate as would apply upon a decree of the Court of Session.[58a]

Obligations recently created

19–90   It is incompetent to apply to the Tribunal for variation or discharge of a land obligation which has been created for the first time in a conveyance, deed, instrument or writing not more than two years before the date of the application.[59] It would appear that the Tribunal will be slow to grant an application by one of the original parties to the deed which created the obligation,[60] although they may do so in a proper case.[61]

---

[53] This construction affirmed by Tribunal in *Manz* v. *Butter's Trs.*, *supra* at 4.
[54] Halliday, *Conveyancing and Feudal Reform (Scotland) Act 1970*, 38–43.
[55] 1977 S.L.T. (Lands Tr.) 16.
[56] *McVey* v. *Glasgow Corporation*, 1973 S.L.T. (Lands Tr.) 15; *Robertson* v. *Church of Scotland Trs.*, 1976 S.L.T. (Lands Tr.) 11. See also *Blythswood Friendly Society* v. *Glasgow District Council*, 1976 S.L.T. (Lands Tr.) 29.
[56a] 1972 S.L.T. (Lands Tr.) 34.
[57] 1978 S.L.T. (Lands Tr.) 13.
[58] 1982 S.L.T. (Lands Tr.) 9.
[58a] Law Reform (Miscellaneous Provisions) (Scotland) Act 1980, s. 18.
[59] 1970 Act, s. 2(5).
[60] *Murrayfield Ice Rink* v. *Scottish Rugby Union*, *supra*; *Solway Cedar Ltd.* v. *Hendry*, *supra*; *James Miller & Partners Ltd.* v. *Hunt*, *supra*.
[61] *McVey* v. *Glasgow Corporation*, *supra*.

Contracting out

9–91   Any agreement or provision, however constituted, is void in so far as it purports to exclude or prohibit the operation of the provisions of sections 1 and 2 of the 1970 Act.[62] So the right of a burdened proprietor to apply to the Tribunal for variation or discharge of a land obligation cannot be excluded contractually.

Registration and effect of orders

9–92   An order of the Tribunal varying or discharging a land obligation is binding upon singular successors of the person entitled to enforce it and upon all persons having interest when an extract of it is duly recorded in the Register of Sasines or when the variation or discharge is registered in the Land Register of Scotland.[63] When compensation has been awarded the order does not take effect until the Tribunal have endorsed the order to the effect either that the compensation has been paid or that all persons to whom compensation has been awarded but who have not received payment have agreed to the order taking effect.[64] Where an order varying or discharging a land obligation takes effect, any irritant or resolutive clause or other condition relating to the enforcement of the obligation will be effective, as regards subsequent acts or omissions, to the same extent as if it had been so varied or discharged by the person entitled to enforce it.[65] Any added or substituted obligation will be enforceable in the same manner as the obligation to the variation or discharge of which it relates.[66]

Procedure and appeals

9–93   As to procedure in applications to the Lands Tribunal for variation or discharge of land obligations and in appeals from decisions of the Tribunal to the Court of Session, see the undernoted text.[67]

List of principal decisions by reference to subject-matter

9–94   The following is a list of the principal reported cases and some unreported cases where an order for variation or discharge of a land obligation has been granted or refused by the Tribunal under section 1(3) of the Act, arranged by reference to subject-matter:

---

[62] s. 7.
[63] 1970 Act, s. 2(4) as amended by Land Tenure Reform (Scotland) Act 1974, s. 19; Land Registration (Scotland) Act 1979, s. 18. See *Hughes* v. *Frame*, 1985 S.L.T. (Lands Tr.) 12.
[64] Lands Tribunal for Scotland Rules 1971 (S.I. 1971, No. 218) (S. 35), r. 5(2).
[65] 1970 Act, s. 1(6).
[66] *Ibid.*, s. 1(6).
[67] Halliday, *op. cit.*, 45–49.

Additional buildings

Crombie v. *George Heriot's Trust*, 1972 S.L.T. (Lands Tr.) 40—granted.

Carmichael v. *MacGillivray*, April 26, 1972—granted.

Albert Thain Ltd. v. *Feuars of Waverley Park*, May 4, 1973—granted.

Martin v. *Scottish Amicable Life Assurance Society*, June 29, 1973—granted.

Robinson v. *Hamilton*, 1974 S.L.T. (Lands Tr.) 2—granted.

Gorrie and Banks Ltd. v. *Musselburgh Town Council*, 1974 S.L.T. (Lands Tr.) 5—granted.

Miller Northern Homes Ltd. v. *Feuars of Gartconnell and Ferguston*, November 12, 1974—granted.

Clarke v. *Eagle Star Insurance Co. Ltd.*, February 21, 1974—granted.

Ness v. *Shannon*, 1978 S.L.T. (Lands Tr.) 13—granted.

Bruce v. *Modern Homes Investment Co. Ltd.*, 1978 S.L.T. (Lands Tr.) 34—granted.

Solway Cedar Ltd. v. *Hendry*, 1972 S.L.T. (Lands Tr.) 42—refused.

Clarebrooke Holdings Ltd. v. *Glentanar's Trs.*, 1975 S.L.T. (Lands Tr.) 8—refused.

Mercer v. *MacLeod*, 1977 S.L.T. (Lands Tr.) 14—refused.

Scott v. *Fulton*, 1982 S.L.T. (Lands Tr.) 18—refused.

Alteration of or extension to buildings

McArthur v. *Mahoney*, 1975 S.L.T. (Lands Tr.) 2—refused.

Bachoo v. *George Wimpey & Co. Ltd.*, 1977 S.L.T. (Lands Tr.) 2—refused.

Ashbin shelter

Orsi v. *McCallum*, 1980 S.L.T. (Lands Tr.) 2—refused.

Boatyard

Ross and Cromarty District Council v. *Ullapool Property Co. Ltd.*, 1983 S.L.T. (Lands Tr.) 9—granted.

Coffee house or tearoom

Mackenzie v. *Munro*, January 10, 1974—granted.

Sinclair v. *Gillon*, 1974 S.L.T. (Lands Tr.) 18—granted.

Fish and chip shop

Di Mascio v. *Pickard*, August 7, 1972—granted.

Guest house

Morris v. *Feuars of Waverley Park*, 1973 S.L.T. (Lands Tr.) 6—granted.

Housing development

Keith v. *Texaco Ltd.*, 1977 S.L.T. (Lands Tr.) 16—granted.

Licensed premises
Off-sales
Owen v. *Mackenzie*, 1974 S.L.T. (Lands Tr.) 11—granted.
Co-operative Wholesale Society v. *Usher's Brewery*, 1975 S.L.T.
(Lands Tr.) 9—granted.

Betting shop
Bolton v. *Aberdeen Corporation*, 1972 S.L.T. (Lands Tr.) 26—
refused.

Public house
McVey v. *Glasgow Corporation*, 1973 S.L.T. (Lands Tr.) 15—
granted.

Hotel
Smith v. *Taylor*, 1972 S.L.T. (Lands Tr.) 34—granted.
Manz v. *Butter's Trs.*, 1973 S.L.T. (Lands Tr.) 2—granted.
Leney v. *Craig*, 1982 S.L.T. (Lands Tr.) 9—granted.
Pickford v. *Young*, 1975 S.L.T. (Lands Tr.) 17—refused.

Light industry
West Lothian Co-operative Society Ltd. v. *Ashdale Land and Property
Co. Ltd.*, 1972 S.L.T. (Lands Tr.) 30—granted.

Petrol filling station
Buchanan v. *Forbes*, January 1972—granted.

Schools and homes
Home for Children in Care
Lothian Regional Council v. *George Wimpey & Co. Ltd.*, 1985
S.L.T. (Lands Tr.) 2—refused.

Nursery school
Main v. *Lord Doune*, 1972 S.L.T. (Lands Tr.) 14—granted.

School
Highland Regional Council v. *MacDonald-Buchanan*, 1977 S.L.T.
(Lands Tr.) 37—granted.
Strathclyde Regional Council v. *Mactaggart & Mickel Ltd.*, 1984
S.L.T. (Lands Tr.) 33—granted.
Grampian Regional Council v. *Viscount Cowdray*, 1985 S.L.T.
(Lands Tr.) 6—refused.

School of art
Glasgow School of Art v. *Campbell*, April 24, 1973—granted.

Supermarket
Murrayfield Ice Rink v. *Scottish Rugby Union*, 1972 S.L.T. (Lands
Tr.) 20; affd. 1973 S.L.T. 99—refused.

Variation or discharge of real burdens or conditions by agreement

19–95   Sometimes it may be practicable to obtain a waiver or variation of a real burden or condition by agreement with the superior entitled to enforce it, at least if the operations or use proposed are unobjectionable. In such circumstances a waiver or variation may be granted by the superior, either without consideration other than payment of his conveyancing costs or for an acceptable payment. In such cases the waiver or variation may be obtained more speedily and with less expense than would be involved in an application to the Lands Tribunal under the 1970 Act. The strictly correct technical method of effecting the necessary change in conditions, at least if a substitute condition is being imposed, is by charter of novodamus, but in circumstances where nothing is involved other than waiver of an existing condition a minute of waiver may be adjusted. Any doubt regarding the effectiveness of a minute of waiver against singular successors has been removed by section 18 of the Land Registration (Scotland) Act 1979 which makes it clear that any deed recorded in the Register of Sasines before or after the commencement of the Act whereby a land obligation is varied or discharged shall be binding on the singular successors of the person entitled to enforce the land obligation. A charter of novodamus or minute of waiver should be recorded in the Register of Sasines or, in the case of registered titles, the transaction should be registered in the Land Register in terms of section 2(4)(c) of the 1979 Act.

CHAPTER 20

SERVITUDES

Definition

20–01   The classic definition of a servitude is that in Bell's *Principles*, section 979:

> "A servitude is a burden on land or houses, imposed by agreement—express or implied—in favour of the owners of other tenements, whereby the owner of the burdened or servient tenement, and his heirs and singular successors in the subject, must submit to certain uses to be exercised by the owner of the other or dominant tenement; or must suffer restraint in his own use and occupation of the property. Presupposing those extensions or restraints of the exclusive or absolute right of use which naturally proceed from the situation of conterminous properties, a servitude is a further limitation of that right in favour of the owner of another subject."

Any owner of heritable property is subject to restraints in its use in the interests of adjoining proprietors, *e.g.* a lower tenement must accept water flowing naturally from a higher tenement and subjacent and adjacent properties are liable to provide continued support. These are the natural restraints inherent in the ownership of property: a servitude is something beyond these, an extension of restraint on the use of one's property for the benefit of another property which has been constituted by agreement, express or implied. A servitude attaches to land independently of ownership—it is in the nature of a real right distinguishable from personal licences such as rights of shooting[1] or trout fishing.[2]

Characteristics of servitudes

–02   Certain important characteristics of servitudes must be kept in view in conveyancing practice. These may be summarised briefly as follows:

(1) A servitude is *jus in re aliena* and can be created only over one property in favour of another owned by a different person.[3]

(2) A servitude is a right annexed to the dominant tenement, is inseparable from it and cannot be communicated to any person not connected with the dominant tenement.[4]

(3) A servitude right exists for the benefit of the dominant tenement: it cannot be used for the benefit of another property even although it also belongs to the owner of the dominant tenement,[5] nor used for commercial profit.[6]

(4) The burden imposed upon the servient tenement consists only *in patiendo* and its owner need not take any active step to facilitate the exercise of the servitude right, *e.g.* he does not require to repair a road over which the servitude confers a right of way in favour of the dominant tenement.[7]

(5) The owner of the dominant tenement must exercise the servitude right in the way least burdensome to the owner of the servient tenement,[8] and the owner of the latter may use his property as he wishes so long as he permits the exercise of the servitude.[9]

(6) The burden on the servient tenement may not be increased beyond the extent of the right granted or acquired by prescription.[10]

Classification

–03   Servitudes over land may be classified as urban (relating to buildings) or rural (relating to unbuilt-on land). From a conveyancing aspect, however, the most important classification is that of positive and negative servitudes. A positive servitude is one which entitles the owner of the dominant tenement to exercise a particular right over the servient tenement which is capable of possession in the limited sense of

---

[1] *Beckett* v. *Bisset* 1921 2 S.L.T. 33.

[2] *Patrick* v. *Napier* (1867) 5 M. 683.

[3] *Donaldson's Trs.* v. *Forbes* (1839) 1 D. 449; *Grierson* v. *Sandsting School Board* (1882) 9 R. 437; *Hamilton* v. *Elder*, 1968 S.L.T. (Sh.Ct.) 53.

[4] *Irvine Knitters* v. *North Ayrshire Co-op. Society Ltd.*, 1978 S.C. 109.

[5] *Scotts* v. *Bogles*, July 6, 1809, F.C.

[6] *Murray* v. *Mags. of Peebles*, Dec. 8, 1808, F.C.

[7] *Allan* v. *MacLachlan* (1900) 2 F. 699.

[8] *Ersk.*, II, ix, 34; *Crichton* v. *Turnbull*, 1946 S.C. 52.

[9] *Beveridge* v. *Marshall*, Nov. 18, 1808, F.C.; *Sutherland* v. *Thomson* (1876) 3 R. 485. *Cf. Central Regional Council* v. *Ferns*, 1980 S.L.T. 126; *Fraser* v. *Secretary of State for Scotland*, 1959 S.L.T. (Notes) 36; *Ferguson* v. *Tennant*, 1978 S.C.(H.L.) 19.

[10] *Bell*, *Prin.*, s. 988; *J. White & Sons* v. *J. & M. White* (1906) 8 F.(H.L.) 41; *Watson* v. *Sinclair*, 1966 S.L.T. (Sh.Ct.) 77.

being actively exercised, *e.g.* a right of way or passage or a right to draw water. A negative servitude on the other hand imposes a restraint upon the owner of the servient tenement in operations on or use of his land and is incapable of possession, *e.g.* a restraint upon building beyond a certain height.[11]

CONSTITUTION OF SERVITUDES

(a) Express Grant or Reservation

Form of deed

20–04   A servitude, whether positive or negative, may be created by express grant or reservation contained in the title deeds of either the dominant or the servient tenement, or in a separate probative or holograph deed,[12] or by informal writing followed by *rei interventus*.[13] A positive servitude, if it is to be binding upon a singular successor in the ownership of the servient tenement, must either be recorded in the Register of Sasines or must be within one of the categories of recognised servitudes[14] and followed by such possession as is evident on inspection or discoverable on reasonable inquiry.[15] A negative servitude, being incapable of possession, is binding on singular successors in the ownership of the servient tenement only if it is created by express grant or reservation in a deed which is recorded in the Register of Sasines or, if not so recorded, is in terms which indicate clearly the intention to create a permanent praedial servitude as distinct from a personal agreement.[16] In the case of registered titles a servitude right may be registered in the title of the dominant tenement,[17] but cannot be registered as a burden affecting the interest in the servient tenement although if notified to the Keeper it may be noted on the title sheet of that interest.[18]

Parties

20–05   The granter must be infeft but, where absolute warrandice is given, the absence of infeftment may be cured by accretion.[19] A servitude may also be created by an heir of entail in possession with a power of

---

[11] Bell, *Prin.*, s. 994.
[12] Bell, *Prin.*, s. 992.
[13] See *Macgregor* v. *Balfour* (1899) 2 F. 345.
[14] See para. 20–07.
[15] Bell, *Prin.*, s. 990; *North British Rly. Co.* v. *Park Yard Co. Ltd.* (1898) 25 R.(H.L.) 47; *Campbell's Trs.* v. *Corporation of Glasgow* (1902) 4 F. 752 at 757.
[16] *Cowan* v. *Stewart* (1872) 10 M. 735; *Russell* v. *Cowpar* (1882) 9 R. 660 at 665, 666.
[17] Under s. 2(3)(iii) of Land Registration (Scotland) Act 1979.
[18] R.T.P.B., para. D.1.16.
[19] *Stephen* v. *Brown's Trs.*, 1922 S.C. 136.

sale[20] or by a proprietor who had disponed the servient tenement in security by way of *ex facie* absolute disposition,[21] but not by an estate factor[22] nor by one of several owners of property in common.[23] The grant must be in favour of the proprietor of the dominant tenement: it is incompetent to grant it in favour of a tenant.[24] If the grantee does not yet own the dominant tenement when the grant is made, the right comes into force when he subsequently acquires it.[25]

Subjects which may be dominant or servient tenements

–06   Any land or building may be a dominant tenement, and any land or buildings in private ownership may be a servient tenement but lands held for a statutory purpose cannot be made subject to a servitude which could conflict with that purpose.[26] A servitude continues to exist so long as the tenements can be identified, even although there have been substantial alterations or rebuilding.[27]

Kinds of servitudes which can be created

–07   Since a servitude, whether positive or negative, may be effective against singular successors without registration, it is essential that it falls within one of the categories of recognised servitudes.[28] An attempt to create a servitude which is not within any of those categories is ineffectual,[29] and it is doubtful whether it is competent to add to a known servitude a qualification or exception which takes it outwith that category.[30] The recognised positive urban servitudes comprise *tigni immittendi, oneris ferendi* and'stillicide. The recognised positive rural servitudes are way, access or passage, aqueduct, *aquaehaustus*, pasturage, fuel, feal and divot, discharge of drainage, the taking of sand, gravel, stone, slate or sea-ware, and bleaching linen. The recognised negative servitudes are *non aedificandi, altius non tollendi* and *ne luminibus officiatur*.[31] As to the procedure in making real a right or obligation which is not within one of those categories, see paragraph 20–36 *infra*.

---

[20] *Bowman Ballantine* (1883) 10 R. 1061.

[21] *Union Heritable Securities Co. Ltd.* v. *Mathie* (1886) 13 R. 670.

[22] *Macgregor* v. *Balfour* (1899) 2 F. 345.

[23] *Grant* v. *Heriot's Trust* (1906) 8 F. 647.

[24] *Safeway Food Stores Ltd.* v. *Wellington Motor Co. (Ayr) Ltd.*, 1976 S.L.T. 53.

[25] *North British Rly. Co.* v. *Park Yard Co. Ltd.* (1898) 25 R.(H.L.) 47.

[26] *Ayr Harbour Trs.* v. *Oswald* (1883) 10 R.(H.L.) 85; *Ellice's Trs.* v. *Caledonian Canal Commissioners* (1904) 6 F. 325.

[27] *Irvine Knitters* v. *North Ayrshire Co-op. Society Ltd.*, *supra*.

[28] *Banks & Co.* v. *Walker* (1874) 1 R. 981 at 984, 986; *Alexander* v. *Butchart* (1875) 3 R. 156, 160; *Murray's Trs.* v. *St. Margaret's Convent* (1906) 8 F. 1109 at 1120; 1907 S.C. (H.L.) 8.

[29] *Campbell's Trs.* v. *Corporation of Glasgow* (1902) 4 F. 752.

[30] *Braid Hills Hotel Co. Ltd.* v. *Manuels*, 1909 S.C. 120 at 126.

[31] For further particulars of these servitudes see Walker, *Prin.*, III, 204–208.

Expression of grant

20–08   Practical rules to be borne in mind when a servitude right is being created either by grant or reservation are:

(1) The extent of a positive servitude right is determined by the terms of the grant: the possession which follows is merely the badge, not the measure, of the right.[32]

(2) The dominant and servient tenements must be clearly identified.

(3) Although the stringent requirements as to precision in describing the right which are necessary for the creation of a real burden or condition do not apply with the same force when describing a servitude of a well-known kind,[33] it is desirable that the extent of the servitude right, particularly a positive servitude, be expressed with accuracy. Since a servitude is a restraint upon the use of the servient tenement, it will be strictly construed on account of the presumption in favour of freedom.[34]

(4) In the case of a servitude of way the route and the kind of traffic, whether pedestrian or vehicular, should be specified, perhaps with a statement of minimum width.[35] In the case of an urban servitude of passage where the line of the route has been precisely defined in the grant, the servient owner cannot alter the route save with the consent of the dominant owner,[36] but in the case of a rural servitude the servient owner may substitute an alternative way equally convenient with the authority of the court, and such authority may be given even in the case of an urban servitude if the alteration in the route is relatively slight.[37] In the absence of any provision in the grant as to maintenance of the road of access, the burden of repair falls on the owner of the dominant tenement, but if the grant imposes an obligation of maintenance wholly or partly upon the owner of the servient property that is not part of a known servitude and if it is to be effective against successors of the servient owner it must be created a real burden upon his property.[38]

(5) Where a servitude right of pasturage or cutting peat is created it may be desirable to specify the exact area over which the right is to extend: in the absence of such specification the owner of the servient property may use part of it for purposes which preclude the exercise of the servitude right as regards that part, so long as he leaves unaffected sufficient land, not unreasonably inconveniently situated, to satisfy the servitude right.[39]

---

[32] Bell, *Prin.*, s. 992.

[33] *Lean* v. *Hunter*, 1950 S.L.T. (Notes) 31: *McLean* v. *Marwhirn Developments Ltd.*, 1976 S.L.T. (Notes) 47.

[34] *Clark* v. *Perth School Board* (1898) 25 R. 919; *Hunter* v. *Fox*, 1964 S.C.(H.L.) 95.

[35] *Cooper & McLeod* v. *Edinburgh Improvement Trs.* (1876) 3 R. 1106. See *Millar* v. *Christie*, 1961 S.C. 1; *Scotland* v. *Wallace*, 1964 S.L.T. (Sh.Ct.) 9 (servitude by prescription).

[36] *Hill* v. *McLaren* (1879) 6 R. 1363; *Moyes* v. *McDiarmid* (1900) 2 F. 918.

[37] *Thomson's Trs.* v. *Findlay* (1898) 25 R. 407.

[38] *Allan* v. *MacLachlan* (1900) 2 F. 699. See para. 20–36.

[39] *Fraser* v. *Secretary of State for Scotland, supra; Ferguson* v. *Tennant, supra.*

Style—servitude non aedificandi by constitution in conveyance

0–09 *(At end of dispositive clause before date of entry)* And whereas it has been agreed that the following servitude should be constituted in favour of the said *(disponee)* and his successors in the subjects hereby disponed, Therefore I agree that neither I nor my successors in the ownership of my property *(identify)* situated immediately to the west of the said subjects hereby disponed shall erect on my said property any buildings or structure of any kind within a distance [radius]⁴⁰ of   metres from the west or outer face of the western gable of the building erected on the said subjects hereby disponed, which agreement and restriction is hereby declared to be a servitude in favour of the subjects hereby disponed over my said property.

Style—servitude altius non tollendi by reservation in conveyance

0–10 *(At end of dispositive clause before date of entry)* And whereas it has been agreed that the following servitude should be constituted in favour of me and my successors in the ownership of the property *(identify)* situated immediately to the west of the said subjects hereby disponed *(or as the case may be)*, Therefore it is hereby provided, and the said *(disponee)* by acceptance hereof and signature hereto agrees, that no building or structure of any kind shall be erected by him or his executors or successors upon the said subjects hereby disponed which shall be of a greater height than   metres [feet] above the level of the ground, which agreement and restriction is hereby declared to be a servitude over the said subjects hereby disponed in favour of my said property.

Style—separate deed—servitude of way

0–11 I, AB *(designed)*, whereas I am the heritable proprietor of ALL and WHOLE *(describe so as to identify)* (hereinafter called "Property A") and that CD, *(designed)*, is the heritable proprietor of ALL and WHOLE *(describe so as to identify)* (hereinafter called "Property B") situated immediately to the west of Property A and that I have agreed to allow him and his successors in ownership of Property B a servitude right of way as aftermentioned, Therefore in consideration of the sum of £   paid to me by the said CD I hereby grant and dispone to the said CD and his successors in the ownership of Property B a servitude right of way for pedestrian and vehicular traffic through the existing pend close on Property A as a means of access to and egress from the rear of the building erected on Property B; but declaring that these presents are granted with and under the following conditions, namely:— (1) The said pend close and the walls and roof thereof and the existing gate at the north end of the said pend close fronting   Street shall be kept in proper condition and repair and shall from time to time be repaired at the sole expense of the said CD or his foresaids; (2) The said gate shall be kept locked between the hours of 6 p.m. and 8 a.m. unless and only so long as

---

⁴⁰ See *Clark* v. *Perth School Board, supra.*

in actual use between these hours; (3) No vehicle shall be left stationary in the said pend close at any time nor shall there be deposited or left in the said pend close at any time any articles of any description so that the same may be kept clear of any obstruction at all times; (4) The said servitude has been granted with reference to the present state of Property B and shall not be extended to apply to any substantially different condition thereof so as to increase the burden on my Property A, and the said right shall at all times be exercised so as to cause as little inconvenience as possible to me and my successors in ownership of Property A: (*Stamp clause*) (*To be attested*) (*Stamp as conveyance on sale*)[41]

NOTE. The advisability of granting a permanent servitude of way through an existing property should always be considered carefully: it may inhibit redevelopment of the servient tenement.[42] If there is any possibility of substantial alteration to or redevelopment of Property A in the foreseeable future the use of the close should be granted only as a personal contract terminable on notice. Where there is no such possibility it may be prudent to qualify the grant thus: "Reserving always to me and my successors in the ownership of Property A the right to terminate the servitude hereby granted for the purpose of effecting any substantial alterations or reconstruction or development of or affecting Property A on giving   months' written notice to the said CD or his foresaids."

Registration

20–12 **(1) Register of Sasines.** Where a servitude is constituted by express grant in a conveyance of the dominant tenement or by reservation in a conveyance of the servient tenement, duly recorded in the Register of Sasines, the existence of the servitude will usually but not necessarily be disclosed by a search against either of the properties. If the servitude is created by a separate deed which is not recorded in the Register of Sasines it will not be disclosed by a search but will nevertheless be binding upon and enforceable by singular successors, provided that in the case of a positive servitude there has been possession in exercise of the right. In the case of a negative servitude there can be no possession which advertises its existence, but if expressed in apt terms which clearly demonstrate the intention to create a permanent right it will be effective in questions between singular successors. In order to obviate the risk to such successors, particularly as regards a negative servitude, it is recommended that in practice a separate deed creating a servitude should be recorded.

---

[41] A separate deed creating a positive servitude for consideration is liable to stamp duty as a conveyance on sale of a heritable right. A deed creating a negative servitude does not involve conveyance of a right and is not liable to stamp duty.

[42] See *Armia Ltd.* v. *Daejan Developments Ltd.*, 1979 S.C.(H.L.) 56.

(2) Land Register. A servitude is an overriding interest but only in relation to the servient tenement;[43] in relation to the dominant tenement it is an incorporeal right which is registrable.[44] (i) Where a servitude is constituted by express grant in a conveyance of the dominant tenement it will be disclosed as a pertinent in the title sheet of that interest.[45] Since it is not an overriding interest in relation to the dominant tenement it is inappropriate to refer to it in the sections relating to overriding interests in Part B of Form 1, 2 or 3, as the case may be. If the servient tenement is registered the Keeper will usually note the servitude on the title sheet of the servient tenement.[46] (ii) Where the servitude is constituted by reservation in a conveyance of the servient tenement, it is appropriate in the application for registration of the interest of the proprietor of the servient tenement to refer to the servitude in Part B(3)(*c*) of Form 1 or Part B(1)(*d*) of Form 2 or Part B(3)(*b*) of Form 3, as the case may be, and the Keeper must note the servitude on the title sheet of the dominant tenement.[47] (iii) Where the servitude is constituted by separate deed an application for it to be entered on the title sheet of the dominant tenement should be made on Form 2. Section 6(4)(*b*)(ii) of the 1979 Act applies and there is no need for a separate application on Form 5 to have it noted on the title sheet of the servient tenement. If, however, the dominant tenement is not registered application on Form 5 for noting on the title sheet of the servient tenement is appropriate. Whichever of the above mentioned methods of constituting the servitude is used, if the title to either the dominant or servient tenement remains in the Register of Sasines and it is desired to have the creation of the servitude disclosed in a search of that Register it remains competent to record the relevant deed in the Register of Sasines with a warrant on behalf of the grantee in addition to the application on Form 2 or Form 5. The effect of registration is to vest in the proprietor of the dominant tenement a real right to the servitude, but there is no entitlement to indemnity except in so far as the claim may relate to the validity of its constitution.[48] Even if registration is not effected it remains the law that a servitude right is binding on singular successors if it is properly created by a separate deed and in the case of a positive servitude is followed by appropriate possession.

(b) Implied Grant or Reservation

Servitude implied on severance of properties formerly in same ownership

–13 An implied positive servitude can be created when two properties, previously in the ownership of one person, have been severed in

---

[43] Land Registration (Scotland) Act 1979, s. 28(1).
[44] *Ibid.*, s. 2(3)(iii).
[45] R.T.P.B., paras. C.15, D.1.16, D.1.18.
[46] 1979 Act, s. 6(4)(*a*).
[47] *Ibid.*, s. 6(4)(*a*).
[48] *Ibid.*, ss. 3(1)(*a*) and 12(3)(1).

ownership by disposal of one or both of them and there has been an omission to create a servitude right over one property which is either (i) absolutely necessary for the use of the other, or (ii) necessary for the comfortable or convenient enjoyment of the other. The question whether a servitude right has been created by implication arises most frequently when a proprietor of two properties disposes of one and retains the other,[49] but the principle applies also when the severance occurs by simultaneous conveyances of both properties to different persons.[50]

Distinction between implied grant and implied reservation

20–14   There is an important distinction between a servitude which is absolutely necessary for the use of the property conveyed, *i.e.* a servitude of necessity, and a servitude which is merely necessary for the comfortable or convenient enjoyment of it. Where the owner of both properties conveys one of them it is implied that he does not intend to derogate from the grant, and accordingly there are implied in favour of the grantee of the conveyance not only any servitudes of necessity but also any servitudes that are necessary for the comfortable or convenient enjoyment of the property conveyed. On the other hand, where there has been omission to reserve in the conveyance any servitude rights in favour of the property retained, any servitude that will be implied is restricted to a servitude of necessity without which no enjoyment of the retained property would be possible.[51]

Implied grant

20–15   To establish an implied grant in favour of the part conveyed over the part retained it is necessary that the right claimed is of the kind which could have been created as a servitude and, save in the case of a servitude of necessity, that it was in fact exercised for the benefit of the part conveyed before the severance took place.[52] It is also necessary to show that the implied servitude is either a servitude of necessity or at least is necessary for comfortable and convenient enjoyment of the property conveyed. A right to a positive servitude has been implied as regards drainage,[53] support[54] and access,[55] but was negatived in other

---

[49] Or disposes of one part of a single property which has been divided into two parts.
[50] Bell, *Prin.*, s. 992.
[51] Bell, *Prin.*,·s. 992.
[52] *McLaren* v. *City of Glasgow Union Rly. Co.* (1878) 5 R. 1042; *Cullens* v. *Cambusbarron Co-op. Society Ltd.* (1895) 23 R. 209; *Shearer* v. *Peddie* (1899) 1 F. 1201.
[53] *Ewart* v. *Cochrane* (1861) 4 Macq. 117.
[54] *Caledonian Rly. Co.* v. *Sprot* (1856) 2 Macq. 449.
[55] *Walton Bros.* v. *Mags. of Glasgow* (1876) 3 R. 1130; *Rome* v. *Hope Johnstone* (1884) 11 R. 653; *Union Heritable Securities Ltd.* v. *Mathie* (1886) 13 R. 670.

cases[56] relating to access, generally on the ground that other means of access were available. A test of what is necessary for comfortable enjoyment is whether, if the right had been withheld, the purchaser would not have bought.[56a] The extent of the right implied is limited to its extent at the time of severance.[57] A negative servitude cannot be created by implied grant: an express grant is necessary.[58]

Implied reservation

4–16   A servitude can be implied in favour of the retained part of a property after severance only if it is absolutely necessary for the property to be used at all, as where it is landlocked and the only practicable access is through the part that has been disponed. The principle, as so restricted, has been recognised in English and some Scottish decisions.[59] Where a servitude right is desired over property conveyed in favour of property retained, it should be reserved expressly in the conveyance: the circumstances in which a servitude by reservation will be implied seldom occur.[60]

(c) Other Methods of Creation

Acquiescence

4–17   Bell states[61] that a servitude right may be conferred by acquiescence, *e.g.* in circumstances where a proprietor has permitted substantial works on his land for the benefit of a neighbouring property he and his successors will be barred by their acquiescence from contending that a servitude right to retain and use the works has not been created. The clearest illustration of the principle is the decision in *Robson* v. *Chalmers Property Investment Co. Ltd.*[62] where a dam, tank and water-supply pipes were constructed upon land belonging to a neighbouring proprietor with his approval. The principle was recognised in *Macgregor* v. *Balfour*,[63] although in that case the fact of acquiescence by the proprietor of the allegedly burdened land was not established. In a case where a common water main served four houses and a plea of

[56] *Gow's Trs.* v. *Mealls* (1875) 2 R. 729; *McLaren* v. *City of Glasgow Union Rly. Co.* (1878) 5 R. 1042; *Campbell* v. *Halkett* (1890) 27 S.L.R. 1000; *Fraser* v. *Cox*, 1938 S.C. 506; *McEachen* v. *Lister*, 1976 S.L.T. (Sh.Ct.) 38.
[56a] *Gow's Trs.* v. *Mealls*, *supra*; *McLaren* v. *City of Glasgow Union Rly. Co.*, *supra* at 1048.
[57] *Louttit's Trs.* v. *Highland Rly. Co.* (1892) 19 R. 791, at 797.
[58] *Dundas* v. *Blair* (1886) 13 R. 759; *Inglis* v. *Clark* (1901) 4 F. 288.
[59] *Wheeldon* v. *Burrows* (1879) 12 Ch.D. 31 at 49; *Union Lighterage Co.* v. *London Graving Dock Co.* [1902] 2 Ch. 557; *Union Heritable Securities Co. Ltd.* v. *Mathie* (1886) 13 R. 670 at 676; *Fergusson* v. *Campbell*, 1913 1 S.L.T. 241.
[60] See *Ellice's Trs.* v. *Caledonian Canal Commissioners* (1904) 6 F. 325 at 333; *Murray* v. *Medley*, 1973 S.L.T. (Sh.Ct.) 75.
[61] *Prin.*, ss. 946, 947; *Cowan* v. *Lord Kinnaird* (1865) 4 M. 236 at 243.
[62] 1965 S.L.T. 381.
[63] (1899) 2 F. 345 at 351, 352.

acquiescence was proposed a proof before answer was allowed, but since none of the proprietors might have been aware of the existence of the pipe, which was underground and not visible, it seems doubtful whether acquiescence could have been established.[64] It is a precondition of the creation of a servitude by acquiescence that there has been approval by the owner of the servient tenement or that the works have been so substantial that they were evident to him and to singular successors; otherwise there will be no permanent servitude right, although in certain circumstances there may have been a personal bargain.[65]

Description and facts and circumstances

20–18   There are two decisions[66] where a servitude of access over a lane was held to be established by the terms of feu grants of land bordering upon but excluding the lane followed by use of the lane for a period less than the period of positive prescription along with facts and circumstances indicating an intention that the feuars should have access by the lane. The *ratio* of these decisions lies between implied grant and acquiescence and was explained thus[67]: "The question is rather in the region of contract than of strict property law and that evidence of acts done by the feuar in the assertion of the right is admissible to interpret the title, or at least to bar the superior from disputing the interpretation of the title which has been acted on with his knowledge, and presumably with his consent." An earlier decision to the contrary effect[68] was distinguished in *Boyd* v. *Hamilton*.[69]

Positive prescription

20–19   In relation to positive servitudes prescription operates in two ways:

(1) It renders unchallengeable a servitude right founded on a deed sufficient in respect of its terms to constitute the servitude except on the ground that the deed is *ex facie* invalid or was forged.[70]

(2) It may create a servitude right by exercise of the right for the period of positive prescription without the need of any grant express or implied.[70a]

It is necessary that possession of the servitude has continued openly, peaceably and without judicial interruption for a period, formerly of 40 years and now of 20 years. The title to claim the right is infeftment in

---

[64] *More* v. *Boyle*, 1967 S.L.T. (Sh.Ct.) 38.
[65] Gloag, *Contract*, 170, 171; *Brown* v. *Baty*, 1957 S.C. 351 and earlier decisions there cited.
[66] *Argyllshire Commissioners of Supply* v. *Campbell* (1885) 12 R. 1255; *Boyd* v. *Hamilton*, 1907 S.C. 912.
[67] *Boyd* v. *Hamilton*, *supra*, *per* Lord McLaren at 921.
[68] *Shearer* v. *Peddie* (1899) 1 F. 1201.
[69] *supra* at 920, 921.
[70] Prescription and Limitation (Scotland) Act 1973, s. 3(1)(*b*).
[70a] *Ibid.*, s. 3(1)(*a*).

the dominant tenement,[71] even if the title is a bounding title since a servitude is by definition *jus in re aliena*.[72] The possession must be as of right and not ascribable to any licence or tolerance[73] and peaceably rather than in the face of opposition, and without judicial interruption: in such circumstances the possession will not be ascribed to tolerance unless there is something in its origin or otherwise to indicate the contrary.[74] Since a servitude is an obligation upon the servient tenement in favour of the dominant tenement, the possession founded upon may be by any person who has in fact been in possession of the latter.[75] The possession which has been enjoyed is the measure of the right—the rule is *tantum prescriptum quantum possessum*.[76]

TRANSMISSION OF SERVITUDES
CONVEYANCES OF DOMINANT AND SERVIENT TENEMENTS

Transmission of servitudes

-20   A servitude is a burden upon the servient tenement for the benefit of the dominant tenement and continues to subsist notwithstanding changes in the ownership of either so long as both tenements do not come into the ownership of one person.[77] No assignation of the servitude right is required: the title to enforce it is simply ownership of the dominant tenement.[78]

(a) Titles recorded in Register of Sasines

Sale of servient tenement

-21   Upon the sale of the servient tenement the servitude right should be disclosed in the contract of sale and should be excepted in the dispositive clause of the disposition and from warrandice. It has been held that a seller was entitled to have a servitude right excepted in both the dispositive and warrandice clauses,[79] but it is thought that if the servitude is excepted in the dispositive clause it is strictly unnecessary to except it also in the warrandice clause since the latter warrants only what has been conveyed. It is not correct, however, merely to except

---

[71] Bell, *Prin.*, s. 993, Ersk., II, ix, 3.

[72] *Beaumont* v. *Lord Glenlyon* (1843) 5 D. 1337.

[73] *McInroy* v. *Duke of Atholl* (1891) 18 R.(H.L.) 46; *McGregor* v. *Crieff Co-op. Society* Ltd., 1915 S.C.(H.L.) 93.

[74] *Grierson* v. *Sandsting School Board* (1882) 9 R. 437 at 441; *McGregor* v. *Crieff Co-op. Society Ltd.*, *supra* at 98.

[75] *Drummond* v. *Milligan* (1890) 17 R. 316.

[76] *Pirie & Sons* v. *Earl of Kintore* (1903) 5 F. 818; (1906) 8 F.(H.L.) 16; *J. White & Sons* v. *J. & M. White* (1906) 8 F.(H.L.) 41; *Carstairs* v. *Spence*, 1924 S.C. 380 at 385; *Kerr* v. *Brown* 1939 S.C. 140.

[77] See para. 20–27.

[78] *Braid Hills Hotel Co. Ltd.* v. *Manuels*, 1909 S.C. 120.

[79] *North British Rly. Co.* v. *Mags. of Edinburgh* (1893) 20 R. 725.

the servitude from warrandice: the dispositive clause is the measure of
the grant and technically an adverse real right should be excluded
therefrom.

Purchase of servient tenement

20–22   If the servitude has been created by express grant the deed which
constituted it should be examined both as to its validity and the extent
of the right granted, since the deed is the measure of the right and that
may be greater than appears from the extent to which it has yet been
exercised by possession. Even though no servitude created by express
grant is disclosed, if inspection of the property indicates that some
servitude right may exist which could have been constituted by implied
grant, acquiescence or prescription, inquiries should be made and, if
there is any doubt, an express warranty of immunity from any servitude
may be sought from the seller.

Purchase of dominant tenement

20–23   If the servitude has been constituted by express grant the validity of
the deed which created it should be verified as part of the examination
of title, and it may be necessary also to ensure that the right has not
been lost by non-use for the period of negative prescription or by any
change of circumstances that may have resulted in its extinction.[80] If
the servitude has been created by implied grant, acquiescence or
positive prescription and there is any doubt as to its constitution or
subsistence there should be obtained, if practicable, a probative
admission from the servient owner that the right subsists. In any event
it is desirable to include an express conveyance of the servitude right in
the disposition of the dominant tenement which will be duly recorded.
These matters are of peculiar importance where the purchase is of a
part of the dominant tenement and developments are contemplated on
the subjects purchased or on the retained part: the result of the
developments may be to increase the burden of the servitude and it
may be necessary to have it reconstituted by express agreement in
probative form by the owner of the servient tenement.

(b) Registered Titles

Sale and purchase of servient tenement

20–24   If the servitude has been noted in the burdens section of the title
sheet of the servient property and still subsists it is unnecessary to refer
to it in the disposition. If it is not noted in the title sheet, then it should
be expressly excepted in the dispositive clause of the disposition in

---

[80] See paras. 20–28 to 20–30.

terms which describe it fully with specification of the dominant tenement. It will then be noted in the burdens section of the title sheet of the servient property when the disposition is submitted for registration of the transfer of the interest in that property.[81]

Purchase of dominant tenement

-25   If a servitude has been entered in the title sheet of the dominant tenement there is no need to inquire as to the validity of its constitution since that is guaranteed,[82] but it may be prudent to verify that nothing has happened that might have discharged or extinguished it. No reference need be made to the servitude in the disposition. If the servitude subsists but for any reason has not been entered in the title sheet of the dominant tenement it should be expressly created, with full particulars of it, including specification of the servient tenement, in the dispositive clause of the disposition which transfers the interest of the proprietor of the dominant tenement, duly signed also by the owner of the servient tenement as granting or consenting to its creation or subsistence, or alternatively created or confirmed by a separate deed of servitude granted by the owner of the servient tenement which may be submitted for registration by an application on Form 2. If the seller contends that a servitude exists but that is not admitted by the owner of the servient tenement, application should be made on Form 2 accompanied by any deed or deeds alleged to constitute it or evidence of other facts, *e.g.* possession for the period of positive prescription, which establish its creation. Any question that arises as to the existence or extent of a servitude or the Keeper's decision on an application to register it may be resolved by decision of the court or the Lands Tribunal for Scotland.[83]

EXTINCTION OF SERVITUDES

Express discharge

-26   A servitude may be extinguished by express discharge in a deed, holograph or probative, granted by the owner of the dominant tenement.[84] As to a style of discharge, see paragraph 20–33 *infra*.

Confusio

-27   A servitude is extinguished *confusione* when both the dominant and servient tenements come into the ownership of the same person—*sua*

---

[81] Land Registration (Scotland) Act 1979, s. 6(4).
[82] *Ibid.*, s. 12(3)(*l*).
[83] *Ibid.*, s. 25.
[84] Bell, *Prin.*, s. 998; *Macdonald* v. *Mags. of Inverness*, 1918 S.C. 141.

res nemini servit.[85] If the tenements subsequently come into the ownership of different persons, the former servitude does not revive but has to be reconstituted.[86] There is an exception, however, where the estates are held on separate titles and a subsequent separation of the two tenements is to be anticipated independently of the will of the proprietor.[87] If there are no separate titles, reconstitution of the servitude may occur on subsequent severance of ownership of the two tenements by implied grant.[88]

Negative prescription

20–28　　A positive servitude may be extinguished by non-use for the period (20 years) of negative prescription.[89] A negative servitude may be lost by failure on the part of the owner of the dominant tenement to challenge an infringement of the right for a period of 20 years.[90] A negative servitude may be thus lost even if it appears in the title deeds of both the dominant and servient tenements,[91] since it is only a real right of *ownership* in land which is imprescriptible.[92]

Acquiescence and abandonment

20–29　　A servitude right may be lost by conduct on the part of the owner of the dominant tenement which indicates an intention to abandon it,[93] or is such as to bar him personally from enforcing it.[94] Acquiescence in limitation of a servitude right does not extinguish it but merely curtails it to the extent of the limitation acquiesced in.[95]

Change of circumstances

20–30　　If either tenement ceases to exist the servitude right is extinguished,[96] or if the purpose of the servitude fails the right ends.[97] So a servitude of necessity ceases with the necessity.[98]

Discharge by Lands Tribunal

20–31　　A servitude is a land obligation and may be discharged by the Lands Tribunal for Scotland.[99]

---

[85] *Baird* v. *Fortune* (1861) 4 Macq. 127; *Donaldson's Trs.* v. *Forbes* (1839) 1 D. 449.
[86] *Union Bank of Scotland Ltd.* v. *Daily Record* (1902) 10 S.L.T. 71.
[87] *Donaldson's Trs.* v. *Forbes, supra.*
[88] See paras. 20–13 *et seq.*
[89] Prescription and Limitation (Scotland) Act 1973, s. 8.
[90] *Ibid.*, s. 8; *Wilkie* v. *Scot* (1688) Mor. 11189.
[91] *Graham* v. *Douglas* (1735) Mor. 10745.
[92] 1973 Act, Sched. 3.
[93] *Muirhead* v. *Glasgow Highland Society* (1864) 2 M. 420; *Douglas* v. *Hozier* (1878) 16 S.L.R. 14; *Mags of Rutherglen* v. *Bainbridge* (1886) 13 R. 745.
[94] *Davidson* v. *Thomson* (1890) 17 R. 287. *Cf. Stevenson* v. *Donaldson*, 1935 S.C. 551.
[95] *Millar* v. *Christie*, 1961 S.C. 1.
[96] Bell, *Prin.*, ss. 995, 996.
[97] *Winans* v. *Lord Tweedmouth* (1888) 15 R. 540 at 568.
[98] Rankine, *Land-Ownership*, 431, 443.
[99] Conveyancing and Feudal Reform (Scotland) Act 1970, s. 1; *Devlin* v. *Conn*, 1972 S.L.T. (Lands Tr.) 11.

Extinction by statute

0–32 Servitudes over land acquired compulsorily under statutory powers may be extinguished on payment of compensation.[1]

Style—express discharge

0–33 I, AB (*designed*), heritable proprietor of (*describe dominant tenement so as to identify it*)[a] (hereinafter called "the dominant tenement") Whereas the dominant tenement enjoys a servitude (*describe character of servitude and sufficient particulars to identify it*) over (*describe servient tenement so as to identify it*)[a] belonging to CD, (*designed*), (hereinafter called "the servient tenement") And whereas [in consideration of the sum of £   paid to me by the said CD of which sum I hereby acknowledge receipt] I have agreed to discharge the said servitude, Therefore I renounce and discharge, and declare the servient tenement to be disburdened of, the said servitude in favour of the dominant tenement whether constituted under (*specify deed of constitution, if any*) or under any other deed or deeds, or by prescription or otherwise howsoever: And I grant [absolute warrandice] *or* [warrandice from fact and deed only] (Stamp clause, if necessary). (*To be attested*) (*Stamp as conveyance on sale if price: otherwise nil.*)

NOTE
[a] Describe by reference to deed recorded in Sasine Register, or by number of Land Certificate if registered in Land Register.

Registration of discharge

0–34 If the title to the servient tenement is recorded in the Register of Sasines the discharge should be recorded therein with a warrant on behalf of the owner of the servient tenement. If the title to either or both of the tenements has been registered in the Land Register, the discharge should be submitted to the Keeper (Form 5) when the Keeper will enter particulars of the discharge in the burdens section of the title sheet of the interest in the servient property and remove the entry relating to the servitude if it has been entered in the title sheet of the dominant property.[2]

There may be events, not appearing in any deeds, which may create a servitude, *e.g.* creation by implication on a severance, or which may extinguish a servitude, *e.g. confusio*, abandonment or non-use for the period of negative prescription. In the case of titles registered in the Land Register notification should be made to the Keeper of the occurrence of any such event, when the Keeper will inform all persons whose interests are likely to be affected. If any question arises as to

---

[1] Lands Clauses Consolidation (Scotland) Act 1845, ss. 93–98; Housing (Scotland) Act 1966, s. 51; New Towns (Scotland) Act 1968, s. 19. See *Largs Hydropathic Ltd.* v. *Largs Town Council*, 1967 S.C. 1.
[2] Land Registration (Scotland) Rules, r. 7: R.T.P.B., para. H.2.09.

whether the servitude has been created or extinguished, the issue will be decided by the court or the Lands Tribunal for Scotland. After the interested parties have been so informed and, in the event of challenge, the issue has been determined by the court or the Lands Tribunal, the Keeper will make the appropriate amendments on the title sheets of the dominant and servient tenements.[3] It should be noted that the Keeper *must* note the existence of a servitude in the title sheet of the interest affected if it is disclosed on any document accompanying an application for registration in respect of that interest,[4] but he has a discretion with regard to noting a servitude where an application to do so is made on behalf of the proprietor of the dominant or servient tenement: he *may* note it but cannot be required to do so.[5]

REGISTRATION OF SERVITUDE RIGHTS

Registration of servitude rights—general principles

20–35   Under the sasine system, recording of a deed creating a servitude was not essential to make the servitude a real right. The value of having the deed recorded was that it gave public notice of the existence of the servitude. The law remains substantially unchanged under registration of title: entry or noting of a servitude is not required to render the right real.[6] There are, however, certain benefits under the latter system. Once a servitude has been disclosed on the Land Register the proprietor of the dominant tenement is entitled to indemnity so far as the claim relates to the validity of its constitution,[7] but there is no guarantee that the servitude remains enforceable or has not been extinguished. Further, indemnity may be payable where the Keeper has omitted to note, or has made an error in noting, a discharge of or freedom from a servitude in terms of rule 7 of the Registration of Title Rules.[8] The system of registration of title also makes possible publication of the existence of servitudes which have not been created expressly in a deed, *e.g.* by prescription or implied grant,[9] or of their discharge otherwise than by express deed,[10] information which is not publicly available under the sasine system.

---

[3] 1979 Act, ss. 6(4)(*b*) and 9; see R.T.P.B., paras. H.2.04 to H.2.08.
[4] 1979 Act, s. 6(4)(*a*).
[5] *Ibid.*, s. 6(4)(*b*)(ii).
[6] 1979 Act, s. 3(2).
[7] *Ibid.*, s. 12(3)(1).
[8] R.T.P.B., para. H.2.07.
[9] *Ibid.*, para. H.2.04.
[10] 1979 Act, s. 9(3)(*a*).

OTHER CONVENTIONAL RESTRICTIONS ON LAND

Restrictions which are neither servitudes nor real burdens

–36   Sometimes agreements are made which purport to impose restrictions on land that are intended to be real, but the deeds fail to achieve that object because the restrictions are not within any of the categories of known servitude and do not satisfy the requirements for the creation of a real burden.[11] If the restrictions satisfy the requirements for the creation of a real burden except that they do not enter the infeftment of the burdened property but are within the definition of land obligations,[12] they may now become real by recording the agreement or deed creating the restrictions in the appropriate Register of Sasines or, in the case of registered titles, having the restrictions registered or noted in the Land Register.[13] Accordingly, if there is any doubt whether a restriction is within the category of a known servitude, or when a servitude is basically a recognised servitude but has special provisions which may take it out of that category, the safe course is to embody them in a deed of conditions with the precision essential to a proper real burden and have the deed recorded or the restrictions registered as may be appropriate.

PUBLIC RIGHTS OF WAY

Nature, constitution, variation of route and extinction

–37   Public rights of way may concern conveyancers as a burden on land acquired or, less commonly, as a convenient means of access to such land. They are distinct in legal character from private servitudes[14] although they may serve a similar purpose to that of a servitude of access. They may be created by grant or prescriptive use, most commonly the latter.[15] The requisites for the constitution of a public right of way are, briefly, that it proceeds from one public place to another along a continuous and definite route and that there has been continuous use of it by the public as of right for 20 years or more.[16] It is not easy for the proprietor of the land affected to obtain from the courts a variation or diversion of the line of route,[17] but planning

---

[11] *Campbell's Trs.* v. *Glasgow Corporation* (1902) 4 F. 752; *Botanic Gardens Picture House* v. *Adamson*, 1924 S.C. 549. For other illustrations see Burns, 433.

[12] Conveyancing and Feudal Reform (Scotland) Act 1970, s. 1(2).

[13] Land Registration (Scotland) Act 1979, s. 17.

[14] As to the distinction, see *Thomson* v. *Murdoch* (1862) 24 D. 975 at 982.

[15] *Mann* v. *Brodie* (1885) 12 R.(H.L.) 52; *Macpherson* v. *Scottish Rights of Way and Recreation Society Ltd.* (1888) 15 R.(H.L.) 68.

[16] *Rhins District Committee* v. *Cuninghame*, 1917 2 S.L.T. 169 at 170; Prescription and Limitation (Scotland) Act 1973, s. 3(3); *Marquis of Bute* v. *McKirdy & McMillan Ltd.*, 1937 S.C. 93; *Richardson* v. *Cromarty Petroleum Co. Ltd.*, 1982 S.L.T. 237.

[17] *Hope* v. *Inveresk Parish Council Landward Committee* (1906) 8 F. 896.

authorities may do so under the powers conferred by statute.[18] A right of way may be extinguished by non-use or acquiescence in its obstruction for the period of negative prescription,[19] by the fact that one or other of its termini have ceased to be a public place or by the exercise of statutory powers.[20]

---

[18] Countryside (Scotland) Act 1967, s. 35 as amended by Countryside (Scotland) Act 1981, s. 5 and Local Government and Planning (Scotland) Act 1982, s. 9 and Scheds. 1 and 4.

[19] Now 20 years—Prescription and Limitation (Scotland) Act 1973, s. 8.

[20] *e.g.* Roads (Scotland) Act 1984, s. 68; Countryside (Scotland) Act 1967, s. 34, as amended; Town and Country Planning (Scotland) Act 1972, s. 108.

CHAPTER 21

EXAMINATION OF TITLE AND SEARCHES

PROTECTION OF PURCHASERS

Statutory protections for purchasers   21–98

Obligations of seller of heritable property

21–01   In a transaction of sale of heritable property the obligations of the seller, subject to any qualifications in the contract of sale, are:

(1) to exhibit or deliver within a reasonable time a marketable title to the property sold which contains no provisions or conditions, express or implied by law, inconsistent with the contract of sale;

(ii) to exhibit or deliver searches in the property and personal registers (sasine titles) or an appropriate report from the Keeper (registered titles) confirmatory of the seller's title and disclosing no incumbrances or diligences prejudicial thereto; and

(iii) to deliver a valid disposition of the property sold. The first two of those obligations are considered in this chapter: the third is dealt with in Chapter 22.

Marketable title

21–02   A marketable title may be described as one which satisfies the following requirements:

(a) Purchaser's title to be recorded in the Register of Sasines. A deed, not *ex facie* invalid or forged, recorded in the Register of Sasines, which is sufficient in respect of its terms to constitute in favour of the seller or an author of the seller a title to the property sold or to land of a description habile to include that property together with, where necessary, a valid progress of titles connecting the title of the seller to that deed, and evidence of possession of the property by the seller and his authors founded on and following that deed for a continuous period of 10 or 20 years (whichever is relevant)[1] openly, peaceably and without judicial interruption.[2]

(b) Transactions inducing first registration in Land Register. The requirements as in (a) above plus the furnishing of such documents, with a plan and any other evidence, as the Keeper may require to enable him to issue a land certificate in the name of the purchaser as registered proprietor of the whole property sold containing no exclusion of indemnity and disclosing no entry, deed or diligence prejudicial to the purchaser's interest other than such as are created by or against the purchaser or have been disclosed to and accepted by the purchaser prior to the date of settlement of the transaction.

---

[1] See para. 21–05.
[2] Prescription and Limitation (Scotland) Act 1973, s. 1.

(c) Title already registered in Land Register. A land certificate in name of the seller or an author of the seller as registered proprietor of the whole property sold containing no exclusion of indemnity together with (where necessary) valid links in title evidencing the seller's ownership of the registered interest plus such documents and any other evidence as the Keeper may require to enable him to issue a land certificate in name of the purchaser as in (b) above.

In addition, it is essential that in cases (a) and (b) above there are no conditions, burdens or rights whether contained or disclosed in the progress of titles or otherwise constituted which are inconsistent with the terms expressed or implied by law in the contract of sale and are prejudicial to the interests of the purchaser. In case (c) above it is sufficient to check that there are no such inconsistent or prejudicial burdens, rights or conditions disclosed in the land certificate.

These requirements are considered in detail in paragraphs 21–05 to 21–72 *infra*.

Searches and reports

1–03   (a) In the case where the purchaser's title is to be recorded in the Register of Sasines, the obligation of the seller is to exhibit or deliver searches in the Register of Sasines against the property sold for a period of 40 years or such lesser period as may be acceptable to the purchaser and searches in the Register of Inhibitions and Adjudications for a period of five years prior to the date of entry against all persons interested in the property, such searches to disclose no burdens, incumbrances or diligences prejudicial to the seller's title other than those which are expressed or implied by law in the contract of sale.

(b) In the case where the transaction of sale induces first registration in the Land Register, the obligation of the seller is to exhibit or deliver to the purchaser a Form 10 report brought down as nearly as practicable to the date of settlement of the transaction (normally by a Form 11 report) and showing no entries adverse to the seller's interest in the property sold.

(c) In the case where the seller's title has already been registered in the Land Register the obligation of the seller is as in (b) above, save that the report will be a Form 12 report (normally brought down to a date near settlement by a Form 13 report).

As to searches in the Companies Register of Charges and Company Files in circumstances where limited companies have been interested in transactions affecting the property during the period of the prescriptive progress and inquiries by the Keeper where a limited company is a party to the deed inducing first registration or effecting a dealing with a registered interest, see paragraphs 21–87 and 24–33 *infra*.

Production of marketable title within a reasonable time

21–04   If there is a stipulation in the contract of sale as to the time within which a title must be produced, failure by the seller to implement it within the period stipulated will entitle the purchaser to resile.[3] In the absence of express stipulation the court will determine what in the circumstances is a reasonable time. Three years' delay was held to be unreasonable,[4] but not six months.[5] However, no definite period can be laid down: the question is one which depends on the facts of each individual case and the actings of the parties.[6] In practice, if a seller delays unduly in producing a marketable title the purchaser should intimate that if the title is not produced within a stated reasonable period, the purchaser may resile. What is a reasonable period is a matter of judgment in the circumstances of the particular transaction.

SASINE TITLES

EXAMINATION OF TITLE DEEDS

(1) The Foundation Writ

Foundation deed

21–05   The examination of title begins with the last title to the property which was recorded in the Register of Sasines prior to the commencement of a period of 10 years before the date of settlement of the current transaction. If the property first came into existence as a separate subject by the subdivision of a larger area or as a feu of part of a larger estate within that period of 10 years the foundation deed is the last title to the larger area or estate recorded prior to the commencement of that period. Where the property consists of or includes foreshore or salmon fishings the period is 20 years.[7]

21–06   **Validity and quality of foundation deed.** The former conveyancing statutes described the foundation deed as "an *ex facie* valid irredeemable recorded title."[8] The relevant provisions of those statutes are now superseded by the Prescription and Limitation (Scotland) Act 1973, which adopts a different terminology and refers to a deed which is "sufficient in respect of its terms to constitute a title to" the interest in particular land or in land of a description habile to include the

---

[3] *Hutchinson & Son* v. *Scott* (1830) 8 S. 377.
[4] *Fleming* v. *Harley's Trs.* (1823) 2 S. 373.
[5] *Raeburn* v. *Baird* (1832) 10 S. 761.
[6] For illustrative cases see *Hunter* v. *Carsewell* (1822) 1 S. 248; *McNeill* v. *Cameron* (1830) 8 S. 362; *Dick* v. *Cuthbertson* (1831) 5 W. & S. 712; *Kelman* v. *Barr's Tr.* (1878) 5 R. 816; *Carter* v. *Lornie* (1890) 18 R. 353; *Gilfillan* v. *Cadell & Grant* (1893) 21 R. 269.
[7] Prescription and Limitation (Scotland) Act 1973, s. 1(4).
[8] Conveyancing (Scotland) Act 1874, s. 34; Conveyancing (Scotland) Act 1924, s. 16.

particular land. The principal difference between the two versions is
that the requirement of the irredeemable quality of the deed is now
absent, with the results that (i) positive prescription now applies to
deeds creating a security, and (ii) even a deed which is *ex facie*
redeemable may be sufficient foundation if the right of redemption has
been subsequently cut off, which is made express in relation to a
decree of adjudication for debt when prescription commences upon the
expiry of the legal.[9] The deed need not necessarily be a conveyance: a
judicial decree or an instrument of sasine, notarial instrument or notice
of title, without production of the warrants, is sufficient.[10] It is
necessary that the interest in land to which the deed relates is one the
title to which can competently be recorded,[11] and as a foundation writ
it must in fact have been recorded.[12] For the purposes of section 1 of
the Act, "interest in land" does not include a servitude[13]; separate
provision for servitudes is made in section 3 of the Act. The description
of the subjects in the deed may be of the particular property or of
lands habile to include it: if the description is capable of being
construed so as to include the particular property as defined by
subsequent possession it is habile to include it[14] unless excluded by the
terms of a description which created a bounding title.[15] It is doubtful
whether the specific reference to a judicial decree, without qualification,
in the absence of the requirement of irredeemability supersedes the
principle of the decision in *Bruce* v. *Stewart*,[16] where a decree of
irritancy which had been obtained in absence and had not become final
was held to render the title unmarketable. A recorded extract of such a
decree does not become final for 20 years, but *quaere* whether that is
an intrinsic qualification of the deed which renders it insufficient to
constitute the foundation of a title?

1–07   As regards validity, the foundation deed must be free from *intrinsic*
defects; *extrinsic* defects such as irregularities in prior deeds affecting
the right or title of the granter do not destroy the effectiveness of the
deed as a foundation for positive prescription. Even where a deed
contained an indication in the narrative clause that the destination in
the dispositive clause might be erroneous it was held that, since the
question could be determined only by a reference to prior deeds, the
destination in the ruling dispositive clause was unchallengeable once

---

[9] 1973 Act, s. 1(3), superseding *Hinton* v. *Connell's Trs.* (1883) 10 R. 1110.

[10] *Ibid.*, s. 5(1).

[11] *Ibid.*, s. 1(2).

[12] Recording must be in the proper register (*Brechin Town Council* v. *Arbuthnot* (1840) 3 D. 216),
but if it *may* have been recorded in the proper register that is sufficient for a foundation deed
(*Ramsay* v. *Spence*, 1909 S.C. 1441).

[13] 1973 Act, s. 15(1).

[14] *Auld* v. *Hay* (1880) 7 R. 663 at 666, 681; *Cooper's Trs.* v. *Stark's Trs.* (1898) 25 R. 1160 at 1167;
Troup v. *Aberdeen Heritable Securities Co. Ltd.*, 1916 S.C. 918 at 923.

[15] *North British Rly. Co.* v. *Hutton* (1896) 23 R. 522; *Brown* v. *North British Rly. Co.* (1906) 8 F.
534.

[16] (1900) 2 F. 948.

the period of positive prescription had run.[17] So a recorded conveyance which creates or transfers a title in unqualified terms, even if not granted in good faith, is a sufficient foundation deed: a disposition *a non domino* is frequently used in practice to provide a foundation for a prescriptive title.[18]

21–08 **Practice.** In examination of the title to subjects which are being purchased or taken in security the requirements of the foundation deed may be summarised.

(1) The deed must be in proper form appropriate to its nature and free from any intrinsic defect.

(2) It must constitute a title to the particular subjects or subjects habile to include them.

(3) It must be properly executed according to the type of deed. In the case of a conveyance, instrument of sasine, notarial instrument or notice of title it should be executed in probative form. If there has been any informality of execution but the appropriate court has subsequently declared in pursuance of section 39 of the Conveyancing (Scotland) Act 1874 that it was subscribed by the granter or maker and witnesses, it is deemed to be validly executed with retroactive effect.[19]

(4) It must be adequately stamped: if there is any doubt it should be submitted for adjudication of stamp duty.

(5) It must have been recorded in the appropriate Register of Sasines within any time limit for recording specified in the deed.

(6) An extract of the deed from the Books of Council and Session or the Register of Sasines is acceptable in lieu of the principal deed itself.[20]

(2) Progress of Titles

Validity of steps in title

21–09   Each deed or link in the progress of title from the foundation deed up to and including the title of the seller or borrower must then be examined as to its validity and sufficiency. In the examination of these documents the purchaser's or lender's solicitor is concerned with both intrinsic and extrinsic defects and any burdens or continuing conditions which they impose or contain. Some of the relevant subjects of examination or inquiry are outlined in the succeeding paragraphs.

---

[17] *Cooper Scott* v. *Gill Scott*, 1924 S.C. 309. See also *Fraser* v. *Lord Lovat* (1898) 25 R. 603; *Simpson* v. *Marshall* (1900) 2 F. 447.

[18] See para. 18–88.

[19] 1973 Act, s. 5(2).

[20] Registration Act 1698; Conveyancing and Feudal Reform (Scotland) Act 1970, s. 45.

(A) Matters affecting Parties

Names and designations of parties

1–10   The names and designations of parties to deeds included in the progress should be correct and, if different from their names or designations in a preceding deed or link, should be properly connected in the following deed. If the name of an incorporated company has been wrongly stated, however, the error is more serious since only the company in its registered name has legal entity and a deed by or to a company in any other name is ineffective and cannot be validated by a connecting reference in a subsequent deed between different parties: a supplementary corrective deed is required. If the error was in the name of a company which granted a deed and the company has subsequently been wound up, the company will not have been effectively divested of ownership of the subjects concerned which will normally have fallen to the Crown as *bona vacantia* under section 354 of the Companies Act 1948 (now section 654 of the Companies Act 1985), and the Queen's and Lord Treasurer's Remembrancer will usually be prepared on explanation of the circumstances to grant a supplementary corroborative deed on payment of his conveyancing charges.

Capacity of parties

1–11   It is necessary as regards each deed after the foundation writ to check that the granter or granters had the capacity to grant it and that, where any procedures are required, they have been correctly followed. As to capacity of parties see Volume I, Chapter 2.

Death of party

1–12   (a) *Prior to September 10, 1964.* In the diminishing number of cases where a prescriptive progress of title has commenced and the death of a party has occurred before the Succession (Scotland) Act 1964 came into operation, it is necessary to check the validity and sufficiency of the relevant documents or decrees under the pre-1964 law. In testate succession the will or other testamentary deed must be examined as to its validity, the appointment of trustees or executors and their powers of sale or disposal of the relevant property.[21] In intestate succession heritable property descended to heirs in accordance with the former law, the title to heritable property being completed by extract decree of special service duly recorded or extract decree of general service which could be followed by a recorded notice of title or used as a link in title.[22] It was held in *Sibbald's Heirs* v. *Harris*[23] that a decree of

---

[21] See Vol. I, paras. 2–40 *et seq.*

[22] Within the prescriptive progress the warrants for any notice of title must be examined; s. 5(1) of the Prescription and Limitation (Scotland) Act 1973 applies only to the foundation deed.

[23] 1947 S.C. 601.

general service was a sufficient link in a progress of title and by parity of reasoning a decree of special service in proper form is likewise acceptable as a link. Claims for terce or courtesy could have arisen only upon deaths before September 10, 1964. Nevertheless, as continuing claims upon annual income from land, they may still be prestable *quoad* annual payments due within 20 years preceding the transaction of purchase, since they are not cut off by the short negative prescription and so are only lost after the expiry of the long negative prescription of 20 years.[24]

21–13   (b) *On or after September 10, 1964.* Where a proprietor of the property has died during the prescriptive period and the succeeding deed has been granted by his executor(s) the confirmation should be examined to ensure that the property is included; if not, an eik which contains it should be procured. In the case of executors-nominate it is normally unnecessary to examine the testamentary deed on which the confirmation proceeded, at least when a sale by the executors or a person deriving title directly from the executors to a purchaser in good faith for value has followed, since the purchaser's title is protected against reduction of the confirmation[25] or against the sale having been at variance with the terms or purposes of the testamentary deed.[26] There is some doubt whether a legatee having a direct bequest of the property can complete title and grant a disposition: the safe course is that title should be obtained through the executors.[27] An English or Northern Irish probate or letters of administration are sufficient links in title to Scottish heritage although they do not normally mention any particular property or asset,[28] and they do not require to be resealed in Scotland.[29]

21–14   Capital transfer tax. Estate duty has been replaced by capital transfer tax with effect after March 12, 1975,[30] and Scottish heritable property is not itself subject to any Inland Revenue charge in respect of unpaid capital transfer tax, although where the property has been disposed of any other property representing it is subject to such a charge.[31] Accordingly, a prospective purchaser of heritable property from the executor of a person who has died after March 12, 1975, is not affected by any liability to capital transfer tax which may have arisen on the death.

21–15   Estate duty. Where a death occurred on or before March 12, 1975, a

---

[24] Prescription and Limitation (Scotland) Act 1973, Sched. 1, para. 2(*f*) and s. 7.
[25] Succession (Scotland) Act 1964, s. 17.
[26] Trusts (Scotland) Act 1961, s. 2.
[27] Opinion of Professors of Conveyancing, (1965) 10 J.L.S. 153.
[28] Succession (Scotland) Act 1964, s. 15(1) proviso, as amended by Law Reform (Miscellaneous Provisions) (Scotland) Act 1968, s. 19. See Currie on *Confirmation*, 246, 247.
[29] Administration of Estates Act 1971, s. 3.
[30] Finance Act 1975, s. 49. For lifetime transfers the relevant date is March 26, 1975.
[31] *Ibid.*, Sched 4, para. 20(4); Capital Transfer Tax Act 1984, s. 237(4).

rateable part of the estate duty on an estate, in proportion to the value of any property which did not pass to the executor as such, formed a charge on the property, but the charge was not leviable against a *bona fide* purchaser for valuable consideration without notice. In terms of section 8(2) of Finance Act 1894,[32] however, any such charge ceases to be effective, at latest, 12 years after the date of death: if that period has not elapsed at the time when the title is being examined, a clearance certificate as regards the property which has been obtained under section 11(1) of Finance Act 1894 or the now repealed section 19(7) of the Succession (Scotland) Act 1964,[33] should be required.

–16 Destinations. Where any of the title deeds within the prescriptive progress has contained a destination which has been evacuated it is necessary to confirm that it was evacuable and has been properly evacuated in conformity with section 30 of the Succession (Scotland) Act 1964. If the title has devolved in accordance with a destination to a named survivor which could not competently have been evacuated, evidence of the death of the predeceaser should be produced. If the title has devolved in accordance with a destination to an unnamed person whose identity has to be established, then (a) it should be confirmed that the destination, if capable of evacuation, has not in fact been evacuated, and (b) the executor of the deceased institute should include the property in the confirmation to the estate as estate held in trust and then convey it (or transfer it by docket) to the person entitled to succeed under the destination, when he and any person subsequently acquiring the property in good faith and for value from him have the protection given by section 17 of the 1964 Act.[34,35]

–17 Gratuitous alienations and unfair preferences. Where a progress of titles contains a disposition or conveyance of the property or any interest in it made gratuitously or for an apparently inadequate consideration, or if a security over the property has been granted, and the granter has subsequently become insolvent, the deed may be vulnerable to challenge as a gratuitous alienation or an unfair preference. The relevant law relating to such challenge has been altered by the Bankruptcy (Scotland) Act 1985 which came into operation on April 1, 1986.

(a) *Sequestration of granter before April 1, 1986.* The circumstances in which a deed may be challengeable as a gratuitous alienation or fraudulent preference are conveniently summarised in the undernoted text.[36]

(b) *Sequestration of granter on or after April 1, 1986.* Sections 34 and

---

[32] Applying Customs and Inland Revenue Act 1889, ss. 12–14, to estate duty.
[33] Repealed by Finance Act 1975, Sched. 13.
[34] ss. 18(4), 17, 36(2).
[35] The construction of destinations is considered in Vol. IV.
[36] Gloag and Henderson, 789–794.

36 of the Bankruptcy (Scotland) Act 1985 restate the law as to challenge of gratuitous alienations and unfair preferences.

As regards alienations, section 34 provides that the alienation may be reducible if made to an associate[37] within five years, or to any other person within two years, before the granter (a) was sequestrated, (b) granted a trust deed for his creditors which had become a protected trust deed,[38] or (c) died and within 12 months after his death his estate has been sequestrated or a judicial factor appointed to administer it under section 11A of the Judicial Factors (Scotland) Act 1889. The challenge may be made by a creditor of the granter or the permanent trustee in sequestration, the trustee under the trust deed or the judicial factor on the estate. The onus rests on the grantee of the deed which effected the alienation of proving that (i) immediately after the alienation or subsequently the granter's assets were greater than his liabilities, (ii) the alienation was made for adequate consideration, or (iii) the alienation was a birthday, Christmas or other conventional gift, or was made for a charitable purpose to a person who was not an associate of the granter, which it was reasonable for the granter to make, with the general proviso that any right or interest acquired in good faith and for value by a third party from or through the grantee is not prejudiced. In examination of title it should be confirmed that any disposition or conveyance is not vulnerable to reduction under those provisions.

As regards unfair preferences created within six months before any of the three events (a), (b) or (c) mentioned in the immediately preceding paragraph occurred, section 36 of the 1985 Act makes such preferences open to reduction unless they were transactions in the ordinary course of business, non-collusive payment in cash of debts which had become payable, non-collusive transactions involving the undertaking of reciprocal obligations or certain mandates authorising payment by the arrestee of arrested funds. If the current transaction in respect of which the examination of title is being made is the acquisition of a heritable security otherwise than in good faith and for value, it should be confirmed that there is no risk of its reduction under these provisions. If the transaction is a purchase of a property from the creditor in the security under his power of sale the title of the purchaser will normally be protected as an interest acquired in good faith and for value.[39]

These provisions of the 1985 Act apply *mutatis mutandis* to alienations or unfair preferences by companies.[40]

---

[37] As defined in s. 74 of the Act.
[38] As defined in Sched. 5, para. 8 to the Act.
[39] 1985 Act, s. 36(5) (proviso).
[40] Companies Act 1985, ss. 615A and 615B as added by the Bankruptcy (Scotland) Act 1985, Sched. 7, para. 20.

-18 Bankruptcy. Where the proprietor of the property or any interest in it was sequestrated during the period covered by the prescriptive progress by an award made before April 1, 1986, it is essential to ensure that the appropriate procedure under the relevant sections of the Bankruptcy (Scotland) Act 1913 was correctly followed in a sale by the trustee or a heritable creditor.[41] The 1913 Act has been repealed by the Bankruptcy (Scotland) Act 1985 and a much simpler procedure for sale of heritable property is now contained in section 39 of the new Act, with the helpful qualification that the validity of the title of a purchaser is not challengeable on the ground that there has been a failure to comply with a requirement of the section.[42] In the case of a sale by the permanent trustee[43] of a family home[44] or a matrimonial home,[45] however, sections 40 and 41 of the 1985 Act impose certain requirements for the protection of the family or the non-entitled spouse, and it must be checked that these requirements have been complied with since there is no qualification with regard to the validity of the title of a purchaser acquiring in good faith for value. Broadly (1) in the case of a sale of a family home by the permanent trustee either a relevant consent[46] or the authority of the court is required,[47] or (2) in the case of a sale of a matrimonial home the permanent trustee has a duty to inform the non-entitled spouse of the award of sequestration of the entitled spouse's estate and of the right of the non-entitled spouse to petition the court within a limited period specified.[48] The requirements of sections 40 and 41 apply only to sales by the permanent trustee: they do not apply to sales by a judicial factor appointed on the estate of a deceased person on the petition of a creditor or creditors under section 11A of the Judicial Factors (Scotland) Act 1889,[49] but the Court of Session has power to regulate the mode in which he shall proceed in realising the funds of the estate.[50]

-19 Trust deeds for creditors. Where a trust deed was granted in favour of a trustee for creditors before April 1, 1986, the matters to be checked are (a) that there was no effective diligence against the property before the trustee completed title to it,[51] (b) that the trust deed was not reduced as a security for prior debts by a non-acceding creditor, which might be done if the debtor had been rendered notour bankrupt before or within

---

[41] The relevant sections of the 1913 Act are 108–116: see Vol. I, paras. 2–86 to 2–88.
[42] 1985 Act, s. 39(7). As to sale where the property is burdened by a heritable security, see para. 22–24.
[43] Defined *ibid.*, s. 3.
[44] Defined *ibid.*, s. 40(4).
[45] Defined in Matrimonial Homes (Family Protection) (Scotland) Act 1981, s. 22 as amended by Law Reform (Miscellaneous Provisions) (Scotland) Act 1985, s. 13(10).
[46] Being the consent of a person specified in s. 40(4)(c) of the Bankruptcy (Scotland) Act 1985.
[47] *Ibid.*, s. 40(1).
[48] *Ibid.*, s. 41(1).
[49] Added by Sched. 7, para. 4 to Bankruptcy (Scotland) Act 1985.
[50] *Ibid.*, Sched. 7, para. 4 (new s. 11B of 1889 Act).
[51] *Gibson* v. *Wilson* (1841) 3 D. 974.

six months after the granting of the trust deed,[52] or (c) that the trust deed was not superseded by sequestration.[53] Where the trust deed for creditors has been granted on or after April 1, 1986, the provisions of Schedule 5 to the Bankruptcy (Scotland) Act 1985 apply. That Schedule introduced the concept of the protected trust deed.[54] As regards heritable property being purchased from a trustee under a trust deed for creditors, the purchaser should check that (a) a notice has been recorded in the Register of Inhibitions and Adjudications in accordance with paragraph 2(1) of the Schedule to ensure that no deed granted by the debtor can prevail against a disposition by the trustee, (b) the trust deed has become a protected trust deed, and (c) no petition for sequestration by a non-acceding creditor has been presented within the period of six weeks after the date of publication of the *Gazette* notice of the granting of the trust deed.[55]

Companies

21–20   If the progress of titles contains a deed granted by an incorporated company in favour of a person dealing with the company in good faith, any transaction decided on by the directors is deemed to be one which is within the capacity of the company to enter into and the directors' power to bind the company is deemed to be free of any limitation under the company's memorandum and articles of association, and the party transacting with the company is presumed to have acted in good faith unless the contrary is proved.[56] If the transaction was entered into after the 1972 Act and was apparently at arm's length for an adequate consideration and several years have passed subsequently it is reasonably safe to assume that it was *intra vires*: if, however, the transaction was recent and there is any doubt whether by reason of relationship of the parties or otherwise the protection afforded by section 9(1) of the 1972 Act or section 35 of the Companies Act 1985 would apply, it may be advisable to seek confirmation that the transaction was within the powers of the company and the directors and was carried out in accordance with any procedure required by the articles of association. As to gratuitous alienations and fraudulent preferences by companies, see paragraph 21–17 *supra*.

21–21   **Liquidators.** Evidence of appointment should be seen, and it should be

---

[52] *Mackenzie* v. *Calder* (1868) 6 M. 833; Bankruptcy Act 1696 (c. 5), as amended by Companies Act 1947, s. 115(3).

[53] *McAlister* v. *Swinburne* (1874) 1 R. 958; *Salaman* v. *Rosslyn's Trs.* (1900) 3 F. 298.

[54] Bankruptcy (Scotland) Act 1985, Sched. 5, paras. 5, 6, 7 and 8.

[55] *Ibid.*, Sched. 5, paras. 5 and 7(1)(*a*).

[56] European Communities Act 1972, s. 9(1). See vol. I, paras. 2–101, 2–102. S. 9 of the 1972 Act is now repealed by Companies Consolidation (Consequential Provisions) Act 1985, Sched. 1, but the provisions of s. 9(1) are re-enacted in s. 35 of the Companies Act 1985.

verified that the transaction concerned was within the powers of the liquidator.[57]

–22 Receivers. Evidence of the validity of the floating charge and of the receiver's appointment should be seen[58] and it should be confirmed that the property formed part of the assets embraced in the relevant floating charge. The powers of the receiver may be given in the instrument which created the floating charge and, in addition, he has powers given by statute, but a person dealing with a receiver in good faith need not inquire whether the receiver is acting within his powers.[59]

22A Administration orders. Where an administration order has been made by the court in relation to a company, no steps may be taken to enforce any security over its property except with the consent of the administrator or the leave of the court and the administrator may dispose of any property of the company which is subject to a floating charge as if it were not so subject, but the holder of the floating charge has the same priority over any property of the company directly or indirectly representing the property disposed of as he would have had over the property subject to the charge. As regards property of the company which is subject to any other security, *e.g.* a fixed security, the administrator, if authorised by the court on application made by him, may dispose of the property as if it were not subject to the security but must apply the net proceeds of the disposal, or any greater sum determined by the court which would be realised on a sale in the open market by a willing vendor, towards discharging the sums secured by the security. The administrator may grant a disposition to the purchaser in implement of the sale and when the purchaser completes his title to the property by recording in the Register of Sasines or registration of his interest in the Land Register, the effect is to disencumber the property of the security.[60] In examination of title a purchaser should check the validity of the administrator's appointment and the adequacy of the procedure leading to sale of the property but it is thought that he has no duty to check the distribution of the price by the administrator.

---

[57] See Vol. I, paras. 2–103 to 2–110. With regard to paras. 2–107 and 2–108 it should be noted that after the Bankruptcy (Scotland) Act 1985 is in force the references to the Bankruptcy (Scotland) Act 1913 in s. 623(1)–(5) of the Companies Act 1985 are replaced by references to s. 37(1)–(6) (effect of sequestration on diligence) and s. 39(3), (4), (7) and (8) (realisation of estate) of Bankruptcy (Scotland) Act 1985 by para. 21 of Sched. 7 to the last-mentioned Act.

[58] If the appointment is invalid the court may order the holder of the charge to indemnify the person appointed from liability arising from the invalidity of the appointment—Insolvency Act 1985, s. 61.

[59] Companies Act 1985, s. 471(3) as amended by Insolvency Act 1985, s. 57.

[60] Insolvency Act 1985, ss. 27–43, particularly ss. 30(3) and 34 and Sched. 3. These provisions come into operation on a date yet to be announced.

Spouses—matrimonial homes—occupancy rights

21–23   The Matrimonial Homes (Family Protection) (Scotland) Act 1981, which came into operation on September 1, 1982, as now amended by the Law Reform (Miscellaneous Provisions) (Scotland) Act 1985, s. 13 (applicable from December 30, 1985), confers upon a non-entitled spouse[61] rights of occupancy in the matrimonial home[62] or family residence together with any child of the family. In terms of section 6 of the 1981 Act these rights are not prejudiced by a dealing with the house by the entitled spouse and the other party to the dealing is not thereby entitled to occupy the house or any part of it. "Dealing" includes a sale, a lease or renunciation of a tenancy, the grant of a heritable security or the creation of a trust, but excludes a conveyance under section 80 of the Lands Clauses Consolidation (Scotland) Act 1845. The protection thus given to the non-entitled spouse, however, is not effective if (1) the non-entitled spouse in writing consents or has consented to the dealing in a prescribed form or renounces or has renounced his or her occupancy rights in the property, (2) the court has made an order under section 7 of the Act dispensing with the consent of the non-entitled spouse to the dealing, (3) the dealing occurred, or implements, a binding obligation entered into by the entitled spouse before his or her marriage to the non-entitled spouse or before September 1, 1982, or (4) in the case of a purchase of a matrimonial home (a) the third party purchasing has acted in good faith, and (b) at the time of the dealing there is produced to the third party by the seller (i) an affidavit sworn or affirmed by the seller declaring that the subjects of sale are not a matrimonial home in relation to which a spouse of the seller has occupancy rights, or (ii) a renunciation of occupancy rights or consent to the dealing which bears to have been properly made or given by the non-entitled spouse.

21–24 **Non-disclosure on registers.** The 1981 Act introduces a species of occupancy right which is not disclosed in the Register of Inhibitions and Adjudications nor in the Register of Sasines.

21–25 **Dealing.** The principal transactions which constitute a dealing for the purpose of the 1981 Act have already been described.[63] The phraseology of the Act indicates that only voluntary dealings are affected. So the occupancy rights of the non-entitled spouse do not affect adjudication by a creditor, irritancy of a lease of the matrimonial home by the landlord, or compulsory acquisition of it by an authority having power to do so. Arrangements for sequestration or adjudication designed wholly or mainly to defeat the occupancy rights of the non-entitled

---

[61] As defined in s. 1, as amended by the Law Reform (Miscellaneous Provisions) (Scotland) Act 1985, s. 13(2)–(4).

[62] As defined in s. 22, as amended by the Law Reform (Miscellaneous Provisions) (Scotland) Act 1985, s. 13(10).

[63] See para. 21–23.

spouse may be restrained by the court.[64] In the case of a sale of a matrimonial home by the trustee in sequestration of the entitled spouse, section 10 of the 1981 Act required the trustee to notify the non-entitled spouse of the award of sequestration within seven days of the date of the act and warrant: in cases where the award of sequestration is made on or after April 1, 1986, the period within which notification must be made is 14 days and the non-entitled spouse may within a limited period petition the Court of Session for recall of the sequestration or an order to protect his or her rights if the court is satisfied that the purpose of the petition for sequestration was wholly or mainly to defeat the occupancy rights of the non-entitled spouse (Bankruptcy Act 1985, s. 41). A sale of the home by a heritable creditor in exercise of the powers contained in his security is not affected by the occupancy rights of the non-entitled spouse, provided that the security has been validly constituted.[65]

Practice

–26 *(a) Sales.* Upon the sale of a matrimonial home the seller will require to produce either (i) a consent to the dealing by the non-entitled spouse in the statutorily prescribed form, either separate or incorporated in the conveyance to the purchaser,[66] or (ii) a formal renunciation by the non-entitled spouse of his or her occupancy rights which should be sworn or affirmed before a notary public.[67] If the non-entitled spouse refuses to consent or to renounce his or her occupancy rights, the entitled spouse may in appropriate circumstances obtain an order from the court dispensing with the consent.[68] Where a sale is of a dwelling-house which is not a matrimonial home, the purchaser will require an affidavit sworn or affirmed by the seller that the subjects are not a matrimonial home in relation to which a spouse of the seller has occupancy rights.[69] If the spouses are estranged or there is any reason to doubt that the non-entitled spouse will consent to the sale, his or her consent should be sought before negotiations for sale are commenced.

If there is no doubt that the non-entitled spouse will concur in the sale, his or her consent may be incorporated in the disposition to the purchaser. It is preferable that the consent be so incorporated since it establishes conclusively that it was produced to the purchaser at the time of the dealing and obviates the need for a separate document. Where the documentation is in the form of a separate consent or a renunciation of

---

[64] See 1981 Act, ss. 10, 12. S. 10 is now replaced by the Bankruptcy (Scotland) Act 1985, ss. 40, 41.
[65] As regards the validity of the constitution of the security in relation to occupancy rights of a non-entitled spouse, see para. 21–28.
[66] As to styles, see para. 21–29.
[67] For a style, see para. 21–30. As to persons outwith Scotland before whom swearing or affirmation may be made, see the Law Reform (Miscellaneous Provisions) (Scotland) Act, 1985, s. 13(4). As to the various circumstances in which such documentation is required, see para. 24–20(3).
[68] As to the circumstances in which the court may make such an order, see 1981 Act, s. 7.
[69] 1981 Act, s. 6(3)(e) as amended by Law Reform (Miscellaneous Provisions) (Scotland) Act 1985, s. 13(6)(b). For a style, see para. 21–31.

occupancy rights by the non-entitled spouse or an affidavit by the entitled spouse or seller, it may be registered in the Books of Council and Session and an extract furnished to the purchaser, although the need for this precaution may now be less in view of the prescription of occupancy rights referred to in paragraph 21–35 *infra*.

21–27 *(b) Leases or renunciations of tenancy.* The procedure in relation to the granting of a lease or the renouncing of a tenancy of a matrimonial home is similar to that already outlined in respect of a sale. Where the sale is of a matrimonial home which is subject to a let which cannot be terminated by the selling landlord at or before the date of the purchaser's entry, the seller must ensure that the necessary renunciation of the tenancy is given with the consent of the non-entitled spouse of the tenant.

21–28 *(c) Heritable securities.* Section 8 of the 1981 Act as amended by section 13 of the 1985 Act provides that the interest of a creditor in a secured loan over a matrimonial home in relation to non-performance of any obligation under the loan shall not be prejudiced by reason only of the occupancy rights of the non-entitled spouse. That provision applies only where (a) the lender in granting the loan acted in good faith, and (b) before the delivery of the deed creating the security there was produced to the lender by the entitled spouse either (i) an affidavit sworn or affirmed by the granter of the security declaring that the subjects are not a matrimonial home in relation to which a spouse of the granter has occupancy rights, or (ii) a renunciation of occupancy rights or a consent to the granting of the security which bore to have been properly made or given by the non-entitled spouse. The provision outlined above applies when the security was granted on or after December 30, 1985: if the security was granted before that date the conditions stated in section 8(2) of the 1981 Act (broadly similar but with verbal differences) apply.

It is suggested that the non-entitled spouse should sign the standard security as a consenter and that any separate consent or renunciation of occupancy rights, duly attested, or affidavit, as the case may be, should be registered in the Books of Council and Session and an extract delivered to the lender. The application of the Act to further advances upon a security for a loan of an indefinite amount made before the commencement of the Act without the consent of the non-entitled spouse or made after the Act with the consent of the non-entitled spouse is not altogether clear. It is thought that so long as the further advances are reasonably within the scope of those contemplated when the security was granted, *e.g.* increases in the debit balance by ordinary drawings on a current account, no further consent by the non-entitled spouse is required. If, however, an "all moneys" security over a matrimonial home is being utilised as security for a new and special advance of significant amount, the safe course is to create a new security with the consent of the non-entitled spouse. Where a house is being purchased for use as a matrimonial home and is subject to an existing security created by a previous proprietor, the conveyancing procedure should not be by way of taking over the existing security: it should be discharged and a new security constituted with the appropriate consent or renunciation by the non-entitled spouse.

–29

CONSENT by NON-ENTITLED SPOUSE
(prescribed by The Matrimonial Homes (Form of Consent) (Scotland) Regulations 1982[70])

(a) *Incorporated in Deed effecting Dealing*
with the consent of AB (*designed*), the spouse of the said CD, for the purposes of the Matrimonial Homes (Family Protection) (Scotland) Act 1981.

NOTE. The consenter signs the deed, the signature being duly attested.

(b) *Separate*

I, AB (*designed*), spouse of CD (*designed*), hereby consent for the purposes of the Matrimonial Homes (Family Protection) (Scotland) Act 1981 to the undernoted dealing of the said CD relating to (*here describe the matrimonial home or the part of it to which the dealing relates*)

Dealing referred to
(*Here describe the dealing*) (*To be attested*)

–30

RENUNCIATION OF OCCUPANCY RIGHTS BY NON-ENTITLED SPOUSE

I, A (*designed*), spouse of B (*designed*), hereby renounce the occupancy rights to which I am or may become entitled in terms of the Matrimonial Homes (Family Protection) (Scotland) Act 1981 in the property known as   [being] [intended to become] a matrimonial home as defined in the said Act; And I hereby [swear] [affirm] that this renunciation is made by me freely and without coercion of any kind; And I declare these presents to be irrevocable.
Given under my hand at   this   day of
19   in the presence of   (*designed*), Notary Public, and in the presence of these witnesses

.... (*Witness*)
.... (*Full Name*) .... A
.... (*Address*)
.... (*Occupation*)
.... (*Witness*) .... Notary Public
.... (*Full Name*)
.... (*Address*)
.... (*Occupation*)

---

[70] S.I. 1982 No. 971 (S. 129).

21–31   AFFIDAVIT BY ENTITLED SPOUSE

I, AB (*designed*), do hereby solemnly and sincerely swear [affirm] that as at the date hereof the property known as   is not a matrimonial home in relation to which a spouse of mine has occupancy rights, all within the meaning of the Matrimonial Homes (Family Protection) (Scotland) Act 1981 as amended by the Law Reform (Miscellaneous Provisions) (Scotland) Act 1985.

Sworn/Affirmed by the above-named AB at   on the day of   19   before me   (*name and designation of notary public*)   .... AB

....
Notary Public

in presence of these witnesses

.... (*Signature*)
.... (*Full Name*)
.... (*Address*)
.... (*Occupation*)

.... (*Signature*)
.... (*Full Name*)
.... (*Address*)
.... (*Occupation*)

21–32 Jointly entitled spouses. Where the matrimonial home is in joint names of the spouses the protection given by section 6 of the Act is extended to either of the two jointly entitled spouses against dealings by the other with his or her part.[71] The Act does not affect the practice when both spouses enter into a dealing with the matrimonial home: that may be carried out as formerly simply by the relevant deed being executed by both parties. The right of either spouse to obtain a decree of division and sale is now subject to postponement in the discretion of the court.[72]

21–33 Executors and testamentary trustees. In certain circumstances it may be necessary for the executor or testamentary trustees of a deceased person to procure a consent, renunciation or affidavit under section 6 of the 1981 Act in connection with a dealing with a dwelling-house which forms part of the deceased's estate. Upon the death of any person his estate vests by virtue of confirmation in his executor for the purposes of administration,[73] but at the same time a right of beneficial ownership of a dwelling-house which forms part of the estate may vest in an individual, *e.g.* as legatee under a direct testamentary bequest of the dwelling-house or as surviving spouse having prior rights or as heir in intestacy. Unless a sale of the property is necessary to meet the liabilities of the deceased, the duty of the executor will be to convey

---

[71] 1981 Act, s. 9.
[72] 1981 Act, s. 19.
[73] Succession (Scotland) Act 1964, s. 14.

the property to the individual who is entitled to it and a sale of the property by the executor will only be at his or her behest so that the sale will in effect be a dealing by the beneficial owner of the property. If at the time of the sale the property is the matrimonial home of the beneficial owner the consent of his or her non-entitled spouse will be necessary; if the property is not a matrimonial home an affidavit by the beneficial owner to confirm that fact will be required. The position is similar where testamentary trustees are directed to hold a dwelling-house for the liferent use of an individual beneficiary. There will, however, be many cases in which no right of occupancy of a dwelling-house will arise on the death of its owner, *e.g.* where testamentary trustees are authorised to sell the estate and the interest of beneficiaries is in the residue so that no beneficiary is entitled to require conveyance of any specific asset of the estate. If, on a death, a right of beneficial ownership of a dwelling-house vests in two or more persons (not being spouses) there will be no right of occupancy under the 1981 Act.[74]

-34 **Time of dealing.** In relation to the sale of a matrimonial home the consent, renunciation or affidavit must be produced at the time of the dealing, now defined in transactions on or after December 30, 1985, as the date of delivery to the purchaser of the deed transferring the title.[75] In relation to a heritably secured loan the consent, renunciation or affidavit must be produced before the granting of the loan, now defined in transactions on or after December 30, 1985, as the date of delivery of the deed creating the security.[76] The specification of those periods of time for delivery of the documentation causes problems in cases where there has been an omission to do so timeously, since the granting of the appropriate consent, renunciation or affidavit subsequently does not constitute compliance with the Act. It is suggested that in such circumstances the consent, renunciation or affidavit, expressed as applicable at or before the time of the dealing, should nevertheless be granted by the non-entitled spouse or the entitled spouse, as the case may be, since it will have evidential value.

-35 **Prescription of occupancy rights.** In terms of section 13(6)(*c*) of the Law Reform (Miscellaneous Provisions) (Scotland) Act 1985 the occupancy rights of a non-entitled spouse in a property which has been sold are excluded if the entitled spouse permanently ceased to be entitled to occupy the matrimonial home and at any time thereafter a continuous period of five years has elapsed during which the non-entitled spouse has not occupied it. It is unclear whether this prescription applies to all sales effected at any time after September 1, 1982 (the commencement of the 1981 Act), if the period of five years

---

[74] s. 6(2)(*b*).
[75] 1981 Act, s. 6(3)(*e*): 1985 Act, s. 13(6).
[76] 1981 Act, s. 8(2) as amended by 1985 Act, s. 13(8).

ended after December 30, 1985 (the commencement of the 1985 Act), or applies only when the relevant sale was made after the latter date. It is thought that the former alternative is correct.

21–36 Evidence of occupancy rights. In the examination of a title to a dwelling-house or subjects capable of being or containing a dwelling-house there should be produced in respect of any sale which occurred after September 1, 1982, and not more than five years prior to the date of entry in the current transaction, a consent to the sale, or a renunciation of occupancy rights, by the non-entitled spouse, or an affidavit by the entitled spouse granted at the date of delivery of the disposition which gives effect to that transaction. The production and examination of the relevant document (or an extract thereof) is required in respect of any such sale made or consented to by (i) an individual person, (ii) an executor-nominate or testamentary trustees in circumstances where an individual was entitled to occupancy rights in a dwelling-house which formed part of the deceased's estate, or (iii) an executor-dative where an individual was entitled to a dwelling-house with a right of occupancy thereof either as the person entitled to succeed thereto on intestacy or as surviving spouse having prior rights (since the surviving spouse might remarry before the sale). Where the dealing is by a curator bonis to an incapax, the Keeper does not require the production of an affidavit.

21–37 Divorce and alimentary actions. Section 6 of the Divorce (Scotland) Act 1976 (applicable from January 1, 1977), substantially re-enacting section 27 of the Succession (Scotland) Act 1964, contained anti-avoidance provisions which enabled a spouse who had applied to the court claiming an order for payment by the other spouse of a periodical payment or capital sum to apply to the court within one year after the disposal of such a claim for an order reducing or varying any settlement or disposition of property by the other spouse in favour of a third party made at any time within three years before the making of the claim on the ground that it was made with a view to defeating an obligation to make financial provision for the claimant. Section 18 of the Family Law (Scotland) Act 1985 (applicable from a date yet to be announced), with certain variations in wording, alters the provisions of section 6 of the 1976 Act (which is repealed) to the effect of extending the anti-avoidance provisions to apply to all actions of aliment, not only those between spouses, and increasing the period during which the transaction with a third party was made to five years before the making of the claim. Any disposition, settlement or transfer of property occurring in a progress of titles which is still vulnerable to reduction or variation under any of these Acts may render the title technically unmarketable. The risk is reduced by provisions in the Acts which protect a third party who has acquired the property in good faith for value or has derived title from any person who has done so, and so in effect the risk of reduction arises only where the acquisition was not so made.

(B) Validity and Sufficiency of Deeds

Quality of deeds

-38 Any deed which is redeemable or has been granted in circumstances which render it vulnerable to reduction is not acceptable as a step in the prescriptive progress. Examples are a deed by a minor which is challengeable within the *quadriennium utile*, a decree in absence which has not become final,[77] a decree of adjudication for debt which is redeemable within the legal,[78] a conveyance which is open to reduction as a gratuitous alienation or unfair preference upon the bankruptcy of the granter,[79] or as a disposition to a third party designed to defeat a claim for aliment or an obligation of financial provision on divorce.[80] On the other hand, a deed which is *ex facie* regular where there are no circumstances to indicate that it is liable to reduction or challenge is acceptable.[81]

Form and execution

-39 All deeds connecting the title of the grantee of the foundation writ to that of the present owner, including unrecorded links, must be sufficient in respect of their form and execution to constitute valid conveyances or transmissions of the right to the property. As to the writings which may be used as midcouples or links in title and the practice in the use of the facility, see the paragraphs undernoted.[82] As to the form and execution of deeds see Volume I, Chapters 3 and 4: some of the defects which may be found in a progress of titles are considered in the succeeding paragraphs.

-40 **Errors in deduction of title.** Under section 3 of the Conveyancing (Scotland) Act 1924 a clause of deduction of the title of an uninfeft granter of a disposition may be in or as nearly as may be in the terms of Form No. 1 of Schedule A to the Act.[83] In examination of title it is necessary to check that (i) the granter of the disposition containing the clause is a person who may competently deduce title under the section, and (ii) the clause conforms in all material matters to the style of Form No 1 to Schedule A to the Act. As to persons who may deduce title

---

[77] *Duke of Devonshire* v. *Fletcher* (1874) 1 R. 1056; *Bruce* v. *Stewart* (1900) 2 F. 948.
[78] *Hinton* v. *Connell's Trs.* (1883) 10 R. 1110.
[79] See *McManus's Tr.* v. *McManus*, 1978 S.L.T. 255. See also para. 21–17.
[80] See para. 21–37.
[81] *e.g.* a decree of general service (*Sibbald's Heirs* v. *Harris*, 1947 S.C. 601).
[82] paras. 22–08 and 22–54.
[83] See para. 22–54.

and the form of clause, see the paragraphs undernoted.[84,85] Where a purported deduction of title by a person who cannot use the facility is contained in a disposition in a prescriptive progress it is necessary to obtain a corroborative conveyance from the person last properly infeft in the subjects or having a right to the subjects within the meaning of the section. A different and less serious problem may be encountered where a disposition by a person who could properly deduce title contains a clause of deduction of title which does not conform in a material respect to the statutorily prescribed form. Errors or omissions which are material and not within the latitude permitted by the "as nearly as may be" wording of section 5, include failure to name and design correctly the person last infeft or to specify the recording date of his or her title or omission to specify a necessary link in the chain of deeds whereby the right to the subjects devolved from the person last infeft to the granter of the disposition. Such a material defect renders the clause of deduction of title inept with the result that the disponee is not properly infeft, but the disposition remains an effective conveyance of the right to the subjects and so the disponee or any person to whom he may subsequently have conveyed the subjects may deduce title correctly from the person last infeft in any further disposition. The clause deducing title may be expressed in alternative form:

> which subjects are now vested in me, my title thereto being recorded in the (*specify Register of Sasines and date of recording of the possibly defective title of the granter*), or otherwise which subjects were last vested in (*name and designation of last properly infeft proprietor*) whose title thereto was recorded in the (*specify Register of Sasines and date of recording*) and from whom I acquired right by (*specify all links by which right acquired by granter from person last properly infeft*).

If it is necessary to complete title in circumstances where no new disposition is being prepared, *e.g.* when a feu or lease is being granted, a notice of title in Form No. 1 of Schedule B to the 1924 Act may be expede with a deduction of title from the last properly infeft proprietor.

21–41   **Errors in execution of deeds.** Every deed in a progress of titles must be validly executed. The possible categories of defects in execution as being (i) minor, (ii) incurable and invalidating, or (iii) remediable informalities have already been described.[86] A material irremediable defect in execution invalidates a deed of conveyance of land with the result that the granter or his executors have not been divested of ownership and remain *in titulo* to grant a corroborative conveyance. Where the granter of such a defective deed was a company which has subsequently been wound up the corroborative deed may be granted

---

[84] paras. 22–07 and 22–09.
[85] For deeds or writings which may be used as links in deduction of title, see 1924 Act, s. 5.
[86] Vol. I, paras. 3–41 to 3–45.

by its liquidator or, if he has been discharged, may be obtained from the Queen's and Lord Treasurer's Remembrancer.[87]

Stamp duty

-42 All deeds within the prescriptive progress which are liable to stamp duty must be appropriately stamped. It is not permissible for a purchaser to be barred by agreement from objecting to insufficiency of stamp duty on a deed.[88] Any unrecorded conveyance on sale must have been produced to the Stamp Office and bear a PD stamp.[89]

(C) Identity of Subjects

Description

-43 Each deed in the prescriptive progress should convey the subjects of the current transaction or larger subjects which include them.[90] If the deed is a special conveyance the description of the lands must be sufficient to enable title to be completed by recording in the Register of Sasines or registration in the Land Register, as the case may be. A conveyance of "all right and interest" in lands is not an appropriate form of description in a disposition; the lands themselves should be conveyed.[91] If the description of the subjects in a deed in the progress does not establish that it includes the whole subjects of the current transaction, it is competent in any action for determining the question to lead parole evidence.[92]

Minerals

-44 If an examination of title reveals that minerals (other than coal or minerals worked in association therewith which have vested in the National Coal Board[93] or petroleum ownership of which is now vested in the Crown[94]) have been reserved and the current contract of sale contains no exception of minerals, then the purchaser may resile on the ground that he is not being given a title to the whole subjects purchased,[95] unless knowledge of the reservation at the time of purchase can be imputed to the purchaser.[96] If in terms of the contract

---

[87] See Vol. I, para. 4–04.
[88] Stamp Act 1891, s. 117.
[89] Finance Act 1931, ss. 28 and 35(*w*).
[90] As to description of lands, see Chap. 18.
[91] *Hay* v. *Corporation of Aberdeen*, 1909 S.C. 554.
[92] *Macdonald* v. *Newall* (1898) 1 F. 68. See also *Houldsworth* v. *Gordon Cumming*, 1910 S.C.(H.L.) 49.
[93] See para. 19–08.
[94] See Vol. I, para. 8–59.
[95] *Whyte* v. *Lee* (1879) 6 R. 699; *Todd* v. *McCarroll*, 1917 2 S.L.T. 127; *Gall* v. *Gall*, 1918 1 S.L.T. 261; *Campbell* v. *McCutcheon*, 1963 S.C. 505.
[96] *Crofts* v. *Stewart's Trs.*, 1927 S.C.(H.L.) 65; *Mossend Theatre Co.* v. *Livingstone*, 1930 S.C. 90. It is not sufficient that the purchaser has knowledge that there are mineral reservations in the area: there must be knowledge of the actual reservation.

of sale the minerals were included in the sale only so far as belonging
to the seller the opinion is expressed that in the absence of any special
knowledge of the purchaser a reservation of minerals with a provision
for reasonably adequate compensation for subsidence damage might be
presumed, but if examination of the title discloses a reservation of
minerals with right to enter on the surface, or to withdraw support
from the surface without or with significantly limited compensation,
the purchaser is entitled to resile. The description of the subjects
purchased in the contract of sale may elide the presumption that
minerals are included. The purchase of a ground flat in a tenement
would on the basis of common law include the underlying minerals, but
quaere if an upper flat is purchased unless knowledge of the purchaser
of a practice in the district of making the solum *pro indiviso* property
of all the proprietors of flatted property can be established?

(D) Tenure and Burdens and Conditions

Tenure

21–45   The original feu grant of the subjects, which will frequently be
earlier in date than the foundation writ of the prescriptive progress,
should always be examined: although feuduty may no longer be
payable it is essential to identify the superior for the purpose of serving
notice of change of ownership. Moreover, the original feu grant will
normally impose conditions of tenure which are still enforceable.

Burdens and conditions

21–46   All deeds of whatever date which impose burdens or conditions
upon the subjects should be examined. If any are inconsistent with the
terms of the contract of purchase, the purchaser may be entitled to
resile. Conditions which may be relevant to the purchaser's use or
development of the subjects should be brought to his notice in
reporting on the title.

21–47   **Real burdens.** When title is being examined on the occasion of a
purchase of the subjects any existing allocated feuduty or ground
annual will be redeemed by the seller in terms of the Land Tenure
Reform (Scotland) Act 1974.[97] The subjects will continue to be
burdened by an unallocated proportion of feuduty or ground annual.
In earlier decisions[98] it was held that where the missives of sale stated
that feuduty was of a certain amount the fact that it proved to be an
unallocated part of a larger *cumulo* feuduty entitled the purchaser to
resile from the bargain. Since a feuduty which in terms of the missives

---

[97] See paras. 17–49 *et seq.*
[98] *Bremner* v. *Dick*, 1911 S.C. 887; *Morrison* v. *Gray*, 1932 S.C. 712.

of sale is to continue to burden the subjects must now be unallocated and the purchaser may have it allocated by using the procedure contained in the Conveyancing and Feudal Reform (Scotland) Act 1970,[99] the substratum of those decisions has been substantially removed. If examination of title discloses a burden of an unallocated portion of feuduty or ground annual, inquiry should be made as to the condition of the other properties over which the ground burden is secured since, if these are derelict or demolished, a larger proportion of the original burden may be imposed on the subjects of purchase.[1]

‑48   Limit of time for feudalising. Feu grants frequently impose a time limit for recording. If that has not been complied with, a probative minute of waiver should be obtained from the superior and recorded.

‑49   Clauses of pre-emption or redemption. As to any such clauses, whether occurring in the original feu grant or in any subsequent disposition, see paragraphs 17–68 to 17–80 *supra*.

‑50   Building conditions. If the buildings on the ground *prima facie* conform to the building conditions in the title deeds and have existed unchanged for a considerable time, it may be assumed that the conditions of title have been complied with. If the buildings have been erected or structurally altered comparatively recently, say within 10 years before the current transaction, the seller should be asked to provide a certificate or letter from the superior or other party by whom the condition was imposed that the building conditions of the title have been complied with. Any fee charged for the provision of the certificate may reasonably be borne equally by the seller and the purchaser. Superiors are not always willing to grant such a certificate or may, in the case of a company, have been wound up: in such circumstances an inspection of the buildings may sufficiently indicate that there has been compliance with the building conditions.

‑51   Obligations and restrictions. The examination of conditions of title which impose obligations or restrictions involves several related matters, the more important of which are considered below.

‑52   *(a) Nature and scope of the condition.* Conditions which are consistent with the structure and use of the existing buildings and do not impose unacceptable restrictions on any proposed development or use of the subjects do not give cause for concern, but may be explained for the information of the purchaser in a report on the title.

‑53   *(b) Enforceability.* Any condition which may impose unacceptable restraints may no longer be enforceable by the superior or other

---

[99] See para. 17–40.
[1] *Barr* v. *Bass Ltd.*, 1972 S.L.T. (Lands Tr.) 5.

persons owing to lack of interest. Inquiry as to relevant circumstances may be necessary.[2]

21–54 *(c) Inconsistency with contract of sale.* If any conditions of title impose restrictions which are inconsistent with a provision, express or necessarily implied, in the contract of sale the purchaser may require the seller to procure a waiver or alternatively may resile from the transaction. The fact that a condition has been made express indicates that it is material,[3] and breach of a material condition by one party entitles the other party to resile. In *McConnell* v. *Chassels*[4] the purchaser stated that he intended to apply for a liquor licence and the seller stipulated for an additional payment if the licence was obtained. When it was discovered that the title deeds contained a prohibition against the sale of liquor the purchaser was held to be entitled to resile, since it was an implied condition that the subjects could be used as licensed premises.

21–55 *(d) Unusual or unduly onerous conditions.* "When a person purchases property by missives in which the property is described in general terms, he is taken to have purchased it with the incidents which usually attach themselves to property of the kind in the surrounding circumstances."[5] If, however, upon examination of the title deeds a burden or condition which is unduly onerous is discovered, the purchaser may withdraw from the transaction. Examples are the purchase of a vacant piece of ground where the titles disclose a prohibition of building,[6] a purchase of ground upon which the seller had created a prohibition against the erection of steam engines and sold to a third party without mentioning the restriction[7] and the purchase of a cottage where the title deeds prohibited the opening of windows in the rear of the building.[8] This general proposition may be subject to qualification if (i) the purchaser had knowledge of the restriction at the time of exchange of missives,[9] or (ii) the missives had stipulated that the property was sold subject to the whole conditions in the title deeds (although such a provision would not safeguard the seller against a restriction created otherwise than in the titles, such as a positive servitude acquired by prescription). As to the effect of a provision in the contract of sale that the title be taken as it stands, see paragraph 15–86 *supra*.

21–56 *(e) Servitudes.* Positive or negative servitudes burdening or benefiting

---

[2] See paras. 19–41 to 19–59.
[3] *Standard Life Assurance Co.* v. *Weems* (1884) 11 R.(H.L.) 48 at 51.
[4] (1903) 10 S.L.T. 790.
[5] *Crofts* v. *Stewart's Trs.*, 1926 S.C. 891, per Lord Sands at 902.
[6] *Louttit's Trs.* v. *Highland Railway Co.* (1892) 19 R. 791.
[7] *Urquhart* v. *Halden* (1835) 13 S. 844. See also *Robertson* v. *Rutherford* (1841) 4 D. 121.
[8] *Smith* v. *Soeder* (1895) 23 R. 60.
[9] *Robertson* v. *Rutherford, supra*; *Mossend Theatre Co.* v. *Livingstone*, 1930 S.C. 90 (the plea of bar by knowledge in relation to a mineral reservation clause failed on the facts, but the qualification was impliedly admitted).

the property may not be disclosed in the progress of titles or by the search in the Property Register. A servitude burdening the property should be mentioned in the contract of sale, but if not so mentioned but later discovered the right of the purchaser to resile would depend upon the materiality of the burden. A servitude of way which affects the exclusive possession and privacy of the garden ground of a private residence may justify rescission,[10] and a right of access through the property which inhibited development contemplated in the missives would do so.[11] The constitution and continuing validity of any servitude rights which benefit the property purchased should be checked by examination of the constituting deeds or evidence of their establishment by prescription.[12] As to procedure in relation to servitudes on sale and purchase of the dominant or servient tenement see paragraphs 20–21 to 20–23 *supra*. As to a public right of way affecting private properties see the undernoted cases.[13]

(E) Heritable Securities

Discharge

1–57 It is necessary to confirm that any heritable securities which formerly burdened the subjects have been effectively discharged and no longer affect the title. If a discharge of a security which bears to be granted by a person entitled to do so has been duly recorded more than five years before the date of the current transaction, the title of a person acquiring an interest in the land *bona fide* and for value, *e.g.* a purchaser or lender, is not challengeable after five years from the date of recording of the discharge by reason only of the recording of an extract decree of reduction of the discharge.[14] In effect, therefore, it is unnecessary to examine the validity of writs whereby a former heritable security was assigned, transmitted or discharged if the search discloses a discharge by the person *prima facie* entitled to grant it which has been duly recorded more than five years ago. As regards a security which a search discloses as having been discharged within the five-year period, the examiner should verify the effectiveness of any deeds by which the security was assigned, transmitted and discharged, but technical irregularities in the form of those deeds are unimportant so long as the security has been discharged by the creditor entitled to do so, since a document of receipt by him extinguishes the security and, when recorded, clears the record in the Register of Sasines.[15] If any

[10] *Welsh* v. *Russell* (1894) 21 R. 769 (although the point was not decided since the wrong remedy was sought).

[11] *Armia Ltd.* v. *Daejan Developments Ltd.*, 1979 S.C.(H.L.) 56.

[12] See *More* v. *Boyle*, 1967 S.L.T. (Sh.Ct.) 38; *Murray* v. *Medley*, 1973 S.L.T. (Sh.Ct.) 75.

[13] *Norrie* v. *Kirriemuir Magistrates*, 1945 S.C. 302; *Strathclyde (Hyndland) Housing Society Ltd.* v. *Cowie*, 1983 S.L.T. (Sh.Ct.) 61; *Cowie* v. *Strathclyde Regional Council*, 1985 S.L.T. 333.

[14] Conveyancing and Feudal Reform (Scotland) Act 1970, s. 41(1).

[15] *Cameron* v. *Williamson* (1895) 22 R. 293.

securities remain undischarged it is essential to procure their discharge in the course of the current transaction.[16]

Conveyances by heritable creditors

21-58   If any of the links in the prescriptive progress of the property title is a conveyance by a heritable creditor in exercise of a power of sale and the exercise of that power was *ex facie* regular, the title of a *bona fide* purchaser for value is not challengeable on the ground that the debt had ceased to exist, unless that fact appeared on the Register of Sasines or was known to the purchaser prior to the payment of the price, or on the ground of any irregularity relating to the sale or in any preliminary procedure thereto.[17] For comment upon the conditions upon which and the extent to which this protection is available to purchasers, see the undernoted text.[18] Where the progress contains a decree of foreclosure by a heritable creditor, the title of the creditor is not challengeable on the ground of any irregularity in the proceedings for foreclosure or on calling-up or default which preceded it.[19]

(F) Bona Fides

Bona fides of purchasers or lenders

21-59   A purchaser of heritable property *in bona fide* on the faith of the record is not affected by personal obligations of the seller or borrower, and he takes the title free of any burden or incumbrance not disclosed by a search in the appropriate registers,[20] other than a servitude or occupancy rights of a non-entitled spouse in a matrimonial home. If, however, the purchaser was aware of some right of a third party in the subjects not disclosed by the search or, although not actually aware of such a right, he had knowledge of facts which should have put him on his inquiry with regard to the possible existence of it, then the title he receives is not secure from challenge.[21] Circumstances which may put a purchaser on his inquiry are knowledge of a prior agreement to sell the subjects to a third party, when the duty of inquiry is not elided by an assurance from the seller that the prior agreement is no longer enforceable,[22] or knowledge of a latent trust affecting the seller's title,[23] or the existence of buildings or works on the subjects erected by

---

[16] See para. 23–10(1).
[17] Conveyancing (Scotland) Act 1924, s. 41(2), as substituted by Conveyancing and Feudal Reform (Scotland) Act 1970, s. 38, applicable to dispositions recorded on or after November 29, 1970.
[18] Halliday, *Conveyancing and Feudal Reform (Scotland) Act 1970*, paras. 5–20, 5–21.
[19] Conveyancing and Feudal Reform (Scotland) Act 1970, s. 28(8).
[20] See paras. 21–73 to 21–88.
[21] Bell, *Prin.*, s. 889.
[22] *Marshall* v. *Hynd* (1828) 6 S. 384; *Petrie* v. *Forsyth* (1874) 2 R. 214; *Rodger (Builders) Ltd.* v. *Fawdry*, 1950 S.C. 483.
[23] *Mags. of Airdrie* v. *Smith* (1850) 12 D. 1222.

a third party.[24] The right of the third party (other than a right of occupancy in a matrimonial home) must be such that it is capable of becoming a real right in the subjects.[25] Even if the disposition to the purchaser has been recorded, the requirement of *bona fides* may result in its reduction.[26] The requirement of *bona fides* applies also to lenders who take a heritable security in circumstances where they had knowledge of the possible existence of a right in third parties.[27] The application and scope of the principle of *bona fides* in relation to the position of a heritable creditor where leases had been granted or assigned by the debtor has recently been considered by the courts in the *Trade Development Bank* cases.[28] The first of those (*Warriner & Mason*) was complicated by specialties and has been criticised,[29] but it was held that the sub-tenants whose right was successfully challenged by the heritable creditors of the tenants were not in good faith by taking a sub-lease without having obtained the prior consent of the pursuers or instituted a search of the Register of Sasines, and a plea of excusable ignorance was negatived both in the *Warriner & Mason* and *Haig* decisions. As regards the heritable creditors, however, it was recognised in the *Crittall Windows* case that if they had knowledge that some sort of right capable of becoming real had already been conferred upon the defenders, the latter could on the broad principle of dealing in good faith prevent the creditors from exercising their rights under the recorded security.

Good faith expressly required by statute

1–60   In certain transactions good faith is expressly required as a condition of protection or rights conferred by statute. Examples are: (1) A transaction with a limited company.[30] (2) The acquisition of a title to an interest in or security over heritable property from an executor or a person deriving title directly from an executor.[31] (3) A purchase from a heritable creditor selling the security subjects in the exercise of a power of sale.[32] (4) The purchase of heritable property which has been subject to a heritable security discharged more than five years previously.[33] (5) The protection against the effect of a decree of

[24] *Lang* v. *Dixon*, June 29, 1813, F.C.; *Stodart* v. *Dalzell* (1876) 4 R. 236.
[25] *Wallace* v. *Simmers*, 1960 S.C. 255; *Trade Development Bank* v. *Crittall Windows Ltd.*, 1983 S.L.T. 510.
[26] *Morrison* v. *Somerville* (1860) 23 D. 232; *Stodart* v. *Dalzell*, *supra*; *Rodger (Builders) Ltd.* v. *Fawdry*, *supra*.
[27] *Trade Development Bank* v. *Crittall Windows Ltd.*, *supra*.
[28] *Trade Development Bank* v. *Warriner & Mason* (Scotland) Ltd., 1980 S.C. 74; *Trade Development Bank* v. *David W. Haig (Bellshill) Ltd.*, 1983 S.L.T. 510; *Trade Development Bank* v. *Crittall Windows Ltd.*, *supra*.
[29] K.G.C. Reid, 1983 S.L.T. (News) 169, 189.
[30] European Communities Act 1972, s. 9(1): repealed but re-enacted by Companies Act 1985, s. 35.
[31] Succession (Scotland) Act 1964, s. 17.
[32] Conveyancing (Scotland) Act 1924, s. 41(2) substituted by the Conveyancing and Feudal Reform (Scotland) Act 1970, s. 38.
[33] Conveyancing and Feudal Reform (Scotland) Act 1970, s. 41(1).

reduction given to a purchaser for value who has acquired right to land or a lease or heritable security between the pronouncement of the decree and the recording of an extract of it in the Register of Sasines.[34] (6) The right to rectification of a defectively expressed document or a title sheet in the Land Register.[35] (7) The protection given to a person who has acquired property from or through the grantee in a gratuitous alienation in a case of bankruptcy.[36]

(G) Statutory Titles

Special titles under statute

21–61   There are anomalous cases under particular statutes where title to heritable subjects is conferred with or without judicial proceedings and with or without the need to record the title in the Register of Sasines. Some of the more important to conveyancers are:

(1) Lands Clauses Consolidation (Scotland) Act 1845. Many statutes whereby lands may be acquired compulsorily incorporate the procedure prescribed by this Act and a schedule conveyance in the form authorised by section 80 of and contained in Schedule A to the Act or a notarial instrument authorised by section 76 of the Act may be used. The effect is to create an anomalous type of tenure which is virtually allodial. The Schedule A conveyance must be recorded within 60 days from its last date.

(2) Local Government (Scotland) Act 1973. Heritable property belonging to the former local authorities was transferred by virtue of section 222 of the Act by the Local Authorities (Property etc.) (Scotland) Order 1975,[37] which provided that the property would be transferred to and vest in the new district or regional or islands council having the duty of discharging the function for which the property was wholly or mainly used. The effect of the Order is to transfer the right to the property: the transferee council may deduce title through the Act and Order in any subsequent disposition of the property or obtain infeftment by a notice of title using the Act and Order as links.

(3) Burgh Police (Scotland) Act 1892. Sections 197 and 200 of this Act provided for the sale of ruinous buildings in burghs where the owners could not be found and for completion of the purchaser's title by recording in the Register of Sasines of a decree by the sheriff. The title of the purchaser is unconnected to that of any predecessor and is independent of any known feudal tenure.[38] In modern practice

---

[34] Conveyancing (Scotland) Act 1924, s. 46 as construed in *Mulhearn* v. *Dunlop*, 1929 S.L.T. 59.
[35] Law Reform (Miscellaneous Provisions) (Scotland) Act 1985, s. 9(3).
[36] Bankruptcy (Scotland) Act 1985, proviso to s. 34(4).
[37] S.I. 1975 No. 659 (S. 92).
[38] *Young's Trs.* v. *Grainger* (1904) 7 F. 232 at 238.

properties which have been repaired or demolished by a local authority where the owner cannot be found are acquired compulsorily by the authority under section 15 of the Building (Scotland) Act 1959.

(4) Nationalisation statutes. The transfer of heritable property upon nationalisation of an industry may be effected by two methods: (a) by vesting of ownership in a national corporation of particular property when infeftment is effected by notice of title using the statute as a link in title,[39] or (b) by acquisition of all the shares and securities of the companies or bodies whose enterprises are acquired by the State when no conveyancing procedures are required to complete title to heritable property.[40]

(5) Railways, docks and waterways. The title to land acquired by railway companies normally is in name of the company which originally acquired it. Title to a particular property may be deduced or completed using as links any schemes of amalgamation whereby ownership of the land was transferred to a larger railway company, the Transport Act 1947 which transferred ownership to the British Transport Commission and the Transport Act 1962 and relative vesting order which transferred ownership to the British Railways Board, British Transport Docks Board or British Waterways Board, as the case may have been.

(6) Private legislation. When land is acquired by virtue of a Provisional Order and Private Act under the Private Legislation Procedure (Scotland) Act 1936 it is usually conveyed by a special disposition in favour of the acquiring body or person in implement of the Act and Provisional Order.

(7) Statutes vesting land to the effect of giving a recorded title. Occasionally, but less commonly, a statute may enact a transfer of land to the same effect as if a disposition had been granted and recorded, *e.g.* Church of Scotland General Trustees Order Confirmation Act 1921. In such cases the transferee body is infeft by virtue of the statute without the need of any other recorded title.

1–62   Effect of statutory acquisition upon burdens and conditions. One of the many uncertainties resulting from the unhappy draftmanship of the Lands Clauses Consolidation (Scotland) Act 1845 is the effect of a timeously recorded Schedule A conveyance upon burdens and conditions of the former title. It seems reasonably clear, however, that they are extinguished, certainly if the special Act has provided for compensation to the persons entitled to enforce them.[41] The Act which authorises acquisition may contain express provisions which have that

---

[39] *e.g.* Coal Industry Nationalisation Act 1946.
[40] *e.g.* Iron and Steel Act 1967; Aircraft and Shipbuilding Industries Act 1977.
[41] See article, 1964 S.L.T. (News) 205.

effect, and in particular the Town and Country Planning (Scotland) Act 1972 extinguishes or overrides all previous rights or servitudes in or relating to the land acquired.[42]

(H) Examination of other Titles

Superiority title

21–63   Where the subjects have been feued within the period of positive prescription it is necessary to examine the superiority title back to the deed last recorded before the commencement of the prescriptive period with the same particularity as the other deeds included in the progress of titles of the subjects of purchase or security and to see clear searches over the superiority: in such circumstances the superiority title to that extent forms part of the prescriptive progress.

Boundary features

21–64   The title under examination may specify a boundary as the centre line or the outer or inner face of a wall or other physical feature. It is normally impracticable to establish that there has been exclusive possession of the boundary feature and there is a risk that the title to the adjoining property may contain an inconsistent description of the line of boundary. The basic title of the adjoining property, if recorded before that of the subjects of examination, will prevail. It is not usual practice to examine the title of the adjoining property, but if the precise line of the boundary is important in relation to possible development or for any other reason, examination of the title to the adjoining property is a sensible precaution.

Tenements

21–65   Rights of ownership in and obligations for the maintenance of certain parts of a tenement of flatted property, such as the roof, outer walls and solum, may be regulated by the common law of the tenement but are frequently made the subject of express provisions of title having a different effect.[43] Inconsistencies in such matters contained in the titles of individual flats are of distressingly frequent occurrence.[44] It is not usual in practice to examine the titles of flats other than that which is the subject of the current transaction, but if there are circumstances which indicate the possibility of conveyancing error, such as a history of disposal of various flats for the first time by different persons over a considerable period, it may be prudent to make inquiry.[45] It is one of

---

[42] ss. 108, 117. See also *Largs Hydropathic Ltd.* v. *Largs Town Council*, 1967 S.C. 1.
[43] See paras. 18–20 to 18–22.
[44] See, *e.g. Duncan* v. *Church of Scotland General Trustees*, 1941 S.C. 145. See also article (1968) 13 J.L.S. 90.
[45] Earlier dispositions of flats may have contained an obligation to insert similar burdens or conditions in any subsequent dispositions of other flats in the tenement.

the advantages of a deed of conditions applicable to the whole tenement that it significantly diminishes this risk.

Cost and maintenance of mutual boundary features

1–66   The obligation of a neighbouring proprietor to contribute to the cost of construction or maintenance of walls, fences or gables which in terms of the title to the subjects of the current transaction appear to be common or mutual may not have been effectively created as a real burden in the title deeds of the adjoining property. The usual inquiry as to the absence of any outstanding liability in respect of such costs will normally, but not necessarily, disclose the existence of any such problem. Special inquiry should be made in circumstances where a property has been subdivided and the appropriate right has been conferred in the conveyance of the part sold: it should be verified that the corresponding burden has effectively been created real in any subsequent conveyance of the remaining part by being incorporated at length in the conveyance of it.

(I) Negative Prescription

Imprescriptible rights and obligations

1–67   Certain rights and obligations in relation to heritable property cannot be extinguished by negative prescription, notably a real right of ownership of land, the right of a tenant under a recorded lease, a right exercisable as *res merae facultatis*, or the right of an heir to take steps for making up or completing title to land.[46]

Prescriptible rights and obligations

1–68   Rights to and obligations for payment of arrears of feuduty, ground annual, rent and periodical payments from land or under a land obligation prescribe after five years,[47] servitudes are extinguished by non-use after 20 years and the rights to heritable securities are extinguished both as to principal and interest in the absence of a relevant claim or acknowledgment for 20 years.[48]

(J) Positive Prescription and Possession

Title and period of possession

1–69   The nature of the foundation deed for positive prescription has already been described.[49] The period of possession required in order to

---

[46] Prescription and Limitation (Scotland) Act 1973, Sched. 3.
[47] *Ibid.*, Sched. 1, para. 1(*a*).
[48] *Ibid.*, ss. 7, 9, 10.
[49] See para. 21–06.

render a title unchallengeable by the operation of positive prescription is 10 years, except that when the subjects are foreshore or salmon fishings and prescription is pled against the Crown as owner of the regalia the period is 20 years.[50] The period is computed from midnight at the end of the day on which the foundation deed was recorded until the last day of the relevant period of 10 or 20 years or, if the latter day was a holiday, the next succeeding day which is not a holiday, and any time during which the person against whom prescription is pled was under legal disability is reckoned as if he were free from that disability.[51] If the foundation deed is a decree of adjudication for debt the period commences only after the expiry of the legal.[52] If a decree of declarator of the expiry of the legal is obtained and recorded it seems clear that the adjudger's right becomes unchallengeable when followed by the appropriate possession for 10 years thereafter, since the effect of the decree of adjudication plus the decree of declarator of expiry of the legal, taken together, is to provide a recorded deed which on the face of the Register of Sasines is sufficient in respect of its terms to constitute a title to the land on which positive prescription may run. If no decree of declarator of expiry of the legal is obtained it is arguable whether the title is secure after 10 years from the date of expiry of the legal by virtue of positive prescription or only after 20 years when the negative prescription operates.[53] I express the view that the former is correct, mainly on the grounds that (i) whatever may be the theoretical arguments based on former decisions the matter is now regulated by the Prescription and Limitation (Scotland) Act 1973 which clearly treats positive prescription as applicable to adjudications, and (ii) subsection (3) of section 1 of that Act refers simply to "the expiry of the legal" which on a straightforward construction is a matter of fact not necessarily evidenced by a decree of court. Nevertheless the careful conveyancer (since caution is the badge of all his tribe) will advise the adjudger to obtain and record a decree of declarator of expiry of the legal. If the subjects are allodial or the title deed, although unrecorded, was sufficient foundation for prescription[54] the period is 20 years.[55]

Continuity and interruption of possession

21–70   The possession must be continuous, openly and peaceably without any judicial interruption.[56] Judicial interruption is defined as appropriate

---

[50] Prescription and Limitation (Scotland) Act 1973, s. 1.

[51] *Ibid.*, s. 14(1). For definition of "holiday" see s. 14(2).

[52] *Ibid.*, s. 1(3).

[53] See G.L. Gretton, 1983 J.R. 177.

[54] *e.g.* a deed granted before the Register of Sasines was established, as in *Wallace* v. *St. Andrews University* (1904) 6 F. 1093. For other examples see Walker, *Law of Prescription and Limitation of Actions*, 33.

[55] 1973 Act, s. 2.

[56] *Ibid.*, ss. 1(1)(*a*) and 2(1)(*a*).

proceedings in a court of competent jurisdiction in Scotland or elsewhere and if in the Court of Session the summons must have been called, not merely served, and initiated by any person having a proper interest to make a claim which challenges the possession of the defender, or any arbitration in Scotland or in any other country if the award would be enforceable in Scotland, the date of interruption in arbitration proceedings being defined.[57]

Nature of possession

1–71   Where the subject is land the possession must be exclusive, and adverse to any competing right. It must be consistent with the title founded upon[58] and cannot fortify a title to land which is outwith the limits of a bounding title,[59] although it may establish a right to pertinents beyond such limits.[60] The possession must be referable to the title founded upon and not attributable to a lesser right of occupation.[61] If the extent of the lands is unclear from the description in the title, possession for the prescriptive period may explain the ambiguity and determine the extent of the lands conveyed (explicative prescription).[62] Possession must be as complete as the nature of the subject permits. In the case of the foreshore in which the public have inalienable rights of use the taking of sand and gravel and sea-ware are sufficiently indicative of a right of ownership,[63] in the case of minerals some reasonably continuous working of the minerals is necessary,[64] or in the case of salmon fishings a regular exercise of the right by any legal method such as by net and coble or even by rod and line.[65] Where one of several joint proprietors of a loch claimed the sole right of fishing it was held that the fact that she alone had been in the habit of fishing did not establish an exclusive right: she could not have prevented the other proprietors from fishing, so that an adverse joint right was not excluded.[66]

Evidence of possession

1–72   Possession may be natural, *i.e.* physical occupation by the person maintaining the right, or civil, as by a vassal for the superior or by a

---

[57] *Ibid.*, s. 4. For a more detailed account see Walker, *op. cit.*, 19, 20.

[58] *Officers of State* v. *Earl of Haddington* (1830) 8 S. 867; *Duke of Argyll* v. *Campbell*, 1912 S.C. 458.

[59] *North British Rly.* v. *Hutton* (1896) 23 R. 522.

[60] *Earl of Fife's Trs.* v. *Cuming* (1830) 8 S. 326; *Cooper's Trs.* v. *Stark's Trs.* (1898) 25 R. 1160.

[61] *Houstoun* v. *Barr*, 1911 S.C. 134.

[62] *Auld* v. *Hay* (1880) 7 R. 663; *Lord Advocate* v. *Wemyss* (1899) 2 F.(H.L.) 1, 9.

[63] *Agnew* v. *Lord Advocate* (1873) 11 M. 309. See also *Luss Estates Co.* v. *B.P. Oil Grangemouth Refinery Ltd.*, 1982 S.L.T. 457.

[64] *Forbes* v. *Livingstone* (1827) 6 S. 167; *Cadell* v. *Allan* (1905) 7 F. 606; *Millar* v. *Marquess of Lansdowne*, 1910 S.C. 618. See also *Lord Advocate* v. *Wemyss, supra.*

[65] *Duke of Richmond* v. *Earl of Seafield* (1870) 8 M. 530; *Warrand's Trs.* v. *Mackintosh* (1890) 17 R.(H.L.) 13; *Maxwell* v. *Lamont* (1903) 6 F. 245.

[66] *Meacher* v. *Blair Oliphant*, 1913 S.C. 417 at 439.

tenant for the proprietor, and may be proved by any competent evidence. In *Anderson* v. *Dickie* evidence based on the Ordnance Survey plan was accepted in the Outer House to assist in identifying ground possessed described as a lawn.[67]

(3) Searches

Property Register

21–73   The primary objective of a search against the property in the appropriate division of the Register of Sasines is to ensure that within the period covered by the prescriptive progress all registrable deeds affecting the property have been duly recorded and that there are no recorded deeds affecting the property which have not been examined. For that purpose the search should extend over the period from the recording of the foundation deed up to the date of settlement of the current transaction. A further objective is to confirm that there are no recorded deeds of whatever date which impose continuing burdens or securities upon the property. For that purpose a search which commences before the date of recording of the foundation deed may be necessary and the period of 40 years, originally recommended by a Joint Committee of Legal Societies in 1938,[68] is still appropriate. The underlying reason for that recommendation remains valid, namely, that an earlier heritable security may have been kept alive by payment of interest although no deed relating to it has been recorded within the period of the prescriptive progress, whereas it is improbable that such a security will have continued in force for 40 years without some deed relating to its transfer or transmission entering the Register. Frequently, however, a search over this longer period may safely be dispensed with in the circumstances of the particular title. For example, if the foundation deed is one of many feu grants made in the course of development of a large estate it is improbable that all the solicitors acting on behalf of numerous feuars have overlooked the existence of a security over the superiority, or if there have been several purchases of the property within the period of the prescriptive progress or shortly before it that the existence of a security will not have been disclosed by demands for payment of interest.

Personal Register

21–74   The purpose of a search in the Register of Inhibitions and Adjudications is to ensure that there is no diligence directed against the owner of an interest in heritable property which will preclude him from effectively dealing with that interest. The pursuer in an action

---

[67] 1913 2 S.L.T. 198.
[68] 1939 S.L.T. (News) 8.

against, or a creditor of, the owner may restrain him by appropriate personal diligence duly recorded in the Register from transacting with the property to the prejudice of the pursuer or creditor. The principal forms of diligence with which the conveyancer is concerned are (i) notices of litigiosity, (ii) inhibitions, and (iii) abbreviates or awards of sequestration.

1–75 Notices of litigiosity. It is competent for the pursuer in a depending real action such as an adjudication or reduction of a title to land to register a notice of litigiosity in the Register of Inhibitions and Adjudications. The calling of such an action does not of itself render heritable property litigious; to achieve that result the registration of the notice is required.[69] The style of notice is prescribed by statute.[70]

The notice states the names and designations of the pursuer(s) and defender(s) in the action. Formerly it did not describe the property affected, but now it does so.[71] It creates litigiosity only in respect of the property to which the notice relates and does not restrict the freedom of the defender in the action to deal with other property belonging to him, nor does it affect the conclusion of a transaction by the defender in respect of the property to which the notice relates if a binding contract of sale or loan has been entered into before registration of the notice. So, if a search discloses a notice of litigiosity, it is necessary to check whether (a) the property to which the current transaction relates is part of or includes that specified in the notice, and (b) binding missives have been completed before registration of the notice. If the property which is the subject of the transaction has been effectively rendered litigious by the notice, any title taken in disregard of the notice is reducible at the instance of the person who has registered it.

1–76 Inhibitions. The diligence of inhibition is competent either in execution or in security or on the dependence of an action having pecuniary conclusions.[72]

(a) *In execution or in security.* Letters of inhibition may be obtained in execution where the creditor holds a liquid document of debt or in security where the creditor holds an illiquid document of debt and the debtor is *vergens ad inopiam* or *in meditatione fugae*. The creditor presents the document of debt with a bill in the Petition Department of the Court of Session and the Clerk of Court issues letters of inhibition in prescribed form.[73] The letters are signeted, served on the debtor and thereafter entered in the Register of Inhibitions and Adjudications.

---

[69] Conveyancing (Scotland) Act 1924, s. 44(2)(*a*).

[70] Titles to Land Consolidation (Scotland) Act 1868, s. 159 and Sched. RR as amended by Law Reform (Miscellaneous Provisions) (Scotland) Act 1985, Sched. 2.

[71] Law Reform (Miscellaneous Provisions) (Scotland) Act 1985, Sched. 2, paras. 4, 5.

[72] It is also competent, on cause shown, in actions of aliment or actions in which a claim is made for an order for financial provision—Family Law (Scotland) Act 1985, s. 19.

[73] Titles to Land Consolidation (Scotland) Act 1868, s. 156 and Sched. QQ.

(b) *On dependence.* It is competent to obtain a warrant to inhibit on the dependence of an action having pecuniary conclusions. If the action is in the Court of Session a warrant to inhibit may be craved in the summons and included in the warrant of service and, after service of the summons on the defender, the inhibition may be registered in the Register of Inhibitions and Adjudications. If the action is in the sheriff court application for a warrant to inhibit may be made to the Court of Session and will be granted on production of the initial writ or a certified copy of it.

21–77 *Notice of inhibition.* Where the creditor intends to inhibit the debtor either by letters of inhibition or on the dependence of an action it is competent to register a notice of inhibition and if the inhibition is duly registered within 21 days from the date of registration of the notice it takes effect from the date of registration of the notice, but otherwise only from the date of registration of the inhibition itself.[74]

21–78 *Effect of inhibition.* An inhibition is a personal prohibition at the instance of a creditor restraining the person inhibited from contracting voluntarily any future debt or granting any deed whereby his heritable property or any part of it may be alienated or burdened to the prejudice of the inhibitor. It strikes only at future voluntary deeds, whether onerous or gratuitous, posterior to the date of its registration, is personal to the inhibited debtor and, unless followed by adjudication, gives no real right or active title to the inhibitor.

21–79 *Subjects affected by inhibition.* Inhibitions affect only heritable property but are effective whether or not the right of any person inhibited has been completed by infeftment.[75] Inhibitions do not affect *acquirenda* such as lands acquired by a person inhibited after the date of registration of the inhibition unless the lands at that date were destined to the debtor by a deed of entail or by a similar indefeasible title.[76] Arrears of rent or interest are not affected by an inhibition since they are moveable,[77] and ordinary acts of administration such as the collection of rents or of interest on a heritable debt are not precluded by an inhibition. There are older authorities for the view that an inhibition does not affect the granting of leases of ordinary duration for an adequate rent, but not leases of inordinate length, at least if the rent or the terms of the lease are unduly favourable to the tenant.[78] It is thought, however, that a tenant would not be in safety to enter into a long lease by an inhibited proprietor without obtaining the consent of the inhibitor. An inhibition against a tenant strikes at voluntary

---

[74] 1868 Act, s. 155—form of notice is prescribed in Sched. PP.
[75] *Dryburgh* v. *Gordon* (1896) 24 R. 1.
[76] 1868 Act, s. 157.
[77] *Scot* v. *Coutts* (1750) Mor. 6988.
[78] *Wedgwood* v. *Catto*, Nov. 13, 1817, F.C.; *Gordon* v. *Milne* (1780) Mor. 7008.

assignation by him of the lease where in terms of the lease the tenant had full power to assign it. The position is otherwise if the lease is assignable only with the consent of the landlord, since the lease could not be the subject of adjudication.[79]

1–80 *Persons affected by inhibition.* An inhibition is strictly personal to the debtor inhibited. As regards persons deriving right or title from the inhibited debtor:

Executors and testamentary trustees. Where the inhibited debtor dies after the inhibition takes effect his executors or testamentary trustees are not precluded by the inhibition from selling the debtor's heritable property. There are old authorities[80] to the effect that an inhibition against a debtor must after his death be renewed against his heir and, although the law of succession to heritage has been fundamentally changed, it seems that the principle, depending as it does upon the personal character of an inhibition, remains valid as regards executors.[81] Since the search may not technically be clear it is advisable for the executor or trustees, when selling, to stipulate that the inhibition will not form a ground of objection to the title. If the inhibition is executed after the death against the executor or trustees as such it is effective and will require to be discharged before a sale is effected.

Trustee in sequestration. Where the date of sequestration was before April 1, 1986, an inhibition against the bankrupt does not restrain his trustee from selling but the trustee must give the inhibitor an appropriate preference over posterior creditors in the ranking.[82,83] Where the date of sequestration was after April 1, 1986, no inhibition which takes effect within the period of 60 days before the date of sequestration is effectual to create a preference for the inhibitor and any relevant right of challenge by the inhibitor and any right to receive payment for discharge of the inhibition vest in the permanent trustee.[84] As regards inhibitions which were effective before that period, the permanent trustee may sell the property but must give effect to the inhibitor's preference in the ranking.

Liquidator. Where a company has been inhibited a liquidator appointed by the court or in a creditors' voluntary liquidation is now in the same position *quoad* inhibitions as a trustee in sequestration[85] and may sell notwithstanding the inhibition. In the case of a members' voluntary liquidation the point is academic: the company is solvent and all its creditors will be paid in full.

---

[79] *Fraser* v. *Marquis of Abercorn* (1835) 14 S. 77.

[80] Bell, *Comm.*, ii, 141; *Roberts* v. *Potter and Reid* (1829) 7 S. 611.

[81] The point is seldom of practical importance. If the debtor's estate is solvent the inhibiting creditor will be paid in full; if not, it will be administered as a sequestrated estate or by a judicial factor.

[82] Bankruptcy (Scotland) Act 1913, s. 100.

[83] As to the calculation of the preference, see *Baird & Brown* v. *Stirrat's Tr.* (1872) 10 M. 414.

[84] Bankruptcy (Scotland) Act 1985, s. 37(2).

[85] *Ibid.*, Sched. 7, para. 21.

Receiver. Conflicting views have been expressed as to the effect of an inhibition of the debtor company upon the power of a receiver to sell its heritable property, whether the inhibition was registered before or after the creation of the charge.[86] It appears to the writer that (1) if the inhibition was registered before the charge was created, the granting of the charge, being a voluntary deed, is struck at by the inhibition and the receiver cannot effectively sell in disregard of it, but (2) if the creation of the charge antedated the registration of the inhibition the receiver is free to sell notwithstanding the inhibition, since it was competent for the company to create the charge and its subsequent crystallisation on the appointment of the receiver and a subsequent sale by him are not voluntary acts of the inhibited company. Since doubt remains, however, the receiver should stipulate in the contract of sale that the inhibition will not be a ground of objection to the title.

Trustee under trust deed for creditors. A trust deed for creditors granted by an inhibited debtor is *prima facie* struck at by the inhibition. The inhibitor may be personally barred from objecting to a sale of heritage if he accedes to a protected trust deed,[87] but an argument based on personal bar does not clear the search of the inhibition and so in all cases the written consent of the inhibitor to a sale by the trustee should, if practicable, be obtained.

Heritable creditor. If the heritable creditor's security has been created prior to the registration of an inhibition against the debtor, the heritable creditor is not restrained from selling the security subjects under the power of sale in the security: that is not a voluntary act of the inhibited debtor. If the heritable creditor is himself inhibited then:

(i) The inhibition strikes at voluntary assignation, otherwise than at the debtor's behest, of the security.

(ii) It also strikes at the sale of the security subjects under power contained in the security.

(iii) It does not affect the right of the creditor to accept repayment of the secured sum and to grant a discharge or, if the debtor requests it, an assignation of the security to a new lender.[88] However, the inhibitor may give notarial intimation of the inhibition to the debtor in which case no discharge of the security will be effectual, and probably also no assignation of the security at the instigation of the debtor, except by way of action to which the inhibitor is cited.[89] It is not clear that an inhibited creditor in a security constituted by way of *ex facie* absolute disposition can grant a reconveyance to the debtor on repayment without the consent of the inhibitor. The general practice is to search against a creditor who has sold or is selling under a power of sale or

---

[86] Articles, 1983 S.L.T. (News) 145 and 177.
[87] As to protected trust deed, see Bankruptcy (Scotland) Act 1985, Sched. 5.
[88] *Mackintosh's Trs.* v. *Davidson & Garden* (1898) 25 R. 554.
[89] Act of Sederunt, Feb. 19, 1680.

has conveyed or reconveyed the security subjects as *ex facie* absolute proprietor, but otherwise it is unusual to search against heritable creditors who have discharged or are discharging a security over the subjects of search within the period of five years before a discharge is rendered unchallengeable by section 41 of the Conveyancing and Feudal Reform Act 1970.

A special problem with regard to heritable creditors is the effect of an inhibition upon post-inhibition advances by the creditor under an existing heritable security which covers future advances. Where the security was granted for periodic advances to be made from day to day, as by operations on a current banking account, it is settled that, if the security is in the form of a cash credit bond the inhibition does not strike at subsequent advances.[90] That decision to some extent depended upon a special provision in the Debts Securities (Scotland) Act 1856,[91] that infeftments taken upon cash credit bonds would be equally valid and effectual as if the whole sums advanced had been paid prior to the infeftment thereon, but the view was expressed[92] that there would be no difference between the case of a cash credit bond and a security constituted by an absolute disposition with a personal cash bond unrecorded. It would appear, although there is no direct authority, that the position is similar where the security is in the form of a standard security and it makes practical good sense—as it was put by Lord Cowan in the case cited[93]: "It is not the purpose of a bank-credit to transact an immediate loan, but to enable a person to draw out money as he may have occasion for it in trade." On the other hand it would appear that the inhibition would strike at subsequent advances by a bank beyond the amount of a previously set limit of credit or a special advance for a new project, and likewise would affect a further advance by a building society. (In practice some building societies make further advances without the precaution of making a search but usually with the protection of a general insurance indemnity).

Spouses—Matrimonial Homes (Family Protection) (Scotland) Act 1981. The occupancy rights of a non-entitled spouse cannot be the subject of an adjudication and so are not affected by an inhibition.

Proprietors of common property. Prima facie an inhibition affects a proprietor having a *pro indiviso* right of ownership in heritable property, which in effect makes the whole property unsaleable. It appears, however, that the inhibition cannot prevent any other of the common proprietors from pursuing an action of division and sale, which is an existing right enforceable, if the inhibited proprietor

---

[90] *Campbells' Tr.* v. *De Lisle's Exrs.* (1870) 9 M. 252.
[91] s. 7.
[92] at 255.
[93] at 257.

declines to sign the disposition to a purchaser, by execution of the disposition by the clerk of court under authority given by the court.[94]

21–81 *Preference of inhibitions and competition between inhibitions and other diligences.* The preference of inhibitions over post-inhibition debts is part of the law of diligence rather than of conveyancing, but the principles of double ranking are explained in the undernoted authorities.[95] The ranking of inhibitions in relation to other diligences likewise is a matter for the law of diligence—for conflicting decisions upon competition with post-inhibition arrestments see the recent decisions undernoted.[96]

21–82 **Abbreviate or award of sequestration.** The Bankruptcy (Scotland) Act 1985 (applicable where the date of sequestration was after April 1, 1986)[97] repealed the Bankruptcy (Scotland) Act 1913 but made provisions with regard to the effect as a diligence of an order of the court awarding sequestration and the prescription of such diligence similar to those made by section 44 of the Conveyancing (Scotland) Act 1924 in respect of an abbreviate of sequestration under the 1913 Act. In effect, when title is being examined, the provisions of the 1913 Act with regard to an abbreviate of sequestration apply if the date of sequestration was earlier than April 1, 1986 and the corresponding provisions of the 1985 Act with regard to an order awarding sequestration apply if the date of sequestration was after April 1, 1986.

(a) Abbreviate of sequestration. In terms of section 44 of the Bankruptcy (Scotland) Act 1913 it was obligatory for the person applying for sequestration to register in the Register of Inhibitions and Adjudications an abbreviate of the petition and first deliverance within two days after the deliverance was given, with the effect of an inhibition and citation in an adjudication of the debtor's estate. That effect expired five years after the date of registration of the abbreviate but had to be renewed by the trustee on the expiry of that period (if he had not been discharged) by registering a memorandum in prescribed form which subsisted for a further five years.

(b) Award of sequestration. Under the 1985 Act[98] the clerk of court must forthwith send a certified copy of the order awarding sequestration to the Keeper of the Register of Inhibitions and Adjudications, with the effect of an inhibition and of a citation in an adjudication of the debtor's heritable estate. That effect expires

---

[94] *Campbell* (1893) 1 S.L.T. 157. See also Law Reform (Miscellaneous Provisions) (Scotland) Act 1985, s. 17. As to a jointly-owned matrimonial home see para. 21–32.

[95] Bell, *Comm.*, ii, 141, 408; Graham Stewart, *Diligence*, 557–560; *Baird & Brown* v. *Stirrat's Tr.* (1872) 10 M. 414.

[96] *George M. Allan Ltd.* v. *Waugh's Tr.*, 1966 S.L.T. (Sh.Ct.) 17; *McGowan* v. *A. Middlemas & Sons Ltd.*, 1977 S.L.T. (Sh.Ct.) 41; *Bank of Scotland* v. *Lord Advocate*, 1977 S.L.T. 24; *Abbey National Building Society* v. *Shaik Aziz*, 1981 S.L.T. (Sh.Ct.) 29; *Ferguson & Forster* v. *Dalbeattie Finance Co.*, 1981 S.L.T. (Sh.Ct.) 53; *Halifax Building Society* v. *Smith*, 1985 S.L.T. (Sh.Ct.) 25.

[97] Bankruptcy (Scotland) Act 1985 (Commencement) Order 1985 (No. 1924) (C. 47).

[98] s. 14.

after three years from the date of sequestration (not five years as under the 1913 Act) but the permanent trustee (if not discharged) must before the end of that period send a memorandum in prescribed form to the Keeper of the said Register to be recorded in it which renews the effect above mentioned for a further period of three years, but that effect is only preserved thereafter if such a memorandum is so recorded before the expiry of every subsequent period of three years, unless the trustee has previously completed his title to the land or recorded in the Register of Sasines a memorandum in the form of Schedule 0 to the Conveyancing (Scotland) Act 1924.[99]

As regards *acquirenda*, *i.e.* estate which is acquired by the bankrupt between the date of sequestration and the effective date of the debtor's discharge and which would have vested in the trustee if it had been part of the bankrupt's estate at the date of sequestration, the provisions of the 1913 Act and the 1985 Act differ. Under the 1913 Act *acquirenda* did not automatically vest in the trustee under the sequestration, but the trustee could obtain an order vesting *acquirenda* in him and was required within one month after the vesting order to record in the Register of Sasines a memorandum in the form of Schedule 0 to the Conveyancing (Scotland) Act 1924 which published the order on record.[1] Under the 1985 Act any estate which is *acquirenda* vests in the permanent trustee as at the date of its acquisition by the bankrupt, who must immediately notify the trustee, and any person who holds such estate must convey or deliver it to the trustee. A person who has conveyed such later acquired estate to the bankrupt or to anyone on the instructions of the bankrupt in good faith and without knowledge of the sequestration is not liable to the trustee but must account to him for any proceeds of the transaction which are in his hands.[2]

–83 Extinction of personal diligences. Any personal diligence may cease to be effective by:

(i) *Discharge* by the creditor who effected it, normally by a probative discharge which is recorded in the Register of Inhibitions and Adjudications; or

(ii) *Recall or restriction* by the court when the decree authorises the Keeper of the Register to mark the Register appropriately; or

(iii) *Prescription.* The Conveyancing (Scotland) Act 1924 provides that all notices of litigiosity and inhibitions registered in the Register prescribe and are of no effect after the lapse of five years from the date on which they took effect and in the case of notices of litigiosity on the expiry of six months after final decree is pronounced in the action

---

[99] Conveyancing (Scotland) Act 1924, s. 44(4)(*a*) and (*b*) as amended by Bankruptcy (Scotland) Act 1985, Sched. 7, para. 5.

[1] Bankruptcy (Scotland) Act 1913, s. 98: Conveyancing Amendment (Scotland) Act 1938, s. 7(1)(*a*).

[2] Bankruptcy (Scotland) Act 1985, s. 32(6) and (7).

which created litigiosity.[3] After an inhibition has prescribed the debtor, if he has not been re-inhibited is free to alienate his heritable property, but if he has done so while the inhibition was still effective, does the expiry of the five-year period without the inhibitor having taken steps to reduce the alienation result in the loss of his right to reduce? The point has not been determined by any post-1924 authority, but in practice a five years' search is regarded as sufficient.

21–84 Period of search. The principal objective of the provisions in section 44 of the Conveyancing (Scotland) Act 1924 was to secure that a search for five years prior to a transaction in heritable property would disclose any diligences which remained effective. It is now the settled practice to search in the Register of Inhibitions and Adjudications for that period, despite the doubt which may exist whether a violation of an earlier inhibition founds an action of reduction when the inhibition has prescribed without court proceedings having been instituted.[4]

21–85 Persons searched against. The parties to be searched against in the personal register are all those who have within the period of the prescriptive progress had proprietorial rights in the property which is the subject of the current transaction, whether such rights have been completed by infeftment or not, so long as they could have been made the subject of an adjudication. These parties include (1) consenters to dispositions, (2) executors or trustees who have granted or consented to dispositions, (3) a heritable creditor who has sold the property under a power of sale, (4) a heritable creditor under an *ex facie* absolute disposition who has conveyed or reconveyed the property and also the beneficial owner who was the true proprietor, (5) a partnership, the trustees who held the property on its behalf and all the partners, whether trustees or not, (6) a trustee in sequestration but not the bankrupt, (7) a liquidator of a company but not the company being wound up, (8) a receiver and the debtor company, and (9) a trustee under a trust deed for creditors and the debtor who granted it. If a proprietor has been searched against for five years prior to the transaction by which he has been divested of his interest in the property and no incumbrances or diligences have been disclosed thereby, it is unnecessary to search further against such proprietor. In order to ensure the identification of a person searched against, all known designations of the person, such as changes of address, should be stated when the search is being instructed.

21–86 Clear search. A search in the Register of Inhibitions and Adjudications is not clear if it discloses any subsisting diligence prejudicial to the current transaction, unless it is evident from a public register or

---

[3] s. 44(3)(*a*).
[4] See para. 21–83.

document that the diligence is no longer so prejudicial. So a search is clear:

(i) where the transaction is a sale by a trustee in bankruptcy although it discloses an inhibition against the bankrupt, or

(ii) where the transaction is a sale by the liquidator of a company although it discloses an inhibition against the company, or

(iii) where an inhibition or notice of litigiosity was registered more than five years ago and has not been renewed, or

(iv) where an inhibition was against the granter of or a consenter to a disposition or standard security which was recorded before the inhibition was registered.

The position is otherwise if the fact that a diligence does not prejudice the current transaction is ascertainable only from examination of a private document: a purchaser who has contracted for production of a clear search cannot be compelled to assess the effectiveness of the document in negativing the restraint which the diligence imposed.[5] An example of common occurrence is the registration of an inhibition against a seller after binding missives of sale have been completed but before delivery of a disposition on settlement. Although the disposition is not a voluntary conveyance since the seller is contractually bound to grant and deliver it, the search is not clear. Various practical arrangements may be made to overcome the difficulty but if the inhibitor is unco-operative intimation should be made to him that an action will be raised against him for declarator that the inhibition does not affect the sale and, since the action will have been rendered necessary by the recalcitrance of the inhibitor, he may be found liable in expenses.[6]

Register of Charges and Company Files

1–87 In transactions which involve a sale by an incorporated company or a loan to such a company additional searches are required.

(i) Sales. In strict theory it is unnecessary to search the Register of Charges in the case of an outright sale of a company's heritable property. Any fixed security over its heritable property will have been disclosed by the search in the Register of Sasines, and a floating charge of its nature does not prevent the company from selling its heritable property. Nevertheless it may be prudent to instruct a search in the Register of Charges. Some floating charges, however inappropriately, contain a prohibition of sale of the company's heritable property without the consent of the holder of the charge. Although that may not effectively preclude a sale without such consent it would constitute a breach of the bargain between the company and the holder of the

---

[5] *Duke of Devonshire* v. *Fletcher* (1874) 1 R. 1056; *Dryburgh* v. *Gordon* (1896) 24 R. 1.
[6] For a fuller discussion of possible courses of action, see para. 23–15.

charge and may precipitate the appointment of a receiver and so render the precautions aftermentioned against such an appointment peculiarly important.

It is necessary to search the company's file in the Register of Companies to guard against certain eventualities, *viz.*—

(a) Liquidation. In a winding-up by the court a copy of the winding-up order must be forwarded "forthwith" to the Registrar of Companies,[7] and in a voluntary winding-up the liquidator must within 14 days of his appointment deliver to the Registrar of Companies notice of his appointment.[8] Two risks remain, namely, (i) there is no requirement for a copy of the winding-up order or the notice of appointment of the liquidator to be entered in the Register of Charges, and (ii) failure by the liquidator in a voluntary winding-up to deliver the notice of his appointment timeously may render the liquidator liable to a fine[9] but does not invalidate his appointment. It is therefore necessary to search the company's file.

(b) Floating charges and receivers. (i) A floating charge may have been created by the company shortly before settlement of the sale transaction but registered within 21 days of its creation,[10] a date which may be after settlement of the sale transaction. (ii) A receiver may have been appointed by the holder of a floating charge or by the court shortly before settlement of the sale transaction but registered in the Register of Charges within the permitted seven days,[11,12] a date which may be later than the settlement of the transaction. Again it does not appear that failure to deliver the certified copy of the instrument of appointment or interlocutor timeously affects the validity of the appointment as at the date of the instrument of appointment or the interlocutor,[13] as the case may be.

In order to provide safeguards to the purchaser against such risks the practice is to stipulate for and obtain an obligation by the selling company's solicitor to clear any entries appearing in the Register of Charges within 22 days and in the company's file within 16 days after the date of settlement of the sale transaction, and also to obtain an assurance in writing from the directors or a director of the company that no steps have been taken by any person to wind up the company and that no new undisclosed charges have been created by the company

---

[7] Companies Act 1985, s. 525(1).

[8] *Ibid.*, s. 600(1).

[9] *Ibid.*, s. 600(2).

[10] *Ibid.*, s. 410(2).

[11] If appointed by instrument a certified copy of the instrument must be delivered to the Registrar of Companies within seven days of its execution, who enters particulars of it in the Register of Charges—1985 Act, s. 469(1) and (5).

[12] If appointed by the court a certified copy of the interlocutor must be delivered by the petitioner to the Registrar of Companies within seven days of its date or such longer period as the court may allow for registration in the Register of Charges—1985 Act, s. 470(3).

[13] 1985 Act, ss. 469(6), 470(5).

prior to settlement and that there are no circumstances known whereby any proceedings for winding up the company or appointment of a receiver of any of its assets will be commenced by any person within 30 days after the date of settlement. The selling company's solicitor may be unwilling to undertake personal liability as regards searches in the Register of Charges and in the company's file, particularly where the consideration is substantial, but the assurances from the directors or a director should be obtainable. A further precaution may be to obtain a letter from the holders of any floating charges that these have not crystallised nor are there existing circumstances known to the holders which render it likely that a receiver will be appointed within the period of 30 days mentioned.

(ii) Secured loans. In such a transaction it is necessary to search in the Register of Charges to ensure that there is no subsisting floating charge which prohibits the creation of any subsequent charge or security ranking prior to or *pari passu* with it.[14] Further, since much the same risks as to liquidation or the creation of a recent floating charge or appointment of a receiver exist in relation to a transaction of loan, the same procedures and safeguards already outlined in relation to a sale should be followed and obtained.

Register of Entails

–88   As to searches in the Register of Entails, see Volume IV.

REGISTERED TITLES

First registration

–89   Where the transaction induces first registration[15] or where voluntary registration is being sought the procedure in examination of title is similar to that already described in paragraphs 21–05 to 21–62 *supra*, subject to the additional matters aftermentioned.

–90   **Information to be furnished on application.** Since the title will also be examined by the Keeper for the purposes of first registration it is essential that the foundation writ, the prescriptive progress of titles, any deeds imposing burdens on the subjects and all unrecorded links in title be furnished to the Keeper with the application, together with the information required in Form 1 and relevant supporting documents.[16]

–91   **Possession.** In order that the Keeper may issue a land certificate without exclusion of indemnity possession for the relevant prescriptive period is required. If any person is in possession of the subjects or any

---

[14] As to ranking of floating charges and fixed securities, see Companies Act 1985, s. 464.

[15] As to transactions inducing first registration, see Land Registration (Scotland) Act 1979, s. 2.

[16] For further details of documents to be furnished, see para. 24–19.

part of them adverse to the interest of the applicant, that must be disclosed in the reply to Question 1 of Part B of Form 1. If a judicial challenge has been made of the applicant's right of possession the Keeper should be informed in the reply to Question 10 of Part B of Form 1.

21–92 Searches and reports. Searches in the property and personal registers are not required since they are replaced by the Form 10 report (with a Form 11 report to be instructed nearer settlement), and the Form 10 report should be available when examination of the title is being made.[17] The Form 10 and Form 11 reports relate to the Register of Sasines, the Land Register and the Register of Inhibitions and Adjudications, but, if a company is granting the conveyance or a loan, searches in the Register of Charges and Company Files should be instructed separately.[18]

Dealings with registered interests

21–93 When a title has been registered without exclusion of indemnity it is unnecessary for the solicitor acting for a purchaser or lender to examine the sufficiency or validity of any deed which has led to an entry in the title sheet. He is concerned only with deeds or links in title later in date than that of the last registration which have not been entered in the title sheet. Discharged security writs need not be examined if they are not disclosed as charges in the charges section of the land certificate. Any undischarged security deeds whether in the Register of Sasines or the Land Register, together with any relevant links in title and a draft discharge (if the security is to be discharged in the current dealing), will require to be examined. In effect the documents which a purchaser's solicitor need examine are (1) the land certificate,[19] (2) any charge certificate, (3) draft discharges of any outstanding heritable securities, (4) any links in title connecting the proprietor as shown in the proprietorship section of the title sheet with the present seller or relating to an outstanding heritable security, (5) any dealings with the registered interest which have not been registered, (6) a Form 12 report (with a Form 13 report to be instructed nearer settlement), and (7) any Form P 17 report.[20]

Where the title has been registered with an exclusion of indemnity, prior titles so far as relating to the exclusion require to be examined in the usual way.

21–94 Reports. A Form 12 report should be obtained from the date of issue

---

[17] As to the procedure in obtaining Form 10 and Form 11 reports, see paras. 23–19 and 23–20.
[18] See para. 21–87.
[19] Where the land certificate in respect of a previous recent transaction is not yet available, a request may be made to the Keeper to expedite its issue.
[20] R.T.P.B., paras. G.3.09, G.3.10.

of the land certificate in order to disclose any subsequent entries in the Land Register and in the Register of Inhibitions and Adjudications against the parties disclosed in the proprietorship section of the title sheet and any other party in respect of whom a search is ordered on application for the Form 12 report. If there has been any significant delay between receipt of the Form 12 report and settlement of the transaction, continuation of the Form 12 report may be obtained by instructing a Form 13 report.[21]

DEFECTIVELY EXPRESSED DOCUMENTS

Rectification

–95   In terms of section 8 of the Law Reform (Miscellaneous Provisions) (Scotland) Act 1985 the Court of Session or the sheriff having jurisdiction may order the rectification of (1) a document intended to give effect to an agreement which fails to express accurately the common intention of the parties to the agreement at the date when it was made, or (2) a document intended to create, transfer, vary or renounce a right, not being a document falling within (1) above, which fails to express accurately the intention of the granter of the document at the date when it was executed.[22] When the court orders rectification of a document (the original document) under the above provision it may also, at its own instance or on an application made to it, order the rectification of any other document intended for any of the above-mentioned purposes which is defectively expressed by reason of the defect in the original document.[23] Subject to the protective provisions in section 9 of the Act,[24] the rectification is retroactive to the original date of the document and, if recorded in the Register of Sasines and the order is also recorded, to the original recording date of the document.[25] It is competent to register in the Register of Inhibitions and Adjudications a notice of application for rectification of a deed relating to land if authority for service or citation has been granted in respect of the application and the land to which the application relates is rendered litigious as from the date of registration of the notice. The notice must specify the names and designations of the parties to the application and the date when authority for service or citation was granted, and must contain a description of the land to which the application relates.[26] As to any necessary rectification of the Land Register to give effect to an order rectifying a deed and exclusion of indemnity arising therefrom, see paragraphs 24–49 and 24–53(*p*), *infra*.

---

[21] R.T.P.B., paras. F.12, F.13.
[22] s. 8(1).
[23] s. 8(3).
[24] See para. 21–96.
[25] s. 8(4) and (5).
[26] s. 8(7) and (8).

Protection of other interests

21–96   The court will grant an order for rectification of a document only where it is satisfied that either (a) the interests of a person (other than a party to the agreement or the granter of the document) who has acted or refrained from acting in reliance on the terms of the document or on the title sheet of an interest in land registered in the Land Register to which the document relates would not be adversely affected to a material extent by the rectification, or (b) such person has consented to the proposed rectification.[27] That protection will not be given to a person who knew or ought to have known at the time when he acted or refrained from acting in reliance on the terms of the document that the document or the title sheet failed accurately to express the common intention of the parties to the document or of the granter of it or whose reliance on its terms was otherwise unreasonable.[28] The court may, for the purpose of protecting the interest of any such third party, order that the effective date of rectification of a document or of its recording in the Register of Sasines may be later than the original date of the deed or of its recording.[29]

Reduction and prescription of rectification

21–97   Where a third party is adversely affected to a material extent by a rectification of which he was unaware, the Court of Session may either reduce the rectifying order or require the person who applied for it to pay compensation to that third party, provided that application for reduction or compensation is made within five years after the making of the rectification order or two years after the making of the order first came to the notice of the third party affected, whichever of these two periods is the earlier.[30] Section 44(3)(*a*) of the Conveyancing (Scotland) Act 1924 is amended appropriately to apply the five years' prescription to rectification orders, and section 46 of the 1924 Act is made applicable to rectification of a document in the same way as it applies to the reduction of a deed.[31]

PROTECTION OF PURCHASERS

Statutory protections for purchasers

21–98   **(1) Trusts (Scotland) Act 1961, s. 2.** In transactions entered into on or after August 27, 1961, in which trustees under any trust deed enter into a transaction with any person under which the trustees purport to do in

---

[27] s. 9(1) and (2).
[28] s. 9(3).
[29] s. 9(4) and (5).
[30] s. 9(7) and (8).
[31] Sched. 2.

relation to the trust estate or any part thereof an act of any of the descriptions specified in paragraphs (*a*) to (*ee*) of subsection (1) of section 4 of the Trusts (Scotland) Act 1921 (which include sales of heritable property, feus and leases) the validity of the transaction and of any title acquired by the second party under it is not challengeable by the second party or any other person on the ground that the act is at variance with the terms or purposes of the trust.[32] Nothing in the section affects any question of liability between any of the trustees and any co-trustee or any of the beneficiaries. It may be observed that the protection afforded by the section is not dependent upon the person who transacts with the trustees having acted in good faith. The reasoning which prompted the enactment of the section was that it was inequitable that a person transacting with trustees for value should require to peril the validity of the title he received upon his construction of the powers, express or implied, of the trustees and that any question on that matter should be left as an issue between the trustees and the beneficiaries. Since in many cases the person transacting with the trustees would be aware from examination of the relevant trust deed that some doubt existed whether the proposed transaction was at variance with the terms or purposes of the trust, a requirement of good faith on his part would have significantly limited the value of the protection. In the case of a transaction by a trustee who acts under the supervision of the Accountant of Court the section applies only if the Accountant has consented to the transaction. The section has no application to trustees under non-Scottish trusts.

(2) Protections dependent upon good faith. See paragraph 21–60 *supra* for examples of transactions in which protection under various statutes is conditional upon good faith of the person to whom the protection is given.

---

[32] See Vol. I, para. 1–24.

CHAPTER 22

DISPOSITIONS

History and development

22–01   The evolution of the disposition in its modern form has been outlined in Chapter 16: for a more detailed account see the undernoted text.[1]

STRUCTURE

Clauses

22–02   In its modern form the disposition comprises the following:

(1) Inductive clause, specifying granter, grantee and consideration.

(2) Dispositive clause containing words of conveyance, any destination, description of property, subject to any reservations, burdens and conditions incorporated by reference to earlier deeds in which they were created or specified at length if constituted for the first time in the disposition itself.

(3) Entry clause.

(4) Clause of deduction of title, if required.

(5) Assignation of writs. ⎤

(6) Assignation of rents. ⎬ These clauses now generally unnecessary.[2]

(7) Obligation of relief. ⎦

(8) Warrandice clause.

(9) Attestation clause.

22–03   Inductive clause.[3] If the granter of a disposition is infeft he will normally be described as "heritable proprietor of the subjects hereinafter disponed"; if he is uninfeft he is usually described as "proprietor" or "having right to" the subjects.[4]

22–04   Dispositive clause. This is the ruling clause of a conveyance of land and if clear is the sole measure of the property conveyed, the person to whom it is conveyed and the real burdens and conditions which affect it.[5]

22–05   Clause of entry. This clause determines the date from which, in a question between the granter and the grantee, the latter acquires the right to possess the property and its rents or fruits. If the disposition omits to state the date, entry is at the first term of Whitsunday or Martinmas after the date or the last date of the disposition, unless it appears from the terms of the deed that another term of entry was intended.[6]

---

[1] Craigie, *Heritable Rights*, Chap. V.
[2] Land Registration (Scotland) Act 1979, s. 16.
[3] See Vol. I, para. 4–02.
[4] As to deduction of title by uninfeft granters, see paras. 22–06 to 22–11, 22–53 and 22–54.
[5] See Vol. I, para. 4–26. As to description of property see Chap. 18, and as to reference to burdens see Chap. 19.
[6] Conveyancing (Scotland) Act 1874, s. 28.

–06 Deduction of title clause. A person having right to land but whose title thereto has not been recorded may grant a disposition in which he deduces his title from the person last infeft in or as nearly as may be in terms of Form No. 1 of Schedule A to the Conveyancing (Scotland) Act 1924.[7] When the disposition is recorded in the appropriate Register of Sasines the title of the disponee is completed as if it had been completed by a recorded notarial instrument under the pre-1924 practice.[8]

–07 *(1) Persons who may deduce title.* The facility of deducing title is available to persons who have a right to land of such a character that they could at their own hand without the intervention of any other person have completed title to the land. So title may be deduced by (1) an executor-nominate or an executor-dative in whom the heritable property of the deceased has vested for the purposes of administration,[9] (2) trustees under a trust deed which contains a general conveyance of estate which includes land, (3) a judicial factor on a trust estate which contains land,[10] or (4) a person holding an unrecorded special disposition in his favour. Title may not be deduced, however, by (1) a person who has a right to land under completed missives of purchase (who still requires a conveyance by the seller before he can complete title), or (2) a legatee to whom testamentary trustees or executors have been directed to convey heritable property forming part of the trust estate. The right must be one which is capable of transfer to another person: an unrecorded writ of *clare constat*, which is personal to the grantee, could not have been assigned to another person and so is not a right which can be used as a basis for deduction of title.

–08 *(2) Midcouples or links in title.* It is competent to use as midcouples or links in deduction of title any statute, conveyance, deed, instrument, decree or other writing whereby a right to land or to any estate or interest in land is vested in or transmitted to any person, or in virtue of which a notarial instrument or notice of title could be expede, or which could be used as a midcouple or link of title in expeding such instrument or notice, or any minute of a meeting at which any person is appointed to any place or office if such appointment involves a right to land or to an estate or interest in land. A copy or excerpt from such a minute certified as correct by the chairman of the meeting or other person duly authorised to sign the minute or give excerpts therefrom, or by a solicitor or notary public, is *prima facie* evidence of the terms of the minute.[11] The terms "conveyance" and "deed" are defined

---

[7] s. 3. As to the principle involved, see para. 16–56.
[8] See para. 22–10 as regards deduction of title in transactions inducing first registration in Land Register and dealings with registered interests.
[9] Succession (Scotland) Act 1964, s. 14.
[10] Conveyancing Amendment (Scotland) Act 1938, s. 1.
[11] Conveyancing (Scotland) Act 1924, s. 5(1).

widely and include extracts and office copies[12] and probate or letters of administration or exemplifications thereof issued by any court of probate in England or Northern Ireland, which are equivalent for the purpose of deduction of title to the will or settlement on which they proceed.[13] Extracts of deeds registered in the Books of Council and Session or sasine extracts of deeds recorded in the Register of Sasines are equivalent to the originals.[14] It is unnecessary to narrate the contents of any deed or writing included as a midcouple or link,[15] but it is desirable to insert a brief narrative of any fact or circumstance which makes the devolution of the right readily intelligible, *e.g.* the death of one of two or more persons jointly entitled.

22–09 *(3) Practice.* The statutory form of the clause in Form No. 1 of Schedule A to the 1924 Act and detailed rules as to the practice in use of the facility of deduction of title are fully considered later.[16]

22–10 *(4) Registered titles*
(a) Dispositions inducing first registration. A disposition by an uninfeft granter in a transaction which induces first registration in the Land Register should contain a clause of deduction of title,[17] and any midcouples or links connecting the granter to the last recorded title should be included in the deeds sent to the Keeper with the application for registration.

(b) Dealings. A disposition conveying property held on a title already registered, however, does not require a clause of deduction of title. Many of the transactions or events which would be unrecorded links in a title recorded in the Register of Sasines are registrable in the Land Register,[18] *e.g.* confirmation of executors, deeds of assumption of or minutes of resignation by trustees, minutes of meetings appointing new trustees, dockets transferring land under section 15(2) of the Succession (Scotland) Act 1964 or a certificate of incorporation on change of name of a company.[19] All that is necessary is to produce to the Keeper with the application for registration of the dealing any midcouples or links in title which have not been registered, and sections 3 and 5 of and Form No. 1 of Schedule A to the 1924 Act are disapplied.[20]

---

[12] *Ibid.*, s. 2(1)(c).
[13] Conveyancing (Scotland) Act 1874, s. 51; Conveyancing (Scotland) Acts (1874 and 1879) Amendment Act 1887, s. 5. See also Succession (Scotland) Act 1964, s. 15(1) proviso added by Law Reform (Miscellaneous Provisions) (Scotland) Act 1968, s. 19.
[14] Registration Act 1698 (c. 4); Writs Execution (Scotland) Act 1877, s. 5; Registration Act 1617 (c. 16); Titles to Land Consolidation (Scotland) Act 1868, s. 142; Conveyancing and Feudal Reform (Scotland) Act 1970, s. 45.
[15] 1924 Act, s. 2(3).
[16] See para. 22–54.
[17] R.T.P.B., para. D.1.17.
[18] Land Registration (Scotland) Act 1979, s. 2(4)(c).
[19] R.T.P.B., para. D.1.15.
[20] 1979 Act, s. 15(3).

2–11 *(5) Deeds in which deduction of title competent.* The facility of deducing title is available in terms of section 3 of the 1924 Act in dispositions and deeds relating to the assignation, discharge or restriction of heritable securities. The facility is also available in standard securities.[21] In other deeds which in accordance with feudal principles require infeftment of the granter, *e.g.* feu grants and leases, it is incompetent to deduce title. Moreover certain deeds of conveyance of land, which are broadly equivalent in effect to dispositions, such as a Schedule A conveyance under section 80 of the Lands Clauses Consolidation (Scotland) Act 1845 or a notarial instrument under section 74 or 76 of that Act, are required by the Act to be recorded on behalf of the acquiring body and cannot be used as unrecorded links of title, either in a disposition to be recorded in the Register of Sasines or a disposition inducing first registration in the Land Register.

2–12 **Clause of assignation of writs.** The statutory clause "And I assign the writs" in a disposition is defined as importing, unless specially qualified, an absolute and unconditional assignation to the writs and evidents in an inventory annexed to the disposition, and to all open procuratories, clauses and precepts (if any) therein contained, and to all unrecorded conveyances to which the disponer has right.[22] Section 16(1) of the Land Registration (Scotland) Act 1979 renders it unnecessary to incorporate in any deed conveying an interest in land executed on or after April 4, 1979, a clause of assignation of writs, and provides that any such deed shall, unless specially qualified, import an assignation to the grantee of the title deeds and searches and all deeds not duly recorded and shall (a) impose an obligation on the granter or any successor to deliver all title deeds and searches relating exclusively to the interest conveyed and to make forthcoming to the grantee and his successors at his or their expense any title deeds and searches which remain in the possession of the granter or any successor and which relate partly to the interest conveyed, (b) import an assignation to the grantee of the granter's right to require any person having custody thereof to exhibit or deliver any title deeds or searches remaining undelivered, and (c) impose on the grantee or any successor an obligation to make forthcoming on all necessary occasions to any party having an interest therein any deeds and searches which have been delivered to the grantee but which relate partly to interests other than the interest conveyed to the grantee. The statutory effect of a disposition which omits the clause of assignation of writs is consistent with the previous expression of the clause inserted in normal cases, and now it is usual to omit the clause, leaving the rights and obligations of parties in relation to writs to be regulated by the statutory provision. In

---

[21] Conveyancing and Feudal Reform (Scotland) Act 1970, s. 12. As regards heritable securities, see Vol. III.
[22] Titles to Land Consolidation (Scotland) Act 1868, s. 8 and Sched. B.

exceptional cases where some qualification is desired the clause might run:

> And I assign the writs to the same effect as is provided by section 16(1) of the Land Registration (Scotland) Act 1979 if the clause of assignation of writs were omitted subject to the qualification that . . .

There may still be circumstances, *e.g.* where there are numerous undelivered writs creating complex or special rights, to include a clause of assignation of writs and an inventory of writs with notation of custody in accordance with former practice.[23]

22–13 **Clause of assignation of rents.** The statutory clause "And I assign the rents" in a disposition is defined as importing, unless specially qualified, an assignation to the rents to become due for the possession following the term of entry, according to the legal and not the conventional terms, unless in the case of forehand rents, in which case it shall be held to import an assignation to the rents payable at the conventional terms subsequent to the date of entry.[24] In the case of dispositions executed on or after April 4, 1979, section 16(3) of the Land Registration (Scotland) Act 1979 renders it unnecessary to incorporate a clause of assignation of rents and provides that any such disposition shall, unless specially qualified, import an assignation of the rents payable (i) in the case of backhand rents, at the legal terms following the date of entry, and (ii) in the case of forehand rents, at the conventional terms following that date. No express provision is made by the 1979 Act for rents which are neither backhand nor forehand, but in law the purchaser will be entitled to the rents payable for the possession following the term of entry. The legal terms for payment of rent are (a) for urban subjects the end of the period of possession for which they are due, *e.g.* entry Whitsunday 1987, first half-year's rent payable Martinmas 1987, (b) for arable farms (including farms predominantly arable)[25] when entry is normally at Martinmas, first half-year's rent at Whitsunday after sowing and second half-year's rent at Martinmas after reaping, and (c) for pastoral farms (including farms predominantly pastoral) when entry is normally at Whitsunday after lambing when stock can most readily be valued, first half-year's rent at Whitsunday when entry is taken and next half-year's rent at Martinmas following. Both sets of statutory provisions are broadly similar in effect and in most cases result in the purchaser receiving the first rent payable at the term following his date of entry. The only difference in effect appears to be in the case of backhand rents of arable or pastoral subjects (backhand rents of urban property are virtually unknown).

---

[23] See R.T.P.B., para. C.99.
[24] Titles to Land Consolidation (Scotland) Act 1868, s. 8 and Sched. B.
[25] *Mackenzie's Trs.* v. *Somerville* (1900) 2 F. 1278.

The provisions of the 1868 Act define the rents which the purchaser receives as those "to become due for the possession following the term of entry according to the legal and not the conventional terms," with the result that where the rents are conventionally backhand the purchaser does not receive the half-year's rent payable six months after his date of entry and the first rent he receives is that payable one year after entry. The 1979 Act, however, deals specially with backhand rents and provides that the purchaser will receive the rents payable at the conventional terms following the date of entry, with the result that the purchaser receives the rent actually payable at the first term following his date of entry regardless of the period of possession in respect of which it is conventionally payable. In order to avoid questions it may be advisable to insert in a disposition of a landed estate an express clause of assignation of rents defining the rents which the disponee is to receive by reference to an annexed schedule of the let properties and recoverable rents with a statement of the first rents which will be receivable by the disponee.

2–14 **Obligation of relief.** The clause in the statutory form "And I bind myself to free and relieve the said disponee and his foresaids of all feuduties and public burdens," unless specially qualified, imports an obligation to relieve of all feuduties payable to the superior and of all ground annuals and public, parochial and local burdens due from or on account of the lands conveyed prior to the date of entry.[26] In the case of dispositions executed on or after April 4, 1979, it is unnecessary to insert the clause; if it is omitted the disposition implies, unless there is some special qualification, an obligation on the granter to relieve the grantee of all feuduties, ground annuals, annuities and public, parochial and local burdens exigible in respect of the interest in the land conveyed prior to the date of entry.[27]

Feuduties and ground annuals. Where the disposition is granted on the occasion of a sale and the feuduty or ground annual has been allocated it will be compulsorily redeemed and the only relevance of the clause if expressed or the obligation if the clause is omitted is to preserve the right of recourse of the grantee against the granter if for any reason the court permits the superior or holder of the ground annual to recover from the grantee under section 5(7) of the Land Tenure Reform (Scotland) Act 1974. If the feuduty or ground annual is unallocated the obligation of the granter is to relieve the grantee of the proportion of the burden exigible from the subjects conveyed in respect of the period prior to the date of entry calculated on the basis that it accrues *de die in diem*. If the date of entry occurs between payment term dates the purchaser should deduct from the price the proportion

---

[26] Titles to Land Consolidation (Scotland) Act 1868, s. 8 and Sched. B.
[27] Land Registration (Scotland) Act, s. 16(3).

of the burden due by the seller. Where the disposition is granted in favour of an authority possessing compulsory purchase powers the feuduty or ground annual, whether allocated or not, will be redeemed by the acquiring authority.[28]

Standard charge. The position is the same as in the case of a feuduty or ground annual. If the feuduty or ground annual was redeemed voluntarily prior to the sale the standard charge will have remained unredeemed, but an allocated standard charge must be redeemed on sale.[29]

Local rates. Payable for year to March 31, and will normally be apportioned by rating authority on request when entry and possession occurs on an intermediate date. Alternatively the parties may apportion rates at settlement. Water rates, if separately assessed, may be dealt with similarly.

Annuities or other continuing burdens. These are apportionable from day to day in respect of time.[30]

22–15 **Clause of warrandice.** Warrandice should always be expressed in a disposition. As to the appropriate degree of warrandice, the statutory import of warrandice in conveyances and necessary qualifications, see Volume I, paragraphs 4–30 to 4–39. In dispositions granted for valuable consideration by persons who are not beneficial owners of the subjects conveyed such as trustees, executors, judicial factors or receivers the grant of warrandice will be qualified usually to the effect of restricting the warrandice of the granter to fact and deed and binding the beneficial owner in absolute warrandice.[31]

SPECIALTIES AS TO PARTIES

Capacity and description of parties

22–16 The capacity and powers of parties to grant deeds relating to heritage have already been considered in Volume I, Chapter 2, and the form of deeds to and in favour of particular parties in Volume I, Chapter 4. For the convenience of readers the relevant paragraphs of these chapters applicable to particular parties are indicated in relation to each party; additional matters applicable to dispositions by and to each party are dealt with in this chapter.

22–17 **Personal capacity—foreign element.** The general rule is that a person's capacity to deal with heritable or immoveable property is regulated by

---

[28] Land Tenure Reform (Scotland) Act, s. 6.
[29] *Ibid.*, ss. 4(7) and 5(12).
[30] Apportionment Act 1870, s. 2.
[31] See styles in paras. 22–48, 22–50.

the *lex situs* rather than by the law of his domicile.[32] The rule has not always been consistently adopted,[33] and the safe course is to assume that a foreigner has capacity to deal with Scottish heritage only if such capacity is imputed to him both by Scots law and the law of his domicile.[34] If there is any doubt on the matter, as in the case of a pupil or minor domiciled abroad, an application may be made by his guardian to the Court of Session for authority to sell or deal with the heritable property.[34]

2–18 **Pupils.**[35] Although the father and mother of a pupil have equal rights and authority to hold the office of tutor which may be exercised by either without the other,[36] it is preferable in an important transaction such as the sale of the pupil's heritable property that the disposition be granted by both parents although it is not a valid objection if a disposition by one parent only is offered.

2–19 **Minors.**[37] Where the disposition is granted by a minor having a curator the power of disposal is in the minor and the consent of either parent as curator is sufficient.

2–20 **Trustees**

Granters.[38] A disposition by trustees of an *inter vivos* trust should be granted by the trustees (with designations) currently acting specifying the trust deed with the name and designation of the truster and the date and (if registered) registration date of the deed. Any changes in the personnel of the trustees since the last infeftment in the subjects should be contained in the clause of deduction of title. A disposition by testamentary trustees should be granted by the trustees currently acting specifying the confirmation by reference to its date and the sheriff court from which it was issued with, where necessary, a clause of deduction of title in appropriate terms. In dispositions for valuable consideration warrandice by the trustees will be from fact and deed only, the trust estate and the beneficiaries therein being bound in absolute warrandice.

Grantees.[39] A disposition in favour of trustees under an *inter vivos* trust should be granted in favour of the trustees named and designed as trustees acting under the trust deed identified by name and designation of the truster and date and, if registered, registration date of the deed

---

[32] *Bank of Africa Ltd.* v. *Cohen* [1909] 2 Ch. 129.

[33] See Anton, 392–394 and authorities there cited.

[34] *McFadzean*, 1917 S.C. 142; *Collins*, 1921 2 S.L.T. 36.

[35] As to capacity and powers of tutors, see Vol. I, paras. 2–05 to 2–08, 2–27, 2–29. As to form of deed, see Vol. I, paras. 4–12, 4–15.

[36] Guardianship Act 1973, s. 10.

[37] As to capacity and powers, see Vol. I, paras. 2–21, 2–23, 2–27, 2–29. As to form of deeds, see Vol. I, para. 4–13.

[38] As to capacity and powers, see Vol. I, paras. 2–40 to 2–52. As to form, see Vol. I, para. 4–07.

[39] As to capacity and power to purchase heritage, see Vol. I, paras. 2–53 to 2–55.

"and their successors in office and the survivors and survivor of them all as trustees foresaid and their assignees."

22–21 **Executors.**[40] Dispositions by executors are granted by the executors designed acting under the confirmation identified by the date and court of issue with, if necessary, a clause of deduction of title in appropriate terms. If the subjects disponed have been contained in an eik to confirmation, the eik should be specified also.

22–22 **Foreign trustees and executors**

(1) Title. An English or Northern Irish probate or letters of administration, or an exemplification thereof, may be used to complete title to Scottish heritage[41] or as a midcouple or link of title in deducing title in a disposition thereof.[42] Probate or letters of administration issued by any court outwith the United Kingdom and sealed in Scotland under section 2 of the Colonial Probates Act 1892 may also be used as links or midcouples in deduction of title.[43] Judgments of a court of a contracting state within the European Economic Community which have been registered in Scotland as authorised under an application to the Court of Session will be recognised in Scotland,[44] and it would appear that a decree or order of a court of a contracting state appointing executors when so registered would constitute a link of title to Scottish heritage.

(2) Capacity and power. As to the capacity and power of foreign trustees or executors to deal with Scottish heritage, see Volume I, paragraph 2–75.

(3) Execution. It is advisable that the disposition be executed in a way which satisfies the requirements of execution of deeds of the laws of both the foreign country and Scotland.[45]

22–23 **Judicial factors.** As to capacity and power to grant dispositions, see Volume I, paragraphs 2–80 to 2–83. In the case of a factor *loco tutoris* or a curator bonis to an incapax the disposition will be granted by the factor with his designation specifying the name and designation of the pupil or ward and the decree appointing the factor; if the pupil or ward has a completed title no deduction of title is required, but, if not, the title of the pupil or ward should be deduced but *not* that of the factor who does not require to connect himself to the title.[46] A disposition by

---

[40] As to capacity and powers, see Vol. I, paras. 2–76 to 2–79.
[41] Conveyancing (Scotland) Act 1874, s. 51; Conveyancing (Scotland) Acts (1874 and 1879) Amendment Act 1887, s. 5.
[42] Conveyancing (Scotland) Act 1924, s. 5(2) as amended by Succession (Scotland) Act 1964, s. 15(1) and Law Reform (Miscellaneous Provisions) (Scotland) Act 1968, s. 19.
[43] 1924 Act, s. 5(2).
[44] Civil Jurisdiction and Judgments Act 1982, s. 4.
[45] See Burns, 313, 314.
[46] *Scott* (1856) 18 D. 624.

a minor who has a curator bonis is granted by the minor with consent of the curator specifying the decree of his appointment but again only the title of the minor, if he is not infeft, need be deduced. On the other hand if the judicial factor has been appointed to administer a trust estate or the estate of a deceased person under section 163 of the Bankruptcy (Scotland) Act 1913 or under section 11A of the Judicial Factors (Scotland) Act 1889,[47] the factor requires to connect himself with the title; the disposition is granted by the factor specifying the decree of his appointment and his title will be deduced using that decree as a link.[48] In all dispositions for value the judicial factor's warrandice will be from fact and deed, the pupil, minor or incapax or the beneficiaries in the trust estate, as the case may be, being bound in absolute warrandice.

2–24 **Trustees in sequestration**
(a) Under Bankruptcy (Scotland) Act 1913. The power of a trustee in a sequestration under the 1913 Act (where the date of sequestration was before April 1, 1986) to sell the heritable property of the bankrupt and the description of the trustee in the disposition to the purchaser have already been considered.[49] As to the style of disposition, see paragraph 22–48(1) *infra.*

As regards the persons who may purchase from the trustee, section 116 of the 1913 Act authorises a purchase by any creditor but prohibits a purchase by the trustee or commissioners or any law agent employed by the trustee in connection with the sequestration or any partner of such law agent. The section is expressed in relation to a public sale, but it is thought that the permission given to a creditor to purchase applies also in private sales,[50] and likewise the prohibition of purchase by the trustee or other interested parties named in the section also applies in private sales since the possibility of preferential treatment arises *a fortiori* in sales by private bargain.

Section 112 of the 1913 Act requires the trustee to make up a scheme of ranking and division of the claims of heritable and other creditors on the price of heritable estate sold, which has to be reported to the court, and provides that the judgment thereon shall be a "warrant for payment out of the price against the purchaser of the heritable estate". That does not mean that the purchaser is bound to await the judgment of the court before making payment to the trustee: he may do so without judicial warrant.[51]

(b) Under Bankruptcy (Scotland) Act 1985. In terms of section 39 of the 1985 Act (applicable where the date of sequestration was on or after April 1, 1986) the permanent trustee may sell the bankrupt's estate by

---

[47] Added by Bankruptcy (Scotland) Act 1985, Sched. 7, paras. 3 and 4.
[48] Conveyancing Amendment (Scotland) Act 1938, s. 1.
[49] Vol. I, paras. 2–86 to 2–98; para. 4–09.
[50] For the reasoning leading to this conclusion, see Burns, 319.
[51] *Callum* v. *Goldie* (1885) 12 R. 1137.

either public sale or private bargain. Where any part of the bankrupt's heritable estate is subject to heritable securities which are preferable to the permanent trustee's right, the trustee may sell that part only with the concurrence of every heritable creditor unless he obtains a price sufficient to discharge every such security. If the trustee has intimated to a heritable creditor that he intends to sell, the creditor is precluded from taking steps to enforce his security, but on the other hand if a heritable creditor has intimated to the trustee that he intends to commence procedure for sale the trustee is precluded from commencing such procedure. If either the permanent trustee or the heritable creditor who has first given intimation to the other of his intention to sell unduly delays in proceeding with the sale, the other, if authorised by the court, may either sell or enforce his security, as the case may be.[52] The validity of the title of a purchaser is not challengeable on the ground that there has been a failure to comply with a requirement of section 39.[53] Neither the permanent trustee nor an associate[54] of his or any commissioner may purchase.[55] As to the sale of the family home or the matrimonial home of the bankrupt see paragraph 21–18 *supra*. For a style of disposition see paragraph 22–48(2) *infra*.

(c) Foreign elements. As to powers of sale by a Scottish trustee in sequestration of immoveable estate of the bankrupt situated abroad, see Volume I, paragraphs 2–95 and 2–96. The Bankruptcy (Scotland) Act 1913 has now been repealed but is replaced by the Bankruptcy (Scotland) Act 1985. As regards immoveable estate of the bankrupt, the definition of the whole estate of the bankrupt now appears in section 31(8) of the 1985 Act and comprehends the whole estate of the bankrupt, wherever situated. Provisions for the reciprocal enforcement in England and Northern Ireland of orders in bankruptcy pronounced by the Scottish courts and the enforcement in Scotland of orders in bankruptcy made by English and Northern Irish courts are made by sections 121 and 122 of the (English) Bankruptcy Act 1914.[56]

22–25 Trustee under trust deed for creditors. See paragraph 21–19 *supra* as to the matters to be checked when a disposition is being granted on a sale by a trustee acting under a trust deed for creditors executed before and after April 1, 1986. Subject thereto, he has the powers of sale outlined in Volume I, paragraph 2–99.

22–26 Liquidators. As to the capacity and power of its liquidator to sell the heritable property of a company, see Volume I, paragraphs 2–104 to

---

[52] Bankruptcy (Scotland) Act 1985, s. 39(3) and (4).
[53] *Ibid.*, s. 39(7).
[54] Defined *ibid.*, s. 74.
[55] *Ibid.*, s. 39(8).
[56] The specific provisions of s. 97 of the Bankruptcy (Scotland) Act 1913 are now repealed, but the provisions of the (English) Bankruptcy Act 1914, ss. 121, 122 remain in force—Insolvency Act 1985, Sched. 10, Pt. III.

2–110, but in paragraph 2–108 (sale by a liquidator of property burdened by securities) the reference in section 623(4) of the Companies Act 1985 to sections 108 to 113 and 116 of the now repealed Bankruptcy (Scotland) Act 1913 has no application to sales by a liquidator in a winding-up which commenced on or after April 1, 1986, when a reference to subsections (3), (4), (7) and (8) of section 39 of the Bankruptcy (Scotland) Act 1985 should be substituted.[57] For a style of disposition by a liquidator, see paragraph 22–49 *infra*.

2–27 **Receivers.** As to the powers of a receiver to sell and grant a disposition of heritable property included in the assets falling under the charge by virtue of which he is appointed and the limitations of those powers, see Volume I, paragraphs 2–111 to 2–115 and paragraph 21–22 *supra*. For a style of disposition by a receiver, see paragraph 22–50 *infra*.

2–28 **Partnerships.** As to the powers of trustees for a firm to sell and grant dispositions of its heritable property, see Volume I, paragraph 2–127 *supra*. As to the form of such dispositions see Volume I, paragraph 4–11 *supra*. For a style, see paragraph 22–47 *infra*.

If any one or more of the trustees infeft in the property on behalf of the firm survive, he or they may grant a disposition without the need to deduce title since the trust infeftment so far as in favour of any deceased trustees will have automatically accresced to the infeftment of the survivors or survivor. If all the trustees having a recorded title to the property on behalf of the firm have died, the trust has lapsed and it will be necessary to obtain a title in one or other of the following ways:

(i) Where the last surviving trustee died on or after September 10, 1964, his executor, whether nominate or dative, may expede confirmation or an eik to confirmation containing a statement of the property as estate held in trust, and a disposition may then be granted by the executor *and* the present partners of the firm. The disposition should narrate that it is granted at the request and with the consent of and by the present partners being the parties beneficially entitled to the subjects disponed, the title of the executor should be deduced through the confirmation and, where appropriate, the eik, and warrandice should be granted by the executor from fact and deed only and by the partners absolutely.[58] The participation of the present partners in the disposition is necessary since section 6 of the Executors (Scotland) Act 1900 as amended merely provides a title linkage and authorises the executor to transfer the property to the beneficiaries entitled thereto, so that the right to sell is in the present partners as such beneficiaries and sale can be effected only at their behest and with their consent.

(ii) Alternatively, or where the procedure under (i) above is not available, the partners may apply to the Court of Session for

---

[57] Bankruptcy (Scotland) Act 1985, Sched. 7, para. 21.
[58] Executors (Scotland) Act 1900, s. 6 as amended by Succession (Scotland) Act 1964, Sched. 2, para. 13.

appointment of a new trustee or trustees[59] who may then grant a disposition deducing title through the decree of appointment.

(iii) Another possible course is for the partners to apply to the Court of Session under section 24 of the Trusts (Scotland) Act 1921 and record or register the extract decree. The partners will then be entitled to grant a disposition.

It appears that if the last surviving trustee died before September 10, 1964, service of his heir will not normally be competent[60]; the enabling provision of section 6 of the Law Reform (Miscellaneous Provisions) (Scotland) Act 1980 is available where the heir of the last surviving trustee has been called as such, but that is an unusual destination in a partnership title: method (ii) or (iii) above should be used.

22-29 **Spouses—matrimonial home.** As to the requirements for consent of the non-entitled spouse to a disposition of a matrimonial home or part thereof, or for an affidavit by the entitled spouse if the property is not a matrimonial home, see paragraphs 21–23 to 21–26 *supra*.

22-30 **Local authorities.** As to capacity and power to grant dispositions see Volume I, paragraph 2–118, and as to mode of execution see Volume I, paragraph 3–10. The former requirement for sale of heritable property forming part of the common good of a burgh by public roup[61] no longer applies.[62]

22-31 **Other special bodies.** As to the powers to deal with heritable property of chartered incorporations, public or statutory corporations, unincorporated associations, friendly societies, trade unions, industrial and provident societies and building societies, see Volume I, paragraphs 2–116, 2–117 and 2–119 to 2–123. Where title to heritable property is taken in the name of an incorporated body, dispositions will be granted by or in favour of the body; where the title to heritable property is taken in name of trustees for the body, dispositions will be granted by or in favour of the trustees. In all cases the constitution or rules of the body must be considered.

Stamp Duty

(1) Conveyance on sale—rates

22-32 Dispositions of heritable property on sale are liable to *ad valorem* stamp duty, subject to exemption for transactions where the amount or

---

[59] Trusts (Scotland) Act 1921, s. 22.
[60] *Browning*, 1976 S.L.T. (Sh.Ct.) 87.
[61] Town Councils (Scotland) Act 1900, s. 98.
[62] Local Government (Scotland) Act 1973, Sched. 29 repealing the 1900 Act: see s. 222(2) of 1973 Act for a general direction as to the administration of property part of the common good.

value of the consideration does not exceed £30,000 and an appropriate certificate of value is contained in or endorsed on the deed. The current rates of duty are: (1) where the amount or value of the consideration is £30,000 or less and the disposition is certified to that effect no stamp duty is payable, or (2) where the amount or value of the consideration exceeds £30,000 stamp duty is payable at the rate of £1 for every £100 or part of £100 of the consideration.[63]

(2) Certificate of value

2–33   The form of the certificate of value is:

"I/We certify that the transaction hereby effected does not form part of a larger transaction or of a series of transactions in respect of which the amount or value or the aggregate amount or value of the consideration exceeds £30,000."

In the case of dispositions where the value of the subjects conveyed is doubtful the Stamp Office may accept a shortened form of certificate:

"I/We certify that the transaction hereby effected does not form part of a larger transaction or of a series of transactions."

The certificate should be incorporated in the disposition, normally immediately before the testing clause, but if there has been omission to do so may be endorsed on the deed and signed by the parties to the deed.

(3) Computation of consideration

2–34   **Building plot.** The assessment of stamp duty on a disposition of a building plot may present difficulties. Where the seller of the land and the builder are independent persons the consideration paid for the building does not attract duty even where the landowner and the builder habitually act together and even where the building has been partly or wholly erected before the disposition is granted.[64] Even where the builder was the seller of the land but there were two separate contracts, the building contract being expressed as conditional upon completion of the purchase of the site, it was held that there were two contracts and the consideration for the building did not attract duty.[65] But where the builder and a company under his control on the same date entered into contracts for a feu of the ground and the building of a house and the house was built before a feu of the ground was granted, it was decided that stamp duty was payable upon the total of the value of the ground and the price of the house.[66]

---

[63] Finance Act 1984, s. 109. If the consideration does not exceed £500 and certification is not possible, the rate of stamp duty is 50p per £50 of the consideration.
[64] *Paul v. Inland Revenue, Span v. Inland Revenue* and *Blair v. Inland Revenue*, 1936 S.C. 443.
[65] *Kimbers & Co. v. I.R.C.* [1936] 1 K.B. 132.
[66] *McInnes v. Inland Revenue*, 1934 S.C. 424.

Goodwill. Where the contract of sale includes goodwill which is heritable in character duty is payable on the price of both the property and the goodwill, but extra-statutory concessions are sometimes given by the Revenue.

Disposition where liability for heritable security forms part of consideration. Where a disposition is granted for a consideration which consists wholly or partly of the grantee undertaking liability for a heritable security burdening the subjects, stamp duty is payable upon the price paid, if any, plus the amount due under the security.[67]

Dispositions on sales at discount by local authority. The consideration on a sale of a dwelling-house under the provisions of the Tenants' Rights, etc. (Scotland) Act 1980 is the price paid by the purchaser, even although that is less than the pre-discount value and the transaction is subject to the contingency that part of the discount is repayable if the house is sold within five years.[68]

Series of transactions. If several transactions of purchase are interdependent, stamp duty is payable on the aggregate amount of the consideration. However, even if several lots of property are purchased contemporaneously by the same purchaser from the same seller and individual dispositions of each lot are executed of the same date it does not follow that they constitute a series of transactions,[69] but if several properties are purchased in a single transaction and the purchase is then effected by separate dispositions of each property the total consideration forms the basis for assessment of stamp duty.

(4) Time of stamping

22–35   A disposition should be stamped either before execution or, if executed in the United Kingdom, within 30 days after the first execution. If a disposition is first executed abroad it may be stamped without penalty within 30 days after its receipt in the United Kingdom.[70]

(5) Adjudication

22–36   The Commissioners of Inland Revenue may, if required, adjudicate the stamp duty on any disposition which is submitted to them with any necessary evidence as to the circumstances of the transaction. In order to avoid the possibility of penalties the deed should be submitted within the permissible time for stamping. Section 5 of the Stamp Act 1891 requires all material facts relevant to stamp duty to be set out in the deed, but in practice the deed may omit a full statement of the

---

[67] Stamp Act 1891, s. 57.
[68] Finance Act 1981, s. 107; Finance Act 1984, s. 110.
[69] *Attorney-General* v. *Cohen* [1937] 1 K.B. 478.
[70] Stamp Act 1891, s. 15.

consideration provided that the relevant facts are disclosed to the Stamp Office when the deed is submitted for adjudication. When the stamp duty has been adjudicated and paid, the adjudication stamp impressed on the deed is conclusive evidence that the proper duty has been paid.

(6) Exemptions and reliefs

22–37   Certain dispositions are exempt from stamp duty. The more important are (1) dispositions where the consideration is certified as not exceeding £30,000, (2) dispositions in favour of charities,[71] and (3) dispositions by a company in favour of an associated company.[72]

Other dispositions formerly liable to *ad valorem* stamp duty are liable only to stamp duty of 50p, namely, (1) dispositions effecting a gift *inter vivos*,[73] (2) dispositions by which property is conveyed from one party to a marriage to the other executed in pursuance of an order of court made in relation to a decree of divorce, nullity of marriage or judicial separation or an agreement of parties in connection with the dissolution or annulment of the marriage or judicial separation,[74] (3) dispositions made in pursuance of a deed of family arrangement executed within two years after a death,[75] or (4) dispositions by an executor in satisfaction of a legacy, prior rights, *jus relictae* or *jus relicti*, legitim or residue or a share thereof.[76] Dispositions of the kinds mentioned in (1), (2) and (3) above require to be submitted for adjudication of the stamp duty.[77]

STYLES[78]

Disposition of detached dwelling-house

22–38   I, A, (*designed*), heritable proprietor of the subjects and others hereinafter disponed, in consideration of the price of £   paid to me by B, (*designed*), hereby (*Insert consent of non-entitled spouse, if appropriate*) dispone to the said B (*Insert any special destination*), heritably and irredeemably, ALL and WHOLE that plot of ground containing   square yards [square metres] or thereby in the City of Edinburgh and County of Midlothian described and disponed in and delineated within red boundaries on the plan annexed to Feu Charter by C in favour of D dated and recorded in the Division of the General Register of

---

[71] Finance Act 1982, s. 129.
[72] Finance Act 1930, s. 42; Finance Act 1967, s. 27(2).
[73] Finance Act 1985, s. 82 applicable on or after March 26, 1985.
[74] Finance Act 1985, s. 83, applicable on or after March 26, 1985.
[75] *Ibid.*, s. 84(1)–(3), applicable on or after March 26, 1985.
[76] *Ibid.*, s. 84(4)–(7), applicable on or after August 1, 1985.
[77] *Ibid.*, ss. 82(5) and 84(9).
[78] These styles are appropriate to dispositions to be recorded in the Register of Sasines or which induce first registration in the Land Register. For styles of disposition of interests already registered in the Land Register, see paras. 22–62 to 22–65.

Sasines for the County of Midlothian on   both days of
          1926; Together with the dwelling-house known as Number
26   Road, Edinburgh and garage and other erections on the
said plot and the fixtures and fittings therein, the parts, privileges
and pertinents of the whole subjects hereby disponed and my
whole right, title and interest, present and future, therein; But
always with and under so far as valid, subsisting and applicable the
whole reservations, burdens, conditions and others specified in the
said Feu Charter dated and recorded as aforesaid[79]: With entry and
vacant possession on   [as at   notwithstanding the
date hereof][80]: And I grant warrandice: (*Stamp clause where
required*) (*To be attested*)

*Disposition of tenement flat where deed of conditions—first conveyance
of flat*

22–39   We, X Construction Company Limited, (*designed*), heritable
proprietors of the subjects hereinafter disponed, in consideration
of the price of £   paid to us by B, (*designed*), hereby dispone
to the said B (*Insert any special destination*), heritably and
irredeemably, ALL and WHOLE that dwelling-house being the
westmost flat on the second floor above the ground floor of the
tenement No.   Bellshill Street, Coatbridge, in the County of
Lanark which tenement is erected on ALL and WHOLE that plot
of ground containing   square yards or thereby in the said
County described and disponed in Feu Charter by James Smith in
favour of John McLean dated   and recorded in the Division
of the General Register of Sasines for the County of Lanark on
          both days of   18   ; Together with (1) the whole
rights of property, rights exclusive, mutual and common and
whole other rights so far as effeiring to the said dwelling-house
specified and contained in Deed of Conditions by us the said X
Construction Company Limited dated   and recorded in the
said Division of the General Register of Sasines on   both
days of   19   ,[81] (2) the whole fixtures and fittings in the
said dwelling-house so far as belonging to us, (3) the parts and
pertinents of the subjects hereby disponed and (4) our whole
right, title and interest, present and future, therein; But always
with and under so far as valid, subsisting and applicable the whole
reservations, burdens, conditions and others specified in (1) the
said Feu Charter and (2) the said Deed of Conditions respectively
dated and recorded as aforesaid[82]: With entry and vacant possession
on   [as at   notwithstanding the date hereof][83]: And
we grant warrandice.
(*Stamp clause if required*)   (*To be attested*)

---

[79] Specify in chronological order any other deeds imposing burdens or conditions.
[80] Alternative when disposition executed after date of entry.
[81] See para. 22–59.
[82] See n. 79.
[83] See n. 80.

Disposition of tenement flat where no deed of conditions[84]

22–40   I, A, (*designed*), heritable proprietor of the subjects hereinafter disponed, in consideration of the price of £   paid to me by B, (*designed*), hereby (*Insert consent of non-entitled spouse, if appropriate*) dispone to the said B (*Insert any special destination*), heritably and irredeemably, ALL and WHOLE that dwelling-house being the eastmost flat on the first floor above the ground floor of the tenement number   Gorgie Road, Edinburgh in the County of Midlothian (hereinafter called "the Flat"), which tenement is erected on that plot of ground containing   decimal or one hundredth parts of an acre or thereby in the said County described and disponed in and delineated within the boundaries coloured red on the plan annexed to Feu Disposition by C in favour of D dated   and recorded in the Division of the General Register of Sasines for the County of Midlothian on both days of   19   ; Together with (1) the lock-up garage number 2 being the second garage counting from the east in the block of garages situated to the south of the said tenement and the *solum* of the said garage,[85] (2) the storage cellar number 2 being the second cellar counting from the east of the row of cellars at ground level also situated to the south of the said tenement and the *solum* of the said cellar,[85] (3) servitude rights of access over and through the other flats in said tenement for the purpose of carrying out repairs to and maintenance of the Flat and through the hatchway leading to the roof for the purpose of cleaning vents and all other necessary purposes, (4) the fixtures and fittings in the Flat and said garage and storage cellar, (5) the parts, privileges and pertinents of the subjects hereby disponed and (6) my whole right, title and interest, present and future, in the subjects hereby disponed; and together also with a right in common with the other proprietors of flats in the said tenement to (1) the *solum* and foundations of the said tenement, (2) the entrance passage and stairway of the said tenement, (3) the water tanks, water, soil, waste disposal and other pipes, gas and electricity pipes and cables, all so far as common to and serving the said tenement, [and the communal television aerial and connecting leads], with right of access thereto when required, (4) the unbuilt on ground surrounding the said tenement included in the said plot of ground [with the access roads, paths and parking areas thereon] and the walls or fences enclosing the same and (5) the whole other parts of the said tenement (but excluding the roof and main outer walls) used in common by the proprietors of the flats therein (which whole parts in which said right in common subsists are hereinafter called "the common parts"); declaring that when the proprietors of a majority of the flats in the said tenement consider it desirable to have any repairs to or maintenance of the common parts executed, they shall have power to order the same to be done, and

---

[84] This style leaves the ownership and liability for maintenance of the roof and main walls to be regulated by the common law of the tenement, but departs from it in certain respects, *e.g.* by making the *solum* and foundations of the tenement common property. The provisions regarding certain of the common parts substantially express those which would be implied by the common law of the tenement but are inserted for the sake of clarity.

[85] Alternatively the *solum* of the garage and cellar may be made common property.

they and the other proprietors of flats in the said tenement, whether consenters or not, shall be bound to pay the expense thereof, such expense to be borne by the proprietors in equal one-eighth shares thereof; But always with and under so far as valid, subsisting and applicable the whole reservations, burdens, conditions and others specified in the said Feu Disposition dated and recorded as aforesaid[86] [declaring that the amount of the annual feuduty of £   per annum payable in terms of the said Feu Disposition hereby apportioned on the subjects hereby disponed is £   per annum payable half yearly at Whitsunday and Martinmas by equal portions beginning the first term's payment at the term of   19   for the half year preceding, with interest at 5 per cent per annum from the terms when the same becomes payable until actual payment thereof:][87] And also with and under (a) the burden of payment of one-eighth of the expense of repair or maintenance of the common parts and (b) a servitude right of access in favour of the proprietors of other flats in the said tenement over and through the Flat for the purpose of carrying out repairs to and maintenance of the flats belonging to them respectively, which further burdens are hereby declared to be real burdens and conditions on the subjects hereby disponed and shall be inserted or effectually referred to in all future conveyances, transmissions and investitures thereof otherwise the same shall be null: With entry and vacant possession on   [as at notwithstanding the date hereof]:[88] And I grant warrandice. (*Stamp clause if required*)

(*To be attested*)

Disposition of tenement flat which has already been conveyed separately

22–41

I, A, (*designed*), heritable proprietor of the subjects hereinafter disponed, in consideration of £   paid to me by B, (*designed*), hereby (*Insert consent of non-entitled spouse, if appropriate*) dispone to the said B (*Insert any special destination*), heritably and irredeemably, ALL and WHOLE that dwelling-house being the southmost flat on the second floor above the ground floor of the tenement number   Road,   in the County of Fife being the dwelling-house described and disponed in Disposition by AB Limited in my favour [in favour of C] dated   and recorded in the Division of the General Register of Sasines for the County of Fife on   both days of   19   ; Together with (1) the whole rights of property, rights exclusive, common and mutual and whole other rights so far as effeiring to the said dwelling-house specified and contained in [Deed of Conditions by the said AB Limited dated   and recorded in the said Division of the General Register of Sasines on   both days of   19   ] [the said Disposition dated and recorded as aforesaid]; (2) the whole fixtures and fittings in the said dwelling-house so far as belonging to me, (3) the parts and pertinents of the whole subjects hereby disponed and (4) my whole right, title and interest, present and future, therein; But always with and under so

---

[86] See n. 79.
[87] Applicable where feuduty has not been redeemed.
[88] See n. 80.

far as valid, subsisting and applicable the whole reservations, burdens, conditions and others specified in the said [Deed of Conditions] [Disposition] dated and recorded as aforesaid[89]: With entry and vacant possession on   [as at   notwithstanding the date hereof][90]: And I grant warrandice. (*Stamp clause if required*)

(*To be attested*)

Disposition of part of villa on first subdivision[91]

-42 I, A, (*designed*), heritable proprietor of the subjects hereinafter disponed, in consideration of the price of £   paid to me by B, (*designed*), hereby (*Insert consent of non-entitled spouse, if appropriate*) dispone to the said B (*Insert any special destination*), heritably and irredeemably, ALL and WHOLE (*describe as in para. 18–58*); But always with and under so far as valid, subsisting and applicable, the whole reservations, burdens, conditions and others specified in the said Feu Disposition dated and recorded as aforesaid,[92] declaring that the amount of the annual feuduty of £   per annum payable in terms of the said Feu Disposition hereby apportioned on the subjects hereby disponed is £ per annum payable half yearly by equal portions beginning the first term's payment at the term of   19   for the half year preceding, with interest at 5 per centum per annum from the terms when the same becomes payable until actual payment thereof][93]: With entry and vacant possession on   [as at notwithstanding the date hereof][94]: And I grant warrandice. (*Stamp clause if required*)

(*To be attested*)

Disposition of part of villa on first subdivision—another form[95]

-43 I, A, (*designed*), heritable proprietor of the subjects hereinafter disponed, in consideration of the price of £   paid to me by B, (*designed*), hereby (*Insert consent of non-entitled spouse, if appropriate*) dispone to the said B (*Insert any special destination*), heritably and irredeemably, ALL and WHOLE the dwelling-house comprising the [main door and basement flat] [upper flat] forming the dwelling-house number [26] [26A]   Road, Airdrie, which dwelling-house, ground and others hereby disponed form parts of ALL and WHOLE that piece of ground containing   square yards or thereby Imperial Measure in the County of

---

[89] See n. 79.

[90] See n. 80.

[91] This style is appropriate where there is a clear vertical subdivision of the building into two houses with exclusive rights to the ground lying in front of and to the rear of the respective houses and separate accesses and services. Where there is subdivision horizontally into two flats with exclusive and common rights to specified parts of the relative ground, see style in para. 22–43.

[92] See n. 79.

[93] Applicable where feuduty has not been redeemed.

[94] See n. 80.

[95] This style is appropriate where there is a subdivision horizontally into two flats with exclusive and common rights to specified parts of the relative ground and sharing of certain common services. In a division of this kind it is peculiarly important to maintain adequate buildings insurance cover over *both* houses, and the insertion of a provision for a common insurance policy should be considered.

Lanark described and disponed in and shown within the boundaries coloured red on the plan annexed to Feu Contract between C and D dated   and   and recorded in the Division of the General Register of Sasines for the County of Lanark on all days of   19   and of the villa formerly known as 26   Road, Airdrie erected thereon; Together with (one) (a) the exclusive right of ownership of the [ground] [two/three pieces of ground] coloured [green] [blue] on the plan annexed and subscribed as relative hereto [and the garage and other erections thereon], [(b) the [internal] [external] stairway leading to the said upper flat and the railings thereof and upper [landing] [porch]][96] and (c) a servitude right of access over and through the said [upper] [main door and basement] flat for the purpose of executing repair and maintenance work on the dwelling-house hereby disponed and the common parts aftermentioned, (two) a right of ownership in common with the proprietor of the [upper] [main door and basement] flat in and to (a) the area(s) of ground coloured brown on the said last mentioned plan and the driveway and pathways thereon which area(s) shall be kept open and unbuilt upon in all time coming, (b) the *solum*, foundations and outside walls of the building containing the said upper and main door and basement flats, (c) the roof, rhones, chimneyheads, rainwater and soil pipes, gas, electricity and telephone pipes and cables and other service connections serving both of the said flats, [(d) the front steps [and railings thereof] and the hall or vestibule on the ground floor][97] and (e) the walls, fences or railings enclosing the said piece of ground (so far as belonging to me) and the pavement and one half of the roadway so far as included in the said piece of ground (which parts owned in common are hereinafter collectively called "the common parts") and (three) the fixtures and fittings in the said dwelling-house hereby disponed, the whole parts, privileges and pertinents of the subjects hereby disponed and my whole right, title and interest, present and future, therein: But always with and under so far as valid, subsisting and applicable the whole reservations, burdens, conditions and others specified in the said Feu Contract dated and recorded as aforesaid[98]; And also with and under the following additional burdens, conditions and others, namely, (One) my said disponee and his successors in ownership of the subjects hereby disponed shall be liable for one half of [(a) the feuduty of £   payable in terms of the said Feu Contract at the terms after the date of entry hereinafter specified with interest as provided in the said Feu Contract until payment[99] and (b)] the expense of maintaining in good order and repair the common parts[1] and (Two) the subjects hereby disponed are disponed under burden of a servitude right of access in favour of the proprietor of the said [upper] [main door and basement] flat for the purpose of executing repairs and maintenance work on the said [upper] [main door and basement] flat and the common parts, all which foregoing additional burdens, conditions and others are hereby declared to be real burdens and conditions and are

---

[96] Applicable where upper flat conveyed.
[97] Applicable where access to both flats is by common front door and hall or vestibule.
[98] See n. 79.
[99] Applicable where feuduty not redeemed.
[1] See n. 95 *re* insurance.

appointed to be recorded as part of these presents in the Register of Sasines and shall be inserted or effectually referred to in all future conveyances, transmissions and investitures of the said subjects or any part thereof otherwise the same shall be null; And I bind myself to insert similar conditions in any disposition or other original conveyance granted by me of the said [upper flat] [main door and basement flat]: With entry and vacant possession on   [as at   notwithstanding the date hereof:]² And I grant warrandice. (*Stamp clause if required*)

(*To be attested*)

PLAN

(*To be docketed as relative and signed*)

Disposition of superiority

—44   I, A, (*designed*), heritable proprietor of the subjects and others hereinafter disponed, in consideration of the price of £   paid to me by B, (*designed*), hereby dispone to the said B (*Insert any special destination*) heritably and irredeemably, ALL and WHOLE that area of ground containing   [hectares] [acres] or thereby in the County of   described in Disposition by C in [my favour] [favour of D] dated   and recorded in the Division of the General Register of Sasines for the County of   on   both days of   19   ; Together with the teinds so far as I have right thereto and my whole right, title and interest, present and future, in and to the subjects and others hereby disponed; But always with and under so far as valid, subsisting and applicable the whole reservations, burdens, conditions and others specified in (*specify any deeds imposing burdens or conditions on the land conveyed*): With entry at the term of   19   : And I assign the rents and the feuduties [and I declare that the feuduties hereby assigned include those specified in the list thereof annexed and signed as relative hereto without prejudice to these presents in all respects but the same does not create any allocation of feuduties]³: And I bind myself to free and relieve my said disponee and his successors of all over-feuduties (if any) and public burdens exigible in respect of the subjects hereby disponed prior to the date of entry: And I grant warrandice but excepting all feu rights⁴ granted by me or by my predecessors or authors but without prejudice to the right of the said B or his successors to quarrel or impugn the same on any ground in law not inferring warrandice against me or my successors: (*Stamp clause if required*).

(*To be attested*)

[List of feuduties referred to in the
foregoing Disposition

Subject	Feuar	Feuduty

]

(*To be signed*)

---

² See n. 80.
³ The inclusion of this clause marks the disposition as a conveyance of a superiority.
⁴ See *Ceres School Board* v. *McFarlane* (1895) 23 R. 279.

Disposition of landed estate

22–45 I, A, (*designed*), heritable proprietor of the subjects hereinafter disponed, in consideration of the price of £   paid to me by B, (*designed*), hereby (*Insert consent of non-entitled spouse, if appropriate*) dispone to the said B (*Insert any special destination*), heritably and irredeemably, ALL and WHOLE the lands and estate of X in the County of   (*describe as in either of the styles in paragraph 18–60*); But always with and under so far as valid, subsisting and applicable the whole burdens, conditions and others specified in (*specify any deed(s) imposing burdens or conditions on subjects conveyed*): With entry at the term of 19   ; And I assign the rents and feuduties and I declare that the rents and feuduties hereby assigned include those specified in the list thereof annexed and signed as relative hereto without prejudice to these presents in all respects but as regards feuduties the same does not create any allocation thereof: And I grant warrandice excepting the current leases and rights of tenancy and all feu rights[5] granted by me or my predecessors or authors but without prejudice to the right of the said B or his successors to quarrel or impugn the said leases, rights of tenancy and feu rights on any ground in law not inferring warrandice against me or my successors; declaring that the said B and his foresaids shall be bound, as by acceptance hereof they bind themselves, to free and relieve me and my successors of all claims which may become exigible by tenants after the date of entry for improvements, (whenever the same were made), taking over stock, disturbance and others and whether arising under their leases or otherwise.[6] (*Stamp clause if required*)

(*To be attested*)

List of Rents and Feuduties referred to in the
foregoing Disposition

Subject	Leases Tenant	Annual Rent	Date of Payment of First Rent receivable by Disponee
Subject	Long Leases Lessee	Annual Rent	Date of Payment of First Rent receivable by Disponee
Subject	Feuduties Feuar	Feuduty	

(*To be signed*)

Disposition by pro indiviso proprietors

22–46 We, (first) A, (*designed*), heritable proprietor to the extent of one-half *pro indiviso* of the subjects hereinafter disponed, (second) B, (*designed*), heritable proprietor to the extent of one-fourth *pro*

---

[5] See *Ceres School Board* v. *McFarlane* (1895) 23 R. 279.

[6] Compensation for improvements is payable only on termination of tenancy although the improvements will have been made earlier—see para. 15–132. If tenancy terminates on date of entry compensation is payable by seller—*Waddell* v. *Howat*, 1925 S.C. 484. Claims for taking over livestock, disturbance, etc., also arise only on termination of tenancy.

indiviso of the said subjects and (third) C, (*designed*), heritable proprietor to the extent of one-fourth *pro indiviso* of the said subjects, in consideration of the price of £ paid to us by D (*designed*), in the proportions of £ to me the said A, £ to me the said B and £ to me the said C of which sums we hereby respectively acknowledge receipt hereby dispone to the said D (*Insert any special destination*), heritably and irredeemably (*continue with description of subjects, reference to burdens and date of entry, as appropriate*): And we assign the writs *quoad* our respective interests: And we assign the rents *quoad* our respective interests: And we bind ourselves to free and relieve the said disponee and his successors of all feuduties and public burdens but each only so far as regards our own respective *pro indiviso* shares[7]: And we grant warrandice but only so far as regards our own respective *pro indiviso* shares. (*Stamp clause if required*).

(*To be attested*)

Disposition by and to partnership firm

–47 We, A, (*designed*), and B, (*designed*), partners of the firm carrying on business as at under the firm name of Thomas & White and infeft in the subjects hereinafter disponed as [surviving] trustees for behoof of the said firm with the consent of C, (*designed*), and D, (*designed*), the other partners of the said firm, and we the said A, B, C and D for our respective rights and interests and we all with joint consent and assent[8] in consideration of £ paid to us by the firm of Wilson & Shaw, (*designed*), hereby dispone to E, (*designed*), and F, (*designed*), the partners of the said firm of Wilson & Shaw, as trustees for that firm and the partners thereof present and future[9] and their successors in office as such trustees and the survivor of them [and the heir of the last survivor][10] as trustees and trustee foresaid, heritably and irredeemably, ALL and WHOLE (*continue with description of subjects, reference to burdens: if any special powers other than those conferred on trustees by law are required insert same[11]*): With entry on 19 : And we the said A and B as trustees foresaid and we the whole granters hereof personally and individually and jointly and severally bind ourselves and the said firm of Thomas & White in absolute warrandice. (*Stamp clause if required*).

(*To be attested*)

Disposition by trustee in sequestration[12]

–48 **(1) Under Bankruptcy (Scotland) Act 1913.** For styles of disposition by

---

[7] The clauses of assignation of writs, assignation of rents and obligation of relief are specially inserted to make them applicable *quoad* the respective interests and obligations of the *pro indiviso* proprietors since the statutory provisions in s. 16 of the Land Registration (Scotland) Act 1979 do not deal with that situation.

[8] No deduction of title required—see Vol. I, para. 4–11.

[9] See Vol. I, para. 11–74.

[10] The insertion of a destination to the heir of the last surviving trustee may permit completion of title by service in the event of lapse of the trust—Law Reform (Miscellaneous Provisions) (Scotland) Act 1980, s. 6.

[11] For a possible provision see *Encyclopaedia of Scottish Legal Styles*, Vol. 4, No. 261.

[12] See Vol. I, paras. 2–86 to 2–94.

a trustee in sequestration (a) on sale by auction, (b) with concurrence of heritable creditor and (c) on sale by private bargain, see *Encyclopaedia of Scottish Legal Styles*, Vol. 4, Nos. 283, 284 and 285. These styles are still appropriate to sales by a trustee under the 1913 Act.

(2) Under Bankruptcy (Scotland) Act 1985

I, A, (*designed*), the permanent trustee on the sequestrated estate of B, (*designed*), duly confirmed conform to act and warrant by the Sheriff of   dated at   on   19   , [with the consent and concurrence of C, (*designed*), a creditor having security over the subjects hereby disponed by virtue of (*description of deed which created security*)],[13] [with the consent and concurrence of (*spouse, former spouse or bankrupt where subjects are a family home*)],[14] in consideration of the price of £   paid to me as trustee foresaid by X, (*designed*), [of which sum £   has been paid by me as trustee foresaid to the said C in reduction of the amount due to him under the said (*deed which created the security*)],[13] hereby dispone to the said X (*Insert any special destination*), heritably and irredeemably, (*description of subjects in appropriate form with any necessary reference to burdens and conditions*): With entry at   19   : And I grant warrandice from my own facts and deeds only and so far as I have power to do so bind the said sequestrated estate in absolute warrandice: [And the said C hereby disburdens the said subjects of and from the said (*security deed*)] (*Stamp clause if required*).

(*To be attested*)

Disposition by company in liquidation[15]

22–49   We, AB Limited, incorporated under the Companies Acts and having our registered office at   (hereinafter called "the Company") [in voluntary liquidation conform to (*specify*) in which liquidation C, (*designed*), is liquidator conform to (*specify*) (the said C being hereinafter referred to as "the liquidator")][16] [in judicial liquidation conform to (*specify*) in which liquidation C, (*designed*), is official liquidator (the said C being hereinafter referred to as "the liquidator")][17] [in voluntary liquidation conform to (*specify*) in which liquidation C, (*designed*), is liquidator conform to (*specify*) (the said C being hereinafter referred to as "the liquidator") and the liquidation has been placed under the supervision of the Court conform to (*specify*) but neither by that order nor otherwise has any restriction been imposed by the Court on the liquidator's powers][18] in consideration of the price of

---

[13] Required only if price insufficient to discharge security in full. If price sufficient to repay secured amount in full separate discharge will be granted by creditor. See Bankruptcy (Scotland) Act 1985, s. 39(4).

[14] Bankruptcy (Scotland) Act 1985, s. 40(4). If the subjects are a matrimonial home, notice will have been given to the non-entitled spouse under s. 41 of the 1985 Act and sale may be effected only where the court has not made an order under that section which protects her or his occupancy rights.

[15] See Vol. I, paras. 2–103 to 2–110.

[16] Appropriate to members' or creditors' voluntary liquidation.

[17] Appropriate to judicial liquidation.

[18] Appropriate to voluntary liquidation under supervision of the court.

£   paid to the liquidator by XY Limited, (*designed*), the Company with the consent and concurrence of the liquidator hereby dispone to the said XY Limited, heritably and irredeemably, ALL and WHOLE (*continue with description of subjects, reference to burdens and date of entry*)[19]: And we the Company grant warrandice and the liquidator grants warrandice from his own facts and deeds only. (*Stamp clause if required*).

> (*To be sealed with the company's seal and signed by the liquidator, his signature being attested*).

Disposition by receiver[20]

2–50   We, X & Co. Limited, (*designed*), and I, A, (*designed*), as Receiver aftermentioned, whereas we the said X & Co. Limited granted a [Floating Charge] [Debenture] in favour of Y Bank, (*designed*), dated   and registered in the Register of Charges on   over (*specify ambit of charge*) and that [by Instrument of Appointment by the said Y Bank dated   ] [by Interlocutor of the (*Court*) issued on   on the application of the said Y Bank] I the said A was appointed Receiver of the property of the said X & Co. Limited which was then subject to the said [Floating Charge] [Debenture] which property included the subjects hereinafter disponed, the said appointment being registered in the Register of Charges on   , And whereas I the said A in exercise of the powers competent to me as Receiver foresaid have sold the said subjects to Z & Co. Limited, (*designed*), at the price of £   , And whereas the said Z & Co. Limited have paid to me as Receiver foresaid the said price of £   Therefore we the said X & Co. Limited and I the said A as Receiver foresaid in pursuance of the said powers competent to me as such Receiver hereby DISPONE to the said Z & Co. Limited, heritably and irredeemably, ALL and WHOLE (*continue with description of subjects*); Together with the whole right, title and interest, present and future, therein of us the said X & Co. Limited and of me the said A as Receiver foresaid: But always with and under (*reference to burdens*): With entry on   : (*deduction of title of X & Co. Limited if not infeft*): And we the said X & Co. Limited grant absolute warrandice, and I the said A grant warrandice from my own facts and deeds only. (*Stamp clause if required*).

> (*To be executed by affixing seal of X & Co. Limited and signature of receiver duly attested*)

Dispositions by testamentary trustees and executors to beneficiaries

2–51   Where heritable property is being conveyed by testamentary trustees or executors-nominate to a legatee of the property or to a residuary legatee to whom the property is being conveyed in implement of the testamentary purposes it will normally be simpler to effect the transfer

---

[19] If company infeft no deduction of title required: if company not infeft deduction of the title of the company, *not* the liquidator, should be inserted.

[20] See Vol. I, paras. 2–111 to 2–115. S. 7 of Administration of Justice Act 1977 now replaced by s. 724 of Companies Act 1985.

by use of a docket authorised by section 15(2) of the Succession (Scotland) Act 1964. The docket however, simply constitutes a midcouple or link in title and cannot be recorded *de plano* in the Register of Sasines, so that if infeftment of the grantee is desired it must be followed by a recorded notice of title. Accordingly, where the grantee requires a recorded title, *e.g.* to enable him to grant feus or leases, or where the testator has directed that a bequest of the property is to be subject to real burdens or conditions, or where the testator has bequeathed the property to the legatee with a further special destination, it is preferable to effect the transfer by a disposition in which title is deduced or burdens and conditions imposed.

Disposition by testamentary trustees to legatee

22–52   We, A, (*designed*), B, (*designed*), and C, (*designed*), the Trustees of the deceased D, (*designed*), (hereinafter called "the testator") acting under his Trust Disposition and Settlement dated and registered in the Books of Council and Session on (hereinafter called "the Will") and confirmed as Executors-nominate of the testator conform to Confirmation issued by the Sheriff of   at   dated   , whereas by the Will the testator bequeathed [the subjects hereinafter disponed] [the residue of his estate which included the subjects hereinafter disponed] to E, (*designed*), (*narrate special destination, if any*) Therefore in [implement] [part implement] of the said bequest we the said A, B and C as Trustees and Executors foresaid hereby dispone to the said E (*Insert special destination, if any*), heritably and irredeemably ALL and WHOLE (*continue with description of subjects and reference to existing burdens*) [And also with and under the burdens and conditions following, videlicet, (*impose any burdens or conditions as directed by testator with, if appropriate, declaration creating them real*)]: With entry as at   notwithstanding the date(s) hereof: Which subjects were last vested in the said D [whose title thereto is recorded in the Division of the General Register of Sasines for the County of   on   ][21] [whose title thereto is recorded in the said Division of the General Register of Sasines on   ][22] [as aforesaid][23] and from whom we as Trustees and Executors foresaid acquired right by the said Confirmation: And we the said A, B and C grant warrandice from our own facts and deeds only.

(*To be attested*)
Stamp 50p.

DISPOSITIONS BY PARTIES UNINFEFT[24]

22–53   **Deduction of title.** The Conveyancing (Scotland) Act 1924[25] introduced

---

[21] Where division of Register not already mentioned.
[22] Where division, but not deceased's title, already mentioned.
[23] Where deceased's recorded title already mentioned.
[24] paras. 22–53 and 22–54 are applicable to dispositions to be recorded in the Register of Sasines or which induce first registration in the Land Register of Scotland. For dispositions of interests registered in the Land Register, see paras. 22–61 to 22–64.
[25] s. 3.

a facility to enable dispositions to be granted by owners of heritable property who were not infeft. For the underlying theory of deduction of title see paragraph 16–56 *supra*, and for an account of the persons who may use the facility and the writings which may be used as midcouples or links in title see paragraphs 22–07 and 22–08 *supra*. For the method of correcting errors in deduction of title see paragraph 21–40 *supra*.

–54 Detailed rules

(1) The statutory form of the clause in Form No. 1 of Schedule A to the 1924 Act is:

> "Which lands and others (*or subjects*) were last vested [*or* are part of the lands and others (*or subjects*) last vested] in AB, (*designation of person last infeft*), whose title thereto is recorded in (*specify Register of Sasines and date of recording or if the last infeftment has already been mentioned say* in the said AB as aforesaid), and from whom I acquired right by (*here specify shortly the writ or series of writs by which the right was so acquired*)."

(2) The clause of deduction of title should be inserted in the disposition immediately after the clause of entry.

(3) It commences with the last recorded title to the subjects conveyed or to larger subjects of which they formed part.

(4) The name and designation of the holder of that last recorded title must be stated, specifying the register and date of recording of his title. If such last recorded title has already been mentioned, *e.g.* in the description of the subjects, it is sufficient to say "which subjects were last vested in the said A as aforesaid" but if A has not been designed in the former reference it is necessary either to do so there or, if not, to insert his designation in the clause of deduction of title. If the last recorded title was in the names of several persons, the names and designations of all should be stated; if they were testamentary trustees or executors the names and designations of all should be stated specifying also the name and designation of the deceased, the date of confirmation and the sheriff court by which it was issued.

(5) Then follows in chronological order a list of all the writs connecting the holder of the last recorded title with the granter of the present disposition, each writ being described in sufficient terms to enable it to be identified, specifying where appropriate its date and date of registration (if any). Designations of parties to each writ are unnecessary if the writ can be identified and no narration of contents is required.[26]

(6) The kinds of writs which may be used as midcouples or links are enumerated in section 5(1) of the 1924 Act—see paragraph 22–08 *supra*.

---

[26] 1924 Act, s. 2(3).

(7) As regards transmissions of the property on a death:

(i) In testate succession, specify the confirmation rather than the will.

(ii) In intestate succession, specify the confirmation.

(iii) In any case where the property has been included only in an eik to confirmation, specify the confirmation and the eik.

(iv) Where the property has passed under a special destination to any person which could not be, or has not in fact been, evacuated, mention the destination in referring to the deed which contains it and narrate the death of the predeceaser, *e.g.*—"which subjects were last vested in A, (*designed*), and B, (*designed*), and the survivor of them by Disposition dated   and recorded in the Division of the General Register of Sasines for the County of   on   and from whom the said B acquired right on the death of the said A on   ".[27]

(v) Where the property has passed under a special destination which could not be, or has not in fact been, evacuated, in favour of a person or persons not named therein and the executor has confirmed to the property in order to convey it to the person or persons entitled to succeed under the destination, specify the confirmation and the docket of transfer by the executor[28] in favour of such person or persons.[29]

(vi) In all cases where the executor of the deceased has been confirmed to the property and transferred it by docket to the person or persons entitled thereto, specify the confirmation and the docket. (Where the executor and the person entitled to beneficial ownership of the property on the death is the same individual, confirmation vests the property in the executor only as such for the purposes of administration; a docket of transfer is required as a further link to give that person a right to the property as an individual.)[30]

(8) As regards changes in the personnel of trustees or executors:

Testamentary trustees or executors-nominate

(i) It is unnecessary to specify any revocation of appointment of a trustee, minute of declinature by a person nominated as a trustee or deed of assumption of a new trustee, if made *before* the issue of confirmation.

(ii) It is necessary to specify any minute of resignation or deed of assumption and to mention the death of any trustee or executor if made or occurring *after* the issue of confirmation.

(iii) Where a sole or last surviving trustee or executor-nominate has died after confirmation has been issued but before the property has been transferred on sale or by docket to the person beneficially entitled

---

[27] See Succession (Scotland) Act 1964, s. 36(2).
[28] *Ibid.*, s. 15(2).
[29] *Ibid.*, s. 18(2).
[30] See article, G.L. Gretton, 1980 S.L.T. (News) 257.

thereto, specify the original confirmation and the subsequent confirmation of his executor (whether nominate or dative) which contains a note of the property as estate held in trust.

Executors-dative

(iv) Where an executor-dative has died after confirmation has been issued but before the property has been transferred on sale or by docket to the person beneficially entitled thereto, specify the original confirmation and the subsequent confirmation of his executor (whether nominate or dative) which contains a note of the property as estate held in trust.

Executors ad non executa

(v) Where an executor *ad non executa* has been appointed on the death or incapacity of the original executor, whether nominate or dative, before the property has been sold or transferred to a beneficiary specify the original confirmation and the confirmation *ad non executa.*

Trustees under inter vivos trust deed

(vi) Specify the trust deed and any minute of declinature, minute of resignation, deed of assumption or the death of any trustee who has accepted office.

Trustees for unincorporated bodies

(vii) Where the trustees are named individuals, specify any minute of resignation by or death of a trustee and any minute of meeting or excerpt therefrom or any deed of assumption which effected the appointment of a new trustee or new trustees.[31]

(viii) Where a recorded title to any heritable property held for religious or educational purposes in terms of section 26 of the Titles to Land Consolidation (Scotland) Act 1868 has been taken in the names of office-bearers of the religious or educational body as trustees for behoof of the body, or where a recorded title to heritable property has been taken in the names of the holders of any place or office and their successors in office in terms of section 45 of the Conveyancing (Scotland) Act 1874, deduction of title is not strictly necessary—but the narrative of any disposition by the present holders of the offices should be in appropriate terms, *e.g.*—"We, A, (*designed*), B, (*designed*), and C, (*designed*), the present holders respectively of the offices of Minister, Session Clerk and Clerk to the Congregational Board of the (*name and address of church*) and as the holders of the said respective offices Trustees for the congregation of the said (*church*)." The disponee is

---

[31] As to certification of copies of minutes of meeting or excerpts therefrom, see 1924 Act, s. 5(1).

entitled to require evidence of appointment of the present office-bearers, but technically they are infeft by virtue of statute and are not persons who require to deduce title.

(9) As regards transfers of heritable property by statute, it is sufficient to specify the Act (and preferably the relevant section) provided that the Act itself effects the transfer. If the statute does not specify the transfer of ownership to an identified body but that is done by statutory instrument made in pursuance of the statute, both the Act and the statutory instrument should be specified, *e.g.*

> which subjects were last vested in The Corporation of the City of Glasgow whose title thereto was recorded in the Division of the General Register of Sasines for the County of the Barony and Regality of Glasgow on   and from whom we the City of Glasgow District Council as the Local Authority for the said District under the Housing (Scotland) Acts and Acts amending the same acquired right by section 222 of the Local Government (Scotland) Act 1973 and The Local Authorities (Property etc.) (Scotland) Order 1975.[32]

Transactions inducing First Registration in Land Register

Dispositions inducing first registration

22–55   Dispositions of unregistered interests in transactions which induce first registration in the Land Register of Scotland should be framed in accordance with the styles given in paragraphs 22–38 to 22–51 *supra*, with deduction of title where the granters are uninfeft as explained in paragraphs 22–53 and 22–54 *supra*. However, in circumstances where the description of the subjects is insufficient to enable the Keeper to identify the boundaries on the Ordnance Map a more elaborate description will be desirable. Examples are: (1) A general description of a landed estate which is dependent for its definition on the owner's possession should be elaborated by a description by reference to a plan as suggested in paragraph 18–08 *supra*. (2) A description of subjects which takes the form of a description of larger subjects under exception of parts previously conveyed may not always identify the subjects disponed sufficiently clearly to enable them to be mapped, and so it may be desirable to insert a particular description of the subjects disponed with a further description by reference to the original description of the larger area under exception of the parts previously conveyed.[33] As to description of subjects in a dispositon inducing first registration, see paragraphs 18–64 to 18–70 *supra*. A reference to burdens should be included as in the case of a Sasine title: as to references to deeds of conditions, see paragraph 19–36 *supra*.

---

[32] S.I. 1975 No. 659 (S. 92).
[33] R.T.P.B., para. G.2.31.

DISPOSITIONS OF REGISTERED INTERESTS

Parties

-56   Where either the granter or grantee hold or are to hold the interest conveyed in a fiduciary capacity that should be stated and any special destination should be inserted as in a disposition under Sasine practice. There is no need to describe the granter as "heritable proprietor" or "proprietor" depending upon whether he is infeft or not. It is unnecessary to insert a clause of deduction of title, but all midcouples or links in title connecting the last registered proprietor as disclosed in the title sheet to the granter of the disposition must be produced to the Keeper with the application for registration of the interest conveyed by the disposition.[34]

Description of subjects

-57   As to the description of the interest conveyed, see paras. 18–74 to 18–79 and the *Registration of Title Practice Book*, paragraph G.3.22(iii). It is unnecessary to repeat or refer to incidental rights or pertinents which are already included in the title sheet of the interest conveyed, but if the conveyance effects a dealing with part of a registered interest and new rights are being created in favour of the interest affected by the dealing these must be specified in sufficient detail to enable them to be entered on the title sheet of that interest. Likewise, if interests are being created in favour of the retained part of the subjects, these should be specified in detail.[35] Where the disposition conveys part of a registered interest, other parts of which have previously been conveyed to other persons, (i) if the description of the part conveyed is in the form of a description of the larger subjects under exception of the parts previously sold there is no need to exclude the latter since they will have been removed from the title sheet and the description of the interest now conveyed will carry only the balance then remaining in the title sheet, but (ii) it is preferable to insert a description of the remaining part which is being conveyed.[36]

Burdens and conditions

58   It is unnecessary to refer in the disposition to any real burden or condition or any other provision which has been entered in the title sheet of the interest conveyed.[37] It is necessary, however, to include in the disposition any new burden or condition created or imposed by it. Burdens or conditions created for the first time in the disposition should be set out at length, and any other subjects in favour of which

---

[34] Land Registration (Scotland) Act 1979, s. 15(3).
[35] See R.T.P.B., para. G.3.22 (iv).
[36] See R.T.P.B., para. G.3.22 (v).
[37] 1979 Act, s. 15(2).

they are created should be identified. If a burden or condition affects only part of the interest conveyed, that part should be identified.[38]

Deeds of conditions

22–59   A deed of conditions relating to a flatted tenement or a building estate, which sets out (i) rights, common or exclusive, which attach to each house or plot (the rights) and (ii) the burdens and conditions to which each house or plot is to be subject (the burdens), may present problems in framing subsequent dispositions. The recording of the deed of conditions in the Register of Sasines or the entry of it in the Land Register is not a conveyance of the rights nor, except in the case where the deed was executed on or after April 4, 1979, without express exclusion of the operation of section 17 of the 1979 Act, does it create the burdens real. (Exclusion of the operation of section 17 in the case of a tenement serves no purpose and is rare, but it may be found in the case of a building estate.[39]) When subsequently a disposition of the tenement or the building estate or of a single house or plot has induced first registration in the Land Register it will have been framed in the normal style appropriate to a disposition which is to be recorded in the Register of Sasines and will have contained a conveyance of the rights and have imported the burdens by reference to the deed of conditions. The practice of the Keeper is to insert in the title sheet a summary of both the rights and burdens and to indicate by a note in the burdens section of the title sheet if a deed of conditions does not make the burdens real. Then:

(1) If the disposition which has induced first registration conveyed the whole tenement or estate, any subsequent disposition of a house or plot, (a) should contain a conveyance of the rights[40] and (b) as regards the burdens, (i) if section 17 applies, they are already real and a reference to the title number is sufficient to import them without express reference to the deed of conditions but (ii) if section 17 does not apply, either because the deed of conditions was executed prior to April 4, 1979, or because the section was expressly dissapplied, it is necessary to import the burdens by reference if it is intended that they should apply to the subjects disponed. Any subsequent disposition of the same house or plot need neither convey the rights nor mention the burdens.

(2) If the disposition which has induced first registration was of a particular house or plot, again it will have been in normal Sasine form and will have conveyed the rights and imported the burdens, unless the operation of section 17 has been excluded and it was not intended that the deed of conditions should apply to the subjects disponed. Any subsequent disposition of the same house or plot need neither specifically convey the rights nor import the burdens.

---

[38] See R.T.P.B., para. G.3.22 (v).
[39] See para. 19–36.
[40] See style (1) in para. 18–77.

(3) If by inadvertence a conveyance of the rights or a reference to the burdens has been omitted, a conveyance of the rights by the former proprietor and a deed of acknowledgment of omitted conditions will be required to put matters right.

NOTE. Where the deed of conditions has been entered in the Land Register, any subsequent disposition which conveys the rights should in referring to the deed of conditions specify the title number of the interest in respect of which the deed of conditions has been entered in the Land Register.

Executory clauses

2–60   As in the case of dispositions to be recorded in the Register of Sasines,[41] it is necessary to ensure that the statutory import of the clauses of assignation of writs and rents and the clause containing the obligation of relief are appropriate to the terms of the bargain, in which case the clauses may be omitted. If any variation of the statutory import of any of these clauses is desired, the clause should be inserted in appropriate terms. If an obligation or a right of relief has already been entered in the title sheet of the interest conveyed, it is unnecessary to assign such obligation or right or to narrate the writs by which the granter of the disposition became entitled to enforce the obligation or exercise the right.[42]

Warrandice

2–61   A clause of warrandice in appropriate terms should be inserted in the disposition. As to the effects of warrandice in relation to registered titles, see Volume I, paragraph 4–35 *supra*, and the *Registration of Title Practice Book*, paragraphs H.3.01 to H.3.06. In particular the parties to a disposition of a registered interest should consider the following:

(i) Matters excluded from indemnity. There are many kinds of possible loss which are excluded from indemnity under section 12(3) of the 1979 Act. If the disponee suffers any such loss, he can rely only upon the disponer's warrandice.

(ii) Specific exclusions of indemnity. When an interest has been registered the Keeper may have excluded indemnity as regards the whole or part of it. If the disponer grants absolute warrandice without qualification he may be liable to the disponee if the latter is subsequently evicted from the whole or part of the subjects and he will have no claim for indemnity against the Keeper, and so the disponer should consider whether he should restrict his warrandice to fact and deed

---

[41] See paras. 22–12 to 22–14.
[42] 1979 Act, s. 15(4).

only as regards any part of the subjects in respect of which indemnity has been excluded on registration. It should be kept in view, however, that a restriction of warrandice to fact and deed will not avoid liability where the exclusion of the Keeper's indemnity was due to acts or omissions of the disponer, *e.g.* where indemnity is excluded under section 12(3)(*b*) of the Act and the disponer had accepted and registered a disposition with knowledge that it was a gratuitous alienation or fraudulent preference.

(iii) Lineal measurements. The Keeper's indemnity is excluded as regards loss resulting from inaccuracies in the delineation of boundaries shown in a title sheet which could not have been rectified by reference to the Ordnance Map (effectively a tolerance of nine inches) or, as regards land extending to two hectares or more, loss resulting from failure to enter the area in the title sheet or inaccuracy in specifying the area entered therein.[43] The granter of a disposition of the registered interest does not have that protection, and may be liable for loss resulting from very small inaccuracies in measurements.[44] If the nature of the subjects is such that an inaccuracy of a few inches may be material, the disponer may wish to qualify his warrandice, *e.g.*—"but excepting from warrandice any loss which may result from an inaccuracy in the measurement of any boundary of the subjects hereby disponed as shown on the Title Sheet thereof if such inaccuracy does not extend to more than   inches."[45] In the case of land extending to two hectares or more where an area has been entered in the Title Sheet but by reason of the configuration or irregular shape of the land there may be doubt as to the accuracy of that area the disponer may qualify his warrandice thus: "but excepting from warrandice any loss which may result from a deficiency in the area of the subjects hereby disponed as entered in the Title Sheet thereof if such deficiency does not exceed . . . square [yards] [metres]." A seller may be unwilling to grant warrandice to this extent, in which event the purchaser may instruct his surveyor to check the measurements or area so far as essential to his interest.

STYLES

Disposition of whole registered interest

22–62   I, A, (*designed*), in consideration of the price of £   paid to me by B, (*designed*), hereby (*Insert consent of non-entitled spouse, if appropriate*) dispone to the said B (*Insert any special destination*)

---

[43] 1979 Act, s. 12(3)(*d*) and (*e*).
[44] *Griffin* v. *Watson*, 1962 S.L.T. (Sh.Ct.) 74.
[45] It may be argued that, if the disposition simply describes the subjects by reference to the title number, the purchaser is entitled only to the registered interest conveyed with the inherent limitation of indemnity as to measurements, and that the disponer need not make the suggested qualification of warrandice, but *quaere*? See R.T.P.B., para. H. 3.03.

ALL and WHOLE the subjects (*short description by name and/or postal address of subjects*)[46] registered under title Number(s) [But always with and under (*Insert any newly created burdens or conditions not already entered in Title Sheet*)]: With entry and vacant possession on [as at notwithstanding the date(s) hereof]: And I grant warrandice (*qualified if desired— see para. 22–61*): (*Stamp clause if required*)

(*To be attested*)

Disposition of part of a registered interest—plot of ground

2–63   I, A, (*designed*), in consideration of the price of £ paid to me by B, (*designed*), hereby (*Insert consent of non-entitled spouse, if appropriate*) dispone to the said B (*Insert any special destination*) ALL and WHOLE that plot of ground containing square [yards] [metres] with the dwelling-house No. Road, Paisley, erected thereon [being the plot delineated and edged red on the plan annexed and signed as relative hereto which plot is part of the subjects registered under Title Number] [being the plot numbered plot 25 delineated on the plan of Title Number] [being the subjects (First) registered under Title Number]; [Together with (*specify in full any rights now being created in favour of the subjects disponed, e.g. rights in common to amenity ground of whole development, so as to identify them and the other plots with which they are held in common*);] But always with and under (*insert any burdens or conditions applicable to the plot disponed other than those already made applicable in the main title*) [But declaring that the following burdens and conditions set out in Title Number are not to apply to the subjects hereby disponed, *if appropriate*]: With entry and vacant possession on : And I grant warrandice (*qualified if necessary—see para. 22–61*) (*Stamp clause if required*)

(*To be attested*)

Disposition of part of registered interest—flat in tenement

2–64   I, A, (*designed*), in consideration of the price of £ paid to me by B, (*designed*), hereby (*Insert consent of non-entitled spouse, if appropriate*) dispone to the said B (*Insert any special destination*) ALL and WHOLE (*describe subjects and rights as in style (1) of paragraph 18–77 supra*): With entry and vacant possession on ; And I grant warrandice. (*Stamp clause if required*)

(*To be attested*)

Disposition of part of registered interest—part of larger house on first subdivision[47]

2–65   I, A, (*designed*), in consideration of the price of £ paid to me by B, (*designed*), hereby (*Insert consent of non-entitled spouse, if appropriate*) dispone to the said B (*Insert any special destination*) ALL and WHOLE the dwelling-house comprising the [main door

---

[46] For an example, see para. 18–75.
[47] Appropriate where division is into two flats with exclusive and common rights to specified parts of the relative ground and sharing of certain common services.

and basement flat] [upper flat] forming the dwelling-house number
[26] [26A]   Road, Paisley; Which dwelling-house, ground
and others hereby disponed are part of the subjects registered
under title Number   ; Together with (one) (a) the exclusive
right of ownership of the [ground] [two/three pieces of ground]
coloured   on the plan annexed and subscribed as relative
hereto [and the garage and other erections thereon] [(b) the
[internal] [external] stairway leading to the said upper flat and the
railings thereof and upper [landing] [porch][48] and (c) a servitude
right of access over and through the [upper] [main door and
basement] flat of the building comprising the said flats for the
purpose of executing repair and maintenance work on the subjects
hereby disponed and the common parts aftermentioned, (two) a
right in common with the proprietor of the [upper] [main door and
basement] flat in and to (a) the area(s) of ground coloured brown
on the said plan and the driveway and pathways and all erections
thereon which area(s) so far as unbuilt on shall be kept open and
unbuilt on in all time coming, (b) the *solum*, foundations and
outside walls of the said building comprising the said main door
and basement and upper flats, (c) the roof, rhones, chimneyheads,
rainwater and soil pipes, gas, electricity and telephone pipes and
cables and other service connections serving both of the said flats,
[(d) the front steps and railings and the hall or vestibule on the
ground floor][49] and (e) the walls, fences and/or railings enclosing
the whole ground delineated on the plan of the said Title Number
        so far as the said walls and others belong to me [and the
[pavement] [footpath] and the one half of the roadway included in
the said last mentioned plan] (all of which parts to which a right in
common is hereby disponed are hereinafter collectively referred to
as "the common parts"), and (three) the fixtures and fittings in the
said dwelling-house hereby disponed, the whole parts, privileges
and pertinents of the subjects hereby disponed and my whole
right, title and interest, present and future, therein: But always
with and under [so far as valid, subsisting and applicable the whole
reservations, burdens and conditions specified in the Burdens
Section of the said Title Number   ][50] and the following
additional burdens, conditions and others, namely, (one) my said
disponee and his successors in the ownership of the subjects
hereby disponed shall be liable for one half of the expense of
maintaining in good order and repair the common parts and (two)
the subjects hereby disponed are disponed under burden of a
servitude right of access in favour of the proprietor of the said
[upper] [main door and basement] flat for the purpose of executing
repair and maintenance work on the said [upper] [main door and
basement] flat and the common parts, all which additional burdens,
conditions and others are hereby created real burdens and
conditions affecting the subjects hereby disponed: With entry and
vacant possession on   : And I grant warrandice: (*Stamp
clause if required*)

                                                      (*To be attested*)

---

[48] Applicable where upper flat conveyed.
[49] Applicable where access to both flats is by common front door and hall or vestibule.
[50] Not strictly necessary but inserted for completeness.

Disposition of superiority already registered[51]

2–66 I, A, (*designed*), in consideration of the price of £   paid to me by B, (*designed*), hereby dispone to the said B (*Insert any special destination*) ALL and WHOLE the subjects registered under Title Number   [*if the feuduties recoverable are different from those in the list of feuduties shown in the existing Land Certificate add* declaring that the feuduties now payable in respect of the said subjects are as specified in the List of Feuduties annexed and signed as relative hereto]: With entry on   : And I grant warrandice (*qualified if necessary—see paragraph 22–61*): (*Stamp clause if required*).

(*To be attested*)

[LIST OF FEUDUTIES referred to in
the foregoing Disposition

Subject	Feuar	Feuduty

(*To be signed*)]

CONTRACTS OF EXCAMBION

2–67 An exchange of lands may be effected by a contract of excambion but it is now more usual to have separate dispositions with an appropriate narrative, which for stamp duty purposes should disclose any money passing. Trustees may enter into a contract of excambion.[52] Real warrandice formerly implied in such contracts is now abolished.[53] A contract of excambion may be recorded in the Register of Sasines with two warrants, one on behalf of each of the parties, usually with a clause directing registration for preservation as well as for publication, and two extracts are ordered, one being delivered to each party. An excambion of lands situated in an operational area induces first registration in the Land Register as a transfer for valuable consideration.[54] If lands situated in an operational area are exchanged for lands situated in an area which is not yet operational, the transaction is most conveniently effected by separate dispositions.

Style

It is contracted between A, (*designed*), and B, (*designed*), to make and hereby make the following excambion [in consideration of the sum of £   paid by the said A to the said B] namely: (First) The said A hereby (*consent of non-entitled spouse, if appropriate*) dispones to the said B (*Insert any special destination*) ALL and WHOLE (*description of subjects with or without reference to*

---

[51] See R.T.P.B., para. G.3.22 (b).
[52] Trusts (Scotland) Act 1921, s. 4.
[53] Conveyancing (Scotland) Act 1924, s. 14: Conveyancing Amendment (Scotland) Act 1938, s. 3.
[54] Land Registration (Scotland) Act 1979, s. 2(1)(*a*)(ii).

burdens in form appropriate to sasine title or registered interest, as the case may be) and (Second) The said B hereby (*consent of non-entitled spouse, if appropriate*) dispones to the said A (*insert any special destination*) ALL and WHOLE (*description of subjects with or without reference to burdens, etc., as appropriate*): With entry to the respective subjects as at   : And the said A and B respectively grant warrandice: (*Stamp clause if required*).

(To be attested)

Stamp Duty. If no cash consideration, 50p. If cash consideration, *ad valorem* stamp duty where amount exceeds £30,000.

Chapter 23

PROCEDURE BETWEEN CONTRACT AND SETTLEMENT IN
SALE AND PURCHASE OF HERITABLE PROPERTY

Section C
Dealings with Registered Interests

Section D
Procedural Matters and Problems

Introduction

–01   This chapter contains four sections relating to the procedures and problems from the conclusion of missives until settlement in transactions of sale and purchase of heritable property, *viz.*—

A.   Transactions where the purchaser's title is to be recorded in the Register of Sasines (paragraphs 23–02 to 23–16).

B.   Transactions inducing first registration in the Land Register of Scotland (paragraphs 23–17 to 23–25).

C.   Transactions involving a dealing with an interest already registered in the Land Register of Scotland (paragraphs 23–26 to 23–35).

D.   Procedural matters and problems which may require attention in any of the transactions in sections A, B or C above (paragraphs 23–36 to 23–63).

Each of sections A, B and C contains an illustrative table of procedure applicable to a transaction of sale and purchase where an existing building society loan is being discharged and a new loan is being constituted over the purchaser's interest.

SECTION A

*Transactions where Purchaser's Title is
to be recorded in Register of Sasines*

Table of procedure[1]

–02

SELLER'S SOLICITOR	PURCHASER'S SOLICITOR
1 Frame (a) draft memorandum for continuation of search or of search[3] (b) draft letter of obligation[4] (c) draft discharge of existing heritable security [(d) draft retrocession of life policy assigned in security (if any)][5]	1 Check insurance position[2]

---

[1] This table and the corresponding tables in paras. 23–17 and 23–26 are appropriate to a transaction where the seller is repaying a building society loan [with life policy assigned in security] and the purchaser is obtaining a building society loan [with life policy assigned in security] and the solicitors are respectively acting for both lenders and borrowers.

[2] See para. 23–36.

[3] See paras. 23–03 to 23–05.

[4] See paras. 23–09 and 23–10.

[5] See Vol. I, para. 10–25.

SELLER'S SOLICITOR	PURCHASER'S SOLICITOR
2 Send drafts (a), (b) and (c) and title deeds to purchaser's solicitor	
3 Write for any prior titles required	
	2 Acknowledge titles and drafts
	3 Examine titles[6]
	4 Revise drafts of (a) memorandum for search or continuation of search (b) letter of obligation (c) discharge of heritable security
	5 Frame draft disposition[7]
	6 Return titles, revised drafts (a), (b) and (c) and send draft disposition to seller's solicitor and raise all observations on title and make other relevant inquiries[8]
4 Acknowledge titles and drafts	7 Receive building society's instructions regarding loan to purchaser and communicate to purchaser [and obtain confirmation from purchaser that he will carry out any remedial works required by society]
5 Make necessary investigations to answer observations on title and other inquiries	
6 Revise draft disposition	
	8 [Effect or obtain any life policy to be assigned in security]
7 Reply to observations and inquiries and return draft disposition	

---

[6] See Chap. 21.
[7] See Chap. 22.
[8] See paras. 23–12 and 23–37 to 23–48.

SELLER'S SOLICITOR	PURCHASER'S SOLICITOR
8 Engross discharge of heritable security	9 Consider replies to observations and inquiries
9 [Engross retrocession of life policy]	10 Engross disposition
	11 Send draft disposition and engrossment to seller's solicitor
10 Send discharge [and retrocession] to building society for execution and request note of loan outstanding at proposed date of settlement	12 Frame draft standard security [and assignation of life policy][9]
11 Instruct interim report	13 Engross standard security [and assignation of life policy]
12 Obtain last rates and feuduty receipts from client	
13 Receive prior titles	14 Send standard security [and assignation] to client for signature
14 Send prior titles to purchaser's solicitor	
	15 [Where existing life policy being used as security confirm from assurance company that no encumbrances on policy and that premiums paid to date]
15 Compare engrossment of disposition with draft	
16 Send engrossment of disposition to seller for signature	
17 Return draft disposition to purchaser's solicitor	
	16 Examine prior titles
	17 Return these with any further observations

[9] See para. 7–30.

SELLER'S SOLICITOR   PURCHASER'S SOLICITOR

18 Acknowledge prior titles and
    deal with any further
    observations

19 Return prior titles to custodier

                                      18 Consider replies to further
                                          observations

                                      19 [Where existing life policy
                                          receive confirmation from
                                          assurance company in reply to
                                          15 above]

                                      20 Send report on title and terms
                                          of life policy to building society
                                          and requisition cheque

20 Submit interim report to
    purchaser's solicitor

21 Prepare state for settlement

22 Send state for settlement and
    vouchers to purchaser's
    solicitor

22A [Obtain consent (if not
    incorporated in disposition)
    renunciation or affidavit if
    subjects are or may be
    matrimonial home]

                                      21 Examine interim report and
                                          return it

                                      22 Check state for settlement,
                                          retain copy and return to
                                          seller's solicitor with any
                                          amendments

                                      23 Frame (a) statement for
                                          purchaser showing sum
                                          required for settlement

SELLER'S SOLICITOR	PURCHASER'S SOLICITOR
	including fees and outlays and (b) report on title
	24 Send report on title and statement to purchaser and request payment
23 Receive executed discharge [and retrocession] from building society	
24 Receive executed disposition from seller	25 Receive standard security [and assignation of life policy] from purchaser
25 Obtain keys from seller	
	26 Receive cheque from building society
	27 Receive cheque from purchaser and give receipted statement
26 Arrange settlement	28 Arrange settlement
27 Receive price and give receipted state for settlement	29 Cash cheques from purchaser and building society[10]
28 Deliver (a) keys (b) title deeds falling to be delivered (c) signed disposition and particulars of execution (d) executed discharge with warrant of registration signed (e) letter of obligation with draft [(f) Any matrimonial home document required] [(g) feuduty redemption receipt (if available)]	30 Deliver cheque for purchase price and get receipted state for settlement 31 Check execution of disposition and discharge

---

[10] Where bridging loan involved, see para. 23–61.

SELLER'S SOLICITOR	PURCHASER'S SOLICITOR
29 Repay building society loan	32 Take delivery of items (a) to (e) [(f)] [and (g)] in item 28 of opposite column
30 Account to seller for balance of price less fees and outlays	33 Deliver keys to purchaser

After Settlement

SELLER'S SOLICITOR	PURCHASER'S SOLICITOR
31 Serve notice of change of ownership on superior[11]	34 Complete testing clause of disposition and stamp (if required)
32 [Intimate retrocession of life policy to assurance company]	35 Record (a) discharge (b) disposition (c) standard security
33 Cancel seller's insurance	36 [Intimate assignation of life policy to assurance company]
34 Redeem feuduty or ground annual (if redeemable and not already done)[12]	
	37 Report settlement to building society and return completion particulars form
35 Receive feuduty redemption receipt	
36 Send same to purchaser's solicitor	
	38 Check feuduty redemption receipt
	39 Mark letter of obligation as so far implemented and advise seller's solicitor
37 [Receive from assurance company acknowledgment of intimation of retrocession]	40 [Receive from assurance company acknowledgment of intimation of assignation]

---

[11] Although the feuduty may be redeemed the other obligations of the feu remain and the seller's liability for performance of them should be terminated.

[12] See paras. 17–49 to 17–53.

SELLER'S SOLICITOR	PURCHASER'S SOLICITOR
38 Deliver to seller life policy, retrocession and acknowledgment of intimation]	41 [Purchaser confirms any remedial work required by building society has been completed, instruct society to make final survey and request release of any retained money and, when received, account to purchaser]
39 Receive recorded discharge from Register House	42 Receive recorded disposition and standard security from Register House
40 Send recorded discharge to purchaser's solicitor	
	43 Check discharge
	44 Mark letter of obligation and advise seller's solicitor
41 Receive search from searchers	
42 Check search	
43 Send search to purchaser's solicitor	
	45 Check search
	46 Return letter of obligation marked as fully implemented
	47 Send all title deeds to building society[12a]

Searches

23–03   As to the periods of search in the property and personal registers and the persons against whom search in the personal register should be made, see paragraphs 21–73, 21–84 and 21–85 *supra*. As to searches in the Register of Charges and Company Files in transactions where companies are concerned, see paragraph 21–87 *supra*.

[12a] Some building societies prefer all deeds available at settlement to be sent to them immediately after settlement and disposition and standard security sent when returned from Register of Sasines.

23–04 Memorandum for continuation of search. Where the property sold comprises a single unit in respect of which an existing search is contained in the titles held by the seller, a memorandum for continuation of that search should be instructed from the Keeper or professional searchers. The existing search should be sent accompanied by a memorandum for its continuation.

Memorandum for Continuation of Search

Continue the Accompanying Search

I In the Property Register
against the subjects of
search   From (*last date of completed
                                                search*)
                                       To   date of certificate to show
                                                recording of (*Disposition
                                                to purchaser and Standard
                                                Security*

II In the personal Register
against
A (*full name and all known   For 5 years prior to date of
    designations*)   certificate in Property Register
B (*do*   )[13]

23–05 Memorandum for search. Where a unit of property is being separately conveyed for the first time, the existing search against the larger subjects of which it formed part will be furnished to the searchers with instructions for its continuation *quoad* the new unit. In practice it is convenient to instruct also a separate search against the new unit in order to diminish the occasions for borrowing the common search when the period of positive prescription has expired.

Memorandum for Search

                                       Search
                                       against
                                       ALL and WHOLE (*describe sub-
                                       jects shortly so as to identify*) and
                                       proprietors
I In the Property Register   From May 15, 1986
                                       To date of certificate
                                       showing recording of
                                       [Feu Disposition]
                                       [Disposition] by A in
                                       favour of B (*purchaser
                                       as at Whitsunday 1986*)

---

[13] Where personal search against purchaser is desired (as when heritable security is being granted by him) the purchaser's name and designation will be added by his solicitor when revising the memorandum.

II In the Personal Register
against

A (*full name and all known designations*)[14]	For 5 years prior to date of certificate in Property Register

23–06   Interim reports. An interim report on the search or continuation of search should be instructed at a date as nearly as practicable to the date of settlement. It will disclose all writs relating to the property recorded in the Register of Sasines up to the last date of the completed Register, which will normally be some months prior to the date when the search is instructed, and will disclose entries in the Register of Inhibitions and Adjudications up to 24 hours before the search is made. If any unforeseen delay occurs in effecting settlement of the transaction it may be prudent to have a further interim report, possibly obtained by telex, which will update the original interim report.

23–07   Companies—searches in Register of Charges and Company Files. In addition to the searches in the Register of Sasines and the Register of Inhibitions and Adjudications it is necessary in transactions where the sellers are or include an incorporated company to instruct a search in the Companies Register of Charges and the files of the company.[15] In such cases it is peculiarly important that the searches be continued as nearly as is practicable to the date of settlement.

23–08   Searches—practice

(1) The date from which the continuation of an existing search should commence is the last date to which the search has previously been brought down, not the date immediately following. The existing search, if it is a common search relating also to larger subjects, may have appended to the last entry relative to the subjects of purchase a note, "Grantee's interest not traced," and it is possible that another deed, *e.g.* a heritable security, may have been recorded on the same date but after a disposition in favour of the seller. That contingency is not present where the search relates only to the subjects of the current transaction, but it is simpler to have a practice rule which applies to all cases.

(2) The closing date of the search in the Register of Sasines is that on which the feu grant or disposition implementing the current transaction is recorded. If an existing heritable security is being discharged or a standard security is being granted by the purchaser, it may be useful to indicate when instructing the search that the discharge and/or the new standard security should also be disclosed in the certificate: it is possible that for some reason one or both of these deeds are recorded subsequently to the recording of the feu grant or disposition.

(3) As to the persons against whom the search in the Register of

---

[14] See n. 13.
[15] See para. 21–87.

Inhibitions and Adjudications should be made, see paragraph 21–85 *supra*. If the parties are trustees or executors the practice is to search against them as a body, without naming them as individuals, but specifying the name and designation of the truster or deceased, as the case may be. Searches against a firm should be made against the firm itself, the trustees holding its heritable property and all the current partners, with names and designations of all of them. The importance of specifying all variants of names and all known designations of parties is emphasised.

Obligations for searches

23–09   There is no duty on the seller's solicitor to give at settlement his personal obligation to deliver or exhibit a search showing clear records. Nevertheless it has been the usual practice for such an obligation to be given, although in special circumstances the seller's solicitor may decline to do so. The risk which the obligation covers is that during the period between the date of the interim report and the recording of the disposition to the purchaser some deed which adversely affects the purchaser's interest may be recorded in the Register of Sasines or some diligence may be registered in the Register of Inhibitions and Adjudications. The period may be several months in the case of the Register of Sasines, but the risk is diminished since normally the title deeds during much of the period will be in the hands of the solicitors for the parties, but it is still possible that another deed may be recorded prepared from copies or extracts. In the case of the Register of Inhibitions and Adjudications the period is relatively short if the interim report has been obtained immediately before settlement, but on the other hand the diligence will be at the instance of a third party and outwith the control of the parties to the transaction or their solicitors. In practice—(1) the obligation should be the personal obligation of the seller's solicitor[16]: an obligation expressed on behalf of his client adds little to the seller's warrandice in the disposition; (2) the obligation should be limited to the period of the continuation of search or of the new search, as the case may be; (3) the obligation should be expressed as conditional upon the disposition in favour of the purchaser being recorded within seven days; (4) the period within which the search should be exhibited or delivered should be stated: it should be based upon the interval which is likely to elapse between the submission of the disposition for recording and its appearance on the index; and (5) the obligation should be restricted to deeds or diligences affecting the seller's title. A suggested form might be:

> With reference to the settlement of the above transaction today we hereby undertake to deliver (exhibit) a search in the Property

---

[16] See *Johnston* v. *Little*, 1960 S.L.T. 129.

and Personal Registers continued (obtained) in terms of the draft memorandum adjusted between us and to clear the record of any deeds, incumbrances or diligences disclosed by the continuation (search) prejudicial to the disposition in favour of your client provided it is recorded within 7 days hereof but excluding any created by or against your client.

In some transactions, particularly where the seller is the receiver or liquidator of an insolvent company and there has been a complex of securities and charges, or in circumstances where the potential liability is substantial and the period covered by an obligation is several months, the seller's solicitor may decline to grant a letter of obligation. That poses difficult problems with regard to effecting timeous entry and settlement. In such cases it is for the solicitors for the parties to negotiate the best arrangement practicable, to explain in writing to their respective clients any risks which the arrangement involves but to make clear to the clients that acceptance of those risks is the responsibility of the clients and not of their solicitors.

Obligations on other matters

1–10   Obligations by the seller's solicitor are often given to enable settlement to be effected although certain items remain outstanding.

(1) Discharges or restrictions of heritable securities. In proper practice the discharge of an existing heritable security will be delivered at settlement with a letter to the Keeper instructing its recording and will be forwarded by the purchaser's solicitor along with the disposition in favour of his client. Since the discharge will be returned to the seller's solicitor, he should include in his obligation an undertaking to deliver the recorded discharge. If a necessary discharge of a heritable security or release from it of the property sold is not available at settlement, the seller's solicitor may undertake to deliver it. It is technically improper for this course to be adopted where the purchaser is obtaining a loan from a building society which cannot lend except upon a first security. In many other cases this practice may be adopted without serious risk, but there can be circumstances in which solicitors should be wary of giving or accepting such an obligation. The full amount of principal and interest payable in exchange for discharge of the security or the payment agreed with the heritable creditor for release of the property from his security must be fully covered by the net proceeds of the sale after allowing for payment of any other sums which the seller's solicitor has undertaken to pay therefrom, *e.g.* a bridging loan in respect of the purchase of another property by the seller. From the point of view of the purchaser's solicitor the obligation of the seller's solicitor is vulnerable to the bankruptcy of the latter.

(2) Delivery of disposition. In some areas there is a practice of settling a transaction of purchase and sale before the disposition by the seller is available for delivery, the seller's solicitor undertaking to deliver it within a stated period. This procedure involves significant risks. It should never be adopted unless, prior to settlement, the solicitors for both parties are satisfied that the seller has a valid title. Even so, there remains the risk that the seller becomes bankrupt or, if a company, is liquidated before the disposition has been fully executed, delivered and recorded.[17] For other possible risks see the undernoted text and article.[18]

(3) **Feuduty redemption receipt.** The receipt for the sum payable on redemption of feuduty or ground annual may not be available at settlement. An obligation by the seller's solicitor to produce it may generally be accepted since the amount involved is usually relatively small but the period for its production should be short, not more than one month after settlement.

(4) **Consent of non-entitled spouse.** An undertaking by the solicitor for a seller or borrower to produce a consent by a non-entitled spouse required by the Matrimonial Homes (Family Protection) (Scotland) Act 1981 is not an obligation which is appropriate for inclusion in a letter of obligation. If the necessary consent has not been obtained at settlement the granting of it subsequently is not strictly in compliance with the Act.[19] Moreover, neither the seller nor his solicitor can compel the granting of the consent, so that the latter may be undertaking an obligation which proves impossible of performance.

(5) **Planning consents, building warrants, National House-Building Council insurance, etc.** There may be documents which the seller is obliged to produce by the contract of sale which are not available at the time of settlement. The seller's solicitor may grant an obligation to deliver any such document or an official duplicate thereof within a stated period, but only if he is satisfied that the document was in fact granted or issued.

Obligations—solicitor/client communication

23–11   The usual practice of the profession is to treat settlement obligations as inter-solicitor matters with the technicalities of which clients need not be informed or troubled. In many cases where no significant risk is involved and the solicitor is content to undertake personal responsibility that course is sensible, but if there are serious risks it may be prudent for the solicitor for either purchaser or seller to explain them to his client and to grant or accept an obligation only with the knowledge and approval of his client.

---

[17] See *Gibson and Hunter Home Designs Ltd.*, 1976 S.C. 23.
[18] Professor A.J. McDonald, *Conveyancing Manual*, 321–324: article, (1975) 20 J.L.S. 260.
[19] See para. 21–34.

Defects or unacceptable real burdens or conditions disclosed on examination of title

‑12   Defects or unacceptable real burdens or conditions disclosed on examination of the title of the seller or borrower, and the remedial measures which may be adopted to cure or remove them where that is practicable, have already been considered in Chapter 21 and other chapters. For the convenience of readers, references in the text to some of those which occur relatively often are: (1) lack of capacity or power of parties who have granted deeds in the prescriptive progress (Chapter 2); (2) defects in form of any such deeds (Chapter 4 and Chapter 22, paragraphs 22–02 to 22–15); (3) errors in deduction of title (paragraphs 21–40 and 22–06 to 22–11); (4) informalities of execution of deeds (Chapter 3, paragraphs 3–41 to 3–45); (5) insufficiency of or errors in description of subjects or boundaries (Chapter 18 and, as to remedial procedures, paragraphs 18–80 to 18–86); (6) reservation of minerals (paragraphs 15–56 and 15–57, 19–01 to 19–07 and 21–44); (7) the creation and enforcement of unacceptable real burdens and conditions (Chapter 19, paragraphs 19–13 to 19–62), and the possibility of procuring their variation or discharge (paragraphs 19–64 to 19–95); (8) necessary servitudes in favour of the subjects or unacceptable servitudes burdening them (Chapter 20); (9) consents, renunciations or affidavits required under the Matrimonial Homes (Family Protection) (Scotland) Act 1981 (paragraphs 21–25 to 21–31); (10) discharges of heritable securities and conveyances by heritable creditors (paragraphs 21–57 and 21–58 and Volume III for more detailed treatment; (11) latent unregistered deeds or documents and good faith (paragraphs 21–59 and 21–60); and (12) problems arising from inconsistency with other titles (paragraphs 21–64 and 21–65).

‑13   Differences between the solicitors for the parties as to the existence or legal effect of such defects or unacceptable provisions and as to remedial action where practicable and necessary are frequently resolved in practice by an agreed reference to the opinion of counsel or a professional colleague.[20]

Intervening diligence

‑14   The claims of secured creditors, preferential creditors and, in the case of companies, holders of floating charges in a situation of bankruptcy or liquidation frequently result in the claims of unsecured creditors yielding little or no dividend. As a consequence the use of the diligence of inhibition or arrestment as a possible *tabula in naufragio* for unsecured creditors has markedly increased in recent years.[20a]

---

[20] Professors of Conveyancing are distressingly familiar victims!

[20a] A notice of litigiosity following upon an action of adjudication may also form an impediment but is less frequently used since the adjudication, if it does not proceed upon a heritable security which already secures the creditor's preference, must be based on a liquid document of debt constituted by decree.

When such diligences are used against a seller or borrower on the security of heritable property or his solicitor in the period between conclusion of contract and settlement of the transaction difficult problems may arise and the frequency of their occurrence merits special consideration.

23–15 **Inhibitions.** An inhibition against a seller of heritable property made after the conclusion of a binding contract of sale but before settlement of the transaction is ineffective to prevent its completion, since an inhibition strikes only at *voluntary* deeds or acts. Nevertheless the existence of the inhibition can impede settlement if the contract has contained the usual obligation of the seller to provide clear searches[21] or even where there is no such express obligation since the search is not *ex facie* clear.[22] The problem may be resolved by negotiation amongst the seller, the purchaser and the inhibitor with a view to making one of or a combination of several arrangements, namely: (1) The seller may ask the inhibitor to agree in writing that the inhibition does not affect the conclusion of the transaction under the threat that, if he declines to do so, an action of declarator of that fact will be raised against him with possible liability on the inhibitor for expenses since his refusal to agree has rendered the action necessary. (The weakness is that such an action, if it becomes necessary, may take some time before a decree is obtained and so does not provide a quick solution to the problem.) (2) An action for recall of the inhibition or restriction of it to the effect that it does not impede the sale transaction. (This is a summary process and will be disposed of more quickly but it is technically less correct since the legal position is that the inhibition does not impede the conclusion of the transaction at all.) (3) Settlement of the transaction and retention of a photocopy of the missives by the purchaser plus an obligation by the seller's solicitor to have the inhibition declared ineffective or recalled or restricted. (4) Settlement of the transaction but with retention by the purchaser of the amount of the debt in respect of which the inhibition was used, thus imposing a compulsitor on the seller to have the search cleared of the inhibition promptly. (5) Agreement between the seller and the inhibitor to buy off the latter by making payment to the inhibitor of the debt due to him or an acceptable payment to account of it. (6) Deferment of settlement until the search has been cleared of the inhibition by agreement or court action.

23–16 **Arrestments.** If the purchaser has made a payment to account of the price before the date of settlement, that payment is vulnerable to arrestment in the hands of the seller's solicitor at the instance of a creditor of the seller. The purchaser may insist on settlement on tender

---

[21] *Dryburgh* v. *Gordon* (1896) 24 R. 1.
[22] See the opinion of Lord McLaren in *Henderson* v. *Dawson* (1895) 22 R. 895 at 902.

of the balance of the price but the arrestment may place the seller in an awkward position if he requires the full price to implement the purchase of another property to which he is committed or may prevent the seller's solicitor from implementing an undertaking to apply the net proceeds of the sale in repayment of a bridging loan, although in the latter situation it may be contended that the arrestment is ineffective to divert the proceeds already irrevocably destined to another purpose.

SECTION B

Title to be registered in Land Register—
First Registration

Table of procedure[22a]

3–17

SELLER'S SOLICITOR	PURCHASER'S SOLICITOR
1 Obtain Form 10 report[24] (Form 10A)[24a] if not already obtained[24b] [and Form P16 report (if desired)][25] and examine same	1 Check insurance position[23]
2 Frame	
(a) draft Form 11[26]	
(b) draft letter of obligation[27]	
(c) draft discharge of existing heritable security	
(d) [draft retrocession of life policy assigned in security (if any)][28]	
3 Send Form 10 report [and Form P16 report] and drafts (a), (b) and (c) and title deeds to purchaser's solicitor	
4 Write for any prior titles required	
	2 Acknowledge titles and drafts
	3 Examine titles[29] and Form 10 report [and Form P16 report]

[22a] See n. 1 to para. 23–02.
[23] See para. 23–36.
[24] See paras. 18–72, 23–18 and 23–19 and R.T.P.B., para. G.2.15.
[24a] The report by the Keeper on applications for search reports is usually numbered 10A, 12A, etc., but in the text these reports are referred to simply as Form 10 or Form 12 reports as the case may be.
[24b] It is recommended that a Form 10 report should be obtained before adjustment of the contract of sale.
[25] See para. 18–72.
[26] See para. 23–20.
[27] See para. 23–24.
[28] See Vol. I, paras. 10–22, 10–25 and 10–26.
[29] See Chap. 21—remember titles will also be examined by the Keeper.

SELLER'S SOLICITOR

5 Acknowledge titles, etc.
6 Make necessary investigations to answer observations on title and other inquiries
7 Revise (a) draft disposition and (b) draft Forms 1 and 4

8 Return titles, draft disposition and draft Forms 1 and 4 to purchaser's solicitor and reply to observations and inquiries
9 Engross discharge of heritable security [and retrocession of life policy]
10 Send discharge [and retrocession] to building society for execution and request note of loan outstanding at proposed date of settlement
11 Instruct Form 11 report from Keeper

PURCHASER'S SOLICITOR

4 Revise drafts of
(a) Form 11
(b) letter of obligation
(c) discharge of heritable security
5 Frame
(a) draft disposition[30]
(b) draft Forms 1 and 4
6 Return titles, revised drafts (a), (b) and (c) and send draft disposition and draft Forms 1 and 4 to seller's solicitor and raise all observations on title and make other relevant inquiries[31]
7 Receive building society's instructions regarding loan to purchaser and communicate to purchaser [and obtain confirmation from purchaser that he will carry out any remedial works required by society]
8 [Effect or obtain any life policy to be assigned in security]

9 Consider replies to observations and inquiries
10 Engross disposition
11 Send draft disposition and engrossment to seller's solicitor
12 Frame draft standard security and relative Form 2 [and assignation of life policy]

13 Engross standard security [and assignation of life policy]

---

[30] See Chap. 22.
[31] See paras. 23–12 and 23–37 to 23–48.

SELLER'S SOLICITOR	PURCHASER'S SOLICITOR
12 Obtain last rates and feuduty receipts from client	14 Send standard security [and assignation] to client for signature
13 Receive prior titles	
14 Send prior titles to purchaser's solicitor	15 [Where existing life policy being used as security confirm from assurance company that no encumbrances on policy and that premiums paid to date]
15 Compare engrossment of disposition with draft	
16 Send engrossment of disposition to seller for signature	
17 Return draft disposition to purchaser's solicitor	
	16 Examine prior titles
	17 Return these with any further observations
18 Acknowledge prior titles and reply to any further observations (N.B. Retain prior titles meantime to furnish them to purchaser's solicitor if required by Keeper)	
	18 Consider replies to further observations
19 Receive Form 11 report from Keeper	19 [Where existing life policy receive confirmation from assurance company in reply to 15 above]
20 Send Form 11 report to purchaser's solicitor	20 Acknowledge Form 11 report
	21 Send report on title to building society and requisition cheque
21 Prepare state for settlement	
22 Send state for settlement and vouchers to purchaser's solicitor	
22A [Obtain consent (if not incorporated in disposition), renunciation or affidavit if subjects are or may be matrimonial home]	
	22 Examine Form 11 report
	23 Check state for settlement,

SELLER'S SOLICITOR

PURCHASER'S SOLICITOR

retain copy and return to seller's solicitor with any amendments

24 Frame (a) statement for purchaser showing sum required for settlement including fees and outlays and (b) report on title

25 Send report on title and statement to purchaser and request payment

23 Receive executed discharge [and retrocession] from building society

26 Receive standard security [and assignation of life policy] executed by purchaser

24 Receive executed disposition from seller

27 Receive cheque from building society

25 Obtain keys from seller

28 Receive cheque from purchaser and give receipted statement

26 Arrange settlement

29 Arrange settlement

Settlement

27 Receive price and give receipted state for settlement

30 Cash cheques from purchaser and building society[32]

28 Deliver
  (a) keys
  (b) title deeds falling to be delivered

31 Deliver cheque for purchase price and get receipted state for settlement

  (c) prior title deeds required for exhibition to Keeper
  (d) executed discharge
  (e) executed disposition and particulars of execution

32 Check execution of disposition and discharge

  (f) letter of obligation
  (g) Forms 10 and 11 [and P16] reports
  (h) [any matrimonial home document required]
  (i) [feuduty redemption receipt, if available]

33 Take delivery of items (a) to (g) [(h)] [(i)] in item 28 of opposite column

29 Repay building society's loan

30 Account to seller for balance of price less fees and outlays

34 Deliver keys to purchaser

---

[32] Where bridging loan involved, see para. 23–61.

After Settlement

SELLER'S SOLICITOR	PURCHASER'S SOLICITOR
31 Serve notice of change of ownership on superior[33]	35 Complete testing clause of disposition and stamp (if required)
32 [Intimate retrocession of life policy to assurance company]	36 Send disposition to Keeper with (a) Form 1 (b) Form 4 in duplicate [(c) P16 report (if any)] (d) all relevant title deeds (e) discharge (f) standard security and Form 2 [(g) any matrimonial home document required] [(h) feuduty redemption receipt, if available]
33 Cancel seller's insurance	
34 Redeem feuduty or ground annual (if redeemable and not already done)[34]	
	37 [Intimate assignation of life policy to assurance company]
35 Intimate change of ownership to rating authority	38 Report settlement to building society with completion particulars form
36 Receive feuduty redemption receipt	
37 Send same to purchaser's solicitor	
	39 Check feuduty redemption receipt and send to Keeper
	40 Mark letter of obligation as so far implemented and advise seller's solicitor
38 [Receive from assurance company acknowledgment of intimation of retrocession]	41 [Receive from assurance company acknowledgment of intimation of assignation]
39 [Deliver to seller life policy and retrocession and acknowledgment of intimation]	42 [Purchaser confirms any remedial work required by building society has been completed, instruct society to make final survey and request release of any retained money and, when received, account to purchaser]
	43 Receive land certificate and charge certificate from Keeper with title deeds

[33] See n. 11.
[34] See paras. 17–49 to 17–53.

SELLER'S SOLICITOR	PURCHASER'S SOLICITOR
	44 Check accuracy of certificates
	45 Send both certificates and disposition [and life policy, assignation and acknowledgment of intimation] to building society
	46 Retain delivered title deeds with note that registration has been effected
	47 Send prior title deeds and discharged letter of obligation to seller's solicitor
40 Return prior title deeds to custodier (N.B. These must not be destroyed)	

NOTE. For further details see R.T.P.B., paras. G.2.14 to G.2.46.

Form 10 report

23-18   A Form 10 report is a comprehensive report covering the Register of Sasines, the Land Register and the Register of Inhibitions and Adjudications. It contains (a) a report from the Register of Sasines narrating (i) a prescriptive progress of titles, (ii) a list of undischarged securities recorded within the 40 years prior to the date of the certificate including those recorded outwith the 40 years but intromitted with during that period, (iii) a list of discharges of securities recorded within five years prior to the date of the certificate, and (iv) a list of deeds other than transfers or deeds creating or affecting securities recorded within the 40-year period prior to the date of the certificate, *e.g.* minutes of waiver or deeds of servitude; (b) a report from the Land Register which will disclose whether the interest or any part of it has or has not been registered and, if registered, the relevant title number; and (c) a report from the Register of Inhibitions and Adjudications against the parties listed by the applicant.[35] As to additional searches where a company is concerned, see paragraph 23–33 *infra.*

23-19   **Application for Form 10 report.** Application for a Form 10 report should be made in duplicate on Form 10. One copy of the application is returned with the report and should be retained with it. The subjects concerned must be described sufficiently clearly to enable the Keeper to identify them on the Ordnance Map.[36] Where necessary, a P16

---

[35] See R.T.P.B., para. F.04.
[36] See para. 18–64 and R.T.P.B., paras. E.38, F.06 to F.08, and G.2.15.

report should be instructed when application is made for a Form 10 report.[37]

Form 11 report

–20   A Form 11 report is a continuation of the Form 10 report which updates it nearer to the time of settlement and may be used also to instruct a search in the Register of Inhibitions and Adjudications against parties not specified in Form 10. Application for a Form 11 report should be made in duplicate on Form 11 and need not be accompanied by the Form 10 report.[38]

Obligations as to period between receipt of reports and registration

–21   There will usually be a short period between the date of the Form 10 report or, where obtained, the Form 11 report and the date of registration of the purchaser's interest (normally the date of receipt of the application for registration), which may be covered by an obligation from the seller's solicitor. It is not in the interests of the seller's solicitor, however, that the obligation should cover an uncertain period terminable only as and when the purchaser's interest is registered, so a cut-off period should be stipulated of sufficient length only to allow of registration being effected with reasonable despatch. A period of between seven and 21 days has been suggested,[39] but it is a matter for negotiation between the solicitors for the purchaser and seller when the terms of the letter of obligation are being adjusted. As to an appropriate style of obligation, see paragraph 23–24 *infra*.

Obligations as to information required by the Keeper

–22   The information furnished in Form 1 may have been obtained from the seller some time before the application for registration was lodged with the Keeper and may require to be confirmed as being still accurate. Moreover, the Keeper may require additional information which is within the knowledge of the seller and which the seller is under obligation to furnish in terms of the contract of sale.[40] The clause designed to cover such matters in the style of letter of obligation given in the first edition of the Registration of Title Practice Book[41] would impose an obligation which is too unqualified, *e.g.* it has never been the practice for the seller's solicitor to guarantee personally the situation as to the state of possession of the subjects sold. On the other hand the Keeper is entitled to require up-to-date information with

---

[37] See para. 18–72 and R.T.P.B., para. F.07.
[38] See R.T.P.B., para. F.09.
[39] R.T.P.B., para. G.2.21.
[40] See style of clause in contract—R.T.P.B., para. G.2.08.
[41] para. G.2.20, subcl. (2).

regard to the answers contained in Form 1, the seller is obliged to furnish it to the purchaser in terms of the contract of sale and his solicitor may reasonably be asked to co-operate in confirming the information to the best of his knowledge and belief.[42]

Obligations on other matters

23–23   **(1) Discharges or restrictions of heritable securities.** Where an existing heritable security over the subjects of sale is discharged or restricted at or before settlement, an obligation by the seller's solicitor to deliver the recorded discharge or deed of restriction is unnecessary and inappropriate. If for any reason the discharge is not available at settlement an appropriate addition to the letter of obligation should be made.[43]

(2) Feuduty redemption receipts, etc. The practice in relation to obligations as to feuduty redemption receipts, consent of a non-entitled spouse, planning consents, building warrants, National House-Building Council insurance, etc., is the same as in Sasine Register transactions.[44]

Style—letter of obligation

23–24   With reference to the settlement of the above transaction to-day we hereby (1) undertake to clear the records of any deed, decree or diligence (other than such as may be created by or against your client) which may be recorded in the Property or Personal Registers or to which effect may be given in the Land Register in the period from   to   [45] inclusive (or to the earlier date of registration of the purchaser's interest in the above subjects) and which would cause the Keeper to make an entry on, or qualify his indemnity in, the Land Certificate to be issued in respect of that interest and (2) confirm that, to the best of our knowledge and belief,[46] as at this date the answers to the Questions numbered 1 to 10 in the draft Form 1 adjusted with you (in so far as these answers relate to our client or to our client's interest in the above subjects) are still correct.

Prior title deeds

23–25   When first registration has been effected the Keeper will return the prior title deeds. In certain cases in particular these should be carefully retained, namely, (1) where a coloured plan is referred to and no duplicate plan has been recorded in the Register of Sasines under section 48 of the Conveyancing (Scotland) Act 1924, (2) where there has been any exclusion of indemnity by the Keeper, since the prior

---

[42] See style in para. 23–24.
[43] See R.T.P.B., para. G.2.22 for a suggested style.
[44] See para. 23–10.
[45] See para. 23–21.
[46] See para. 23–22.

titles may be required until the exclusion of indemnity has been removed by the operation of positive prescription or otherwise, and (3) where the prior titles are common to other subjects not yet registered in the Land Register or registered with an exclusion of indemnity. Institutional lenders may not wish to be burdened with the custody of prior titles, in which event the solicitor for the purchaser/borrower should retain them with a note that registration in the Land Register has taken place.

SECTION C

Dealings with Registered Interests

Table of procedure[46a]

-26

SELLER'S SOLICITOR	PURCHASER'S SOLICITOR
1 Obtain Form 12 report[47] (Form 12A)[48] if not already obtained[49] [and Form P17 report (if desired)][50]	1 Check insurance position[51]
2 Examine Form 12 report and P17 report (if any).[52] (Note any exclusion of indemnity in land certificate)	
3 Frame	
(a) draft Form 13[53]	
(b) draft letter of obligation[54]	
(c) draft discharge of existing heritable security	
(d) [draft retrocession of life policy assigned in security (if any)][54a]	

[46a] See n. 1 to para. 23–02.

[47] See paras. 23–27 and 23–28.

[48] See n. 24a.

[49] It is recommended that a Form 12 report be obtained before adjustment of the contract of sale.

[50] A Form P17 report is not normally required since the boundaries of the subjects will appear sufficiently clearly from the plan in the title sheet incorporated in the land certificate—see para. 23–28.

[51] See para. 23–36.

[52] In practice this will have been done when Form 12 report has been obtained before contract, since it may require appropriate provisions in the missives.

[53] See para. 23–29.

[54] See para. 23–32.

[54a] See Vol. I, para. 10–25.

SELLER'S SOLICITOR

PURCHASER'S SOLICITOR

4 Send to purchaser's solicitor
  (i) land certificate
  (ii) any links in title subsequent
       to date of land certificate
  (iii) existing charge certificate
        and draft discharge of
        standard security
  (iv) Form 12 [and P17] reports
  (v) draft Form 13
  (vi) draft letter of obligation

2 Acknowledge items in 4 opposite
3 Examine land certificate (noting
  any exclusions of indemnity)
  and Form 12 [and P17] reports
4 Revise drafts of
  (a) Form 13
  (b) letter of obligation
  (c) discharge of standard
      security
5 Frame
  (a) draft disposition[54b]
  (b) Form 2 or Form 3 (if part
      dealing) and Form 4
6 Return land certificate, links in
  title, revised drafts (a), (b) and
  (c) in 4 above and send draft
  disposition and draft Form 2 or
  3 and Form 4, and raise any
  observations and make any
  relevant inquiries[55]
7 [Effect or obtain any life policy
  to be assigned in security]

5 Acknowledge land certificate,
  etc.
6 Make necessary investigations to
  answer observations and other
  inquiries

8 Receive building society's
  instructions regarding loan to
  purchaser and communicate to
  purchaser [and obtain
  confirmation from purchaser
  that he will carry out any
  remedial work required by
  society]

[54b] See Chap. 22.
[55] See paras. 23–12 and 23–37 to 23–48.

SELLER'S SOLICITOR	PURCHASER'S SOLICITOR

7 Revise
   (a) draft disposition
   (b) Forms 2 or 3 and 4
8 Return land certificate, draft disposition and draft Form 2 or 3 and Form 4 to purchaser's solicitor and reply to observations and inquiries

9 Engross discharge of standard security [and retrocession of life policy]

10 Send discharge [and retrocession] to building society for execution and request note of loan outstanding at proposed date of settlement

11 Instruct Form 13 report from Keeper

12 Obtain last rates and feuduty receipts from client

13 Compare engrossment of disposition with draft

14 Send engrossment of disposition to seller for signature

15 Return draft disposition to purchaser's solicitor

16 Receive Form 13 report from Keeper

17 Send Form 13 report to purchaser's solicitor

18 Prepare state for settlement

19 Send state for settlement and vouchers to purchaser's solicitor

---

9 Consider replies to observations and inquiries

10 Engross disposition

11 Send draft disposition and engrossment to seller's solicitor

12 Frame draft standard security and relative Form 2 [and assignation of life policy]

13 Engross standard security [and assignation of life policy]

14 Send standard security [and assignation] to client for signature

15 [Where existing life policy being used as security confirm from assurance company that no encumbrances on policy and premiums paid to date]

16 [Receive confirmation from assurance company in reply to 15 above]

17 Acknowledge and examine Form 13 report

18 Send report on title and terms of life policy to building society and requisition cheque

SELLER'S SOLICITOR	PURCHASER'S SOLICITOR
	19 Check state for settlement,
20 Receive executed discharge	retain copy and return to
[and retrocession] from	seller's solicitor with any
building society	amendments
21 Receive executed disposition	20 Frame (a) statement for
from seller	purchaser showing sum
	required for settlement
	including fees and outlays and
	(b) report on title
21A [Obtain consent (if not	21 Send statement and report on
incorporated in disposition),	title to client and request
renunciation or affidavit if	payment
subjects are or may be	
matrimonial home]	
	22 Receive standard security [and
	assignation of life policy]
	executed by purchaser
	23 Receive cheque from building
22 Obtain keys from seller	society
	24 Receive cheque from purchaser
	and give receipted statement
23 Arrange settlement	25 Arrange settlement

Settlement

24 Receive price and give	26 Cash cheques from purchaser
receipted state for settlement	and building society[56]
25 Deliver	27 Deliver cheque for purchase
(a) keys	price and get receipted state
(b) executed disposition and	for settlement
particulars of execution	28 Check execution of disposition
(c) land certificate	and discharge
(d) any links in title	
(e) executed discharge with	
relevant charge certificate	
(f) letter of obligation	
(g) Forms 12 and 13 [and P17]	
reports	
(h) [any matrimonial home	29 Take delivery of items (a) to
document required][56a]	(g) [(h)] in item 25 of opposite
26 Repay building society loan	column
27 Account to seller for balance	30 Deliver keys to purchaser
of price less fees and outlays	

[56] Where bridging loan involved, see para. 23–61.
[56a] If feuduty or ground annual has been redeemed before settlement redemption receipt should also be delivered.

After Settlement

SELLER'S SOLICITOR	PURCHASER'S SOLICITOR
28 Serve notice of change of ownership on superior[57]	31 Complete testing clause of disposition and stamp (if required)
29 [Intimate retrocession of life policy to assurance company]	32 Send to Keeper
30 Cancel seller's insurance	(a) form 2
31 Redeem feuduty or ground annual (if redeemable and not already done)[58]	(b) executed disposition
	(c) land certificate
32 Intimate change of ownership to rating authority	(d) any links in title
	(e) executed discharge and relative charge certificate
	(f) Form 2 for registration of dealing effected by creation of new standard security
	(g) the new standard security
	(h) Form 4 to include discharge, disposition, relative links in title and new standard security
	[(i) any matrimonial home documents required][58a]
	33 [Intimate assignation of life policy to assurance company]
	34 Report settlement to building society with completion particulars form
33 Receive feuduty redemption receipt	
34 Send same to purchaser's solicitor	
	35 Check feuduty redemption receipt and send to Keeper
	36 Mark letter of obligation as so far implemented and advise seller's solicitor
35 [Receive from assurance company duplicate acknowledgment of retrocession]	37 [Receive from assurance company acknowledgment of intimation of assignation]
36 [Deliver to seller life policy and retrocession and acknowledgment of intimation]	

[57] See n. 11.
[58] See paras. 17–49 to 17–53.
[58a] Also feuduty redemption receipt, if available.

SELLER'S SOLICITOR   PURCHASER'S SOLICITOR

38 [Purchaser confirms any
   remedial work required by
   building society has been
   completed, instruct society to
   make final survey and request
   release of any retained money
   and, when received, account to
   purchaser]

39 Receive land certificate and
   charge certificate from Keeper
   with any title deeds

40 Check accuracy of certificates

41 Send both certificates and
   disposition and charge
   certificate [and life policy,
   assignation and
   acknowledgment of intimation]
   to building society

42 Retain any title deeds delivered
   with note that registration
   effected

43 Send any undelivered title
   deeds and discharged letter of
   obligation to seller's solicitor

37 [Return any borrowed title
   deeds to custodier]

NOTE. For further details, see R.T.P.B., paras. G.3.08 to G.3.38.

Form 12 report

23–27   Just as the search in sasine procedures discloses the recorded deeds
relevant to the ownership of and burdens or securities upon the
subjects, so under the system of registration of title the land certificate
establishes ownership of the registered interest and burdens and
securities upon it. A Form 12 report in relation to a registered interest
broadly corresponds to an interim report on the search in sasine titles
and discloses any changes after the date of the land certificate. Likewise
a Form 12 report discloses any entries in the Register of Inhibitions
and Adjudications affecting the parties entered in the proprietorship
section of the title sheet and any other parties against whom a search is
instructed in the application for a Form 12 report. Particulars of
applications in course of registration will be included in the Form 12
report with a statement that registration has not been completed.[59] The

---

[59] See R.T.P.B., para. F.12.

response by the Keeper to an application for a Form 12 report depends upon the state of the Land Register as regards the particular subjects at the time. Responses on the following forms are used in different circumstances:

12A–Subjects for which registration has been completed.

12B–Subjects for which first registration has not yet been completed and no land certificate yet issued.

12C–Subjects for which first registration has not yet been completed in the case of a compulsory purchase.

12D–Subjects comprising the whole subjects in a transfer of part in the course of registration, forming part of subjects in a parent title.

12E–As in 12D, but the subjects comprise only part of those in the transfer of part.

A response on Form 12B includes a report of the position on the Register of Sasines brought down to the date of first registration and particulars of the application for first registration: in the case of a response on Forms 12D or 12E a report on the Land Register only is required since the parent title has already been registered. A response on Form 12B involves certain risks to the purchaser, *e.g.* that the seller may withdraw the application for registration of his interest or that the land certificate in respect of that interest, when its registration is later completed, may contain an exclusion of indemnity or a qualification of the Keeper's statement in relation to occupancy rights in a matrimonial home which is unacceptable to the purchaser. It is suggested that these risks should be safeguarded by an undertaking from the seller, supported if obtainable by an obligation from his solicitor, that (1) the seller's application for registration of his interest will not be withdrawn, (2) the seller will furnish to the Keeper any further information or documents required to enable the registration of his title to be completed, and (3) a land certificate in name of the seller will be delivered which contains no exclusion of indemnity which is unacceptable to the purchaser and (where relevant) will contain an unqualified statement by the Keeper that there are in respect of the subjects no occupancy rights of a spouse under the Matrimonial Homes (Family Protection) (Scotland) Act 1981. As to additional searches where a company is concerned, see paragraph 23–33 *infra*.

23–28 **Application for Form 12 report.** Application for a Form 12 report should be made in duplicate on Form 12. One copy of the application is returned with the report and should be retained with it. If the report is required in connection with a transaction concerning the whole registered interest in the land certificate no further description of the subjects is required than specification of the title number, but if the transaction relates to part only of the registered interest a description of the part sufficient to enable the Keeper to identify it must be given in the application. If any doubt exists as to the boundaries of the registered interest or the part being conveyed, a P17 report may be instructed. Where a separate land certificate has been issued in respect of the *pro indiviso* interest of one of the proprietors in common it is necessary, when a Form 12 report is being instructed, to advise the Keeper on the application form of the date down to which the land certificate was last completed.[59a]

Form 13 report

23–29   Where there is an interval between receipt of a Form 12 report and settlement of the transaction, the Form 12 report may be updated by applying for a Form 13 report and the opportunity may be taken of instructing a search in the Register of Inhibitions and Adjudications against any additional party who has not been included in the Form 12 report. Application for a Form 13 report should be made in duplicate on Form 13, and need not be accompanied by the Form 12 report.[60]

Obligations as to period between receipt of reports and registration

23–30   An obligation is normally required from the seller's solicitor to cover the short period between the date of the Form 12 report or, where obtained, the Form 13 report and the date of registration of the purchaser's interest. Similar considerations to those already outlined in paragraph 23–21 *supra* apply in relation to the period from the date of the Form 12 or Form 13 report. As to an appropriate style, see paragraph 23–32 *infra*.

Obligations on other matters

23–31   As to obligations in relation to further information that may be required by the Keeper and other matters, the considerations applicable are much the same as those already rehearsed in paragraphs 23–22 and 23–23 *supra*.

Style—letter of obligation

23–32   With reference to the settlement of the above transaction to-day we hereby (1) undertake to clear the records of any deed, decree or diligence (other than such as may be created by or against your client) which may be recorded in the Personal Register or effect given thereto in the Land Register in the period from   to
          [61] inclusive (or to the earlier date of registration of the purchaser's interest in the above subjects) and which would cause the Keeper to make an entry on, or qualify his indemnity in, the Land Certificate to be issued in respect of that interest, and (2) confirm that, to the best of our knowledge and belief,[62] as at this

---

[59a] See R.T.P.B., paras. E.36, E.40, E.42 and F.14.
[60] See R.T.P.B., para. F.13.
[61] See paras. 23–21 and 23–30.
[62] See paras. 23–22 and 23–31.

date the answers to the Questions numbered [1 to 6] [1 to 11] in the draft Form [2] [3] adjusted with you (in so far as these answers relate to our client or to our client's interest in the above subjects) are still correct.

Transactions involving companies

23–33   Where a transaction of sale by or with consent of a company induces first registration in the Land Register or is a dealing with an interest already registered therein a Form 10 or Form 11 report, or a Form 12 or Form 13 report, as the case may be, does *not* include a search in the Register of Charges or the Company Files. In view of the possible risks involved in relation to such transactions[63] it is recommended that a separate search in the Register of Charges and the company's file be instructed either from the Keeper or from private searchers. The answers to questions relating to companies in the relevant Form 1, 2 or 3 and the investigations which may be made by the Keeper are fully described in paragraphs D.4.36 to D.4.39 of the *Registration of Title Practice Book*, but it is in the purchaser's interest that any matters of inquiry which may be disclosed in the searches recommended above should be ascertained before settlement.

Inhibitions—registered interests

23–34   The Keeper is required to enter in the title sheet of a registered interest any subsisting entry in the Register of Inhibitions and Adjudications adverse to the interest,[64] so that a subsisting inhibition will normally appear on the relevant title sheet and the Keeper's indemnity in respect of any loss resulting from it will be excluded. It appears that the legal position is effectively the same as under sasine procedure; the inhibitor may reduce the title to the registered interest if the transaction has been prejudicial to him, the Register discloses a diligence which is *prima facie* adverse to the seller's interest and the obligation of the seller under missives in the normal form will not have been implemented. Where the inhibition has been made after conclusion of the contract of sale but before settlement of the transaction the same problems as those already discussed in relation to sasine titles arise.[65] Inhibitions which have been effected more than five years before the transactions or, if effected within that period, have been discharged will not appear in the title sheet—they are no longer subsisting.

---

[63] See para. 21–87.
[64] Land Registration (Scotland) Act 1979, s. 6(1)(c).
[65] See para. 23–15. The problems, however, may be less difficult since the Keeper on production of the contract of sale may register the purchaser's title without disclosing the inhibition.

Omission of subsisting inhibition from title sheet, reports or office copies

23–35   (a) If the Keeper by mistake omits to enter in the title sheet an inhibition against a party to a transaction or any party concerned in the transaction against whom a search has been instructed on Form 10, 11, 12 or 13 the position appears to be that the inhibitor cannot enforce his rights against the proprietor of the registered interest since in terms of section 3(1)(*a*) of the 1979 Act the rights of the proprietor of the registered interest are subject only to matters entered in the title sheet and an inhibition is not an overriding interest. In such circumstances it would appear that the inhibitor may claim to be indemnified by the Keeper for any resulting loss, the Keeper being entitled to subrogation to the inhibitor's rights.[66]

(b) If the Keeper omits to enter an inhibition in a Form 10 or Form 11 report the inhibition may still be inserted in the title sheet if it is discovered before registration is completed. If that is done the inhibiting creditor may still enforce the inhibition but the registered proprietor will have a claim for indemnity under section 12(1)(*d*) of the 1979 Act. If the omission occurs in a Form 12 or Form 13 report the legal position is more doubtful depending upon the respective dates of the land certificate, the report and the inhibition: in the various possible situations the rights of parties and the obligations of the Keeper may require to be clarified by judicial decision.

(c) If the omission occurs in an office copy of a title sheet (when the Keeper may not be aware of all the parties against whom a search in the Register of Inhibitions and Adjudications should be made) there is no right to indemnity in respect of any loss due to the omission of an inhibition against any person whose interest is neither disclosed in the Register not otherwise known to the Keeper.[67]

SECTION D

Procedural Matters and Problems

Insurance

23–36   The potential liability of a purchaser of heritable property for loss or damage to it occurring during the period between completion of the contract of sale and possession being taken by him has already been explained,[68] and appropriate steps to procure cover have been suggested.[69] The insurance item included in each of the tables of procedure in paragraphs 23–02, 23–17 and 23–26 *supra* is inserted to remind solicitors of this important matter.

---

[66] 1979 Act, ss. 12(1)(*d*) and 13(2) and (3).
[67] *Ibid.*, s. 12(3)(*k*).
[68] para. 15–116.
[69] para. 15–115.

Matters for investigation or inquiry

3–37   There are several matters which may require investigation or inquiry in the period between the conclusion of a contract of sale and settlement of the transaction. Some of these may not be disclosed by the search procedures either in respect of sasine titles or registered interests. So far as they relate to validity and marketability of title they have for the most part been referred to in Chapter 21, but where first registration in the Land Register is induced by the transaction or where a dealing with a registered interest is involved further comment may be helpful. Further, there are non-title matters upon which inquiry should be made whether in transactions involving sasine titles or registrable or registered titles.

3–38   **Matrimonial homes.** The inquiries to be made and the procedures to be carried out in relation to the occupancy rights of a non-entitled spouse in transactions in respect of matrimonial homes already described in Chapter 21, paragraphs 21–23 to 21–36 *supra*, are applicable either in transactions which induce first registration in the Land Register or are dealings with registered interests. See also paragraph 24–20 *infra*.

3–39   **Reservation of minerals.** Where the title deeds of subjects contain specific information regarding minerals the Keeper will enter details in the property section of the title sheet when the interest of the proprietor of the subjects is first registered. In the absence of any such information it should not be assumed that ownership of the minerals is guaranteed unless the title sheet expressly includes them in the registered interest.[70]

3–40   **Burdens and conditions.** It must not be assumed, because the proprietor's interest has been registered in the Land Register, that the title is necessarily marketable. If the real burdens or conditions disclosed in the title sheet are unduly onerous or inconsistent with the contract of sale, the legal position is as outlined in paragraphs 21–54 and 21–55 *supra*. If the seller's solicitor has any reason to doubt whether a reservation of minerals, or conditions, are usual and acceptable, he should furnish the land certificate or a copy of it to the purchaser's solicitor at the pre-contract stage and contract under burden of them.

3–41   **Servitudes.** Under registration of title a servitude may be registered but only as regards the interest of the proprietor of the dominant tenement.[71] It cannot be registered as a burden on the servient tenement although, if it comes to the notice of the Keeper, he may note it on the title sheet of that interest.[72] Before the Keeper enters the

---

[70] 1979 Act, s. 12(3)(*f*); R.T.P.B., para. C.76.
[71] 1979 Act, s. 2(3)(iii); R.T.P.B., para. C.15.
[72] R.T.P.B., para. D.1.16.

interest of the proprietor of the dominant tenement to a servitude, either separately as a heritable right or as a pertinent of a registered interest of ownership of the dominant tenement, he must satisfy himself that it has been effectively constituted but he cannot be certain that the right has not been lost by non-use for the period of negative prescription or by other circumstances which may have resulted in its extinction,[73] and so any claim by the proprietor of the dominant tenement in respect of a servitude is excluded except in so far as it relates to the validity of its constitution.[74] Inquiries by the purchaser or his solicitor should be made (a) in the purchase of the dominant tenement (i) if the servitude has been entered in the Land Register when he need not be concerned as to the validity of its constitution but should verify that it has not been extinguished, or (ii) if it has not been so entered when he should seek to have it registered by the procedure suggested in paragraph 20–25 *supra*; or (b) in the purchase of the servient tenement (i) it should be verified by inspection or inquiry that no unacceptable positive servitude burdens the subjects, and (ii) if any development of the subjects is contemplated it should be confirmed by inquiry of the seller's solicitor that no negative servitude exists which would frustrate or adversely affect the development proposed. (If the title to any adjoining property which may be the dominant tenement in relation to any such servitude has been registered an office copy of the relevant title sheet may be applied for on Form 15 but that will not necessarily be conclusive; the interest of the dominant tenement in the servitude may not have been registered.)

23–42   Latent rights—good faith. As to sasine titles see Chapter 21, paragraphs 21–59 and 21–60 *supra*. In the case of a registered interest (a) if the possibility of reduction on the ground of a latent right is disclosed to the Keeper on application for registration the Keeper will normally exclude indemnity for any resulting loss, or (b) if the applicant is aware of the possibility of such reduction but fails to supply adequate information on the matter in his application for registration, the Keeper will not be liable to indemnify in respect of any resulting loss.[75] It follows that, if the applicant for registration has reason to apprehend the existence of a competing claim to the subjects, he should make careful inquiry as to the relevant circumstances and disclose the information available to him in the application for registration.

23–43   Heritable securities burdening the subjects. Where an old heritable security over the subjects exists and no deed relating to it has been disclosed in searches but it has been kept alive by payment of interest or relevant acknowledgment it will continue to burden the purchaser's

---

[73] See paras. 20–26 to 20–31.
[74] 1979 Act, s. 12(3)(1).
[75] Land Registration (Scotland) Act 1979, s. 12(3)(*n*).

title in the Register of Sasines. If the period of search is adequate, however, the risk is small. Where a heritable security over a sasine title bears to have been discharged within five years of the transaction, the effectiveness of the discharge and any preceding links in the title of the creditor should be examined—see Chapter 21, paragraph 21–57 *supra*. In the case of a registered interest indemnity is excluded in respect of any amount due under a heritable security.[76] If the Keeper omitted to enter a heritable security in the charges section of the title sheet of the burdened land he would be liable in indemnity under section 12(1)(*b*) of the 1979 Act. If the Keeper by mistake understated the amount due under a security for a fixed sum submitted to him, it is thought that he might be liable in indemnity for any loss resulting, notwithstanding the terms of section 12(3)(*o*).

23–44 Conflict with other titles. As to the need in certain circumstances to examine other titles, see Chapter 21, paragraphs 21–63 to 21–66 *supra*. When application is made for registration of an interest in the Land Register any possibility of conflict with or boundary discrepancies relating to other titles should be disclosed in the application. As to minor discrepancies in boundary measurements of a registered interest which may be material, see paragraph 22–61 (iii) *supra*.

23–45 Physical condition of subjects. The risk of defects in the condition of the subjects of purchase should in good practice have been safeguarded by a pre-contract survey.[77] The risk of damage to the subjects by fire or otherwise should have been placed on the seller by an appropriate clause in the missives.[78] If any serious defect is discovered either before settlement, as when the purchaser has taken entry on making a payment to account, or immediately after settlement when entry is taken, the purchaser may have no redress for the loss, but there can be circumstances in which he may have a remedy on the ground of misrepresentation, *e.g.* if a central heating system has been included in an advertisement as a feature of the property and is found not to be in working order. If any serious defect is discovered the purchaser should inform his solicitor immediately so that a claim, if sustainable, may be intimated forthwith.

23–46 Planning permissions and building warrants. The purchaser should be assured that any recently-erected buildings on the subjects of purchase or additions thereto or any change of use of a building to use as a single dwelling-house have been authorised by planning permission and, where building operations have been involved, by a building warrant issued by the relevant buildings authority, and should have included an appropriate stipulation in the contract of sale.[79] An

---

[76] See R.T.P.B., para. C.84.
[77] See para. 15–60.
[78] See para. 15–116.
[79] See paras. 15–105 and 15–106.

enforcement notice in respect of a breach of planning control may be issued within four years from the date of the breach.[80] The Building (Scotland) Act 1959 does not impose a limitation as to the time within which a notice may be served requiring the execution of operations in order that the building may conform to the current Buildings Standards (Scotland) Regulations, but in practice it is improbable that the existence of the unauthorised buildings or erections will not have been observed within 10 years of their construction. If a clause such as that suggested in note 2 to the style of offer suggested in paragraph 15–136 has been contained in the contract of sale, the purchaser's solicitor should require production of the permission and warrant before settlement; an obligation by the seller's solicitor to produce them is unsatisfactory, since they may not exist or be unobtainable except with conditions which are unacceptable to the purchaser. Even if no such stipulation has been included in the contract of sale the purchaser's solicitor should make the same inquiries as regards buildings or additions to them which have been recently erected or substantially altered; if there has been a breach of planning control or disconformity with building regulations the purchaser may have to carry out any remedial operations required by the relevant authority and he may be entitled to resile if the result is that the subjects will be materially different from those purchased.

23–47 **Dwelling-houses recently constructed.** Where a dwelling-house has been constructed within 10 years before the date of purchase, a stipulation as to production and delivery of a Scottish house-purchaser's insurance policy may have been included in the missives.[81] Even in the absence of such a stipulation, however, the purchaser's solicitor should in an appropriate case inquire whether such a policy is available and request delivery of it; the seller will normally have no interest to withhold its delivery.

23–48 **Redemption of feuduty or ground annual.** If the feuduty or ground annual affecting the subjects has previously been redeemed the receipt should be furnished with the title deeds. If it has not earlier been redeemed but becomes redeemable by reason of the current sale and the seller cannot produce a receipt at settlement, the obligation of his solicitor to do so within a stipulated period, say one month, may be acceptable. Alternatively the purchaser may retain the amount of the redemption money at settlement and thereafter, as now proprietor of the subjects himself, serve a notice of redemption in accordance with subsection (6) of section 5 of the Land Tenure Reform (Scotland) Act 1974 in order to start the two months' period referred to in the subsection running.

---

[80] Town and Country Planning (Scotland) Act 1972, s. 84.
[81] See para. 15–109. In cases where inspection was applied for before Jan. 1, 1980, the protective documentation was in a different form.

Possession

3–49   When subjects have been sold with vacant possession, any circumstance which materially prevents or restricts full possession and enjoyment being given entitles the purchaser to resile. It has been held that either *de facto* possession or a claim to a right of occupancy, if substantial and affecting a substantial part of the subjects, is a ground for rescission.[82] If the subjects or any part of them have been let it is the responsibility of the seller to secure vacant possession by serving on the tenant, where necessary, a valid notice to quit and securing vacant possession for the purchaser on the due date. If for any reason the effectiveness of the notice to quit is challenged by the tenant or vacant possession is not given on the date of entry, the purchaser, if possession is not of importance to him, may show tolerance and defer settlement, but any such concession should be made without prejudice to his rights. The purchaser and his solicitor should not participate in any way in the proceedings or arrangements for securing possession, which should be left as the responsibility of the seller alone.

Statutory restrictions

3–50   There are many statutes which impose restrictions upon the development or use of heritable property. In appropriate circumstances where the applicability of a statute may affect the subjects of purchase it is proper to make inquiry. Clearly it is prudent that such inquiry should be made before the parties are contractually bound but, if that has not been done, it is nevertheless proper to make inquiry before settlement in order that the purchaser should be informed of any restraints before settlement. It is impracticable to prepare a comprehensive list of all possible statutory restrictions, but some of the more important are considered in this paragraph.

(1) Town and Country Planning (Scotland) Acts 1972 and 1977 as amended. Inquiries as to planning control affecting the use or proposed use or development of the subjects at the pre-contract and pre-settlement stages have already been considered.[83] In addition the provisions as to buildings of special architectural or historical interest (listed buildings),[84] trees and tree preservation orders,[85] control of advertisements,[86] maintenance of waste land[87] and compulsory acquisition of land[88] may be relevant to particular subjects.

---

[82] *Stuart* v. *Lort-Phillips*, 1977 S.C. 244.
[83] See paras. 15–106 and 23–46.
[84] 1972 Act, ss. 52–56.
[85] *Ibid.*, ss. 57–60 as amended by Local Government (Miscellaneous Provisions) (Scotland) Act 1981, Scheds. 2, 4.
[86] 1972 Act, ss. 61, 62 as amended by Local Government and Planning (Scotland) Act 1982, Sched. 4.
[87] 1972 Act, s. 63 as amended by Local Government (Scotland) Act 1973, Scheds. 23, 25, 29 and Local Government and Planning (Scotland) Act 1982, Sched. 2.
[88] 1972 Act, ss. 102–110 as amended.

(2) Ancient Monuments and Archaeological Areas Act 1979, which makes special provision as to scheduled monuments and designated archaeological areas.

(3) Building (Scotland) Acts 1959 and 1970. As to pre-contract and pre-settlement inquiries, see paragraphs 15–105 and 23–46 *supra*. The Acts also contain provisions as to unauthorised buildings,[89] powers to require buildings to conform to building standards regulations[90] and to require remedial work on or demolition of dangerous buildings,[91] with supplementary powers of entry and recovery of expenses.[92]

(4) Fire Precautions Act 1971. A fire certificate is required in respect of certain categories of buildings or premises to which members of the public are invited or have access, notably hotels, boarding houses, hospitals, teaching or training establishments or places of work.[93] The fire authority may require structural alterations, sometimes substantial, as a condition of issue of a fire certificate.

(5) Offices, Shops and Railway Premises Act 1963, and

(6) Health and Safety at Work, etc. Act 1974. These Acts impose obligations upon proprietors or tenants of premises in which employees work as to cleanliness, overcrowding, sanitary conveniences, lighting, ventilation, washing facilities, etc. In certain cases compliance with the Acts may involve structural alterations to the premises or expensive internal alterations or installations.

(7) Civic Amenities Act 1967. The Act provides for the designation of certain areas as conservation areas and penalises unauthorised work on buildings of special architectural or historic interest.[94]

(8) Roads (Scotland) Act 1984. The Act contains provisions as to the making up and maintenance of private roads and security for the cost of their construction, and compulsory acquisition of land for the construction, improvement or protection of roads.[94a]

(9) Refuse Disposal (Amenity) Act 1978. The Act imposes restrictions on the dumping of abandoned motor vehicles and other refuse.

(10) Control of Pollution Act 1974. The Act, as amended or with substituted provisions,[95] regulates waste disposal, pollution of water in rivers and coastal waters and in the atmosphere.

---

[89] 1959 Act, s. 10 as amended by 1970 Act, Sched. 1 and Local Government (Scotland) Act 1973, Sched. 15.

[90] 1959 Act, s. 11 as amended by 1970 Act, Sched. 1.

[91] 1959 Act, s. 13 as amended by Local Government (Scotland) Act 1973, Sched. 15.

[92] 1959 Act, s. 17.

[93] ss. 1 to 9 as amended by Health and Safety at Work, etc. Act 1974, s. 78.

[94] The Act has been substantially repealed but its provisions have been largely re-enacted—Town and Country Planning (Scotland) Act 1972, Local Government (Scotland) Act 1973.

[94a] ss. 13–18 and 103–110.

[95] Principally by Water (Scotland) Act 1980, Local Government and Planning (Scotland) Act 1982 and Roads (Scotland) Act 1984.

(11) Water (Scotland) Act 1980. This Act contains further provisions as to misuse, contamination or pollution of water.[96]

(12) Weeds Act 1959. In terms of this Act[97] an occupier of land may be required to take action to prevent weeds from spreading.

(13) Pipe-lines Act 1962. Cross-country pipe-lines may not be constructed without Government approval, nor may a local pipe-line of less than 10 miles be constructed without notice being given to the relevant Government department.[98]

(14) Caravan Sites and Control of Development Act 1960. The use of land as a caravan site is prohibited without a licence from the local authority.[99]

(15) Countryside (Scotland) Acts 1967 and 1981. The Countryside Commission established by the Acts has functions for the provision and improvement of facilities for the enjoyment of the countryside, and the Acts make provision for access agreements or access orders by the local authority to enable members of the public to enter upon designated areas of open country without being treated as trespassers.[1] Access agreements and orders must be recorded in the Register of Sasines.[2] Land required for access to open country may be acquired compulsorily by the local authority with the consent of the Secretary of State where it is impracticable to obtain access by agreement or order.[3]

(16) Rent (Scotland) Act 1984. This Act, consolidating and amending earlier statutes, provides for protected tenancies, secured tenancies, rents under regulated tenancies, fair rents, short tenancies, etc. Its provisions are considered further in Volume III.

(17) Agricultural Holdings (Scotland) Act 1949. The Act, as subsequently amended, contains provisions for the protection of tenants of agricultural holdings as to security of tenure, rights of a tenant on waygoing and compensation for disturbance, etc. The relevant provisions are considered in Volume III.

(18) Crofters (Scotland) Acts 1955 and 1961 and Crofting Reform (Scotland) Act 1976. These Acts regulate security of tenure of crofts, determination of fair rents, resumption of crofts by landlords and acquisition of crofts by tenants. See Volume III.

(19) Wildlife and Countryside Act 1981. The Act empowers the Nature Conservancy Council to issue notices imposing restrictions upon operations on areas of special scientific interest.

---

[96] ss. 70–75.
[97] s. 1.
[98] ss. 1, 2.
[99] ss. 1–5.
[1] 1967 Act, ss. 1–18.
[2] *Ibid.*, s. 16(5).
[3] *Ibid.*, s. 24 as amended by 1981 Act, s. 4.

(20) Highlands and Islands Development (Scotland) Act 1965. The Act established the Highlands and Islands Development Board with powers to acquire land by agreement or compulsorily[4] and to enter upon land for any purpose in connection with the exercise of the Board's functions.[5]

Public rights of way

23–51   A landed estate may be subject to rights of way exercisable by the public.[6] The existence of a public right of way is normally evident on inspection of the subjects, but may not be so if it is a pedestrian track used only occasionally.

Delays in settlement

23–52   It frequently happens that for various reasons settlement of a transaction for the purchase and sale of heritable property is not effected on the date of entry stipulated in the contract of sale. In such cases difficult problems may arise as to the rights of parties, the answers to which depend upon the terms of the contract and the actings of parties or their solicitors. Many of these problems have been discussed in legal journals[7]: the following is a summary of the opinions expressed in relation to various situations as affected by subsequent judicial decision.

23–53   **Special conditions of contract.** In certain circumstances, as when the period between the conclusion of missives and the date of entry and settlement is short and/or when the seller has a special reason for requiring punctual settlement on the pactional date, a clause which makes provision for the possibility of delay in settlement may be inserted by the seller in the missives. The terms of such a clause vary but it often includes one or more of the following elements: (1) punctual payment of the price on the pactional date is an essential condition of the contract; (2) consignation of the price will not be accepted; (3) if the price is not paid on the pactional date the seller may refuse entry but the purchaser will nevertheless be liable to pay interest at a stipulated rate from the pactional date of entry until payment; and (4) if payment of the price is not made within a brief stated period after the pactional date of settlement the seller will be entitled to resile from the contract and hold the purchaser liable in damages for any loss incurred. Such a clause may not be acceptable to the purchaser and negotiations usually follow, the outcome of which

---

[4] s. 4.
[5] s. 10 as amended by Local Government and Planning (Scotland) Act 1982, Sched. 4.
[6] See para. 20–37.
[7] A.G.M. Duncan, *Conveyancing Review*, Vol. III, 189; I.W. Noble, (1979) 24 J.L.S. W vii; J.M. Halliday, 1980 S.L.G. 68; A.J. McDonald, (1980) 25 J.L.S. W 103; I.W. Noble, (1983) 28 J.L.S. 116.

depends upon the relative negotiating strengths of the parties and their anxiety to conclude the bargain. At the very least a qualification should be inserted by the purchaser that the provisions of the clause will be applicable only if there is no delay in the procedure on the part of the seller or for which he or his solicitor is responsible.

23–54 Normal conditions of contract. Often the contract of sale does not contain any such special conditions and provides simply for payment of the price on a stated date of entry in exchange for vacant possession, the delivery or exhibition of a good marketable title, delivery of a valid disposition and the production of clear searches in a form appropriate to a title to be recorded in the Register of Sasines, first registration in the Land Register or a dealing with a registered interest, as the case may be. The problems discussed below arise in the context of a contract in this form unless otherwise stated.

23–55 *Delay on the part of the seller.*

(1) In this case the purchaser may take entry and consign the price in joint names of the parties or their solicitors to await settlement. The seller cannot require interest at a rate higher than that receivable on the consigned price (normally current deposit receipt rate) unless he has stipulated in the contract for payment of a greater rate of interest notwithstanding consignation.[8] (2) Alternatively the purchaser may refuse to take entry and the seller cannot require him to do so if he is not in a position to implement his part of the bargain, nor can he demand interest on the purchase price in respect of the period between the contractual date of entry and the date when entry is actually taken on settlement.[9] (3) Although the seller is not yet ready to settle the purchaser may wish to take entry: that is a matter for arrangement between the parties as to terms, but frequently the purchaser makes a payment to account in exchange for entry. From the point of view of the seller the amount of the payment should be sufficient to meet any expense that may be incurred in resale if for any reason the purchaser fails to pay the balance of the price when the seller is in a position to settle: from the point of view of the purchaser the amount of the payment should be the minimum which the seller will accept, since there is the risk of loss if the seller becomes bankrupt and is unable to give a good title. (4) Again, the purchaser may wish to use the seller's failure to implement his part of the contract timeously in order to resile from the bargain: the procedure which he must then adopt is to intimate that unless settlement is effected within a reasonable period stated he will treat the bargain as at an end and will claim the expenses incurred by reason of the seller's failure to implement his part of the contract. The difficulty, however, is to determine what is a reasonable

---

[8] *Prestwick Cinema Co. Ltd.* v. *Gardiner*, 1951 S.C. 98.
[9] *Bowie* v. *Semple's Exrs.*, 1978 S.L.T. (Sh.Ct.) 9.

period. In some older cases[10] quite lengthy periods were allowed by the court but it is a matter of circumstances in the particular transaction. For example, if the impediment to settlement is procuring confirmation in a sale by an executor, three months might be reasonable, if the cause of delay is the execution of a discharge of a heritable security by the creditor a period of one month might be reasonable, but if the consent of an inhibitor is required a longer period may be necessary. It is suggested that in most circumstances the maximum period that may reasonably be stipulated would be six months. In many cases, *e.g.* where the seller contends that he is offering a marketable title but the purchaser disagrees, the safe course is to have the issue determined by the court.

23–56 *Delay on the part of the purchaser.* More commonly the delay in settlement is caused by the purchaser who is unable to procure the necessary funds in time to make full payment on the contractual date. Various courses of action by the seller are possible. (1) He may allow the purchaser to take entry without payment in which event the purchaser will be liable to pay interest on the price from the date of entry until settlement is ultimately made. That course has obvious dangers for the seller; the purchaser may be unable to settle for a lengthy period or may fail completely to do so, and there may be difficulty in obtaining repossession and a long delay before resale can be effected. The risk to the purchaser is that the seller may become bankrupt and be unable to deliver a disposition. (2) The seller may permit entry in exchange for a payment to account. The dangers to the seller and purchaser are similar to those outlined in (1) above. Moreover as a tactical matter in events (1) and (2) above the pressure on the purchaser to complete quickly is diminished, although that result may be offset to some extent by a stipulation for a high rate of interest on the price or the balance, as the case may be. (3) Entry may be given on partial consignation of the price. Since the delay is due to the fault of the purchaser, the seller need not permit entry on partial consignation. If he does he is entitled to stipulate that there will be no reduction in the rate of interest on the full price. (4) The seller may refuse to give entry until he receives full payment of the price, but in that event he cannot claim interest on the principle that he cannot both enjoy continued possession of the subjects and interest on the price he should have received for them.[11] (5) If the seller offers to give entry but the purchaser declines to take it, it is probable, although not altogether clear, that interest will be payable by the purchaser from the date when entry was offered. The purchaser is not enjoying the fruits of the land, but that is due to his own action. (6) The seller may wish

---

[10] See para. 21–04 and cases there cited.
[11] *Stirling and Dunfermline Rly. Co.* v. *Edinburgh and Glasgow Rly. Co.* (1857) 19 D. 598, 621; *Greenock Harbour Trs.* v. *Glasgow and South-Western Rly Co.*, 1909 S.C.(H.L.) 49.

to terminate the contract. The situation is similar to that already discussed[12] in the case where the delay is on the part of the seller, but where the delay is on the part of the purchaser guidance may be obtained from judicial *dicta*.

> "Nor do I wish it to be thought that an unpaid seller must remain indefinitely at the mercy of a dilatory purchaser . . . It seems to me that there is room for a broad distinction between two types of case. In the one, there is no reason to doubt that the money will ultimately be forthcoming and in such cases, while pressure may be applied, it is right that patience should be shown before matters are brought to a head—it being remembered too that, after entry, interest is running on the price. In the other type of case, there is reason to doubt whether the money will be forthcoming and, in that case, the setting of a time limit may more readily be resorted to. What will justify doubt must always be a question of circumstances, but there are recognised means of seeking assurance with regard to ultimate payment, and, if these means have been tried and found wanting, the seller will be in a strong position to take action."[13]

Upon these observations the following comments may be made: (a) they are applicable in the context that entry had been given to the purchaser, (b) even in the first type of case it is thought that pressure may take the form of the imposition of a reasonable time limit, and (c) the question remains of what is a reasonable time limit. Some assistance on the last point may be obtained from the decision in *Lloyds Bank Ltd.* v. *Bauld*,[14] where settlement was due on December 15, 1974, a deposit of £700 to account of the price of £7000 having been paid on conclusion of the missives, on the request of the purchasers the sellers extended the time for completion to early January, 1975, and on January 13 the sellers called upon the purchasers to pay the balance by January 31, 1975, failing which they would hold the contract as rescinded. The court decided that, when the purchasers failed to pay on that date, the sellers were entitled to a declarator that the contract had been validly rescinded. The broad conclusions are that, if the seller wishes to be free of the bargain because of delay by the purchaser he should either obtain a probative or holograph letter from the purchaser or his solicitor accepting that the contract is cancelled or raise an action in court for declarator that the contract is terminated with a further conclusion for damages. A style of such an action given in the *Encyclopaedia of Scottish Legal Styles*, Volume 8, page 122, has been approved by the court in a recent case.[15]

3-57 *Delay not attributable solely to either party.* It is clear that if entry is taken by the purchaser interest is payable thereafter upon the price or

---

[12] In para. 23–55(4).
[13] *Rodger (Builders) Ltd.* v. *Fawdry*, 1950 S.C. 483 *per* Lord Sorn (Ordinary) at 494.
[14] 1976 S.L.T. (Notes) 53.
[15] *Bosco Design Services Ltd.* v. *Plastic Sealant Services Ltd.*, 1979 S.L.T. (Notes) 33.

the outstanding balance of the price from the date of entry until full payment has been made, on the principle that the purchaser cannot both enjoy the fruits of the subjects and retain the price, or the balance of the price, which he should have paid.[16] Likewise it seems clear that if consignation or partial consignation has been made by agreement of parties interest is payable on the amount consigned only at the rate receivable thereon. Subsequently this situation will resolve itself into one or other of the situations already considered in paragraphs 23–55 or 23–56, depending upon which of the parties is first ready to settle.

23–58 *Rate of interest on price.* The rate of interest payable by the purchaser on the price or unpaid balance of the price has not been determined by relevant judicial decision. It would seem that the old "legal" rate of 5 per cent is not necessarily appropriate.[17] It is suggested that the rate applicable to heritably secured loans on the type of property concerned is reasonable, since the seller is virtually in the position of having security over the subjects because he need deliver a conveyance only on receiving full payment. It may be that where the purchaser is responsible for the delay the rate may be greater,[18] but *quaere?*

23–59 *Consignation.* Consignation must be made in a form which gives the seller some measure of control over the release of the consigned amount.[19] Usually it is made by deposit receipt in joint names of the seller and purchaser or of their respective solicitors.

23–60 *Damages for late settlement.* In the general case where delay in settlement has been occasioned by the purchaser but is ultimately effected, the seller is not entitled to damages other than interest on the price in respect of the period between entry and settlement. In a recent case[20] a claim by the seller of an owner-occupied house (in a transaction of sale which was ultimately settled) for *inter alia* interest on a bridging loan incurred in connection with the purchase of a new house was rejected by the court in circumstances where the seller did not offer to prove how or why the purchaser should have been aware that financial loss of the nature claimed was within the reasonable contemplation of the parties at the time when missives were entered into, it being an extravagant proposition that the necessity of the seller obtaining a bridging loan for the purpose of an alternative residence was something which should be within the reasonable contemplation of any purchaser.[21]

---

[16] See cases cited in n. 11, para. 23–56.
[17] See *Kearon* v. *Thomson's Trs.*, 1949 S.C. 287 (relating to interest on legitim, but see general observations by Lord President Cooper at 292–296).
[18] See *Traill* v. *Connon* (1877) 5 R. 25.
[19] *Grandison's Trs.* v. *Jardine* (1895) 22 R. 925.
[20] *Tiffney* v. *Bachurzewski*, 1985 S.L.T. 165.
[21] In many cases the relevant facts are otherwise: when missives are being adjusted the selection of the date of entry is partly conditioned, to the knowledge of the solicitors for both parties, by the desirability of it coinciding with the date or anticipated date of entry to an alternative residence being purchased by the seller.

-61 *Bridging loans.* In transactions involving the sale of one property and the purchase of another it frequently happens that the price of the latter property becomes due for payment before the proceeds of sale of the former property are available, and a bridging loan from bankers is required. Bankers may be reluctant to provide this facility unless a binding contract for the sale of the former property has been concluded, since the usual procedure is for the party's solicitor to give to the bank an irrevocable undertaking to account to it for the net proceeds of that sale when received. In the case where the amount of the bridging loan does not exceed £15,000 the arrangement must comply with the relevant provisions of the Consumer Credit Act 1974.[22]

Notice of change of ownership

-62 Although the feuduty may have been or is being redeemed it is still necessary for the seller to serve a notice of change of ownership to ensure that, when the purchaser's title is recorded or registered, the seller is relieved of the other obligations of the feu which remain in force notwithstanding redemption of the feuduty.[23]

Communication with client

-63 On the conclusion of a transaction for the purchase of heritable property the purchaser's solicitor should furnish to his client a report on the title. It should contain a summary of the conditions of the title which should be accurate and should omit nothing that may be relevant. In addition it may be proper for the solicitor of either party to keep his client informed during the course of the transaction of any unusual problems or arrangements and take instructions with regard to them. In claims of professional negligence or complaints to the Law Society of Scotland of unprofessional conduct an element which constantly recurs is delay in settlement of a conveyancing transaction and failure of the solicitor concerned to communicate the reasons timeously to his client.

---

[22] See Vol. I, para. 8–26.
[23] Land Tenure Reform (Scotland) Act 1974, s. 5(3).

CHAPTER 24

INFEFTMENT AND REGISTRATION

SECTION A

Sasine Titles

SECTION B

Registration of Title

(1) First Registration

(2) Registered Interests

SECTION A

Sasine Titles

Requirements for infeftment

24–01   In feudal law the classical requirements for infeftment following upon a conveyance of land were, (1) the granter of the deed must himself be infeft, (2) the party taking infeftment must be a disponee under the deed, and (3) the deed had to be a special, as distinct from a general, conveyance. The first of these requirements was modified by the Conveyancing (Scotland) Act 1924 which permitted deduction of title where the conveyance was a disposition[1]: infeftment of the granter is still necessary if the conveyance is a feu grant, although the granter's lack of infeftment may be cured by accretion when he subsequently becomes infeft.[2]

Methods of obtaining infeftment

24–02   Infeftment is normally effected by direct recording in the Register of Sasines of a special conveyance in favour of the grantee. It may also be effected, usually where the right to the property rests on midcouples or links of title which are themselves inappropriate for recording *de plano* in the Register of Sasines, by expeding and recording a notarial instrument[3] or a notice of title.[4] As to automatic infeftment in the case

---

[1] See para. 16–56.
[2] See paras. 24–59, 24–60.
[3] Titles to Land Consolidation (Scotland) Act 1868, s. 19 (as restricted in its application by Succession (Scotland) Act 1964, s. 34(2) and Sched. 3) and ss. 23, 24 and 25 as amended.
[4] Conveyancing (Scotland) Act 1924, ss. 4 and 6.

of survivors under destinations and trustees, see paragraphs 24–09 and 24–10 *infra*.

Effect of infeftment

4–03 Infeftment by the recording of a special conveyance or a notarial instrument or notice of title in the Register of Sasines converts the personal right of the grantee into a real right of property. Infeftment is still required for the granting of certain deeds, *e.g.* a feu grant or lease, and where infeftment is necessary the court cannot dispense with the requirement.[5] Such recording, however, does not establish the validity or marketability of the title of the person appearing on the Register as proprietor; that depends also upon the sufficiency of the progress of titles leading to the recorded deed, at least until positive prescription has fortified the recorded title.

Grantees

4–04 It is essential that, before a real right can be obtained by infeftment, the grantee is named or identified in the deed which is recorded. It should be noted that, where the proprietor is an individual person or persons, the recorded deed should be framed in his or their favour, not in favour of factors or commissioners for the true proprietor or a judicial factor who administers his estate.[6]

4–05 **Named disponees.** Ordinarily the grantee of the conveyance is named and designed in the deed. There may be cases, however, where there is omission to design the grantee in the deed or the name or designation of the grantee has changed before it is recorded, when the omission may be supplied or the alteration specified in the warrant of registration.[7]

4–06 **Descriptive disponees.** In older practice, dispositions were occasionally granted in favour of persons not named but described so as to enable them to be identified, "the heir of A," or "the children of the marriage between A and B." Once the identity of the disponee(s) was established, as on the death of A or the dissolution of the marriage A and B, the disposition could be recorded with a warrant of registration in appropriate terms, *e.g.*—"Register on behalf of X, (*designed*), the heir of the within named A, in the Register of the County of   ," or "Register on behalf of X (*designed*), Y (*designed*) and Z (*designed*), the children of the marriage between the within named A and B in the Register of the County of   ." In addition, it was recommended that a declaratory service was taken for the purpose of identifying the

---

[5] *Campbell* (1890) 18 R. 149.
[6] *Scott* (1856) 18 D. 624.
[7] Conveyancing (Scotland) Act 1924, s. 10(2): See Burns, 250.

disponee(s).[8] In the case of a disposition granted on or after September 10, 1964, a declarator of service may not be competent,[9] but it is thought that the recording of the disposition with a warrant of registration which identifies the disponee(s) *prima facie* effects infeftment. In the event of a subsequent sale of the subjects before the title has been rendered unchallengeable by the operation of positive prescription there may be a problem in providing evidence which establishes the identity of the disponee(s), but the problem is largely of academic interest since post-1964 dispositions of this kind to descriptive disponees are rarely encountered.

24–07 Vesting, interposed liferents and fiduciary fees, institutes and substitutes. Problems which may result from more complex destinations in conveyances involving such matters belong more appropriately to the field of completion of title, and are considered in Volume IV.

Special conveyance—description of subjects

24–08 In feudal theory a special, as distinct from a general, conveyance of lands was one which contained an identifying description of the lands and the proper feudal clauses, so that it constituted a sufficient warrant to the grantee to obtain infeftment directly by recording the deed in the Register of Sasines or by expeding and recording an instrument of sasine. A general conveyance was one which lacked any of those elements.[10] The distinction remains today but, as the result of the simplifications in the style of a special disposition by modern statutes, the only significant question as to the sufficiency of a special conveyance now relates to the adequacy of the description of the subjects. The requirements of a sufficient description have already been considered.[11]

Survivorship infeftment

24–09 Where a conveyance is in favour of two or more persons and the survivor or survivors, no procedure is required to give the survivor or survivors a completed title to the whole subjects when one dies. It is not necessary for the destination to the survivor or survivors to be mentioned in the warrant of registration.[12] In three special cases some qualification may be required: (1) In the unusual situation where each of the grantees has taken infeftment separately, or by recording the deed with separate warrants in respect of each, it may be necessary on the

---

[8] Montgomerie Bell, 646; Burns, 250.
[9] The sections of the Titles to Land Consolidation (Scotland) Act 1868 providing for services were repealed by the Succession (Scotland) Act 1964, Sched. 3 *quoad* successions opening on or after September 10, 1964, and the partial revival of service procedures by the Law Reform (Miscellaneous Provisions) (Scotland) Act 1980, s. 6, applies only to trust services.
[10] *Studd* v. *Cook* (1883) 10 R.(H.L.) 53, 59.
[11] In paras. 18–05 to 18–16.
[12] Conveyancing (Scotland) Act 1924, s. 10(3).

death of one of them to re-record or to expede and record a notice of title narrating the fact of survivorship. (2) If one of the grantees has died before the deed is recorded the survivor or survivors may take infeftment by recording the deed with a warrant narrating the fact of survivance. In neither of these cases is any procedure required to evidence the fact of survivorship; production of a death certificate is enough. It is possible, where the destination to the survivor could have been evacuated, that the predeceaser has done so but no competing right appears on the record or is intimated. In such a case it would appear that a subsequent purchaser from the survivor or survivors has no duty of inquiry.[13] (3) If the destination to the survivor or survivors is subject to a qualification, *e.g.* on failure of issue of the predeceaser or after a prior substitution of issue of the predeceaser, the position is different: evidence of failure of the issue or the substitute would be necessary.

Continuity of trust infeftment

4–10   In conveyances to trustees a destination to the survivors or survivor of them is usually expressed, but even in the absence of such a destination the rule of accretion in joint property operates to give complete infeftment in the whole subjects to the survivors or survivor.[14] Certain special statutory provisions may be noted:

(1) A recorded conveyance of lands acquired for religious or educational purposes taken in the names of office-bearers of, or trustees appointed or from time to time to be appointed for, the relevant religious or educational body has the effect of automatically giving a completed title to their successors in office. It is not necessary for a destination to successors in office to be included in the deed. The appointment of the successors may be in any manner provided or referred to in the deed or if no mode of appointment is so provided then the appointment may be in terms of the rules or regulations of the body.[15] A purchaser would be entitled to evidence, such as an extract from the minutes of the meeting at which the appointment was made, which, it is suggested, should be certified in the manner provided by section 5 of the Conveyancing (Scotland) Act 1924. The provisions of the 1868 Act apply also to leases, whether registered or not.

(2) Where in terms of a recorded conveyance the office of trustee is conferred on the holder of any place or office or the proprietor of any estate and his successors therein any person subsequently becoming a trustee by succession to the place or office or estate is deemed to have a valid and complete title by infeftment as if he had been named in the

---

[13] Burns, 259.
[14] *Gordon's Trs.* v. *Eglinton* (1851) 13 D. 1381; *Oswald's Trs.* v. *City of Glasgow Bank* (1879) 6 R. 461.
[15] Titles to Land Consolidation (Scotland) Act 1868, s. 26.

recorded title without the necessity of any deed of conveyance or other procedure.[16] A destination to successors in office must have been contained in the recorded deed and the statutory provision applies to feudal property, not leaseholds.

Some statutes provide expressly for the vesting of heritable property in successors of trustees. For example, the Friendly Societies Act 1974[17] provides that property belonging to a friendly society shall vest in the trustees *for the time being* of the society. Purchasers from the trustees should be satisfied as to the trustees having been properly appointed by production of a copy of the relevant minutes of meeting duly certified.[18] There may be a question whether such a provision vests merely the right to the property or effects infeftment: the safe course is to regard it as only vesting the right and to complete or deduce the title of the trustees as may be necessary for the granting of any subsequent deed by the trustees.

Liferent infeftments

24–11   Infeftment may be taken by a proper liferenter, as where a conveyance is granted in favour of A in liferent and B in fee. The warrant of registration need not refer to the nature of the interest of the proprietor in liferent or fee, since the qualities of the destination are presumed to be imported into the warrant.[19] It may be in favour of the liferenter or both liferenter and fiar, *e.g.* (1) "Register on behalf of the within named A in the Register of the County of   ," or (2) "Register on behalf of the within named A and B in the Register of the County of   ." In the more usual case where the liferent is protected by a trust, infeftment in heritable property is taken in the names of the trustees who hold for the benefit of liferenter and fiars. It is incompetent to effect infeftment in the assignee of a liferenter, even a proper liferenter, since a liferent right is intransmissible as such.[20]

Clause of direction

24–12   Where a conveyance contains material which it is not desired to record in the Register of Sasines the parts of the deed which are to be recorded may be specified in a clause of direction inserted immediately before the testing clause.[21] A style of a clause of direction is provided[22] and runs:

---

[16] Conveyancing (Scotland) Act 1874, s. 45.
[17] s. 54.
[18] See *Mitchell v. St. Mungo Lodge of Ancient Shepherds*, 1916 S.C. 689, 693; Conveyancing (Scotland) Act 1924, s. 5(1).
[19] Conveyancing (Scotland) Act 1924, s. 10(3).
[20] *Ker's Trs. v. Justice* (1868) 6 M. 627, 631; *Scottish Union and National Ins. Co. v. Smeaton* (1904) 7 F. 174, 178; Ersk., II, ix, 11.
[21] Titles to Land Consolidation (Scotland) Act 1868, s. 12.
[22] *Ibid.*, Sched. F.

And I direct to be recorded in the Register of Sasines the part of this deed from its commencement to the words [*insert words*] on the   line of the   page [and also the part from the words [*insert words*] on the   line of the   page to the words [*insert words*] on the   line of the   page] [*Or*, I direct the whole of this deed to be recorded in the Register of Sasines, with the exception of the part [*or* parts, *as the case may be, specifying the part or parts excepted, as above*].

The use of such a clause requires care. For example, (i) a part of the deed may be omitted which is essential to render intelligible the part recorded, (ii) the name or designation of a person may be inadvertently omitted, (iii) all real burdens and conditions must be included at length or duly referred to in the part to be recorded, or (iv) in the case of a deed creating a heritable security the powers of the the creditor with reference to the property should be expressed in order to give notice on record to creditors who may take postponed securities.

Warrants of registration

24–13   Forms of warrants of registration to be endorsed on conveyances are prescribed in Schedule F to the Conveyancing (Scotland) Act 1924. Designations of the person or persons on whose behalf the conveyance is being recorded are not necessary if the designations are contained in the deed and have not been changed. Nor is it necessary to specify the quality of the grantee's infeftment, *e.g.* as trustees or as liferenter or fiar, nor to mention destinations to a survivor. Examples of warrants are:

(1) *Individual named and designed in deed*
"Register on behalf of the within named A in the Register of the County of   ."

(2) *Individual named but not designed in deed*
"Register on behalf of the within named A, (*designation*), in the Register of the County of   ."

(3) *Individual not named or designed in the deed*
"Register on behalf of A, (*designed*), the heir (*or otherwise as the case may be*) of the within named B, in the Register of the County of   ."

(4) *Individual wrongly named or designed in deed*
(a) "Register on behalf of John Smith, (*designed*), being the within named James Smith, in the Register of the County of   ."

or

(b) "Register on behalf of the within named A, now residing at   , in the Register of the County of   ."

(5) *Individual grantee in liferent*
"Register on behalf of the within named A in the Register of the County of   ."
Note. Reference to the liferent is unnecessary.

(6) *Individual grantees in liferent and fee respectively*
"Register on behalf of the within named A and B in the Register of the County of   ."
Note. Reference to liferent and fee is unnecessary.

(7) *Two or more individuals with destination to survivor or survivors*
"Register on behalf of the within named [A and B] [A, B and C] in the Register of the County of   ."
Note. Reference to survivorship is unnecessary.

(8) *Trustees with destination to survivors and survivor*
"Register on behalf of the within named A, B and C as in the Trustees within mentioned in the Register of the County of   ."

(9) *Changes in designations in case (5), (6), (7) or (8)*
If there are any changes in the designations of parties, insert new designations as in 4(b) above.

(10) *Clause of direction*
"Register in terms of the clause of direction herein contained on behalf of the within named A in the Register of the County of   ."

(11) *Registration in two or more counties*
"Register on behalf of the within named A in the Registers of the Counties of   and   [and   .]."

(12) *Notice of title recorded along with special conveyance*
Where a notice of title in Form No. 2 of Schedule B to the Conveyancing (Scotland) Act 1924 is being recorded along with the special conveyance the warrant of registration on the notice of title runs: "Register on behalf of the within named A in the Register of the County of   along with the disposition docqueted with reference hereto."

The disposition will be docqueted: "Docqueted with reference to the notice of title in favour of A recorded of even date herewith."[23]

Warrants of registration are signed by the grantee of the conveyance or his solicitor.
As to registration for publication as well as for preservation (or preservation and execution in appropriate deeds) or for publication and preservation but not for execution see Volume I, paragraph 4–75.

SECTION B

Registration of Title

Introduction

24–14   The Land Registration (Scotland) Act 1979 introduced a new system of registration of interests in land by the establishment of the Land

---

[23] Conveyancing (Scotland) Act 1924, s. 4(2), Sched. B, Note 7, and Sched. F, Note 5.

Register of Scotland with detailed rules as to its operation and the legal effects of registration therein. The essential characteristics of the system are:

(1) A register of interests in land, including any estate, interest, servitude and other heritable right in or over land and any heritable security and long lease subject to such burdens or conditions as are set out on the register.

(2) Registration of an interest vests in the registered proprietor a real right therein and to any right, servitude or pertinent forming part of it, subject only to the effect of any matter entered on the title sheet of the interest as adverse to the interest and any overriding interest, and also makes any registered right or obligation relating to a registered interest a real right or obligation.

(3) Accurate identification of the land and its boundaries by a plan based on the Ordnance Map.

(4) The issue to the registered proprietor of a land certificate which contains a facsimile of the title sheet of the register including the plan identifying the land, which will broadly take the place of prior title deeds and largely avoid the need for their examination.

(5) The right of the proprietor of a registered interest is guaranteed by a Government indemnity subject only to certain statutory exclusions from indemnity and any exclusion expressly entered in the title sheet of the interest.

(6) The provision of simple forms of deeds relating to registered interests using an identifying title number of the interest.

(7) The provision of an official search service which covers entries in the Register of Sasines, the Land Register and the Register of Inhibitions and Adjudications.

(8) The preservation of the public character of land registers in Scotland by the express provision to that effect in section 1(1) of the 1979 Act and the availability on request of office copies of entries in the Land Register.

This chapter treats of the more important provisions of the 1979 Act so far as relating to the registration of the interests of proprietors of estates in land and related servitudes, burdens and obligations: registration of titles to heritable securities and leases is dealt with in Volume III. Practitioners will have available the invaluable *Registration of Title Practice Book* prepared by the Joint Consultative Committee of the Law Society of Scotland and the Department of the Registers of Scotland: constraints of space restrict the contents of this work to the main principles and machinery of practice with references to the *Practice Book* for further details.[23a] References to the "Act" in this section are to the Land Registration (Scotland) Act 1979.

[23a] Reference may be made to the series of articles by the Keeper, (1979) 24 J.L.S. W xlvii, W liii, W lxi, W lxxix, and lxxxv; (1980) 25 J.L.S. W 93, W 98, W 105, W 129, W 139, W 151, W 157 and W 173; (1981) 26 J.L.S. W 181, and by Mr J. Robertson (now Deputy Keeper), (1982) 27 J.L.S. W 286, W 307, W 322 and W 327, and (1983) 28 J.L.S. W 333, W 351, W 358 and W 394. The articles by the Keeper are substantially reproduced in Part C of R.T.P.B.

The Registers

24–15   The 1979 Act[24] established the Land Register of Scotland, a new register of interests in land under the control of the Keeper of the Registers of Scotland. The Land Register is located in the same premises as the General Register of Sasines, also under the control of the Keeper; the two Registers will operate in parallel and the information contained in each will be co-ordinated. Registration of title in the Land Register is being introduced area by area, each area broadly corresponding to an existing division of the Sasine Register, and as areas become successively operational the Land Register will gradually supersede the Sasine Register as the principal record of rights in land. At present the areas which have become operational are the counties of Renfrew, Dumbarton, Lanark and Glasgow.[25]

Compulsory registration

24–16   Once an area has been designated a compulsory registration area in terms of section 30 of the Act (an operational area) certain transactions, including the grant of a feu and a conveyance on sale, induce compulsory registration in the Land Register.[26] As to the registration of interests where the deeds are delivered shortly before or after an area becomes operational in a transaction which would induce first registration see the *Practice Book*, paragraph D.1.05, and as to registration of writs relating to subjects which are partly within and partly outside an operational area see the *Practice Book*, paragraphs D.1.07, D.1.21 and D.1.22.

Voluntary registration

24–17   The Keeper in his discretion may accept for registration an interest in land which lies in an operational area even though it is not compulsorily registrable.[27] Normally the Keeper will accept applications for voluntary registration of such interests, subject to administrative pressures on his staff or if a complicated examination of title is involved.[28] The facility is peculiarly valuable where an area is about to be developed and numerous feus or dispositions of parts are contemplated, or where it is desired to test the validity of a doubtful title.[29] Application may also be made for voluntary registration of an interest in subjects which lie outwith an operational area, but in

---

[24] Act, s. 1.
[25] As to the extent to which the provisions of the Act apply to operational and other areas, see R.T.P.B., para. A.1.03.
[26] Act, ss. 2, 3 and 8(4). For a full list of transactions which do and do not induce first registration, see R.T.P.B., paras. D.1.01, D.1.02 and D.1.03.
[27] Act, s. 2(1)(*b*).
[28] R.T.P.B., para. D.1.11.
[29] R.T.P.B., para. D.1.12.

general the Keeper will accept such an application only if the subjects are situated in an area which is next due to be declared operational.[30] Preliminary inquiry may be made of the Keeper whether an application for voluntary registration is likely to be accepted, and that should be done before any Form 10 report is instructed.[31] Once an interest has been registered voluntarily all subsequent writs relating to it will be registered in the Land Register.

Recording in the Sasine Register

-18 Recording in the Register of Sasines remains appropriate where the subjects are situated in an area which has not yet become operational. Once an area has become operational most transactions will lead to registration in the Land Register either because they induce first registration or are dealings with an interest already registered, but recording in the Register of Sasines is still appropriate in a limited number of transactions.[32] Eventually, in order that maximum information regarding interests in land in a specified area are entered in the Land Register, the Secretary of State may require by order that interests in land in that area which have not yet been registered in the Land Register will be included in the Land Register, and thereafter recording in the Register of Sasines of deeds relating to subjects within that area will cease to be competent.[33]

(1) First Registration

Application for registration

-19 The conveyancing procedures and form of deed in respect of a transaction leading to first registration in the Land Register are similar to those in a transaction leading to recording in the Register of Sasines except that no warrant of registration is placed on the feu disposition, disposition or other final unrecorded writ which gives effect to the transaction save in the special case where the writ relates to subjects partly within and partly outwith an operational area.[34] An application for first registration is made by submitting a completed Form 1 to the Keeper together with the relative writs listed in an Inventory (in duplicate) on Form 4. The writs sent should comprise (1) a sufficient progress of title with all unrecorded links up to and including the deed giving effect to the current transaction, (2) all prior writs outwith the prescriptive progress whereby rights, burdens or conditions affecting the subjects are created, varied or discharged, (3) all outstanding

---

[30] R.T.P.B., para. D.1.13.
[31] R.T.P.B. paras. D.1.11 and F.04.
[32] For examples of such transactions, see R.T.P.B., para. D.1.20.
[33] Act, s. 2(5).
[34] R.T.P.B., paras. D.1.21 and D.2.01.

securities and transmissions, restrictions and discharges of outstanding securities and of securities discharged within the past five years, (4) any deed not already included in (1) or (2) containing a full description of the subjects and particularly any deed plan together with any additional information which will enable the Keeper to identify the subjects on the Ordnance Map, (5) any relative redemption receipt for feuduty or ground annual, (6) any Form P16 report, and (7) documents or evidence required in relation to possible occupancy rights of a non-entitled spouse under the Matrimonial Homes (Family Protection) (Scotland) Act 1981.[35,36] If any writs are not available when the application is made they should be included in Form 4 and marked "to follow." Common writs applicable to several subjects need not be submitted with the application; the Keeper may already have examined these in connection with another application and, if not, he will call for their production. In terms of section 4(3)(*b*) of the Act and Rule 11 of the Land Registration (Scotland) Rules 1980[37] the Keeper may, without rejecting an application, return any document relating to the application which requires amendment, normally the deed giving effect to the current transaction, which on examination is found to contain remediable errors or omissions.[38] Where practicable the necessary amendments should be effected by alterations, duly authenticated, to the deed rather than by drawing a new deed since the latter procedure involves the risks of (i) the date of execution of the new deed being after the date of registration of the interest (normally the date of receipt of the application by the Keeper), and (ii) a discrepancy between the new date of the deed and the reference to it in a standard security which is being registered contemporaneously plus the same risk that the date of registration of the standard security may be prior to the date of execution of the disposition in favour of the debtor.

The application (Form 1) must be signed by the person in whose favour the real right is to be completed or his solicitor. If a standard security by the purchaser is being submitted for registration of the interest of the heritable creditor at the same time as the application for registration of the purchaser's interest two application forms are required, one (Form 1) in respect of the purchaser's interest as proprietor, and one (Form 2) in respect of the interest of the heritable creditor.[39]

The date of registration is the date when the application, properly completed and signed, is received by the Keeper, subject to the

---

[35] As to the requirements and procedure in relation to possible occupancy rights of a non-entitled spouse, see para. 24–20.

[36] As to completion of Form 1 generally, see Notes and Directions for Completion of Forms 1, 2, 3 and 4 reprinted in R.T.P.B., para. B.3.01. See also R.T.P.B., paras. D.1.22 (case 2), D.2.03, and D.2.06 to D.2.13.

[37] S.I. 1980 No. 1413 (S. 114).

[38] R.T.P.B., para. D.2.18.

[39] R.T.P.B., para. D.2.07.

qualifications that (1) if the application is not signed or any fundamental deed requires amendment the date of registration will be that on which the Keeper receives the application duly signed or the deed appropriately amended, and (2) if documents or evidence essential to completion of registration are not furnished within 60 days of request by the Keeper the application may be rejected and registration may be effected on a later date when the amended documents and evidence are provided.[39a]

Reference may be made to paragraphs D.2.18 to D.2.21 of the *Practice Book* as to the Keeper's practice with regard to the correction or rejection of an application.

4–20 **Matrimonial homes.** It was observed by Lord President Cooper[40] "This decision belongs to a tract of cases . . . in which the Courts, confessedly acting upon 'relaxed notions,' embarked upon the perilous enterprise of mitigating the supposed rigour of feudal theory by engrafting upon it equitable rules borrowed from the law merchant. Such a process is liable to create two new problems for every one which it solvès." The Matrimonial Homes (Family Protection) (Scotland) Act 1981,[40a] based upon social considerations for the protection of a non-entitled spouse in relation to occupancy of the matrimonial home, has engrafted upon land law new rules in the field of family law, with the result that it has created a host of new problems for every one which it solves. In particular it has involved additional procedure and documentation, and has created new and often difficult problems, for both the Keeper and the legal profession, both on the first registration of an interest and dealings with a registered interest.

(1) Legal nature of occupancy rights. An occupancy right under the 1981 Act is an overriding interest and is not noted in the Land Register.[41] Nevertheless, in order to preserve the principle of "faith of the records" rule 5(*j*) of the Land Registration (Scotland) Rules 1980,[42] as amended by the Land Registration (Scotland) (Amendment) Rules 1982,[43] requires the Keeper to insert in the proprietorship section of the title sheet a statement that there are in respect of the interest in land no subsisting occupancy rights, in terms of the 1981 Act, of spouses of persons who were formerly entitled to the interest, if the Keeper is satisfied that there are no such subsisting rights.

(2) Documentation. In order that the Keeper may be satisfied that there are no such subsisting rights he requires to see one of the

---

[39a] In practice the Keeper will permit retention of the original date of registration only if the superseded deed is submitted with the new deed.

[40] In *Pall Mall Trust* v. *Wilson*, 1948 S.C. 232 at 241.

[40a] As now amended by the Law Reform (Miscellaneous Provisions) (Scotland) Act 1985, s. 13.

[41] 1981 Act, s. 6(4).

[42] S.I. 1980 No. 1413 (S. 114).

[43] S.I. 1982 No. 974 (S. 132).

documents listed below (a) in the case of a first registration, in respect of every person, other than the applicant, who has been entitled to the interest since September 1, 1982, and (b) in the case of a dealing with a registered interest, in respect of the proprietor disclosed in the land certificate and any person, other than the applicant, who was subsequently entitled to the interest. In this context "entitled" is not restricted to persons having a recorded or registered title: it embraces any person who has had a right to the interest, whether completed by infeftment or not. The Keeper requires production of one of the following documents or assurances: (i) a consent to the dealing by the non-entitled spouse, (ii) a renunciation by the non-entitled spouse of her or his occupancy right in the interest, (iii) an order by the court dispensing with such consent, (iv) an assurance that the transaction or dealing divesting the entitled spouse implements a binding obligation entered into either before September 1, 1982, or before the marriage, (v) an affidavit by the entitled spouse that the subjects are not a matrimonial home in respect of which a spouse of the seller has occupancy rights, or (vi) evidence of the death of the entitled person.[43a]

(3) Circumstances in which documentation is required. Production of one of the documents listed above is necessary where (i) the subjects are a dwelling-house which is, or is capable of being, a matrimonial home, (ii) the subjects are industrial, commercial or agricultural properties, which, although not primarily residential, may contain residential accommodation, (iii) the person is a tenant under a registered lease of subjects in either of the categories (i) or (ii) above, (iv) a right of ownership of the subjects has vested in an individual on the death of a former proprietor,[44] (v) a person who enjoyed a liferent of the subjects has died leaving a widow (the document required being a certificate of death of the liferenter), (vi) the title to the subjects is in the name of a nominee, when the consent or renunciation should be granted by the spouse of the true proprietor, or (vii) the subjects had been let to a tenant under a non-registrable lease so that the spouse of the proprietor had no occupancy rights,[44a] or the entitled spouse was entitled to occupy the subjects along with a third party[45] when the appropriate document is an affidavit by the entitled proprietor that the subjects are not a matrimonial home in respect of which a spouse of the seller has occupancy rights.

One of the above documents is *not* required where (i) the proprietor is a limited company or other body corporate, (ii) the proprietor is a

---

[43a] As to forms of consent, renunciation or affidavit, see paras. 21–29, 21–30 and 21–31.
[44] See para. 21–33.
[44a] In such a case the lease may have been renounced in order to enable the seller to obtain vacant possession, and the purchaser should ensure by inquiry that the non-entitled spouse of the former tenant had consented to the renunciation.
[45] 1981 Act, s. 6(2).

body of trustees or an executor (save in the case mentioned in (iv) or (v) of the preceding subparagraph), or (iii) the relevant transaction is a compulsory sale, *e.g.* by a heritable creditor selling under a power contained in a security which has been validly constituted in circumstances where the creditor's right prevails over the occupancy rights of a non-entitled spouse under section 8 of the Act. In a sale by a heritable creditor, although the documentation is not required in respect of the sale, it is required in connection with the heritable security under powers in which the sale proceeds. As to procedure required on sale of a matrimonial home by the permanent trustee in sequestration, see section 41 of the Bankruptcy (Scotland) Act 1985.

(4) Time of consent. In the case of a sale of a matrimonial home the Keeper will require an assurance that any necessary consent, renunciation or affidavit was produced to the purchaser at or before the date of delivery of the disposition and in the case where the transaction was the creation of a heritable security the Keeper will require an assurance that the necessary consent, renunciation or affidavit was granted before the date of delivery of the deed creating the security.[46]

(5) Qualification of title sheet. If the Keeper is not satisfied regarding occupancy rights of a non-entitled spouse he will qualify the statement in the title sheet thus:

> "The Keeper is satisfied that there are in respect of the subjects in this title no occupancy rights in terms of the Matrimonial Homes (Family Protection) (Scotland) Act 1981, of spouses of persons who were formerly entitled to the said subjects, [except AB (*designed*) who ceased to be entitled on   and in respect of whose entitlement no evidence of the non-existence of an occupancy right has been produced *or* no evidence has been produced to the keeper that the affidavit by the said AB (*or* the consent or renunciation by the spouse of the said AB) was produced to the purchaser at the time of the dealing in terms of Section 6(3)(*e*) of the above Act]."

The qualification will be removed on the subsequent submission to the Keeper of evidence that the occupancy has terminated, *e.g.* on the death of either spouse, divorce, the death of the former proprietor whether married or not, or failure to exercise the occupancy right for a period of five years from the divestiture of the entitled spouse when the right will have been extinguished.[47] Evidence of the death of the non-entitled spouse before the relevant dealing by itself is insufficient; an affidavit by the entitled spouse is required.

(6) Indemnity. Although the occupancy right is an overriding interest,

---

[46] See para. 21–34.
[47] Law Reform (Miscellaneous Provisions) (Scotland) Act 1985, s. 13(6)(*c*).

the indemnity of the Keeper is not excluded under section 12(3)(*h*) of the 1979 Act,[48] so that (a) the right of a registered proprietor or the secured creditor, as the case may be, will prevail over an occupancy right if the appropriate consent, renunciation or affidavit has been granted under section 6(3)(*e*) in the case of a sale or under section 8(2) of the 1981 Act in the case of the grant of a heritable security, but (b) if for any reason the protection given by either of those subsections is not available and the Keeper has registered the interest without the qualification as to occupancy rights the right of the non-entitled spouse will prevail but the registered proprietor or secured creditor will have a claim for indemnity.[49]

24–21 Mapping. The description of subjects contained in the title deeds submitted with an application for first registration and, if necessary, any other information required to enable the Keeper to delineate the subjects and their boundaries accurately on the plan contained in the title sheet of the interest are discussed in paragraphs 18–64 to 18–73 *supra*. The practice and procedure of the Keeper in the preparation of plans and delineation thereon of boundaries are explained in detail in Part E of the *Registration of Title Practice Book*.[49a]

24–22 Title sheet. Upon first registration the Keeper will prepare a title sheet of the interest[50] consisting of a property section, a proprietorship section, a charges section and a burdens section.[51] Details of the matters to be inserted in each section are prescribed in the Rules.[52]

(1) Property section. The principal matters to be inserted in this section are the title number of the interest, the nature of the interest, *e.g.* as proprietor, a description of the subjects (with an indication, if information is available from the titles submitted, of the position as regards minerals), a plan based on the Ordnance Map with the reference number of the O.S. plan sheet and the date of first registration of the interest.[53] Normally the deed relating to the interest, or larger subjects which include it, will previously have been recorded in the Register of Sasines and shown on a search sheet, and in effect the interest is transferred from the search sheet to a title sheet and an appropriate marking of the transfer will be made on the search sheet. Where the area of land appears to extend to two hectares (approximately five acres) or more, the Keeper is required by section 6(1)(*a*) to insert the area as measured by him but the area as stated in the title sheet is excluded from indemnity.[54]

---

[48] rule 5(*j*).
[49] As to occupancy rights in matrimonial homes, see article by J. Robertson, (1982) 27 J.L.S. W 308 and article (1985) 30 J.L.S. 486.
[49a] See further, para. 24–57.
[50] Act, s. 5(1)(*a*)(i).
[51] Act, s. 6.
[52] Land Registration (Scotland) Rules 1980 (S.I. 1980 No. 1413) (S. 114), rr. 3–7.
[53] For a full list of matters to be inserted see r. 4 (R.T.P.B., para. B.2.04).
[54] Act, s. 12(3)(*e*).

(2) Proprietorship section. The principal matters to be inserted in this section are the name(s) and designation(s) of the proprietor(s) of the interest, the date of registration, the consideration, and the date of entry with an appropriate statement as to occupancy rights in relation to a matrimonial home.[55] Any subsisting entry in the Register of Inhibitions and Adjudications adverse to the registered interest will also be inserted in this section.[56]

(3) Charges section. The principal matters to be inserted in this section are particulars of any heritable security over, or other debt affecting, the registered interest.[57] Particulars of any subsisting floating charge which is an overriding interest may fall to be noted.[58] It may be observed that certain statutory charges such as charging orders under the Building, Housing or Water Acts, absolute orders under the Land Improvement Acts and notices of statutory grants should also be inserted.[59]

(4) Burdens section. The principal matters to be inserted in this section are particulars of any subsisting real burden other than one falling to be entered in the charges section, any overriding interest, other than a floating charge, which falls to be noted under section 6(4) of the Act, any probative discharge of (a) an overriding interest, other than a floating charge or the right of the proprietor of the dominant tenement in a servitude, but only where the overriding interest has been recorded in the Register of Sasines and the applicant for registration has requested that the particulars be noted, and (b) the right of the proprietor of the dominant tenement in a servitude.[60]

4–23 Land certificate. On completion of registration the Keeper issues a land certificate, which is a copy of the title sheet, and returns to the applicant all the deeds and documents and other evidence which have been submitted in support of the application.[61] The Keeper first makes copies of those which he may require for the issue of office copies under section 6(5) of the Act and of such others as he requires as an authority for an entry on the title sheet.[62] In effect the land certificate supersedes the title deeds prior to its issue and the need for their repeated examination in future transactions largely disappears.

4–24 Title deeds. Useful guidance as to the retention or disposal of title deeds after registration of an interest is given in paragraphs G.2.46 and G.2.47 of the *Practice Book*. See also paragraph 23–25 *supra*.

---

[55] See para. 24–20(5).
[56] For a full list of matters to be inserted, see r. 5 (R.T.P.B., para. B.2.05).
[57] For a full list, see r. 6 (R.T.P.B., para. B.2.06).
[58] Act, s. 6(4) and r. 6(2).
[59] R.T.P.B., para. C.35.
[60] For a full list see r. 7 (R.T.P.B., para. B.2.07).
[61] Act, s. 5(2). For an example of a land certificate see R.T.P.B., section D, App. 1.
[62] R.T.P.B., para. D.3.11.

(2) Registered Interests

Application for transfer of the whole of a registered interest

24-25   In a subsequent transaction which effects a transfer of the whole of an interest already registered in the Land Register application for registration of the transferee's interest should be made on Form 2, unless the transaction is the grant of a feu or a lease when it is treated as a transfer of part. Form 2 is appropriate where (i) the transfer, whether for valuable consideration or not, is of *the whole* registered interest, *e.g.* where the deed is a disposition on sale or otherwise of the whole interest, (ii) the creation of a standard security, liferent or incorporeal right over *the whole* or *part* of the registered interest, (iii) a deed of conditions over *the whole* or *part* of the registered interest or (iv) any transmission or discharge of a heritable security whether secured over *the whole* or *part* of the registered interest.[63] The application should be accompanied by (i) the relevant land certificate (unless production of it is excused under rule 18[64]), (ii) any relevant charge certificate but only in cases where the transaction affects the heritable security, (iii) the document whereby the transaction is effected, (iv) any necessary links in title, and (v) any other document containing new information relating to any matter already entered on the title sheet or which will lead to a new entry on the title sheet.[65]

Application for dealing with part of a registered interest

24-26   In a transaction which affects part only of a registered interest application for registration should be made on Form 3. Form 3 is appropriate where the transaction is, for example, (i) the transfer, whether for valuable consideration or not, of part only of the subjects of a registered interest, *e.g.* where the registered interest is of a tenement containing several flats and one of the flats is being sold, (ii) the grant of a feu or long lease of *the whole* or *part* of the registered interest.[66] The documents to be furnished with the application are the same as those listed in paragraph 24–25 *supra* with the addition of sufficient information to enable the Keeper to identify the part on the Ordnance Map.[67] It may not always be practicable in dealings with a part of the registered interest to furnish the land certificate, as where several feus have been granted in a developing estate or several flats in a tenement are being sold but in such cases office copies of the title sheet may be obtained and furnished to the purchaser, and the land certificate may be deposited with the Keeper and the deposit number quoted in the application for registration of the transfer of part.[68]

---

[63] R.T.P.B., para. D.2.16.
[64] *Ibid.*, para. D.3.08.
[65] *Ibid.*, para. D.3.07. See also para. 24–27.
[66] Ibid., para. D.2.17.
[67] *Ibid.*, para. D.3.07. See also para. 24–27.
[68] *Ibid.*, paras. D.3.08 and D.3.09.

Matrimonial homes

24–27 In transactions effecting a transfer of or dealing with an interest in subjects which are, or are capable of being, a matrimonial home there must also be submitted with an application for registration relating to the whole or part of the registered interest one of the documents listed in paragraph 24–20(2) *supra* in respect of the proprietor disclosed in the land certificate and any person, other than the applicant, who was subsequently entitled to the interest.

(3) Particular Matters

Pro indiviso proprietors

24–28 As regards the registration of interests of *pro indiviso* proprietors the practice of the Keeper is:

(a) Where the proprietors hold on one title, only one land certificate is issued unless each proprietor requests otherwise.

(b) On a subsequent transfer of one of the *pro indiviso* shares a separate land certificate is issued to the transferee.

(c) Where the *pro indiviso* proprietors hold on separate titles, separate land certificates are issued to each proprietor.

Where a *pro indiviso* share is held as an adjunct of other property, such as a share in curtilage ground of property, parts of which are owned by several separate proprietors, no separate title sheet will be opened for the *pro indiviso* share which will be registered as a pertinent in the title sheet of the main subject.[69]

Adjudication in execution

24–29 A decree of adjudication for debt is not an absolute title but is merely a *pignus praetorium* redeemable within the legal (10 years). When such a decree is pronounced the entry of the debtor in the proprietorship section of the title sheet remains, but a further entry is made showing the adjudger as proprietor, the latter entry being subject to an exclusion of indemnity. An entry is also made in the charges section in respect of its character as a security which will establish its ranking in relation to other securities. When an extract decree of declarator of expiry of the legal is registered the entry relating to the debtor will be deleted from the proprietorship section, the exclusion of indemnity will be removed from the adjudger's title and the entry in the charges section will also be removed, since the adjudger is now absolute proprietor. If no declarator of expiry of the legal is registered

---

[69] R.T.P.B., paras. D.4.10 to D.4.12.

but the adjudger can prove that he has had possession for the period of positive prescription after the expiry of the legal then, on application being made to the Keeper, the exclusion of indemnity and the entry in the charges section will be removed and the entry of the debtor as proprietor will be deleted from the proprietorship section. On the other hand if the adjudger neither obtains a declarator of the expiry of the legal nor completes his right by prescriptive possession the negative prescription (20 years), commencing from the date of expiry of the legal, will cut off the security right of the adjudger and so will operate in favour of the debtor as proprietor.[70]

Adjudication in implement

24–30   A decree of adjudication in implement gives the adjudger an absolute title and on production of the extract decree the entry of the former proprietor will be deleted and the adjudger will be entered as proprietor in the proprietorship section.[71]

24–31   **Application for registration of decrees of adjudication.** Application for registration of a decree of adjudication, whether in execution or in implement, should be made on Form 2 with an inventory (in duplicate) on Form 4. The adjudger will not normally hold the land certificate but the Keeper under rule 17 may require the holder to exhibit the land certificate to him. After registration, where the adjudication is in execution, the amended land certificate will be returned to the holder and a land certificate will also be issued to the adjudger. Where the adjudication is in implement the Keeper will not issue an amended land certificate to the previous holder but will deliver it to the adjudger, who is now the proprietor, unless the certificate was obtained from a heritable creditor in which event the amended certificate will be issued to that creditor.[72]

Liferents

24–32   **(a) Proper liferents.** The creation of a proper liferent is registrable but only if it is over a registered interest.[73] A separate title sheet is not opened for a liferent and no certificate of title is issued in respect of it.[74] A proper liferent existing at the time when the interest of the proprietor of the subjects concerned is first registered must be noted on the title sheet of the interest, since otherwise the interest would no longer be subject to the liferent. If for any reason the liferent is not so noted the liferenter in possession may apply for rectification of the

[70] R.T.P.B., paras. D.4.13 and D.4.14. The underlying theory has been criticised—see G.L. Gretton, 1983 J.R. 177, 186, 187—but it makes practical sense as a matter of procedure.
[71] R.T.P.B., para. D.4.15.
[72] *Ibid.*, para. D.4.16.
[73] Act, s. 2(2) and (3).
[74] Act, s. 5(1).

Register in his favour, failing which he may have a claim for indemnity, but the mere noting of the liferenter's interest does not *per se* create that interest real; for that the liferenter must apply on Form 2 for registration of his interest when it will be entered on the title sheet of the interest of the proprietor of the subjects over which it subsists.[74a] If the liferent is created for the first time over an interest already registered the liferenter should apply on Form 2 for registration of his liferent interest in order to constitute it as a real right.[75] As to the procedure on termination of a registered liferent interest see the *Practice Book*, paragraph D.4.35.

(b) Legal or beneficial or trust liferents. Liferent rights of this kind, as where trustees hold property for the liferent use of a beneficiary, are not registrable. The trustees will be entered as fiduciary proprietors of the subjects.

Transactions involving a company

4–33   Where any party to a dealing, whether involving first registration or transfer of the whole or a part of a registered interest, is a company registered under the Companies Acts, certain questions particularly relating to the company are included in the relevant form of application for registration of the dealing. These questions and the inquiries which the Keeper may make with regard to the replies thereto are described in paragraphs D.4.36 to D.4.38 of the *Practice Book*. It should be noted that the Keeper will not necessarily be aware of the appointment of a receiver or the winding-up of the company subsequent to the registration of the company's interest, and so, when an office copy or report is subsequently issued or when the certificate of title is updated, parties to a transaction with the company should search the Register of Charges and the Company Files.[76]

(4) Overriding Interests

Introduction

4–34   There is a vast miscellany of rights and restrictions, temporary or of longer duration, which can affect heritable property but which may not be disclosed by a search in the Register of Sasines. In the system of registration of title these are comprehended in the phrase "overriding interests."[77] In certain respects the Land Register is more informative

---

[74a] The text states the practice of the Keeper (see R.T.P.B., para. D.4.34) and is procedurally convenient, but its logic seems dubious. If the proprietor of subjects submits a disposition containing a reserved liferent in an application for first registration of his interest, it would seem logical that when the liferent burden is noted it becomes real.

[75] R.T.P.B., paras. D.4.32 to D.4.34.

[76] See para. 21–87.

[77] For a definition, see para. 24–35.

with regard to overriding interests than the Register of Sasines, *e.g.* certain overriding interests must or may be noted in the Land Register and also discharges of them,[78] but there is no indemnity for loss arising from an error or omission in doing so.[79]

Definition

24–35   The various interests which are included within the term "overriding interest" are specified in section 28(1) of the Act. They comprise, in relation to any interest in land, the right or interest over it of:

(a) the lessee under a lease which is not a long lease;

(b) the lessee under a long lease who, prior to the commencement of the Act, has acquired a real right to the subjects of the lease by virtue of possession of them;

(c) a crofter or cottar within the meaning of section 3 or 28(4) respectively of the Crofters (Scotland) Act 1955, or a landholder or statutory small tenant within the meaning of section 2(2) or 32(1) respectively of the Small Landholders (Scotland) Act 1911;

(d) the proprietor of the dominant tenement in a servitude;

(e) the Crown or any Government or other public department, or any public or local authority, under any enactment or rule of law, other than an enactment or rule of law authorising or requiring the recording of a deed in the Register of Sasines or registration in order to complete the right or interest;

(ee) the operator having a right conferred in accordance with paragraph 2, 3 or 5 of Schedule 2 to the Telecommunications Act 1984 (agreements for execution of works, obstruction of access, etc.);

(f) the holder of a floating charge whether or not the charge has attached to the interest;

(g) a member of the public in respect of any public right of way or in respect of any right held inalienably by the Crown in trust for the public;

(gg) the non-entitled spouse within the meaning of section 6 of the Matrimonial Homes (Family Protection) (Scotland) Act 1981;

(h) any person, having a right which has been made real, otherwise than by the recording of a deed in the Register of Sasines or by registration; or

(i) any other person under any rule of law relating to common interest or joint or common property, not being a right or interest constituting a real right, burden or condition entered in the title sheet of the interest in land under section 6(1)(*e*) of the Act or having effect by virtue of a deed recorded in the Register of Sasines,

---

[78] See paras. 24–36 and 24–38.
[79] Act, s. 12(3)(*h*).

but does not include any subsisting burden or condition enforceable against the interest in land and entered in its title sheet under section 6(1) of the Act.

Note that in the case of a servitude the interest of the proprietor of the dominant tenement is an overriding interest in relation to the servient tenement. In relation. to the dominant tenement it is a registrable interest, but since it is an incorpreal heritable right it is not registrable on its own (section 2(2)) but only as a pertinent of the dominant tenement if that interest is itself registered.

Noting of overriding interests

4–36 An overriding interest is not registrable under section 2 of the Act but may be noted on the title sheet of the interest which it affects. The interest of a lessee under a lease other than a long lease, however, will not be noted in the Land Register; short-term leases are numerous and transitory in character and their notation in the Register would increase the work of registration to an unacceptable extent. Under section 6(4) of the Act:

(1) The Keeper *must* note an overriding interest in the title sheet of the interest affected by it if the overriding interest is disclosed in any document accompanying the application for registration of the affected interest. Where the overriding interest affects several properties, however, as in the case of an "all assets" floating charge granted by a company which owns more than one property, the floating charge will be noted in the charges section of the title sheet of the interest in the particular property which is the subject of the application for registration but there is no obligation on the Keeper to trace the other properties owned by the company and note the floating charge on the title sheets relating to them.

(2) The Keeper *may* note an overriding interest—

(a) If an application is made to him to do so.[80] The application should be made on Form 5. An example is where a servitude has been granted over a registered interest and the proprietor of the dominant tenement wishes to have its existence noted on the title sheet relating to the servient tenement.

(b) If the overriding interest is disclosed in *any* application for registration of an interest.[81] So, for example, if application is made for registration of the dominant tenement in a servitude over a registered interest, the Keeper may note the existence of the servitude on the title sheet relating to the servient tenement.

(c) If the servitude otherwise comes to the notice of the Keeper.[82]

---

[80] Act, s. 6(4)(*b*)(i).
[81] Act, s. 6(4)(*b*)(ii).
[82] For an example see R.T.P.B., para. H.2.04(iv).

Where a registered proprietor wishes an overriding interest to be noted on the title sheet when an application is being made on Form 1, 2 or 3 for registration of an interest he may request the Keeper to note the overriding interest and it is unnecessary to make a separate application for that purpose.[83]

Effect of noting

24–37   The rights or restrictions now included in the term "overriding interests" are of a kind which did not require recording in the Register of Sasines to ensure their effectiveness as real burdens or as burdens or conditions running with the lands. The noting of overriding interests in the Land Register is in a similar position; its purpose is publication in order to make the Register as informative as possible.

Discharge of, or freedom from, overriding interests

24–38   A discharge of an overriding interest may be entered in the relevant title sheet under section 6(1)(*g*) of the Act and application for noting the discharge, or freedom from, an overriding interest may be made on Form 5 accompanied by such documents or other evidence as are required to support the application. Normally the Keeper in such cases will simply remove the relevant entry from the title sheet, except that, where an overriding interest which has either been recorded in the Register of Sasines or noted on the title sheet is discharged by a probative deed and the applicant requests that the particulars of the discharge be noted, the particulars of the discharge will be so noted. The exception does not apply, however, to a discharge or memorandum of satisfaction of a floating charge, when the original entry will simply be removed. Further, in the case of a probative discharge of a servitude, the discharge will be noted on the title sheet, whether or not the original grant of the servitude was recorded in the Register of Sasines or noted on the title sheet.[84]

Indemnity

24–39   Loss arising from any error or omission in a land certificate or charge certificate in the noting of an overriding interest, whether the noting has been required under section 6 of the Act or not, is excluded from indemnity.[85] Nevertheless indemnity may be payable if the Keeper has omitted to note, or has made an error in noting, the discharge of or freedom from, an overriding interest.[86]

---

[83] R.T.P.B., para. H.2.05.
[84] See R.T.P.B., paras. H.2.08 and H.2.09.
[85] Act, s. 12(3)(*h*).
[86] R.T.P.B., para. H.2.07.

(5) Ranking Provisions

Ranking of recorded and registered titles

4-40   Section 7 of the Act provides that, without prejudice to any express provision as to ranking in any deed or any other provision as to ranking in, or having effect by virtue of, any enactment or rule of law, (a) titles to registered interests shall rank according to the date of registration of those interests, (b) a title to a registered interest and a title governed by a deed recorded in the Register of Sasines shall rank according to the respective dates of registration and recording, and (c) where the date of registration or recording of the titles to two or more interests in land is the same, those interests shall rank equally.

Change in former law

4-41   Formerly writs recorded in the Register of Sasines ranked in order of presentment with the qualification that writs received by the same post were deemed to be presented and recorded *pari passu*.[87] As from April 6, 1981,[88] the criterion of preference in ranking, both as regards registration in the Land Register and recording in the Register of Sasines, is the day, regardless of the hour of presentment or receipt, of the application or writ.[89]

(6) Continuing Effectiveness of Recording in Register of Sasines

Non-operational areas

4-42   Under the law prior to the Act, real rights or real obligations relating to land were normally created by recording of the relevant deeds in the Register of Sasines although certain rights or obligations, *e.g.* servitudes, could be created otherwise. The law remains the same as regards subjects situated in areas which are not yet operational, but once an area has been designated as operational the role of the Register of Sasines is much reduced.

Operational areas

4-43   When an area has become operational most real rights or real obligations affecting registrable or registered interests in land can be created only by way of registration in the Land Register,[90] since the Keeper is prohibited from accepting for recording in the Register of

---

[87] Land Registers (Scotland) Act 1868, s. 6.

[88] When s. 7 of the Act came into force—Land Registration (Scotland) Act 1979 (Commencement No. 1) Order 1980, (S.I. 1980 No. 1412) (C. 58) (S. 113).

[89] See amendments to earlier statutes relating to recording in the Register of Sasines in Scheds. 2 and 4 to the Act.

[90] Act, s. 8(1).

Sasines any deed other than those permitted by section 8 of the Act.[91] Recording in the Register of Sasines may still be effected in operational areas in relation to the following:

(a) an interest in land which is to be transferred or otherwise affected by

(i) an instrument[92] which, having been recorded before the commencement of the Act in the Register of Sasines with an error or defect, or

(ii) a deed which, having been recorded before the commencement of the Act in the Register of Sasines with an error or defect in the recording,

has not before such commencement, been re-presented, corrected as necessary, for the purposes of recording of new under section 143 of the Titles to Land Consolidation (Scotland) Act 1868;

(b) a registered interest in land which has been absorbed, other than by the operation of prescription, into another interest in land the title to which is governed by a deed recorded in the Register of Sasines; or

(c) anything which is not registrable under subsections (1) to (4) of section 2 of the Act and in respect of which, immediately before the commencement of the Act, a real right or obligation could be created or affected by recording a deed in the Register of Sasines.[93]

As regards these three cases:

(a) *Recording of new.* It was permissible to correct an error in a notarial instrument or notice of title and record it of new since such an instrument did not create or transfer a right in land but merely feudalised an existing right. In the case of a deed, which could have such an effect, recording of new was competent only to correct an error in the recording of it. Clearly the correction of such errors in instruments or deeds recorded before the commencement of the Act can most easily be done by recording of new in the Register of Sasines.

(b) *Absorption.* The most familiar example is the consolidation of the *dominium utile* with the superiority of land when the higher superiority title has been recorded in the Register of Sasines but the interest in the *dominium utile* has been registered in the Land Register. See further paragraphs 17–118 to 17–121 *supra*.

(c) *Non-registrable matters.* There may be a property which, although situated in an operational area, has not yet become the subject of a transaction which induces first registration so that the title to it remains in the Register of Sasines. Accordingly a standard security over such a property, or a notice of title to it, or a gratuitous conveyance of it, or a deed of declaration of conditions affecting it, will be recorded in the Register of Sasines.

---

[91] Act, s. 8(4).
[92] As defined in the Titles to Land Consolidation (Scotland) Act 1868, s. 3.
[93] Act, s. 8(2).

(7) Positive Prescription

Amendments to the Prescription and Limitation (Scotland) Act 1973

24-44 The Act amends section 1 of the 1973 Act in order to adapt its provisions relating to positive prescription to registration of title. Section 1 of the 1973 Act as so amended is reprinted in *The Parliament House Book*.

Positive prescription in relation to registered interests

24-45 Since an interest registered in the Land Register without exclusion of indemnity is valid from the date of its registration and needs no fortification by positive prescription, the function of the prescription is in effect limited to cases where there has been an exclusion of indemnity. In such cases where the running of the period of prescription has rendered the matter in respect of which the exclusion was made no longer challengeable the Keeper will, on production of evidence of exclusive and uninterrupted possession by the registered proprietor, *e.g.* affidavits made before a notary public, remove the exclusion of indemnity.[93a]

(8) Rectification of the Register

Background

24-46 The report of Lord Reid's committee[94] and the Henry report[95] recommended provisions for rectification of the Land Register following the precedent of the system of registration of title in England with the complementary remedy of indemnification for loss, but the extent of rectification to the prejudice of a proprietor in possession is severely restricted as also are the losses for which indemnity can be claimed when rectification takes place.

Rectification by the Keeper[96]

24-47 The Keeper may, whether on being so requested or not, rectify any inaccuracy in the Register by inserting, amending or cancelling anything therein, but if rectification would prejudice a proprietor in possession the power to rectify is exercisable by the Keeper only where:

(i) the purpose of rectification is to note an overriding interest or to correct any information in the Register relating to an overriding interest[97];

[93a] See R.T.P.B., para. C.63.
[94] (Cmnd. 2032) July 1963, para. 114.
[95] (Cmnd. 4137) October 1969, Pt. I, para. 47.
[96] Act, s. 9(1) and (3).
[97] Overriding interest in s. 9 of the Act excludes the interest of a lessee in a lease which is not a long lease and of a non-entitled spouse within the meaning of the Matrimonial Homes (Family Protection) (Scotland) Act 1981—s. 9(4)(*b*) of the 1979 Act as amended by the 1981 Act.

(ii) all persons whose interests in land are likely to be affected by the rectification have been informed by the Keeper of his intention and have consented in writing;

(iii) the inaccuracy has been caused wholly or substantially by the fraud or carelessness of the proprietor in possession; or

(iv) the rectification relates to a matter in respect of which indemnity has been excluded under section 12(2) of the Act.

24–48   Commentary on section 9(3) of 1979 Act

(i) *Overriding interests.* Since an overriding interest exists whether noted on the Register or not,[98] and since there is no entitlement to indemnity in respect of loss arising from an error or omission in noting an overriding interest,[99] rectification of the Register in respect of an overriding interest merely corrects the information on the Register with regard to it and effects no change in the legal position.

(ii) *Consent of parties.* The persons whose rights are likely to be affected include the registered proprietor, so that rectification cannot be made without his written consent.

(iii) *Fraud or carelessness of proprietor in possession.* Fraud would plainly include forgery and possibly even undue influence or *mala fides* in failing to disclose the existence of a competing title in the information furnished to the Keeper on application for registration. Carelessness would comprehend an inaccuracy in the information given to the Keeper on an application for registration on a matter which was overlooked by the applicant or which could have been verified on proper inquiry. In such cases rectification of the Register to the prejudice of the proprietor in possession would not entitle him to indemnity or may result in reduction in the amount of the indemnity.[1]

(iv) *Indemnity excluded by Keeper.* The Keeper may have registered an interest in respect of which indemnity has been excluded under section 12(2) of the Act, *e.g.* disposition *a non domino* or the precise position of a particular boundary. If the registered proprietor thereafter possesses the whole land, or possesses it up to the line of the dubious boundary, continuously, peaceably and without judicial interruption for the relevant period of positive prescription, the Keeper may on an application made by the registered proprietor rectify the Register by cancelling the exclusion of indemnity. On the other hand, if the validity of the registered proprietor's title to the land or to the land up to the dubious boundary has been decided against him before positive prescription has operated in his favour, the Keeper may rectify the Register against him.

Any application for rectification of the Register should be made on Form 9.

---

[98] Act, ss. 3(1)(*a*) and 28(1).
[99] Act, s. 12(3)(*h*).
[1] Act, ss. 12(3)(*n*) or 13 (4).

Rectification by order of the court or the Lands Tribunal

24–49 Any court having jurisdiction in questions of heritable right or title or the Lands Tribunal for Scotland may order the Keeper to rectify any inaccuracy in the Register on any of the four grounds listed in paragraph 24–47 *supra* with the exception of ground (ii) (consent of all proprietors) where such an order would be inappropriate.[2] The court or the Tribunal may also order any rectification of the Register that is consequential on the making of an order under section 8 of the Law Reform (Miscellaneous Provisions) (Scotland) Act 1985 authorising rectification of a defectively expressed document, and where rectification of the Register for that purpose is made the entry concerned is rectified with retroactive effect to the date on which the entry was originally made.[2a]

(9) Indemnification

Claims for indemnity—general principles

24–50 It is a fundamental principle of a system of registration of title that ownership of a registered interest is vested in the person registered as proprietor, but inevitably there will be cases where the ownership of a registered proprietor will be lost or restricted, when he may be entitled to claim indemnity. It is by no means in all cases, however, that a registered proprietor will be so entitled. The statutory provisions, mainly contained in section 12 of the Act, set out the circumstances in which a claim to indemnity will and will not be competent to a registered proprietor or other person. It is impossible to subsume under a general heading the various circumstances in which indemnification is available but, very broadly, they are confined to cases where loss is attributable to error or omission or carelessness on the part of the Keeper or his staff, but not otherwise.

Cases where claims to indemnity may be competent

24–51 These are stated in section 12(1) of the Act as being cases where a person suffers loss as a result of:

(a) a rectification of the Register made under section 9 of the Act;

(b) the refusal or omission of the Keeper to make such a rectification;

(c) the loss or destruction of any document while lodged with the Keeper; or

(d) an error or omission in any land certificate or charge certificate or in any information given by the Keeper in writing or in such other manner as may be prescribed by rules made under section 27 of the Act.

---

[2] Act, ss. 9(1), (3)(1)(*b*) and (4)(*a*).
[2a] Law Reform (Miscellaneous Provisions) (Scotland) Act 1985, Sched. 2, para. 21.

Illustrations of circumstances in which indemnification may be claimed under these headings are given in paragraph C.68 of the *Practice Book*.

Cases where claims to indemnity are expressly excluded

24-52   Section 12(2) of the Act empowers the Keeper on registration in respect of an interest to exclude, in whole or in part, any right to indemnity as regards anything appearing in or omitted from the title sheet of the interest. Where the exclusion is partial the matter in respect of which indemnity is excluded will normally be specified in the land certificate. Examples are (a) absence of or material defect in a document in the progress of titles submitted with an application for first registration, or (b) dubiety as to the precise location of a boundary of the subjects.

Cases where claims to indemnity are excluded by the Act

24-53   These are specified in section 12(3) where:

(a) The loss arises as a result of a title prevailing over that of the claimant in a case where (i) the prevailing title is one in respect of which a right to indemnity has been partially excluded under section 12(2), and (ii) such exclusion has been cancelled but only on the prevailing title having been fortified by prescription. For an example see paragraph C.71 of the *Practice Book*.

(b) The loss arises in respect of a title which has been reduced as a gratuitous alienation or fradulent preference, or has been reduced or varied by an order under section 6(2) of the Divorce (Scotland) Act 1976 or by an order made by virtue of section 29 of the Matrimonial and Family Proceedings Act 1984 or has been set aside or varied by an order under section 18(2) of the Family Law (Scotland) Act 1985. This paragraph of subsection 12(3) negatives a right to indemnity of proprietors who have acquired title by gratuitous alienations or fraudulent preferences to the prejudice of creditors in bankruptcy proceedings who have no equitable right to protection. The same reasoning applies to proprietors who have acquired title by a deed designed to defeat the obligations to make financial provision for a spouse on divorce, now extended by the 1985 Act to apply to all actions of aliment.[3] Purchasers in good faith and for value are protected under both Acts,[4] so that the exclusion of indemnity affects only parties to the avoidance device.

(c) The loss arises in consequence of the making of a further order under section 5(2) of the Presumption of Death (Scotland) Act 1977 (effect on property rights of recall or variation of decree of declarator

---

[3] Family Law (Scotland) Act 1985, s. 18 and Sched. 1.
[4] See para. 21–37.

of presumed death). Under section 5(5) of the 1977 Act the right of a person who has acquired property in good faith and for value as a result of a decree of declarator of presumed death is unchallengeable when the decree is recalled or varied, so that indemnity is excluded only in the case of a registered proprietor who has acquired property gratuitously as a result of the original decree. That is reasonable: the subsequent decree of variation or recall establishes that he should not have had an unqualified or any right to the property in the first place.

(d) The loss arises as a result of any inaccuracy in the delineation of any boundaries shown on a title sheet which could not have been rectified by reference to the Ordnance Map unless the Keeper has accepted responsibility for the accuracy of that delineation. The principle is that there is no right to indemnity if the Keeper could not have been aware of the inaccuracy by reason of the limitations imposed by the scale of the Ordnance Map.[5]

(e) The loss arises, in the case of land extending to two hectares or more, as the result of the Keeper's failure to enter the area in the title sheet or any inaccuracy in the specification of the area if he has entered it. The quality of the title is not affected by the failure to state the area in such cases; if the Keeper does state the area wrongly then, because of the problems in specifying a large area accurately,[6] the exclusion of indemnity means in effect that the statement of area should be regarded as demonstrative and not taxative.

(f) The loss arises in respect of an interest in mines and minerals and the title sheet of any interest which is or includes the surface does not expressly disclose that the interest in mines and minerals is included in that interest. If the titles submitted demonstrate to the satisfaction of the Keeper that the minerals are included in the interest to be registered he will enter in the property section "with minerals"; if they disclose that minerals are excepted he will enter "the minerals are excepted." If there is no satisfactory evidence of the position regarding the minerals neither of those entries may be made, in which case indemnity is excluded as regards them and registration of an interest as proprietor of the surface does not guarantee ownership of the subjacent minerals on the *a coelo usque ad centrum* principle.

(g) The loss arises from inability to enforce a real burden or condition entered in the Register, unless the Keeper expressly assumes responsibility for its enforceability. The Keeper will be aware of the existence and the terms of burdens and conditions as disclosed in the relevant title deeds. What he will not know is whether they have ceased to be enforceable from absence of interest to do so, etc.,[7] and so the right to indemnity is excluded if burdens or conditions appearing

---

[5] See R.T.P.B., para. C.74.
[6] See R.T.P.B., para. C.41.
[7] See paras. 19–51 to 19–59.

on the Register turn out to be unenforceable, unless he has expressly assumed responsibility for them being so.[8]

(h) The loss arises in respect of an error or omission in the noting of an overriding interest. While the Keeper must or may note overriding interests[9] there can be no certainty that all such interests may have come to his notice or that there has been some subsequent variation in those which have been noted.

(j) The loss is suffered by (i) a beneficiary under a trust in respect of any transaction by its trustees or in respect of any title granted by them the validity of which is unchallengeable by virtue of section 2 of the Trusts (Scotland) Act 1961 or section 17 of the Succession (Scotland) Act 1964, or (ii) a person in respect of any interest transferred to him by trustees in purported implement of trust purposes. In all the circumstances postulated a remedy is available to the beneficiary or person against the trustees; it is not appropriate that he should have also an indemnity from the Keeper, who is not obliged to examine the trust purposes and decide whether the trustees have observed them.[10]

(k) The loss arises as a result of an error or omission in an office copy as to the effect of any subsisting adverse entry in the Register of Inhibitions and Adjudications affecting any person in respect of any registered interest in land and that person's entitlement to that interest is neither disclosed in the Register nor otherwise known to the Keeper. The reasons for exclusion of indemnity in this case are fully explained in paragraph C.80 of the *Practice Book*.

(l) The claimant is the proprietor of the dominant tenement in a servitude, except in so far as the claim may relate to the constitution of that servitude. A servitude right may be lost in various events[11] and the Keeper cannot be required to investigate whether any such event has occurred. The Keeper must, however, be satisfied that a servitude has been validly constituted when he enters it as a pertinent of a registered interest, and so any error by the Keeper as regards its constitution founds a claim to indemnity.

(m) The claimant is a superior, a creditor in a ground annual or a landlord under a long lease and the claim relates to any information (i) contained in the feu writ, the contract of ground annual or the lease, as the case may be, and (ii) omitted from the title sheet of the interest of the superior, creditor or landlord (except in so far as the claim may relate to the constitution or amount of the feuduty, ground annual or rent and adequate information has been made available to the Keeper to enable him to make an entry in the Register in respect of such constitution or amount or to the description of the land in respect of

---

[8] Which, being a prudent chap, he is seldom likely to do!
[9] See para. 24–36.
[10] See R.T.P.B., para. C.79.
[11] See paras. 20–26 to 20–32.

which the feuduty, ground annual or rent is payable). The reasons for exclusion of indemnity in this case are explained in paragraph C.82 of the *Practice Book*.

(n) The claimant has by his fraudulent or careless act or omission caused the loss.[12] If the claimant has contributed to the loss by fraud or carelessness the indemnity may be reduced appropriately.[13]

(o) The claim relates to the amount due under a heritable security.[14]

(p) The loss arises from a rectification of the Land Register consequential on the making of an order under section 8 of the Law Reform (Miscellaneous Provisions) (Scotland) Act 1985.[14a]

Section 12(4) of the Act

4-54 The Keeper need not enter in the title sheet any over-feuduty or over-rent exigible in respect of the relevant interest in land, but he may do so.[15] If he elects to omit those, a claim for indemnity may be competent. Likewise, if the Keeper omits to insert in the property section a right alleged to be a real right on the ground that it is unenforceable and so he has no duty to insert it in a title sheet,[16] then a claim for indemnity may be made if loss results from the omission.[16a]

Expenses of claimant for indemnity

4-55 Under section 13(1) of the Act the Keeper is required to reimburse expenditure reasonably and properly incurred by a claimant for indemnity in connection with any claim disposed of by the Lands Tribunal or the court provided that it was a *prima facie* well-founded claim. This is a generous concession to claimants; contrast the position as to expenses in unsuccessful claims under warrandice.[17] The Lands Tribunal or the court may, however, make an order for payment of expenses which will supersede the statutory provision.

Subrogation

4-56 If the Keeper settles any claim for indemnity he is subrogated to all rights which would have been available to the claimant to recover the loss indemnified, and may require the claimant as a condition of payment of his claim to grant at the Keeper's expense a formal assignation to the Keeper of such rights.[18]

---

[12] As to what may constitute fraud or carelessness, see para. 24–48 (iii).
[13] Act, s. 13(4).
[14] See under heritable securities in Vol. III.
[14a] See para. 24–49.
[15] Act, s. 6(3).
[16] Act, s. 6(1)(e).
[16a] Act, s. 12(4).
[17] Vol. I, para. 4–50.
[18] Act, s. 13(2) and (3).

(10) Maps and Plans

Procedure in preparing plans in relation to registered interests

24–57   The procedure adopted by the Keeper as to preparation of plans to be included in the title sheet of a registered interest, the description of the interest, the guarantee of the boundaries of the land, the facilities for identification of the subjects and the special arrangements for building developments by approved estate layout plans are fully described in Section E of the *Practice Book*.

(11) Public Character of Land Register

Office copies and reports

24–58   The Act continues the long-established tradition that information contained in Scottish land registers is public and available to any interested person. Several provisions of the Act facilitate the furnishing of such information to members of the public. Parties to transactions or proposed transactions, may obtain reports as to the state of the Register of Sasines, the Land Register and the Register of Inhibitions and Adjudications by appropriate applications on Forms 10 and 11 (unregistered interests)[19] or Forms 12 and 13 (registered interests).[20] Other persons may obtain information as to particular subjects by application on Form 15 for an office copy of a title sheet,[21] although indemnity is excluded as regards information with regard to persons not disclosed in the title sheet nor in the Form 15 application,[22] or an application on Form 14 in order to ascertain whether subjects have been registered in the Land Register. The holder of a land certificate who wishes to ensure that it is up-to-date with the Register may submit an application on Form 8 in circumstances where there is no current transaction (when the desired information will be available in a Form 12 report).[23]

SECTION C

Accretion

Accretion in titles to land

24–59   The principle of accretion in relation to land rights has its most important application in the subsequent infeftment of the granter of a

---

[19] R.T.P.B., para. E.38.
[20] *Ibid.*, para. E.40.
[21] *Ibid.*, paras. B.2.24, C.35, D.3.09, D.3.11 and F.16.
[22] *Ibid.*, para. C.80.
[23] *Ibid.*, paras. F.10 and F.11.

conveyance who did not have a completed title when the conveyance was granted. The principle operates to the effect that such subsequent infeftment draws back to the date of the conveyance and validates it as if the granter's title had then been complete. Although the principle finds its most frequent illustrations in feudal conveyancing it is not distinctively feudal in origin but rests on equitable principles applicable to conveyances of any kind cf property. In relation to a conveyance of land with absolute warrandice, whether express or implied, an uninfeft granter who subsequently becomes infeft is deemed *fictione juris* to have been infeft when the conveyance was granted, and the benefit of his later infeftment accrues to the grantee without the need of any supplementary conveyance or other deed. It may be added that accretion operates even where the granter of a conveyance had at the time of granting no title whatever but subsequently acquired one.[24]

Parties between whom accretion operates

4–60　It has long been settled that the benefit of accretion is available, not only to the grantee of the conveyance, but also to all persons who derive right from the common author whose title was originally defective. So a lease granted by an uninfeft landlord was, on his subsequent infeftment, binding in a question between the tenant and a disponee to whom the landlord subsequently conveyed the subjects, since the retroactive effect of accretion validated the lease with effect before the disposition was granted.[25] Again where several dispositions had been granted by a proprietor who remained uninfeft until after all the disponees had taken infeftment, on the granter subsequently becoming infeft the disponees were preferred in the order in which they had themselves respectively become infeft.[26] The retroactive effect of accretion, however, applies only in questions between those acquiring right from the same granter; as between competing titles derived from different sources, one which was completed before accretion had operated to cure the other would prevail.[27]

Accretion after changes in the person of the grantee or the granter of a conveyance

4–61　If infeftment of the granter of the conveyance takes place only after the grantee has died, accretion nevertheless operates to validate the title of his heir or executor.[28] Similarly it operates in favour of disponees, tenants or heritable creditors who derived right from the original grantee of the conveyance upon the subsequent completion of

---

[24] *Swans* v. *Western Bank* (1866) 4 M. 663.
[25] *Neilson* v. *Menzies* (1671) Mor. 7768.
[26] *Neilson* v. *Murray* (1738) Mor. 7773.
[27] *Munro* v. *Brodie* (1844) 6 D. 1249.
[28] *Lockhart* v. *Ferrier* (1837) 16 S. 76.

title of the granter of it. On the other hand where infeftment was subsequently obtained, not by the person who had granted the conveyance himself, but by persons representing him, accretion does not operate.[29] Again, where the conveyance was granted by an uninfeft trustee, the subsequent completion of title by the truster did not validate the title of the grantee of the conveyance.[30] Likewise, completion of title by assumed trustees does not accresce to and validate conveyances by original trustees none of whom ever became infeft.[31]

Where accretion inapplicable

24–62   Since accretion is based on absolute warrandice it has no application where the warrandice in a conveyance is qualified, *e.g.* simple or fact and deed only,[32] although possibly, if the conveyance included all right, title and interest, present and future, accretion would operate.[33] It is said by Erskine[34] on the authority of two old cases[35] that, where a title to the lands conveyed is subsequently acquired by a consenter to the conveyance, accretion does not operate to perfect the title of the grantee, but in neither of these cases does it seem that absolute warrandice was granted by the consenter or implied against him and in principle, if the consenter grants absolute warrandice, there seems no reason why accretion should not operate. A judicial conveyance, such as adjudication from a person having a defective title, is not validated by subsequent acquisition of a right by him, since the judicial conveyance merely transmits any right then vested in the debtor and imposes on him no obligation of warrandice.[36] If a bankrupt's title to heritable property is completed in his name after sequestration, accretion does not operate to perfect any unperfected right in favour of any person other than the permanent trustee in bankruptcy.[37]

Accretion in relation to registration of title

24–63   The scope of application of the principle of accretion is much reduced under the system of registration of title. If a transaction which induces first registration is effected by a deed which in feudal law requires that the granter be infeft, *e.g.* a feu grant or a long lease, and the superior or landlord did not have a completed title when the deed was granted, the subsequent completion of the title of the superior or

---

[29] *Keith* v. *Grant* (1792) Mor. 7767, 2933.
[30] *Redfearn* v. *Maxwell*, March 7, 1816, F.C.
[31] *Martin* v. *Martin's Trs.* (1841) 3 D. 485.
[32] Stair, III, ii, 2.
[33] *Douglas* v. *Laird of Wedderburn* (1664) Mor. 7748.
[34] II, vii, 4.
[35] *Forbes* v. *Innes* (1668) Mor. 7759; *Stuart* v. *Hutchison* (1681) Mor. 7762.
[36] *Wilson* v. *Webster* (1836) 14 S. 1117.
[37] Bankruptcy (Scotland) Act 1985, s. 31(3).

landlord, either by application for registration of his interest in the superiority or property, as the case might be, or by expeding and recording a notice of title, would obviously assist the Keeper in completing registration of the interest of the feuar or lessee. If for any reason that is not done and the applicant insists upon registration, the Keeper may either require that the title of the superior or landlord be completed or register the interest of the feuar or tenant with exclusion of indemnity, which exclusion may subsequently be removed as and when the superior or landlord completes his title and accretion operates to rectify the defect in the title of the feuar or tenant. There is no need for accretion in relation to an interest which has been registered without exclusion of indemnity: the registered proprietor has a guaranteed real right of ownership.

INDEX

Note
Figures in ordinary type refer to text.
Figures in bold type refer to styles.

ABSORPTION,
  consolidation, registered interests, 17–
    118, 17–119, 17–120, 17–121, 24–43
ACCESS,
  conditions in missives as to, 15–47, 15–
    94, 15–95
  servitude of,
    creation and transmission. *See*
      SERVITUDES.
    servitude of way for access, **20–11**
ACCRETION,
  bankruptcy, excluded as against trustee,
    24–62
  effect of, in land rights, 24–59
  judicial conveyances, excluded in, 24–
    62
  parties between whom accretion
    operates, 24–60
  changes in grantee or granter of
    conveyance, 24–61
  principle of, in relation to land rights,
    24–59
  registration of title, scope in relation
    to, 24–63
  warrandice, based on absolute, 24–62
ADJUDICATION IN EXECUTION,
  decree of, as foundation of prescriptive
    title, 21–06
  decree of declarator of expiry of legal,
    effect in relation to prescription,
    21–69
  registered interests, 24–29
    application for registration of decree
      of adjudication, 24–31
    decree of declarator of expiry of legal,
      24–29
ADJUDICATION IN IMPLEMENT,
  registered interests, 24–30
    application for registration of decree
      of adjudication, 24–31
ADMINISTRATION ORDERS, 21–22A
AGENTS,
  contracts for purchase and sale of
    heritable property by, 15–02
  on behalf of companies to be
    incorporated, 15–02
AGRICULTURAL SUBJECTS,
  contracts for sale and purchase, 15–40
  farms subject to tenancies, 15–132
  farm where tenancy being terminated,
    15–133, 15–134, **15–140**
  farm with vacant possession, 15–130,
    15–140
ALIMENTARY RIGHTS,
  deeds designed to defeat, 21–37
ALLOCATION OF FEUDUTIES,
  agreement, by, 17–37
  augmentation on, 17–37

ALLOCATION OF FEUDUTIES—*cont.*
  effect of, 17–36
  methods of,
    historical, 16–53
    before March 1, 1971,
      actings of superior, 17–38
      charter of novodamus, 17–38
      memorandum, endorsed, 17–38
      memorandum, separate, 17–38
      provisions in feu grant, 17–38
    on and after March 1, 1971,
      compulsory allocation under
        statute, 17–39
      notice of allocation by proprietor,
        17–40
      allocation by Lands Tribunal, 17–
        40
    older methods remain competent,
      17–39
  subdivision of feu, on, 17–34
  total amount of feuduty cannot be
    increased, 17–39
  vassal's risk, 17–35
ALLODIAL AND SPECIAL TENURES,
  church property, 16–14
  Crown property, 16–13
  kindly tenants, 16–17
  statutory tenants, 16–16
  udal tenure, 16–15
ANCIENT MONUMENTS AND
  ARCHAEOLOGICAL SITES, 23–50
APPORTIONMENTS ON SALE,
  electricity, gas and telephone charges,
    15–113
  feuduty or ground annual, 15–111
  fire insurance premiums, 15–115
  local rates, 15–112
  price, of, as between heritable and
    moveable items, 15–68
  rents receivable, 15–114, 22–13
ARRESTMENTS,
  in course of conveyancing transaction,
    23–16
ARTICLES OF ROUP. *See* AUCTION, SALE BY.
ASSIGNATION OF RENTS. *See* RENTS,
  ASSIGNATION OF.
ASSIGNATION OF WRITS. *See* WRITS,
  ASSIGNATION OF.
AUCTION, SALE BY,
  arbitration clause, 15–148
  articles of roup, 15–142, 15–143
  caution, 15–145
  minute of enactment and preference,
    execution of, 15–142
  persons entitled to bid, 15–144
  procedure at roup, 15–144
  special conditions,
    land registration, 15–143

501